Der Fuehrer

Der Fuehrer

Hitler's Rise to Power

BY KONRAD HEIDEN

Author of A History of National Socialism

TRANSLATED BY RALPH MANHEIM

HOUGHTON MIFFLIN COMPANY · BOSTON

The Riverside Press Cambridge

1 9 4 4

PRINTED AND BOUND IN THE U. S. A. BY
KINGSPORT PRESS, INC., KINGSPORT, TENN.

Preface

IT IS TWENTY-THREE YEARS now since I first attended a National Socialist meeting, saw (without particular enjoyment) Herr Hitler at close range, and listened to the flood of nonsense — or so it then seemed to me — that he was spouting. It was only gradually that the effects of these speeches made me realize that behind all the nonsense there was unrivaled political cunning.

In 1923, as the leader of a small democratic organization in the University of Munich, I tried, with all the earnestness of youth, and with complete lack of success, to annihilate Hitler by means of protest parades, mass meetings, and giant posters. And so I am entitled to call myself the oldest — or one of the oldest — anti-Nazis now in the United States, for there cannot be many in this country who came into conflict with Adolf Hitler and his handful of followers at so early a date.

Those who experience history and have a share in its making rarely see the enduring threads but only the whirl of exciting and quickly forgotten details. In 1920, and the years following, my friends and I certainly did not view our modest fist-fights and other encounters with the National Socialists as an attempt to put a premature end to the career of the modern Genghis Khan, and I would have jeered at anyone who had prophesied that this was the beginning of a new epoch in world history.

The narrative that follows is based partly on my own observations and experiences then and in later years. However, even the most intimate episodes and reports of private conversations are grounded on documentary evidence or on statements of individuals who seemed to me thoroughly reliable.

This book owes much to that unique collection, the Hoover Library at Stanford University, California. I want to thank Professor Ralph H. Lutz for his permission to use this treasure of documents about recent European history, and Miss Nina Almond, Librarian, and

Mr. Philip T. McLean, Reference Librarian, for the friendly help they gave me in every way. I am indebted, too, to the library of the University of California at Berkeley, and to the valuable private library of my friends Muriel and Joseph Buttinger, New York.

The share the publishing firm of Houghton Mifflin Company had in the making of this book seems to me larger than usual. I cannot leave unmentioned the amount of help, advice, hard work, time, and patience Robert N. Linscott, as an editor, gave to the job; it was a most decisive contribution. Miss Constance Purtell was very helpful with revising and last-hour translating.

Ralph Manheim entered the army before he could finish his translation. The last chapter and part of the chapter before the last have been translated by Norbert Guterman.

K.H.

Contents

Der Fuehrer

Chapter I

THE PROTOCOLS OF THE
WISE MEN OF ZION

ONE DAY IN THE SUMMER OF 1917 A STUDENT was reading in his room in Moscow. A stranger entered, laid a book on the table, and silently vanished. The cover of the book bore in Russian the words from the twenty-fourth chapter of Matthew: 'He is near, he is hard by the door.'

The student sensed the masterful irony of higher powers in this strange happening. They had sent him a silent message. He opened the book, and the voice of a demon spoke to him.

It was a message concerning the Antichrist, who would come at the end of days. The Antichrist is no mythical being, no monkish medieval fantasy. It is the portrait of a type of man who comes to the fore when an epoch is dying. He is a man with a white skin, in everyday clothes, dangerously contemporary, and a mighty demagogue. He will talk with the masses, and at his word the masses will rise up and turn a culture to ashes, a culture which has deserved no better, since it has borne the Antichrist in its own image and for its own destruction. The great Russian philosopher Soloviev described him. The Antichrist 'does not look like what he is,' and therein precisely lies the danger. He is a young man with a strong personality and seductive power of speech and writing. He is an ascetic and a vegetarian. He will win fame first by a book in which 'respect of the ancient traditions and symbols stands side by side with a bold and thorough radicalism in social and political problems . . . absolute individualism with an ardent fidelity to the common weal. . . .' Then, in Berlin, he will become ruler of the 'United States of Europe'; he will conquer Asia and North Africa; America will submit to him voluntarily. He is an absolute genius, and he may, says Soloviev, wear a small mustache.

This is the demon who speaks out of the book.

'We shall talk with the people on the streets and squares,' says the demon, 'and teach them to take the view of political questions which at the moment we require. For what the ruler says to the people spreads through the whole country like wildfire, the voice of the people carries it to all four winds.

'We' — the demon always says 'We' — 'shall create unrest, struggle, and hate in the whole of Europe and thence in other continents. We shall at all times be in a position to call forth new disturbances at will, or to restore the old order.

'Unremittingly we shall poison the relations between the peoples and states of all countries. By envy and hatred, by struggle and warfare, even by spreading hunger, destitution, and plagues, we shall bring all peoples to such a pass that their only escape will lie in total submission to our domination.

'We shall stultify, seduce, ruin the youth.

'We shall not stick at bribery, treachery, treason, as long as they serve the realization of our plans. Our watchword is: force and hypocrisy!

'In our arsenal we carry a boundless ambition, burning avidity, a ruthless thirst for revenge, relentless hatred. From us emanates the specter of fear, all-embracing terror.'

A gabbling demon, and self-conceited, too:

'We are the chosen, we are the true men. Our minds give off the true power of the spirit; the intelligence of the rest is instinctive and animal. They can see, but they cannot foresee; their inventions are purely corporeal. Does it not follow clearly that Nature herself has predestined us to dominate the whole world?

'We shall not submit the unique greatness of our ultimate plan, the context of its particular parts, the consequences of each separate point, the secret meaning of which remains hidden, to the judgment and decision of the many, even, of those who share our thoughts; we shall not cast the gleaming thoughts of our leader before the swine, and even in more intimate circles we shall not permit them to be carped at.

'We shall paint the misdeeds of foreign governments in the most garish colors and create such an ill-feeling toward them that the peoples would a thousand times rather bear a slavery which guarantees them peace and order than enjoy their much-touted freedom. The peoples will tolerate any servitude we may impose on them, if only to avoid a return to the horrors of wars and insurrection. Our principles and methods will take on their full force when we present them in sharp contrast to the putrid old social order.

'Outwardly, however, in our "official" utterances, we shall adopt an opposite procedure and always do our best to appear honorable and co-operative. A statesman's words do not have to agree with his acts. If we pursue these principles, the governments and peoples which we have thus prepared will take our IOU's for cash. One day they will accept us as the benefactors and saviors of the human race.

'If any state dares to resist us; if its neighbors make common cause with it against us, we shall unleash a world war.'

And then the demon spreads his wings, conceals the sky, darkens the world:

'By all these methods we shall so wear down the nations that they will be forced to offer us world domination. We shall stretch out our arms like pincers in all directions, and introduce an order of such violence that all peoples will bow to our domination.'

Who is this 'we'? Who is it that brags so absurdly?

To the student it is not absurd. It sounds fantastic, but it is not a mere tissue of lies. He turns back the pages and discovers that all this accursed wisdom, all these diabolical plans, were hatched out by a group of old Jews, who met together in a back room in Basel, Switzerland, in the year 1897. The demon aiming to devour the world is a Jewish club. It stands there in black and white, described at length, with place and date. Twenty years had passed before this knowledge found the right man. And thus *The Proto-*

cols of the Wise Men of Zion, since become so famous, fell into the hands of Alfred Rosenberg.

A mysterious occurrence. Rosenberg himself has often told how the unknown suddenly stepped into the room, laid down the book, and silently departed. To Rosenberg it was a sign from heaven. Both the place and the hour were significant. Moscow, 1917. Far to the west, the German-Russian phase of the First World War was drawing to an end in crumbling trenches; in the streets of the capital, the Russian Revolution was ebbing and flowing. Alfred Rosenberg, the son of a shoemaker, born in Reval (Tallinn) on the Baltic, was then twenty-four years old; he was of German descent but as an Esthonian, he was a subject of the Russian tsar. He had been raised in the German and Russian languages; he had first studied engineering and architecture at Riga, also on the Baltic; then, when the German army occupied Riga, he had fled. Now he was studying in Moscow.

The globe was afire. The tsar's empire was crumbling. Perhaps there would never again be peace. Perhaps this book would tell him why. The demon, who had incited the nations against each other, had spoken. Perhaps he, Alfred Rosenberg, understood him better than others; for in his own soul he could feel more strongly than others the mesh woven by hatred and love between the nations. He came from the tsar's Baltic, German provinces. He could scarcely say whether he was more Russian or more German. But today there were greater things concerning which he must achieve clarity. Here in Russia's holy city, in Russia's language, he had received a message. Judah, a book has brought forth thine innermost thoughts! He, the student, would close his eyes and believe it all his life, as firm as a rock. Was a new epoch of world history beginning in Moscow at that hour? Surely one of the most astounding, far-reaching, and bloody conspiracies of all time was bound to that hour. He who could read would go far.

'The nations,' says the demon, 'love and honor audacity in statesmen. Faced with an act of violence, they say: that was vile but clever! A scoundrel's trick, but wonderfully executed! With what insolence! Our leaders must move toward their goal with unparalleled boldness. Then we shall break all resistance in our path.'

The vision sends forth an icy chill and a breath of deadly truth.

The demon of world domination has spoken. He has proclaimed the great secret: the world can be dominated. Bowed with weariness, the peoples demand subjection. And those who resist will be tamed by terrible blows and sufferings. Modern society is charged with a magical current which in all men creates the same thoughts. The masses expect great things of their rulers. And for that reason, great things are easy.

This is the true sense of the secret writings which we today know as *The Protocols of the Wise Men of Zion*. Everything else in them develops from the basic idea that world domination is possible in our time: with sovereign contempt it is shown with what relative ease it can be achieved. Later, at third, fourth, and fifth hand, these profound thoughts were woven together with a figment of forgeries and purposeful lies which confused and obscured the whole document to the point of unintelligibility. But precisely in that condition it could be swallowed without understanding by millions of readers, and this gave it its great effect.

Today we are in a position to re-create the original content of the document. Its content is how to establish dictatorship with the help — and abuse — of democratic methods. The genesis of Caesarism is described. We are told that democracy, if carried to its extreme conclusion, provides the usurper with his best weapons. Furthermore, democracy, in the international field actually offers a dictator, who has firmly entrenched himself in one country, the possibility of world domination. This is the true content of the famous *Protocols*.

Three generations ago a brilliant thinker wrote this secret formula for the achievement of world domination. We know little concerning his life. He was a French lawyer named Maurice Joly. He was, at the time he wrote his little book, a conservative, legitimist and monarchist. He had no thought of writing a secret document; on the contrary, he had in mind a satire against Napoleon III, then emperor of the French. Whether he ever perceived that he was leaving behind him the prophecies of a great seer; whether he ever guessed that his book embraced a political doctrine of world-shaking force, we do not know.

The work was published in Brussels in 1864, by A. Mertens et Fils, as an illegal propaganda pamphlet; it was written in French and bore the title: *Dialogue aux enfers entre Machiavel et Montesquieu, ou la politique de Machiavel au XIXᵉ siècle, par un Contemporain.* (Dialogue in hell between Machiavelli and Montesquieu, or the politics of Machiavelli in the nineteenth century by a contemporary.) His anonymity did not avail the author. The police of the French emperor discovered him, he was sent to prison for fifteen months. His book was published in a second edition, then it was forgotten, and today scarcely any copies of it can be found.

For the author had seen the secret disease of his epoch, and that is something which men do not like. Today we read Joly with quite different eyes. Today the evils are no longer secret. To us, living in the present day, some of the sentences of this forgotten book seem like a lightning flash, bathing the present in dazzling light. They are unpleasant truths, but great truths, and they come down to us from great sources. Joly gathered his wisdom from Machiavelli and Montesquieu; the Italian political philosopher of the fifteenth, the French political philosopher of the eighteenth century, step forward in his book and utter the ideas of their great works, *Il Principe* and *L'Esprit des Lois.* Chiefly the ideas of Machiavelli were retained in the book's later form, *The Protocols of Zion.* Joly applied these ideas to the technique of dominating the modern masses; that was his contribution. In the final version the conception is broadened to cover the masses of whole continents, of the entire globe.

This brings us to world domination. It is a secret necessity inherent in the mechanism of our existence; it lives in our minds as a secret goal; it stands in the sea of the future as a magnetic mountain, inexorably attracting the ship of modern society. The modern world is a unit. China and England may not pray to the same God, but a telephone bell means the same thing to the yellow man as to the white; a telegraphic transfer of pounds sterling or dollars buys in Asia the rice which is eaten in Europe or America. Such a world would be perfect under the leadership of a central mind, informed over a thousand wires, seeing through millions of electric eyes, aided by the best brains; a mind which would know the needs of the world and satisfy them with all the means which a dominated earth holds at the disposal of the knowing.

Is this the truth? Who has spoken? Perhaps it is only a half truth, but even in its halfness it is of enormous import, which is not seen by most men. The demon has spoken — or shall we say the spirit of the age — or, in still other words — the new type of man, who is imprinting his features on this age. History is the most skeptical of all sciences; it knows no absolute truths. It does not matter whether things really are as the demon says; what matters is to know whether there are men who see them that way; and whether these men are important.

This is the meaning which our age breathes into the teachings of Machiavelli. At its base, however, lies an eternal pessimistic wisdom which teaches that men are easily satisfied, hence easy for a clever mind to dominate. These two elements, the modern truth and the timeless wisdom, give the book a terrifying power which shines through the varnish of superimposed lies.

Maurice Joly had understood the meaning of domination. He knew the modern mass and its state of mind. He had seen a master guide it. The master was Napoleon III, conspirator, usurper, and for nearly twenty years emperor of the French; at once nationalist and socialist, democrat and tyrant, pacifist and conqueror, dictator by virtue of bayonets and the plebiscite; applauded by the masses whom he had politically raped. Joly had written his book with him in mind. He was meant when the demon spoke: we shall stultify the people, we shall promote disturbances in Europe and elsewhere, we shall create a mighty central power, we shall commit crimes, and the people will admire us for them. If gallstones had not made a wreck of this third Napoleon, he might have died in power and glory.

Joly's magnificent portrait of modern tyranny underwent a strange fate. After thirty years of oblivion, its great day came. It was discovered by a group of Russian conspirators. Not, to be sure, by the Russian revolutionaries of that day, the Nihilists, Social Democrats, or Social Revolutionaries; but by a few crafty agents of the counter-revolution, members of the Ochrana, the tsar's secret police. They wanted to frighten the tsar and drive him to bloodshed. To this end they persuaded him that the Jews of the whole world had devised a secret conspiracy to achieve domination, first over Russia, then over the whole world.

Claims of this sort were not new; they lay to a certain extent in the air. In the nineteenth century the Jews had nearly everywhere — though not in Russia — achieved civil equality and thus taken their place in modern society. Some had amassed great wealth, a few — for example, the house of Rothschild — had even attained real influence, and inspired a venomous anti-Semitism. Soloviev, for example, quotes a French priest who wrote 'that he lived by anticipation of that glorious day when, the skin stripped off . . . the Jews will be used for making cheap carpets.'

This epoch lies behind us. Today Rothschild is a memory, no longer a power. Anonymous, massive concentrations of power in industry and finance have relegated the Jewish bankers and big merchants — once so impressive — to second or third rank. There is a Jewish problem; this book will not attempt to deny it. As a modern Jewish leader, Theodor Herzl, said, 'The Jewish question exists wherever Jews live in any considerable number. . . . The longer anti-Semitism lies dormant, the more furiously it must break out.' Nevertheless, painful as it is, it principally concerns the Jews themselves; it is not and never was the chief problem of society as a whole, which has other and graver worries. But in the nineteenth century, it was possible for imaginative minds to be frightened by the aura of political power surrounding certain Jewish names. In 1868, Hermann Gödsche, a German signing himself Sir John Retcliffe the Younger, wrote a novel entitled *Biarritz*. In it twelve rabbis from all corners of the earth meet in the Jewish cemetery in Prague. There they set up a cry of Satanic glee, for through accursed gold, through its mighty bankers, Judah has conquered the world, bought kings and the princes of the Church; Judah is wallowing in vice and glory. The rabbis represent the twelve tribes of Israel and speak Chaldaean. Subsequently this chapter, somewhat revised, was printed in pamphlet form and translated into foreign languages. And now, lo and behold, we have an 'authentic document,' proving the existence of a Jewish world conspiracy.

Gödsche's text was childish and none too convincing. But suppose you take these rabbis conspiring in their cemetery and give them the worldly wisdom, the contempt for humanity, the seductive power of Joly's tyrant. Don't just make them avaricious braggarts; make them subtle and crafty: make them speak the accursed satirical wisdom of Machiavelli, but in deadly earnest; finally, confound the fabulous nocturnal conspiracy with an international Jewish congress which actually did convene to discuss such sober matters as the problem of emigration. Then we have before us, in all its bloody romantic horror, the demon of Jewish world domination gathered in a congress and fixed in a protocol.

That is what happened. The group of Russian conspirators dug up Joly's forgotten book; they were also familiar with the horror story about the Jewish cemetery in Prague; they knew by the newspapers that in 1897 the Jewish Zionist Movement had very publicly been founded at a congress in Basel; finally, they knew only too well the golden awe emanating from the ancient fame of the Rothschilds. The ingredients of a magnificent conspiracy lay at hand, requiring only to be mixed.

The Ochrana, the tsarist secret police, furnished the means and the brains. First General Oryevsky, one of its heads, had a pamphlet prepared, based on the rabbis' conspiracy in Gödsche's story. The novelty was that the pamphlet was written in the form of protocols; this gave it a much more serious look. The pamphlet served as a frame to which Joly's ideas were embroidered in glowing colors. This was the work of General Ratchkovsky, the leader of the French division of the Ochrana. For the Ochrana had divisions for all countries. Everywhere it tracked down the activities of Russian, and not only Russian, revolutionaries. It was a kind of world conspiracy; a net of spies, intriguers, bribe-givers, and political agitators, which Russian tsarism had cast over the world.

With his eye for conspiracy, Ratchkovsky saw the explosive power inherent in Joly's timeworn and seemingly harmless work. It described modern dictatorship, its secret and yet so open methods; laid bare its cogs and springs. A real tyrant would never have spoken so self-revealingly; only a hostile satirist could have put such words of braggadocio into his mouth. The effect was a terrible

self-indictment of modern dictatorship. This presumably is why
the material appealed so strongly to these conspirators of dictatorship. They were confronted with their own image.

They could scarcely have pondered the matter very deeply, but
it is precisely in the unconscious acts of men that history is most
clearly revealed. The Ochrana men knew that this was good material, that they could make use of it. That was enough. In one or
two evenings, over a pipe and a cup of tea, you could adapt this
colorful but rather anonymous document for any purpose, put any
label on it. Where Joly speaks in the first person singular, puts
his speeches in the mouth of Machiavelli, means Napoleon III, and
is actually denouncing modern Caesarism as such — just substitute
'We Jesuits,' 'We Freemasons,' 'We Englishmen,' or 'We Jews' —
the result would be a fragment of perverted truth, hence not entirely
incredible. As for Ratchkovsky and his clique, they were interested
in the Jewish angle.

Their plan was more than a simple palace conspiracy. It was the
first great attempt at a mighty national counter-revolution against
the democratic and socialist revolution of the nineteenth century.
The plan was to fuse the passion of the people and the cold power
of the state into a mighty, counter-revolutionary force that would
shake society to its foundations. If the movement had succeeded,
it would most likely have transformed the old autocratic tsarism
profoundly from within, made it a hundred times more powerful.
In Holy Russia, at the beginning of the twentieth century, it would
probably have created a new phenomenon in many respects resembling the later fascist dictatorships. Society in Russia was further advanced in its spiritual disintegration, inwardly more prepared for revolution than anywhere else in the world; at the same
time the state power was stronger than anywhere else. Hence, it is
understandable that this first attempt at a state-directed revolution
should have been made here. It is in any case worth thinking
about. Through this conspiracy, Russia became the spiritual mother
country of modern fascism, as it later became the world center of
communism.

As nucleus of the counter-revolutionary popular movement, a new
party was formed. A certain Butmy was its leader. This party was

military in organization. Its storm troops rode through the country, performing 'propaganda by action.' Chief among their activities was a bloody persecution of the Jews, the aim being to call attention to the Jews as the ostensible cause of bad conditions. Always strike the minority was their principle — for when a minority is punished, it is guilty in the eyes of the masses. The name of the movement was 'The Black Hundreds,' which meant simply: the black guard. *The Protocols of the Wise Men of Zion* became the program of this movement; with it they were born, and with it they grew. Even the primitive version, based on Gödsche's nocturnal conspiracy of rabbis, had a terrible effect. It was circulated widely, and in 1903 gave the signal for the Kishenev pogrom, in which several thousand Jews were massacred.

By its very nature every fascist movement strives to harness both the people and the state power to its will. The men who cooked up the *Protocols* wanted not only to stir up the masses, but also to take in the credulous tsar. To this end, they gave the book a political timeliness. A first version had been prepared toward the end of the nineties by Golovinski and Manuilov, two journalists in the service of Ratchkovsky. This version included Joly's most impressive bits. For some reason or other the bombshell was left unused for a few years. It was not hurled until political developments offered a particularly grateful target. In 1904-05, the pamphlet was refurbished as an attack on Prince Svatopulk-Mirski, minister of the interior, and Count Witte, the finance minister, who were too liberal for the Ochrana. A pamphlet on financial policy, by a certain Sharapov, attacking Count Witte was appended. References to the unfortunate Russo-Japanese War and to Witte's rôle as peacemaker were woven in. All this, of course, beneath the paper-thin trimming of a Jewish conspiracy. Other propaganda works represented the Jews as warmongers; now, on the contrary, they had to be peacemongers; for if Witte made peace with the Japanese, he did so — say the *Protocols* — on the instigation of the Jews, who were opposed to a Russian victory. They did not want a Russian victory, because it would have thwarted their plan for world domination.

This is the origin of the supposed textbook of Jewish world domination. Today the forgery is incontrovertibly proved, yet some-thing infinitely significant has remained: a textbook of world domination pure and simple. The leaders of the Black Hundreds had written this great method of demagogy, the tsar's secret police had given it plastic form. Or, to call this clique of political officials, venal writers, conspiratorial officers, by their proper name: the armed intellectual [1] was out to seize power over the masses. He denied it, to be sure; he said: no, no, this was not my work. The Jew devised these plans; I only stole them and brought them to light for the salvation of mankind. But today we know better. An impartial court has established the truth, even anti-Semitic propa-gandists have today dropped the myth of the Jewish conspiracy in Basel and admitted Joly's authorship. At first the anti-Semites comforted themselves with the idea that Joly was a Jew and that a 'Jewish spirit' had impelled him to write his book; but then Joly's baptismal record was found, exploding this last hope; since then, some anti-Semites have declared merely that the *Protocols* are 'deeper wisdom,' beyond any possibility of documentary proof. Actually they do contain a deeper truth; but the demonstrable his-tory of their origin shows that this truth involves not a Jewish but a fascist world conspiracy.

[1] The word 'intellectual' makes it necessary, for the first and the last time in this book, to bother the reader with a footnote. The German 'Intellektueller' and the English 'intellectual' do not mean the same thing. The German word has (espe-cially in recent times) taken a broader meaning and is frequently used merely to designate people with an education above the average; either academic or technical. But the difficulty does not stop here. This book deliberately uses the word 'intellectual' to designate a group, or rather a type, characterized, not by a common economic or material interest, but a common outlook. It comes close to the type of the pragmatical and mechanistically minded modern man, product of mass education, whose sole criterion is: Will it work? Such a man may be, for example, an executive, dentist, or engineer, but whatever his occupation, he will have a sense of class superiority due to an education above the average. In Germany it was this type, restless and disillusioned, that gravitated most readily to the Nazis and formed the backbone of the movement.

The term 'bohemian,' which occurs later, can best be defined as the 'intel-lectual' who has not found his place in society; who was 'uprooted and disinherited' by the economic upheavals of the twenties and thirties, and unable — owing to the stricter class consciousness of the European — to slide comfortably down into the ranks of the proletariat. He has been perfectly described by Karl Marx, in his *The Eighteenth of Brumaire of Louis Bonaparte,* where he calls the scum of all classes which carried through the *coup d'état* of Napoleon III 'creatures of whom the best that can be said is that they are men of ill repute . . . each a noisy *bohème,* out for looting the state.'

At first the concept of conspiracy is purely symbolical. The human mind, with its tendency to personify great objective phenomena, interprets surprising objective contexts as a personal plan. World history becomes a moral drama; the eternal struggle between man and society becomes the struggle between good and evil; the lofty ruthlessness of history seems bearable only when it is humanized. Thus we give it a mythological form: the great hereditary enemy, the Antichrist, the destroyer, and finally, the conspirator. The nineteenth century in Europe was indeed full of conspirators, from the German Burschenschaften, the Italian Carbonari, the Irish Fenians, to the Russian Nihilists and Socialists. Behind all this, our imagination seeks a world context, a world conspiracy aiming at world domination. Where is the kernel of historical truth in the fantasy of a Jewish world conspiracy? It lies in the great world struggle for human equality to which the Jews owe their admission to modern society; this is the historical fact standing in the broad daylight of truth, whence it casts weirdly magnified, indistinct, and unfathomable shadows into the background of fantasy. On the opposing side, the great principle of inequality fights to preserve its rule; the ruling class philosophy of a natural hierarchy, of innate differences between men. Once this principle is expressed in the form of historical events, it also soon assumes an aspect of conspiracy. The coup d'état of Napoleon III on December 2, 1851, and *The Protocols of the Wise Men of Zion* were not hatched out by the same mind. But they are acts of one and the same psychological type; only this made it possible for history to combine one with the other by the thin red thread of a documentary connection.

The spirit of the *Protocols,* therefore, contains historical truth, though all the facts put forward in them are forgeries. Hence its influence on such varied times and peoples. When they were published, their deeper, genuine content beneath the varnish of falsification found a receptive mood in many sections of the Russian people — a mood of decadence and despair. The Russian literature of the period from Tolstoi to Sologub bears witness to this mood. The superstitious tsar permitted himself to be frightened and influenced by wonder-working monks. Serious religious people were oppressed by the warnings of Soloviev. He associated the materialism and silly optimism of modern culture with the approach of the Antichrist as a modern demagogue; his book, to some extent, is an attack on Tolstoi. Soloviev's Antichrist finally disappears in a battle against the desperate Jews, many of whom he had massacred before. But one of his disciples makes the Antichrist himself a Jew: this was a certain Sergei Nilus.

Nilus was a religious writer. It is hard to say whether he was an honest visionary or an intriguing swindler. At all events, he became the tool of the Ochrana in a picturesque palace intrigue, which was part of the above-mentioned general fascist plan. The purpose of the intrigue was to remove a foreign wonder-worker, the French magnetic healer Philippe, from the tsar's entourage. Ratchkovsky's clique wished to replace the Frenchman by Nilus as their creature. Why Nilus? He had written a book, under the influence of Soloviev, on the theme of the Jewish Antichrist. Its title: 'Small signs betoken great events. The Antichrist is near at hand.' The book is one of hundreds of documents attesting a forgotten mood, and would today be quite lost sight of were it not for a noteworthy change made in the second edition. This second edition was sponsored by the Ochrana and published in 1905 in the Imperial state printing shop in Tsarskoye Selo. Its appendix includes *The Protocols of the Wise Men of Zion*. This was the first publication of the *Protocols* in their present form, and it was claimed by Nilus that these *Protocols* were the minutes of speeches and debates which were made at the founding congress of the Zionist Movement in Basel, Switzerland, in 1897.

This much was true, that in 1897 in Basel the Jewish Nationalist Movement of the Zionists was born. The goal of this group, to put it simply, was to lead the Jews back again to Palestine; to state it more exactly, to create for those Jews who were leading an intolerable life of oppression, especially in Russia, a 'legally assured homestead' in Palestine. In order to disappear in that little corner on the eastern shore of the Mediterranean they had, as Theodor Herzl, the founder of the movement, put it, 'to make the Jewish problem . . . a question of world politics.'

This was the purpose of the Basel congress. But, if we believe

Nilus, its true, secret aim was just the opposite; that is, the foundation of an uncontested world domination by the Jews. He claimed that the public congress was a mere blind for a number of far more important secret sessions. In these secret sessions the Zionist leaders set forth their plan for Jewish world conquest. It was there that those speeches allegedly were made: 'We shall everywhere arouse ferment, struggle, and enmity — we shall unleash a world war — we shall bring the peoples to such a pass that they will voluntarily offer us world domination.'

These speeches were taken down in shorthand and entered in the minutes. A courier of the congress was supposed to bring the terrible papers from Basel to the German city of Frankfurt am Main, to be preserved in the secret archives of the Rising Sun Lodge of Freemasons. But the courier was a traitor. On the way he spent the night at a little city in Baden. Some officials of the Ochrana were waiting for him there with a staff of scribes, and that night the *Protocols* were copied in a hotel room. This was Nilus's story in 1905; but in a later edition he has quite a different version; the mistress of a French Zionist stole the papers from him and delivered them to the Ochrana. In later editions he gives still other versions. There is but one point to which he always adheres: that he himself had received the papers from a certain Suchotin, marshal of nobility in the district of Chernigov, who had received them from Ratchkovsky.

The book was laid on the tsar's table. Its effect was strong but not lasting. At first the tsar was shaken, praised the book's wealth of ideas, its mighty perspective, and believed it all. But Ratchkovsky had gone too far. At that time, perhaps, the deepest sources of the forgery were not discovered; but it soon became clear to the Russian public, who for a hundred years had been only too familiar with the methods of the secret police, that such documents from the hand of the Ochrana did not carry much weight. Minister Stolypin even succeeded in convincing the tsar of the forgery. The tsar gave orders that the book should no longer be used as propaganda, for 'we must not fight for a pure cause with unclean weapons.' Not Nilus but Rasputin became the tsar's confessor.

Nonetheless, the Ochrana did its best to spread its product among

the masses. Butmy, the leader of the Black Hundreds, also published a version of the *Protocols*. In 1917, during the World War
and after the tsar's downfall, Nilus published the last edition of his
book, with the *Protocols* in the appendix. This time it was: 'He is
near, he is hard by the door.' It is this edition which was placed
on Alfred Rosenberg's table. It was from this edition that the
loquacious and seductive demon of world domination spoke to the
young man.

Rosenberg believed in the secret session of Basel, at least he did
then. For this we cannot be too hard on a lad of twenty-four. For
beneath the heavy coating of a clumsily exaggerated forgery, the
Protocols contain a genuine element which might well carry a
strong, mysterious appeal to the modern intellectual. This element
is their radicalism. The *Protocols* are the work of a decadent, unscrupulous group of intellectuals, who pondered the problem of
dominating the masses. They saw the modern mass in revolutionary
motion. They set themselves the task of weaning the masses from
their revolutionary leaders. See what these socialist agitators had
succeeded in doing with a few revolutionary phrases and little
apparent thought! Why couldn't we learn to do as well? We
academicians would surely be a match for a band of trade-union
secretaries! There is a technique of dominating the masses, and in
principle technical problems can always be solved. The intellectual's envy of the demagogue gave birth to a new political technique.

And here history turns over a new leaf. The conspirators did
not need to invent anti-Semitism; no, what they did was to create
anti-Semitism as a weapon in the class struggle; something quite
apart from the hostility which, since the beginning of the nineteenth century, had been aroused by the Jewish entrance into the
bourgeois society of Europe. For now, in modern society, a new
Jewish type had made its appearance — the Jewish intellectual;
and it is predominantly he who became the target and victim of the
most frightful outbursts of anti-Semitism in modern history. For
it is his competitor, the non-Jewish intellectual, who incited and
directed this anti-Semitism, and directed it chiefly, not against
Jewish capital (though an outmoded propaganda says so), but

against the Jewish intellectuals — the lawyers, doctors, government officials, and others who had made themselves, by their share in modern education, so influential a part of society.

We are living in the age of technology. Technology is more than the transformation of heat into power. It is, in general, the domination of brute force by trained intelligence. Natural scientists have studied the soul, and vaudeville 'professors' have demonstrated the power of hypnosis. The fakirs are not the only ones who can cast a spell over the masses. Here, this book shows what great things are possible, even with the simplest methods. Alfred Rosenberg is an engineer and architect, a young man who in a few months will take his examinations for registered engineer. The powers have laid this book on his desk and thereby given him the watchword that was to govern his life, the open sesame of technology: everything is possible.

With the book in his bag, he fled at the beginning of 1918 to his native city of Reval, later called Tallinn. German troops took the city. Rosenberg remembered that he was a German. He volunteered for the German army, to fight against the Bolsheviki who for some months had been in the saddle in Petersburg and Moscow. The German commandant distrusted the German Russian and rejected him. He remained a civilian, earning his living as a drawing instructor at the *Gymnasium*. His eyes were still fixed on Russia. The Bolsheviki had disbanded the Constituent Assembly, proclaimed the dictatorship of the proletariat and the advent of socialism, but at the same time had given the poor peasants land, or rather summoned them to take it; they had brutally suppressed all political freedom, all opposition parties. Those affected resisted; there were plots and assassinations. The Bolsheviki, in a desperate life-and-death struggle, always in power but always on the brink of catastrophe, struck down their enemies by ruthless, barbaric terror. They acted in accordance with the recommendations of *The Protocols of Zion*. Were they not themselves the Wise Men of Zion? Hadn't they Jewish leaders? Isn't Lenin, their top leader, a Jew? In this, to be sure, Rosenberg was mistaken. Lenin was no more a Jew than Rykov, Kalinin, Krassin, Bucharin, and other Bolshevik leaders of the old guard; but Trotzky, Zinoviev, Radek were Jews.

The Bolsheviki exterminated the Jewish bourgeoisie of Russia as heartlessly as the Christian; from time to time some little Jewish community cursed and excommunicated a Bolshevik leader who arose in its midst; for Rosenberg, however, Russia was ruled by the Jewish Antichrist which Nilus had prophesied. Rosenberg himself has a little drop of Jewish blood in his veins; let us assume that he did not know it at the time. The world in which his great experiences took place remains in any case Russia. It was there that he met the demon. It was there that the dice governing the destiny of nations were falling. There the Antichrist held sway over a field of corpses. From there the plague was moving on Europe. It was on Russia that we should march, when the time came, to tumble Satan from his throne. Our life work was to summon Europe to avenge our exile.

For at the end of 1918, Rosenberg was forced to leave Reval with the remnants of the withdrawing, disbanding German army. The Bolsheviki pressed after them, occupied Reval, took Riga, approached the German border. He fled from them, crying: The plague is coming! An infected army, on the point of mutiny, flowed homeward, carrying him along. Thus he left Russia, came to Germany, bearing with him a treasure, the message of the Russian Antichrist, the *Protocols*. In a swarm of Russian fugitives, officers, intellectuals, barons and princes, Rosenberg reached Berlin, then Munich. At the same time other refugees reached Constantinople, London, Paris; Russians, Germans, but also Englishmen, Frenchmen, even Americans, members of those Allied expeditionary armies who, after the outbreak of the Bolshevik revolution, had occupied, for a time, Russian territory in Siberia, in the North, in the Crimea. And with this flow of fugitives not a few copies of the *Protocols* reached Western Europe.

A pity that General Ratchkovsky never lived to see the day. The shadow of Russia fell over Europe. From the Kremlin, Lenin exhorted the world to revolution, holding aloft the *Communist Manifesto*. Rosenberg comes, a humble fugitive, with the textbook of world domination in his battered suitcase.

Chapter II

THE ARMED

INTELLECTUALS

IN MUNICH, TOO, THERE WAS A REVOLUTION; here, too—or so it seems to Rosenberg—the Wise Men of Zion had seized the helm. But already the saviors were silently gathering. Conspirators had found one another; secretly they were amassing arms, preparing to overthrow the revolutionary, though legal governments. Rosenberg found his way into these circles, and became acquainted with two men: a young officer by the name of Rudolf Hess and Dietrich Eckart, an elderly writer. The group of conspirators had learned from the Wise Men of Zion. Outwardly they were an innocent club, studying and declaiming old Germanic literature. They even called themselves the Thule Society, after the legendary kingdom of Nordic mythology. Thule was the ancient—and scientifically more than questionable—homeland of the German race, which was supposed to have come down from the North.

Rosenberg brought the conspirators of Thule the secret of world domination and therewith their program. *The Protocols of the Wise Men of Zion* appeared in German. A certain Ludwig Müller signed his name as publisher. The impression on German intellectuals was extraordinary. Edition followed edition; the little volume was given away and widely distributed; the good cause found backers who preferred to remain anonymous. Not only in

Germany did it become the book of the hour. A respectable British newspaper, the *Morning Post,* devoted a series of articles to it. Even the *Times* demanded an investigation to determine what truth there was in the *Protocols.* The same occurred in France. In Poland the Bishop of Warsaw recommended the book's dissemination. The *Protocols* were published in America, in Italy, in Hungary, in Turkish and Arabic. The story of the circulation of *The Protocols of the Wise Men of Zion* would seem to indicate the existence of an international network of secret connections and co-operating forces, the actual aims of which did not become known to the world until twenty years later. And yet this network is described clearly enough in the *Protocols* themselves.

Now the Thule Society prepared to act. They decided to kill Premier Eisner. Kurt Eisner was a Socialist writer, the leader of the Bavarian Revolution. On November 6, 1918, he was virtually unknown, with no more than a few hundred supporters, more a literary than a political figure. He was a small man with a wild gray beard, a pince-nez, and an immense black hat. On November 7 he marched through the city of Munich with his few hundred men, occupied parliament and proclaimed the republic. As though by enchantment, the king, the princes, the generals, and ministers scattered to all the winds. When the news came, the minister of war cried out: 'Revolution, oh, my God, and here I am, still in uniform!'

Unlike Lenin, Eisner really was a Jew. Like Lenin, he had the peasants and workers on his side, but all the educated classes, the officers, officials, students against him; in such a case, there is no difference between Christian and Jew. Belatedly the intellectuals grew ashamed of their cowardice; they grew ashamed when they perceived that there was no danger. Their radical hatred found its embodiment in leagues like the Thule Society. While the Rosenbergs, the Hesses, the Eckarts, and others whose names have been forgotten were still planning — such an act, after all, was dangerous — a man whom they had insulted and cast aside got ahead of them. The League had rejected Count Anton Arco-Valley, a young officer, for being of Jewish descent on one side. Determined to shame his insulters by an example of courage, he shot Eisner down in the midst of his guards on the open street. A second later he himself lay on the ground, with a bullet through his chest. Eisner's secretary, Fechenbach, sprang forward and saved the assassin from being trampled by the boots of the infuriated soldiers. A mass insurrection broke out, a soviet republic was proclaimed. The Communists seized power — without bloodshed. In the place where Eisner fell, his picture was pasted to the wall; a Red Army man stood beside it, and all passers-by had to salute the picture. The members of the Thule Society soaked a bag of flour in the sweat of two bitches in heat, someone 'accidentally' dropped the bag in front of the picture, the flour clung to the ground and the walls; dogs gathered by the dozens, the picture and the guards silently vanished. This repulsive story is told here only because those responsible publicly boasted of it.

An army marched against revolutionary Munich. It was a motley troop; remnants of disbanding regiments; free corps, newly formed of unemployed soldiers and young people eager for adventure. In a village south of Munich a labor battalion of Russian war prisoners, forgotten though peace had been signed with Russia months before, fell into their hands. Russians? Must be Bolsheviki. What else would they be? Fifty-three Russian prisoners met their death in a sandpit over this misapprehension. In another village, a lieutenant asked the priest on whom he was billeted if he didn't know a few Red suspects in his community. Oh, yes, he knew some, and he named twelve, all of whom, as came to light in a later trial, were quite harmless individuals, who in the troubled times had somehow frightened the priest. On its march the troop dragged along twelve workers, drove them into the courtyard of the Munich slaughterhouse, and shot them against a wall with several hundred other unfortunates. The slaughter lasted for several days.

For on May 2, 1919, Munich had fallen to the White Army, the so-called government troops. The Red régime had survived but a few weeks. With a single exception, its record was free of blood. This exception regards the Thule Society, which had formed a small underground free corps of its strongest members, to work behind the Red lines. The free corps was armed and thus constituted what since the Spanish civil war (1936) has been called a fifth column. The conspiracy was discovered, a number of Thulists arrested; according to martial law, they were liable to the death penalty, but the Red government could not make up its mind to sentence them. In the last hours of the collapsing régime, news came that the White troops were shooting prisoners. Munich was embittered. In vain the army commander, the poet Ernst Toller, intervened. A fanatical subordinate, to whom the prisoners were entrusted, had a number of them shot, among them a woman; with them a few others who had nothing to do with the Thule Society and who had been arrested for tearing down government posters and other trifling offenses. Those shot included — in view of the subsequent legend, this is not unimportant — a Jew; all in all, ten persons. It remains a hideous deed, but the fifth-columnists of Thule were only bearing the consequences of their conspiracy; it is not true, as Rightist propaganda later claimed, that any hostages were murdered. In the courtyard of the Munich slaughterhouse hundreds of victims paid with their lives for the shooting of the Thulists. Many, if not most of them, were innocent. The drunken soldiery arrested, by mistake, Catholic workers, loyalists, enemies of the revolution and the republic; they murdered twenty-one persons in a cellar by order, or at least with the connivance, of their captain. 'The soldiers,' an eye-witness said later in court, 'many in a drunken condition, tramped around on the prisoners, struck them down indiscriminately with their side-arms, and thrust about so wildly that one of the bayonets bent and the victim's brain splattered all over. In this way they killed fourteen more people and then looted the corpses. Five prisoners were severely wounded. The corpses looked ghastly. The nose of one had been bashed into his face, half of another's skull was missing. If one of the wounded still showed sign of life, the soldiers beat him and stabbed him. Two soldiers grasped one another around the waist and carried on an Indian dance beside the corpses, screaming and howling.'

When the White troops entered Munich, they went to the Nineteenth Infantry barracks and found a body of soldiers which an eye-witness later called 'a wild Red rabble.' Every tenth man, chosen at random, was stood up against the wall and shot. Only one was set aside from the very first to be spared. His position was only too clear. When the high officers of the Munich Reichswehr fled before the radical uprising, they had left this man behind, to observe and report. A dangerous commission, requiring courage — but ugly. A few months previous, this man had attracted the attention of his officers in a strange way. 'They all noticed him,' one of them later recollected, 'because his salutes were so punctilious as to be provocative' in those revolutionary months when most of the soldiers defiantly refrained from saluting at all. When the government troops stormed Munich, his comrades wanted to help defend the city; he made a speech dissuading them. His comrades had suspected him of being a spy, and during the soviet régime he barely escaped arrest. Now he became the executioner. After May 2 an examining commission sent hundreds of men to the slaughterhouse wall. This man soon came to the attention of the commission, which used him as an informer. He delivered his reports in writing and later boasted of them. 'When he was ordered before the examining commission,' wrote one of his friends, 'his indictments cast a merciless clarity upon the unspeakable disgrace of the military treason practiced by the Jewish dictatorship of Munich's soviet period.' By rank this stool-pigeon was a corporal; by nationality, strange to say, an Austrian. His stated profession was painter and architect. His name was Adolf Hitler.

For these men the World War was not at an end. They did not recognize defeat. In any case, they said, we were stabbed in the back. But we do not accept this peace, we shall not reconcile ourselves to this revolution. The German army fights on in Germany. Every period has its methods. The thing for you to do is to sit down at an inn, watch the people, listen to them, get acquainted with them and win their confidence. It is a strange period of silent civil war. Two armies are fighting one another, almost unseen by the public; they are building up secret arsenals, and the problem in this war of position is to steal the enemy's arms by bold forays. The greatest danger is that the Allied victors of Versailles should find out what is going on, for then the weapons will inevitably fall into their hands. Hence we must sound the people out, find out if they know anything about hidden arms; and if they do know, whether they are disposed to pass their knowledge on. We give them a little encouragement; they open their hearts. And then the time comes. One night we get into an automobile together. Two comrades 'happen' to be along. Out into the woods; we raise our gun to the fellow's head, and boom. That is how we fight against traitors.

The struggle was nourished on a wild hatred from man to man. During a communist uprising near Merseburg the leader of a police detachment learned that a troop of seventy rebels had been seen in the vicinity; the soldiers jumped on their bicycles and rode out against the enemy. An encounter followed, and 'all the rebels fell,' according to a later printed report. No quarter was given, no prisoners taken. From a dark thicket in the Black Forest, Erzberger, the minister who induced Germany to sign the Treaty of Versailles, was shot. One night a few young men swore a mortal oath over their wine and beer; next morning, feverish and overwrought, they drove out in a car, overtook another car, and shot Minister Rathenau with an automatic. Deputy Gareis planned to attack the army of secret murderers in the Bavarian parliament; the night before the session he came home late. As he was opening the door, two shots rang out in the darkness. Gareis was dead, his murderers were never found. Men vanished without trace; how many corpses the woods concealed can only be guessed; a woman was found dead at the foot of a tree, over her head a note was pinned with the words: 'Lousy bitch, you've betrayed the fatherland. So you are judged by the Black Hand.' One Pöhner was president of the Munich police, a brilliant official, an extraordinary jurist; later he became a judge of the highest court in Bavaria. Someone said to him that beyond a doubt there were organizations of murderers at large. With an icy glance through his pince-nez, Pöhner, the judge, replied: 'Yes, but too few!'

In the Bavarian ministry of justice sat a high official, appointed to solve these murders. Actually he had been put there not to solve them and not to find the murderer; that was his unwritten task. His name was Franz Guertner, and he was a man of no ordinary abilities. A few hundred steps away, in police headquarters, sat a colleague, also a high government official, whose official function was likewise to prosecute political murderers; but he, too, had his unwritten orders, he, too, discovered nothing. More than that, it was later proved that he had murderers directly in his service. His name was Wilhelm Frick.

But who gave the unwritten orders? Who sent out the murderers, held back the police, commanded the judges? At first this force was an *esprit de corps,* inspiring a large circle of officers, officials, and other intellectuals; not all, or even most of them — but a blood-thirsty minority which forced its will on a startled and trembling majority. They killed and lied for the German army. This army had been defeated on the battlefield; its formations had disinte-grated, its soldiers had thrown down their arms and packs, and had gone home, weary and desperate. The revolution had triumphed over the army. But the ideal lived on in the hearts of two hundred thousand officers.

A hundred and ninety thousand had been forced to doff their uniforms; but in civilian life, whether in secure positions, menial occupations, or actual want, most of them remained officers at heart. The republic reduced its army to two hundred thousand men, and the peace treaty forced them to halve this number; patri-otic revolts broke out, which in reality were the class struggles of discharged officers. In March, 1920, a *putsch* was attempted; the government had to flee from Berlin for a few days; but in a five-day general strike the German workers forced the officers to their knees. Twice, in 1918 and in 1920, the German officers' corps capitu-lated to the German workers, and this is something they will never forget.

The revolutions of the twentieth century gave rise to a new militarism. For in these revolutions the soldier rose up against the army, the armed civilian broke open the front of which he was supposed to be a part. The army as such was attacked, the army as such defended itself. It was a new kind of struggle, and from it developed a new kind of army.

On the whole, the leaders of this army were neither noble junkers nor rich men. Before the World War of 1914-18, the main body of these leaders lived modestly and without glory on meager pay, often in proud poverty. If they reached the post of lieutenant-gen-eral, they were rewarded with personal nobility, but this did not mean admission to the noble caste. If this officers' corps combated the revolution, it was not fighting for an existing social order. A professional soldier was defending his profession. It was the officers' class struggle.

The German Revolution of 1918 to 1923 was not the great experience of the German people, but it was the great experience of its officers. A strange gray terror rose from the trenches and overpowered them. They began to study this terror and turn it to their own ends. Army and revolution entered upon a struggle for the source of power in modern society: the proletariat.

The educated worker, the intellectual of the fourth estate, is the strength of present-day armies. This proletarian worker, who more and more is becoming the actual intellectual of the technical age, is the human reservoir of modern society. Any militarism which does not want to die of malnutrition is dependent on him. The modern army is an army of technicians. The army needs the worker, and that is why it fights against the revolution; not for the throne and not for the moneybags, but for itself.

The army devours the people. A fatherland rises up within the fatherland. Germany: it is no longer the soil on which Walter von der Vogelweide, Luther, or Goethe trod; it is not the Cathedral of Bamberg, the *Nibelungenlied* or the Rhine, the people on the wharves of Hamburg or the learned men of the Prussian academy of sciences; Germany is: a tank park, a line of cannon, and the gray human personnel belonging to them. 'I find,' wrote one of those two hundred thousand officers in his autobiography, 'that I no longer belong to this people. All I remember is that I once belonged to the German army.'

The words are by Ernst Röhm. This Röhm, more than any other in his circle, is the key figure we were seeking when we asked: Who sent out the murderers, who gave the judges their orders? A young officer in his mid-thirties, a captain like a thousand others, the kind who might gladly and easily disappear in the mass, he stood modestly aside in the dazzling parades where generals and marshals, personally responsible, perhaps, for the loss of the war, were applauded by a misguided patriotic youth. Röhm was only an adjutant to the chief of the infantry troops stationed in Bavaria, a certain Colonel von Epp. But from this modest post he established, in defiance of the law and against the will of every minister in Berlin and Munich, a volunteer army of a hundred thousand men, calling themselves modestly the *Einwohnerwehr* (citizens' defense). When this armed mass was finally disbanded by orders from above, he formed new nuclei. New organizations kept springing up, with all sorts of names, under constantly changing official leaders, all having ostensibly nothing to do with the Reichswehr. Actually all were an extension of the Reichswehr, under the command of Röhm.

Röhm was a professional soldier of petty-bourgeois origin. His father was a middling railway official in Ingolstadt, Bavaria, where Ernst Röhm was born on November 28, 1887. The boy became an excellent soldier, the embodiment of personal bravery. In 1906 he joined the army, in 1908 became a lieutenant. Three times wounded in the war, he returned each time to the front. Half his nose was shot away, he had a bullet hole in his cheek; short, stocky, shot to tatters, and patched, he was the outward image of a freebooter captain. He was more a soldier than an officer. In his memoirs he condemns the cowardice, sensuality, and other vices of many comrades; his revelations were almost treason against his own class.

A gigantic arsenal had been left behind by the fallen German army. In the peace treaty Germany had promised to destroy it. The Allies supervised the process by control commissions, sitting in the large cities of Germany and traveling through the country. These arms had to be saved. In Bavaria Röhm undertook this task.

He was able to persuade a few of the Allied officers that these old armored cars and rusty machine guns could be of no use in serious warfare, but would come in handy for combating the world revolution which was moving, through Germany, toward the Rhine. This strange collaboration with the Allied organs must have been very close; in his memoirs Röhm indicates as much in passing, praising certain British officers and mentioning an Italian, Major Grammacini. He succeeded in surrounding the Allied officials with a dense net of counter-spies; men wishing to report a secret arsenal were prevented from reaching the foreigners; they fell into the hands of a German, masquerading as an officer of the

Entente, who with a straight face, stammering broken German, listened to their reports, and then delivered the traitors to eager assassins.

'We will transfer them from their rascally lives to death,' Röhm used to say in such cases. 'That is the soldier's law of self-defense.' Many years later, generals might from time to time appear as witnesses before courts and parliamentary committees, raise their right hands and swear that they had known nothing of the murders, and had no idea who the murderers were. The job was done by Röhm and his henchmen, the Heineses, Neunzerts, Schweikharts, and Ballys — to mention only a few of all those who have been half or totally forgotten. He was not the only such leader in the Reich. There was Lieutenant Rossbach in Pomerania, Captain von Pfeffer in the Ruhr; there was Captain Ehrhardt who marched through the whole of Germany with his armed band, and at the height of his career instigated the *putsch* which was stifled by the general strike. Röhm was more conscious of his goal than any of the others; his career was the most successful, his end the most tragic.

In any case, it was the officers of middle rank, captains, or at most majors, who relieved the generals of their responsibility, ostensibly without their knowledge, often actually against their will. They shoved their generals aside, in the end openly combated them, and during the whole period grimly despised them for their cowardice and inertia. The officers' class struggle became the struggle of the lower against the higher officers. When the German Republic disbanded the army, more generals retained their posts than the English army has in peacetime; those who were discharged received pensions they could live on. The well-paid generals became easily reconciled to the republic; they were not grateful enough to admit it openly, nor courageous enough to deny it. But the lieutenants and captains saw no place for advancement in the tiny army of a hundred thousand men; they saw themselves reduced to the level of armed élite proletarians; many, with no official position at all, marched through the land at the head of mercenary bands, subsidized by heavy industrialists and landowners to protect their factories or estates from the specter of communist revolution.

This seemed the end of the lordly life to which the German intellectual youth had grown accustomed during the war. Their school course had been broken off ahead of time; their examinations had been made easy for them. After a short period of active service, they were sent to an officers' training course and soon they were lieutenants with a monthly salary of three hundred gold marks. It was a dangerous existence, but one full of pride and pleasure. The material level of life was high enough to permit of a hard fall, when, as Röhm put it, 'peace broke out.' He adds in his autobiography: 'Since I am an immature and bad man, war appeals to me more than peace.' But peace had come.

These armed intellectuals were the German army, they preserved its spirit, upheld its tradition. Even before the First World War, it had ceased to be the army of Prussian junkers, which foreigners held it to be. Its most brilliant mind, its leader in the World War, was Erich Ludendorff, a man of bourgeois origin, like most of the important German generals in the World War, such as von Mackensen, von Kluck, Groener, Max Hoffmann, Scheer. When the Kaiser offered him nobility, Ludendorff declined, saying he wished to bear the same name as his father. Since the broad mass of the lower officers gives an army its character, the German Army of the World War could be called an army of armed students. And since these intellectuals in uniform found no career and no bread in the breakdown after the peace, their officer days remained for many the high point of their existence; the hope for a return of the golden days remained their secret consolation.

Among these bright-colored, though plucked birds, Röhm was conspicuous by his simplicity; he had the nature of a leader, not of an aristocrat. This freebooter captain was inspired by an almost worshipful love for his subordinates; he was the type of superior officer who lives and dies for his troop and is constantly fighting his superior officers in their behalf. 'Respect and affection for your subordinate, not the praise of your superior, is the highest ideal,' he wrote as a young lieutenant. In general, obedience was not his strong point. 'The thinking subordinate is the natural enemy of his superior,' is another of his maxims.

And this fatherly soldier was a homosexual murderer.

We shall not go into the apparent contradictions in Röhm's

nature. He was the secret head of a band of murderers. For his arsenal, he had men killed without the slightest qualm. In his inconspicuous position, he spent four years in Bavaria, secretly building up an army; or, more accurately, he kept building up new armies, for this secret army often disbanded. It was scattered by commands from above, torn by internal struggles. It allowed itself to be used for different purposes by political leaders who the next day abandoned them. But somehow Röhm always kept his army in hand, for he disposed of the arms and maintained a bloody guard over them.

It was this atmosphere that led him personally astray. Many sections of this secret army of mercenaries and murderers were breeding places of perversion. One of these was Rossbach's free corps. Rossbach and his adjutant, Heines, seem to have brought Röhm to the path which ultimately led to his destruction.

It is no contradiction that this misled leader should have been attached to his soldiers and thought more about them than most of his comrades did. Röhm was the type of officer who fights with the revolution for the soldier's soul. He grasped the great truth that the new army should not destroy the revolution but use it. 'The revolutionary school of communism prepares the German worker for the struggle for national freedom,' he writes. He never wearies of praising the communists and their military qualities. Once he had him in his company, he assures us, he could turn the reddest communist into a glowing nationalist in four weeks.

The future workers' army passes through the school of civil war. These freebooters do not complain about the inner conflict in their fatherland. There are too many soft and rotten elements among the people, wipe them out! Röhm calls them the 'philistines,' and by that he means everything mediocre: in spirit, in passion, in possessions; sometimes he seems to mean everyone who has a family. He praises the have-nots without office and property, the raw warriors. They are the stuff the new army needs, for the new army must wage war in Germany, to wean the workers from the parties.

To this end, Röhm founded the National Socialist German Workers' Party. It might be said to have existed before him, first under the simpler name of the German Workers' Party. But that was a club, sitting in the back rooms of little restaurants, talking. At all events, a mere idea. And an idea it remained until the club, seeking to win over the German workers, became the party of soldiers. This was Röhm's work. He discovered the club, joined it—an officer among workers! And not he alone. With commands he forced his soldiers, with pleas he drove his comrades into it. Thus the party became a political troop. Whole Reichswehr companies marched through the streets in civilian clothes as National Socialists! Thus arose the formation which later, as the SA, became the basic party formation.

They hunted down the Jews and beat them. Were they not the Black Hundreds of southern Russia, risen from the dead after fifteen years? At all events, they employed the same methods. They thought the same thoughts; for all these soldiers had read *The Protocols of the Wise Men of Zion,* or read about them at least. And, indeed, they were practically the same men.

A colony of Russian émigrés—aristocrats, generals, industrialists, scholars, artists, students—had settled in Munich as in almost every other big city throughout the world. They stood as martyrs of the great Bolshevik terror which kept the post-war world a-tremble, and made Europe skip a heartbeat when in 1920 a Bolshevik army appeared before Warsaw and nearly changed the course of history.

From this Russian legion, Rosenberg stepped forward. With his new friends of the Thule Society, with Dietrich Eckart, with Rudolf Hess, with an engineer named Gottfried Feder, he approached the German Workers' Party. First he delivered lectures about the Wise Men of Zion, the Jewish peril, the Jewish wirepullers behind Bolshevism. This was still a far cry from an organized party. Rosenberg repeated the same lectures before a dozen similar groups and grouplets, all in obscure back rooms and small beer halls. But then Röhm sent in his soldiers from the other side. The grouplet became a piece of that German Reichswehr which then was a gigantic political party under arms, though without a program and without a leader.

Rosenberg supplied the program. It had already been tested, the idea of the Wise Men of Zion had gripped millions throughout the world. Rosenberg pointed eastward. From Russia the Antichrist was sending forth his new armies, after moving his cannon to the Rhine under the tricolor of France.

The German Army was undergoing a revolution, a profound spiritual and physical metamorphosis. The impact upon this army of a foreign, supra-national world policy, conceived in gigantic Russian images, gave birth to the great movement which has been known ever since as National Socialism. A captain from the German provinces and a Russo-German student had to meet before the power of Germany and the world-embracing fantasy of the East could combine into an explosive mixture. Personally Röhm always rejected Rosenberg's distant perspectives and probably never took them seriously. 'Europe and the rest of the world,' he says, 'can perish in flames. What is that to us? Germany must live and be free.' Such a sentiment is the antithesis of any broad world policy. From the outset the two men sensed that they were foreign to one another; they hated one another throughout their collaboration. But their work was stronger than they.

The Röhm type surely did not recognize the ironical textbook of world domination in the *Protocols*. To him it sufficed that it was an effective pamphlet against the Jews. The defeated German officers' corps needed such a book. For an army that wants to maintain its prestige among the people must not be defeated. For forty years this army had been trained to defeat the French; it could not accustom itself to failure. The *Protocols* offered consolation: 'It was not the French who defeated us but the Jews.'

At all times and among all nations, crafty and strong personalities have recognized the simple secret of rule by violence. Four hundred years ago, an Italian gave it the theoretical form which today seems to us the most valid. A Frenchman adapted these thoughts to the modern age. But it took a band of Russian conspirators to transform the theories into a practical program. And in Germany the program was to be consciously applied for the first time. German officers took the idea of world domination seriously.

Those who wish to transform the world must be able to transform themselves. Every real revolutionary deed begins with one's own person. After his last unsuccessful *putsch* in 1923, General Ludendorff, for long years the idol and leader of all national revolutionary movements in Germany, said in court: 'Events have taught me, and it pains me to own, that the leading stratum of our society is incapable of giving the German people the will to freedom.'

Röhm says it more simply: 'Only he who is without possessions has ideals.'

A broken people, a broken army, broken men. The new movement rises out of wreckage. Ideals had to fall into the mire, destinies to be shattered, characters to sicken, before something new could be born. For this thing was new, and from the very beginning it was frightful. Rosenberg lost his home, Röhm his people; the type which now fell in with them, bringing them their greatest strength, had nothing to lose.

The gilded troop met in feebly lighted beer halls, smelling of cold smoke. Officers became conspirators. And they were no longer alone — that was the decisive factor. Now they were with workers. Not with the main body of the workers, with the mighty masses from the factories, but with the flotsam, the stragglers living on the fringe of their class, the workers at odd jobs and the unemployed. The declassed of all classes came together; those of the upper and the lower classes made common cause. In all times this has been the way of counter-revolution: an upper layer that has lost its hold in society seeks the people and finds the rabble. The officers were out to find a demagogue, of whom it could be said that he was a worker. They would cry out to him: Leader, command us, we shall follow.

In their class struggle the officers were forced by circumstances to create a workers' army; they found their leader in the lowest mass of their subordinates, and commanded him to command. The spirit of history, in its fantastic mockery, could not have drawn an apter figure. It was the man who had sent his comrades to the slaughterhouse wall after the overthrow of the Munich soviet. A human nothing, a gray personality even among soldiers, 'modest and for that very reason inconspicuous,' as a superior has characterized him; not even a German, but a homeless derelict from the Viennese melting-pot. The army in which he was a soldier was charged with energy, laden with possibilities, but he descended to the most dubious level, that of *agent-provocateur;* even in that field he was no leader, but an unsavory tool of the political counter-espionage; an *homme de main,* entrusted with necessary but loathsome tasks; happy when he could obey and, by his own admission, knowing no higher goal than 'to follow his superior blindly and contradict no one.' His exterior was without distinguishing marks, his face without radiance; there was nothing unusual in his bearing. He was one of those men without qualities, normal and colorless to the point of invisibility. They can be forgotten beneath the broadest spotlight, even while they are present. The void, it might be said, had disguised itself as a man.

The leadership of the new military party in Munich was given over to this human object. The officers wanted a tool. They sent him through the country on speaking tours, used him in their press bureau to write releases, sent him into political meetings to hear what he could hear. At length, as propagandist orator for the German Workers' Party, he seemed to have found his niche in the world. He was a man of the people, at home amid the most sordid poverty, hence familiar with the heart of the poor. To speak in the language of his employers, accustomed to the military trade and embarrassed in the presence of the people: that trap of his will come in handy.

For in this unlikely looking creature there dwelt a miracle: his voice. It was something unexpected. Between those modest, narrow shoulders, the man had lungs. His voice was the very epitome of power, firmness, command, and will. Even when calm, it was a guttural thunder; when agitated, it howled like a siren betokening inexorable danger. It was the roar of inanimate nature, yet accompanied by flexible human overtones of friendliness, rage, or scorn.

The contradiction between the lamentable appearance and the mighty voice characterizes the man. He is a torn personality; long reaches of his soul are insignificant, colored by no noteworthy qualities of intellect or will; but there are corners supercharged with strength. It is this association of inferiority and strength that makes the personality so strange and fascinating.

Adolf Hitler, the man, is portrayed here as most of his contemporaries and many of his own supporters saw him in his beginnings; and the picture is basically true. As a human figure, lamentable; as a political mind, one of the most tremendous phenomena of all world history — this is a contradiction which occurs in every man of genius, from the stuttering Moses to Bonaparte, the strange, unglamorous artillery captain; but few of those historic figures united so many contradictions, such lack of distinction, and such superhuman strength.

Chapter III

'HE IS BOTH TERRIBLE

AND BANAL'

ADOLF HITLER CAME FROM A REGION ON THE north shore of the Danube, about fifty miles above Vienna, an impoverished out-of-the-way section. His father was the illegitimate son of a poor peasant girl. The family relations, so restricted as to border on incest, may be somewhat clarified by the accompanying genealogical chart. It shows how the present form of the name Hitler developed comparatively recently from a medley of different sounds and spellings. There are Jewish Hitlers, though the name is rather rare. This has led to a search for a Jewish strain in Adolf Hitler. There is no proof, however; all the facts and internal evidence at our disposal argue against the idea.

Adolf Hitler's maternal line is settled and stable. From its first appearance the name remains unchanged in the form of Pölzl, and down to Hitler's mother the family stayed four generations on peasant holding Number 37 in the village of Spital. The paternal line, however, is unsettled almost to the point of vagrancy. The spelling of the name varies; and the residence changes three times in three generations: Walterschlag, Spital, Strones, Leonding; and the lives of the individuals show a deep unrest.

Johann Georg Hiedler, grandfather of the future chancellor, wandered without steady residence through Lower Austria, in one place leasing a mill, in another officially inscribed as an 'unemployed

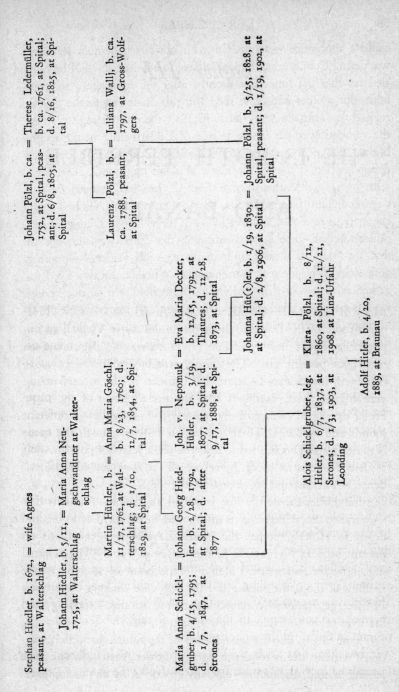

miller's apprentice' — an artisan with obvious bohemian leanings, wandering from one small, poor village to another. In 1824 he married for the first time; five months after the marriage a son was born, but mother and child died (all this according to the church registers). Thirteen years later, in 1837, the church registers find the wandering miller in the village of Döllersheim. In the neighboring village of Strones, Anna Marie Schicklgruber, a peasant's daughter, bore a son by the name of Alois on June 7, 1837. Five years later, in 1842, this woman, now 47 years old, married the still vagrant Johann Georg Hiedler, now a man of fifty, who had again changed his residence and was living in the village of Dürenthal as a miller's helper. The laconic entries in the church registers are all that we know of these grandparents of Adolf Hitler — supposing both sides to be his real grandparents. Whether the two lived together as man and wife and kept a household, we do not know; we are rather inclined to suppose the contrary. After the death of his wife (1847), the vagrant miller vanishes for three whole decades. For many years Alois, the son, did not legally bear the name of Johann Georg Hiedler, but his mother's maiden name of Schicklgruber.

Alois Schicklgruber grew up in the village of Spital in the house of a brother of Georg Hiedler's. The name of this brother is written as Hütler; and in accordance with the local custom conferring even the strangest names from the holy calendar in full, this uncle and foster-father of Alois was called: Johann von Nepomuk Hütler. Johann von Nepomuk is the national saint of the Czech people; this indicates a possible Czech strain in Adolf Hitler's forebears, who actually did reside in a German-Czech border section. In this Johann von Nepomuk Hütler we observe a trait which sharply distinguishes him from his brother: while Johann Georg seems to have lived without discipline and done pretty much as he pleased, never settling down or assuming any firm ties, Johann von Nepomuk, after leaving his native Walterschlag, married a peasant girl fifteen years older than himself in the village of Spital and remained a peasant in Spital till the end of his life.

It was here that Alois Schicklgruber spent his childhood. He learned the shoemaker's trade from a relative by the name of Ledermüller. A little anecdote has come down to us which characterizes the temperament of the whole family: one day in a rage the young man threw his change purse out of the window. It contained his whole pocket money consisting of a kreuzer. If he didn't have any more money than that, he cried out, he didn't need the kreuzer either.

It will probably be impossible to find out whose son he was considered by those who knew or should have known; but in the eyes of the village he apparently passed as a child of the Hiedler or Hütler family. To judge by his character as we see it in the meager documents, it is probable that the odd man who wandered about Lower Austria as a miller's helper actually was the grandfather of the odd man who later became a scourge and mystery to the world. It has also been suggested that not Georg Hiedler but his brother, Johann von Nepomuk Hütler, was the father of Alois Schicklgruber, and thus the grandfather of Adolf Hitler. This is an hypothesis defying proof. But there is one curious fact which cannot be argued away: the later National Socialist racial legislation requires everyone desiring to pass as an Aryan to prove four Aryan grandparents; if brought before strict judges, Adolf Hitler might have difficulty proving the identity of his paternal grandfather.

The young Alois Schicklgruber does not seem to have been happy in his home. Apparently he was not treated as a legitimate child and was without expectation of inheritance. His son later related that his father left his native village fully determined not to return 'until he had made something of himself.' This 'something,' in accordance with small peasants' conceptions, was a profession of command: the police career. At eighteen he became a border policeman in the Austrian customs service near Salzburg. He guarded the national border and hunted smugglers — in a word, he became a man-hunter. An honorable profession, but scarcely friendly to man. In many countries it is the children of poor, out-of-the-way country sections who, from inborn hardness and contempt of humanity, choose the police profession. This illegitimate son of a small peasant took up his rifle and stalked the borders for human prey. The people in his native village must have looked on him with timid amazement when they first saw him in his shiny gold buttons, stamped with the imperial two-headed eagle, his pistol at his belt. The records show a young border patrol-man: 'Alois Schicklgruber, surnamed Hitler.' At the age of twenty-seven he was well enough established to found a family. Eleven days after his promotion, in 1864, he married Anna Glasl-Hörer, adoptive daughter of a customs collector — distinctly a higher station in life. She brought him some money and was fourteen years his elder — he was twenty-seven, she forty-one years; the same pattern as with his foster-father (or father?), Johann von Nepomuk Hütler: marriage to a wealthier, much older girl. The woman was sickly and bore him no children; in 1880, after sixteen years, the marriage was dissolved — in so far as this was possible according to the law of Catholic Austria. Three years later, the woman died of tubercu-losis at the age of sixty, when her husband was forty-six. Alois Schicklgruber spent sixteen years of this unfertile and presumably melancholy marriage as a customs official in Braunau am Inn, a little city on the German-Austrian border. According to the accounts of contemporaries, he must have been an impressive personality in his way, 'hungry for education and well versed in words and letters'; his wife's means, it seems, had procured the ill-paid official the luxury of books and travel.

Apparently convinced that he had 'made something of himself,' he resumed, after his marriage, relations with his 'native village.' Johann von Nepomuk Hütler was still alive. All parties may have reckoned with the approaching end of Alois Schicklgruber-Hitler's first wife. Johann von Nepomuk's daughter, Johanna, who was married to a certain Pölzl, bore him in 1860 a granddaughter by the name of Klara; for Alois Schicklgruber-Hitler this child was the daughter of a cousin — and conceivably, if rumors are correct, the daughter of a half-sister, hence a niece. His own marriage was childless and so he took little Klara into his house in place of a daughter.

The developments in the internal relations of this family can only be presumed; but these presumptions are based upon events which really took place — though years later. We can assume that Schickl-gruber's marriage with the sick woman fourteen years older than himself finally ceased to be a marriage; and that, as he approached his forties, the man slowly conceived the idea of taking his growing foster-daughter as a wife as soon as his first wife should die — which was to be expected in a reasonable time. In the Austrian law of those days, a separation would not have allowed remarriage, but death made it possible and legitimate. It is conceivable that all concerned were agreed on the question and probable that Klara's parents and grandparents expected this solution. Many years later, Alois Schicklgruber told a friend that Johann von Nepomuk Hütler — that is, his own foster-father and at the same time Klara's grandfather — had wanted to mention him, Alois Schicklgruber, in his will; but had demanded that it be established beyond any doubt that Alois was legally entitled to bear the name of Hütler, or Hiedler, or Hitler — as the names of brothers and sisters, fathers and sons, sometimes in fact the name of one and the same person, appear in the carelessly kept church registers. This change of name and the matter of the will fall in the year when Klara Pölzl became sixteen.

Whoever Alois Schicklgruber-Hitler's natural father may have been, it was definite that Georg Hiedler married his mother in 1842. And thus the vagrant miller's helper rises again from obscurity. This event is mentioned in a few existing documents, of which the most interesting is a memorandum of the Diocesan Court of Sankt Poelten (Lower Austria) of March 29, 1932. As the Bishop's archives show, an old man who called himself Georg Hitler — hence no longer Hiedler — appeared before the notary in the little city of Weitra on June 6, 1876. But according to his statement, he was one and the same man to whom the peasant maid, Maria Anna Schicklgruber, had in 1837 borne the illegitimate son, Alois, and the same who five years later had married the mother, but had forgotten to recognize Alois expressly as his son. At the age of eighty-four, he now declared to the notary, in the presence of three witnesses by the name of Rameder, Breiteneder, and Pautsch, that he was the father of the illegitimate child, Alois Schicklgruber, born on June 7, 1837. Why he had failed to legitimize Alois when marrying his mother does not appear from the records. Under what circumstances he did so in 1876, what sort of life Georg Hiedler-Hitler was then leading, on what terms he was with his son, and what occasioned this tardy legitimation are also absent from the records. The act of legitimation went into actual force in the parish office at Döllersheim whither Georg Hiedler-Hitler's declaration to the notary was sent from Weitra. In Döllersheim on November 23, 1876, Josef Zahnschirm, the parish priest, in a rather irregular form which later gave rise to doubts, changed Alois Schicklgruber's name to Alois Hitler in the baptismal record. Legally the whole occurrence was the repetition of an act which should have occurred when the marriage was concluded in 1842; in the official language of the Austrian Church it was called: *'legitimatio per matrimonium subsequens.'*

Thus, from 1876 on, Adolf Hitler's father bore the name of Hitler; the future chancellor was thus entitled to his name from birth. Georg Hiedler acknowledged paternity in legally adequate form; and Alois actually bore this name during most of his life. His famous son, Adolf Hitler himself, was never called Schicklgruber. The obscure spot in his ancestry indicates in all likelihood not a strain of outside, hence conceivably foreign origin, but an incestuous mixture within his own family. The degree of this incest can only be surmised.

Apparently the ailing life of Alois Schicklgruber-Hitler's first wife dragged on much longer than her husband had expected. He took up relations with a young hotel cook by the name of Franziska Matzelsberger, and this broke up his marriage and family. His wife obtained a separation in accordance with the Austrian 'bed-and-board' law of the time, and moved into a dwelling of her own; his relation with Klara Pölzl was also severed; the twenty-year-old girl left the house and went to Vienna as a servant. Alois Hitler lived with his new wife in a relation similar to marriage; she bore him, during the lifetime of his first wife, a son, whom he likewise called Alois. When his first wife at last died in 1883, he married the second; after a few months she bore him a daughter named Angela. After a marriage of one year, in 1884, this second wife died, also of tuberculosis.

In the last months of her life she, too, moved away from her husband. Klara Pölzl reappeared and kept house for Alois Hitler — her stepfather or fiancé. Half a year after the death of his second wife, on January 7, 1885, Alois Hitler married his third: his ward, twenty-three years younger than himself.

In the first marriage, a young man of twenty-seven had married a woman fourteen years his senior; now, at the age of forty-eight, he took a wife twenty-three years younger than he. According to church law, it was a marriage between relatives ('collateral relationship of the third degree, bordering on the second'). An episcopal dispensation was necessary for the marriage. This marriage resulted in five children, three of whom died at an early age: a son, Gustav, born in 1885, died in 1887; a girl, Ida, born in 1886, died in 1888; a son, Edmund, born in 1894, died in 1900. Another daughter, Paula, born in 1896, survived, learned applied art, and later led a modest life in Vienna; the only one of Adolf Hitler's full brothers and sisters to survive. A half-brother and a half-sister, children of Franziska Matzelsberger, also survived: Angela, born in 1883, later married to an official by the name of Raubal, after his death lived in Vienna as a cook and housekeeper, and for a time worked in a Jewish charity kitchen; and the half-brother, Alois Matzelsberger, born in 1882, later legitimized as Alois Hitler. Alois, Jr., had a more than troubled life. He was a waiter by profession. In 1900, he received five months in jail for theft; in 1902, eight months, again for theft. Later he went to Germany; on March 7, 1924, the provincial court in Hamburg sentenced him to six months in prison for bigamy. Then he disappeared to England, established a family and later left it. In the thirties he opened an inn, much frequented by National Socialists, in a Berlin suburb; later he moved his establishment to one of the busiest squares in Berlin, and it became fashionable.

The family life in the house of Adolf Hitler's parents in the first years is described by acquaintances and neighbors as harmonious and friendly. An old inhabitant of Braunau, who worked as a servant girl in Alois Hitler's house, spoke of harmony reigning in the house; the sole note of unpleasantness was created by a 'haughty, lazy, and not quite normal sister of Frau Klara,' who frequently came to help out.

Could this 'unpleasantness' have been connected with the above-mentioned matter of inheritance? It might seem so, for in 1888 Alois Hitler suddenly bought a farm in the village of Wörnharts, near Weitra, and gave it to his unmarried sister-in-law, Johanna

Pölzl, to run. The farm was situated in his home village of Spital, more than a hundred miles from Braunau, his place of service. Thus Alois Schicklgruber-Hitler was apparently preparing his return to the home sod.

On April 20, 1889, at half-past six in the evening, at the Hotel zum Pommer in Braunau, another son was born, in the fifth year of his third marriage. Two days later, at a quarter after three in the afternoon, this child was baptized by the name of Adolfus. This was Alois Hitler's fourth child, the second from his marriage with Klara Pölzl. The godparents were a couple by the name of Prinz (possibly of Jewish descent) from the Löwengasse in Vienna. The little son of the Austrian border official spent his first years on German soil in the border city of Passau, not far from Braunau.

Then some quarrel must have broken out in the family and Alois Hitler abandoned the idea of returning home. He had himself transferred to Linz, the capital of Upper Austria, and there he retired on pension at the strikingly early age of fifty-eight (1895). There now began a restless period. He bought and sold farm after farm in the little townships around Linz; it looked more like land speculation than any idea of settling down. At length he established himself for the last years of his life in Leonding, a suburb of Linz.

The school reports of his son, Adolfus, have been preserved from these years. On April 2, 1895, the six-year-old entered the public school in the village of Fischlham; two years later he was sent to the cloister school at Lambach; then followed a year at public school in Leonding. His report cards from these years show only marks of 'excellent,' with an occasional exception in singing, drawing, and gymnastics.

A six-year-old boy — a sixty-year-old father. A thirty-seven year-old mother. Adolfus grew up in a violently, unnaturally divided world. To his mother — this we can feel from his own account — he was deeply devoted, and she in turn was devoted to the point of weakness to the self-reliant, stormy son. Was he self-reliant? Light and shade alternate strangely in this character. Reports of teachers, fellow pupils, and neighbors concur in their description: a big 'Indian chief,' a rough-neck, an eloquent, loud-voiced ringleader in children's games, planning a trip around the world with his comrades, bringing knives and axes to school with him; if he gets a licking from his comrades in school, he may not complain to his father, but must help himself. His own narrative again shows how he forces his will on his weak mother, lovingly uses her and exploits her — and how completely his victorious nature falls apart when he finds himself face to face with his father, whom age has made hard and stern.

His father was a short-tempered old man, grown prematurely inactive. He had fought a bitter struggle with life, had made the hardest sacrifices, and in the end things had not gone according to his will. He goes walking about Leonding, usually holding his gold-bordered velvet cap in his hand, looks after his bees, leans against the fence, chats rather laconically with his neighbors. He looks on as a friend erects a little sawmill and sourly remarks: such are the times, the little fellows are coming up, the big ones going down. His lungs are affected, he coughs and occasionally spits blood. In political conversations it develops that he 'can't stomach the Prussians': he is of extremely Austrian mind, a witness relates.

Not so his son. He was not Austrian, he was not a dutiful son, he was not loyal and obedient, he was not even very conscientiously devoted to the Catholic religion of his country; a persistent legend relates that at the age of fourteen he spat out the Host at communion in protest. Though this sacrilege has never been proved, it fits into the period and its passionate atmosphere, and jibes with the human type, enraged against the god of his fathers. An embittered rebellion against the authority of Church and State was simmering among the intellectuals of Austria, particularly in the country sections outside Vienna. The European national revolution shook the old empire for decades; the Germans of Austria also had a part in it, with their rebellious battle-cry and banner; the battle-cry was, 'Home to the Reich!' which meant, away from the Habsburgs to the new Prussian German Reich. The banner was black, red, and gold, the old German colors from the Napoleonic period, dream colors from the days when the educated classes of Germany, drunk with Hegel's world spirit, dreamed of their future state. And sometimes on the black, red, and gold background a strange sign appeared; a kind of wheel with an axial cross in the middle, but the circle is cut in four places so that four scythe blades seem to swing in a circle around the cross. Anyone who sees this strange shape involuntarily recognizes the Swastika.

This movement was closely related to a second one, the battle-cry of which was '*Los von Rom!*' (Away from Rome!) It was the same rhythm as '*Heim ins Reich*' (Home to the Reich). And that was exactly what it meant. It was a spiritual uprising against the Pope in Rome, but at the same time a rebellion against the Catholic Emperor in Vienna, his 'Apostolic Majesty,' the old man who, on Corpus Christi, walked in the procession with a candle in his hand. These German intellectuals in Austria were rising against the Italian Vicar of God in the foreign country beyond the mountains and against the emperor of the Czechs, Poles, and Hungarians. Sunday after Sunday, German and Czech students fought in Prague, and in the German provincial cities of the empire bands of students, encouraged by a part of their professors, marched through the streets with black, red, and gold caps and insignia; in Linz, for example, they paraded across the Franz Josef's Platz and the Landstrasse. 'I, too, bore the black, red, and gold insignia and was often beaten for it,' Hitler later related.

Beaten by whom? By political adversaries? Only by them? It seems that he was beaten by his father, too. He himself hints that this occurred in the struggle over his future profession. But his father's image runs like a dark shadow through his whole self-portrait; an authority which always harshly intervened when contradicted. This father had been proud to be an Austrian official and he wanted his son to be an Austrian official, too. But his son wanted to be a painter.

Why a painter? Was Hitler a visual mind? At the end of the nineteenth century, the painter or the poet was a kind of king; the Renaissance figures of the poet-prince and the royal artist dominated society. Makart in Vienna, and Lenbach in Munich — two painters little known abroad and by now half forgotten in their own country — were in their time more impressive rulers than the true princes, giving laws to society and form to human lives, and in return receiving fame and earthly goods in abundance. Young

Adolf Hitler wanted to become something of this sort. The sharp, suspicious paternal eye may have penetrated the lack of seriousness of the youthful plan and wanted to anchor his son's frivolous mind in a serious profession.

This was the source of the fights between father and son — this, and probably all the other conflicts which can create strife between a twelve-year-old son and a father of sixty-four. It was Adolf Hitler's first great struggle, and by his own admission he conducted it with great fears, with lies and secretiveness, and with a degree of scheming that was almost suicidal. The struggle was not exactly glorious, but it did bring some success: ' . . . since, of course, I drew the short end, the old gentleman began the relentless enforcement of his authority. In the future, therefore, I was silent . . . ' He avoided blows. And why not, he reflected twenty-five years later: 'I had, to some extent, been able to keep my private opinions to myself; I did not always have to contradict him immediately. My own firm determination never to become a civil servant sufficed to give me complete inner peace.' He did not always have to contradict immediately! He fought his father with lies and trickery; but this does not seem to have been clear to the mature Adolf Hitler when he inscribed the story of his childhood in pages full of self-praise and self-pity at the beginning of *Mein Kampf*. He decided, so he tells us, to punish his father by becoming frivolous and lazy: 'What gave me pleasure I learned; what . . . was otherwise unattractive to me, I sabotaged completely.' Perhaps this is true; it is certainly true that his brilliant beginnings in school were soon reversed. In 1900, he entered a secondary school in Linz, and in the very first year made such a poor showing that he was not promoted. To judge by his son's story, the father must have been greatly grieved. One son was already in prison, and now the second was doing badly. But his weak mother took the son with the disquieting good-for-nothing propensities under her protection.

On the morning of January 3, 1903, shortly before ten o'clock, Alois Hitler suddenly collapsed in the street while taking his morning walk. A friend found him and brought him to a near-by inn, the hostess ran into the kitchen for wine and water, blood filled his mouth, and Alois died quickly and peacefully in the arms of his neighbor, Ransmaier. The Leonding death records report: 'Died suddenly of pulmonary hemorrhage.' Later his son sadly accused himself: 'His most ardent desire had been to help his son forge his career, thus preserving him from his own bitter experience. In this, to all appearances, he had not succeeded.' Alois Hitler died in melancholy doubts concerning the future of his son.

When Alois Hitler died, it seemed as though his line — rich in uncommonly strong temperaments and characters, violently bursting forth from narrow circumstances and striving upward — had fallen into sudden decadence. Children upon children — but most of them had died, and most of the others had turned out badly. The sudden shift into city life seemed to be bad for these small peasants.

The 'Waldviertel' in Lower Austria, from which both the Hitler and Pölzl families came, is a gloomy, remote, impoverished section; like many such regions, it has no lack of superstitions and ghost stories. The ancestors were mostly poor peasant people; 'small cottager' often stands in the church registers. Then comes the strange break in the series with the gypsy-like character of Georg Hiedler, the grandfather; a break which continues in the person of Alois Schicklgruber-Hitler and drives his children in turn on the most unusual and varied paths. In a picture, old Alois Hitler strikingly resembles the aged Field-Marshal Hindenburg; not only the same mustache, but also the same lurking eyes, the same cheeks, mouth, and chin; the head represents the same unmistakable square. There must have been something avid and speculative in the man who in his old age sold farm after farm, and in his youth had married a well-to-do woman fourteen years older than himself — a case which occurs no less than three times in Adolf Hitler's ancestry.

A lavish yet destructive vitality dominates the paternal line. Children appear and die *en masse*. The number of Alois Hitler's legitimate children is seven, only four survive; but already, with regard to Georg Hiedler, the meager data permit all possible suppositions in addition to his legal offspring. The striking mortality in the third marriage indicates a predisposition to weakness, originating perhaps in the mother's blood; her picture shows a young woman of delicate type. The same sickness creeps strangely through the whole family: Alois Hitler's first and second wife die of consumption, he too succumbs to a lung ailment.

Is any other hereditary taint discernible? Certainly neither Georg nor Alois Hitler was mentally balanced; both clearly bordered on the abnormal. A sister of Adolf Hitler's mother is characterized by a neighbor as 'lazy and not quite normal.' A son from Alois Schicklgruber-Hitler's second marriage turned out to be a black sheep. Eccentricities enough for one family; yet they suffice only to cast a somewhat sharper light on the picture of Adolf Hitler as we already know it.

With the death of Alois Hitler the family begins to disintegrate. Brother Alois already has his prison terms behind him, and perhaps his father in dying feared that Adolf had his ahead of him. And Adolf for the moment did little to dispel such a concern. He was now free from the paternal discipline, and his mother offered no resistance. He spent five more years with her in 'downy softness' and 'in the hollowness of comfortable life' — in his own story there is a note of smugness in his self-reproaches. He changed his school, attended a secondary school in the near-by city of Steyr; his laziness remained unchanged. His last school report for the fourth class of the *Staatsrealschule* in Steyr, issued on September 16, 1905, may give an approximate picture of Adolf Hitler, the scholar:

	First Semester	Second Semester
Moral conduct	satisfactory	satisfactory
Diligence	unequal	adequate
Religion	adequate	satisfactory
German language	inadequate	adequate
Geography and history	adequate	satisfactory
Mathematics	inadequate	satisfactory
Chemistry	adequate	adequate
Physics	satisfactory	adequate
Geometry and geometrical		inadequate*
drawing	adequate	adequate**
Free-hand drawing	laudable	excellent
Gymnastics	excellent	excellent
Stenography	inadequate	....
Singing	....	satisfactory
External form of written work	displeasing	displeasing

* Repetitive examination permitted. ** In consequence of repetitive examination.

It would surely be meaningless to draw up a case against Adolf
Hitler, the 'poor scholar.' We desire only to know how this
strange soul gathered the brutal strength which it later poured forth
on the world. All the documents and personal records indicate
that during the first thirty years of his life this power lay positively
dormant. He took fright at the thought of work, bent aside like a
feeble stream in the face of obstacles, hid from any serious responsibility beneath a beggarly existence. If we look into his laziness, it seems to have concealed fear of his fellow men; he feared
their judgment and hence shunned doing anything which he would
have had to submit to their judgment. Perhaps his childhood
furnishes an explanation. The data at our disposal show Adolf
Hitler to be a model case for psychoanalysis, one of whose main
theories is that every man wants to murder his father and marry
his mother. Adolf Hitler hated his father, and not only in his subconscious; by his insidious rebelliousness he may have brought him
to his grave a few years before his time; he loved his mother deeply,
and himself said that he had been a 'mother's darling.' Constantly
humiliated and corrected by his father, receiving no protection
against the mistreatment of outsiders, never recognized or appreciated, driven into a lurking silence — thus, as a child, early sharpened by hard treatment, he seems to have grown accustomed to the
idea that right is always on the side of the stronger; a dismal conviction from which people often suffer who as children did not find
justice in the father who should have been the natural source of
justice. It is a conviction for all those who love themselves too
much and easily forgive themselves every weakness; never are their
own incompetence and laziness responsible for failures, but always
the injustice of the others.

In any case the outward circumstances are not responsible. The
young Adolf Hitler had sufficient material means for an adequate
education, provided he lived modestly. After his father's death, his
mother lived with her two children, Adolf and Paula, in simple
but comfortable circumstances in the suburb of Urfahr, near Linz.
For three years Adolf worried his way through school, sullen and
unsuccessful; his tuition was paid regularly by relatives in Spital,
no attempt was made to obtain a scholarship. At the age of sixteen,

the young man fell violently ill with a lung ailment, his schooling was broken off, and the patient sent to Spital, his mother's home village, to recover; there he lived with his aunt, Theresa Schmidt, a peasant woman. He was described at that period as a big, pale, lean youth. A Doctor Karl Keiss, from near-by Weitra, treated him and said to his Aunt Theresa: 'Adolf will never be healthy after this sickness.' Yet his father, from whom he had inherited the predisposition, had lived to be sixty-six with the same disease.

Whether it was his sickness or his constant lack of success in his studies — in any case in September, 1905, Adolf managed to leave school ahead of time without any final examination. Then follows an episode which — like many others — for unclear reasons he conceals in his autobiography: in the fall of the same year, 1905, he went to Germany for a few months, his first visit. In Munich he attended a private art school in Blütenstrasse, directed by a Professor Gröber, and studied drawing. Photographs from this time have been preserved, showing a sickly figure with a soft, round, smallish head; the nose and eyes and even the famous hair lock are unmistakable, however. According to accounts of fellow pupils, he was quiet, reserved, almost shy; but occasionally there were outbreaks in which he made much noise and fuss. He spoke much with his hands, and the short, angular, brusque motions of his head were conspicuous — characteristics which were noticed a few years later by comrades in Vienna.

But he spent most of the time at home, doing absolutely nothing. In Linz he was often in the house of a comrade whose father was a high government official. Here he found a well-equipped library, discovered Richard Wagner's prose writings, read the master's thundering accusation against the *Jews in Music,* his gloomy views on *Decay and Regeneration.* Perhaps it was then that Wagner's picturesque condemnation of meat-eating made its first impression on him, and perhaps also his doctrine that the whole of history has been a tragedy of the noble races; yet Hitler denies having known anything about anti-Semitism in Linz. There was a daughter in the house; the young man admired her in silence but ventured no utterance. For, he later told a friend in Vienna, she was the daughter of a high official, and his father had been only

a middle customs officer; on the whole he was somewhat surprised
that these people admitted him, the poor boy, to their house.

After October, 1907, he lived in Vienna, supported by his mother
and other relatives, preparing himself to attend the Academy of
Fine Arts and for the rest enjoying the city in his own boyish way:
theater, museums, parliament. He registered with the Vienna
police, sometimes as a student and sometimes as a painter. Once
he indicated that he 'was studying to be a writer.'

To gain admission to the Academy's school of painting, one had
to submit a number of drawings. If they were halfway acceptable,
the candidate had to take an examination in drawing which was
held each year in October. Freshly arrived from his province,
young Adolf, apparently with great self-confidence, headed straight
for his goal; the result was shattering and unexpected. The classification list of the Academy for the school year 1907-08 contains the
following entry:

> Composition exercises in drawing. First day: expulsion from
> paradise, etc. Second day: episode from the deluge, etc. . . . The
> following took the test with insufficient results, or were not ad-
> mitted: . . . Adolf Hitler, Braunau a. Inn, April 20, 1889, German,
> Catholic. Father civil servant. 4 classes in Realschule. Few heads.
> Test drawing unsatisfactory.

He was rejected. He does not seem to have mentioned this failure at home; in his autobiography he passes it over in complete
silence. He remained in Vienna as an art student, rejected but still
self-confident, lodging in attics looking out on palaces; certainly
despising the teachers who had failed to appreciate him; measuring
the imperial city of Vienna with the eye of a conqueror. For he
did not give up, but prepared to begin anew, the royal artist still
unrecognized, scorned, and insulted, but confident that victory
would come. Thus began his struggle against the city of Vienna;
after his struggle with his father, his second big conflict with life.

For the first year he lived on the money sent to him by his mother
and relatives and practiced drawing. Then, in October, 1908,
another examination at the Academy's School of Painting; the result was even more crushing. This time the classification list reads
simply:

> The following gentlemen performed their test drawings with in-sufficient success or were not admitted to the test: . . . 24. Adolf Hitler, Braunau, a. I. Twentieth of April, 1889. German, Catholic, civil servant, 4 Realschulein. Not admitted to the test.

In other words, the drawings he had brought were of such a nature that the examiners did not regard a test as necessary.

This was the second and final rejection. It was such a blow that even in his own account he could not pass it over in silence. According to his version, he went to the director of the Academy and asked the reasons for his rejection; the director allegedly told him that his drawings showed him to be much better suited for architecture and advised him to apply for admission to the Architectural School. But the road to this Architectural School, Hitler goes on to say, was closed to him because it required a high-school diploma, and this he did not have.

At that time perhaps he felt something akin to consciousness of guilt. He had dodged this diploma, had shunned work, learned nothing, and not even attempted his final school examination, but had regarded himself as an artistic genius, far above hard work and sweat. This was the same mistaken idea of genius that idlers have always had. And this was the punishment. In the judgment of these people, he was no artistic genius. They consoled him, he says, by telling him that he was gifted for architecture — yes, if he had only studied more! And even this story is not true. Hitler does not give an honest account of his failure. He could have entered Architectural School even without examination and diploma; the school regulations contained a loophole. There was a case in which examination and diploma could be disregarded: the case of 'great talent.' Did he lack confidence in this talent? Or did the professors fail to recognize it? Probably he did not even make the attempt.

At home his mother was dying of cancer of the breast. Five years previous his father had died in the conviction that his son, Adolf, was a good-for-nothing. Now the son was forced to confess to his dying mother that actually five years full of artistic dreaming and lazy floundering had led him to the edge of nothingness. On December 21, 1908, Klara Hitler died, and was buried in Leonding beside her husband. In Spital, Adolf took leave of his relatives. As his father had done, he declared to his aunt, Theresa Schmidt, that he would not return to Spital or even write until he had made something of himself. This was to require thirty years. A spoiled boy who learned nothing, achieved nothing, and could do nothing, was facing the void.

For four years he strove to prove to his relatives at home, to the haughty professors of the Academy of Art, to the heartless city of Vienna, and above all to himself, that in spite of everything Heaven had chosen him to be an artist-prince. He drew and painted — for the shopkeeper on the corner he made a poster in oil, advertising a talcum powder; a Santa Claus selling bright-colored candles, and Saint Stephen's Church over a mountain of soap. For four years he carried on these and similar anonymous art exercises with unchanging meager success. Hundreds of his art products from these days are probably still available in the houses of Vienna citizens or in tradesmen's shops — their owners unaware of their treasures. Makers of wooden furniture in those days used to attach little 'works of Art' to the backs of sofas and chairs, often a floral goddess or two little angels on a cloud. Hitler could not furnish this kind of thing; he was not able to draw a human form or even a head from nature. But sometimes, instead of the flower girls or angels, there was a view of Vienna with stiff, angular lines — and these he could make; though not directly from nature, but painfully and fussily copying from other pictures. His products are precise stereotypes, rather geometric in effect, not always with a very happy distribution of light and shade. The human figures sometimes thrown in are a total failure. They stand like tiny stuffed sacks outside the high, solemn palaces.

With such pictures he made the rounds of furniture-makers and dealers and manufacturers of picture frames, who bought his products to fill their empty frames. Some of them could remember him years later. He was always terribly unshaven, they reported, ran around in a long coat resembling a caftan. His conduct was shy, almost crawling — in his own account he calls himself 'earnest and still.' It struck one witness that he seldom looked people in the eye except when he was in 'ecstasy'; and this occurred as soon as the conversation turned to politics. Then he went up 'like a flame.' One cannot vouch for every word of these reports, but it is safe to visualize the young Adolf Hitler of those days going about like an eccentric and unkempt saint. There also are more precise reports.

A year after his mother's death, he sank into the bitterest misery. He had no more money and was obliged, in November, 1909, to give up his last real lodging, a furnished room in the Simon Denk Gasse. For a few nights he wandered around without shelter, sleeping first in cafés, then on park benches. He learned how it felt to be awakened by policemen and chased away from your bench. One night in despair he begged a well-dressed drunk for money; the drunk raised his stick and wanted to beat him. This experience deeply embittered him; later he told the story several times to comrades, who simply asked him if he didn't know better than to beg of a drunken man.

The downward path of the twenty-year-old ended in the beginning of November, 1909, in a lodging-house in the suburb of Meidling. A light blanket on a hard spring, his own clothes for a pillow, his shoes wedged beneath the leg of the bed lest they be stolen, to left and right of him his companions in misery — thus Adolf Hitler passed the next months. In the cloister of Gumpendorfer Strasse he had free soup every day; in the evening his comrades in the lodging-house gave him a piece of horse sausage or a crust of bread. When the first snow fell, he hobbled out with his sore feet a few times to shovel snow on one of the Danube bridges, but the hard work in the cold soon proved too much for him. He had no overcoat. He trudged through the snow with his comrades to the suburb of Erdberg or the district of Favoriten; there they hung around the 'warming rooms' where the homeless took refuge from the cold and found soup and bread to still their hunger. These warming rooms were a charity of Baron Königswarter, a man of Jewish origin. Occasionally Hitler stood outside the West Station, and carried travelers' suitcases for a few pennies. Then he wanted to apply for some digging work, advertised in the Favoriten section. But a newfound friend told him not to, saying that once he took to manual labor, the upward path would be very difficult. Hitler followed his advice.

The man who characterized himself by this shrewd warning was Reinhold Hanisch, later an artist; somewhat older than Hitler, he was living in the same misery, and he was an expert in the ups and downs of life. At that time he thought fit to conceal his real name, calling himself Fritz Walter. Like Hitler he had been on the downgrade for several years; but Hitler had come to a turning point. The vagabond scholar, the artist-prince of his childhood dreams, had reached the hopeless depths in which bitter self-knowledge scornfully announced to him: now nothing can help you but work. Hitler nevertheless decided not to work. This may be called character.

He himself, it is true, related that he made a living as a hodcarrier. People who knew him well at that time later expressed certainty that the sickly young man lacked the strength for hard work; a fragile little fellow whom any foreman would have sent away at once; they also said that at that time he never spoke of this work. These doubts do not suffice to refute his own version entirely, but he may at any rate have embellished it. According to his own report, if for the moment we accept it, his attempt at manual labor could only have lasted a short time. Then — and this can be seen from his own report — such quarrels arose, through his belligerence and inability to get along with the other workers, that he had to leave the job.

No, the unrecognized artist-prince did not work, and his new friend, Hanisch-Walter, only strengthened him in this determination. Wasn't his half-sister, Angela, married in Linz? Wasn't she drawing a monthly pension as the daughter of the late customs official, Alois Hitler? Adolf in his pride ('you won't hear from me until I've made something of myself') wanted no part of the money, but Hanisch, with his worldly cynicism, told him not to be foolish. He pressed him for several days, Adolf struggled, and finally gave in. A letter was sent to Linz, and at Christmas fifty kronen (about ten dollars) arrived; what a treasure in the lodging-house! Hitler had spent two months in this dreadful hole; now with his fifty kronen he moved into a 'Home for Men' in the Meldemann Strasse; also a poor dismal place. 'Only tramps, drunkards, and such spent any time in the Home for Men,' said Hanisch later, and he must have known, having spent a few months there himself; Adolf Hitler stayed on for three years.

For three years an unrecognized artist-prince. To Hanisch he confided that he was an 'academic painter.' Hanisch found this amazing and wonderful and seems to have believed that in Hitler he had made the great find of his life. It had business possibilities: pictures could always be sold, for small sums, perhaps, but it ran into money if the artist worked quickly and conscientiously. Adolf answered that he was tired and wretched, and wanted to rest. Hanisch replied with an outburst of rage: 'Lazybones, aren't you ashamed, etc.?' Yes, he could paint beautiful pictures, said Hitler, but what good was that? To whom could he sell them? He couldn't show himself anywhere as an artist, because his clothes were much too shabby. Hanisch explained that it wasn't a question of great works of art, but of modest little picture postcards which could be peddled in taverns and fairs for a few cents; the secret of this business was to work very hard and sell cheap with a big turnover. But for that, Adolf objected, you had to have a permit from the police, and he didn't have one; he would certainly be arrested and put in jail. He was looking for difficulties, and Hanisch may well have thought that the fallen artist-prince still had much to learn in the hard school of life. Just paint your little cards, he said, and let me worry about the rest. Hitler painted or rather drew his lifeless, rather dark pen-and-ink copies of the Burgtheater, or the Roman ruins in Schönbrunn Park; and Hanisch, little worried about permit or police, peddled them around in the taverns.

A profound hostility toward work runs through the whole life of this young man. It is a hatred of work arising not from lack of strength, but from excess of passion. At great times he was capable of great exertions; but the idea of having to pay for the air he breathed, the water he drank, the bread he ate, the room he lived in, with the constant sacrifice of his own person and abilities, of enslaving himself to labor, deeply wounded his pride. The purchase of life by regular activity — this is basically what Richard Wagner had hated in the society possessed by the economic ideal; for this hatred and pride he had forgotten duties, led a vagabond's life, and at last achieved his royal triumph. Every great creator has once ventured this risk, but it seems to have been the example of the venerated Wagner which particularly strengthened the young Adolf Hitler in his decision to look on economic society as his enemy, to regard the need of working as a disgrace, and to take his strong inclination for doing nothing as a proof of his higher calling. He hated the whole great sphere of human existence which is devoted to the regular transference of energy into product; and he hated the men who had let themselves be caught and crushed in this process of production. All his life the workers were for him a picture of horror, a dismal gruesome mass, and his thoughts about the working rabble were not far different from those of a Shakespearean aristocrat; everything which he later said from the speaker's platform to flatter the manual worker was pure lies. 'The workers are an indulgent mass, they know nothing but their belly, booze, and women,' he said to Hanisch; and those unwilling to accept Hanisch as a witness need but to glance through Hitler's later public utterances, and they will find confirmation enough.

Observe, for instance, how he portrays the workers, whom he supposedly knew on the building; how at first he kept aloof from them, for 'my clothing was still more or less in order, my speech cultivated' — what an illusion! — 'and my nature reserved,' and if it had been up to him, he would 'not have concerned myself with my new environment.' With the horror and revulsion of the man regarding himself as a higher type, he here saw for the first time the 'human dragon,' the human mass monster of manual labor, which knows no ideals, which 'rejected everything' that young Adolf has learned to honor: ' . . . the nation as the invention of the capitalistic classes, the fatherland as an instrument of the bourgeoisie for the exploitation of the working class; the authority of law as a means for oppressing the proletariat; the school as an institution for breeding slaves and also slave-holders; religion as a means of stultifying the people and making them easier to exploit; morality as a symptom of stupid, sheeplike patience.' In Hitler's opinion the worker had such thoughts because he was the embodiment of materialistic selfishness; and though in his public utterances he usually adds that this is purely the result of seduction by Jewish Marxism, he privately owns that in his conviction the baseness of human nature is to blame. 'The whole mass of workers,' he said twenty years later (1930) to his rebellious follower, Otto Strasser, 'wants nothing else but bread and games; they have no understanding for any ideals.' Otto Strasser triumphantly publicized those words and Hitler did not deny them, for all his companions knew what he thought and they felt the same. One of his friends and advisers, Gottfried Feder, when challenged, wrote in profound embarrassment that 'the core of this utterance, supposing it really to have been made, must in a certain sense be recognized as correct.' 'No false humanity!' Hitler added. Thus thinks the intellectual thirsting for power who, again in Hitler's words, feels himself to be the 'new master class' which 'on the basis of its better race has the right to rule, and which ruthlessly maintains and secures this domination over the broad masses.' In order to understand the rise of the youth, Adolf Hitler, from the vagabond art student to the master man, we must understand what inborn distaste divides the master man from mere physical labor. All his life Hitler remembered Reinhold Hanisch's advice; fifteen years later, as a mature man he called the Socialist movement a 'movement of men who either possessed no clarity of thought or in the course of time have grown alien to all intellectual work. A gigantic organization of working beasts without intellectual leadership.' Ten more years later, when he was Chancellor, he asserted that it was necessary only to give the 'primitive' mass enough to eat; they did not demand more.

Consequently, all Hanisch's little anecdotes about young Adolf's hostility to work are credible and convincing. The conversations also sound genuine. Did the worker know no idealism? Hanisch, who himself had formerly been a worker, was hurt and objected that workers had proved their idealism by making many European revolutions. Hitler answered contemptuously that some people didn't seem to know that the European revolution of 1848, for example, had been made by students. Hanisch bitterly accused his friend of not knowing the real workers, since those he saw around him in the Home for Men were mostly idlers and drunkards; the respectable workers, however, preferred to live in furnished rooms, seeking family connections; they liked to tinker on their nights off, to try and invent something; they liked to read and try to improve their education. How many of the great engineers and industrialists had started out as workers! Hitler: 'Well, those are the exceptions, master men . . .'

In the age which had invented the 'religion of labor,' the young artist-prince wouldn't let himself be fooled. That was a sugary swindle for the masses who didn't want to and had no right to improve their lot; but a young artist waits in princely idleness for the dream-gift of inspiration, and 'can't work like a coolie after all.' This is his answer to his partner, Hanisch, when he comes running impatiently for new merchandise and finds the artist with his nose deep in the newspaper. Newspaper reading was his favorite occupation; there he sits in the gloomy reading-room of the Home for Men, bending over the page, gripping two other newspapers fast under his arms; and if for a change he really does start to work on a drawing, someone only has to leave a fresh newspaper on the table beside him — he snatches at it and his work flies under the table. Artist, cries Hanisch, you an artist? A hunger artist, at most, a dauber, and a lazybones in the bargain. And he didn't even know how to take care of his few pennies, Hanisch reproached him; if he earned a few kronen, he didn't do a stroke of work for days, but sat around a cheap café reading newspapers, eating four or five cream puffs one after another. Yet he spent next to no money on alcohol, none at all on tobacco; even his critical friend had to admit that.

The young man with the affected lungs had never smoked and had almost never taken drink. His father had drunk and his son's abstinence may be regarded as an unconscious protest against his father, just as his protest against work was a conscious protest. Yet all external influences, accidents, educational methods do not bring out of a man what was not in him to begin with; when Hitler father and son fought, the personality type lying at the base of the whole family was fighting with itself; the self-dissatisfaction, expressed in abrupt restlessness, which we suspect in Georg Hiedler, clearly recognize in Alois Schicklgruber, and can literally touch in Adolf Hitler, is the real source of the quarrel. They all broke out of the traditional life. Georg Hiedler led the life of a gypsy; Alois

Schicklgruber took his gun in hand and went on the man-hunt, to make himself 'something better'; and if, as a young man, Adolf Hitler didn't want to work, it was with the half-conscious realization that the higher man just does not work. His youthful failure is a stubborn and frightened protest against the whole normal world of order and service into which his gray-haired, alien father wanted to drive him with a big stick. From deepest natural predisposition, he distrusted this world of toil and sweat which breaks the man and cuts him up for its purposes, disfigures the body and paralyzes the spirit. In this world young Adolf became an idler, and this had a deep significance. If the time of the 'intelligent herd-beast prepared for obedience' — as Nietzsche puts it — is dawning, the time of the intellectual with the cast-iron soul, dominated by the ideal of 'it works' — then high above the herd and the cast-iron soul, there must nevertheless be the soaring master soul which does not let itself be adapted or stamped into shape, which obeys only itself and commands only the others.

Idlers all about! In the Home for Men, he finds himself with a certain Neumann, a Jew from Hungary, a man by the name of Greiner, with Hanisch. Work? The thing is to invent something! For instance, something to prevent window-panes from freezing over; some ointment that can be sold to shopkeepers. In the winter, the purchasers would notice the swindle, so the merchandise had to be got rid of in summer, and besides, 'you've got to have the gift of gab.' Hanisch claims to have heard this from Hitler. In any case it fits in with his whole nature. His imagination helped him to find the unusual beneath the rubble of his daily life; but he always lacked the small amount of sober ability and skill to do anything with his discovery. Apparently he fascinated several of his comrades at that time, and himself was fascinated by some: Neumann, a Hungarian Jew and old-clothes dealer, furnished him with shirts and the caftan-like black coat, Hitler praised Neumann's goodness in warm tones. When in 1910 Neumann left Vienna for Germany, Hitler nearly went along. By a hair's-breadth history escaped the drama of Hitler making his entry into Germany by the side of a Hungarian-Jewish old-clothes dealer.

He learned to know humanity from the dregs; the lodging-house schooled him for the world. He copied his pictures from other pictures and studied society in its caricature. In this world of the declassed and fallen, he also encountered the declassed peoples and the fallen races. For this human scum was at the same time the scum of the twelve nations which made Imperial Austria a mouldering heap of disintegration; each one in itself a fragment of national revolution with wings of freedom, but within the empire a corrosive poison. The stubble-bearded drunken human wreck at the next table is a Czech; the crook who came in yesterday evening and sold us a used razor blade for a new one was a Pole; the fellow over there with bedbugs crawling down his neck in broad daylight — an Italian, of course! Unwashed scoundrels, the whole lot of them, these South Slavs and Slovaks; but the most unwashed and malignant of all are, of course, the thirteenth race: the Jews.

For in this Austria filled with hostile nationalities the Jews, too, are a kind of nationality, or stand in the place of one. In the western parts of the country, to be sure, they disappear as inconspicuously among the population as in many other countries, and even the suspicious eye of the young German patriot, Adolf Hitler, could no longer detect them among the other inhabitants of his home city of Linz, because 'in the course of the centuries their exterior had become Europeanized and human'; later he finds this very surprising. But the Jews from the eastern Polish section of the country have their own strange culture, clothing, speech; great masses of them had settled in Vienna, and the sight of them seems to have pursued the newly arrived artist from Linz like a bad dream: 'Wherever I went, I began to see Jews, and the more I saw, the more sharply they became distinguished in my eyes from the rest of humanity. Particularly the Inner City and the districts north of the Danube Canal swarmed with a people which even in their exteriors had lost all resemblance to Germans.'

As a national minority among twelve other national minorities, the Jews of Austria had their full part of the seething hatred with which these minorities, or at least their radical, intellectual strata, battled with one another. This is something different from the 'Jewish question' as it exists throughout the world. The anti-Semitism of Austria was wilder and bloodthirstier than that of Germany. In the Czech and Hungarian sections there were state's attorneys willing to prosecute Jews for alleged ritual murder, and a German deputy in the Vienna parliament demanded a law 'granting the liberty to shoot at Jews.' In Austria, anti-Semitism was one of the many national hatreds and that is what gave it its murderous power.

Among the Germans of Austria, the party with the program of 'Home to the Reich' and 'Away from Rome' had a third slogan: 'Out with the Jews!' This movement called itself Pan-German. Toward the beginning of the century, a small, radical, and anti-Semitic group broke loose from it, and in 1904 called itself the 'German Workers' Party.' In 1913, this group debated whether to call itself the National Socialist Party of Austria and in 1918 did so. A much greater development was that of a second anti-Semitic movement embracing the mass of the German petty-bourgeoisie and parts of the working class, but also having many supporters among the numerous Czech population of Vienna: this was the Christian Social Party, led by an intellectual who had arisen from modest circumstances: Doctor Karl Lueger. A strong personality, a powerful tribune of the people, a party despot who made himself the all-powerful mayor of Vienna. Young Hitler admired him greatly, handed out leaflets for the Christian Social Party, stood on street corners and made speeches. Lueger had the young sons of his supporters parade through the streets with music, banners, and the beginnings of a uniform, and Hitler said to Hanisch that this was right, the youth could not be given political training early enough.

Later, Hitler was regretfully forced to criticize this 'mightiest German mayor of all times' for not having understood the racial question despite his anti-Semitism; for him a baptized Jew was a Christian — what folly! Lueger was a good Catholic Christian, persecuting the enemies of Christ as he saw fit; an armed sentry guarding Peter's Rock, obedient and devoted to the Holy Father in Rome whom young Hitler already consciously hated, because he was always an Italian and hence an enemy of the German people. Lueger was a loyal subject of the old emperor, a true son of the great paternalistic Austria; with his Christian Social movement he hoped to breathe new strength into the sickened empire. He was not interested in nationalities; he was no Pan-German; he wanted neither to go away from Rome nor home to the Reich. And yet one could learn from him. How well this unknown, nameless man had fought his way to power, almost to omnipotence! With his 'rare knowledge of men' he took — as Hitler describes him — good care 'not to see people as better than they are' — the young student of life from the lodging-house could agree with a burning heart. And Lueger had put his profound knowledge of human affairs into a form 'corresponding to the receptivity of the broad masses which is very small'; yes, Lueger knew the great brainless working beast. There were in particular two secrets of success which Hitler thought he had learned from him: Lueger put the chief emphasis 'on the winning of classes whose existence is threatened,' because only such classes carry on the political struggle with passion; secondly, he took pains in 'inclining powerful existing institutions to his use.' In Lueger's case, this was the all-powerful Catholic Church; in another case, it might have been the German Army or the Bank of England; and no one will ever have any success in politics who overlooks this obvious fact.

But whatever Hitler learned or thought he had learned from his model, Lueger, he learned far more from his opponent. And this opponent, whom he combated from the profound hatred of his soul, is and remains plain ordinary work. Organized, it calls itself labor movement, trade union, Socialist Party. And, or so it seems to him, Jews are always the leaders.

The relatively high percentage of Jews in the leadership of the Socialist parties on the European continent cannot be denied. The intellectual of the bourgeois era had not yet discovered the workers, and if the workers wanted to have leaders with university education, often only the Jewish intellectual remained — the type which might have liked to become a judge or government official, but in Germany, Austria, or Russia simply could not. Yet, though many Socialist leaders are Jews, only few Jews are Socialist leaders. To call the mass of modern Jewry Socialist, let alone revolutionary, is a bad propaganda joke. The imaginary Jew portrayed in *The Protocols of the Wise Men of Zion* ostensibly wants to bend the nations to his will by revolutionary mass uprisings; the real Jewish Socialist of France, Germany, and Italy, however, is an intellectual who had to rebel against his own Jewish family and his own social class before he could come to the workers.

Karl Marx, the prototype of the supposed Jewish labor leader, came of a baptized Christian family, and his own relation with Judaism can only be characterized as anti-Semitism; for under Jews he understood the sharply anti-Socialist, yes, anti-political Jewish masses of Western Europe, whom as a good Socialist he coldly despised.

The Jewish Socialist leaders of Austria in Hitler's youth were for the most part a type with academic education, and their predominant motive was just what Hitler at an early age so profoundly despised, 'a morality of pity,' an enthusiastic faith in the oppressed and in the trampled human values within them. The Jewish Socialist, as a rule, has abandoned the religion of his fathers and consequently is a strong believer in the religion of human rights; this type, idealistic and impractical even in the choice of his own career, was often unequal to the test of practical politics and was pushed aside by more robust, more worldly, less sentimental leaders arising from the non-Jewish masses. An historic example of this change in the top Socialist leadership occurred in Soviet Russia between 1926 and 1937 when the largely Jewish leaders of the revolutionary period (Trotzky, Zinoviev, Kamenev) were bloodily shoved aside by a dominantly non-Jewish class (Stalin, Voroshilov, etc.); the last great example of the humanitarian but impractical Socialist leader of Jewish origin was Léon Blum in France.

It was in the world of workers, as he explicitly tells us, that Adolf Hitler encountered the Jews. The few bourgeois Jews in his home city did not attract his attention; if we believe his own words, the Jewish 'money domination' flayed by Wagner made no impression upon him at that time. But he did notice the proletarian and subproletarian figures from the Vienna slums, and they repelled him; he felt them to be foreign — just as he felt the non-Jewish workers to be foreign. With amazing indifference he reports that he could not stand up against either of them in political debate; he admits that the workers knew more than he did, that the Jews were more

adept at discussion. He goes on to relate how he looked into this
uncanny labor movement more closely, and to his great amazement
discovered large numbers of Jews at its head. The great light
dawned on him; suddenly the 'Jewish question' became clear. If
we subject his own account to psychological analysis, the result is
rather surprising: the labor movement did not repel him because it
was led by Jews; the Jews repelled him because they led the labor
movement. For him this inference was logical. To lead this broken,
degenerate mass, dehumanized by overwork, was a thankless task.
No one would do it unless impelled by a secret, immensely alluring
purpose; the young artist-prince simply did not believe in the
morality of pity of which these Jewish leaders publicly spoke so
much; there is no such thing, he knew people better — particularly
he knew himself. The secret purpose could only be a selfish one —
whether mere good living or world domination remained for the
moment a mystery. But one thing is certain: it was not Rothschild,
the capitalist, but Karl Marx, the Socialist, who kindled Adolf
Hitler's anti-Semitism.

No justice, no equal rights for all! One of Hitler's most characteristic reproaches to the labor movement is that in Austria it had
fought for equal rights for all — to the detriment of the master
race chosen by God. At the beginning of the century the Austrian
parliament was organized on the basis of a suffrage system which
for practical purposes disenfranchised the poor. This assured the
more prosperous German population a position of dominance. By a
general strike the Social Democrats put an end to this scandal
and twenty years later Hitler still reproached them for it: 'By the
fault of the Social Democracy, the Austrian state became deathly
sick. Through the Social Democracy universal suffrage was introduced in Austria and the German majority was broken in the
Reichsrat' — the Austrian parliament.

The power and strategy of this movement made an enormous impression on the young Adolf Hitler, despite all his revulsion. An
impressive model for the power-hungry — for the young artist-
prince in beggar's garb will never let anyone convince him that the
labor movement owed its existence to anything but the lust for
power of Jewish wirepullers. A new labor party would have to be

founded, he told Hanisch, and the organization would have to be copied from the Social Democrats; but the best slogans should be taken from all parties, for the end justifies the means. Adolf Hitler saw with admiration how an unscrupulous intelligence can play with the masses, for him this was true of the Austrian Social Democrats as well as their opponent, Karl Lueger.

Adolf Hitler was born to regard men as base matter for the strong and dexterous hands of — to quote Nietzsche again — 'power philosophers, and artist tyrants.' From his father and grandfather he inherited a gypsy-like trait of disloyalty and human coldness; also a tendency toward sly calculation which did not shrink back from humiliation. In his struggle against his father, he discovered with a sure instinct the truth suited to his own nature, that no holds were barred, and that the end justifies all means; in the school which leaves the most lasting impression — that is, his own family — he learned that the right of the stronger prevails, contested at most by the right of the craftier. Having achieved this gloomy wisdom, he was hurled into the abyss where broken, uprooted men develop the worst qualities of the wolf and the fox; into a mass community of unhappy souls, the best of whom long passionately to get out of this community into the old life which formerly divided them so far from one another. A class consciousness of pathological intensity was the only thing that kept many of these declassed individuals — whether former counts or former workers — afloat. From this abyss each one looked up to his own stars; the lack of solidarity is the great characteristic of this class in which the fallen artist-prince unexpectedly found himself. He had a sharp eye for this lack of loyalty in the class of the declassed; it jibed with his previous idea of the human species. He had pitilessly discerned the faults of the working class. But the great virtue of the worker type, proletarian solidarity, he had not understood; he had only been insulted when it reached out to him. In his narrative, which is not above suspicion, he tells us that the building workers wanted to force him into a union; he had sharply refused, and this had been the beginning of hostility. To be sure, there is ground for suspicion that Hitler copied this whole fine story with small changes from the autobiography of his later political friend, Anton Drexler, *Mein Politisches Erwachen*

(My Political Awakening), which appeared in Munich in 1920; but the attitude it expresses is nevertheless genuine and his own.

It was not among the oppressed, but among the shipwrecks, that Adolf Hitler came to know the people. The class concepts of the labor movement can be regarded as true or false; but beyond a doubt they are based on pride, self-respect, and sense of strength. But in the lodging-house there is no self-respect or sense of strength, but only unreliability and distrust. A common striving for contradictory aims is the way of this degenerate community; to help one another up and then push one another down; to hold together and then cheat one another. This human chaff molded the precocious Hitler's conceptions of human worth. Here for the first time he saw the mass, the later object of his politics; and yet this would have no decisive significance if it could not be said of this disloyal, loveless man that in it he saw himself.

In his own self-portrait Hitler uttered not a word of this oppressed, impotent vegetating life amid the human wreckage; and in general this self-portrait is a masterpiece of unreliability, concealment, occasional false claims, self-praise and self-pity. Neither the lodging-house nor the Home for Men is found in it, neither the advertising drawings nor his friend Hanisch, not to mention his Jewish friend, Neumann. The melting-pot of Vienna at that time teemed with sub-proletarian Jews, and Hitler, whether he liked them or not, belonged among them. He wore the long coat given him by Neumann, and a stiff, greasy, black derby; his matted hair hung down over his collar, his fuzzy beard formed a thick ruff around his chin — if we may believe Hanisch's report and the drawings which Hanisch later did from memory, he constituted 'an apparition such as rarely occurs among Christians.' Cynically his comrade said to him, 'Your father must have been out when you were conceived,' and your shoes are also 'of the nomad brand.' Neither in Adolf Hitler's physical appearance nor in the history of his family is there any serious suspicion of Jewish strain, and yet among the unkempt Jews of Vienna, he looked like an unkempt Jew of Vienna. Such is the force of environment. On the basis of these few who outwardly resembled him, he formed his opinion about them all. From these figures of the Vienna slums, unwashed like himself, he derived the opinion that one could recognize a Jew with one's eyes shut by the smell — supposing this was really his opinion; from the wretched suspender peddlers (like himself), failures (like himself), petty swindlers (like himself), he formed a picture of the whole race — as from the non-Jews who (like himself) shared their lot, he formed his picture of the common people.

And through this whole dismal, vicious life runs the desperate struggle against the city, the fatherland, the world which has not recognized the artist-prince in him, and whose judgment has made him shy of humanity. With Hanisch — or Walter as he actually called himself — he constantly argued about his rank as an artist. This little peddler, who later learned to draw better than Hitler, was out to develop a thriving picture trade; but Hitler sat in the reading-room of the Home for Men, paying no attention to the unfinished drawing in front of him, wildly brandishing his ruler, and roaring speeches at an astonished audience. Sometimes he made a deep impression, sometimes people simply laughed at him, and then Hanisch would have to console the weeping boy in the evening. When the shouting grew too loud, the porter rushed up and ordered quiet, threatening to throw the disturber out; then Hitler would pull down his arms and crouch over his drawing like a model child. He was always quiet and well-behaved when the other was clearly the stronger; in Vienna he acquired a wild fear of the police which he has never lost.

The friendship between Hitler and Hanisch finally ended in a quarrel, grave accusations and a lawsuit. Hitler denounced Hanisch, accusing him of embezzlement, and perhaps Hanisch was none too precise about his accounts — so the court in any case decided. Hanisch, in turn, not quite so effectively, accused his former friend of having injured him and prejudiced his clientèle by his laziness and megalomania. Laboring several days, Hitler had done a drawing of the Vienna parliament, a stiff and insignificant copy of a copy; but he was firmly convinced that such a work of art must bring in a hundred kronen. Actually, when Hanisch sold it, it brought in ten kronen and — the piece was still extant a few years ago — it was certainly not worth more. Hanisch was condemned to seven days' imprisonment; later he called this an injustice, but today there is no way of getting to the bottom of the matter. In one thing he was certainly right: that Hitler thought too highly of his pictures and expected far too much money. For us the lawsuit is interesting because the record of it is one of the very few remaining documents concerning Hitler's youth; because its few details confirm the main points of Hanisch's story and strongly indicate its credibility. Since Hitler himself conceals and falsifies the story of his youth, a few extracts from the records of this little trial may not be amiss here.

At Hitler's request one Löffner, a Jewish inmate of the Home for Men, had located the vanished Hanisch, and had him arrested. His testimony is preserved in the records; the passage important to us runs:

Royal and Imperial District Police Commissariat of Wieden

Z 18370   August 4, 1910

Reinhold Hanisch
Embezzlement, False Registration.

Siegfried Löffner, Salesman, XX Meldemann Strasse 27, declares:

> I have learned from a painter in the Home for Men that the arrested party sold pictures for him and embezzled the money. I do not know the painter by name, only from the Home for Men, where he always sat with the arrested party. . . .

Thus Hitler (the 'painter') 'always sat' with Hanisch (the 'arrested party'). The close friendship which Hanisch boasts is no invention.

One more record:

Royal and Imperial District Police Commissariat

Brigittenau   August 5, 1910.

Adolf Hitler, artist-painter, born in Braunau, 20/4, 1889. Permanent address, Linz. Catholic, single. Now resident XX Meldemann Strasse 27, declares:

> It is not correct that I advised Hanisch to register as Walter, Fritz. I knew him only as Fritz Walter. Since he was destitute, I gave him the pictures I painted to sell. He regularly received fifty per cent of the proceeds from me. For about two weeks Hanisch

has not returned to the Home for Men, and stole from me the picture of parliament, valued at fifty kronen, and a watercolor, valued at nine kronen. The only document of his that I ever saw was the working booklet in question in the name of Fritz Walter. I know Hanisch from the lodging-house in Meidling where I once met him.

(signed)   Adolf Hitler

The record bears the same signature as his numerous drawings from that time. Today the case does not especially interest us; but it does confirm that Hitler lived in the lodging-house and later in the Home for Men, and thus offers an interesting trace of his past over which he later in his autobiography spreads a veil of generalities and high-flown unlikelihoods. One detail must be added: In a trial taking place on August 11, 1910, Hitler under oath partly changed his testimony; he admitted he had received money for the second picture ostensibly purloined by Hanisch.

The lawsuit and the whole affair with Hanisch made a great impression on Hitler. Years later he told new friends in Munich that the Jews in Vienna had wanted to defraud him out of the fruits of his labor. Hanisch came of a Catholic working-class family in Sudeten Germany.

Hitler spent three whole years in the Home for Men in the Twentieth District of Vienna, and the style of his existence remained unchanged; so much can be gleaned from the extremely meager indications of his own version, and the sparse data provided by chance acquaintances. For in those terrible years he seems to have had no closer friends. According to what he later told friends in Munich, he seems to have spent the years after his break with Hanisch in the most terrible loneliness; totally limited to the most superficial contacts with room neighbors and business friends. His family in Linz and Spital heard nothing of him; for years they thought him dead.

Was there no woman during all this time? This is a special chapter. All sorts of abnormalities have been attributed to him, from perversion to indifference. In the purely biological or medical sense, he is as normal as anyone could wish; but here, as in all other human relations, his distorted soul tormented and thwarted him. Hanisch in his simple way has perhaps come closest to the truth when he says that Hitler was basically so shy that he simply didn't dare to approach women. He tells us that in conversations Hitler described at length how easily women were to be 'had'; among the most effective tricks, according to the wisdom of the youthful man of the world, was to pull your hat far down over the back of your head, leaving your face free — this was fascinating and seductive. Just because it was so easy, it was wrong to take advantage of the poor things' weakness; the man of mature mind must have himself in hand. As an example he relates a rural experience of his own in a cow barn: at the last moment he mastered his passion, so that the damage was limited to an upset milk pot. In listening to these stories, Hanisch had the impression that Hitler was quite decent in this respect. And Hitler's principles really were decent; their chief basis, however, seems to have been timidity.

After three wretched years he left Vienna forever. He was a total failure, nothing had turned out right. He had proved to no one that he was a future prince in the realm of art; no one had taken any notice of him. The imperial city had not surrendered to him; he himself later attested that it had grown 'repugnant' to him: 'Repugnant this whole national mixture of Czechs, Poles, Hungarians, Ruthenians, Serbs, Croats, etc.; and above all, as the eternal disintegrating fungus of humanity — Jews and again Jews. This giant city seemed to me the embodiment of blood outrage.' He does not tell us the exact cause of his departure; but if we believe that no accidental causes but deep unconscious necessities guide men, the case of Adolf Hitler takes on a clarity transcending all possible details: he had to leave. Vienna was his failure, and he was faced with the choice of total destruction or flight.

Perhaps flight saved him from ruin; it did not bring him forward.

Early in the summer of 1913, a young student of technology from Vienna rented a room in the station quarter of Munich. The landlady told him that she had had to put out the former lodger because he had not paid his rent for a long time. During this conversation the poor dismissed lodger came in; he, too, was an Austrian. He took courage and asked his compatriot for permission to spend at least one more night in his room — on the sofa. The new lodger was good-hearted, took the poor devil out for a glass of beer, and they arranged that for the present he should sleep on the sofa until he should have money enough to pay for his share of the room. The two remained roommates for over a year: the young engineer from Vienna and his guest on the sofa, the designer of advertisements, Adolf Hitler from Linz.

According to the police register, Hitler left Vienna in May, 1913. Until then he had scraped along in the Austrian capital by selling his watercolors and drawings. In Munich he did not fare much better; here he designed posters for business houses. Outwardly his existence was perhaps even lonelier than in Vienna — an intimidated stranger amid the bustle of a gay city. At the age of twenty-four he made a sickly, haggard, unathletic impression. 'At first positively repulsive, somewhat nicer on further acquaintance,' he was described by an observer in this period.

Here, too, he was without friends. And here, too, he avoided contact with women almost fanatically, he had none of the gaiety of youth. With his insistent seriousness, he oppressed and embittered the mood of others. His roommate, who enjoyed life, had several girl friends, and wanted to saddle Hitler with one of them for Sunday. Hitler exploded and rejected the proposition in no uncertain terms, flinging violent reproaches at his astonished friend: it wasn't right to turn the poor girls' heads, they took it all seriously, and afterward felt betrayed.

He had no girl friends, but no men friends either. Neither he nor others mention any closer human relationship; later, in fact, he even boasted of having been so lonely that no one bothered about him at all. He was unfit to be a human being.

But with uncanny certainty he found his way out of his loneliness to the masses; even then when totally unknown. The unknown were closest to him; in taverns he spoke from behind his beer mug and with almost playful ease created his public. It was impossible to go to a Social Democratic meeting with him because he could not restrain himself from shouting interruptions. As soon as the conversation in a small circle turned to politics, he began to scream and hold endless lectures; and a certain precision and clarity were apparent in his style. He loved to prophesy and predict political developments; he was convinced of the impending downfall of Austria. His new Austrian roommate made the same observation as Hanisch had made: as soon as there was any mention of politics, Hitler abandoned any work, however urgent. He sat in the 'Schwemme,' the low-price room in the Hofbräuhaus, made speeches to anyone available and soon had many listeners.

An eccentric, screaming in taverns, a hermit among six hundred thousand people; without wife, friend, family, or home. In Austria, for a time, the military authorities regarded him as a deserter; for three years he simply did not report for the prescribed supplementary examinations; he was entered in the list as 'illegal' and 'address unknown.' Then he seems to have become aware of the dangerous and ambiguous aspect of this conduct; on February 5, 1914, he went to the Austrian border city of Salzburg and had himself examined. To his relief the doctor's findings were: 'Too weak for armed or auxiliary service, unfit to bear arms.' 'Not fit for service' was the verdict of the commission. Now he was through with Austria.

Now he had achieved what had been his unconscious goal through all the years of misery in Vienna: obscurity. He had disappeared from his family, shunned close friendships, shyly avoided the eyes of people he spoke with; then he had left the hated land of his fathers and dissolved his last relations with it. Now he was living in Germany, the land of his longing, yet only tolerated, not actually belonging to it. He went about his beloved city of Munich like a visitor in a museum on Sunday when the admission is free. He was a stranger in his world and his time; and even if he had asked himself honestly, he would always have had to answer: this alien condition was the only one in which he felt secure against life. It was the haven of his failure. Since he could not have been great, the only tolerable thing for him was to be nothing. The greatness of the historical phenomenon which was one day to step forth from this human shadow cannot be contested; but human nonentity is actually the premise and one of the explanations for the superhuman power of the phenomenon. It was not lack of success and resultant poverty that made him into such an overpowering nonentity. He might have been great in the contempt of outward success; instead he passionately worshiped it. Success in his eyes is the ultimate standard of human worth — yet what a minute particle he is, vegetating beside his own standard. And as a nonentity he is by no means modest; in his lonely hours he has been filled with an exuberant megalomania since childhood; but he pays dearly for these hours with the feeling of pitiful doubt in himself which attacks him again and again in the presence of strange people. He is not modest — that is, conscious of his worth and therefore not insisting on it; no, left alone with himself, he finds everything within him, but in the presence of men, he feels himself to be nothing. And thus he moves among them in an obscurity which has become a mask; and except in moments of special excitement, this obscurity expresses itself in a strange shrinking of his physical aspect. In good times it is his aims, his plans, his desires that give him life and energy; but people are only a burden, an exertion to him; every new face is in a sense a new task, something that must be conquered and subjugated — discouraged by his terrible failure in youth, he does not feel equal to this task. As for his finer feelings — tenderness, affection, friendliness — he devotes them chiefly to himself.

Here, be it noted, we are speaking of a young man of twenty-five and his private aspect; this private aspect has a poverty of feeling that robs his relations to men of all color and charm. Richard Wagner had written that the study of history must create hatred of mankind, and in exactly this sense Hitler, even in his youth, saw man only as a fragment of current history. The living world around him is for him nothing, consequently he is nothing for it; hence the shadow of hostile nothingness about him, rendering him almost invisible. Hence his unconscious demand for a new world in which, as he himself expressed it, he would be permitted to do nothing but 'respect his superior, contradict no one, blindly obey.'

Heaven sent this new world to him and many of his like in August, 1914. In Berlin, Vienna, Paris, St. Petersburg, enthusiastic masses, filled with a sense of happiness mysterious to us today, marched through the streets, singing *Die Wacht am Rhein,* the

Marseillaise, Gott erhalte, Gott beschütze; shouting, '*A bas l'Alle-magne!*' '*Nieder mit Serbien!*' '*Es lebe der Krieg!*' This stormy mass exultation at the outbreak of the World War of 1914, observed in all the capitals of Europe and repeated in America in 1917, is totally strange to the generation of 1942; nowhere, not even in Germany, was anything similar seen at the outbreak of the Second World War. In 1914, if Hitler is to be believed, the war 'was not forced on the masses, but desired by the whole people.' There must have been many Hitlers who, enclosed in the mass, felt relieved from a painful and issueless state of peace, and, like Hitler, 'overpowered by stormy enthusiasm fell down on their knees and thanked Heaven from an overflowing heart.'

In Munich, on August 1, 1914, such a mass overpowered by enthusiasm stood on the Odeons Platz in front of the ornate Feld-herrn Halle and listened to the reading of a proclamation announcing the declaration of war. The people sang patriotic songs; at a window stood a photographer. Ten or twelve years later, this photographer ran across one of the pictures taken on this occasion and published it. Among the many hundred heads he discovered a face which, despite the conspicuous ordinariness of his features, seemed illumined by an emotion unusual even in this crowd. It was a haggard, sickly face; the broad bushy mustache gave it an artificially wild look; the protruding, hyperthyroid eyes sent forth an exaggerated gleam, as though the face were addressing someone in Heaven and saying: Take notice of me, O Lord! The man to whom this face belongs stands apparently alone in the crowd; even in this hour of mass frenzy he seems solitary; the mouth is opened to sing, and we may believe that the words of the song are the first that have crossed his lips that day.

Thus Adolf Hitler experienced the outbreak of the First World War. In this World War he at last found his home. He volunteered for the Bavarian Army.

Chapter IV

HITLER FINDS HIS HOME

ON APRIL 26, 1896, IN ALEXANDRIA, EGYPT, A SON was born to Friedrich Hess, a wholesaler and exporter. The boy was named Rudolf. Friedrich Hess was a German; his family came from the town of Wunsiedel in northern Bavaria. One branch of the Hess family is resident in Switzerland. Friedrich Hess is one of those numerous Germans who, by origin or career or both, are connected with foreign countries. Up to his fourteenth year, his son lived with him in Alexandria. Then the apparently not too gifted boy was sent to a German school in Godesberg on the Rhine. He studied business in Hamburg and French Switzerland, though he would rather have gone in for mathematics. At the outbreak of the war in 1914, he volunteered. He was twice wounded; a bullet passed through his lung. He wanted to become an aviator; and achieved his aim against great difficulties. The infantry regiment in which he fought until 1916 was a special kind of troop, consisting in large part of students and other intellectuals who had volunteered for service. In German war history it is known as the List Regiment, after its first commander, Colonel von List. Under incompetent leadership the regiment incurred staggering losses in 1914. The flower of Bavaria's intellectual youth was mowed down, and the List Regiment achieved a mournful immortality. Everyone who escaped with his life could consider himself fortunate, enjoying the special protection of Providence. Hess came out alive. One day he reported to the regimental commander who succeeded List, a Lieutenant-Colonel Tubeuf. Beside Tubeuf stood his orderly.

Hess and the orderly looked one another in the eye, two survivors of the great hecatomb. How could they have suspected the adventurous future? The orderly's name was Hitler.

In the world of peace Hitler had been a foreigner. In the world of war he felt at home. Later he recalled that he never received presents from home. This is not literally true; half-strangers sometimes sent him something out of sheer pity and then complained that he was slow in thanking them; he once answered with the lame excuse — the postcard still exists — that his letter 'probably got lost.' But it is true that he had no real friend; no sweetheart. When the war came to an end, he tells us, he wept for the first time since the death of his mother. Now this is an outright lie — tears came easy to him; but it is true that, since the death of his mother, he had loved only one thing, war. How he loved it, we shall see from a letter addressed to a near-stranger, a tailor from whom he had rented a room in Munich. It is a lively letter, effusive and often passionate; it describes — one might almost say it rejoices in — the terrible slaughter of the List Regiment:

> Honored Sir . . . I am glad that you received my last card and hasten to thank you heartily for the kind letter you wrote in answer. I should have written you a long letter before, but will now try to catch up. First of all, I must tell you that on December 2, I received the Iron Cross. Thank God there was plenty of opportunity. Our regiment was not, as we had expected, assigned to the reserve. Early in the morning of October 29 we were sent into battle; since then we have been in those fellows' hair without interruption; if not as attackers, as defenders.

The letter describes the journey to the front, the unloading of the troop near Lille, and goes on:

> • . . . We passed the night in the courtyard of the stock exchange. A pretentious building, not yet completed. We had to lie down with full packs — prepared for an alarm — I couldn't get a wink of sleep. Next day we changed our quarters. . . . During the day we drilled some, took a look at the city. We were filled with admiration for the tremendous army apparatus which has put its imprint on all Lille, and rolled before our amazed eyes in its gigantic forms. At night there was singing, for many it must have been

the last. At two o'clock on the last night, the alarm came, and at three we left our assembly point in field step. . . . Then morning came. We were far outside of Lille. The thunder of the cannon had grown a little stronger. Like a giant snake our march column twined its way forward. . . . We went on till eight at night. The regiment had vanished, dissolved into its companies, and each man in the companies had taken cover against planes. At nine o'clock we pitched camp. I couldn't sleep. Four steps from my bundle of straw lay a dead horse. The beast was already half decayed. Besides, there was a battery of German howitzers right behind us; every fifteen minutes it sent two grenades flying over our heads, off into the black night. They howled and hissed through the air, and then far in the distance you heard two dull thuds. Every man of us listened. We had never heard that sound before. . . .

Just as we were getting our marching orders, Major Count Zech rode by: 'Tomorrow we're attacking the English!' At last! Every man of us was overjoyed. After this announcement the major took the head of the column, on foot. . . .

Out there the first shrapnel were flying over us, bursting at the edge of the woods, and tearing apart the trees like so much brushwood. We looked on curiously. We had no real idea of the danger. None of us was afraid. Each man was waiting impatiently for the command: 'Forward!' The show was getting hotter and hotter. We heard that some men had been wounded. Five or six fellows brown as clay suddenly appeared from the left, and all of us broke into a cheer: six Englishmen and a machine gun! We shouted to the escort. They were marching proudly behind their catch. The rest of us had to wait. We could hardly see into the foggy, seething witches' caldron before us. At last the command rang out: 'Forward!'

We swarmed out and chased across the fields to a little farm. To left and right the shrapnel were bursting, and in between the English bullets sang. But we paid no attention. For ten minutes we lay there, and then we were again ordered forward. I was way out in front, ahead of our squad. Squad-leader Stoever had been hit! Good God, I had barely time to think, now things are starting. But since we were in the open, we had to dash forward. The captain was at the head. The first of our men began to fall. The English had set up machine guns. We threw ourselves down and crawled slowly forward through a gutter. From time to time a man was hit and couldn't go on, and the whole column was stuck. Then we had to lift the man out of the ditch. We kept on crawling until the ditch stopped, then we were in the open field again. We ran fifteen or twenty yards, then we came to a big pool of water. One after another we splashed into it, took cover, and caught our breath. But it was no place to lie still. So we dashed out quick, and double-quick, to a forest that lay about a hundred yards ahead of us. There we found each other after a while. But the woods were beginning to look pretty thin.

By this time we had only a second sergeant commanding us: that was Schmidt, a big tall splendid fellow. We crawled on our bellies to the edge of the woods. Over us the shells were howling and whistling, splintered tree trunks and branches flew around us. And then again grenades crashed into the wood, hurling up clouds of stones, earth, and roots, and stifling everything in a yellowish-green, stinking, sickening vapor. We couldn't lie there forever, and if we were going to be killed, it was better to be killed outside. Then our major came up. Again we went forward. I jumped up and ran, as fast as I could, across meadows and turnip fields, jumping over ditches, over wire and living hedges. Then I heard someone ahead of me shouting: 'Everybody in! Everybody in here!' A long trench lay before me; a moment later I had jumped into it. Before me, behind me, to the left and right others followed. Beside me were Württembergers, under me dead and wounded Englishmen.

The Württembergers had stormed the trench before us. And now I knew why I had landed so soft when I jumped in. Between 240 and 280 yards to the left of us, there were still English trenches; to the right, the road to Leceloire was still in their possession. An unbroken hail of iron was whistling over our trench. Finally at ten o'clock, our artillery opened up in the sector. One — two — three — five — and so on. Again and again a shell burst in the English trenches ahead of us. The fellows swarmed out like ants, and then we rushed them. We ran into the fields like lightning, and after bloody hand-to-hand fighting in different places, we threw them out of one trench after another. Many of them raised their hands. Those who wouldn't surrender were knocked down. In this way we cleared trench after trench.

At length we reached the main highway. To right and left of us was a young forest. Forward we went, straight into it! We drove them out in whole packs. Then we came to the place where the forest ended and the open road went on. To the left of us lay several farms, they were still occupied, and we went through a withering fire. One man after another collapsed ahead of us. Our major came up, fearless and calmly smoking, with his adjutant, Lieutenant Piloty. The major took in the situation at a glance and ordered us to assemble to right and left of the highway for an assault. We had no more officers, hardly any non-coms. So every last one of us, that was still more or less in one piece, ran back to get reinforcements. When I came back the second time with a troop of scattered Württembergers, the major lay on the ground with his breast torn open. A heap of corpses lay around him.

By this time there was only one officer left, his adjutant. We were boiling with fury. 'Herr Lieutenant, lead us at them!' we all shouted. So then we went forward and leftward into the wood; on the road we could not advance. Four times we went forward and were forced to retreat; of my whole detachment only one man was left aside from myself, and finally he too fell. A shot tore off the whole left sleeve of my tunic, but by a miracle I remained untouched. Finally at two o'clock, we advanced a fifth time, and this time we occupied the edge of the forest and the farm. At five in the afternoon we assembled and dug in a hundred yards from the road.

For three days we fought on like this, and on the third day the Britishers were finally licked. The fourth evening we marched back to Werwick. Only then did we see what our losses had been. In four days our regiment of thirty-five hundred men had melted away to six hundred. There were only thirty officers left in the whole regiment. Four companies had to be dissolved. But we were all proud of having licked the Britishers. Since then we have been in the front lines the whole time. I was proposed for the Iron Cross, the first time in Messines, the second time in Wytschaete by Lieutenant-Colonel Engelhardt, our regimental commander. Four others were proposed at the same time. On December 2, I finally got it.

I am now carrying dispatches for the staff. With regard to dirt, conditions are a little better here, but it is also more dangerous. In Wytschaete alone, on the day of the first attack, three of us eight were shot off, and one badly wounded. We four survivors and the wounded man were cited for distinction. And this saved our lives.

For while the list of those proposed for the 'Cross' was being discussed, four company commanders came into the tent, or dugout. Due to lack of space, the four of us had to step out. We hadn't been outside for five minutes when a grenade struck the tent, gravely wounded Lieutenant-Colonel Engelhardt and killed or wounded all the rest of the staff. It was the most terrible moment of my life. We worshipped Lieutenant-Colonel Engelhardt.

I am sorry, I have to close now. . . . Day after day we are under the heaviest artillery fire from eight in the morning to five in the afternoon. In time, that shatters even the strongest nerves. I often think of Munich, and every man of us has the single wish that the gang out here will soon have their hash settled once and for all. We want an all-out fight, at any cost, and we hope that those of us who have the good fortune to see their homeland again will find it purer and more purified of foreignism. That through the sacrifices and sufferings which hundreds of us go through every day, that through the stream of blood that flows here day after day against an international world of enemies, not only Germany's enemies abroad will be crushed, but that our internal internationalism will also be broken. That would be worth more than any territorial gains. With Austria it will come as I have always said.

Again I express my heartfelt thanks and remain your most devoted and grateful

ADOLF HITLER.

This is the letter of an impassioned warrior. In it there is not the slightest soft spot. He sees only the enemy whom he hates, and strikes down in a true frenzy. He is brave and attaches no value to his life, as his regimental commander later attested. But there is also, clearly expressed, the belief that he owes his own life to a miracle or rather to a chain of miracles; that the bursting shells spared him, time and again; that, while three quarters of his regiment were sacrificed, he really enjoyed the special protection of Providence.

In March, 1932, Hitler brought a lawsuit in the Hamburg provincial court, as plaintiff against a newspaper which had accused him of cowardice as a soldier. His attorney submitted a number of written affidavits, attesting the contrary. Lieutenant-Colonel Engelhardt, mentioned in Hitler's letter, wrote:

As commander of the 16th Regiment of Bavarian Infantry at the Battle of Ypres in the period from November 10 to November 17, 1914, I came to know Adolf Hitler as an exceedingly brave, effective and conscientious soldier. I must emphasize the following: As our men were storming the wedge-shaped forest (later known as Bayer-Wald), I stepped out of the woods near Wytschaete to get a better view of developments. Hitler and the volunteer Bachmann, another battle orderly belonging to the 16th Regiment, stood before me to protect me with their bodies from the machine-gun fire to which I was exposed. . . . Munich, February 29, 1932, signed, Engelhardt, Major General (retired).

The Iron Cross referred to in Hitler's letter was of the second class, but on August 4, 1918, he was awarded the Iron Cross first class, one of the highest distinctions to which a common soldier in the German army could aspire. He is supposed to have received it for an astounding feat; a witness described it as follows in the above-mentioned trial:

On his way to the battalion staff, Adolf Hitler, regimental orderly, was caught in a barrage. He thought that the battalion was behind a hill, ran over the top and fell into a shell-hole occupied by Englishmen, who at once demanded his surrender. Hitler was armed only with a pistol. He drew it out and not only held the Englishmen at bay, but took them prisoner and led them to his regimental staff. An officer, a sergeant and thirteen men!

A comrade named Schmidt, it is true, describes the episode somewhat differently:

. . . In the spring or summer of 1918, Hitler received the I.C.1 for his extraordinary accomplishments as a dispatch carrier in the big offensive of 1918, especially for having personally taken prisoner a French officer and about fifteen men, whom he suddenly ran into while carrying dispatches, and who, as a consequence of his decision and presence of mind, laid down their arms. . . .

In this version they are Frenchmen instead of Englishmen. This contradiction does not necessarily disprove the story. But it does seem strange that none of his superiors had apparently heard of the dramatic exploit. The official history of the List Regiment does, to be sure, recount similar feats by other members of the regiment who consequently received far higher distinctions; but the history does not mention Hitler's fifteen English or French prisoners.

Even so, it cannot be denied that Hitler was a brave soldier. Why, then, did this enthusiast remain an eternal gray private? The German Army needed leaders; the need for them became more and more acute as the war progressed; yet Hitler never became a leader. One of his superiors, Reserve-Lieutenant Horn, maintained in the same trial: 'If Adolf Hitler had been promoted to the rank of sergeant, he could not have remained a battle orderly and the regiment would have lost one of its best dispatch carriers.' It has also been claimed that Hitler did not want to be a leader, but insisted on remaining a dispatch carrier. And his letter shows what delight he took in simple, uncomplicated soldiering. One of his superiors, it is true, is said to have declared that he did not want Hitler to become a non-com on account of his mental instability.

Although Hitler was a good soldier, he was not always a good comrade. He impressed — and not favorably — his fellows by never complaining about the length, the hardships, and the general nonsense of the war; by never grumbling nor getting bored. 'We all cursed him and found him intolerable,' one of them later said. 'There was this white crow among us that didn't go along with us when we damned the war to hell.' It was actually the war that interested him, not his own life as a soldier. 'News came of Hindenburg's great victory over the Russians,' he wrote home; ' . . . three cheers . . . long live our great marshal . . .' — and he did not add, as most of them would have done: 'And now let's hope that the whole thing will be soon over, and in your next parcel, please send some salami. . . .'

It has often been said that the sudden escape from domestic ties into the virile world of war has a singular attraction for many men. But this was certainly not true of Hitler, for he had had no domestic life. It was the business of war itself; the burning desire for victory and the destruction of the enemy that shaped this human nonentity into a figure of super-personal strength.

If personality is like a shell which covers our inner world of dreams and keeps them from flooding the world of reality, then there rarely has been a thinner shell than the personality of Adolf Hitler, and a less protected world. In his dreams he is always supreme. Among the marble palaces, statues, museums, and half-royal, half-artistic glitter of Vienna, he had been the unknown prince of art; now, in the world of guns, assaults, pincer movements, commands, organization, plans, he becomes the unknown general, weaving around his dirty little world of trenches, mud, stench, and death the great, glorious dream-world of Adolf Hitler and his war. An inconspicuous orderly, he fought as if he were responsible for the 'working' of the whole affair. In the midst of escapists who tried to make the best of an unpleasant situation, he was always the serious-minded warrior.

Hitler entered the war with a contempt for the masses: he left it with an equal contempt for the leaders. He felt that these leaders trembled before what he called the rabble; in later years he was still scornful of the timidity of this upper class who handled with kid gloves those they should have trodden under their feet. That they did not slaughter ten or twelve thousand socialist agitators by poison gas seemed to him the greatest blunder of the German leaders.

He goes to great length to tell in detail how these leaders were unable to make the mass understand the meaning of the war; and to counter the superior Allied war propaganda; how they were hopelessly outclassed by shabby trade-union officials in the art of influencing people. This is the central point of accusation the self-appointed general brings against the officially appointed generals. They might be experts in military science, but they had no conception of the decisive task: to inspire a whole people with the willingness to die for a cause.

In October, 1918, Hitler was badly gassed and was blind for several days. He was transported to the rear and finally reached a military hospital at Pasewalk, a small town northeast of Berlin. Early in November, 1918, the German Revolution broke out; beginning with a mutiny in the Navy. Sailors' delegations traveled throughout the country; one came to Pasewalk. At first they did not dare to agitate openly for mutiny, but made secret propaganda for insurrection. A group of these sailors spoke to Hitler. It would have been his duty to report them — later he was not squeamish in this respect. Why he neglected to do so in Pasewalk is not quite clear; he himself said: 'I didn't denounce them, for even then I felt that the collapse was near.' He did not write this unusual admission in *Mein Kampf*; it occurred in his defense plea in the 1924 trial. Lost in the world, reduced to inactivity, he looked on at the death of the war which had been his fatherland.

Chapter V

THE BURNING HEAVENS
ARE REFLECTED IN
A MUD PUDDLE

THE GAS SLOWLY VANISHED FROM LUNGS AND EYES, but its traces remained. A strange hoarseness of the voice seems to be an inheritance the war has left to Adolf Hitler, an obstacle in the throat which has to be overcome by an effort when he talks a long time. Speaking was to mean fighting to him from now on, and this fight against his acquired weakness penetrates the whole man — a fight he had been unable to put up against his natural weaknesses of laziness and timidity. The amount of force he has now to put into the simple action of speaking may at least have contributed to the impression of power which seems to stream even from his insignificant utterances. Although the power of this thundering voice certainly was there before the gas enhanced it, hidden sources of his personal strength probably have been brought to life by the almost deadly touch of the poison. The experience of war and defeat stirred up qualities in Adolf Hitler which peace had left slumbering; the physical remnants of the gas in his body were at least an everlasting memo of this experience.

After his discharge from the hospital, Hitler went to Bavaria, lived for a time with the replacement battalion of his regiment in the Upper Bavarian town of Traunstein, and later in the Munich infantry barracks, where on May 2, 1919, every tenth man was stood up against the wall. He lived, struggled, killed, with these soldiers simply because he had no other place to go; no other job to do.

Meanwhile, that other remnant of the vanished army, spared by fate from the blood-letting of the List Regiment, tried to find his way back. In the fall of 1918, Hess had passed his aviator's examination. Just as he seemed to have reached the climax of his military career, peace broke out. Hess was neither a professional soldier like Röhm nor a man without home and family like Hitler, but he felt the downfall. He was just twenty-two years old.

The consequence: Thule Society. Conspiracy. Plans for murder. Remember the club which had planned to shoot Premier Eisner, and Count Arco who had fired the shot. One day leaflets were handed out, the next day grenades were thrown. A young officer in the civil war, he took part in the punitive expedition which overthrew the Red régime in Munich on May 2, 1919. While Tubeuf's old orderly, the gray *agent-provocateur,* was sending his victims to the slaughterhouse wall, Hess lay in the hospital with a bullet in his leg. They must have met in the small circle of armed conspirators in Munich, for everyone knew everyone else. But an unknown in his own circle, Hitler was so inconspicuous that Hess retained no memory of him from those days.

No, the war had not perished completely. There was an army that was still carrying it on at home, and to this army Hitler belonged. He was now a so-called civilian employee with the District Army Command in Munich, the authority governing all troops stationed in Bavaria. It was a military authority, but also far more; it was a center of that armed political grouping which had turned against their own people the war lost on the battlefield, with the aim of overthrowing the new state to which they had just pledged loyalty. We are looking for the mysterious circumstances that transformed the unknown prince of art, the inconspicuous gray soldier into the best known and most conspicuous figure of this disloyal army. After the experience of poison and defeat, here is another reason: the very disloyalty of this army; an army the loftiest aim of which it was to disobey. This at last was the kind of world in which Hitler could follow the pattern that had been familiar to him since childhood: — hatred of authority.

In those months a transformation took place in Hitler. Up to that time he had acted only under orders. In a decisive moment, when he should have acted, he had done nothing: he had failed to denounce the revolutionary sailors. That, on an insignificant scale, was the same crime that Wilhelm II had committed in failing to put down the revolution and in fleeing to Holland. To him, Hitler, such a thing would not happen a second time.

He worked in the political department of the District Army Command. This office called itself press and news bureau, which was tantamount to propaganda and espionage center. As an employee of this bureau he had to participate in the manifold attempts the Munich Reichswehr made to find the ideal form for their projected political movement. For some time Hitler belonged, with Ernst Röhm, to an officers' and soldiers' group which called itself 'The Iron Fist,' tried to terrorize loyal followers of the republican régime, and very probably had its share in many of the secret murders. The real reason for this political activity was by no means clear to most of the men from the beginning, perhaps to none of them. During this activity, Hitler fell — by accident, he says — among a small grouplet called grandiloquently the 'German Workers' Party'; it was so much to his liking that he joined it and ultimately became its leader.

'In the year 1919' — he said, ten years later — 'when I met the handful of men who held their little meetings under the name of German Workers' Party, there was neither a business office nor any employee. There was no paper with letterhead; in fact, even rubber stamps were lacking. The entire property of this seven men's club consisted of a briefcase, in which the incoming and outgoing mail were kept, and a cigar box which served as cash-box. This portable party office in the form of a briefcase traveled under the arms of party comrade Harrer, our 'president'; into every conceivable beer hall and café, in which the party committee — which at that time was the party itself — met.'

The grouplet at this time was in a pitiable state. But although the members, and even more the so-called leaders, were, strictly speaking, nobodies, the grouplet itself had been something more in its time. It was now a remnant of a large movement which, during the war, had counted hundreds of thousands of followers: the pan-German movement of the 'Fatherland Party,' favored by the High Command, paid by the big industrialists, pleading for a 'strong peace' with conquests and annexations. The German Workers' Party had tried, as part of the Fatherland Party, to win the workers for the idea of the 'strong peace,' but this had been a perfect failure as the founder of the small grouplet, Anton Drexler, frankly admits in his autobiography.

Thus the German Workers' Party, although the influence of its members amounted strictly to nothing, had preserved, from old days, the backing of several more important outsiders. When he first entered the party Hitler does not seem to have known that (for instance) Ernst Röhm had become a member some time before. Now Dietrich Eckart, the journalist and poet from the Thule Society and a friend of Röhm and his superior, General von Epp, also joined. For months he had been going around with the plan of forming a new 'middle-class party,' and looking for a leader.

The fourth to join them was Gottfried Feder, the engineer, a man with a real, though questionable, political idea: he wanted to do away with 'big money' or high finance. It was a time of Socialist ferment; for the broad masses capital was the root of all evil, and for the purposes of the new party, Feder had a very fitting answer to the great Socialist question of the day: yes, abolish that part of capital which is totally superfluous, to wit banking capital, which creates no values, but only lays its clutches on interest; but productive capital, expressed in objective values, mines, factories, machines, must be retained. These four men, Röhm, Eckart, Feder, and Hitler, now took the German Workers' Party in hand. With their help Hitler made his way, rather arduously at first, against the resistance of the timid and unimaginative little men who constituted the party leadership. Looking back on this period at a later date, he forgot the entire plot, except for the personal bickering and irritations, made picturesque by their dwarfish dimensions.

'In this year of 1919 my first struggle in the Party began. After long negotiations I put through the acquisition of three rubber stamps. I also succeeded in having our little invitations to meetings hectographed. When, in addition to all that, I pressed for larger meetings, Harrer couldn't follow me. He retired, and that gave me a free path. . . .'

Imagine that thundering voice, demanding three rubber stamps! And the speeches in behalf of hectographed invitations! Hitler was just thirty years old. To judge by all of his own accounts and those of others, he was a human nothing; consistently, he began his historical career as a political nothing. All his life he has loved to describe the tininess of those beginnings. He himself has indirectly admitted that a sure instinct led him among the smallest fellows — because only there could he hope to be greatest. But never has he uttered so much as a word to the effect that he performed all this political work as a political employee of the Reichswehr; that as a paid 'political soldier' he started the first mass meeting of his soldier-party.

'We ourselves were horrified at our boldness. Would one of us be able to speak in this hall? Would he get stage-fright and start to stammer after the tenth sentence and be shouted and whistled down? That is why this hall is holy to us and eternal in our memory, because we did succeed that time. When we came in, the hall was full of opponents, Red trash and some so-called "neutrals," but actually all enemies. The first speaker was Doctor Dingfelder. Then I had the honor of speaking to a big crowd for the first time. I hadn't been talking ten minutes when they began to yell interruptions at me from all sides. A small troop of my most faithful supporters intervened from time to time; here and there there was a gleam of side-arms. After two hours we managed to assert ourselves. I will never forget the time when we read our program for the first time and flung this challenge at the people: Now, if you dare, come out against it! All that happened since then was not as hard as this first step. . . .'

This is his own later report of the first public meeting held by the party. It took place on February 24, 1920, in the Hofbräuhaus in Munich. Hitler was not the chief speaker, but the homeopathic physician, Johannes Dingfelder. Nor was Hitler the party leader. The leader, after the retirement of the above-mentioned Harrer, was

Anton Drexler: a bespectacled, modest man, by trade a toolmaker, but without doubt the intellectual father of the whole movement; for it was he who, in the middle of the war, had been inspired with the idea of founding a nationalist-minded workers' party, which would be 'at the disposal of the general staff.' The party did not yet bear the name National Socialist, the term was still unknown. But the most revealing item in Hitler's report is that he was surrounded by a body of personal supporters; that these supporters 'intervened' against interrupters, and that they had side-arms. In other words, a troop of armed soldiers founded the National Socialist Party. The employee of the political bureau of the Munich District Army Command had come with a squad of Reichswehr soldiers; according to reports from a hostile source, they belonged to a company of mine-throwers. First he had his political opponents driven out with cold steel — this is the meaning of 'intervention,' as everyone knows who ever attended a National Socialist meeting in those years. Then he shouted at the terrorized crowd: If anyone else dares, let him speak up against the program. Before the meeting, he was not sure whether he was an orator or not, but he did feel sure of his side-arms.

Later he said aptly: 'When I finally closed the meeting, we were not alone in feeling that a wolf had been born which was destined to break into the herd of the swindlers and misleaders of the people.'

Thus the National Socialist Movement was born, under the sign of the sword. Its program, which Hitler put forward on that February 24, 1920, consisted of twenty-five points. It was written by Hitler, Anton Drexler, Gottfried Feder, and Dietrich Eckart.

The first point is Hitler's. It expresses his revolt against his Austrian fatherland; shows the new National Socialist Movement as a belated descendant of the great European revolt of nations: 'We demand that all Germans be gathered together in a Greater Germany on the basis of the right of all peoples to self-determination.'

This is a demand without end. There are Germans all over the globe — that is, people of German language and descent, for that is how the word is meant. In some places they live densely settled, as in southern Russia, South Africa, southern Brazil; not to mention

Milwaukee or Cincinnati. There are six great nations on the earth, large parts of which live outside the political jurisdiction of the mother country: Indians, Chinese, Japanese, Spaniards, Italians, and finally, Germans. The principle of the 'right of nations to self-determination' has transformed these national splinters scattered throughout the earth into political dynamite, charged with intense peril whenever a power-loving and belligerent mother country tries to use them as a weapon for its world policies. The National Socialists were later to maintain that in Europe alone there were thirty-three millions of such Germans, though they arrived at this figure by placidly counting foreign peoples such as the Dutch.

The idea of self-determination originated in old Austria, where Germans, Hungarians, Italians, and Slavs, of different language and nationality, lived under one crown and fought one another bitterly. After the war it became a world slogan. Woodrow Wilson had taken it up; it had served as a yardstick for the Peace of Versailles. To all European nations the same right of self-determination had been granted — except to defeated Germany. Regions inhabited by Germans had been given to foreign countries without plebiscite, consequently without self-determination — German South Tyrol to Italy, the so-called Sudeten Germans to Czechoslovakia; and even the desire for union with Germany expressed by the German parts of Austria in 1919 had been coldly rebuffed. From the democratic right of self-determination Hitler forged one of his sharpest and most effective weapons in a struggle for power, whose ultimate aims went far beyond any right of self-determination.

The program goes on demanding 'equal rights for the German nation,' 'abrogation of the peace treaties of Versailles and St. Germain,' 'land and soil [colonies]'; for the former German colonies in Africa had been taken away by the Versailles Treaty.

'Only a racial comrade' — so the program goes on — 'can be a citizen. Only a person of German blood can be a racial comrade, without regard to religion. Consequently no Jew can be a racial comrade.'

Here the program shows that it means business. And it means 'Jewish' capital when it demands in point 11: 'Abolition of all income obtained without work or pains; interest slavery must be broken.'

Then follows two strange paragraphs. Point 13 runs: 'We demand that all corporate enterprises [trusts] be taken over by the state.' And point 17: 'We demand a passage of a law for confiscation without remuneration of land for communal purposes, abolition of land rent and the prevention of all speculation in soil.'

Points 11, 13, and 17 can be called the Socialist part of the program. They embrace two central ideas: the destruction of finance capital and the protection of the creative industrial personality. They also embody a less pronounced tendency to attack large property-holdings as such. The idea that the power of finance capital could be broken by the abolition of capital interest originated with Gottfried Feder. In the beginning, this plan made a tremendous impression on Hitler; not because he approved it from the economic point of view — about such things he admittedly understood nothing — but because Hitler regarded all finance capital as Jewish capital. Point 13 is intended to protect small business. 'Taken over by the state' sounds strongly Socialist, but the main emphasis is not on this; the real meaning of the clause is that the corporations should be eliminated from private business and replaced by small individual enterprises. Needless to say, none of these points ever has been achieved.

The program then coined some fine-sounding slogans. It affirmed that the party upholds the standpoint of a positive Christianity (few people realized that this meant a non-Biblical, non-ecclesiastical Christianity); and that the ethical principle of the movement was: 'The common good before the individual good.' Finally: 'In order that all this may be carried out, we demand the creation of a strong central power in the Reich, unconditional authority of the political central parliament over the whole Reich and its general organization: chambers representing the corporations and trades shall be constituted. . . .'

The word 'parliament' is striking. Apparently the founders of the party were not yet clear or not yet agreed concerning one of their chief aims: the replacement of democracy by dictatorship. The original founders, the Drexlers and Harrers, actually did not want a dictatorship. The example of Soviet Russia was too terrifying. They occasionally referred to their party as a 'party of the Left.'

But in demanding a strong central power in the Reich, Hitler impressed his absolute will on his comrades. In the next few years this became one of the decisive party problems. Up to 1918, Germany had consisted of relatively independent federative states; formally, only foreign policy and war came within the sphere of the Reich. When the princes fell, taking with them the historical glamour of the old political subdivisions, the republic ruthlessly broke the old independence of these subdivisions, particularly in the realm of tax and finance. Of course, this aroused violent local opposition; in parts of the Reich an embittered discontent against Berlin arose, particularly in proud and volatile Bavaria. The German counter-revolution consciously exploited this local discontent. An armed uprising was organized amid the tumult and trumpets of national festivals. Rheumatic old officers still regarded themselves, not as leaders of the Reichswehr, but as colonels in the Royal Bavarian Army. A deep-seated, often humorous hatred for the more progressive, more industrial, far larger, richer, more powerful, and predominantly Protestant Prussia, which for generations had been leading Germany, was one of the oldest national sentiments of Catholic Bavaria. There were influential political figures who wanted it under certain circumstances to secede from the Reich altogether, perhaps to join Austria; some even wanted to form a new Danubian state under French protection; at the very least, these men wanted to restore Bavaria's king and its old independence of Berlin.

During the next three years, the future of Bavaria became a question of life and death for Germany and for Hitler. In his personal propaganda he unscrupulously exploited all opposition to Berlin, but in his politics he combated it. He spoke Bavarian at meetings, but his thoughts were Pan-German. In this respect he differed from many fellow members and sympathizers. It was self-evident that he would demand a strong central power, some day he wanted to be that central power himself. Therefore, point 25 sounds as though a sentence from *The Protocols of the Wise Men of Zion* had been ringing in Hitler's ears: 'For modern society, a colossus with feet of clay, we shall create an unprecedented centralization, which will unite all powers in the hands of the government. We shall create a hierarchical constitution, which will mechanically govern all movements of individuals.'

Three weeks after the party's first public meeting the goal seemed reached, the struggle won, the new party already obsolete. The military *putsch* of March, 1920, which failed in the greater part of the Reich, succeeded in Bavaria; the Reichswehr overthrew the government, put in a new cabinet enjoying their confidence, under Premier Gustav von Kahr, installed their own men as ministers and police presidents. During the *putsch,* Hitler flew to Berlin in a small plane to entreat the Prussian generals to hold out, as Bavarian assistance would soon be forthcoming. For Berlin it was too late; but in Munich events seemed to have gone almost ahead of Hitler. The Reichswehr, a short time before a rebellious faction, now had become the state; Hitler, still a rebel, had to give up his desk in the District Army Command (April 1, 1920).

Nevertheless, the Reichswehr went on supporting its child and, if possible, guiding its steps. There was a little weekly in Munich, originally nothing but a rather suspect, scandal-mongering enterprise, called *The Munich Observer* (*Münchner Beobachter*); a gossip sheet, not more. After the war it slowly turned anti-Semitic, changed its name into *Racial Observer* (*Völkischer Beobachter*); on account of internal and personal quarrels the paper was rather cool toward Hitler and his friends. Now Major-General Franz von Epp, commander of the Bavarian infantry troops, and the body to which Röhm was the right hand, bought the *Völkischer Beobachter* for the National Socialists; rather he raised a fund among wealthy persons and gave it to Dietrich Eckart to buy a paper. To be sure, the rich men were little inclined to support a party calling itself Socialist. But Hitler publicly set them straight:

'For National Socialists it goes without saying that industrial capital, since it creates values, will remain untouched. We combat only Jewish international loan capital. . . .'

As a matter of fact, it was, above all, the material and financial organization of the new party that kept Hitler busy in these first months, when the Reich was shaken by tremendous uprisings. All his life he has had a possessive sense, as far as his party was concerned; far more than for his own person. This is how he tells the story:

'At the beginning of 1920, we succeeded in renting the council chamber of the Sternecker brewery in Sternecker Alley as a business office. It was a small, vaulted, dark room with brown wooden paneling, about six yards long and three broad. On overcast days everything was dark.

'We brightened up the walls with posters announcing our meetings, and for the first time hung up our new party flag. When we held a meeting, it was spread out on the table — in short, it remained always before our eyes.'

In this dark back room, Hitler delivered his hour-long speeches several times a week to fifteen or twenty persons; a few party comrades and the friends they brought along. There he stood amid the cigarsmoke in his gray soldier's uniform. He coughed out of his gas-corroded throat, and shouted: the day will come, 'when the banner of our movement will fly over the Reichstag, over the Castle in Berlin, yes, over every German house.'

Among the audience was that twenty-three-year-old student, formerly a war aviator, a volunteer in the List Regiment. He saw the twenty men, he saw the gray speaker, and he asked himself — as he later reported: Was this man a fool, or was he the man who would save all Germany? He decided the latter. The thundering voice shook Rudolf Hess, and carried him away. He became a party member and soon a close friend of the speaker's.

Hess was originally a purer type than most of the avid and broken figures in this armed Bohemia. All the greater was his determination to think his way into their life and activity. To him violence was not an urge, but a principle. Nature had created him to be the mirror and sloganizer of other men's savagery; lending his approval where strong men entered upon dubious ventures; lending encouragement where difficulties caused their determination to flag; and finally lending even his hand, when a harder man had transformed his ideas into a command.

This flying, shooting, leaflet-distributing student, mathematician and later geographer embodied in his longing and his attitudes the intellectual who is becoming the new ruler of our age. A lone engineer stands in his control room, high above the mighty gleaming machine; he presses a button, and the machine begins to roar with its hundred pistons. He pulls a lever, and it stands still as a rock. We want a state that can be regulated as smoothly as that, a state for mechanics. *Heil* the chief engineer!

Hess drew up a political program for the German intellectual, and at the same time drew his portrait. A wealthy South American had endowed a prize at the University of Munich for a thesis entitled: 'How must the man be constituted who will lead Germany back to her old heights?' Hess wrote the thesis and won the prize. He had drawn a picture of his beloved Hitler and described his future path.

The Wise Men of Zion had prophesied:

> We shall speak with the people in the streets and squares. . . . Our Right lies in might. In a state where might is badly organized, we will create a new Right, by seizing the government in accordance with the Right of the stronger. . . . An autocratic personality will assume the leadership. Without unlimited power no civilization can survive; this power does not repose in the masses, but in their leader, whoever he may be. The mass consists of barbarians. . . . By effective executions, we shall uphold the reign of terror and force blind, unconditional obedience. The knowledge that we are merciless will suffice to eliminate any disobedience. . . . The highest principle of every successful political art is the strictest concealment of all undertakings. . . . Our leaders must move toward their goal with unparalleled boldness. Then we shall break all resistance in our path. . . . Imperceptibly the last traces of all constitutional Justice will vanish, and finally the time will come when we can openly seize all state power in the name of our autocracy. . . . We shall arouse ferment, struggle and enmity in the whole of Europe, and thence in other continents. . . .

Hess writes:

> For the sake of national salvation the dictator does not shun to use the weapons of his enemy, demagogy, slogans, street parades, etc. Where all authority has vanished, only a man of the people can establish authority. This was shown in the case of Mussolini. The deeper the dictator was originally rooted in the broad masses, the better he understands how to treat them psychologically, the less the workers will distrust him, the more supporters he will win among these most energetic ranks of the people. He himself has

nothing in common with the mass, like every great man he is all personality. . . . When necessity commands, he does not shrink before bloodshed. Great questions are always decided by blood and iron. And the question at stake is: Shall we rise or be destroyed?

Parliament may go babbling, or not — the man acts. It transpires that despite his many speeches, he knows how to keep silent. Perhaps his own supporters are the most keenly disappointed. . . . In order to reach his goal, he is prepared to trample on his closest friends. . . . For the sake of the great ultimate goal, he must even be willing temporarily to appear a traitor against the nation in the eyes of the majority. The lawgiver proceeds with terrible hardness. . . . He knows the peoples and their influential individuals. As the need arises, he can trample them with the boots of a grenadier, or with cautious and sensitive fingers spin threads reaching as far as the Pacific Ocean. . . . In either case, the treaties of enslavement will fall. One day we shall have our new, Greater Germany, embracing all those who are of German blood.

The portrait culminates in an unexpected perspective:

The work must not be cut to the towering dimensions of its builder, or the whole will totter at his decease like the state of Frederick and Bismarck. New independent personalities, to guide the steed of Germania remounted in the future, do not thrive under the dictator. Therefore, he performs his last great deed: instead of drinking his power to the dregs, he sets it down and stands aside as a loyal adviser.

This is Hitler, drawn by himself, for Hess is his *alter ego*; a flattering self-portrait, painting more his wishes than his features, but for that very reason authentic, though not entirely true. He exposes his most secret aspiration: a carefree private life as the goal of a magnificent career, as the reward for joyous struggles and disgraceful acts excused by patriotism. Just in this weakness it is the true program of that particular variation of the armed intellectual: the armed bohemian.

Dietrich Eckart had introduced Alfred Rosenberg, the young fugitive from Russia, to the party. But for the time being the recognized spiritual leader of this small group was Eckart, the journalist and poet, twenty-one years older than Hitler. He had a strong influence on the younger man, probably the strongest anyone ever has had on him. And rightly so. A gifted writer, satirist, orator, even (or so Hitler believed) thinker, Eckart was the same sort of uprooted, agitated, and far from immaculate soul. Born of well-to-do parents in a little town of northern Bavaria, he had been a failure as a law student because he had drunk too much and worked too little. Then in Berlin — already in his forties — he had led the life of a vagrant who believes himself to be a poet. He could tell Hitler that he (like Hitler himself) had lodged in flop houses and slept on park benches because of Jewish machinations which (in his case) had prevented him from becoming a successful playwright. He had grown to be a morphine addict and had spent some time in an asylum for the mentally diseased, where his theatrical gifts finally found a haven, for he had staged plays there and used the inmates as actors. Now he was the grand old — and often drunk — man of the young Nazi Movement. It would be interesting to know how and in which member of the circle the realization dawned that *The Protocols of the Wise Men of Zion* was not a pamphlet at all, but a secret textbook of world domination. Nothing contradicts the assumption that, in any event, Hitler secretly and with sealed lips conceived the idea that he himself would become the 'king' and 'ruler' of the world prophesied in the *Protocols*. He was now — 1921 — in his thirty-third year, exactly the year in which the diabolical vocation, preceded by a short blindness, comes to Soloviev's Antichrist.

The Antichrist first appeared in the form of an utter ne'er-do-well. He is the human scum of all classes. He is the sort of man who in a normal civilized world is totally useless and unsuccessful, but who in a disintegrating society conquers and seizes all. The burning heavens are mirrored in a mud puddle. A world revolution has blown these uprooted existences from all directions to a table in a Munich beer hall; from the wreckage of dead classes arises the new class of intellectuals, and at the head march the most ruthless, those with the least to lose, hence the strongest: the armed bohemians, to whom war is home and civil war fatherland.

Chapter VI

'ARYANS OF ALL
NATIONS, UNITE'

THE NEW ARMY SOON WENT INTO BATTLE; AND
had there not been a war, this army would have created it. The
army might have been called Röhm's army, if its actual builder
and military leader at that time had been mentioned; and the
name of the war, Hitler's war. For it was the war of the new
army against their own people, and nobody defined the necessity
of this war so clearly and sharply as Hitler did.

Bavaria was the center of this military enterprise and, with some
ups and downs, remained so until the end of 1923. The sullen hostility of this southern country against Prussia in the north created
an atmosphere in which all preparations of the counter-revolution
matured faster than elsewhere. The régime of Prime-Minister
Gustav von Kahr and his Police-President Pöhner was already the
counter-revolution in power. Many of their Prussian leaders had
taken refuge in Bavaria; the first of them General Ludendorff.

Thus, in the summer and fall of 1920, an illegal but by no means
secret army was established, chiefly by Röhm. On paper this army
numbered as many as 200,000 men, and it may have had more
than 100,000 actual effectives. Although it was based on Bavaria,
it had ramifications through the whole of Germany and even in
Austria, and a loosely knit organization connected the Bavarian
nucleus with the more clandestine organizations in northern Ger-

many. The name of the army, 'Citizens' Defense' (*Einwohnerwehr*), stated clearly that this body was directed only against the 'Red' enemy within; against the Communists first, but possibly also — this was more secretly whispered — against the republican régime of the Reich.

But many of the leaders would not admit this, would not even believe it. They claimed that the real purpose of the Citizens' Defense was to be a protection against the enemy without; not just against the far superior French army on Germany's western frontier, but against Bolsheviks in the northeast; against Lithuanians, who wanted to take away the German city of Memel and later really did; especially against the Poles. If the Berlin government tried to do away with these illegal troops and 'free corps,' their leaders would have accused the government of depriving the country of its last remnants of protection; and quite a few of them would have been sincere. Even a man like Röhm, as much as he hated the new state, expected that one day his army would fight the enemy on the border of the Reich.

It was Hitler, and almost Hitler alone, who had a much clearer conception of the political situation and the immediate issue. He insisted on the absolute necessity of fighting the new state first, of overthrowing the republican government before undertaking any ventures against the foreign enemy. 'Civil war — no foreign war' — this formula of Hitler's policy shows that he really was a man with a political idea. The foreign enemy itself, to be sure, did not want to take any risks. The Allies demanded that this army be dissolved, as contrary to the provisions of the Treaty of Versailles. With the consent of England, French and Belgian troops occupied the cities of Duisburg and Düsseldorf on the Rhine, March, 1921, and England subjected Germany to a killing export duty. A great English paper, the *Morning Post,* wrote that this policy would tear the German Reich apart once and for all, and prevent it from ever again becoming a menace to all Europe. The so-called London ultimatum (May 5, 1921) set the total sum of the political debt to be paid by Germany as indemnity for war damage to the Allies, at 132 billion marks. Lloyd George, the British premier, said: 'We wish to state clearly once and for all that the German responsibility for the war will be treated as a *"cause jugée."* '

At the same time a bloody war was being fought between bands of German and Polish volunteers in the province of Upper Silesia on the Polish border. The peace treaty stipulated that a plebiscite decide whether Upper Silesia, one of Germany's three great coal provinces, should belong to Germany or Poland. The plebiscite in Upper Silesia gave (March 20, 1921), a clear German majority (707,000 to 479,000), though by far not so pronounced as in the German-Polish border provinces of West and East Prussia, one time before. Poland sought to seize the province by means of an illegal army (the so-called 'insurrectionary leagues'). Germany sent her illegal army against them, among them the most active groups of the Bavarian Citizens' Defense. Hitler cried: 'We have lost our first coal province, the Saar on the German French border, to the French; we shall lose the second and largest, the Ruhr, for it lies within the range of French cannon; the third and last, Upper Silesia, must be lost unless our illegal army [Citizens' Defense] defends it.' But he added — and this is his true political line: 'This is possible only if the pigsty of Jewish corruption, democratic hypocrisy, and Marxist deception is swept out with an iron broom.'

An internal crisis was approaching in the Reich. The German government, under Foreign Minister Doctor Walter Simons, an outstanding jurist but less of a diplomat, tried to overcome the home crisis by a solution of the foreign questions, and to gain strength for the solution of the foreign questions by overcoming the home crisis. Simons, willing in principle to carry out the peace treaty, regarded the economic section, providing for an indemnity in the scores of billions, as impracticable; in this view the German government had the support of John Maynard Keynes, the eminent British economist. It wanted to negotiate with the Allies; but it did not want to obey commands and suffer penalties for an indefinite time. In other words, the Allies treated Germany as a defeated, and, therefore, still reluctant, enemy; the German government wanted to be treated like a party that had concluded a negotiated peace — although, in their eyes, a definitely unfavorable and unjust one.

Thus, the German government agreed, though only half-heartedly, to the dissolution of the illegal army, thus hoping to gain better control also over the legal army, which still was too closely connected with that illegal army, especially in Bavaria. It also tried to force, upon these bands of legal and illegal soldiers, recognition for the new black, red, and gold flag of the republic. Any of these great and petty causes seemed likely to touch off the explosion which would send all Germany up in flames.

In March, 1921, the worst of all happened: the Communists succeeded in starting a revolt in central Germany. This seemed to give Simons some justification for the illegal army. But the majority of parliamentarians regarded resistance against the combined will of France and England as hopeless. On May 10, 1921, Simons and the whole government fell. A new government, led by Reich Chancellor Doctor Joseph Wirth and Foreign Minister Doctor Walter Rathenau, made a new, almost heroic attempt to arrive at a true peace with France and England. Rathenau tried to convince German public opinion that France really had some claims for a German indemnity. The new government accepted the London ultimatum. It demanded that Bavaria dissolve the Citizens' Defense. The menace of civil war hung like a black cloud over Germany. Hitler was exultant; he believed that his hour had already struck:

> We will incite the people, and not only incite, we will lash them to a frenzy. We will preach struggle, the inexorable struggle against this parliamentary brood, this whole system which will not cease before either Germany has been totally ruined or else one day a man with an iron skull appears. His boots may be dirty, but he will have a clear conscience and a steel fist, he will put an end to the speeches of these matinée heroes and show the nation some action.

But his hour had not struck yet. The civilian elements were still too strong. Bavaria herself was not united. The leaders of the bourgeois parties began to be horrified at the illegal army, and for this Hitler's threats may have been partly responsible. Bavaria gave in. On June 29, the Reich government dissolved the Citizens' Defense, and the Bavarian government looked on in silence. This was the political death of Premier Kahr; he finally resigned on September 21, 1921.

Civil government was trying to take over, even in Bavaria. It strove to exclude the Reichswehr from power; disbanded the armed parties and patriotic murder clubs. On the surface, it seemed to have succeeded, but not in actuality. This secret army fighting for its existence could not be destroyed by decrees; such a force can be destroyed only by force. Up to this point, Hitler had been the secret army's spokesman, its attorney before the public; the crisis made him one of its leaders.

Thus far, we have viewed Hitler as a piece of his element, a part of the German counter-revolution, a flake amid a mighty foam, a bubble that slowly swells up and becomes strangely iridescent. But to regard him only as the political *enfant terrible* of our epoch, as merely a great adventurer, a great demagogue, or a great dictator would be to underestimate the significance of the man. He is something much more basic. In his qualities, in his destiny, and in his acts he is an image, a product, and an executant of a social revolution, which has spread in great waves throughout the globe; the greatest probably since the fall of the Roman Empire. In terms of modern sociology we have attempted to interpret this revolution as the organization of modern society by the intellectual. This new social type has a different face in every country; in the lands of Europe, broken by the First World War, his face is always topped by a soldier's cap.

In the maelstrom of the German counter-revolution, dozens of hitherto nameless figures suddenly rose to the surface, founded and led so-called defense leagues, and with them conquered cities and provinces. Hitler started out as one of these, but soon distinguished himself from all the others. All of them strove to gain control of the key points of power. But Hitler recognized more clearly than any other that in time of disorganization the true source of power lies in public opinion. 'Only a man of the people can create authority,' says Hess. No one has better understood the advice of the Wise Men of Zion to speak with the people 'in the streets and squares' than this man from the Viennese lodging-house. None took so much pleasure in just that. Others had friends, a wife, profession; he had only the mass to talk to. Silent in a circle of three, sullen and sluggish in conversation, without interest in his own private life, this miserable human nothing could think only in public terms, feel only the feeling of the mass, and when the nothing spoke with the people, it was as though the voice of the people were speaking.

What Hitler told the people about the depravity of the Jews, he could say just as effectively about the Prussian junkers, the Pope in Rome, or the high English nobility. His revelation of a world conspiracy of Jews achieved its extraordinary effect, not because of the Jews, but because of the world conspiracy. The sentiment that our modern society had arrived at a breaking point, that millions and millions would be crushed in the impending collapse, tormented every man's soul. With unerring sureness Hitler expressed the speechless panic of the masses faced by an invisible enemy and gave the nameless specter a name. He was a pure fragment of the modern mass soul, unclouded by any personal qualities. One scarcely need ask with what arts he conquered the masses; he did not conquer them, he portrayed and represented them. His speeches are day-dreams of this mass soul; they are chaotic, full of contradictions, if their words are taken literally, often senseless, as dreams are, and yet charged with deeper meaning. Vulgar vilification, flat jokes alternate with ringing, sometimes exalted, phrases. The speeches begin always with deep pessimism and end in overjoyed redemption, a triumphant happy ending; often they can be refuted by reason, but they follow the far mightier logic of the subconscious, which no refutation can touch. Hitler has given speech to the speechless terror of the modern mass, and to the nameless fear he has given a name. That makes him the greatest mass orator of the mass age.

He grew in the decay of his own cause. Röhm set out to reorganize the suddenly broken army with the greatest possible speed. Things had to be done less openly than before. Clubs with harmless names were founded; they were all private armies of varying sizes. Hitler himself was given a private band, Röhm producing the personnel, the arms, the officers. In place of the little group of soldiers from the Hofbräuhaus, Hitler could soon muster companies and even regiments. The troop was given (August, 1921) the supposedly harmless but quite transparent name of 'Gymnastics and Sports Division.' Its first recruiting proclamation said:

The N.S.D.A.P. (*Nationalsozialistische Deutsche Arbeiterpartei*: National Socialist German Workers' Party) has formed its own gymnastics and sport division within the framework of its organization. It will embody and propagate the military idea of a free nation. . . . It will instill a boundless desire for action in the hearts of our young members, hammer and burn into their brains that history does not make men, but men history. And that the man who lends himself defenseless to the chains of slavery deserves the slave's yoke. In it, we will continue to cultivate loyalty between comrade and comrade, and joyful obedience to the leader. . . .

It was at this time that the corporal from the List Regiment first met the man who one day should be his second in power. This occurred in the thick of the struggle over the Citizens' Defense, at one of those great demonstrations on a public square which raise passions to fever heat but lead only to defeat. A former captain of the *Luftwaffe*, at that time a private citizen unconcerned with politics, was an onlooker. Hitler, by this time widely known and a center of much controversy, was leaning silently against a pillar, not far from the former captain. The demonstration was drawing to an end. Voices arose: Let Hitler speak! A man stepped up and asked Hitler if he would like to say a few words. Only then did Göring see who was standing next to him. He had heard a good deal about Hitler. Hitler said in his firm, thundering voice: 'If I spoke, I would destroy the unity of the meeting. I don't want to do that!' That was all. But the captain went home and said to his wife that he had seen and heard this man for the first time and had carried away an indelible impression; he believed in Hitler. This was a later story, perhaps somewhat exaggerated; but Hermann Wilhelm Göring was neither the first nor the last whom Hitler's astonishing voice had hypnotized with an insignificant remark.

Göring, born January 12, 1893, in Rosenheim, Bavaria, son of a German diplomat at that time consul-general in Haiti, might actually be called a foster-child of the Prussian Army. He spent part of his youth in the house of a Jewish friend of the family in Austria; later he grew up, far from home and family life, in several boarding-schools; finally in the officers' school of Lichterfelde, near Berlin. At this time, as he later told the story, he often envied his luckier classmates, who had a family and who, therefore, were invited to attend parties at the emperor's court. He was brought up as a soldier, and he became a soldier by profession.

He had begun the World War as an infantry officer, and then, in defiance of his superiors, made himself into an aviator by taking flying lessons from a friend by the name of Lörzer. He was a good combat pilot, sparing neither himself, his subordinates, nor his planes. At the end of the war he was leading a pursuit squadron, which Baron von Richthofen, the most famous of German World War aviators, had commanded before him. He was decorated with the *Pour le Mérite,* the highest distinction accessible to a soldier of his rank. But medals were not the only pay he obtained for his achievements. The German front-line fliers had great influence in the choice of planes and engines; manufacturers sought to win this influence in their own way, and all aviators did not resist these temptations, which began with golden cigarette cases concealed beneath their napkins at banquets. In partnership with Prince Philipp of Hessia, a fellow officer, he established a shoe factory for army orders — in the midst of the war. His friendship with Prince Philipp later took on prime importance for Göring, when the prince became son-in-law to the king of Italy. Again and again he had startling luck in his personal encounters. During the war he was quartered for a time at Stenay on the Maas. In near-by Charleville the crown prince had his dissolute and justly notorious headquarters. Göring made the acquaintance of Friedrich Wilhelm, and this, too, was to prove profitable.

He was on top of the world. Everything that an ambitious man can hope to have at the age of twenty-five had fallen to Göring's lot. He had fame, money, connections, future, and, best of all, pride in his own accomplishments. More important than his private career, he had a small share in the domination of the world. Since Napoleon I, no group of European men had looked forward to such brilliant careers as offered themselves to the young leaders of this German Army, which from the English Channel to the Black Sea and the Euphrates seemed to have conquered a world empire by the force of its arms.

In every respect they were on top of the world, and yet Göring required artificial exaltation. Life in the flying corps was perilous, though in many ways pleasant. The aviators were the coddled and petted darlings of the Army, with frequent rest periods, the best of food, and every possible consideration; the accomplishment of the individual was more conspicuous, less immersed in the squadron than twenty years later. Nerves suffered in this up and down between death and champagne; some took to drugs. Göring became a morphine addict. Up to 1932 his vice never left him completely. Later he seems to have overcome it; this rare feat of will characterizes the man.

From these giddy heights there came a fall: the eleventh of November, 1918. From the first this meant a bitter struggle for daily bread. After the peace, Germany was permitted no military, and very few commercial, planes. German aviators emigrated to near-by countries. Göring became a transport pilot in Denmark and Sweden, carrying passengers and mail bags. One winter day he set out from Stockholm with a single passenger, Count Eric von Rosen. They flew to Rosen's estate of Rockelstadt, where they landed on a frozen pond in front of the castle. Göring was hospitably received and Count Rosen's whole family turned out to be friends of Germany. These Swedish aristocrats had intermarried with North-German families; they had relatives who were serving or had served as officers in the German Army. Göring's host spoke with enthusiasm of Germany's future and even sang German songs to the accompaniment of the lute. Two large swastikas adorned the hall. The lady of the house, it transpired, had a sister, Carin von Kantzow, née Baroness Fock. She had an eight-year-old son, but was unhappily married and spent most of her time with her relatives. She was beautiful and charming, but suffered from epilepsy. Carin von Kantzow soon dissolved her marriage and married the German transport pilot, Hermann Göring.

His marriage brought Göring a certain amount of money. He returned to Germany and enrolled as a student of economics in Munich. Up to that time he had stood aside from politics and had taken no part in the various armed activities of the German counter-revolution. Now he became a National Socialist. The corporal and the captain soon developed a liking for one another. A year later (1922) Göring was leader of the new party army. Hitler might have had better trained and more experienced officers than this aviator. But with a sure instinct, he preferred this wild, unrestrained fellow, because he was more compatible with Hitler and the whole movement. Moreover, he was a bridge to good society, and politically that was of the greatest importance. Perhaps it was not entirely without bearing that Göring occasionally, in private and *sub rosa,* lent his leader money; this pecuniary aid began with millions, then rose to billions and finally trillions, for the inflation was raging through Germany.

With it raged murder, the most hideous and, for a time, the most effective weapon of the counter-revolution. The very moment the Citizens' Defense and its offspring had to go underground, they became the army of the murderers again, more so than ever. Matthias Erzberger, former Reich Minister of Finance, fell while taking a walk in the Schwarzwald on August 26, 1921, and the killers escaped through the dark woods. On November 11, 1918, Erzberger had signed the armistice in Marshal Foch's railway coach, because the military leaders lacked the courage to seal their defeat with their own signatures. As a man and as a political figure, he was not beyond reproach; but he had at least one deed of historic importance to his credit: he had given Germany a unified financial administration after the war, had made the 'federal states' financially dependent on the Reich and so helped to break down their semi-sovereignty. By this financial and political unification of the German Empire, point 24 of Hitler's program (strong central power) had to a large extent been taken care of thirteen years before Hitler came to power. It was for this — and because he was too able, too successful, briefly, too dangerous — that Erzberger was killed by Hitler's own men. The first leader of Hitler's private army, Johann Ulrich Klintsch, most probably an accomplice, was in prison for a while; but in the end the killing of Erzberger was another of those deeds of the secret murderers' army that was never avenged.

'The man who leads the German people leads it with his head, and his head is a pledge,' said Hitler at a public meeting in October. Promptly more revolvers went off, this time against a leader of the

Munich Social Democrats by the name of Auer; the darkness of night saved the intended victim, but, as usual, his assailants as well. The Social Democrats were up in arms and decided to put an end to the National Socialists once and for all. Early in November, they marched several hundred strong to the Hofbräuhaus, where Hitler was scheduled to speak. Hitler ordered his gymnastics and sport division to throw the visitors out by force. When a Socialist ventured an interruption, shouting the word 'Liberty!,'[1] the National Socialists under the leadership of Rudolf Hess jumped on him. A brawl ensued. The National Socialists were inferior in numbers and would probably have got the worst of it, if President Pöhner's police had not, as always, come to their assistance. From that day on, the National Socialist private army was known as the *Sturmabteilung* (Storm Division), or S.A.

It was the time when Hitler had just had a unique stroke of luck: he had proved to be the successful prophet of the nation's doom, justified by events. His forecast that Germany would lose the coal basin of Upper Silesia, despite her success in the plebiscite, came true, October 20, 1921. The Allies, basing themselves on a League of Nations' report, gave the larger part of the small border country to Germany, but that part, with about four fifths of the heavy industry and most of the coal mines, was given to Poland — a decision, by the way, made against the will of England.

From now on for twelve years the National Socialist Movement was to be the negative barometer of Germany's fate in the world; it was bound to grow with the decline of the country, to fall with its rise. This was the picture of Hitler's success: disaster attracted the crowds; the crowds attracted money. Financial backing came when the enterprise began to look promising.

Success and money finally won for Hitler complete domination over the National Socialist Party. He had grown too powerful for the founders; they — Anton Drexler among them — wanted to limit him and press him to the wall. But it turned out that they were too late. He had the newspaper behind him, the backers, and the growing S.A. At a certain distance, he had the Reichswehr

---

[1] The word *Freiheit* (liberty) was used by the German Social Democrats as a greeting and cheer. (Trs.)

behind him too. To break all resistance for good, he left the party for three days, and the trembling members obediently chose him as the first, unlimited chairman, for practical purposes responsible to no one, in place of Anton Drexler, the modest founder, who had to content himself with the post of honorary chairman (July 29, 1921). From that day on, Hitler was the leader of Munich's National Socialist Movement.

But he failed in his attempt to force the 'leader principle' upon other anti-Semitic, 'racial,' or 'German Socialist' groups over the rest of Germany. A nation-wide convention of these groups in Munich, January, 1922, rejected Hitler's plea for absolute power — tiny groups, little men, but they did not accept a dictator.

These men — anti-Semitic, reactionary, militarist, as they certainly were — probably were completely at a loss to understand the meaning of the new movement. Not a few may have shivered inwardly when Hitler in his speech coldly declared: 'I thank Messrs. Klintsch and Maurice [Klintsch's aide] for their activity in the organization of the storm troop. Even if Klintsch has been in prison for suspicion of the Erzberger killing, we did not shake him off as certain other parties would have. On the contrary: when he came back we carried him through the hall on our shoulders.'

They may have asked themselves, 'What's the good of it all?' when they heard Hitler shout: 'We want nothing to do with parliaments. Anyone who goes into a swamp sinks into the muck. The big things have always been done in opposition to parliaments. . . .' And possibly they found that Hitler was expecting too much from them when he said: 'A minority suffices to overthrow a state when the majority of the population has gone soft and lost its direction.' He even despised what they considered the greatest achievements of German history: '. . . And we do not want the thing they call unity, which includes everything that is rotten; what we want is struggle; struggle against Jewish democracy, which is no more nor less than a machine for the elimination of genius . . . we do not want millions of indifferent rabble, we want a hundred thousand men — headstrong, defiant men. Our success will force the millions to follow us.'

With such speeches Hitler frightened away those who would have liked to share his leadership, and this may have been his intention. But this was just the bait which hooked a certain type of the masses; those lonely minds who believe themselves (mistakenly) to be an élite. Hitler did not hesitate a moment; he immediately gave up the idea of becoming a leader over all of Germany and contented himself with absolute authority over his followers in Munich and later in Bavaria. Instead of risking a doubtful struggle on unknown terrain, he kept to the comparatively small field where he was sure of success — sure of the masses, sure of protection by the state power, sure of men and money.

The Reichswehr lent soldiers, and when the soldiers shot and beat their victims, Police President Pöhner's men saw nothing; but if the victims defended themselves, they were arrested for disorderly conduct. Money poured into the treasury. 'The party,' Hitler claimed later, 'was financed almost exclusively by my meetings. The membership dues stood in no relation to the money brought in by my speeches. To be sure, the party did have one big backer at that time; our unforgettable Dietrich Eckart.' The unforgettable, in turn, had backers of his own, General von Epp, Bechstein, the piano manufacturer, and others. And these backers and backers of backers — most of them outsiders themselves among the rich — were able, with comparatively small means, to buy for Hitler more and more of this stock of passion and daring that was embodied in the party. It was the time when murder could be had for small change.

Some facts about Hitler's resources in these first years were found out later by an investigating committee of the Bavarian diet. The spenders mostly were headstrong individualists, lone wolves among the big administrators of Germany's wealth; as a rule, small or medium-sized industrialists, not seldom half-broke themselves. In Germany, big money for political purposes used not to come from individual backers, but from corruption funds which were administered by the big associations of manufacturers, employers, bankers. Up to the last day before he finally came to power, for the most part, Hitler had access to these funds only when he was associated with other and more moderate groups — that is, when he seemed to come with tied hands. Sometimes Hitler was not ashamed to promise his backers utter obedience toward 'capital' when he should come to power; at other times he was proud, especially if the game did not seem worth the candle.

'In the summer of 1921,' Hitler continues, 'work in the business office had grown impossible. So many people kept milling around in the narrow room that organized activity was out of the question. Everybody was in everybody else's way. Slowly there began to be consequences which I have since then often observed in similar circumstances: our people grew nervous. Finally, the summer of 1921 brought a drastic change in the business management of the party. . . .'

In the whole management. This was when Hitler won the leadership. At the head of its business administration he placed a man in whom he had unlimited personal confidence, who was responsible only to him, and who, by his extreme brutality and unpleasantness, made himself so detested in the whole party that only Hitler's authority kept him in his post. But he was an effective business manager. This man was Hitler's former war comrade, Max Amann, a second sergeant in the same regiment: 'On my request, party comrade Amann took over the position of party business manager. He told me at once that further work in this office was absolutely impossible. And so, for a second time, we went out in search of quarters, and rented an old abandoned inn in Corneliusstrasse, near the Gärtnerplatz. . . . A part of the old taproom was partitioned off and made into an office for party comrade Amann and myself. In the main room, a very primitive wicket was constructed. The S.A. leadership was housed in the kitchen. . . .' At this time the party already had large, double-doored, steel cabinets.

This homey comfort was suddenly endangered. A new government had come in, a new police too; and these new Pharaohs did not want to know too much of Joseph. Up to this time Hitler and his gang had been able to beat up their enemies without interference from the state. Now the state began to open its eyes. For breaking into a hostile meeting with one of his gangs and chasing the speaker off the platform with a club, a court sentenced Hitler to three months' imprisonment. Two of the months were suspended: that is, he would not have to serve them if in the future he refrained from all acts of violence. For months he pleaded with the government to stretch a point and suspend the third month too. But the new government had no such intention; it even considered a punishment which would have been far greater than three months' imprisonment. Technically Hitler was a foreigner; his conviction for a felony gave the government the right to deport him. For ten years this threat of deportation hung over Hitler's head, and it is doubtful whether he ever feared anything more in all his life. Count Lerchenfeld, the new Bavarian premier, a distinguished gray-haired gentleman, whose manners were far too good for an age of murderers, intimated in parliament that such inciters to passion and disunity did not necessarily have to be tolerated in the country (April, 1922).

Hitler replied in an open letter to the count:

> . . . I admit that by the letter of our present Jewish law, I really am a 'foreigner.' I might argue, Your Lordship, that my birthplace is only two hundred and fifty yards from the Bavarian border, that it was Bavarian territory a hundred years ago, and, as I hope, will be returned to the German Reich in less time than that. . . . Blood is thicker than water, Your Lordship, and by blood I am not only proud to be a German, but even prouder that fortune permitted me to stake my blood for my Germanism. At that time, it would have been child's play for me, Your Lordship, to win citizenship. I neglected to do so, because I ventured to retain my unshakable hope in a greater Germany, and also my conviction that a day would come when a German's right to work with his people would not be judged by papers and certificates, Your Lordship, but exclusively by his blood and by his worth. . . .

If Hitler attacks a count in writing, he will never fail to call him 'Your Lordship' in every third line. But in this letter he was fighting more than some accidental count. He was fighting the whole new course of affairs that began late in 1921, with the induction of the Wirth-Rathenau government. This government had adopted a new attitude toward the peace treaty: the only way was to try to live with it. Wirth and Rathenau wanted to stop protesting against the treaty and to fulfill it, believing that the very attempt to carry out its provisions would demonstrate their impossibility.

By this they hoped to achieve peace and understanding at home. The Lerchenfeld government in Bavaria nourished the same hopes and stopped the fight against Berlin. Even the popular question of a return to the Bavarian monarchy would for the moment be shelved. The political domination of the majors and murder clubs must be ended.

In April, Wirth and Rathenau set out for Genoa. At a conference of all great powers except the United States, a true peace was at last to be prepared. Lloyd George, the British Premier, was its author. His aim was to devise an economic plan as a basis for a normal world. Saving the world by economics was a favorite idea of all British governments from Lloyd George in 1922 to Ramsay MacDonald in 1933. In 1922, German leaders shared the same faith. 'Economics is destiny,' Rathenau had said. Regretting his part in the Peace of Versailles, Lloyd George was to spend twenty years combating it. In 1922, he still clung harshly and firmly to the letter of the treaty, but strove to attenuate it by economic understandings. This might have led to a German-British front against France; but Germany was not strong enough for such a policy, and Lloyd George himself was not politically strong enough in his own country. The sensation of Genoa was the Bolsheviki, who, led by Foreign Commissar Chicherin, appeared for the first time at a conference. During the Genoa Conference, Rathenau, to the amazement of the world, concluded the Treaty of Rapallo with the Russians. In the face of France's hardness and refusal to compromise, Rathenau wanted to show that Germany, too, could carry on a strong policy. This would have meant something if Russia had been strong, but internationally she was almost as impotent as Germany. The conference ended in formal as well as practical failure.

Yet there had been a beginning of international conversations. Germany no longer sat at the council table purely in the rôle of a conquered country. Perhaps Rathenau would be the man to lead Germany back into the ranks of the great powers?

Rathenau, the Jew! And perhaps tomorrow the savior of Germany! Hitler was not yet important enough to be in this play; but nevertheless, here was his dilemma. Could he wish to see Germany saved by a Jew? If he was sincere: he could not.

It was at this time that he began to believe in his own God-given mission. It was no accident that — in his own words — he 'learned from the Bible with boundless love how our Lord and Saviour seized his whip,' and marched on Jerusalem. Was not he himself armed with a heavy crocodile whip, marching through the streets of his beloved Munich, which he sometimes called the 'Mecca' of National Socialism? A short time previous, it is true, he had admitted in a chastened mood to his friend Georg Schott: 'All of us are nothing but little Saint Johns. I am waiting for a Christ.' But the period of modesty was drawing to a close. Were not all the signs by which Heaven customarily announces its prophets being fulfilled in him? The fanatical faith of the disciples, the rejoicing of the masses, the hostility or contempt of those in high places — and now wasn't he going through a sort of Golgotha? His Golgotha, to be sure, was nothing more impressive than the month in prison which he wished so fervently to avoid; but before going in, he took leave of his people with the words: 'Two thousand years ago the mob of Jerusalem dragged a man to execution in just this way.'

Then the prison gate closed behind him. For a month he sat furious and silent in Stadelheim near Munich. In this month happened the inevitable: Germany was saved from being saved by a Jew. Right-Wing fanatics, just the common type that believed itself to be an élite, shot Walter Rathenau from a speeding car (June 24, 1922). The measure seemed full. The workers rose in great demonstrations; for a whole day things looked like a new revolution. But the revolution was spent before it began; the movement found no leaders. The counter-revolution, which had crawled into its corner for a moment, emerged and breathed easy. The only tangible result of the revolutionary move was that the Reichstag in Berlin passed a 'Law for the Defense of the Republic' as a supposed curb to extremist agitation on the Right. The gesture was more than feeble. The law led to a few more or less serious prison sentences for agitators who called the state a Jewish republic, the Social Democratic President Friedrich Ebert (without the shadow of justification), a brothel-keeper, and the banner of the republic, a filthy rag. Nowhere in the world would such a law attract attention. But the murder party fumed about state tyranny, the strangling of democracy, dictatorship. In Bavaria the Right radical movement (the disbanded, but nevertheless growing and thriving, murderers' army), again threatened revolt. The otherwise co-operative Bavarian government feared a restriction of its sovereignty by Berlin. In defense of this sovereignty, Munich assumed an attitude of defiance toward Berlin and, half against its will, was driven forward by the Right radicals. The half-century-old hatred of the Bavarian South for the Prussian North gushed forth in a sizzling jet of hatred.

Amid this tumult, Hitler was released from prison. He immediately spoke to the masses. The resultant speech was one of his most notable and casts a considerable light on his own person.

He strove to make clear the deeper contexts underlying the events of the day. He related the secret history of world domination, describing with many images how the power struggling for world domination concealed itself behind opposite pretexts and ideologies; here assuming a national, there an international, guise, today capitalistic, tomorrow anti-capitalistic, but always seeking the most suitable means of approaching one step closer to world domination. He says expressly that the struggle is international, not concerned with any one nation. He finds a name, now familiar to all, for the social type with which he identifies himself and for whose victory he is fighting; he calls this type the 'intelligentsia' or, more graphically, the 'brain-worker,' hinting at the close relationship between the modern intellectual and the modern educated proletarian. In broad and prolix periods, he summons this intelligentsia to take up the struggle against the world domination of Jewry; now and then a narrow rent in the tissue of his oratory permits a glance at his own future world domination; in later speeches the rent grows wider. The speech runs in part:

> Today we all of us feel that two worlds are struggling with one another, and not alone in our country, but everywhere we look, in oppressed Russia, in Italy, in France, and England, etc. An inexorable struggle between the ideals of those who believe in a national people and the ideals of the intangible, supra-national international. . . .
>
> It is a struggle that dates back nearly one hundred and twenty

years. It began at the moment when the Jew obtained the rights of citizenship in the various countries of Europe. The political emancipation of the Jews was the beginning of a madness. For by it the European states gave to a people which by race was much more clearly and sharply delimited than all others — which always had constituted, and always will constitute, a state within a state — full civil rights and equality. . . . In the end a people, which in the eighteenth century seemed totally strange, possessed the same political and civil rights as we ourselves.

And in the economic sphere exactly the same thing happened! The immense industrialization of the nations meant that great masses of workers streamed together in the cities. . . . Parallel to this ran a tendency to turn all labor to money. There was a sprouting of stocks and bonds, and little by little the stock exchange began to run our whole national economy. And the owners of this institution, then as today, were without exception Jews. I say without exception; for the few who do participate in the guise of non-Jews are in the last analysis nothing but a front, false Christians, who are needed to make the broad mass think that these institutions have a base in the character of all nations and in their economy, while in reality they are institutions compatible only with the nature of the Jewish people from which they arise. . . .

At that time Europe stood at the crossroads. The continent began to divide into two parts, Western Europe on the one hand, Central and Eastern Europe on the other. At first, Western Europe took the lead in industrialization. Especially in England, throngs of rural workers, the sons of peasants and peasants who had been ruined, streamed into the cities, where they constituted a new fourth estate. But the significant part of all this is a face which we have never given the attention it deserves. Like France, this England had relatively few Jews. The consequence was that the great masses concentrated in the cities did not come into immediate contact with this foreign nation, and that for this reason the otherwise inevitable feeling of revulsion against them did not find sufficient nourishment. In the end it was child's play for the Jews of England, numbering hardly fifty thousand to sixty thousand heads, so to 'Europeanize' themselves that they remained hidden to the primitive eye of the ordinary fellow national; they became 'economic leaders,' big capitalists, and as such they no longer seemed to be foreigners — but actually appeared to be Englishmen! For

this reason anti-Semitism in those countries could achieve no elemental force; and the same was true of France. And this is exactly what made the institution we have been taught to call
democracy possible in those countries. Only in those countries was
it possible to set up a form of government which necessarily implies
the herd-like domination of intelligence and true energy by the
numbers of the dead mass. In other words: the Jewish intelligentsia
was enabled by its small numbers to vanish completely amid the
British people; it was inevitably child's play for them to work upon
the broad masses in such a way that they, unaware whom they
were obeying, ended by working in the sole service of this small
group. By press propaganda and educational work, they succeeded
in forming the big classical parties. Even then, they cleverly
formed two or three groups which apparently combated one
another, but actually hung by the same gold thread, all attuned to a
single trait of the human character: the fact that man easily
wearies of a thing that he has possessed for a long time. He wants
something new, and that's why two parties are needed. One runs
the country and the other carries on opposition. When the first
one makes a mess of things, the opposition party takes control and
the government party goes into opposition. After twenty years the
new party has made a mess and the game starts in again. In
reality the whole thing is nothing but a clever mill, in which the
interests of the nation are ground to dust. As everybody knows,
this is called 'popular self-government.' . . .

Then Jewry took a step which showed political genius. This
capitalist people, which had brought the most unscrupulous exploitation into the world, found a way to lay hands on the leadership of the fourth estate. The Jew founded the Social Democratic,
the Communist Movement. And with extraordinary dexterity he
gathered the leadership little by little into his own hands. This
was done by two methods. One was employed on the Right, the
other on the Left; in other words, the Jew had his apostles in both
camps. On the Right, he attempted to intensify all existing wrongs
to such an extent that by emphasizing as strongly as possible those
qualities which were repugnant to the man of the people, the poor
devil would be provoked beyond measure. It was the Jew who
raised the avidity of these classes to the highest possible degree. It
was he who fostered the idea that the unscrupulous use of all
methods in business dealings was a matter of course, and by his

competition forced others to follow suit. It was he who brought hard-heartedness in the ruthless application of these methods so far that the saying, 'Business passes over corpses,' came to be regarded as perfectly self-evident. . . .

On the Left, he was the common demagogue. Two means enabled him to disgust the national intelligentsia with leading the workers. First, the international viewpoint in itself. Well he knew that, once he taught the workers the international viewpoint as a self-evident premise of their existence and their struggle, the national intelligentsia would shun the movement. For here they cannot follow. . . . And then there was a second means: Marxist theory as such. As soon as the Jews declared that property as such was theft; in other words, as soon as they departed from the self-evident formula that only natural resources can and should be common property, but that what a man honorably creates and earns is his own; from that moment on, the nationally minded economic intelligentsia was again unable to follow; for they could not help but say that this theory must inevitably involve the total collapse of all human culture. And so the Jew succeeded in bringing about the isolation of the new movement from all national elements. And he furthermore succeeded, by a brilliant exploitation of the press, in influencing the masses to such an extent that the errors of the Left were viewed by the people on the Right as the errors of the German worker, while to the German worker the errors of the Right seemed nothing other than the errors of the so-called bourgeoisie. And neither of the two noticed that the errors of both sides were the calculated result of diabolical foreign agitation. Only now do we begin to understand the monstrous joke of world history, the irony that stock-exchange Jews could become the leaders of a German workers' movement. A gigantic swindle such as world history has rarely seen. [Stormy applause.]

In all this, we can see at all times how wonderfully they work together, the stock-exchange Jew and the labor leader, the stock-exchange journal and the labor press. Both pursue a single direction and a single aim, whether we are dealing with the *Frankfurter Zeitung* and the *Münchener Post*, the *Berliner Tageblatt*, the *Freiheit* or the *Rote Fahne*. While Moses Kohn sits in the directors' meeting, advocating a policy of firmness — that is, hostility in the face of the workers' demands — his brother, Isaac Kohn, stands in the factory yard, stirring up the masses: take a good look at them; all they want is to oppress you. Cast off your chains, etc. And upstairs his brother is helping to forge those very chains. On the one side the stock-exchange organ tries incessantly to arouse the fever of speculation; these people speculate on the broadest possible scale with grain and all the foodstuffs of the people beyond comparison: on the other hand, we find the workers' organ busy getting the masses' hair up. Bread has gone up, they say, and this and that has gone up, too; don't stand for it; rise, proletarians ... Down with ... [Throws up his arms in a gesture of dramatic fury. Merriment.]

Yet how long can this process go on? It implies not only the destruction of economy alone, but the destruction of a whole nation. It is perfectly clear that this fourth estate was not organized by the Jews to guarantee them the fruits of their toil; it is perfectly clear that the Jew Isaac Kohn does not stand in the factory yard out of love for the workers; it is self-evident that all these apostles who talk their tongues out for the people, but spend their nights in the Hotel Excelsior, travel in express trains, and go to Nice for their vacations — it is perfectly clear that these people do not go to all their pains out of love for the people. No, their idea is not to help the people, but to make them dependent on these leaders. The idea is to make the people break the backbone of their own independence, their own economy, and fall inevitably into the golden chains of eternal interest slavery to this race.

How long can this process of race betrayal go on? — It can go on until from out of this mass one man suddenly rises up, who seizes the leadership, finds other comrades, and little by little fans the rage of the people, which has so far been restrained, into a flame against the betrayers. This is the great peril that lurks in wait, and against this there is only one guarantee for the Jews: to do away with the national intelligentsia. [Cries of: 'Russia!'] This is the irrevocable, final aim which the Jew pursues with his revolution. And he must pursue this aim. He knows full well: no good will come of his administration; he is not a people of masters, he is a people of exploiters and rascals. He has never founded a culture, but has destroyed hundreds of cultures. He possesses nothing of his own to which he can point. Everything that he has is stolen. He lets foreign peoples, foreign workers, build his temples; it is foreigners who work and create for him; foreigners who bleed for him. He knows no 'people's army,' only paid mercenary slaves who are ready to go to their death for him. He has no art of his own; little by little it has all been stolen from other nations, or copied. Yes, and he doesn't even know how to preserve this costly treasure. In the twinkling of an eye, it becomes dirt and filth in his hand. He knows, too, that he cannot keep a state for any length of time. There is a difference between him and the Aryan. Certainly, the Aryan, too, has dominated other peoples. But how? He went in, cleared the forests, built up civilizations from deserts; he didn't use other peoples for his own ends, he fitted them into the state in accordance with their ability, and as a result, art and science flourished. In the last analysis only the Aryan has been able to create states and lead them toward a future!

Of all this the Jew is incapable. And because he cannot do these things, all his revolutions have to be 'international.' They must spread as a disease spreads. He cannot build a state and say: 'Look. Here it stands, an example for all. Build one like it!' His effort must be to keep the plague from dying out, to prevent it from dying out, to prevent it from being restricted to one spot, because otherwise this hearth of disease would burn itself out. Hence he must cause everything he does to spread internationally. How long will it be before the whole world falls to ruin and draws him to destruction with it! . . .

This speech was about what he called Jewish world domination; and he appealed to the world. Germany was condemned to pay 132,000,000,000 marks? Do some poor devils in France or England believe that therefore they will be the richer? Goodness, no. 'It is not the people who reap the profit of this slave labor, but the swindling middlemen, who transfer the reparations from Germany abroad: the Jews.' Therefore they threw Germany into a revolution; and by what means? 'That was a part of the plan of this race. That is why they strove to lay hands on the food traffic; they brought about the revolution by starvation. No worker wanted to destroy his fatherland, but the Jew created hunger to make revolution — that is, *his* revolution; he followed the directions of the Wise Men of Zion exactly.'

Moreover, it is German youth that first is called on to carry through the struggle against the common enemy of mankind. 'Hail to you, my boys! You are only eighteen or nineteen, and you have the good luck to be hated by the greatest of scoundrels. What others must fight for through a life of toil, this highest treasure, the distinction of the honorable man from the bandit, falls into your lap in your youth.'

But when Hitler speaks to his German boys, he nevertheless looks far beyond the walls of a smoky beer hall. There are other nations, other boys who today believe that Germany is the enemy; but one day they will understand that there is only one common enemy of them all, disguised in the masks of Moses and Isaac Kohn. Why did England go to war against Germany? 'A large-scale propaganda campaign against Germany was launched in the press. But who was the chief of this commercial press? One name crystallizes out: Northcliffe — a Jew.' Alfred Harmsworth, Lord Northcliffe, was no Jew, nor even of Jewish descent. But Hitler goes on: 'What cause did America have to go to war with Germany? Well, with the outbreak of the war, all the Jewish firms in the United States began to sell war materials. The venal press, dependent on the stock-exchange kings, launched an unprecedented propaganda campaign. A gigantic organization of press lies was built up. And again it was a Jewish concern, the Hearst Press, which laid down the tone of the agitation against Germany.' William Randolph Hearst is neither Jewish nor of Jewish descent. But since Jewish propaganda is at the roots of everything in contemporary world history, we, the armed intellectuals, shall answer them with our own propaganda everywhere. And thus Hitler one spring day in the little Bavarian country town of Tölz, before a gathering of beer-drinking and pipe-smoking peasants and lumbermen, launched his battle-cry to the five continents:

Aryans and anti-Semites of all nations, unite in the struggle against the Jewish race of exploiters and oppressors of all nations!

Which means: Arise; master race of the globe!

Chapter VII

THE DEATH OF MONEY

IN THE SUMMER OF 1923, HITLER TOLD A STORY in a large meeting: 'We have just had a big gymnastic festival in Munich. Three hundred thousand athletes from all over the country assembled here. That must have brought our city lots of business, you think. Now listen to this: There was an old woman who sold picture postcards. She was glad because the festival would bring her plenty of customers. She was beside herself with joy when sales far exceeded her expectations. Business had really been good — or so she thought. But now the old woman is sitting in front of an empty shop, crying her eyes out. For with the miserable paper money she took in for her cards, she can't buy a hundredth of her old stock. Her business is ruined, her livelihood absolutely destroyed. She can go begging. And the same despair is seizing the whole people. We are facing a revolution. . . .'

This was the story of the end of the world — seemingly the story of an old woman, but really, in seven or eight phrases, the story of the destruction of German, indeed of European, self-reliance and dignity. The truths which had seemed most certain, the multiplication table and the difference between good and evil, vanished before the eyes of the uncomprehending individual. First it was the story of the German inflation, which reduced the supposedly eternal value of the German mark from \$0.24 to \$.000,000,000,024; or, in other words: an object which had previously been worth twenty-four cents, now cost a sum which would formerly have equaled three times the national wealth. To a lesser degree, it was also

the story of the blowing away of money in other countries, Austria,
Poland, Hungary, France, Italy, Spain; and later, there were be-
ginnings of the process in England, and even the United States.
This was the twilight of the age of progress: the death of money.

On Friday afternoons in 1923, long lines of manual and white-
collar workers waited outside the pay-windows of the big German
factories, department stores, banks, offices: dead-tired workingmen
in grimy shirts open at the neck; gentlemen in shiny blue suits,
saved from before the war, in mended white collars, too big for
their shrunken necks; young girls, some of them with the new
bobbed heads; young men in puttees and gray jackets, from which
the tailor had removed the red seams and regimentals, embittered
against the girls who had taken their jobs. They all stood in lines
outside the pay-windows, staring impatiently at the electric wall
clock, slowly advancing until at last they reached the window and
received a bag full of paper notes. According to the figures inscribed on them, the paper notes amounted to seven hundred thousand or five hundred million, or three hundred and eighty billion,
or eighteen trillion marks — the figures rose from month to month,
then from week to week, finally from day to day. With their bags
the people moved quickly to the doors, all in haste, the younger
ones running. They dashed to the nearest food store, where a line
had already formed. Again they moved slowly, oh, how slowly,
forward. When you reached the store, a pound of sugar might have
been obtainable for two millions; but, by the time you came to the
counter, all you could get for two millions was half a pound, and
the saleswoman said the dollar had just gone up again. With the
millions or billions you bought sardines, sausages, sugar, perhaps
even a little butter, but as a rule the cheaper margarine — always
things that would keep for a week, until next pay-day, until the
next stage in the fall of the mark.

For money could not keep, the most secure of all values had become the most insecure. The mark wasn't just low, it was slipping
steadily downward. Goods were still available, but there was no
money; there was still labor and consumption, but no economy;
you could provide for the moment, but you couldn't plan for the
future. It was the end of money. It was the end of the old shining

hope that everyone would be rich. The secular religion of the nineteenth century was crumbling amid the profanation of holy property.

Germany had financed her war by means of loans. The state had borrowed from its citizens approximately eighty billion marks, about a third of the so-called national wealth, and shot them into the air — without result, for the war had been lost. Every citizen had been forced to lend, even the propertyless out of their meager wages. Great fortunes and petty savings had been thrown down the gullet of war. And then, suddenly, the mark lost its value. The war loan was worth nothing. Savings of a lifetime were worth nothing. The great radical cure, ruthless equalization, was going into effect. It was a process which would affect the distant future, but most men failed even to suspect its full significance, for they saw only the beginnings, the first symptoms. The great prophecies of the nineteenth century were beginning to be fulfilled. A man who thought he had a small fortune in the bank might receive a politely couched letter from the directors: 'The bank deeply regrets that it can no longer administer your deposit of sixty-eight thousand marks, since the costs are out of all proportion to the capital. We are therefore taking the liberty of returning your capital. Since we have no bank-notes in small enough denominations at our disposal, we have rounded out the sum to one million marks. Enclosure: one 1,000,-000-mark bill.' A canceled stamp for five million marks adorned the envelope.

The state wiped out property, livelihood, personality, squeezed and pared down the individual, destroyed his faith in himself by destroying his property — or worse: his faith and hope in property. Minds were ripe for the great destruction. The state broke the economic man, beginning with the weakest.

From Russia, the explosion of 1917 had resounded throughout the world. Over one seventh of the earth's surface it had made private property questionable, and ultimately, after years of struggle and experiment, destroyed it. Like a sea, receding for a moment, then wildly surging through all dikes, a counter-movement, inspired by fear, had swept across the world. Anti-Bolshevik propaganda bureaus, clubs, newspapers were launched. Perhaps the strangest monster nurtured by this movement was *The Protocols of the Wise Men of Zion.*

Nowhere, with the exception of Russia, did the state destroy property as radically as in Germany. And it was not the workers who did it. Not the Social Democrats, who in 1918 had proclaimed the republic; or the Communists, who reviled the Social Democrats as 'traitors to the working class,' and for years kept disturbing the peace with vain, hopeless attempts at revolt. The workers had no intention at all of destroying property. Plans to this effect stood in the party programs, but nowhere else. For the proletarian is a component of the capitalist economy, and what he wishes is not to abolish exploiting capitalism, but to exploit it himself.

On November 9, 1918, Philipp Scheidemann, the Social Democratic leader, proclaimed the republic in Berlin, saying, 'The German people has been victorious all along the line'; but a week later, the leaders of the German working-class, who had been victorious all along the line, concluded a pact with the leaders of the German employers 'for the maintenance of our economic life.' And both sides solemnly declared 'that the reconstruction of our national economy requires the pooling of all economic and intellectual forces and the harmonious collaboration of all.' It could not have been said more clearly: to save capitalism from the crushing vise of war socialism was the aim of the workers as well as the capitalists.

At this time Socialist demonstrations were swarming through the capital; as the masses passed through the Tiergarten, the great park in the middle of Berlin, a voice is said to have cried out: 'Comrades, preserve revolutionary discipline! Don't walk on the grass!' A legend, perhaps. But how apt!

Actually the leader of German capitalism after the war, Hugo Stinnes, destroyed far more private property than all the German Socialists. Mammoth industrialist with super-capitalist dreams of domination, he unconsciously sought after super-capitalist forms. Such was the magnitude of the property he amassed, and such the methods by which he amassed it, that the very concept of property burst asunder. Between 1920 and 1923, Stinnes was the most powerful man in Germany — in so far as we may speak of power in those dissolved, anarchic times. By bold combination of widely ramified interests (mines, electricity, navigation, hotels, newspapers, book publishing) he exerted an influence on the whole country, financed parties and politicians, and in all his activities was guided by the feeling that Fate had called him to rebuild Germany. The first step in this reconstruction was a process of destruction. At the outset the masses misinterpreted it as nothing more than a scandalous rise in prices; only later, under the name of inflation, the process was correctly comprehended as the downfall of money.

While Walter Rathenau was still foreign minister, a group of American bankers visited Germany to study the causes of the German inflation. In some quarters it had been maintained that Germany hoped the devaluation of her currency would cause her political debts to evaporate. It is doubtful whether anyone ever cherished so naïve a hope, and surely it was never realized. In reality the inflation was largely caused by the efforts of German industry to regain its position in the world market. Rathenau and Stinnes sat down with the Americans, and Stinnes, according to his own report, gave them the following harsh explanation for the German inflation:

'I informed the gentlemen that after the lost war Germany had been obliged to develop regular working habits in the four million men who, in the army, had lost the habit of regular work; for this, I told them, raw materials and employment were necessary. In order to obtain raw materials and a market for our products, in order to preserve the life of the nation, we had been obliged to sacrifice parts of our capital; there was no other way. For if the masses had remained without employment, Bolshevism would assuredly have seized Germany. . . . I further informed the gentlemen that the weapon of inflation would have to be used further, without regard to the resultant extraordinary losses of capital, because this was the only possibility of providing the population with the ordered regular activity which was necessary to secure the life of the nation.'

The specter of Bolshevism overpowered the holiness of property. That money was obsolete could be no more dismally proved than by this suicide for fear of death. As a defense against Bolshevism, the destroyer of private wealth, private wealth was destroyed. Germany, like all countries, had been bled white by the war, and this real decline in wealth was inevitably followed by a decline in nominal titles to wealth, in the form of currency. Germany's money had been turned to cannon and hand-grenades. The grenades produced corpses, the cannon fell into the hands of the enemy, the national wealth was turned to dust. Germany had scarcely anything left.

But after the war, even the little that remained was flung away, to preserve at least political peace in the land. While Stinnes, on his royal-industrial throne at Mühlheim on the Ruhr, calmly took it upon himself to destroy private property in Germany, Hitler stamped furiously back and forth on his platform in the ill-lit beer hall and shouted: 'You had no right to make the whole economy, state as well as private enterprises, unprofitable, by overfilling them with workers at a time when the market was stagnant and there was a shortage of raw materials!' He spoke like a learned doctor of economics, and just this sounded quite incredible in his mouth; but then the beer-hall orator expressed an idea, far surpassing Stinnes in political wisdom: the chaos should have been exploited for a transformation of the German economy. He censured the government, because, 'when the soldiers streamed back from the front, it did not distribute them among much-needed projects [public works and housing], but sent them back to the places from which they had been called to the colors.'

He understood that the old *laissez-faire* economy could not be restored. He understood that the old liberal Germany could not be rebuilt. He early realized what his friend Rudolf Hess wrote, many years later: 'For Adolf Hitler the revolt of 1918 was a necessity of Fate, for, despite its criminal leadership, it swept away many survivals of a time that was outlived, survivals that would have created obstacles to the National Socialist revolution.' He knew how much he owed to the chaos. At the height of the year 1923 it was the chaos which literally fed him and his followers; for the decay of the mark blew small financial contributions, made in substantial foreign currency by friends in Czechoslovakia, Switzerland, the United States, up to gigantic sums in marks; a person could live comfortably for a week on a dollar at that time, and for a hundred dollars one could buy a minor revolution. It was a decisive turn in Hitler's career when his friend and admirer, Ernst Hanfstaengl, scion of an old-established, wealthy printer's family, himself half-American by descent, borrowed for him the fabulous sum of one thousand dollars. This money enabled Hitler to set up, in February, 1923, the *Völkischer Beobachter* as a daily paper.

He said: 'The government calmly goes on printing these scraps, because, if it stopped, that would mean the end of the government. Because once the printing presses stopped — and that is the prerequisite for the stabilization of the mark — the swindle would at once be brought to light. For then the worker would realize that he is only making a third of what he made in peacetime, because two thirds of his labor go for tribute to the enemy.'

And just that made inflation a 'necessity of Fate.' It shattered public faith in property, and nothing was more necessary for Hitler than the shattering of this faith. And so he prophesied and described the destruction which was to pave his road to power: 'Believe me, our misery will increase. The scoundrel will get by. But the decent, solid businessman who doesn't speculate will be utterly crushed; first the little fellow on the bottom, but in the end the big fellow on top too. But the scoundrel and the swindler will remain, top and bottom. The reason: because the state itself has become the biggest swindler and crook. A robbers' state! . . .'

The whole demagogical debate was actually a fight between two thieves over the corpse of the national economy. Stinnes flung away the national wealth to banish poverty and with it Bolshevism; but Hitler screamed: 'And what if even greater misery descended on us! Let us have misery! . . . The greatest misfortune would be so-called prosperity. We would forget all our disgrace. If we were getting along, we would stop hating France!' He meant it; for he went on to explain: 'In present-day Germany, sad to say, people do not lament over the loss of our world position and world respect, not over the loss of Alsace-Lorraine and Upper Silesia, Schleswig-Holstein and the other ravished territories — all they complain about is the exorbitant prices. If today there were a French dictator in Berlin and the physical needs of the German people were secured by him and his officials, we may be convinced that a majority of our fellow countrymen would resign themselves to their fate. This sheds full light on the demoralization into which we have fallen, and concerning which, sad to relate, no one wastes any tears.'

Therefore, let us have misery. Therefore, chaos was a necessity of Fate; therefore, prosperity would have been a misfortune. This was the destructive, and at the same time creative, idea of a brilliant have-not, a good-for-nothing, with nothing to lose. Let us have misery! The economy is dying. Let it die, and no tears shed, for it has only plunged us into misfortune: 'The pure scientists are misled. An economy exists only because a strong national people creates it. An economy without political power is a temptation for foreign conquerors. Hence today we have a slave-economy.' The old bourgeois parties 'are to blame, for they have trained us to be merely an economic people. If economic development had gone on like that, we would have developed an innumerable mass of factory workers, crippled in body and mind' — Richard Wagner in his time had accused Germany's ruling class of letting the German worker degenerate in hunger, vice, and crime. For Hitler, Germany was stifling in the morass of peace: 'Nobody wants to die for business deals. But a man dies gladly for a political ideal!' This lost world war did Germany some good by casting it into an abyss, from which, in Hitler's opinion, it could not save itself by mere economic means: 'To liberation belongs more than economic policy; more than sweat. To make us free, we need pride, will, defiance, hate, hate, and again hate!'

And so, let us have misery! Let the people despair of the economy. Let them cease to believe in their own labor. There stood these men, pressed tightly between the tables of an overfilled beer hall. Their cheeks were sunken, their gray suits — remade uniforms — were shabby and threadbare; under their arms some held a bundle of food, arduously and illicitly acquired. The speaker fixed his eyes on one of these poverty-stricken figures and said: soon you will starve completely unless you blindly follow me, wherever I lead you. Citizens reckoning in billions, said Hitler, will die of hunger, because the farmer will stop selling his grain or butter for the worthless billions, 'with which he can paper his outhouse on the

manure heap. And don't go complaining: how mean of the farmer!
Will one of you step forward and say he is willing to give away his
work of many months for nothing?' The money you offer the
farmer 'is no longer a note on work done, it is a note on a swindling régime. And that means hunger!' On this Hitler set his great
hope, on the 'revolt of starving billionaires.' The revolt against the
parliamentary régime in Germany was inevitable, and hunger
would bend the masses under dictatorship: 'If the horrified people
notice that they can starve on billions, they must arrive at this
conclusion: we will no longer submit to a state which is built on
the swindling idea of the majority, we want dictatorship!'

To repeat the same in the words of the Wise Men of Zion: 'By
envy and hatred, by struggle and warfare, even by spreading hunger, destitution, and plagues, we shall bring the people to such a pass
that their only escape will lie in total submission to our domination.'

Adolf Hitler is a true child of the old German self-contempt.
At all events, the German people was one of the first to witness the
decay of those material values which a whole century had taken as
the highest of all values. The German nation was one of the first
to experience the death of the unlimited free property which had
lent such a royal pride to modern humanity. Money had lost its
value — what, then, could have any value? Of course, many were
accustomed to having no money; but that even *with* money you
had nothing — that was a twilight of the gods, as horrible as anything Wagner could have foreseen. When a mark was no longer a
mark, the period of nihilism foreseen by Nietzsche seemed to be
at hand. First the Kaiser had gone, then the silver coins with his
likeness had gone, and unknown faces, sometimes distorted to
frightful grimaces by eccentric artists, stared at you from worthless
paper notes. The world's aim was changing. A cynical frivolity
penetrated men's souls; no one knew what he really possessed and
some men wondered what they really were. This could not be compared to any depreciation of currency in the past, with the assignats
of the French Revolution, for example; for at that time the mass of
real property was not even touched by the depreciation. But in
modern times wealth largely consists of claims and credits, which
have value only as long as the state protects and secures them.

Men understood this with terrible clarity when the state stopped protecting and securing their wealth.

Man had measured himself by money; his worth had been measured by money; through money he was someone or at least hoped to become someone. Men had come and gone, risen and fallen, but money had been permanent and immortal. Now the state had managed to kill this immortal thing. The state was the conqueror and successor of money. And thus the state was everything. Man looked down at himself and saw that he was nothing.

In this state of self-contempt, insults aroused the enthusiasm of the masses. 'The German people,' Hitler told them, was 'made up of children, for only a childish people would accept million-mark bills.' To hear these flattering words, the people were even willing to pay a few millions in admission. 'True, a third of the German people are heroes, but another third are fools, and the last third are cowards.' When a French firing squad in Düsseldorf shot a patriotic German saboteur by the name of Albert Leo Schlageter, Hitler cried out: 'The German people didn't deserve this sacrifice. . . . The German people of today is truly not worthy to possess a Schlageter.'

The majority of the people were 'the broad mass of the undecided, the stand-asiders, the lazy, the cowardly'; and without being dragged off the platform, he could say to a meeting of five thousand persons: 'True strength is a quality of few men, or else we would not have the word hero. The masses consist of average men, democrats. But a hundred blind men do not make one seer, a thousand cowards do not make a hero, a hundred thousand parliamentarians do not make a statesman. Cowardly men choose the most cowardly as their leaders, so that they won't have to show courage; and they choose the stupidest among the stupid, so that everyone can have the feeling that he's a little better than the leader. A people subjected to the decisions of the majority is on the road to ruin.' He wanted every single one of his listeners to feel that this applied to him, and said so plainly: 'There is a delusion in the political thinking of the broad masses. They think: anyone can govern. Every shoemaker or tailor, they think, is capable of running a state. . . .' And, slapping an intimidated audience full in the face: 'We have become so cowardly that the democratic poison threatens to penetrate everywhere. No one in the parliamentary majorities wants to accept responsibility. . . . Nations that have lost their character and honor deserve no good fortune, no happy life. . . . The German people is going the same way that the ancient peoples went: it is a people passing little by little into decay. . . . The expression, a great nation cannot go under, is nothing more than an attempt to cloak cowardice. Great nations have vanished from the surface of the earth before this, nothing has remained but ashes. . . .'

In this disorganized, drifting, doubt-torn state, Hitler tried to give the German people a new strength, which might be regarded as a substitute for the vanishing national character: that system of political prayers, soliloquies of encouragement and command, which has been designated by the inadequate word propaganda. It was the artificial building of a new national character, an *ersatz* character, an attitude created in accordance with an artificial plan. The people dream and a soothsayer tells them what they are dreaming. This continuous, domineering yet intimate conversation with the people could only have been carried on by a man who was people and enemy of the people in one; a torn personality who felt himself a trampled fragment of the people in his own downtrodden miserable nonentity, and rebelled with the people against this destiny, but who at the same time was convinced of the absolute necessity of trampling, coercing, and shaking the master's fist. Rebellious slave and ruthless tyrant in one — there have been plenty of slaves who would have liked to be masters; but rare are the natures which are really both. With equal power of conviction Hitler could summon people now to rebel, now to obey. He could deal in endless contradictions without becoming entangled, because he was able to put power into every contradiction. At only a few days' interval, he could make the two following statements:

'First the Reich must be headed by heroes who carry the people along, lash them on to resistance! Because such men were lacking, we lost the war, and we are experiencing the same thing now. The spirit of resistance must be kindled from above!'

And — or — but — however:

'Salvation must come from below! From above we can expect nothing. The people must redeem themselves, when the others fail!'

At first when his opponents wanted to depreciate Hitler, they accused him of 'always saying the same thing.' When later, somewhat chastened, they comforted themselves: oh, well, he was nothing but a propagandist, though 'a very clever one, to be sure,' then they thought they had made a profound discovery when they declared his 'always saying the same thing' to be the essence of his cleverness. Hadn't Hitler himself called attention to his constant repetition and 'hammering'? But here Hitler is mistaken about himself, and his opponents, with their sweet-and-sour praises, have misunderstood him completely. He by no means always says the same thing. After he had mocked the masses long enough, earned their applause by calling them inferior, cowardly, stupid, blind, and degenerate, he suddenly changed his tune. His public had long consisted of intellectuals or those who liked to consider themselves as such. But in the spring of 1923, a few hundred workers, driven from the occupied Rhineland by the French military occupation, came to Munich. Hitler tried to recruit these homeless, unemployed, uprooted proletarians for his storm troops and did succeed in inciting them to attack Socialist newspapers and party houses. In addressing this new class of people, he slavishly adapted himself to their old habits of thought — the eternal opportunist. Yes, earlier he had boasted: 'We want no majorities. For the truth is always recognized and upheld by minorities. Every new invention has been a protest of genius against the masses' — even the style of these remarks is imitated from Nietzsche. But now: 'We are suffering from overeducation. We respect only knowledge. But the bookworms are enemies of action. What we need is instinct and will. Most people have lost both by their so-called "education." Yes, we have a class of people who are intellectually high, but they are poor in energy. If by overemphasis on mechanical knowledge we had not gone so far from popular feeling, the Jew would never have made his way into our nation. . . .' Not a word about the élite and the forceful minority, nothing about the leading rôle of the national intelligentsia, nothing about 'genius versus the mass'; no reference to the dullness and cowardice of the majority, only praise and admiration of its power. Hitler had flattered the middle class that it was the real national class, for 'those on the Left [read:

workers] have been led astray by agitators.' Now, with the suppleness of an actor, he flattered those on the Left.

'Without the boundless stupidity and blindness of our bourgeoisie [formerly "national intelligentsia"], the Jew would never have
become the leader of the German working-class. Stupidity was
joined by pride. The "better class" thought it beneath its pride to
descend to the "plebs." The millions of German fellow nationals
would not have been alienated from their people if the leading
classes had troubled themselves about them. Relinquish the hope
that we can expect anything from above for the freedom of the
German people! The most elementary requirements are lacking:
the will, the courage, and the energy. Where, then, lies the power of
the German people? It lies, as it always has, in the broad masses.
There the energy lies slumbering, waiting for the man who can
rouse it out of its slumber and hurl it into the fight for the destiny
of the German race.'

What's that? Where is the power? In the 'broad mass of the undecided, the stand-asiders, the lazy, the cowardly'? In the broad
mass that lives in the lunatic delusion that every shoemaker
and tailor can govern? In the 'broad mass of mentally and physically crippled factory workers'? In the broad mass, two thirds of
which consist of fools and cowards and which as a whole is made
up of 'average men, democrats'? Yes, indeed! Only in the broad
masses is there hope and power, to them alone belongs the future
— once they condescend to fill Hitler's meeting halls. Then he
assures them: 'It is the same as it has always been: liberation does
not come down from above, it will spring up from below.' Who re-
members that 'the spirit of resistance must be kindled from above'?

No, evidently propaganda is not just the trick of 'always saying
the same thing' — that would be too simple. True, Hitler's adversaries thought so because they took him for a fool; he himself said
so because he wanted to be taken for an iron character with immutable principles. Actually, propaganda changes and irradiates
like swamp water in changing weather. The facts must constantly
be interpreted, invented, falsified anew; overnight, friend must become foe; good, evil — and always the force of faith must gleam
through the veil of shifting truths. Without this power of faith,

the propagandist cannot make people believe even the simplest truths, much less a tissue of contradictions and lies!

A word must now be said concerning our source for these speeches. They are taken from the old issues of the *Völkischer Beobachter,* Adolf Hitler's own newspaper, edited by Alfred Rosenberg and Dietrich Eckart. The texts were examined and approved by Hitler. In 1923, Rosenberg and Eckart decided to publish the speeches in book form and entrusted Adolf Viktor von Körber, a member of the newspaper's staff, with the editorial task. Hitler told Körber certain events from his life, and Körber wrote a little biography as an introduction. At the end of 1923, he published a small volume of some one hundred and fifty pages, containing selected speeches, and entitled *Adolf Hitler, sein Leben und seine Reden* (Adolf Hitler, His Life and Speeches). Subsequently several new editions of the book appeared; and it is sometimes strange to note how the speeches changed in the course of the years.

In the *Völkischer Beobachter* text, these speeches stand before us in all their freshness, just as they were delivered. In these very words they resounded from the platform; in these very words the *Völkischer Beobachter's* reporter took them down and brought them to the print-shop that very night, charged with all the power, the hatred, the self-reliance, the factual and grammatical mistakes of an agitated hour. This is what makes them such reliable testimony. Days or weeks later, the speaker re-reads his own words; he is uncertain and suspicious, as often when relaxed. Could I have said that? Perhaps Rosenberg or Körber is alarmed: the old boy has blundered again. It can't stay like this. We'll have to change it or throw it out.

Hitler has uttered a hasty word about America. The paper carries it just as it slipped out: '... Those phrases about reconciliation were a lie. If Wilson hadn't been a swindler, he would not have become President of America. In our country we had one of these apostles of reconciliation, Herr Scheidemann' — first premier of the German Republic. 'Today we feel the results of their pacifist activity only too clearly, though both prophets have vanished from their posts. In accordance with parliamentary custom, the peoples have to pay the bill.' In the 1923 edition the whole passage is reduced to one brief sentence: 'If Wilson hadn't been a swindler, he would not have become president of a democracy.' In the edition of 1933, the entire quotation is omitted.

Sometimes Hitler could not make up his mind whether to heap the blame for everything on France or on the Jews. So he said in one of his speeches (newspaper version): 'Between Germany and France there is a rift that cannot be leveled by pacifist telegrams or cowardly submission. The attitude of France toward the Reich is the same today as it was four hundred, three hundred, two hundred, one hundred and fifty years ago. . . . No chance to mend this rift. . . .'

But in the same speech he said (book version): 'Between Germany and France there was a fundamental rift that could not be leveled by pacifist telegrams or cowardly submission. Before the war both countries could live beside each other in arms only. True, for Germany the war of 1870 closed a century-old hostility. But in France flaming hatred against Germany was cultivated with all methods of newspaper propaganda, in textbooks, on the stage, in the movies. . . . Who croaked the ugliest calumnies? . . . All the Jewish newspapers of France. To bring about bad feeling and exploit it was, as everybody can see, the aim of World Jewry.'

Thus the prophet falsifies his own words. With the deepest conviction he contradicts his deepest convictions. It is as though the various heads of a many-headed beast were biting one another.

The truth is irremediably buried beneath these deceptions and contradictions. How, then, can the speaker expect to put through a single incisive, suitable lie, when from speech to speech, from sentence to sentence, he changes even the lies? Whom does he expect to persuade that he himself believes a single one of these mutually contradictory lies? And to what purpose does he try to spread an opinion among the people, when on the very next day he is going to sacrifice that opinion?

Such questions are asked by those who do not understand propaganda, who regard propaganda as the art of instilling an opinion in the masses. Actually it is the art of receiving an opinion from the masses.

The usual conception of the great propagandist is the commanding, purposive mind, who by magic suggestion subjects an empty animal mass to his will; Marc Antony, who in a single speech makes a thousand friends out of a thousand enemies. It is in this light that most of our contemporaries view the greatest propagandist of our day, Adolf Hitler, and this is Adolf Hitler's own idea of himself. With the authority of success, he has put over a false theory on the world: the theory that he dominates the minds of millions by tirelessly hammering the same simple statement into them. But this only shows that he never listened to himself very closely, and was never too eager to illuminate his own success. He did not hammer the same simple statement into the minds of millions; on the contrary, he played with the masses and titillated them with the most contradictory assertions. It is this art of contradiction which makes him the greatest and most successful propagandist of his time. He does not dominate the minds of millions, his mind belongs to them. Like a piece of wood floating on the waves, he follows the shifting currents of public opinion. This is his true strength.

The true aim of political propaganda is not to influence, but to study, the masses. The speaker is in constant communication with the masses; he hears an echo, and senses the inner vibration. In forever setting new and contradictory assertions before his audience, Hitler is tapping the outwardly shapeless substance of public opinion with instruments of varying metals and varying weights. When a resonance issues from the depths of the substance, the masses have given him the pitch; he knows in what terms he must finally address them.

Rather than a means of directing the mass mind, propaganda is a technique for riding with the masses. It is not a machine to make wind, but a sail to catch the wind. The mass, however, is a phenomenon of deepest world importance — this leveled conglomeration of fools and wise men, heroes and cowards, proud and humble, the unusual and the average. This mass, with its anonymous intellectual pressure, its unexpected moods and unconscious desires, mirrors and echoes the commanding force of prevailing conditions; it embodies and personifies the necessities and resistances of the objective world; it expresses the silent command of Fate in a mysterious murmur. It is the art of the great propagandist to detect this murmur and translate it into intelligible utterance and convincing action. If he can do this, his utterances and actions may be full of contradictions — because the contradictions lie in the things themselves; they may be deceptive and misleading. The lies of propaganda reveal the deeper truth of the whole world's cynicism and dishonesty. By his lies the great propagandist involuntarily shows himself to be an honest, self-revealing prophet of the Devil.

Hitler's profound, rapacious, avid eye for the weakness of this intellectual age, awaiting only the man who can master it, is revealed in the natural affinity between a depersonalized soul and a depersonalized world. The more passionately Hitler harps on the value of personality, the more clearly he reveals his nostalgia for something that is lacking. Yes, he knows this mass world, he knows how to guide it by 'compliance.' He is like the crafty dope addict who manages to get his poison despite all efforts of his physicians and guards to prevent him. Hitler's mind directs a personality without center, a restlessly pulsating force without constancy and firmness, oscillating like the needle of a magnet, trembling and dancing, but always finding the — momentary — north.

Hitler never wearied of studying his own experiences and the world about him to discover the secrets and conditions of this world! He did not have a plan and act accordingly; he acted, and out of his actions a plan arose. At first he sincerely believed that *The Protocols of the Wise Men of Zion* were the instructions for establishing Jewish world domination. Later, when the time came for him to formulate his own aims, he was forced to recognize that they were laid down in this supposed Jewish book.

With a detachment of Reichswehr soldiers he founded his party, because this party had to be based on power. Accustomed to military discipline, his men shouted *'Heil!'* as their leader entered the meeting hall; after certain phrases, the speaker learned to make a barely perceptible pause and give a silent sign of which he himself was barely conscious, and the troop, with quick understanding, again broke out in a *'Heil!'* Then, one day, they, for the first time, clubbed off the platform a hostile speaker, who had innocently believed in the promised freedom of speech; after another meeting they marched, for the first time, four abreast through the city, singing: 'When Jewish blood gushes from our knives, things will be better.' And Hitler learned from his followers. He learned that this kind of troop possesses more than the power of its fists; it possesses an almost irresistible power over men's souls. The troopers tramped through the streets like the state itself. Five hundred marching storm troopers expressed more power and authority than ten mounted policemen. In the onlooker, doubts arose; was this marching monster rebellion, or was it already state power?

These men had to learn through accidents to create a distance between themselves and other men, to distinguish themselves by threats. At first Hitler merely knew that his men were disguised soldiers, a fragment of the Reichswehr like himself; and so he demanded a military salute, hand to their caps. But the enthusiastic, adventurous young men who began to gather round the hardened old soldiers had never known real military training. To them the regular military salute with its bent elbow was a strain. They took to greeting their comrades with a simple wave of the hand, which soon stiffened into an abrupt thrust. Thus the so-called Fascist or Hitler salute was born. The new storm-troop salute developed shortly after the appearance of the first Fascist symbols in Italy. A whole system of gestures, cries, songs, attitudes, insignia, and flags came into being; and this multicolored, many-voiced expression of an inner attitude made it clear that these people had more than a program, that they had more than an objective aim: the symbols embodied a whole manner of being and feeling. A definite type of men had come together; and it was by their totality and likeness that they produced an effect. Seldom could any of them say what they really wanted; but they wanted it with a determination which was expressed in their symbols. The original mind, who had contributed most to creating these symbols, was the Italian poet, Gabriele d'Annunzio, co-founder of the Fascist Movement, later forced aside by his robuster rival, Benito Mussolini. But d'Annunzio did not create the most original emblem of the new movement — the swastika.

What the swastika first meant, whence it came — that is one of those questions which never will find a definite answer. Some decades ago it penetrated white civilization as a symbol of religious or semi-religious cults, which used it in order to exhibit some sort of connection with Buddhism. Since the swastika can be followed back for countless centuries in countries ranging from India to Scandinavia, it seemed to confirm the existence of a national bond between far distant lands — a common possession of that Aryan race which, as one of their prophets, Houston Stewart Chamberlain, admitted, might not exist, but which should exist in the future. Many decades before the appearance of National Socialism, German national leagues in Austria bore the swastika as their insignia. But it is also found in purely Mongolian countries, as in China; and in all innocence it used to grace British stamps from Hong Kong. It is found among the American Indians. It is an official emblem in Finland and Estonia, whence presumably the German Free Corps, who in 1918-19 fought the Bolsheviki in the Baltic, brought it back to Germany.

A brigade of these troops was led by the former naval captain Ehrhardt. This Ehrhardt was a sort of forerunner of Hitler, or rather Röhm; it was he who chased the Reich government out of Berlin in 1920, until a general strike put down the military *putsch*. With the swastika on their tin hats, Ehrhardt's soldiers marched into Berlin. After their defeat, the troop was broken up. Many of the officers fled to Munich, and Röhm enrolled them in Hitler's S.A., of which they formed the real nucleus. It was they who brought the swastika to the National Socialists. It was originally a spider-like figure with thin lines; but the printer who made up the National Socialist leaflets and posters used heavy bars for better visibility. This new type ultimately became the official emblem of National Socialist Germany. It has the effect of an iron octopus, a monster, aggressively reaching out in all directions — hence its menacing and frightening effect. In 1921, Hitler's new red banner with a black swastika in a white disk was unfurled in the open for the first time. The effect was so inflammatory that Hitler himself was surprised and pleased.

In the swastika historical accident gave Hitler one of his mightiest magic weapons. It was a lucky find. The old German Workers'

Party had not come across it; Italian Fascism was denied a symbol of such strength. One of its strongest qualities became apparent only in the course of time: every child could draw it, and its expressive form encouraged people to draw it — even those who did not know what it meant. An uncanny power emanated from the mysterious sign; Hitler could point at it and calmly say: 'It is not knowledge that helps us. But faith.' Amid general disintegration he raised his banner: 'Everything around us is dying. We must make our movement a living force.'

A banner means more to an army than a printed program. And more essential than a banner is the battle-cry: knives unsheathed — guns cocked! A great event was needed if the swelling movement was not to fall apart. 'Moral rebirth,' Hitler prophesied, 'can only be the consequence of a great event. It will come to us at the moment when the struggle breaks out between Swastika and Soviet Star.' The first blood means more than speeches, more than symbols, more even than marching: 'With fanatical fury we will make the people national again. . . . Our slogan must be: If you don't want to be a German, I'll bash your skull in. . . . People, learn to be silent, grit your teeth and think of revenge, and again revenge! Learn how to settle with the men who hurled you into the abyss! This is no time for reconciliation. The Jew and his stooges within our people remain our eternal enemies. We know this: if they take the helm, our heads will roll in the sand. But we also know that if we get the power in our hands, then God help you!'

Head against head; two enemies, but, fundamentally, only one method. Tomorrow we will do the very thing for which we attack the enemy today; we have studied *The Protocols of the Wise Men of Zion,* and now we apply them. The intellect and the culture of a people, the *Protocols* teach us, rest on the leaders, not on the barbaric mass. Hitler drew the consequence: 'If we are able to raise such leaders out of the mass of our people, then a nation will once more crystallize around them.' He could not have said it more clearly. 'Is the leader personality we need with us?' he asked. In 1923, he was at a loss for an answer. 'It is not our task to seek after personalities. Either a personality is sent from Heaven, or there is none.' He had an idea whom Heaven had in mind. In speaking to the masses, however, he had to content himself with saying that the dictator did not exist for the people, but the people for the dictator: 'It is our task, when the dictator comes, to give him a people that is ripe for him.'

The generation which had led Germany into the war and lost the war was beginning to step aside. The famous and defeated generals were being pensioned, the captains and majors were taking their places in the key posts, Hitler's generation was climbing upward; and as their spokesman he cried: 'The force which will conquer in the end is the fire of German youth. They will have to uphold the state that they themselves have created. Today new claimants to power are arising in Germany, men who have shed their blood for Germany and are convinced that this blood flowed in vain, through the fault of the men who ran the government.'

The new claimants: A youth creating for itself a new state. A new species of man — the army of the armed bohemians, of heroes and murderers by conviction. Since 1919 it has been flowing back and forth through Germany, splitting like quicksilver into innumerable fragments or gathering into a heavy mass, but always present as a social factor of decisive power; too big to vanish in the general disintegration; too strong and influential to be extinguished by force. It was 'the beautiful old freebooter class of war and post-war times,' as later one of the leaders of this band, Lieutenant Gerhard Rossbach, declared in melancholy reminiscence. Rossbach, friend of Röhm, resembling him in many ways, including his unnatural inclinations, less hard and reliable, but just as outspoken and self-critical, gave a frank picture of this murderers' army: '. . . organizing masses and losing them just as quickly; tossed this way and that way just for the sake of our daily bread; gathering men about us and playing soldiers with them; brawling and drinking, roaring and smashing windows — destroying and shattering what needs to be destroyed. Ruthless and inexorably hard. The abscess on the sick body of the nation must be cut open and squeezed until clear red blood flows. And the blood must be left to flow for a good long time till the body is purified. . . .'

Hitler was practically a mollycoddle when he said that he didn't want to train his young freebooters 'for aesthetics and humanitarianism and not for preaching or heroism with the mouth.' For what, then? For the urge that was within them, pressing to come out: for destruction. They were the model of the human type which had lost everything, possessions and ideals, which nothing could impress but ruthless violence. The vagrant from the Vienna lodging-house said: 'In the ranks of us National Socialists the disinherited of Right and Left must come together. All of them must learn that there is one place in Germany where faith in the future is far from lost. We need the uprooted as fighters to rebuild the coming Germany!' The disinherited of Right and Left, the uprooted. . . .

Perhaps Hitler had just been hearing his friend Röhm say that 'only the man without possessions has ideals.' Göring, the friend of princes, leading the unemployed: this was the spirit of the movement, these were the uprooted of Right and Left. Hitler was a realist and knew that the great good-for-nothings are sometimes the best fighters. He himself had been an outstanding soldier — a man without home, friends, family, or employment. Years later, his friend Hess half-consciously described the type of his leader: 'It is a known fact,' he said, 'that many men stood up best in the field who were everything but suited for normal peacetime bourgeois life. In critical situations, the front-line companies were glad to have such men at their disposal. . . .'

This type, so proficient at war, is now mustering its forces to dominate the peace. The armed bohemians, grown homeless through the downfall of war, conjure up the dead war in peacetime life and force it on the sighing peoples. Hess, consistently, says: 'In the struggle against Marxism we cannot choose our leaders for their company manners and respectability. . . . I know that our corps of leaders contains a sprinkling of those who, according to some, should be dismissed. But I also know that in the hard years of struggle, these leaders stood up. And more: that we largely owe our success to them.'

The success was owed to them — to those 'figures' who were worth so little in bourgeois life; who 'were tossed in all directions — just for their daily bread'; who as murderers let the clear red blood of the people flow, and as bohemians 'brawled and drank, roared and smashed windows.' The bourgeois, even the Nationalist press, began to take fright and talk of 'Bolshevism'; and Hitler himself boasted: 'In our movement the two extremes come together: the Communists from the Left and the officers and the students from the Right. These two have always been the most active elements, and it was the greatest crime that they used to oppose each other in street fights. The Communists were the idealists of socialism; through years of persecution they saw their mortal enemy in the officer; while the officers fought the Communists because they inevitably saw the mortal enemy of their fatherland in the proletarian led astray by the Jew. Our party has already succeeded in uniting these two utter extremes within the ranks of our storm troops. They will form the core of the great German liberation movement, in which all without distinction will stand together when the day comes to say: The nation arises, the storm is breaking!'

At the Paris Peace Conference, Woodrow Wilson said to Clemenceau and Lloyd George that Germany in 1919 was an alliance between junkers and Bolsheviks. That it was not. But Wilson had sensed something. The alliance was in the air; the German leaders of 1919 rejected it; Hitler seized on it in his own way. He led the uprooted proletarians and the uprooted intellectuals together. And this gives rise to a new man: 'Neither of the two could exist without the other. Both belong together, and from these two a new man must crystallize — the man of the coming German Reich.'

Gerhard Rossbach assures us, almost with tenderness, that his drinkers and killers were 'a new troop of light-seeking fighters for freedom. . . . Some day, dedicated to death, they will have to fight on native soil for the life of the nation.' On native soil — for the armed bohemians fight to subjugate their own people. Hitler had meant nothing else when he prophesied that the fight against the Soviet Star — the fight of German against German — would renew the nation.

This brings us to the great cleft that divides Hitler, and with him his cause, in two. He summons the Aryans and anti-Semites of all countries to the struggle against Soviet Star and Judaism. He even accuses Judaism of having driven the European nations into

a useless struggle against each other. But all the same, he is ready
to resume this useless struggle as soon as possible, for 'Germany will
not be free until the first German grenadiers are back on the
Ruhr and the Rhine.' (At that time French soldiers were standing
guard on the Ruhr and Rhine.) It is the task of the Uprooted
and Disinherited to drive them from German soil. And would he
stop then? No. To him Bismarck in Versailles, crowning the
German emperor over the corpse of the defeated foe, remains one
of the highest goals of German history: 'Compare the coronation
in Versailles to that scene of disgrace in the Forest of Compiègne.
In those days Bismarck was Germany. Then came Erzberger, the
fat paunch. Marshal Foch was amazed: "Is this the Germany before which a thousand times we almost went down in defeat?" he
asked. No, that was not Germany! It wasn't Germany that you
French overran. You didn't defeat Germany; treason put her in
your hands, a defenseless victim.'

Wars are lost by treason; but this means also that wars can be won
by treason. War, in the last analysis, is won or lost at home; the
battlefield is the test ground for the forces that build up the inner
life of a nation. On this test ground you will learn soon that problems and quarrels, which today still loom great, actually have vanished already in the abyss of history. For the fate of Germany has
slipped from the hands of their former ruling classes into the hands
of the Uprooted and Disinherited: 'Today the German no longer
dies for state forms, not for republic or monarchy — and anyone
who tries to make him is a scoundrel; today the German — if he is
prepared to die for anything at all — dies only for the freedom of the
working German people, only for the freedom of his native soil.
The question of state forms will be decided by the people who have
faith in the fatherland, who are ready to go back to the battlefield;
who in victorious battle will return to the place where the old
German Reich was founded and where it was smashed by the slimy
bandits and criminals who set their signatures to the peace treaty;
the only place where a new, more beautiful and greater Reich can
proclaim its state form: that place is Versailles.'

This Hitler said in October, 1923, to a meeting of his armed
men, and the newspaper reports 'stormy applause.' In Versailles,

after another victory over France, the Uprooted and Disinherited would raise their new Germany from the bloody baptismal font. Hitler's young followers shouted *Heil!* till they were hoarse; the lieutenants and captains were moved and fascinated; but the generals, in so far as they took any notice of their former subordinate, remained cool. A war of vengeance against France — no reasonable person could think of such a thing!

Even Hitler did not really think of it. Listen to the overtones in his speeches, and you will perceive that the war against France is not his true purpose. He wants, once and forever, to do away with the old ruling caste; with petrified legitimists, and hollow dignitaries in gold-braided uniforms. And so he asks them: Can you win a war? No, but you have lost one. Why? 'You did not understand how to hammer the national sentiment into the people by teaching and example. Not having understood this duty, the time has come for you to abdicate. . . .' He doesn't mind calling them names: 'You could have stamped out the symptoms of revolt with two or three divisions. Maybe a few thousand deserters would have been stood up against the wall, but the German people would have been saved. But you showed yourself to be cowards, and like cowards you turned the other cheek.'

Thus, briefly, what is war? War is the 'necessity of Fate,' the great historical decision between the traditional governing caste, and the new class of the Uprooted and Disinherited. Therefore, Hitler will be willing to risk this fateful necessity with a light heart, as soon as the inner situation is at stake; for even a lost war finally strengthens the nation that is not killed by it — this is the nucleus of the whole doctrine. Blood does not mean anything, and in this struggle for what he calls the 'German soul' there is no law nor rule: 'We may be inhuman! But if we save Germany, we have accomplished the greatest deed in the world. We may do wrong. But if we save Germany, we have ended the greatest wrong in the world. We may be immoral. But if our people is saved, we have reopened the road for morality.'

Lured and enchanted by their demonic goal, the army of the Uprooted and Disinherited cast off everything that bound them to human morality; they loaded their automatics, tuned up the motors of their death-cars, and didn't even forget the stones to weight down the victims of their fight for freedom. The value of a man's life dwindled to nothing, after the value of his money had vanished. 'The creation of the future Germany — a Germany on a Germanic foundation' — had begun.

But even if the unleashed hordes didn't know it, their leader did: there was far more at stake than Germany. Again conviction was changed for conviction, again the whole world picture changed, again the aims changed. No, the goal was not merely Germany. The goal was the union of the Aryans and anti-Semites of all nations — the world domination, which Nietzsche divined, which Houston Chamberlain prophesied, and for which the Wise Men of Zion indicated the means. The Demon, disguised as an unknown soldier from the Vienna lodging-house, speaks: 'Furthermore, this Germany must be the foundation of an Aryan world order.'

Anyone who has inwardly comprehended such a goal in all its greatness knows that it is attainable. Only unknown greatness terrifies. Little things decay, private life decays, the individual existence becomes hard and hopeless, man becomes impossible. But the mighty mass arises, the mass means everything; infinite greatness becomes necessary and therefore easy. The Demon, knowing no sentiments of happiness, peace, gaiety in his own life, and utterly cold to the life and happiness of others, speaks again: 'We must not ask if it is possible to attain this goal, but whether it is necessary. If it is impossible, we will try it anyway and be destroyed. But if it is necessary and true, we must believe that it is possible just the same. And we need this faith. A thousand years look down on us, the future demands sacrifices of us.'

Hitler spoke these words on September 28, 1922. One month later, on October 27, 1922, Benito Mussolini in Italy established the first Fascist dictatorship in the world.

Chapter VIII

WAR IN THE RUHR

ONE NOVEMBER AFTERNOON IN THE YEAR 1922, Adolf Hitler left the Café Heck, near the Munich Court Garden, where he usually spent the middle of the day sitting with friends. He went directly across the Odeonsplatz, a magnificent broad square enclosed by stone palaces and churches. Perhaps, without any foreboding of the frightful future that was impending, he glanced at the so-called Feldherrn Halle, a shadowy, gray building — an imitation of the Italian town hall decorated with high arched niches — which is at the southern side of the square. He entered, through an inconspicuous little door, one of the old houses which seemed to blink at the beautiful square indifferently, out of dark, deeply sunken windows that resembled half-closed eyes. On the first floor he asked if he might speak to the minister, for the old building housed the Bavarian Ministry of the Interior. It is possible that the official in the foyer asked him impatiently, 'The minister? Yes, and who are you?' Hitler could have answered, 'The most famous man in the city, the most controversial figure in the country, the most enigmatic person of the times, the best beloved and the most hated human of this day,' and the official, suddenly understanding, would very probably have answered: 'That is not possible! I pictured you as wholly different.' For of the millions who had already heard of Hitler, there were only a few hundred, perhaps only dozens, who had seen him close to. For all the rest his form existed only in fantasy. He had no wish to be seen. He slipped through the streets unobtrusively, whenever possible hidden by his escort. When he entered a meeting hall, he darted down the aisle of yelling supporters often with his coat collar turned high; and on the speaker's platform in the hard light of the gas lamps he was a lank figure, gesticulating in his shabby black business suit, hardly recognizable from below. Disfigured for about a year by a pointed beard, his face then in no way suggested the mask that was later to become famous. Photographs of him were not to be seen anywhere.

Once when Heinrich Hoffmann, the photographer, snapped Hitler as he was entering his car, two strong men rushed at the surprised photographer and seized his camera. Hitler approached, polite and embarrassed, and requested Herr Hoffmann not to publish the picture — Herr Hoffmann did not publish it.

Hitler was afraid of being recognized, convinced that a murderer lurked at every corner. Anyone who recognized the inconspicuous figure in the yellow trench coat and stared for so much as a moment would receive a glance, burning with hatred, suspicion, and rage. Hitler was afraid of his fame.

How many victims had he delivered to the muzzles of the firing squads! He knew more about all the murders in the woods and in speeding automobiles at night than any state's attorney ever dared to find out. He wanted lamp-posts full of corpses, and promised to send heads rolling from the scaffold. Through Rudolf Hess, his friend and admirer, he had his own supporters spied upon, their weak and dark points marked down on index cards. At the head of a few hundred followers, he had fallen upon little provincial towns and chased political enemies or unfortunate Jews through the streets. But in between these adventures, he went his ways unknown; a little man, casting a giant shadow on the sky.

The minister had sent for this man. Hitler knew he was going to see his enemy; the minister was Doctor Franz Schweyer, who six months before had wanted to deport him to Austria. Nevertheless he went; it isn't every day that a minister asks you to call, and he knew that the invitation was a sign of respect and fear; fear of the man whom virtually no one knew and who aroused the curiosity of millions. The minister for his part knew that the captains and majors in the Reichswehr were constantly playing with plans for a *putsch*; he knew that these volatile and embittered young soldiers spent their evenings in the back rooms of obscure beer halls near the Munich Cathedral, reckoning how few companies would be needed to arrest a government, to occupy a railway station, to silence a telegraph office, to block six bridges, and place machine guns in the most important corner windows in the center of the city. This was the world in which the younger officers of this army lived, and everyone knew it. And the unknown man in the yellow coat, with the unexpressive mustached face and the murderous eye, was mysteriously involved in all these conspiracies. A passionate force, a confidence of victory, incomprehensible to outsiders, seemed to emanate from him.

All this was known to the minister. He knew that at least one responsible general, Franz von Epp, favored the conspiracies. He also knew that the really active force was Epp's adjutant, Röhm; and he suspected that Captain Röhm and the beer-hall orator Hitler hung together like twins. What kind of state was it which its army did not support but was forever threatening to overthrow! Schweyer, the calm, gray-bearded minister, had written bitter letters to Berlin. Others had written; the Social Democratic president of the Reich had complained. Reluctantly the Reichswehr Minister, a former mayor, had called his generals to account. In the end the Berlin generals had conducted a hasty and inadequate investigation in Munich. They had separated Röhm from his superior, Epp, and had subjected him to the immediate supervision of the general commandant of Bavaria. And to the latter post they appointed a new man, disinclined to adventures: General Otto von Lossow, a skeptical man, diplomatic and sly, believing in nothing but his military profession. Röhm and Epp accused one another of disloyalty; between the two a coolness arose which lasted for years and perhaps exerted a decisive influence on National Socialism. Röhm, the hero of the counter-revolution, was accused of making money on secret armament sales. Apparently nothing could be proved; he himself subsequently claimed to have been rehabilitated; but hardly a year later, in autumn, 1923, he resigned from the Reichswehr. Epp soon followed him.

The new commandant of the Reichswehr in Bavaria, von Lossow, was one of those higher generals who realized what the captains and majors, in their lust for action and recognition, did not and could not realize: that the Reichswehr needed no more *putsches* in Bavaria. It had most of what it required; and the republic could not forever deny its further needs. As for heavy armaments and planes, sternly forbidden by the peace treaty, in the first place they could not be obtained by *putsches,* and in the second place, they were unnecessary for the moment.

General Hans von Seeckt, who commanded the little army of the republic, developed the theory that the war of the future could no longer be carried on with mass armies, since two giant armies of half or badly trained military bunglers would only slaughter each other without profit. He taught that the small, well-trained, highly mobile, superbly armed professional army would cut the numerically superior, ponderous mass armies to ribbons in a lightning attack; and that in defensive operations it would paralyze the numerically superior foe by an aggressive defense, by constant thrusts at the flanks and rear. This ideal army of the future had been forced on the Germans by their unsuspecting foes in Versailles.

Von Lossow and his like had to induce the Reichswehr to accept a policy of silent, inconspicuous organization. The force remained numerically small and offered little opportunity for advancement. The captains and majors were doomed to years of waiting. This was the problem, this was the conflict, this was the dynamite which threatened Germany's inner security: the rebellion of the captains and majors against the generals, the class struggle of the officers under the intellectual leadership of the unknown man from the Austrian lodging-house.

With unshaken confidence, Hitler assured his young followers: 'When the day comes for us to march, no soldier and no policeman will shoot at us. For that day prepare yourselves.'

It was to dispel this illusion that the minister had sent for Herr Hitler. He told him he was mistaken: the police certainly would fire on him if he broke the law. Hitler replied that he would give the police and other organs of state power no cause to shoot: his intention was to smash Marxism, and this would enormously strengthen the authority of the state. What did he mean by the smashing of Marxism? the minister asked. Now he was threatened by a long speech with no clear answer. The minister interrupted Hitler and said: 'If you continue your propaganda in its present form, it will inevitably lead to a violent explosion some day, whatever your intentions. You can't just go on talking for years, some day you will have to act.'

Hitler jumped up from his chair, beat his breast with his right hand, and cried: 'Herr Minister, I give you my word of honor, never as long as I live will I make a *putsch!*' He repeated: 'My word of honor, I will never make a *putsch!*'

The minister replied: 'All respect to your word of honor, but if you go on making such speeches as you have been making, the stream will one day burst loose of its own accord, and you will be faced with the choice of sinking or swimming with it. And you will swim with it.'

Despite its apparent insignificance, the scene is historically memorable. It was Hitler's first pledge of peace. His word of honor. There would be no *putsch!*

The epoch of unknown soldiers was dawning. Mussolini had just shown how you can make yourself dictator with the help of a few thousand ruffians. Hitler passionately admired the 'great man in the south'; the man who had risen from the trenches 'in dirty boots' and attained the highest power. In the whole of central Europe the old concepts of domination or revolution, upper or lower class, lost their historical meaning through the upsurge of new forces, represented by the unknown, hitherto insignificant, yet menacing faces — 'a scourge, making a mockery of all ethical and honorable political activity . . . rabble released from prison for the purpose . . . in close fraternization and intermarriage with the petty officers' groups . . . with the state shutting an eye to murder, arson, and robbery': these were the very words by which an irate collaborator of Hitler, driven from German South Tyrol by the Italian Fascists, described Mussolini's armed bohemia in the *Völkischer Beobachter*. Near Munich dwelt, seemingly in retirement, General Erich Ludendorff, honored by the officers like a god, feared by the republican ministers in Berlin, suspected and admired by foreign governments and peoples. He was the former World War Captain, the great 'Quartermaster General,' who had ruled half Europe and even a piece of Asia and, for practical purposes, virtually dethroned his own Kaiser. This Ludendorff considered himself the coming Leader of Germany, and he saw the day near when, at the head of the captains and majors, he would sweep aside or beat into submission the Seeckts. As early as 1921, he had been willing to meet Herr Hitler; he found him an able speaker, very useful for propaganda purposes, a man of estimable patriotic fervor. This 'useful' Hitler, this legend without a face, was to become 1923's man of destiny; the abysmal force that was in him was to send forth a whirlwind engulfing all traditional greatness, including the Quartermaster General.

In this year the short-lived French domination of the Continent, established in 1919 by the Treaty of Versailles, was shattered. In the autumn of 1922, Lloyd George's government fell in England. The new cabinet of Bonar Law gently but indefatigably moved toward a balance of power: obstruction of French influence; greater leniency toward Germany, which should gradually be restored to the family of nations, from which Versailles had excluded her. The response of France to this British policy was an outburst of violence; for the first and last time, France attempted, independently and on her own, to protect herself against the dangers of whose existence she was firmly convinced.

At the Paris Peace Conference in 1919, Marshal Foch had demanded the left bank of the Rhine for France. President Raymond Poincaré had supported him, but France's true leader, the octogenarian Premier Georges Clemenceau, could not put through this demand, a mockery to the principle of self-determination, against Woodrow Wilson and Lloyd George. Clemenceau then renounced a permanent occupation of the Rhine, when Wilson and Lloyd George promised him that the United States and England would conclude a defensive treaty with France, guaranteeing that both countries would immediately and automatically come to France's aid in case of a German attack. But the alliance did not come into being, for the American Senate tore up Wilson's promise (Clemenceau, like most Europeans, had been surprisingly misinformed as to the President's actual power). After America's withdrawal, England, in accordance with the agreements, was no longer bound by Lloyd George's promise.

France now faced a terrifying alternative: should she strive for a British alliance even without America — or should she try to smash Germany while the enemy was still weak? Clemenceau had at least put through the occupation of the French Rhineland by Allied, chiefly French, troops for fifteen years. This term could be extended indefinitely if Germany did not fulfill the obligations as laid down in the peace treaty. The peace treaty was now literally unfulfillable or could be made so, by subjecting Germany to impossible indemnity payments — figures for the so-called 'reparations' had purposely been omitted from the Versailles Treaty. In a dramatic session of the French cabinet, Poincaré accused Clemenceau of frivolously surrendering the Rhineland. The terms of the treaty, Clemenceau replied, made it inconceivable that France should ever have to evacuate the Rhineland. 'Monsieur le président,' said the octogenarian to the younger president, 'if in fifteen years you will do me the honor to visit my grave, you will be able to tell me that we are on the Rhine, and there we shall remain.'

Not only were they on the Rhine, in the heart of Germany's richest and most cultivated province; but everywhere they menaced the German borders. To the east and southeast of Germany, new states had come to life — 'states against Germany,' to characterize them by their origin. In the east, wedged between Germany and the Soviet Union, lay the new Poland. After almost one hundred and fifty years of repression and non-existence, a nation of nearly thirty-five million souls had arisen — to all appearances, out of the void. Poland was composed of territories which had — unjustly, to be sure — belonged to Russia, Germany, and the Austrian Empire; it comprised — even after Austria's almost complete disappearance — the former territories of two immense, insulted, and injured neighbors who enclosed the country on two sides. A dubious heritage! Eternal unrest was a birthmark of this state. To make matters worse, some of its territories were inhabited by non-Poles: White Russians, Lithuanians, Ukrainians, and Germans. A final misfortune: the Poles possessed no clear outlet to the sea — a cruel trick for history to play on a great people. At Versailles, Wilson and Clemenceau gave them a route to the sea against English resistance. Approximately following the course of the Vistula, a strip of land abutting on the Baltic was cut straight through conquered Germany. It was not an unjust solution: this 'Polish Corridor' actually was inhabited predominantly by Poles. But at the same time, the Corridor did tear Germany apart, cutting off the German province of East Prussia from the rest of the Reich. Moreover, in order that Poland should have a seaport under her own sovereignty, the totally German port of Danzig was taken away from Germany, contrary to the will of its inhabitants, and made into a sort of 'free city,' under League of Nations control. Also, there were numerous Germans living in the Polish Corridor, and about a million of them, often by the harshest measures, were forced out of the country. It must be owned that this policy of Polonization served social progress. It was part of a greater democratic agrarian policy, attempted in the whole of Poland: to divide the large estates among the peasants and thus break the power of feudalism. In this struggle against feudal land tenure, Poland, at least in her western provinces, was more advanced than Germany; the East Prussian junkers remained an island of feudalism in the midst of the agrarian reforms of eastern Europe.

A second 'state against Germany' was Czechoslovakia, the most important fragment blasted out of the Austrian Empire. She was surrounded on three sides by Germany, a wedge between German territories. Of her fifteen million inhabitants, between six and seven million belonged to the dominant Czech nationality, while two and a half to three million were Slovaks, closely related to the Czechs; more than three million were Germans. The German-inhabited territory could not have been separated from the core of the country without great disadvantage to all parties. On the whole, the Czechs treated their German minorities more justly and humanely than the Poles did. Fortunately for both sides, economic relations between Germany and Czechoslovakia (unlike Poland) gave small cause for irritation. But here, too, there were expropriations, resulting in bitter and justifiable German protests. After 1918, Czechoslovakia — like Poland — faced the alternative: to pursue a policy of compromise and conciliation toward defeated but by no means broken Germany, even at the expense of some momentary advantages; or to build on the supposition that Germany never would rise again, at the risk of dire vengeance in the event of having guessed wrong. Both Poland and Czechoslovakia chose the latter policy. They concluded military pacts with France (1921, 1924), thus encircling Germany. Like two daggers Poland and Czechoslovakia thrust into Germany, menacing Berlin at a distance of less than one hundred and forty miles.

But in the south there was a cleft in the system; narrow as a hair at first, it gradually widened. Along the Alps, virtually separating northern and southern Europe into two continents, extended the Republic of Austria, inhabited by eight million German-speaking people, the humble and helpless remnant of a once great empire. In 1918, this fragment wanted to exercise the right of self-determination and join Germany. This the victors of Versailles forbade. The *Anschluss* idea, nevertheless, remained alive. Czechoslovakia was opposed to it, because in the event of *Anschluss,* she would have been almost surrounded by Germany; France was opposed because she feared any enlargement of German power. Italy, too, was against it.

Italy was the existing, yet missing, link in the military chain around Germany. In the World War she had not really fought against Germany, but against Austria; this main enemy had been destroyed, the Italian-speaking provinces of Austria, Trieste, and South Tyrol had been 'redeemed'; for ostensibly strategic reasons, Italy had advanced her northern border to the main Alpine watershed, the Brenner Pass, thus winning sovereignty over a quarter of a million Germans in the northern part of South Tyrol. These Germans — at least in their cultural life, language, habits, even names — were worse oppressed by the Italian Fascists than their compatriots by the Czechs or even the Poles; moreover, Italy was more bitterly opposed to *Anschluss* than anyone else because Austria constituted a buffer against Germany, and totally covered the northern boundary of Italy. Italy might have fitted into France's system of military alliances against Germany if there had not been deeper reasons to the contrary. Though numbered among the victors of

1918, Italy felt herself humiliated by her fellow victors. She had made a poor showing in the World War; the English and French had barely saved her from annihilation at the hands of the enemy. In Versailles she had raised excessive imperialistic claims; for instance, to Dalmatia and parts of the defeated Turkish Empire. In addition, Italy had strong claims against France; among them in the North-African province of Tunisia, which actually did have a large Italian population. In 1915, when Italy entered the still uncertain war, stating her price in businesslike terms, France had made promises concerning Tunisia, and in 1919 they had not been entirely kept.

Among the intellectuals of Italy all these experiences aroused a feeling of national disgrace, which largely contributed to the rise of Italian Fascism. It was a feeling somewhat related to that of post-war Germany and it has even been claimed that the German Free Corps of 1919, the secret army of murderers, were the prototype of the Italian Fascist leagues. There was a difference, however; German fascism — as far as it had its roots in foreign politics — had sprung from a wounded feeling of frustrated self-determination; Italian fascism from frustrated imperialism.

But the deeper cause of these conflicts was older than the Versailles Treaty. It was simply the presence of a first-rate power (France) in the Mediterranean; while England, with Gibraltar, Malta, Suez, and Cyprus, controlled, so to speak, the source and outlet of this sea in which the Italian peninsula swims and breathes like a cell in living plasma. Italy, in the opinion of her intellectuals, would have to achieve absolute domination of the Mediterranean — 'mare nostrum' (our sea) — or remain permanently dependent on France and England. Bismarck had used this Italian problem to forge a German-Italian alliance in 1882; the alliance finally failed, for as long as Austria, Germany's other ally, survived, she remained, despite everything, Italy's prime enemy. Now that the Austrian Empire was dead, Italian ambitions and Italian enmities were focused on the Mediterranean. She began to turn angry eyes on France. If Italy should ever have to choose, her claims against France would outweigh her resistance against the Austrian *Anschluss* — especially if Germany could give her substantial assurance that she would renounce the two hundred and twenty thousand Germans in South Tyrol and would not molest Italy on their account. Immediately after Mussolini's rise to power, a cold, lonely voice in Munich declared, amid a storm of protest, that the issue of South Tyrol must not be allowed to come between Germany and Italy; if Fascist Italy was prepared to oppose France, this represented such a gain for Germany that she might calmly renounce South Tyrol. It was the voice of the unknown Hitler.

This, roughly, was the political situation at the beginning of 1923, when the struggle with France for the Rhine approached its climax. The term of Raymond Poincaré, President of the French Republic, had expired in 1920. Georges Clemenceau had attempted to succeed him, but failed; embittered, he had withdrawn from political life. But Poincaré had returned: in 1922, he became premier and prepared a violent and final settlement with conquered Germany. Germany, too, was arming for a test of strength. Both sides used the question of German reparation payments as a pretext. Germany, without denying her obligations, wanted them to be clearly defined and finally settled, for as long as they were not, the country's balance of payment remained an unknown and unsafe factor, and inflation was there to stay. France maintained that Germany's obligations had been defined and settled by the London plan of 1921, and that there was nothing to settle any more — which was quite true except that the London settlement, with its one hundred and thirty-two billions, certainly exceeded Germany's capability to produce and to pay, and France's capability to receive and to digest.

In Germany the Wirth cabinet which, by its policy of 'fulfilling' obligations that simply could not be fulfilled, had aroused doubts of Germany's sincerity, fell in autumn, 1922. It was replaced by the most conservative and nationalistic government that the German Republic had had up to that time. Doctor Wilhelm Cuno, the new Chancellor, who had been director of the leading German steamship line, tried in vain to reach a definite settlement.

On January 11, 1923, a French army occupied Germany's last and greatest coal province, the industrial heart of the Reich, the Ruhr. A war broke out between France and Germany, in so far as one can speak of war between a first-class military power and a dis-

armed nation. Germany waged war by falling down and passively
submitting to the enemy's blows. Wherever French soldiers appeared, the trains stopped running, machines gathered rust and
dust in empty factories, the coal mines were abandoned. Throughout the west of Germany, occupied by the French, life was at a
standstill, excepting in the Cologne region, where the occupation
was English; from near-by Koblenz, the Americans had previously
departed, regretted by the population. Among the foreign conquerors they alone had given the German population the feeling
that understanding was still possible between victor and vanquished,
a return to peace without bitterness and vengeance.

Poincaré's France did not believe in such an understanding.
Poincaré felt that Germany had not been sufficiently broken by the
defeat of 1918 and wanted to break her for good. Actually Germany did have a certain power. The passive resistance to which the
Cuno government summoned the Ruhr and the Rhineland was
an expression of power, the standstill in western Germany was — at
least in the beginning — a great political achievement. The unions
gave the strike order, and everyone struck, the industrialists included. Let the conqueror find himself with a worthless country,
a dead victim. The French military authorities chased thousands
of inhabitants into the unoccupied territory. For Hitler it was
painful and humiliating that the 'great man in the South' should
also participate in the pillage, sending a company of Italian engineers after the French troops into the Ruhr; for Italy could not
live without the German coal from the Ruhr. England, by contrast, was not in the least enthusiastic over the French seizure of
German coal; for France had always bought a large part of the
coal for her industry from England, and the English mines could
not live without their French purchasers. Besides, England could
not approve the establishment of French rule near the mouth of
the Rhine, hard by that triangle of coasts, river mouths, seaports
leading into the heart of Europe, through which one hundred and
twelve years earlier Napoleon had drawn a military line extending
from Cape Finisterre in Spain to Hamburg, menacing the British
Isles — no, it was a cardinal principle of British policy that this
coast must never belong to a single power. English banks sup-

ported the passive resistance of Germany in the Ruhr by supporting the German mark. For the strike in the western provinces was a new and even heavier drain on the mark; the strikers had to live, the employers cried out for indemnities. The campaign was financed by the Reich treasury. At the bank windows the millions were no longer counted, the piles of notes were measured with a ruler. At the beginning the mark was successfully pegged, but soon English aid proved insufficient. The mark slipped and crashed again, the passive resistance crumbled, the French held out the temptation of wages in good, solid francs, printed specially for the Rhineland. In Germany secret patriotic establishments set to work, forging masses of these Rhineland francs to make them depreciate. All to no avail. The French slowly succeeded in putting the Ruhr back to work and carrying off the coal. With her passive resistance, Germany had harmed herself more seriously than the enemy.

Nevertheless, Germany developed in this 'Ruhr War' a power which she had not shown since 1918; for a short time she had been inwardly steeled and united as she had not been since the outbreak of the World War. To be sure, she was materially paralyzed and impoverished; she was unarmed in comparison to France; but France, too, was permeated with inner conflicts, the break with England was a source of deep anxiety. With all their hearts the French people rejected the Ruhr War — like everything which in any way reminded them of war. Hitler well understood this: 'Today the disproportion between outward power and inner strength in France is greater than ever. France has only the momentary weakness of Germany to thank for her present position of power' — again the profound insight into the weakness of the enemy to which he has owed so many of his successes.

But now Germany, in the Ruhr War, developed a force of will which at the outset was highly effective. Never had Hitler been more afraid than in those days when it looked as if his 'necessary' chaos might suddenly come to an end. What if Germany should overcome her inner weakness? What if the conquered country should unite and reorganize? What if Germany should recover her power — and all this without Hitler? Here lay a true danger. If

Germany should work herself out of the bloody morass of civil war and return to the solid ground of order; if the Uprooted and Disinherited should regain a hold on life; if the general ruin were halted — Hitler was lost. Consequently, the war in the Ruhr must not be won, the civil war must go on.

When the French troops moved into the Ruhr, a storm of national passion rose in Germany; the country was transformed overnight, united by a wild patriotic upsurge. But in Munich a lonely voice repeated: 'No — not down with France, but down with the traitors to the fatherland, down with the November criminals. That must be our slogan.' By the traitors against the fatherland Hitler meant the parties which were organizing strikes for the fatherland in the Ruhr. Perhaps for the first time the Nazis heard cries of shame when they approached a mass demonstration with their swastika banners. Hitler stubbornly persisted in refusing to make common front with the 'traitors,' even in the Reich's greatest need; future history must not report that he had ever forgiven them. It must go down in history that 'all these scoundrels had been called to account, that a divine judgment had broken over them which would be remembered for centuries to come.' Fear of a great national upsurge gave him the strangest ideas; he went so far as to accuse the Jews of war agitation. In his newspaper, Dietrich Eckart wrote: 'It would suit the Hebrews to lash us into an insane war against France — insane because obviously it would be lost with the swiftness of lightning.'

Hitler shouted himself hoarse for civil war and scaffold, and no one wanted to listen. And so — at the end of January, 1923 — he ordered five thousand of his storm troops to Munich, ostensibly to dedicate a flag. If he spoke with this background, people would hear him. He had given his word of honor to Minister Schweyer not to make a *putsch* — why, then, this assemblage of five thousand Uprooted and Disinherited? The minister later described his own attitude: 'I attached no importance to Herr Hitler's word of honor, because, in the handling of police power, one has no business giving or accepting words of honor.' The government forbade the parade — or 'party day,' as Hitler called it — out of hand.

Hitler dashed to the police president and put on an indescribable scene; as the police chief later reported to his superiors, Hitler 'begged on his knees for approval of the parade.' When the police president, like his minister, an elderly, gray-bearded man, stuck to his guns, Hitler foamed at the mouth and cried out that he would march with his men in any case, even if the police should fire; he would march in the front rank and let himself be shot. In answer, the government forbade, not only the demonstration of the storm battalions, but also twelve public meetings at which Hitler was to speak afterward.

Who was Hitler, anyway? Did the state rise and fall with him? Was he really the most controversial person in the country, the most mysterious figure of his day — or was he just a nuisance and disturber of the peace, who could be extinguished by a touch of the trigger without any special repercussions? The question was put to the Reichswehr, for it was the Reichswehr which would have to do the firing. Lossow called his officers together and asked their opinion. Epp fumed: intolerable how the government was treating a national movement like the National Socialists. Röhm openly accused the ministers of treason against the national cause; he would not shoot at these men who were his comrades. Now a remarkable thing happened: the two conspirators encountered opposition. The captains and majors no longer agreed among themselves. A part of them already saw and sensed how the new national army was growing and coming to demand respect; they felt the magnetic force of this inwardly strong force drawing them away from the chaotic murderers' army of the Uprooted and Disinherited. 'How can you combine your attitude with your oath to the flag?' Röhm was asked. Lossow hesitated, dismissed his officers, did not object to the government's measures. The Reichswehr had let Hitler down.

Epp went back to his office, deeply depressed. Röhm, in despair, assembled a few like-minded comrades and stormed into Epp's room. He pleaded with him to gather courage and besiege Lossow again. In the end, he personally dragged the hesitant infantry leader to the supreme commander. Epp went into Lossow's study and spoke with him alone; panting and feverish, Röhm sat in the vestibule. The whole scene was not far from military insubordination. Lossow stepped to the door: 'Can you bring Hitler himself here?' 'Of course!' Röhm hurried away.

A few minutes later, Hitler and Lossow faced one another for the first time. For the first time Lossow looked into the empty, undistinguished face of the legend, faced an embarrassed, over-polite man, striving almost obsequiously to make a good impression. By the quietness of his tone, Hitler strove to convince the general that the government's fear of a *putsch* was absurd. Lossow's appraisal, as he later reported, was: 'Insignificant!' The general could not believe that this man represented a danger. But he did not wish to impair the government's authority unnecessarily. So he proposed to Hitler that he give Minister Schweyer his personal word of honor not to make a *putsch* — then he might be allowed to parade. Now, before Lossow's astonished eyes, occurred a human transformation such as few men can accomplish. Out of the embarrassed nothing there suddenly burst a volcano, filling the room with bad manners and shouting: Hitler roared that he would give Minister Schweyer no word of honor; no, never again; he had given it to him once, and one word of honor was all he had. But he would give His Excellency, the Herr General, his word, that he would make no *putsch* on January 26, 1923. He would report again to His Excellency on January 28. These, at least, were the words in which Hitler himself described the same scene later.

Lossow, again undecided, called the officers a second time and asked them if they would fire on the National Socialists if ordered to. Answer, unanimously: yes. That set his mind at rest. He commissioned Röhm to inform the government 'that in the interests of national defense, he would regret any vexation of the national elements'; he suggested that the government re-examine its decisions. And the government acceded to the armed forces. The police president again sent for Hitler and told him that the prohibition had been withdrawn; merely requested that Hitler voluntarily abandon his open-air demonstration. 'Perhaps,' said Hitler. He would see what could be done. The demonstration took place in the open.

'We have no cause to make a *putsch*,' Hitler scoffed in his speech to his troops. 'The government is so rotten and shaky that sooner or later it will collapse of its own accord.' That was his explanation for his word of honor: I will make no *putsch*. The *putsch* will make itself; assuming, of course — and again there was fear in his words — that the battle of the Ruhr should be lost and Germany collapse. 'The fight in the Ruhr must and will collapse!' he cried. Half a dozen times, in different terms, he declared to his storm troops that Germany was going under. 'Our job is to insure the success of our movement!'

But despite this seeming success, Hitler's relation to the Reichswehr had reached a strange turning point. The Reichswehr had experienced and learned to understand the problem of the proletariat in its own flesh — almost succumbing in the process. That was why the Röhms and Epps had founded their Workers' Party. Hitler was expected to bring the workers to the army — and in the spring of 1923, his employers were forced to admit that this hope had been frustrated. In its place a new hope arose. When the unions in the Ruhr, with machine-like precision, stopped the wheels of industry for the fatherland, a new road to the proletariat seemed to open. It was not Hitler's road.

General von Seeckt in Berlin made an agreement with Carl Severing, the most popular of the Social Democratic leaders, who, as Prussian Minister of the Interior, was in command of the Prussian police, an armed force second only to the Reichswehr. The two men arrived at an agreement: despite Versailles, a secret army must be set up. Severing, to be sure, did not venture to contemplate open warfare against France. The purpose of the new army should be merely to protect the eastern border against any sudden attack by Polish volunteers or similar groups. Shortly after the French invasion of the Ruhr, little Lithuania seized the German border city of Memel by force. This was done, not only against the will of the population, but also against the will of France and England; but there was no help, and Germany was unable to protect her territory against the weakest of her neighbors.

Since there was no legal remedy in the framework of the peace treaties, it would have been surprising, indeed, if no illegal remedy had been found. The 'black' — i.e., secret — Reichswehr came to life. The soldiers were ostensibly 'short-term volunteers.' Most of them were the old, familiar faces from the murderers' army, the

National Socialist storm sections, the Free Corps of Ehrhardt, Rossbach, etc., and other 'defense leagues.' The Socialist leaders could
not have failed to realize that they were arming and nourishing
the murderers of the republic. But they thought it their patriotic
duty to defend the country's borders. Also they believed that the
central Reichswehr command in Berlin, by paying and arming the
'black' soldiers, might 'tie them to the crib' and thus render them
harmless.

Hitler saw things in the same light, and he was embittered.
Röhm — sometimes acting behind Lossow's back — calmly carried
on the trade he knew so well: he amassed more and more weapons
for Hitler's S.A. and raised their numbers, toward autumn, 1923,
to some fifteen thousand. He thought that he was furnishing his
friend with a wonderful implement of civil war. But Hitler recognized that his entanglement in the new army was destroying his
political freedom, putting him back where he was before: a mere
tool of the Reichswehr — yet of a Reichswehr that was cooled and
strangely transformed.

There were bitter scenes, for Röhm did not understand this.
Thus far the National Socialist storm troops had had their own
arms, their own machine guns, and even a few cannon. In form,
to be sure, these implements of murder had always belonged to the
Reichswehr, but the Reichswehr, unable to store them in its own
barracks for fear of the Allied control commission, had been glad
to give the precious weapons to the political leagues for safe-keeping
and maintenance; in fact, the leagues had been created more or less
for this purpose. Little by little, they had come to regard the arms
as their own property. And now came the great blow. After the
outbreak of the battle of the Ruhr, the Reich had half-broken off
diplomatic relations with France. In January, 1923, a control commission barely escaped murder by National Socialists in Munich,
and after that the commissions ceased to function. The Reichswehr
in Bavaria had no more need to hide its arms. And so the leagues
were obliged to return the precious guaranty of their power, the
arms with which they wanted to overthrow the republic. They
received promises that the arms would be returned any time they
asked for them — but these were mere promises.

This agreement had been made by Röhm. To his mind, the goal of all his desires was virtually achieved. His side had a large army for civil war; they had the power; all they needed was the will. But just this was the weak point. The will had to be aroused in the generals. And here Hitler, unlike Röhm, sensed an almost insuperable difficulty: these generals would never want civil war. Hitler was in a desperate position, requiring of them a political decision they had no intention of making, since they no longer thought it necessary. They already had their army.

In these straits, Hitler decided to employ the magnetic force of his voice on Lossow. Perhaps the general could be bewitched. Hitler called on him week after week, and in April, 1923, nearly every day. He besought him to raise the banner of civil war, to summon the entire Reichswehr to revolution, to overthrow the government in Berlin. Lossow later admitted that Hitler's eloquence made a great impression on him — though only for a time. But one thing Lossow could never deny: '. . . that in our conferences of spring, 1923, Hitler never wanted anything for himself. He wanted no position, no government post; all he wanted was to make propaganda and prepare the terrain for him who was to come. . . .'

Who was to come? Directly questioned, Hitler would have replied, perhaps with some embarrassment: Ludendorff, the great Quartermaster General of the World War. He did not yet dare to say: myself. He modestly declared that he was only a drummer who would awaken Germany. In those days Hitler always hid behind this myth of modesty when the influential leaders of the German counter-revolution began to suspect that they were nurturing their own gravedigger.

Meanwhile, in the Ruhr, little troops of men crept at night through the industrial territory. They laid dynamite on railroad trestles, bridges, and junctions. French military trains were blown up. In the canals ships sank, and for days the westward stream of coal was interrupted. The secret army had again found a task. These dynamite squads were led at night by guides who knew the country. The dynamiters were the cream of armed bohemia. The guides, however, were often even more dubious characters, who for

money betrayed the men they guided to the French. In this way
Albert Leo Schlageter met his death at the hands of a French firing
squad, May 27, 1923 — this was the man of whom Hitler said that
the German people was not worthy to possess him. Before the
French military court, Schlageter declared that a desire to make
money had led him to dynamiting; and, involuntarily perhaps, he
betrayed a number of comrades. A number of the most hideous
'Vehmic murders' were committed at just this time.

This was not yet open warfare. But it had also ceased to be
passive resistance, a war of folded arms. The unions began to protest. Severing protested to Seeckt. The Social Democrats wanted
no bloodshed. Suddenly Hitler scented an opportunity for which
he had no longer hoped. If the unions were against war, he would
demand war. As late as the beginning of February, he had accused
the 'Hebrews' of agitating for war. Then he began to shift. 'Did
anyone really believe,' he asked, 'that the French military machine
in the Ruhr could be "idled to death"?'

He cited Georges Clemenceau, the savior of France in the World
War, who had declared that he would fight the Germans before
Paris, he would fight them in Paris, and he would fight them behind Paris. That was what should have been done in the Ruhr.
Weapons? Technical armament? 'That is simple. Child's play.
And even if at first we had nothing but our fists! If sixty million
people had a single will, a fanatical national mind — the arms
would spring forth from our fists!' When he was perfectly sure that
no one would follow his advice, he demanded a mass orgy of
dynamite; the smelting ovens might well be blown up, he said in
August, 1923, when the fight was virtually over; coal mines might
be flooded, houses go up in flames — if only the people were strong
and unflinching, all these things would rise up again. But even
these words seem cold and threadbare, compared with the same
speech, when published months later in book form. Only then
did he really think of all that he might have said, of the mighty,
heroic impression he might have made:

Blow up the furnaces, flood the coal mines, burn the houses to
the ground — provided that behind them a nation arises, strong,

unflinching, prepared for the utmost. For when the German people rise again, the rest will rise again, too. . . . The Ruhr should have become the German Moscow! . . . Behind the burning Ruhr, such a nation would have organized its resistance to the death. If this had been done, France would have proceeded with the greatest caution. And the rest of the world would have realized that Germany had recovered. A reorientation of our foreign policy would have been the first obvious consequence, a consequence welcomed in London. Not out of love for us. No, for the one aim which from time immemorial has guided England's policies: the aim of securing safety and peace, by creating an approximate balance of continental powers. . . . Cuno should have seized on the Ruhr question to harness the rising flame of our national spirit with determination and show France that a new hour was dawning. Furnace after furnace, bridge after bridge had to be blasted! France's army would not have allowed itself to be lashed into the horror of such a world catastrophe. By God, we would be in a different position today!

A speech full of decision and political boldness! It has but one failing: it was never delivered.

Forged words of flame, addressed to his officers and Communists. For this is the constant and secret sense of his propaganda: the Reichswehr is spiritually slipping out of his hands, he must refresh it and renew it constantly with the spirit of adventurism, the spirit of the extremists of Right and Left, the Uprooted and Disinherited. This must succeed in this decisive year of 1923, for thereon hangs his fate for many years to come, and perhaps for good. Germany must not return to order. The chaos must grow, there must be misery; that is a necessity of Fate: 'We have on our side historical truth and the growing misery of the people, which with natural necessity will bring a violent outbreak,' he once said to two thousand persons, by way of balm and consolation.

The possessions, hope, and faith of the German people lay in ruins. They were slipping into a night of despair, and Hitler, the shifting, restless flame, nourished by the gases of putrefaction, sent forth a fascinating glow. Hideous triumph: 'The hungry will cry out for bread, and the twenty million Germans, who, according to Clemenceau, are too many in Germany, will face a terrible destiny.

And each one will have to ask himself: Will you be one of those? Hammer, Sickle, and Star, the Red Banner will rise over Germany, but France will not give back the Ruhr.'

As he wallowed in these images of terror, fear grew in him: fear that the wave which bore him might suddenly break; fear that this creeping catastrophe might end, not with a sudden plunge to ruin, but with a sudden turn for the better, a sudden mustering of energies, a sudden salvation. Hitler lived in dread of a sudden shift of fortune. What he particularly dreaded was that despite his prophecies France should give back the Ruhr.

So he looked desperately for an opportunity to force the Reichswehr into a bloody civil war, before it was too late. The opportunity seemed to come. It was May Day, 1923, 'world holiday of the proletariat.' Trade unions, Social Democrats, and even Communists planned to gather peaceably and respectably in a meadow outside Munich, listen to a few festive speeches, and sing a few of their songs — the traditional, somewhat sleepy workers' holiday as it was celebrated in most countries of the world. It was the dull demonstration of those masses who, as Hitler liked to say, were compounded of stupidity, cowardice, and laziness — of men who, 'working only with their bodies, either possess no clarity of thought, or become disinclined to all brain work. A gigantic organization of work animals, without spiritual leadership.' At all events, a peaceable herd. And just this gave Hitler courage. He called his lieutenants together and declared that under any circumstances this Red demonstration must be broken up. He, together with the leader of other 'combat leagues,' addressed an ultimatum to the government: the May Day celebration must be forbidden, or blood would flow. Leaflets were printed: Women and children, off the streets! One of the subordinate leaders promised that the Reds would be shot down like mad dogs.

But the rifles lay in the barracks. Hitler and his comrades went to Lossow and demanded them. What for? Well . . . there was danger of a Marxist *putsch*. This was a pretext, and a particularly bad one. Defense against a Marxist *putsch*, said Lossow, is something you can leave to me. Hitler grew red in the face and reminded the general of his promise to release the arms any time they were asked

for. Lossow: 'As far as I'm concerned, you can call me a perjurer —
I will not release the arms. And anyone creating disorder in the
streets will be fired on, regardless of who it is.'

This was almost war with the Reichswehr. Hitler now ventured a desperate trick. Trucks drove up to the gates of the barracks, storm troops jumped out, the troops in the barracks didn't
stir — for secretly, behind Lossow's back, Röhm had given orders
to offer no resistance. The storm troopers marched into the barracks as though quite at home there, shouted a few comradely jokes
at the regular soldiers, took the weapons they wanted, threw them
into the trucks and drove off. A daring venture — but it exhausted
Hitler's store of courage. On a meadow outside the city some thousands of Socialists stood beneath their Red banners and quietly listened to their speakers, scarcely suspecting the danger. The danger,
meanwhile — stricken with indecision and discouragement —
marched out the other end of the city. There Hitler assembled his
followers on another meadow known as the Oberwiesenfeld, where
Reichswehr troops were drilling. Hitler hoped to win them over
and incite them against Lossow: the former corporal had gone far,
he had lost his feeling for military discipline. With a steel helmet
on his head, his Iron Cross pinned to his chest, he ran desperately
from one Reichswehr officer to another, growing gloomier from
hour to hour. For, as the hours passed, his hopes dwindled. Lossow
had learned of Röhm's disobedience; a torrent of rage broke over
the captain, and worse was doubtless in store for him. Sharp
orders reached the Oberwiesenfeld. The Reichswehr drew a cordon
around Hitler's troops and demanded that they lay down their
arms. Hitler could only capitulate. He was granted permission to
take the weapons back to the barracks himself, spared the disgrace
of surrendering them in the open. Nevertheless, the whole episode
was an ignominious defeat.

At the decisive moment Hitler had not shown a warrior's heart
— and his men had seen this. Worst of all, the Reichswehr had not
only declined to help Hitler, but had also given him an actual rebuff. More and more clearly the solid core of the army was casting
off the armed adventurers; they were still comrades, they still had
the same past and more or less the same ideals; but their roads

were beginning to part. In the beginning the split was barely visible, for the lower ranks still hung closely, intimately together; the storm troopers still were at the same time 'black' Reichswehr; Hitler still hoped to force his will one day upon the hesitant generals who could not throw him off as easily as they might have wished. But a rift there was; and less than a year later it would be an abyss.

Thus the separation between the moderates and the extremists was on the way. On September 2, the extremists, i.e., National Socialists and several other combat leagues, gathered in Nuremberg. It was a meeting of about one hundred thousand people; the origin of the 'party meetings' of later days. Hitler and Ludendorff met, almost on the same level; but still in the eyes of most Ludendorff was the real leader, Hitler only his aide and tool. The combat leagues and storm troopers formed a loosely knit union, the 'German Combat Union.' It had, in spite of strong-worded proclamations, no definite aims; it was concluded in expectation of the 'national catastrophe' which Hitler had predicted for a long time.

For in the midst of the chaos, amid the disintegration of a million fortunes and careers, Germany was gathering her strength for a new accomplishment. It had grown clear that if the Ruhr War were continued, Germany would bleed to death economically. But it was also known that the French people had no heart for this costly war in peace-time; that they dreaded any armed expedition into the heart of Germany and wanted to keep their soldiers at home; at heart they no longer supported the intransigent Poincaré. Both sides had but one desire, to end the mad struggle; and in the depths of her misery, Germany found a leadership possessing the moral courage to take the first step toward peace, a step which at first sight seemed a capitulation, but which actually led to a series of successes in the field of foreign relations, to an economic upsurge at home, and the restoration of defeated Germany to the ranks of a great power. This policy was, to a large extent, inspired by England. Lord d'Abernon, British ambassador to Berlin, was one of its spiritual fathers. In August the Reichstag overthrew the Cuno cabinet; Doctor Gustav Stresemann, a parliamentarian of the half liberal, half nationalist Right, a former chauvinist, for a time an adversary of the republic, became Chancellor; at the end of a few months he relinquished this post, but remained Foreign Minister, and for years after that remained the political leader of Germany. Stresemann wanted peace and a real *rapprochement* with the victors. To regain her strength, Germany needed peace, and to enjoy peace she would have to resign herself to certain conditions which she might consider unjust. England promised to exert a moderating influence on France; American and English banks promised a large loan to bolster up German finances, for the restoration of German economy and the stabilization of the German currency, which late in the fall of 1923 had reached the low point of 1 : 1,000,000,000,000. On September 24, 1923, the German government broke off the Ruhr War unconditionally.

Unconditional surrender — Hitler's triumph! His forecasts came true, the war on the Ruhr was lost; here was Germany's defeat, by Fate necessary for his victory. Everywhere in Germany the murderers' army leaped to its feet. One day after the end of the Ruhr War, Röhm proposed that the 'German Combat Union' make Hitler its political leader, and this was done. Hitler himself, as always in such crucial hours, did not make a decision immediately, but was ready to take his lead from events that seemed inevitable now. He started an extraordinary propaganda campaign; arranged, for September 26, fourteen mass meetings in Munich alone, ordered his fifteen thousand S.A. men to be ready in full strength. If public opinion was ready — and this he wanted to find out by his fourteen mass meetings — he would march; rather his masses would march and take him with them. Such was his strategy; to be led by events was what he called intuition.

But the Bavarian government parried this slowly flying thunderbolt in time. It set up its own dictator, Gustav von Kahr again, this time with the title of State Commissioner General. Kahr, a short, thickset, dark-haired man, was no inspiring personality; stubborn, but slow of decision; his limitations disappeared for a short time behind a halo of ambition and vanity. His power was greater than his ability, his popularity greater than his daring. But he started well; without hesitation he suppressed Hitler's fourteen mass meetings. In the presence of Hess, Göring, and Röhm, Hitler shrieked, he would answer by a bloody revolution immediately, but he probably knew before that Röhm would be able to talk him out of this senseless plan. Whether Kahr, by habit and tradition a somewhat soft and half-hearted counter-revolutionary and anti-Prussian, this time meant business, he probably even did not know himself; anyhow, in order not to be caught by surprise, Berlin proclaimed a state of siege for the whole Reich; and there they were. Since liquidation of the Ruhr adventure, stopping of the endless flow of money into the 'hole in the West,' and final settlement of the reparation problem and, thereby, stabilization of money were the only sensible things to do, Bavaria in all probability would have given in finally; her businessmen would have seen to that, had it not been for two circumstances.

In the Rhineland, occupied by French and Belgian forces, a movement had arisen, demanding separation of the western provinces; establishment of an independent state; and alliance with or even kind of incorporation into France. Unknown leaders suddenly had thousands of followers, dominated the streets, occupied government buildings, and declared independent governments. It goes without saying that they enjoyed the favor of the French army of occupation. The separatists were an army of the Uprooted and Disinherited, very much like the National Socialist cohorts in the south. Seemingly at one another's throats, they strove for the same aim — chaos. The separatists who then dominated the Rhineland were the same rabble who — as storm troopers — were to torment Germany in 1933. Often they were the same individuals. The danger was that even more serious people, especially businessmen, favored the idea of separation. And Rhineland was the 'heartland' of German industry.

But resistance was too strong, especially among the workers, to whom separatism smelled too much like international big business. The movement did not become really popular. Then England protested against this attempt to create a French vassal state on the Rhine, and after some weeks of seeming success, the separatist movement suddenly collapsed. Even the French army hardly dared to protect its remnants against the popular indignation. One winter's night a little group of armed civilians rowed across the Rhine and broke into a hotel in Speyer where one of the most powerful separatist leaders was dining. They turned off the lights. Shots rang out in the darkness. When the lights were turned on, the intruders had vanished and the separatist leader lay dying beside his table. In the city of Pirmasens, a crowd gathered under the eyes of the French garrison, surrounded the district office where the separatist 'government' was located; a few dare-devils climbed the roof, poured gasoline on the building, and set it on fire. Some sixty of those within met their death in the flames.

But there was more unrest in shaken Germany. A Communist wave arose; the Communist leadership saw a 'revolutionary situation' and believed it would be possible, by a clever combination of legal and illegal procedures, to seize power in at least part of Germany. Communist-influenced and, for all practical purposes, Communist-led régimes gained power in Saxony and Thuringia, in the heart of Germany, just halfway between Munich and Berlin.

This Communist uprising was just that piece of chaos which Hitler needed in order to go on. He demanded a northward march of the Reichswehr from Bavaria, in alliance with his storm troops and the other combat leagues. First they would put down Communism in central Germany; then go to Berlin and, in collaboration with the North-German Reichswehr, overthrow the government which had permitted the existence of Communist régimes in the heart of the country. The march on Berlin became his program for the next months. Troops of the 'German Combat Union' gathered on the Thuringian frontier, ready to invade 'the enemy's country.'

Kahr, too, dreamed of seizing the Communist pretext in order to start, from Bavaria, a counter-revolution over the whole of Germany. There was, besides, a strong dose of Bavarian separatism and anti-Prussianism in his plans; an idea to restore the monarchy in Bavaria. His motives never have become quite clear, probably not even to himself. Anyhow, he induced Lossow not to obey orders from Berlin any more, but to take orders only from him, Kahr. A national split was threatened, although Kahr and Lossow went on assuring that they did not want to get 'away from Berlin'; but 'forward to Berlin.'

Kahr, von Lossow, and the commander of the Bavarian police
troops, one von Seisser, formed a triumvirate with practically unlimited power in Bavaria. The three may have been uncertain for
some time whether they meant to reach an understanding with
the government in Berlin or overthrow it. But they were pretty
well agreed as to one aim: to discipline Hitler and render him
harmless. Not to destroy him entirely, but to reduce him to the level
of a tool. They employed the illusory, halfway methods which
have destroyed so many moderate rulers who thought they could
make pacts with extremists and use them as tools. 'We always
tried,' said Lossow later with childish pride, 'to bring Herr Hitler
back to reality, to the realm of facts, for we had recognized the
healthy core of the Hitlerite movement. We saw this core in the
movement's power of recruiting the workers to a national point of
view.'

Then something decisive happened: the Communist pretext
disappeared. First the Communists shrank from an open uprising;
they did so on orders given by the man who at that time already
practically wielded the strongest influence on the international Communist machine: the secretary general of the Russian Communist
Party, Josef Dugashwili Stalin. By a technical mistake there was an
isolated outbreak in Hamburg (October 26); for three days the
Red workers fired desperately from roofs and windows and for
this folly of their inadequate leadership died in vain. Then Berlin
liquidated what was left. Northern German Reichswehr marched
into Saxony and Thuringia (October 29), deposed the Socialist
and Communist, but nevertheless quite legal, governments by force
and thus put an end to the 'Bolshevist menace.' With it disappeared
Hitler's strongest propaganda weapon; and it is an irony of history
that Josef Stalin had a share in this blow.

This was, for all intents and purposes, the end of the march on
Berlin as the triumvirate of dictators in Bavaria soon found out.
Seisser, in the first days of November, went to Berlin, talked with
General von Seeckt, came back and reported that Seeckt wouldn't
march. The big financial backers lost interest in the counter-revo-
lution. These financial backers, anyway, never had been behind
Hitler, but behind men like Kahr. Even a meeting between the

representative of Hugo Stinnes, Minoux, and Ludendorff ended with a clash: 'you are much too economic for me,' shouted Ludendorff. Hitler's march on Berlin became a march into empty space.

Two separate worlds were at that time fighting each other: a rising world of order, still with tender membranes and limbs, easily hurt, growing and solidifying amid infinite perils — and a world of disintegration and tumult, struggling with wild outbursts against its own ruin. Hitler fought for the perpetuation of the chaos, as five years before he had fought to perpetuate the war; in both struggles he was defending his spiritual home. In a world of normalcy a Nothing, in chaos a Titan — his extraordinary powers did not develop in supporting the tottering edifice; they flowered when it came to giving it one last shove. Swimming amid wreckage, climbing over ruins; that is his gift; and seldom has a man possessed it to a greater degree. With his inner kinship to all disintegration and decay he senses the currents that lead to the abyss and in them he knows how to steer his course. But in them alone. With uncanny acuteness he guesses the hidden weakness of the adversary; but in the presence of tranquil strength his perception and understanding are dulled. All his gifts of oratory, persuasion, planning, suddenly left him once a venture proved really impossible. Unless there was something to be smashed, overturned, subjugated, this strange personality assumed the dull gray tone which continued to amaze observers even after he had achieved the summits of power. A hypersensitive nature, he reacted almost hypnotically to circumstances. This is why he responded to them so effectively. In times of calm, he was sleepy; in tormented times, he lost all restraint; like a flag, he snaps in the storm.

The Nothing put in an appearance as the chaos lifted. Those conspirators enjoying positions of power or other influence withdrew from politics or decided to collaborate with the changed order. And now Adolf Hitler stepped forward to show the world his empty face with the piercing eyes of fiery revolt.

Suddenly his picture appeared on every wall. Heinrich Hoffmann, the photographer, received an order for thousands of picture postcards showing his face. A motion picture was made. In it, Hitler appeared with General Ludendorff as equal beside equal, but

even then it was felt that Ludendorff represented tradition, while
Hitler was youth, the future — hence the true leader, 'Der Führer.'
The term became current at this period, and from the beginning
it meant the Leader of All Germany — at the very least.

The political problem remained as before, the problem which
faces every counter-revolution: to persuade the state power to make
a revolution. The revolution from above never ceased to be the
goal of Hitler's strategy — even after the top leaders had abandoned the idea as superfluous. For Lossow, though for a time he
had been driven by circumstances not of his choosing into a sort
of revolt amounting almost to mutiny against Seeckt, desired only
a return to discipline and order. Röhm resigned from the Reichswehr at the end of September, 1923. His exact reasons are still not
clear. Perhaps the accusations of armament swindling had something to do with it. In any case, his political rôle in the Reichswehr was at an end. He now set all his hopes on a revolution of
the National Socialists, on the revolution and victory of the creature
which he had been building for five years. At about the same time,
Epp went on leave, and tendered his formal resignation a few
months later. Less courageous, less crafty than Röhm, he moved
away from the National Socialists and aimed at a political career
with the moderate bourgeois parties. He did not believe in Hitler's
star.

Meanwhile, the middle officers, the captains and majors, continued
to live in expectation of the *putsch,* for they expected it to bring
an enlarged army, with magnificent posts and promotions. They
saw Ludendorff as their future general; and Hitler as the man
who would carry out the *putsch*. It was their expectations which
goaded Hitler forward. He knew that he was in a desperate way;
he exclaimed: 'I have taken this road, and I will follow it to the
end, even alone and forsaken.'

Since there was no other solution, he ran headlong into the
most insane gamble: an uprising against the Reichswehr.

He began by giving Lossow another of his words of honor not
to *putsch* against the Reichswehr; in order to be believed, he felt
it necessary to add: 'Don't think I'm stupid enough to do that!'
He promised Seisser too: no *putsch* against the police. But later

he quite naïvely expounded to Lossow the crafty means by which he meant to disorganize the Reichswehr: he had enlisted General Ludendorff to be the military head of his uprising, and no soldier or officer would fire on Ludendorff. 'The generals, yes,' he said disparagingly to General von Lossow, 'they might want to shoot, for they cling to their swill pail, their pay-checks; but from major down, no one will fire on Ludendorff.' When Lossow very cautiously and coolly suggested that perhaps Ludendorff was politically not very intelligent, Hitler apparently quite flattered, explained that he needed Ludendorff only for the army; politically he would have nothing to say, for politically, as Lossow couldn't fail to realize, Hitler was for Germany what, in similar situations, Napoleon I and Gambetta had been for France, and of course he was the German Mussolini too.

At that very hour, unknown to Hitler, Captain Göring, supreme leader of the storm troops, was telling a member of Lossow's staff that of course the government must be led by Ludendorff, and 'something or other' would be found for Herr Hitler. At the same time Göring gave bloodthirsty commands to his lieutenants: the revolution will soon break out; you must make yourselves respected by unprecedented terror; in every locality, 'at least one man must immediately be shot dead, to frighten the people.'

Germany was returning to order, but the Uprooted and Disinherited still wanted their *putsch*. They could not yet see the beginning of stability and were still living in absolute despair. 'If someone couldn't get rid of his Jewish roomer, or didn't want to pay his taxes, he would say: "I can't stand it, I'm joining the National Socialists."' Five years later, Hitler used these contemptuous terms to describe the men who supported him in Germany's darkest hour. And these were not the most desperate. Ludendorff sent for Lossow and appealed to his conscience: better strike soon; the ranks of the National Socialist S.A. and the other defense leagues were starving. Soon it would be impossible to restrain them from action.

One of the lesser leaders of the S.A. was a former lieutenant, Wilhelm Brückner, who subsequently became Hitler's personal adjutant. Brückner later gave a classic picture of the army of the Uprooted and Disinherited in court. Officers, he related, had come to him with the reproach: 'You aren't striking! It's all the same to us. Whoever it is that strikes, we'll go along.' And Brückner had begged Hitler to strike soon, for 'the day is coming when I won't be able to hold the men back. If nothing happens now, they'll run away from us.' Action at any price. For Hitler the leap into the void became a bitter necessity. 'We had many unemployed in the S.A.,' Brückner went on, 'men who had staked their last suit, their last pair of shoes, their last cent to be trained as soldiers, and were saying: Soon things will move, we'll be put into the Reichswehr, and that will be the end of our misery.' The uprooted looked on civil war as their bread and butter and for that they drove their Leader on.

Chapter IX

THE BEER HALL PUTSCH

HITLER HAD HESITATED UNTIL HIS HESITATION nearly broke the movement. But then he pulled himself together. From one moment to the next he took an extraordinary decision. The task was to drive the government to revolution. But how? This time it looked as though the orders had come directly from the Wise Men of Zion.

Two refugees from Russia devised the plan, Alfred Rosenberg and his friend, Max Richter. Richter was a German from East Prussia, but he had spent a large part of his life in Russia, in the German Baltic provinces, from which Rosenberg originated. During the Russian revolution of 1905, he had belonged to one of the little private armies set up by landowners and industrialists for defense against the revolution — something on the style of the Black Hundreds. He had married the daughter of a manufacturer whose factory he had guarded. Later he had served in Turkey as a German 'diplomat,' or rather agent, and after the war, still as a German agent, he had been involved in the Russian counter-revolution. Fleeing from Russia, he had found his way to the German counter-revolution. Lossow knew him from the old days and characterized him as a man of dubious honor; Ludendorff esteemed him and vouched for his good character. Of bourgeois origin, he ennobled himself with his wife's family name, calling himself Max Erwin von Scheubner-Richter.

This political schemer of the Russian school, a craftier, more worldly man than his young friend Rosenberg, knew exactly how the Wise Men of Zion make a revolution. The revolution must be 'imperceptible,' say the *Protocols;* 'under an outward appearance of legality, the last traces of legal, constitutional life must gradually be destroyed.' At the end of September, Scheubner-Richter had provided Hitler with a lengthy plan for revolution. 'The national revolution,' he wrote, 'must not precede the seizure of political power; the seizure of the state's police power constitutes the premise for the national revolution'; one must, therefore, strive 'to lay hands on the state police power in a way that is at least outwardly legal.'

This was the type of revolution that the captains and majors had been working on for five years — revolution 'by permission of the Herr Präsident,' it was called in a secret document (one of a number that has come down to us).

In the first days of November, a great celebration, in memory of the war dead, was to be held not far from the Feldherrn Halle. According to plan, the heads of the state would stand in a short, narrow side-street, waiting for the Reichswehr troops to parade past. Kahr, Lossow, Seisser, the real rulers of Bavaria, would be there, and with them nearly all the important ministers. Also present would be Crown Prince Rupprecht, who, except for the revolution of 1918, would have been the king of Bavaria. In the war, Rupprecht had served as a field marshal and led great armies. Among the upper classes of Bavaria, whom Hitler needed, he enjoyed an almost mystical respect. Kahr, the dictator, was himself a convinced monarchist and viewed it as his life's aim some day to proclaim Rupprecht king — for these old civil servants could conceive of revolution only as a restoration of the monarchy. Hitler, it is true, despised the German princes for their cowardly flight in 1918. A few weeks previous he had informed Rupprecht through an intermediary that unless the prince did his bidding he would 'sweep him aside.' But now that the occasion offered, the king seemed to him just the right tool and very welcome.

Scheubner-Richter's and Rosenberg's plan was this: When all the notables were assembled in their little alley, but before the parading troops arrived, a few hundred storm troopers would suddenly descend in trucks, close off the street, covering the approaches with machine guns. Hitler would then approach Prince Rupprecht and Herr von Kahr and politely inform them that the German revolution was on. The overthrow of the monarchy in 1918 would be avenged, the dethroned prince recover his rights; he could then proclaim the German revolution and anything else that seemed suitable. Hitler was delighted with the idea. On the day of the celebration, Rosenberg reconnoitered the side-street in question, and was horrified to find a large and well-armed police guard. The revolution had to be called off.

But the plan was retained and carried out four days later in modified form. On the morning of November 8, Hitler made a visit to Ernst Pöhner, the former police commissioner, who had always protected him so well. Hitler told Pöhner he was going to make his *putsch* that night: 'I have great confidence in you,' he said. 'I have an important post in mind for you — will you help?' Carried away by the conspirator's lighthearted daring, Pöhner assented, and at once rendered a vital service. On the night of November 8, Kahr was to address a mass meeting, and this seemed to be the decisive opportunity to put the 'revolution with the permission of the president' through. It appears that Hitler feared Kahr might make a kind of Bavarian separatist pronunciamento — at least, this fear gave him a pretext to do what he did. All the political leaders of Bavaria — though without the prince — were again assembled in a small space. This time it was in the Bürgerbräu Keller, one of the many great halls in the city, where, in accordance with Bavarian custom, thousands of thirsty souls gathered at rough-hewn tables to drink beer out of big stone mugs. Most political meetings were held in these halls; Hitler had spoken dozens of times in the Bürgerbräu.

Kahr was to make a political speech — on a matter of little importance. Lossow, Seisser, and most of the ministers were present; and about three thousand people, who might well have been considered the leaders of the government, the army, society, and industry. The chief of the Munich police was also there, having delegated his post to a junior official, with whom we are already acquainted: Wilhelm Frick — the man who could not find the murderers. Frick was still blindly devoted and fanatically obedient to Pöhner. The Bürgerbräu, a large building surrounded by a fenced-in garden, hence easy to defend, had an ample police guard. But Frick, at the behest of his former boss, telephoned the commanding officer not to intervene in the event of disorders; but to wait and report all happenings to him.

What happened was that Hitler's armed followers captured three thousand men, representing the entire state power of Bavaria. It was many hours before the nature of the event became halfway clear to the outside world. Hitler's purpose was simply to set his gun at the heads of the dictators and force them to *putsch*. He felt sure he could carry the three thousand away by his eloquence. Six hundred of his storm troops quietly surrounded the building in the dusk. At police headquarters, Frick gave the police commissioner permission for the revolution. The president himself sat in the Bürgerbräu Keller, and Hitler took him prisoner along with the rest.

With his storm troops at their posts, Hitler, seemingly an innocent guest, stood amid the beer fumes in the crowded vestibule and whispered a command to a little middle-aged man with a pince-nez. The little man was Scheubner-Richter. Hitler bade him drive out to Ludendorff's place in the suburbs, inform the general that the *coup d'état* was an accomplished fact, offer him a command in the army, and bring him to the Bürgerbräu at once. All this, of course, with the greatest politeness — yet there was no mistaking that the unknown corporal was giving the general orders and a job.

The trucks bearing storm troopers and machine guns rushed out of the darkness, the illumined entrances of the building were suddenly black with armed men. Inside, Kahr stood unsuspecting on the platform; for half an hour he had been arduously reading from his prepared manuscript. Hitler rushed into the hall, at his left side was Alfred Rosenberg, meditating, perhaps, on the words of the Wise Men of Zion: that the boldest and most treacherous strokes are those that gain the admiration of the peoples. At Hitler's right side a broad-shouldered man with a mighty mustache; this was Ulrich Graf, apprentice butcher, an amateur wrestler and great brawler; he followed Hitler everywhere with the loyalty of a dog, a gun always ready in his pocket. Behind them came Rudolf Hess.

Hitler jumped on a chair, while his men set up a machine gun at the entrance to the hall; he fired a pistol at the ceiling, jumped down, and through the sudden silence strode to the platform. A stony-faced police major, his hands in his pockets, barred the way. Hitler, fearing a shot through the coat, quickly set his gun at the man's head, and screamed: 'Take your hands out of your pockets!' Another police officer pulled his arm away, but Hitler freed himself and mounted the platform where Kahr, pale and confused, had taken a few steps backward. Hitler cried out to the audience: 'The national revolution has begun. The building is occupied by six hundred heavily armed men. No one may leave the hall. Unless there is immediate quiet, I'll have a machine gun placed in the gallery. The Reichswehr and police barracks have been occupied, Reichswehr and police are marching on the city under the swastika banner.' Of this last, not a word was true.

According to a witness, Hitler had the 'expression of a madman.' His nerves were apparently unequal to the excitement. On this point nearly all who saw him that night were agreed. In a loud, raucous voice, he ordered Kahr, Lossow, and Seisser to follow him. A voice in the crowd cried out: 'Don't be cowards as in 1918. Shoot!' Little prevented Hitler and his men from being trampled to death by the crowd. Kahr was helpless. Lossow, who knew what a machine gun meant, held resistance to be useless. He whispered to Seisser — as both he and Seisser later stated: 'Put on an act!' Siesser passed the word to Kahr; amid this whispering they disappeared from the hall, led away as prisoners by the storm troopers.

What if they had refused? Today we know that Hitler's *putsch* would have instantly collapsed. But the three men were not so clear about the situation. Hitler's assertion that the Reichswehr had risen and joined him with cheers could have been true or false. Lossow, doubtless seething with rage and shame, held outward compliance to be the only way of gaining time and freedom of action.

The crowd in the hall was not so docile. Hitler left the hall with his prisoners and a sullen murmur arose. The mood grew menacing. 'Don't worry,' Göring shouted in a voice of thunder, 'we have the friendliest intentions, and anyway, you can be happy, you have your beer.'

Meanwhile, in the adjoining room — a cold, dismal place, full of beer fumes — Hitler spoke to his three prisoners in confused, jumbled snatches. He told them that he had formed a new government with Ludendorff. This was again untrue. Ludendorff knew nothing about it. The three, he continued, had but one choice: to join him. He was the government; in a hoarse voice he stammered: 'Reich government — Hitler; National Army — Ludendorff; Police — Seisser.' Herr von Kahr could be Bavarian 'Provincial Administrator,' a post without power. Pöhner was to be premier with dictatorial powers.

No answer. All three were darkly silent. At the doors and windows stood armed bohemia, pistols at belts, rifles over their shoulders, daggers at their sides — wild men with burning eyes, the ravenous beast, sensing that the cage door is about to open. Hitler raised his pistol and cried out that he knew it was hard for the gentlemen to decide, but that anyone who did not want to collaborate in the post to which Hitler appointed him 'has no right to existence.' They had but one choice: to fight by his side and conquer, or to die. Lossow and Seisser later testified that he staggered round the room half-drunk, though he had certainly taken no alcohol. He brandished his gun in their faces: 'I have four shots in my pistol! Three for my collaborators if they abandon me. The last bullet for myself!' He set the pistol to his temple and said solemnly: 'If I am not victorious by tomorrow afternoon, I shall be a dead man.'

Meanwhile, the three had recovered their nerves. Kahr, with forced indifference, told Hitler to go ahead and shoot him: 'Dying or not dying makes no difference to me. . . .' Hitler, barely listening, roared at Graf: 'Get me a stein!' He wanted beer.

Seisser spoke. He reproached Hitler for breaking his word of honor. Hitler suddenly grew plaintive: 'Yes, I did. Forgive me, but I had to for the sake of the fatherland.' Lossow was still silent. Kahr began to say a few words under his breath to the general. Hitler flew into a rage and interrupted: no talking without his permission. Again hostile silence.

The *putsch* was threatening to collapse. Hitler had an inspiration. He ran from the room, dashed into the hall, faced the silent, sullen gathering and announced that he had just formed a national government with the three men in the next room. Lossow would be Reichswehr minister, Seisser police minister; he himself would be political leader, while Ludendorff would lead the army. 'To-morrow,' he repeated, 'will find a German national government in Germany, or will find us dead!'

Is the meeting agreed? — Hitler asked. When the three thousand heard that Kahr, Lossow, and Seisser were in accord with Hitler, all hearts grew light. With this lie, as a witness put it, Hitler changed the mood of the meeting 'like a glove.' Everyone cheered. Hitler returned to the adjoining room, and Kahr could hear the cheering through the open door. He was as vain as he was timid, and this made a great impression on him.

At this moment, General Ludendorff, punctually delivered by Scheubner-Richter, entered the room. He began at once to speak. He said he was just as surprised as the three gentlemen, but that this was a great national event, and he could only advise the three to collaborate. He now solemnly offered them his hand to shake. This cost Ludendorff almost as much self-control as the three. He felt that Hitler had taken him by surprise and humiliated him and that night he spoke barely five words to him. This didn't trouble Hitler at all. When Ludendorff had concluded, he cried out joy-fully, almost mockingly: 'We can no longer turn back; our action is already inscribed on the pages of world history.'

Suddenly Pöhner appeared and began to argue with Kahr. The little dictator was still resisting: he was a monarchist after all and could act only in the name of his king. Pöhner, a big man, nearly a head taller than Kahr, spoke down to him. 'I, too, am a monarchist,' he declared, 'and that is exactly why I am taking part.' Meanwhile, Ludendorff stood in the middle of the room with outstretched hand; sheer respect demanded that Lossow take the hand of his general. If this was comedy, it was well played. Hitler meanwhile approached Kahr, suddenly changing his attitude. He folded his hands and assumed an unexpectedly humble tone: all he wanted was to repair the injustice suffered by the monarchy. 'If your ex-cellency permits, I will drive out to see his majesty at once and inform him that the German people have arisen and made good the injustice that was done his majesty's late-lamented father.' In all circumstances and with all persons, he found the right words. Now Kahr, too, found his word: he was prepared to co-operate 'as the king's deputy.' He had almost forgotten that he was putting on a comedy.

The accord seemed complete. They all returned to the hall. Kahr spoke; Ludendorff spoke; Lossow spoke; Seisser spoke — the first two with emotion, the others with painful restraint. Hitler and Ludendorff celebrated the greatness of the moment: here in this hall, a German national government had been formed. Hitler repeated that he himself had undertaken the political direction of this government, thus fulfilling 'the oath I swore five years ago as a blind cripple in a military hospital.' As the historian, Karl Alexander von Müller, subsequently related, Hitler was as pleased as a child, 'beaming with joy, overjoyed at his success; he had a child-like, frank expression of happiness that I shall never forget.' Beside Müller sat Max von Gruber, professor of racial hygiene at Munich University, impassioned nationalist and scientist, uncontested authority in racial questions. As a witness, he made the following statement to the state's attorney: 'For the first time I saw Hitler at close quarters. Face and head: bad race, mongrel. Low, receding forehead, ugly nose, broad cheekbones, small eyes, dark hair; facial expression, not of a man commanding with full self-control, but betraying insane excitement. Finally, an expression of blissful egotism.'

The men on the platform all shook hands and swore loyalty to one another. The audience stood on tables and chairs and shouted, overpowered by enthusiasm. Hitler, who had threatened to shoot Kahr but a few minutes before, clasped his hand and said: 'Excellency, I shall stand faithfully behind you like a dog!' — perhaps he meant a watch-dog. Lossow and Seisser, to whom Hitler had broken his word of honor, received new oaths and new words of honor. And to the applauding, cheering throng, Hitler cried out that now there would be a march on Berlin, the 'great sinful Babel,' and there we shall establish a new Reich, a Reich 'of power and glory, Amen!'

Suddenly, amid the merry tumult, a stout, gray-bearded man

stepped up to Hitler — Minister Schweyer: 'Hitler did not honor me with so much as a glance. I stepped up to him, tapped him on the chest with my finger, and said in an emphatic tone: "Now let me tell you something, Mr. Hitler. Do you remember the declaration you made to me in my office a year ago, of your own free will? Do you remember?" — whereupon Hitler fell into a sort of embarrassment and gave me no answer.'

While the others were swearing oaths of loyalty and gazing into each other's eyes, Lossow, with features cast in bronze, went on with his act. Beaming with happiness, Hitler shook everyone's hand and spoke in a warm voice of Germany's dawning glory. Rudolf Hess stood at the exit with a few of his sturdy henchmen and arrested a number of ministers who tried to slip away home unnoticed. Hitler himself, despite all his apparent emotion, never let his three victims, Kahr, Lossow, and Seisser, out of his sight. He was determined to prevent them from leaving the hall. Just then news arrived of a brawl between Reichswehr men and storm troops at one of the barracks. Lossow could easily have settled this, but Hitler didn't trust him. He himself drove to the scene, leaving the beer hall in command of Ludendorff.

The crowd began to break up. The agitated human stream seeped slowly through the narrow door. Most felt exalted and happy, a few dubious and worried; all were moved by the feeling that they had experienced a bit of history behind their beer mugs. Lossow nonchalantly informed Ludendorff that he was going to his office, as there were important orders to be given. With Kahr and Seisser, he vanished in the departing crowd. 'Is it safe to let them go?' Scheubner-Richter whispered to Ludendorff. 'I forbid you to doubt the word of a German officer,' Ludendorff replied sharply. In the vestibule one of Kahr's officials approached and asked what all this meant? The little dictator replied: 'Herr Kollega, I am really despondent. You yourself saw that I was forced to give my consent. That kind of thing simply isn't done.'

Meanwhile, Berlin had learned of the *putsch*. The government met at midnight under chairmanship of President Ebert. The men in Berlin understood the problem of the hour as well as Hitler in Munich. The President asked General von Seeckt: 'Tell us, please, General, whom does the Reichswehr obey? Does it obey the laws and the government, or the mutineers?' Seeckt looked coldly through his monocle and answered: 'The Reichswehr obeys me, Herr Reichs Präsident!' This answer hit the nail on the head and meant that the Reichswehr obeys its own interests. The Munich *putsch* threatened to tear the little army asunder, and therefore had to be crushed. Seeckt's position soon became clear to the others at the meeting; the President transferred to him a sort of dictatorial power, and Seeckt wired to Munich that he would put down the *putsch* if Munich didn't do so by itself.

Munich did it. A few of Lossow's close associates, among them General von Leeb, who later became a field marshal, had no sooner received the first reports from the Bürgerbräu than they placed the troops in readiness. The man who might have prevented this — Franz von Epp — was no longer there. Kahr may have lost his head for a moment, but the generals soon set him right. One of them received the returning Lossow with the sharp question: 'All that was bluff, excellency, was it not?' By 'all that' he meant the oath to the new Germany and the handshake. No misplaced sentimentality, if you please! A civilian, a former corporal, had dragged the general and commandant out of the hall at pistol-point in the presence of three thousand people; according to the code of honor prevailing in the German Army, Lossow was under obligation to strike him down. The general called Lossow a coward, a 'sorry figure.' 'I'd shoot down these dogs with a smile,' said one of his subordinates, referring to the National Socialist storm troopers.

Hitler prided himself on his understanding of the military soul, particularly the mood among the officers from major down. Yet it seems never to have entered his head that his pistol was a bitter affront to the Army's honor.

In high good humor, he returned to the Bürgerbräu. The waitresses were removing the beer mugs from the tables. On the floor, between the table and chair legs, the storm troopers lay sleeping amid their rifles and knapsacks. In one of the smaller rooms, Hitler expected to find General von Lossow in a council of war with Ludendorff; to plan on carrying the revolution to Berlin. But no Lossow was there, nor was there any sign of Kahr or Seisser.

Stunned at the blow, Hitler sank into a chair, stared at the great Quartermaster General and said nothing. He felt that his game had gone amiss, though he did not yet fully admit it to himself.

During the night of November 8, some three thousand storm troopers gathered in Munich. They had machine guns and even some cannon. But for many hours Hitler refused to believe that he would really have to fight. In that night two men were active. Röhm hurried with a small band to Lossow's headquarters where he himself had formerly worked, drew barbed wire around the building, set up machine guns in the windows, and prepared for battle. Rudolf Hess sent gangs to the homes of political opponents, rounded them up and herded them to the Bürgerbräu, aiming to intimidate Kahr and Lossow with the threat of murdering the hostages. For weeks Göring had spoken of nothing but the murder of hostages.

The night was spent in deliberation, hope, fear, hesitation. Meetings were held in the Bürgerbräu and in Lossow's offices occupied by Röhm. Hitler, Scheubner-Richter, Rosenberg, and Ludendorff examined their situation for hours. For a long time they continued to hope that Lossow or Seisser would suddenly reappear and put everything aright. They felt that a crisis, a struggle for a decision, was in progress among their adversaries. They continued to hope for a favorable turn and — partly out of pride and vanity — failed to realize the gravity of their situation. Who would dare to raise a hand against them?

'If we get through,' said Hitler darkly, 'very well; if not, we'll have to hang ourselves.' Röhm was embittered at so much inactivity and showed it. He had appeared with a fully packed soldier's kit, as though going into the trenches for weeks; he lay half asleep on the ground, his head on his knapsack, blinking at the light. Defiant and indifferent, he took no part in the deliberations. Someone suggested that perhaps the Allies, at news of the *putsch,* would send in their soldiers; particularly the Czech army was feared because of its proximity. 'There you see again,' said Hitler, 'what a worthless government we have in Berlin. They ought to have such a hold on the three million Germans in Czechoslovakia that they would rise up at the press of a button and make the whole Czech mobilization impossible.'

He began to shout at Pöhner, his new premier, that he wasn't
doing enough. Patrols should march through all the streets, ring
at every doorbell, and cry out: 'Hang out your banners!' The city
should be bedecked with flags — 'then we'd see some enthusiasm
among the people.' He had a constant flow of plans with which the
others were unable to keep up. Every minute he had some new
idea for winning more support, for bolstering up the ruined venture. Enraged generals had decided to break him so that he would
never rise up again. But Hitler and Ludendorff still believed that
they could melt the souls of the opposing forces, make them open
their fists, and put down their rifles.

In Munich, Hitler commanded a well-armed little troop, numerically stronger than Lossow's Reichswehr and Seisser's police; outside
in the country, he could raise double, perhaps triple, the number.
For a moment he thought of retreating to the open country and
waging real war in his own way, rallying the peasants to his banners, morally crushing the generals, at the same time tearing the
captains and majors away from them. But Ludendorff rejected
the idea, and Hitler himself knew that it was not feasible. Only too
well did he know his Uprooted and Disinherited who revolted to
obtain bread and wages from the Reichswehr. Later he said in
court: 'We had to fear that our men, who had to eat after all,
would plunder.'

And then this inventive mind suddenly had a new plan — mad,
desperate, magnificent in its desperation. He wanted to avoid fighting at any price. The victory which was slipping through his fingers could be salvaged only by a compromise peace — perhaps even
by an apparent capitulation. Ludendorff's personal prestige had
failed him. Lossow had shouted at a messenger from the general
and threatened to shoot even at him. Hitler cold-bloodedly decided to drop the Quartermaster General who had proved useless.
Another figure stood in the background: the pretender, Prince
Rupprecht, since World War days Ludendorff's bitter personal
enemy. Among the sleepy unshaved figures in the Bürgerbräu was
Lieutenant Neunzert, an old armed bohemian, a good friend of
Röhm's and a personal friend to the prince. In the dawn of November 9, Hitler summoned him and ordered him to Berchtes-

gaden, where the prince resided in a large castle. His instructions were to ask the prince to intercede with Kahr and Lossow and obtain a pardon for Hitler and Ludendorff. This would let them out of the affair without bloodshed or criminal proceedings. Hitler still hoped to win by humbling himself. An unpunished *putsch* is a victorious *putsch*. When Hitler gave Neunzert his message, Ludendorff stood by — did not speak a word.

Neunzert went — but how can petty circumstances sometimes change history! He found no car; was forced to go by train and did not reach Berchtesgaden until noon. Meanwhile, Ludendorff took the decision into his own hands. He saw his hour. There was only one way out. This band of three thousand idealists and dubious adventurers, of armed bohemians and plunderers, of believing and avid youth, must face the carbines of the Reichswehr, and the miracle must happen: the carbines must drop. Ludendorff was confident that they would if he marched in the lead. Hitler had thought so, too; but now his courage left him. While Ludendorff prepared his big act, the encounter between armed bohemia and Reichswehr, Hitler lent ear to timorous advisers who made it clear to him that the encounter would be more than an act. He hesitantly approached Ludendorff: 'They will fire on us.' The Quartermaster General replied only: 'We will march!'

Meanwhile, measures had been taken to help the miracle along. Hess packed Minister Schweyer and a second minister into the car, guarded by two sinister-looking individuals with rifles; he himself sat down beside the driver. The car sped southward, toward the mountains, where Hess appears to have had a hide-out; in any case, the two were being held as hostages for the safety of the rebel army and its leader. At a clearing in the woods Hess halted, the little company left the car and marched away from the road — things looked very much like a new forest murder. But this time it was only an act, like everything else connected with the *putsch;* after the two were sufficiently terrified, the journey was resumed. In Munich, Hitler was waiting anxiously for the saving message from the prince, and at length it came — when it was too late. Three thousand men were awaiting the order to march; the carbines that were to decide the day were already loaded. Meanwhile, in the November mist, Rudolf Hess was racing through the mountains with his two victims; more and more in sorrowful doubt whether this was the right thing to do.

The mass of hostages had been corralled in the Bürgerbräu. Göring made them join the marching columns, which in the course of the morning gathered in front of the building. He commanded one of his lieutenants, a certain Knoblauch, to keep a sharp eye on the prisoners during the march, as their life was a pledge for the safety of the whole venture. Knoblauch promised the prisoners that if anything happened to the column, he would have their skulls bashed in with rifle butts. Meanwhile, Göring and Ulrich Graf left the Bürgerbräu and went a few hundred yards toward the center of the city from which the rebels were separated by the Isar River. The bridge was closed by heavily armed police. Göring, magnificent in his black cap and black leather coat, beribboned and bemedaled, stepped up to the commanding officer, put his hand to his cap and said: 'Herr Kamerad, we are marching, and I want to tell you this: the first dead man in our ranks means the immediate death of all the hostages.' Ulrich Graf has given us a faithful picture of the whole scene. How terrible, the officer moaned, that they should begin shooting at one another. Only a little while before he and his comrades had fought shoulder to shoulder with Göring's men, and he couldn't see why they had suddenly become enemies. That, Göring replied coldly, was something he could ask von Lossow and Seisser. After much sighing on both sides the conversation ended with the following proposal from the police officer: 'Very well, Herr Kamerad, if I receive orders to move against you, I will inform you in time for you and your people to take the necessary defensive measures . . . or to withdraw if you wish to.'

At eleven o'clock the storm columns started toward the bridge. The hostages, awaiting death, stood in their ranks. Hitler passed and his eyes fell on the unfortunates. He gave orders to leave them behind — 'I wanted no martyrs,' he said later. The *putsch* was three quarters lost and a massacre of these defenseless men might have cost the leaders their heads. Hitler's courage and spirit of initiative sank from hour to hour. He let himself be driven, and Ludendorff did the driving.

It was a gray November morning. The Isar River separates the quarter in which the Bürgerbräu is situated from the center of the city and the government buildings. At the bridge stood the armed police squad under its benevolent commander. Göring, who for days had been possessed by blood lust, stepped forward, put his hand to his cap, and repeated: 'The first dead man in our ranks means the death of a hostage.' He thought the hostages were still in the column. At this moment the marching mass fell on the policemen, tore their carbines out of their hands, spat on them, and struck them in the face. This was no fraternization, no hopeful beginning.

In the inner city, somewhat to the north of the Feldherrn Halle, lay Lossow's headquarters, which Röhm had fortified with machine guns. Reichswehr troops had surrounded the building and set cannon in place. Neither of the two parties dared to fire. There were the closest comrades and friends on both sides. This drama had gone beyond all politics. It would have been easier for the officers to shoot into a band of unknown storm troopers. But to fire on comrades — this was hard.

And now advanced toward them, through the streets of Munich, leading three thousand more or less dubious figures, that extraordinary soldier who, to the Reichswehr, still seemed the embodiment of all military fame and greatness: the Quartermaster General of the World War. Ludendorff led his troop through the center of the city toward Lossow's headquarters near the Feldherrn Halle, apparently with the intention of liberating the besieged Röhm. He was convinced that the besieging officers and soldiers would not resist the sight of his aquiline face. When he commanded them to fraternize with their adversaries, when he commanded them to disobey Lossow, they would do so.

The column made its way into a narrow, gully-like street, opening out on the broad Odeonsplatz near the Feldherrn Halle. In the first row marched Ludendorff; to his right his personal adjutant, a former major by the name of Streck. On Ludendorff's left side marched Hitler, holding the pistol with which he had sworn to shoot himself in the event of failure. He had slung his left arm through the arm of Scheubner-Richter — an astonishing gesture of uncertainty and helplessness. Directly ahead of Hitler marched Graf, farther to the left Göring; Alfred Rosenberg was in the second row. Dietrich Eckart, a sick man, was missing. A little to one side was a stocky, bald man with hysterically convulsed features, the anti-Semitic agitator, Julius Streicher from Nuremberg. The first ranks were followed by an automobile carrying several machine guns. Then came three thousand men with shouldered rifles, some with mounted bayonets — all singing.

An armed cordon was drawn across the street where it opens into the Odeonsplatz. Perhaps a hundred men — again police and not Reichswehr — against three thousand. If the police wanted to stop the marchers, they had to do it in this narrow pass; once they reached the open square, the revolutionaries could have brought their numerical superiority to bear.

It is still not entirely clear who fired first. It would seem that Streicher leapt at one of the policemen and tried to snatch his carbine. One heard Hitler crying: 'Surrender! Surrender!' This man could bluff from the depths of his soul. At the same moment a Nazi ran forward and cried in terror: 'Don't shoot, His Excellency Ludendorff is coming!' Who can measure the effect of the fraction of a second wasted in muttering the useless word, 'Excellency'? A shot rang out and the man — probably Ulrich Graf — collapsed, wounded. A volley was fired. Göring fell, shot in the thigh. Scheubner-Richter received a fatal wound and fell. So tight was his leader's grip on him that Hitler's arm was dislocated. Hitler lay on the ground. It is not clear whether he was pulled down by Scheubner or was instinctively seeking cover. In any case, it is certain that if he wanted to cow the enemy, he had to remain on his feet.

Ludendorff remained standing. He even advanced. With Streck he passed between the rifle barrels of the police to the open square. If fifty or perhaps even twenty-five men had followed him, the day would have ended differently.

The front ranks of the three thousand returned the fire. They put their machine gun into action. Rosenberg lay on the ground near the front line. Behind him lay a National Socialist whom he did not know, shooting over him. The other side shot back; the ambassador of the Wise Men of Zion covered the unknown warrior. As Rosenberg later related, he found the man's bravery quite superfluous, and yelled at him to stop shooting in the Devil's name. The other took no heed and went on firing. Rosenberg finally crawled to one side; the firing stopped; he stood up and crept backward. Pressed against a house-wall stood Doctor Friedrich Weber, leader of the 'Oberland' Defense League allied with Hitler, weeping hysterically. Göring was carried into a near-by bank by two young storm troopers. The Jewish owner gave him first aid; this made so deep an impression on the two young National Socialists — brothers — that they soon left the party.

The whole exchange of fire had lasted less than a minute. Both sides were horrified and quickly stopped shooting. The narrow bit of street was covered with fallen bodies. Fourteen of Hitler's followers lay dead on the pavement.

Followers . . . it is noteworthy that the leaders in the first row lost only one dead: Scheubner-Richter. The other dead were unknown rank-and-filers; one or two held respected posts in civil life, but were simple privates in the party. The leaders appear to have saved themselves by quickly throwing themselves on the ground, so that the fire passed over them into the onrushing mass, killing thirteen. Three of the police fell.

As soon as the shooting stopped, in the first seconds of stunned silence on both sides, a man rose in the front row, the first of them all to rise, the quickest, perhaps the most terrified, obeying only his instinct of self-conservation. Doctor Walter Schulz, the National Socialist physician, who had marched in the foremost ranks, later told the examining magistrate: 'I saw that Hitler was the first to stand up. Apparently wounded in the arm, he moved back. I hurried after Hitler at once and caught one of our cars which were driving at the end of the column. Hitler was taken to this car.'

Another witness, the National Socialist Doctor Karl Gebhard, mentions the rapidity with which Hitler entered the car and drove away; both stories indicate that Hitler was the first to flee.

A bystander about a hundred yards from the head of the column, not knowing that Hitler and Ludendorff were marching in the lead and certainly not suspecting that there would be shooting in a few moments, saw the following picture: The storm troopers marched in gray or yellow wind-jackets and Norwegian ski caps (from which the S.A. cap was to develop). They carried their rifles over their shoulders and sang, apparently with no thought of fighting; as on parade. Suddenly the sound of firing was heard. It was an unexpected shock, not on the program. Two, perhaps three, volleys were heard, and for a few seconds the heavy rat-tat-tat of a machine gun. The whole thing did not last much more than half a minute. Time enough for the observer to run into a house door. At the same time the long column began to halt, to break up, and to run back in leaderless flight.

Ahead of all the rest the Leader fled. The day before Hitler had taken a long chance, he had risked his head and he knew it; he had done it in high spirits and with good courage. Today he had gone into a venture, lost before it was begun. Unable to avoid it, he had staked his life on an action which he knew to be useless. Now, leaving his men stretched out on the paving stones, he stood up and ran away.

Thus did armed bohemia behave when things became serious and their lives were at stake. Walter Flex, their poet and model, once had said that a man must be capable 'of shooting at the enemy through his own body.' On November 9, 1923, there was none of this. One man who really wanted to fight was commanded by Rosenberg to stop. A few weeks before, Communist workers in Hamburg had kept on shooting; in 1919, the bloody struggles of the proletarians in Berlin had lasted for days; the same was true in Munich in April and May of 1919, in March, 1920, in the Ruhr, later in central Germany. In February, 1934, it took the Austrian Fascists with their cannon days to break the resistance of the workers — not to mention the fight which the Spanish Republicans put up for more than two years against the Fascist generals. These struggles were serious and both sides realized that their heads were at stake. But in Munich it was a different type that faced the fire. We know the professions of the men who fell. Among the sixteen there was a locksmith, a hatter, a headwaiter, and Ludendorff's servant; the others were retired officers, or 'merchants' and 'bank clerks' — in reality, retired officers, temporarily in civilian occupations: armed bohemia. When this type makes a revolution, it is by nature and plan a sham, an armed noise to drown out the whispered betrayal; the seemingly military conclusion of a business deal concluded in advance; a painless indulgence of vanity and a hoax on the audience. This time the act had been a failure, and the actors fled at once.

Two hours later, Röhm capitulated behind his barbed wire. He gave in to the persuasion of Epp, who came as intermediary and angel of peace; apparently a friend, perhaps a traitor; at all events, a faint heart and a gravedigger of the common cause. Of Röhm's men, two had fallen.

Meanwhile, a car with the two hostages was still driving about the mountain roads. Shortly after noon, the news of the collapse in Munich reached the countryside. The lonely motorists heard it while pausing for rest. Schweyer suddenly noticed that the guards had vanished. He gathered new energy and commanded the driver, who suddenly showed himself astonishingly solicitous toward the ministers, to drive them back to Munich in all haste. Rudolf Hess slipped across the border into Austria over a mountain trail.

A few days later, Hitler was under arrest. As he sat there, the German chaos came to an end, and in a pacified world, returned to normalcy, a band of aimless rebels remained behind prison gates. Six days after the shooting at the Feldherrn Halle, the German mark was stabilized; from then on, it stopped sinking and has outwardly remained one of the firmest currencies in the world. In London a committee of international financiers met and decided to help sustain the German economy. Under the guidance of the American financier, Owen D. Young, and the English banker, Sir Josiah Stamp, a plan was worked out which became known as the Dawes Plan after the chairman of the committee. Germany received an international loan of eight hundred million gold marks, secured by the German state railways. At the same time the Allied governments set an approximate limit to the German 'reparations' payments, which had been purposely left vague. The payments were to begin with half a billion marks per annum, rising, within five years, to two and a half billions. An American financier, Parker

Gilbert, of J. P. Morgan and Company, was to supervise the management of German public finances and make sure the foreign capital was not misused. It was an oppressive and humiliating condition, but, in the beginning at least, understandable from the viewpoint of the creditor; for the next few years, Germany flourished under this system.

A period of prosperity, of relaxed nerves and settled living conditions began. This was the great recovery which Hitler had tried in vain to prevent with his last minute *putsch*. But the accomplices of the armed bohemians, the protectors and employers of the murderers' army, still sat in their high state positions, in the ministries and courts. It was these accomplices who were to mete out justice to Hitler.

The judges could scarcely look their victims in the eyes, the jailers did not know whether to guard or wait on their prisoners. To be sure, there were numerous conscientious officials in all departments; and among the accomplices many were enraged against Hitler for exposing them. Epp declared in no uncertain terms that Hitler had broken his word. Yet the leaders of the state were well aware that they were Hitler's accomplices and should have been on trial with him, and their bad conscience certainly weakened the prosecution. The young people who had run so fast from the fire recovered their courage in the presence of the embarrassed police inspectors and state's attorneys. They were seized with righteous indignation. They had marched out for a parade, and instead they had been forced to fight; the state which had already surrendered to them suddenly slipped away. The armed bohemians thought they were Germany; power over society was their prerogative, by virtue of their natural superiority and talents — and then they were fired upon. They were haled into court for proclaiming the violent overthrow of the government, arresting the ministers and leading officials, seizing and threatening to kill men who were totally innocent, plundering private lodgings and stealing banknotes from state printing offices. They scoffed and cursed at their judges, for daring to annoy them over such matters. Hitler in prison heard how his men had recovered their old daring and insolence; this, as he later related, considerably restored his courage.

At first 'I wanted to hear nothing more of this false world'; he threatened to end his life by voluntary starvation; Anton Drexler, founder of the party, visited him, and Hitler — not too reluctantly — let himself be dissuaded.

At the end of February, 1924, he faced a special court with Ludendorff, Röhm, Frick, and others. The trial gave him immense publicity and was a scandal in every respect. With a certain truth Hitler could declare that he had not wanted to rise against the state, for he had thought the state was with him. Gürtner, who had risen to be minister of justice, used his powerful influence to make the judges incline the scales even more than they normally would have.

In the presence of these complaisant judges, Hitler regained all his courage, and his speeches before the court are among his most impressive. He strove to prove his innocence by insisting that he had done only what Kahr, Lossow, and Seisser themselves had wanted. He attempted — and to this he attached far more importance — to explain himself to the world: 'This is my attitude: I would rather be hanged in a Bolshevist Germany than perish under the rule of French swords.' Lossow appeared as a witness and related how Hitler for months had pressed him to act, to set up a military dictatorship. 'Once we take over the government,' Hitler had said, 'the program will come of itself.' When the chairman of the court asked Hitler: 'And how did you conceive of things after that?' — the greatest propagandist of our day replied: 'I thought this: the first thing must be an inconceivable wave of propaganda. That is, a political action which would have had little to do with the other problems of the moment. . . . We would at once have approached the German nation with a great plebiscite.' But he went on to indicate that he did have at least a foreign policy: As Leader of Germany, he would have played England against France. England, he said, had the single desire to 'Balkanize' Europe in order to create a balance of power on the Continent, 'and prevent her world position from being threatened. She is not basically an enemy of Germany. . . . France, however, is Germany's explicit enemy. As England requires the Balkanization of Europe, France requires the Balkanization of Germany.' Whatever government is at the helm in France, its purpose would always be 'to exterminate twenty million Germans and break up Germany into separate states.'

He utilized the occasion to publicize himself in the presence of a hundred attentive reporters from all five continents; and in this he unquestionably succeeded. Lossow had testified that Hitler originally had only wanted to be a 'drummer'; meaning 'at that time Hitler was still modest.'

Hitler replied: 'How small are the thoughts of small men! Believe me, I do not regard the acquisition of a minister's portfolio as a thing worth striving for. I do not hold it worthy of a great man to endeavor to go down in history just by becoming a minister. One might run the risk of being buried beside other ministers. My aim, from the very first day, was a thousand times more than becoming a minister. I wanted to become the destroyer of Marxism. I am going to solve this task, and if I solve it, the title of minister will be an absurdity as far as I am concerned. When I stood for the first time at the grave of Richard Wagner, my heart flowed over with pride that here lay a man who had forbidden any such inscription as: Here lies privy-councillor, music-director, his excellency Baron Richard von Wagner. I was proud that this man and so many men in German history were content to give their names to history, without any titles. It was not from modesty that I wanted to be a drummer in those days. That was the highest aspiration. The rest is a trifle.'

In a gloomy gray suburb of Munich lay an old red-brick structure, its floors and walls in poor repair. It was an officers' training school. In one of its large classrooms the trial was held. It went on for weeks. The unknown stood up and proclaimed to the world: Make no mistake. I am the Leader.

Many times in the course of the trial he was asked directly and indirectly by what right he, a man without origins, title, or virtually any education, arrogated to himself the right to govern Germany, sweeping aside all the generals, presidents, and excellencies. Hitler replied: 'This was not overweening or immodest of me. On the contrary, I am of the opinion that when a man knows he can do a thing, he has no right to be modest. . . . In such questions there are no experts. The art of statecraft is — well, an art, and you've got to be born to it.' Here no doubt the Demon from the masses speaks more democratically than his adversaries in their gold-braided uniforms — but he is only talking. For in the last analysis he is referring only to himself; and what he has in mind is power: 'My standpoint is that the bird must sing because he is a bird. And a man who is born for politics must engage in politics whether at freedom or in prison, whether he sits in a silken chair or must content himself with a hard bench. . . . The man who is born to be a dictator is not compelled; he wills; he is not driven forward; he drives himself forward; there is nothing immodest about this. Is it immodest for a worker to drive himself toward heavy labor? Is it presumptuous of a man with the high forehead of a thinker to ponder through the nights till he gives the world an invention? The man who feels called upon to govern a people has no right to say: If you want me or summon me, I will co-operate. No, it is his duty to step forward. . . .'

In conclusion, he informed the judges that despite everything that had happened they must honor the future state power in him. With unshakable confidence he explained that despite all the moods of the historic moment, despite the temporary reinforcement of the state, despite the apparent discomfiture of the Uprooted and Disinherited by rifle fire, the Reichswehr could not permanently reject an alliance with armed bohemia. For on both sides there was the same human substance, the same ideology, the same attitude toward social affairs; the men on both sides were and remained armed intellectuals. And if the reconciliation could be brought about in no other way, it would have to be done by war, which Hitler declared to be inevitable, necessary, an aim ardently to be desired; with his unchanged manner of speech, expressing an unchanged conviction, he called this reconciling, liberating war, this war so ardently to be hoped for, the 'great divine judgment' to come:

'I believe that the hour will come when the masses, who today stand on the street with our swastika banner, will unite with those who fired upon them. I believe that this blood will not always separate us. When I learned that it was the Green police which fired, I had the happy feeling that at least it was not the Reichswehr which besmirched itself; the Reichswehr stands as untarnished as before. One day the hour will come when the Reichs-wehr will stand at our side, officers and men. . . .'

Chairman: 'Herr Hitler, you say that the Green police was be-smirched. That I cannot permit.'

Hitler: 'The army we have formed is growing from day to day, from hour to hour, and faster. Especially in these days I nourish the proud hope that one day the hour will come when these wild companies will grow to battalions, the battalions to regiments, the regiments to divisions; that the old cockade will be taken from the filth, that the old flags will wave again, that there will be a recon-ciliation at the last great divine judgment, which we are prepared to face. Then from our bones and our graves the voice of that court will speak, which alone is entitled to sit in judgment over us. For it is not you, gentlemen, who pronounce judgment upon us. The judgment is spoken by the eternal court of history which will say what it has to say concerning the accusation that has been raised against us. What judgment you will hand down, I know. But that court will not ask us: "Did you commit high treason or did you not?" That court will judge us, the Quartermaster General of the old Army, his officers and soldiers, who, as Germans, wanted and desired only the good of their people and fatherland; who wanted to fight and die. You may pronounce us guilty a thousand times over, the goddess of the eternal court of history will smile and tear to tatters the brief of the state's attorney and the sentence of the court; for she acquits us.'

The sentence of the judges was not so far from the judgment of history. Intimidated from above, tormented by the conscience of their own accomplices, in fear even of the accused, they trampled on what was most defenseless: justice. Contrary to the clear word-ing of the law, Ludendorff was totally acquitted. Contrary to the clear wording of the law, Hitler, despite the bloody consequences of his crime, received the mild minimum sentence of five years' im-prisonment; contrary to the clear wording of the law, he was made to serve only eight and a half months of his term; contrary to the clear wording of the law, he, a foreigner, who had filled the German streets with fire and corpses, was not deported. Röhm and Frick, though formally condemned, were released at once. Göring had

fled to Italy and later went to his wife's native Sweden. His un-
founded fear of Munich justice kept him for nearly three years
in unnecessary exile. Hess was cleverer; he returned, and an
equally mild and brief sentence brought him to the same so-called
'prison' as Hitler, a sanatorium-like building in the little city of
Landsberg am Lech.

Hitler's cause had collapsed more than he had at first realized.
In May, the French people elected a new parliament. It was a crushing defeat for Poincaré, virtually a revolution of the French people
against the war in the Ruhr, a severe condemnation of French military
policy, a clear 'No' to all aspirations on the Rhine, a renunciation of
the policy of adventures and conquests on German soil. The victorious parties of the Socialist and democratic Left had the power
and determination to overthrow not only Poincaré but Alexandre
Millerand, the President of the republic, who had favored Poincaré's policy. To be sure, elements of domestic policy were also to
blame for the landslide; to be sure, the French people stood as
firmly as ever for security on the Rhine. But for years to come they
were to seek this security by a policy of understanding; not only
with Germany, but also with England, a three-cornered relationship
of peace with the foe under the aegis of a protector. After five
years of vain, costly preparation, France renounced military hegemony over Europe, and withdrew to the line of security and defense. This was the clear will of the French people as expressed by
the French parliamentary majority. In 1918, the 'last' of all wars
had ended; this was the most sacred axiom in all French politics.
When Germany bled economically as a result of the Ruhr, even
when she capitulated, she had made the French military aware
of the limits of their power; thus, in spite of the capitulation, the
Ruhr War was the victory for Germany which Hitler had always
feared, vainly prophesying that it would not come to pass.

In the summer of 1924, at a conference in London, English,
French, and German statesmen met as equals for the first time in
years. Stresemann, shouting and red in the face, argued with
French Premier Edouard Herriot, but they arrived at an agreement. The Dawes Plan was accepted by all parties on August 16,
1924, in London, the French began to evacuate the first places in

the Ruhr; the eight hundred million gold marks flowed into Germany; more hundreds of millions and ultimately billions came from England and America in the years that followed. For Germany, internally pacified, rebuilding her economy, passed now as a place where money could be invested profitably and safely. To be sure, the inflation had cost the masses a fortune which they never recovered; later it became evident that this destruction of money and hence of bourgeois self-esteem was no unique, transitory stroke of misfortune, but heralded a long wave of destruction and annihilation. But for the present, smooth, friendly conditions seemed to be returning, and hearts were filled with an illusory hope that the terrible catastrophe of 1923 would not be repeated, and should, therefore, in God's name be forgotten.

National Socialism was forgotten along with it. Impotent and embittered in his prison, Hitler laid down the leadership, broke with Ludendorff in a harsh and disrespectful manner, drew forth old sheets of manuscript on which he had begun to write in 1922, and dictated to various fellow prisoners, lastly to Rudolf Hess, the continuation of a work of monumental conception to which he later gave the title *Mein Kampf.*

Thirteen years later, Hitler spoke hard words of self-condemnation about his *putsch* of 1923. In 1922, he had given Minister Schweyer his word of honor, never to make a *putsch*. One year later, he might have had the excuse that the circumstances had been stronger than he. But in 1936, he admitted without shame: 'Today I can frankly own that in the years from 1920 to 1923 I thought of nothing else but a *putsch*.' Then he added: 'I can calmly say this: that was the rashest decision of my life. When I think back on it today, I grow dizzy. . . . If today you saw one of our squads from the year 1923 marching by, you would ask: What workhouse have they escaped from? . . . But Fate meant well with us. It did not permit an action to succeed, which if it had succeeded, would in the end have inevitably crashed as a result of the movement's inner immaturity in those days, and its deficient organizational and intellectual foundation.'

What Hitler wanted to say was that thirteen years ago he actually did not know the direction in which he was going. He hardly understood the reasons that were leading him there.

Chapter X

INTERLUDE

ONE MAY MORNING IN 1849, AT DRESDEN, CAPITAL of the kingdom of Saxony, a man climbed across the barricades and went over to the troops of the king. The soldiers, Saxon mercenaries, had been vainly attempting to storm the city, defended by its citizenry. Unable to subdue his own people, the king of Saxony had asked for 'foreign aid,' that is, the troops of the king of Prussia. The foreigners were on their way. That is why the man climbed over the barricades. He went over to the soldiers, who were enemies, but none the less Saxons, and handed them leaflets, which read 'Are you with us against the foreign troops?'

That afternoon, the same man stood on the three-hundred-foot steeple of the Church of the Cross, watched the Prussians marching up in the distance, and dropped slips of paper describing developments to the defenders. Enemy sharpshooters fired at the observation tower; revolutionary sharpshooters, lying behind the breastworks, returned the fire. When the firing grew too violent, a comrade wanted to draw him away. He said with a smile: 'Don't worry, I am immortal!'

He was a man of thirty-five, a conductor at the royal opera, and had composed operas of his own. His contemporaries were not yet aware of it — but in these operas human longing had been expressed in new, enchanted tones; and more than by the shots that spattered round the tower, the century was to be shaken by the swelling, darkly beautiful melody, the immortal cry of rejoicing: 'To thee, O goddess of love, let my song resound. . . .'

That man was Richard Wagner.

All this was a small episode in the great and futile German revolution of 1848-49, a single sigh in the storm that raged through Europe in the middle of the nineteenth century.

Most of the state interests and national boundaries that these men were fighting over have vanished beneath the dust of history. But through these struggles ran a spiritual stream which, in the coming decades, rose higher and higher, a stream which has flooded our present, breaking through all dikes. A man stood on the tower, singing of love without fear of the bullets — justly conscious of his immortality for which he was to fight all his life with good means and bad. But his immortality weighs like resonant bronze on the souls of men, an evil spell that has not yet begun to lift, a poison that men would spew out were it not so sweet. His best, or at least his most popular, music transforms the curse of power into a glamorous song; and destruction — the inevitable fate of unbridled power — resounds in it with tragic beauty. Love of overwhelming disaster — that is his haunting *leitmotiv*.

Such a fateful love is presented in this book. It is an attempt to give a picture of the power-hungry intellectual. He has become a leader in modern life. We shall attempt to observe his beginnings. We shall study the birth of the Antichrist.

The Antichrist arises out of an immense fear; Wagner's soul and Wagner's life combined to a high degree the forces whose struggle created the Demon of our days. It is true that all his life Wagner personally detested the demonic man of power, but he contributed more than he suspected to create the Demon. A pamphlet forged in St. Petersburg did not conjure up the Demon out of nothing; it only drew his picture and publicized him. He did not arise suddenly out of the distant desert to lay waste our civilization. The truth is that with fateful necessity he arose everywhere out of the substance and conditions of our own life. It is his universality, growing like mildew in the soil of modern civilization, that makes him dangerous. The Antichrist is a world-citizen, else he could not be a world-ruler. A Prussian junker with a Baltic horizon could no more be a world-demon than a Cossack chief; the Antichrist is no barbarian, he is refined and civilized. That is why his mightiest embodiment has occurred in Germany, in the midst of a high civilization, bruised in its kernel by a disastrous history. The Antichrist is a rank weed growing out of a wounded culture; and German culture received its wound in the days when Richard Wagner stood on the Dresden steeple, braving a rain of bullets.

Germany was ablaze with rebellion against her thirty-six princes, against the king of Prussia, against the emperor of Austria, or rather his hated, all-powerful minister, Metternich; against the great oppressor of peoples through the whole of Europe: the Russian tsar. She was fighting for her freedom: freedom of speech, press, confession; the rights of man, equality of classes and races, parliamentary representation; she was fighting for that great freedom, which in those days was denied most of the nations east of the Rhine; the freedom to be a single nation, obeying only itself. That is why awakening Germany, robbed of her inner freedom and desiring it in the form of unity, engaged in the most painful and tragic of all the struggles of our epoch, the desperate and futile struggle against France.

In the seventeenth century, Armand Duplessis, Cardinal de Richelieu, established a basic principle of French foreign policy: the security of France demands that Germany must never be united. From then on, the dream of German unity became a vain struggle against superior French strength, against French conquest, even against the French language, which at times forced the German language out of educated German society. France oppressed Germany out of a panic fear, resulting from the Spanish-Habsburg embrace in the sixteenth century. At the beginning of that century, a Spanish king became German emperor; the ruling houses of Spain and Austria (Habsburg) fused, and Spain, vanguard of the Roman Catholic Church in defending its tottering rule over the souls of Europe, used her increasing power to crush rising Protestantism in Germany as well as encircled France. In Germany the attempt succeeded only partially, but for a hundred years France, torn by her own religious parties and powerful nobles, was strangled by the Spanish-Habsburg ring. Spain interfered in France's internal affairs, dictated French policies, maintained parties in France; and France remained Catholic. If France was not utterly defeated, it was because of two factors which came to her aid: first, the rising British sea-power which distracted and paralyzed Spain; second, the Protestant German princes, who were continuously rising up against the Catholic, Habsburg-Spanish emperor, thus immobilizing at least one of his arms. It is understandable that France should henceforth have placed her hope in this strife between German emperor and German princes, and viewed it as the immutable aim of her foreign policy. For two centuries she did her best to tear Germany apart.

The split of European civilization into two enraged religious parties gave France an advantage which her own strength would not have given her. At the end of the sixteenth century she settled her own religious conflicts, while Germany was torn by religious wars, culminating in the most terrible conflict of modern times. For thirty years (1618 to 1648) the soldiers of Europe staged on German soil the most frightful slaughter in modern history, and the German nation nearly bled to death. For thirty years Swedes from the Arctic regions and Spaniards from the south streamed into Germany to fight battles and massacre the population; German cities, situated but half an hour's journey from one another, but worlds apart by reason of religion, fought on opposing sides. Provinces were turned into deserts, covered with heaps of ashes; cities vanished forever from the face of the earth; men died by murder, fire, starvation, and plague; cannibalism was not unknown.

When the thirty years' butchery was over, the number of Germans had fallen from about twelve to four millions. No other modern people has ever experienced anything of the sort. A generation later, the war broke out anew at the western borders of the country: France tried to snatch the left bank of the Rhine from Germany, and when this failed, Louvois, the French Minister of War, gave orders to create an artificial desert in the border province of the Palatinate: 'Brulez le Palatinat' was his order, and the ruins of Heidelberg castle remain a monument to this policy. A century and a half later, the armies of Napoleon, emperor of the French, marched across Europe, and Germany was more torn than ever.

This was the great turning-point in German history; its after-effects are clearly discernible in the Germany of 1940. Napoleon's France, newborn through revolution, possessed a real inner strength, a superiority of spirit and will over the other, despotically governed nations of the Continent; the Caesar of France played these forces with all the refined dexterity later so well described in the *Protocols*. Napoleon broke the millennial German Empire into pieces and built a new Germany. He founded new German states and created new German princes, who were to endure a whole century and determine the course of German history. To him Ludwig van Beethoven dedicated his Third Symphony, the *Eroica;* Goethe cried out contemptuously to German patriots: 'Tug away at your chains, the man is too big for you, you will never break them!' Hegel, the philosopher, saw Napoleon riding through the streets of Jena, and owned that he felt as though he had seen 'the world spirit on horseback.' This son of Corsica, emperor of the French, was incontestably the greatest single figure in German history — perhaps down to our own day. But at the same time his epoch signified French oppression and domination of Germany. France not only swallowed up Holland and Belgium; for a time she annexed North Germany as far as the mouth of the Elbe. She governed and manipulated at will the new states she had created, the kingdoms of Bavaria, Württemberg, Westphalia. She brought modern militarism to Germany and levied armies in Germany with which to conduct her own wars. But above all, in the person of Napoleon I, she brought to Germany the idea of democratic Caesarism, of the conspirator who makes himself a tyrant by the abuse of democracy . . . the living model of the Wise Men of Zion.

Germany learned and imitated. When the French Revolution broke out, the best of the German intelligentsia rejoiced. For a time there were Jacobin republics on the Rhine, under the protection of the French revolutionary armies. The inner reforms in France; the immense power they gave the country which shortly before had been in a state of collapse; the systematic organization by the tyrant of this new spiritual might, made a deep impression on the clearest heads in Germany. What we today call German organization, was first learned from Napoleon, who from army organization to apiculture re-formed his nation; who chose as a symbol of his imperial power the totalitarian bee, dedicated to work and war; who, on the ruins of conquered Moscow, decreed the foundation of a French national theater. From him Germany learned the new methods of raising popular armies; she learned how to arm, train, feed them, move them across country in flexible, widely distributed bands, and then hurl their assembled power at a single point. From France, Germany learned the secret of the new patriotism: organized freedom.

'His aim,' said Johann Gottlieb Fichte, the romantic German philosopher, 'is not to be ruler of France, but ruler of the world; and if he cannot be that, he would prefer not to be at all. He has enthusiasm and an absolute will; only a stronger enthusiasm can defeat him — enthusiasm for liberty!'

Another contemporary of Napoleon, the patriotic Prussian poet, Heinrich von Kleist, asserted that this was the custom in the army of the French enemy, especially in the artillery: the captain of a battery at the beginning of a battle, 'with his left fist grasps an artilleryman by the chest, and with the tip of his sword pointing at a spot on the ground, he says, "You die here!" looking at him all the while; then to the next, "You, here!" and to a third, and fourth, and all the rest, "Here, here, and here!" and to the last, "Here!"' Kleist thought 'that this command to the soldiers to die without any argument had an extraordinary effect,' and the whole business, Kleist, the Prussian, called a 'French experiment that ought to be imitated.'

The Germans learned by plan. In the German masses a democratic longing stirred which actually sprang to the surface decades later; but in the period of Napoleon's domination, Prussian ministers and generals undertook to organize this longing from above. Officially, at least, they released the Prussian peasants from their semi-enslavement to the junkers; they gave their subjects the novel privilege of choosing their own trade; they went so far as to promise a parliament and freedom of the press. In the end, they confronted the French emperor with an army that was almost revolutionary. It was based on general conscription and in a way democratic. Commoners, believe it or not, could rise to be officers. A

German revolutionary chauvinism broke out among the German intellectuals. They hated not only the French, but their princes as well, because most of them favored the French emperor, who had added enormously to their power. The well-informed even despised such a figure as the king of Prussia, who, when for the first time he saw his people's army that was embarking on the fight for freedom, could think of nothing to say but 'Dirty men!' Karl, Baron vom Stein, the mind behind the Prussian reforms, hated by his king and suspected of Jacobinism, went so far as to say that he knew but one fatherland, and that was Germany. Another patriot, Ernst Moritz Arndt, the poet, proclaimed that Germany must extend 'as far as the German tongue is heard.' In 1813, Prussia rose up in a people's war against the domination of the French. It was a German revolution, but a European tragedy. For this people's war — the most intellectual of all wars as the French historian, Ernest Renan, later said — was at the same time a war of European reaction (French kings and aristocrats included) against the French Revolution which Napoleon had not entirely perverted. When in March, 1814, the cannon thundered in Berlin to celebrate the final victory, a man of the people — so Carl Varnhagen von Ense, the writer, tells the story — cried out sadly: 'There you have it, Paris has been taken, the nobles have won!'

The French grenadiers with their bearskin caps vanished, but the emperor's portrait remained hanging on the wall of many a German living-room. The corpse of Saint Helena — the hieroglyph in the ocean, as a German poet put it — became a myth even mightier than the living man had been. In the first half of the nineteenth century, he became for France a symbol of national pride and consciousness of power. For Germany, politically torn, divided, and humiliated by their own miserable rulers, Napoleon became the embodiment of human Titanism, a demigod who had set out to build the Tower of Babel, a hero, a model of intellect and will. Once, when Ludwig van Beethoven wanted to boast, he said: 'If I knew as much about war as I do about music, I would defeat him!'

Thus oppressed Germany admired her oppressor and almost forgave the tyrant his tyranny because of its immensity. Germans became accustomed to the concept of injustice ennobled by genius, of crime justified by greatness, of history elevated above morality. Napoleon Bonaparte, living proof that a man risen from the people could dominate the world, became a powerful motif in the ideas and dreams of the modern era — in Germany as elsewhere.

Fichte, deeply anti-Napoleonic in his feelings, had hoped for a Germany that would be inspired by 'enthusiasm for liberty . . . based on the principle that all beings with a human face are equal.' These words still breathe the spirit of Germany's classic humanism, the spirit of Kant, Goethe, and especially Schiller; and this human- itarian heritage, popularized by Schiller's plays and poems, has been the choicest spiritual heritage of the German people. But here we are not studying those sentiments which lived in the soul of the Germans for a century, but the genesis of their destruction.

Around the divine image of Napoleon, Georg Wilhelm Hegel, a Napoleon of the mind, created a philosophical religion of the state, which became the highest revelation of the 'world spirit.' This world spirit is a true child of the German political fantasy. Its mean- ing is that all worldly happenings are governed by a rational neces- sity and not by blind compulsion. The world spirit is revealed either through a difficult, highly ingenious thought process (dialec- tics), or by deeds; to accomplish such deeds is the task of the great men in history, the 'business agents of the world spirit.' The great historic individuals, Hegel taught, do pursue their selfish purposes in history, but it is their special nature that their 'private purposes contain the substantial, which is the will of the world spirit. . . . The others follow these leaders of their souls, for in them they feel the irresistible power of their own inward spirit.'

Thus German philosophy began to honor historic greatness as a thing in itself, without inquiring whom this greatness might injure. But the hero cult was not the sole product of Napoleon's mighty impression on Hegel. Hegel's contradictory experience with the great foreigner led him to kneel before the hard reality of all history, to an obedient affirmation of everything that was real. Hence his famous saying: 'What is rational is real and what is real is rational.' The 'rational' is the same as what he elsewhere calls 'idea' or 'world spirit.' A great, universal principle of reason underlies the entire world, governing all events, because it is inherent in the things themselves; but to reveal itself or to 'realize' itself, as Hegel says, it must 'appear in an endless wealth of forms, phenomena, and shapes,' until it finally can enter 'conscience'; that is, be grasped by the human mind.

This principle of reason, or the 'world spirit,' is realized in history in successively higher forms, or, as Hegel calls them, 'stages'; one of these stages is the 'national spirit,' but the highest is the state. Hence the state is a thing 'rational in itself'; indeed Hegel calls it 'the moral universe,' and as a philosopher he indignantly rejects any idea of instructing or improving the state. As the highest revelation of the world spirit, the state stands above individuals and their supposed rights, for 'the right of the world spirit is above all special privileges.' And 'world history is no empire of happiness. The periods of happiness are the empty pages of history, because they are the periods of agreement, without conflict.' For history goes on only by conflict between its successive 'stages.'

Hegel is the intellect triumphant on the summit of self-confidence. An exalted and pitiless reason rules the world, and the German intellect aroused by Napoleon thinks history which it cannot yet make. The Antichrist assembles his scattered limbs and begins to take form. The German contribution to this world figure begins at this point. The German Nationalist Movement in the first half of the nineteenth century derives its strength from the classical flowering of German literature and philosophy. The educated classes multiplied enormously. They created the first form of modern national pride in Germany: the democratic belief in equality of all by virtue of education.

But all this dreaming cult of Napoleonic greatness and state omnipotence would not have been possible without the misery of actual German politics. In the mind of most German intellectuals state omnipotence was only another expression for the people's sovereignty in its desperate struggle against Germany's countless petty, shabby, and ridiculous princes.

This German intellectualism was part of an intellectual and at the same time political uprising through Europe. Students, professors, lawyers, writers, journalists, banded into secret societies, and if they were discovered, ended in terrible prisons. Agents of the tsar or the Austrian emperor controlled the police in Germany and Italy, and pursued fleeing democrats from country to country. Foreign monarchs were ruling as princelings over larger or smaller parts of divided Germany: the king of Denmark was duke of Holstein and of the German-speaking parts of Slesvig; an English prince was king of Hanover and, in the best Georgian tradition, broke the sworn constitution of his country; the emperor of Austria was looked upon as a tyrant by his German subjects as well as by his Hungarian, Czech, Polish, and Italian.

An international police despotism ruled over Europe, and the resistance was international. French, Italian, and German revolutionaries greeted one another as brothers. Seldom has the decisive rôle of the intellectual been more clearly discernible. For the national revolution of the nineteenth century was his work. Formal education spread, universities were founded. Young men, predominantly of the poorer classes, studied and were dissatisfied. A stream of democratic students, revolutionary journalists, parliamentarians and bomb-throwers, demagogues and Carbonari, runs through the nineteenth century. The French Revolution had proclaimed the rights of man, and the echo resounded through the big and little nations of central, eastern, and southern Europe. This echo was the rights of nations, for the first right of man is the right to his own nationality. To these nations freedom meant the right to be governed by men of their own language, and translated into central European, democracy meant the right of national self-determination. Two nations marched at the head of this democratic national revolution: Italy and — more important — Germany.

With mingled foreboding and delight, Heinrich Heine, one of Germany's sharpest minds, saw the united German nation storming its way through the future. He saw it trained by German philosophy for world revolution, freed from the restraints of Christianity. 'If some day the taming talisman, the cross, should crumble, the savagery of the old warriors will again burst forth, the insensate berserk rage, about which the Nordic poets sing and say so much. That talisman is rotting, and some day it will lamentably crumble. The old stone gods will rise from the ancient ruins and rub the millennial dust from their eyes. Thor with his giant hammer will

spring aloft and shatter the Gothic cathedrals. When you hear
that stamping and clashing, take care, ye neighbor children, ye
Frenchmen.'

At that time France actually did take fright at the German
Nationalist Movement. If Germany was uniting, let her at least
surrender the left bank of the Rhine to France! Beginning in
1840, French politicians advanced this demand for more than thirty
years on every possible occasion. In Germany it met with angry
protest. Even Heine, son of the Rhineland, rejected the French
demand with the proud and magnificent line: 'I cannot surrender
the Rhine to you Frenchmen, for the Rhine belongs to me personally.'

In 1848, the Nationalist Movement of the German intellectuals
flared into revolution. The best brains in the land assembled in Saint
Paul's Church in Frankfort on the Main, to found a German Reich
and give it a democratic constitution; a minority demanded a republic. The princes were helpless, for a time even intimidated
by bloody uprisings in Berlin, Vienna, and other cities; reactionary
ministers were driven from the country; the people seemed victorious.

But who were the people? New classes had arisen. The proletariat appeared in the large countries. This proletariat, created during the last decades by the new industries, the spinning and weaving mills, the great iron smelteries, machine shops and mines, lived
amid frightful conditions, bordering on starvation and moral decay.
The workers saw little in democracy and national unity. They
wanted to eat. The propertied classes, which had previously been
democratically minded, took fright and sought the protection of the
military reaction; the alliance between property and military force
strangled the revolution and silently drained off the blood of
democracy.

Thus, in 1852, a military and political adventurer was able to
seize power in France, make himself emperor under the title of
Napoleon III, and create the state which was to become the model
for the conspiracy of the Wise Men of Zion. Everywhere world
economy was on its way to creating — in the words of Hegel — a
new 'stage' — the world proletariat. Two German students of

Hegel, Karl Marx and Friedrich Engels, applied the master's doctrine to this world, and in so doing (these were their words) stood Hegel's doctrine, hitherto upside down, on its feet. There was an inner necessity in world history, as Hegel had taught, but it was not the world spirit; according to Marx and Engels, it was something very unspiritual — the material interests of man.

This would have been a feeble discovery had not Marx and Engels broadened and dramatized their hastily conceived world view with the profound method of Hegel, which made their doctrine enormously impressive and compelling. In 1847, the two German revolutionaries wrote a pamphlet in their Brussels exile. It began with the words: 'A specter is haunting Europe, the specter of Communism!' and concluded: 'Workers of the world — unite!' It was — in their opinion — the historical task of the proletariat all over the world to abolish private property, in what they called 'means of production,' from coal mines to needle and thread in a garments sweatshop. Industrial property, they taught, had a natural tendency to concentrate in fewer and fewer hands; inevitably the people would be driven to take this monopolized property back into the hands of society, and thus a society without private property, and therefore without classes, would become the inevitable next 'stage' of history.

To understand the enormous effect of this *Communist Manifesto,* it must be realized that ever since Hegel the entire West had been permeated by a belief in the necessary and meaningful course of history. The world proletariat, instructed by Marx and Engels in the spirit of Hegel, fights for its interests in the conviction that it is thus accomplishing the work of the world spirit. And there was something in it; for the Marxist proletariat was the heir and successor of the European national and democratic revolution. Economics becomes destiny. With telegraph lines, steamships, transatlantic bank drafts, the globe becomes the scene of a commercial activity which seems to be life itself. The merchant views himself as the spiritual leader of his time, far above the soldier or the philosopher; and so does his antagonist, the Marxist proletarian. This belief in the supposed economic kernel of all things was a belief that has had its day in history — and now this day is gone.

Meanwhile, the revolution, abandoned by a part of its supporters, was crushed in hard-fought and bloody struggles (1849), in places with the help of the Russian tsar. It was in one of these lost battles that Richard Wagner threw down his slips of paper from the Church of the Cross in Dresden.

The rise of economic thinking at the middle of the nineteenth century had broken the momentum of the great revolution. When the new economic age began to appear above the horizon, the most ardent souls among the intellectuals lost their glowing confidence that world history in the Hegelian sense would be a progressive self-realization of world reason.

One of the most moving examples of this despair is Heinrich Heine, who in his youth had uttered the most eloquent words in the German language about democracy and socialism. Then came the recoil. Observation of the Parisian masses brought him to the pessimistic conviction that 'the premature triumph of the proletariat would be of short duration and a misfortune for humanity. In their mad intoxication for equality, they would destroy everything that is beautiful and noble on earth and unleash their iconoclastic rage on art and science. . . . The kings vanish, and with them the last poets. . . . The barren work-a-day sentiment of the modern Puritans will spread over all Europe like a gray dusk, foreshadowing rigid winter. . . .'

Heine's backsliding from democracy was more than a personal matter. Others said the same thing with greater thoroughness and depth; but with him it was more than a statement, it was an event; he not only experienced an historic turn; he was that turn. In the person of Heine, the penitent intellectual fell from his proud rational glory, confessed his great sins, and renounced humanity's most regal thought: the equality of all mortals:

As long as such doctrines [he is referring to freedom, equality, and particularly atheism] remained the secret possession of an intellectual aristocracy and were discussed in the refined language of a coterie, incomprehensible to the servants who stood behind us as we bandied blasphemies at our philosophical *petits soupers* — I, too, counted myself among the frivolous *esprits forts*. Most of us resembled those liberal *grands seigneurs* who shortly before the

revolution sought to dispel the boredom of their idle court existence with the new revolutionary ideas. But when I saw that the
raw plebs, the Jan Hagels, were beginning to discuss the very same
topics in their grimy symposia, where wax candles and girandoles
were replaced by tallow and oil lamps, [when the old ideal of his
youth] began to stink of cheese, brandy, and tobacco: then suddenly my eyes were opened, and what I had not understood by my
reason, I now understood by my sense of smell, by nausea and discomfort. . . . We shall gladly sacrifice ourselves for the people;
self-sacrifice is among our subtlest pleasures — the emancipation of
the people was the great task of our life, for it we have struggled
and borne nameless misery, at home as in exile — but . . . I would
wash my hand if the sovereign people honored me with its handshake.

The *'trahison des clercs,'* the betrayal by the intellectuals, as a
French philosopher a hundred years later called it! Public life — all
life in a sense — began to look questionable. In opposition to Hegel,
a gloomy prophet arose: Arthur Schopenhauer. Hegel had taught
that the essence of all things was world reason and that every event
was an act of its self-realization. Schopenhauer angrily replied that
the center of all things is the most irrational thing conceivable, the
blind will, the desire, the urge. It lay at the base of all happenings
in nature, and since it could never achieve fulfillment, its existence
was suffering without end; the function of reason was to recognize
this tragedy and put an end to the suffering by putting an end to
the will, that is, to life. 'Every human life as a whole,' he wrote,
'shows the qualities of a tragedy, and we see that life, in general,
consists only of hopes gone astray, thwarted plans, and errors recognized too late.' Consequently, life is 'something which better were
not; a sort of delusion, knowledge of which should remove us
from it.'

The corner of this sad world in which Arthur Schopenhauer
spent his earthly existence, or, as he would have said, his existence
subject to the will, was an upper-class house in the city of Frankfort
on the Main. From its high windows he viewed the ships on the
Main, the white façades and tall pointed towers of the city, the
crowd in the narrow medieval streets, and, in language ringing
with the fury of the prophets, painted the emptiness of human

striving and the beauties of absolute renunciation. When twelve
o'clock struck from the near-by cathedral tower, he laid down his
goosequill, took up a walking-stick with a silver handle, and be-
took himself — a little old man with wild gray hair and a faintly
apelike countenance, a well-known and much-ridiculed city character — to the Swan Hotel, where he consumed astonishing quantities of the finest foods. He expressed the hope that some day a
wise man would succeed in boring a hole in the earth and sinking
enough powder into it to blow the whole planet to bits. The most
ruinous expression of human nature was for him sexual love;
'sexual desire,' he maintained, 'particularly when concentrated into
love by fixation on a particular woman, is the quintessence of all
the swindles of this noble world: it promises so unspeakably, infinitely, immeasurably much, and delivers so wretchedly little.'

As for human progress, the greater happiness of the mass, Schopenhauer would not even have understood the question, since he
was interested only in the possibility of insight into the nature of
things (or behind the veil of Maya, as he put it) by a well-equipped
individual mind. To him the world spirit on horseback, so admired
by Hegel, was only 'the bandit Buonaparte.' The 'great' acts of
history were just an accumulation of crimes and follies. If a nation
arrogated to itself an heroic or spiritual world mission, it was unquestionably a swindling pretext for common robbery and mass
murder — he expressly had Jews and French in mind.

In his lifetime, Schopenhauer remained virtually unheard by the
German Hegelian generation, and this contributed no little to his
embitterment. But over the succeeding generation his philosophy
of death swept like a tidal wave, washing away all Hegel and all
faith in world reason. Amid all its material successes and despite
all its vigor, the educated German bourgeoisie consoled itself in
Schopenhauer's grim, sullen wisdom: 'Pass this world by, it is
nothing!'

In dealing with the influence of thinkers and poets on their age,
we do not mean that these men determined the spirit of their time.
They are what Hegel might have called the 'bookkeepers of the
world spirit'; they understood the laughter and tears of their time better than others and expressed it with greater clarity and force. After

the defeat of the great ideals in 1849, shame, gloom, discouragement, led men to affect a lofty contempt for freedom and the masses. It was generally said that politics ruined the character; a pitiable philistinism spread — the dusty ashes of spent ideals. 'It is no mean accomplishment to read through world history and retain one's love of the human race,' writes Richard Wagner, twenty years after his act of light-hearted, confident defiance atop the Church of the Cross in Dresden.

The new reality was world economy. This might seem rational to Hegel's misguided students, Marx and Engels, to the cotton manufacturers of Lancashire, or to Baron Rothschild. But the demonic intellectuals found that Europe had succumbed to a leaden winter's sleep, to a puritanical 'work-a-day sentiment,' as Heine had called it. Wagner has a similar image: 'With all our far-flung state and national economy, we seem to be caught in a dream; first it lulls, then it frightens, and in the end it oppresses. We are all eager to waken. But the strange thing about this dream is that, as long as we are in it, we regard it as real life and struggle against awakening as against death.' He found that all political parties in Germany from Left to Right in reality served only economic interests. Not an original discovery in itself; but Wagner had the remarkable insight and foresight to view these supposedly so vital interests as phantoms and figments of the brain, concealing the far nobler, but also harder, reality.

Wagner exerted an enormous influence on history that cannot be measured in numbers of opera performances. A dilettante without thorough — at all events without scientific — education, he gave the impetus to a philosophy of history which, after decades of hesitant knocking at the portals, is shaking the world in our days. Without knowing or intending it, he contributed some of the most important sentences to the message of the Antichrist.

In a purely outward sense, this begins with the fact that Wagner conducted a lifelong, embittered struggle against the Jews. Two years after the episode in Dresden, he wrote a long essay entitled *Jews in Music*. The grim earnest in Wagner's attack was this: 'The Jew, in the present state of the affairs of this world, is more than emancipated: he rules and will rule so long as money remains the power before which all our acts and efforts lose their force.' In other words, the world domination of economics is the world domination of Jewry. Wagner later translated this idea into poetry and music. In his *Ring* trilogy, he tells the story of the treasure of the Nibelungs, treating the old legendary motif of the curse of gold as a political allegory. In a prose commentary he tells us what he has in mind: that in the present era 'the fateful ring of the Nibelungs takes the form of a stockbroker's wallet,' and thus we have 'a gruesome picture of the ghastly world overlord' (read Jew).

Wagner was a man of repellent egotism, disarming by virtue of its very magnitude. He felt himself to be the spiritual center of the world — a terrifying example of artistic madness, even in a great creative artist. He took a polemical, partisan stand on all controversial issues of his time, though he remarked naïvely that the issues in themselves did not really interest him, but that all his fighting and writing were intended only to serve 'his art.' But what is this art? It is a great epic about the decline and death of nobility in this world. The love-death of Tristan and Isolde, the twilight of the old gods — all Wagner's images are aspects of the one terrible vision: the exalted values of an earlier day perish in the rising flood of mediocrity. And what actually does he mean by 'mediocrity'? 'Where do our German barbarians sit?' he asked. And answered. 'We find them in parliaments chosen by universal suffrage.'

Wagner is a true child of Germany's great disillusionment and exhaustion in the latter half of the nineteenth century. To be sure, Germany's outward successes in the same period seemed to overshadow this mood. In the sixties a group of Prussian junkers built up the army which has filled the world with fear and suspicion ever since. This army came into being against the express will of the majority of the Prussian people. For four whole years the Prussian statesman, Otto von Bismarck, had to deal dictatorially with the Prussian parliament in order to create an army. These years (1862-1866) mark the birth of modern Prussian militarism. It was the product of a diplomatic defeat which Prussia had suffered after the years of the German revolution when the combined superiority of Russia and Austria forced Prussia to resign political leadership in Germany — the Treaty of Olmütz, 1850; in addition there was the fear of the newly growing military power of France under Napoleon III and of the French desire to annex the western provinces of Germany. At that time, as soon as a strong foreign power crossed Germany's borders, it might hope to win over to its side a part of the sovereign German states, as in the time of Richelieu. To make impossible such a coalition between a foreign power and a section of Germany against Prussia, Bismarck made German unity his goal. In 1866, Prussia, strengthened by the economy of the industrial Rhine province, waged a victorious war against the other half of Germany, and thus forced a new unity on a part of the old German Empire. Austria with her German provinces was thrust aside. The dreams of 1848 were not fulfilled, but the Prussian success was, after all, a success. As always, economy obeyed political power. Bismarck cleverly managed to represent the disruption of Germany as unification. The rest of Germany accepted Prussian domination because it seemed to be the only means to protect the country against being attacked and torn apart by two strong neighbors: France and Russia.

For the imperial ruler of France, Napoleon III once more demanded purely German parts of the left bank of the Rhine; he demanded them of Bismarck (1865) and of Austria, too (1866); both were unscrupulous enough to put Napoleon off with promises and appeasement, even to concede him a rôle of arbiter in Germany's internal affairs. Later, by making Napoleon's demands public (he had demanded Belgium, too), Bismarck aroused anti-French feelings, not only in Germany, but also in England; the final outcome was a declaration of war by Napoleon in 1870.

The Emperor, haunted by the specter of a unified Germany, had attempted to lead a coalition of all Europe against Prussia and to attract to his side even the South German states and Austria. This latter plan misfired completely, and Bismarck's skillful diplomacy was able to prevent the European coalition — a diplomacy much more successful and farsighted than that of his successors forty and sixty years later. Napoleonic France was shattered by the war. Prussian Germany won a *Blitzkrieg* against the usurper, who had been the living model for the Wise Men of Zion and was so hated by the radical democrats of Europe that even Marx and Engels, though bitter enemies of Prussia, desired a Prussian victory.

This German 'unification on the field of battle' was completed in 1871 when the King of Prussia was crowned German Emperor. Even Richard Wagner, who had long ceased to be a revolutionary, was unhappy about the 'constant readiness for a new war' which was, in his opinion, one of the characteristics of the new empire. He accused Bismarck of having missed the opportunity for a genuine reconciliation with France, complained of the annexation of Lorraine by Germany ('Germany's new unity shows its hungry teeth everywhere'), and said it was a scandal that inside Germany the army, which, after all, was based on 'German labor,' nevertheless was used to 'protect the propertied against the non-propertied.' And the curse of this age was 'war civilization.'

This was the better future he saw and expected for Germany: 'The Germans, by their special gifts, are destined to become not rulers, but ennoblers of the world. . . . With the help of all related Germanic peoples, we could permeate the world with the products of our special culture, without ever becoming rulers of the world.' Never let them become rulers, for this is the road to inevitable destruction. History, he said, shows man to be 'a beast of prey developing through constant progress. The beast of prey conquers countries, founds great realms by the subjugation of other subjugators, forms states and organizes civilizations, in order to enjoy his booty in peace . . . Attack and defense, suffering and struggle, victory and defeat, domination and servitude, all sealed with blood; this is the entire history of the human race. . . .'

In support of his gloomy faith, Wagner always sought out suitable prophets. In the prime of his life, it was Schopenhauer who helped to destroy his pleasure in humanity; in later years, it was a personal friend, the Frenchman, Count Arthur de Gobineau. Gobineau provided an ostensibly scientific system into which he could fit his race despair, a biological basis for the twilight of the gods. From Gobineau's *Essai sur l'inégalité des races humaines,* Wagner learned, as he himself said, 'that the human race consists of irreconcilably unequal races. The nobler of these can dominate the others; by mixture, however, they cannot make the others like themselves, but can only make themselves less noble.' This is the essence of the whole doctrine. As the noble race, Gobineau and Wagner designate the white race. But 'the ruination of the white race is that it is incomparably less numerous than the lower races, and was forced to mix with them.' And thus the higher, nobler minority of the white race must decline with the force of a natural law; 'the tragic character of this realization must not close our eyes to it.' The particular tragedy of modern society in its racial decay is that in their midst there always remains, undamaged, the Jew; 'the most astonishing example of race consistency that history ever has provided.' This, in Wagner's eyes, is 'an amazing, incomparable phenomenon; the plastic demon of the decay of humanity enjoys triumphant safety.'

The white sons of the gods decline, and this decline cannot permanently be prevented. Valhalla sinks into the twilight of the gods, and in this tragedy the gods are not blameless, for their realm was based on force, on the domination of the beast of prey. But though the whole downward course of the world cannot be stopped, it can, for a time, be halted in certain details, and the degeneration combated by a 'regeneration.' Wagner hoped that Germany would give the world this temporary regeneration if she renounced power politics and permeated the world with her culture: 'Even if the Holy Roman Empire were to go up in smoke, We would still have sacred German art,' sings Hans Sachs in the *Meistersingers.*

Germany's bright and dark souls met in Wagner's breast. Just as he was wearying of Bismarck's cannon-and-stock-exchange-state, large sections of the German people were beginning to ask themselves: Did we really want this? Lulled for a moment by the thunderous spectacle of 1871, they now began to strain against the shackles of Prussian might. The German workers' movement, an angry protest against soulless Prussian force, grew to be the largest and most powerful movement of its sort in the modern world, though the German workers never became conscious of their power. As a part of the European workers' movement, the German movement was a rebellion against capitalism, but as a German movement, it was a rebellion against the Prussian military state; Bismarck saw the danger for his creature so clearly that, at the time he fell from power, he was planning to provoke artificial disorders among the workers (in the style of Napoleon III), as a pretext for crushing the movement in blood.

Under pressure of circumstances, Bismarck had won for Germany several colonies overseas, but he did it against his convictions. His most enduring political creation was the German military machine; what, for decades, the world has called Prussian militarism. Bismarck did not conceive this militarism as an instrument of world domination, for in his eyes Germany was simply not strong enough for 'world rule.' To the end of his life he was much more conscious of her weakness than of her strength.

This nervous fear has left its deep imprint on German thought. The most far-reaching voice of modern German philosophy bears its mark. We refer to Friedrich Nietzsche, who cursed 'nationalism and race hatred . . . the national heart-itch and blood-poisoning on account of which the nations of Europe today are bounded off and secluded from one another, as by quarantine.' For this modern European nationalism he held Bismarck's system largely responsible; a system that must 'plant itself between two mortal hatreds lest its own creation should collapse.' His final opinion about his own nation (like every great spirit Nietzsche did not hold the same opinions throughout his life) might be summed up in his words: 'Wheresoever Germany penetrates she ruins culture.'

Therefore, Wagner's 'degeneration' was quite true for Germany, but it was a 'death dream' peculiar to Germany and not applicable to the human type of the future which Nietzsche sometimes called the 'good European,' sometimes the 'Superman'; 'a daring, dominant race based on an extremely intelligent herd,' which will overcome nations and particularly the German nation.

For in our time 'it has been made possible for international racial leagues to arise, which set themselves the task of cultivating a race of masters, the future masters of the earth; a new and mighty aristocracy, based on the hardest self-legislation, in which the will of philosophical despots and artist tyrants will endure for thousands of years; a higher type of men, who, thanks to their surplus of will, knowledge, wealth, influence, use democratic Europe as their most supple and mobile tool, to lay hands on the destinies of the earth. . . .'

Democracy as tool! — for if you look closely it is democratic mass education which transforms human beings into tools for the new ruler: 'He who has retained and cultivated a strong will at the same time as a broad spirit has better chances than ever. For man's capacity for training has become very great in this democratic Europe; men who learn easily, who easily adapt themselves, are the rule: the herd beast, who may even be highly intelligent, is created. He who can command finds those who must obey. . . . The modern mass intelligence easily slips down the road to mass slavery; it lacks the bigoted resistance of the "strong and unintelligent will." '

And what would the philosophical despots and artist tyrants do with the earth? Nietzsche replies: 'They would mold man as an artist would.' The task is to 'achieve that immense energy of greatness, to mold the future man by breeding, and, at the same time, by destroying, millions of bungled humans — we must not be deterred by the suffering we create, the equal of which has never been seen!'

Here the German intellect had withdrawn to the wild beast's den; it no longer represents its nation. This philosophy is quite foreign to the sentiment of the popular mass. During the fifty years of the German Empire's existence, a people's movement had grown up, demanding democracy. A movement of the rabble, Nietzsche would have said. But where was the superman to lead this 'intelligent herd'?

Wilhelm II, by God's grace German Emperor and King of Prussia, took himself to be this ruler. He promised the German nation to lead it toward glorious times; and swore to crush anyone opposing him. He was the son of an English princess, the grandson of Queen Victoria, and spoke English as well as German. What Napoleon had meant a century before to the soul of Germany, the British Navy and colonial empire meant to Wilhelm's soul; they were the measure of greatness, to which at all costs he meant to raise Germany. And so he built a German fleet and tried to found a German colonial empire. Most of these plans bogged down in the execution. Wilhelm's most fatal achievement in foreign policy was that he replaced Bismarck's complicated system of peace through alliances by the simple system of peace through the sword. He dropped Germany's alliance with Russia and based Germany's delicate security in the heart of Europe on the excessively increased German armament; an effort that could be accomplished only by a nation at a high technical level.

Everything came too late to Germany. Democracy came too late, national unity came too late — and now technology came too late. About a hundred years before, the nation had first become conscious of its unity through a great literary and philosophical movement; but this movement had been powerless to create a political unity; violence and war had then forged a dubious, superficial unity, but now a new national experience descended on Germany: the consciousness of a great technical achievement, the building of German industry between 1870 and 1910. Industry was expanding in other countries, but nowhere did it develop such national self-confidence as in the land to which Bach, Kant, Goethe, Beethoven, had not given sufficient strength and pride. The steel of Krupp's cannon in Essen, the optical lenses in Jena, the high tension lines along the Rhine, the chemical products of Mannheim and the lower Rhine — all this, taken together, was a great national campaign against English, Belgian, and even French industry, which up to the twentieth century had dominated the German market. Now, step by step, the foreign industries were forced out, pursued into the world market, and there, too, undersold and defeated.

This was the time when the acquisition of African colonies was explained to the nation with arguments like this: some 60,000,000 Britishers owned 13,500,000 square miles or almost a fourth of all land on the globe; about 130,000,000 Russians lived (at that time) on more than 8,500,000 square miles; why should 70,000,000 Germans be locked up in 200,000 square miles?

On February 21, 1902, the Emperor of this technological nation received a remarkable letter in his 'New Palace' at Potsdam. A friend and admirer wrote these words of encouragement and exhortation: 'We have arrived at a turning-point in world history. Never, as far back as history takes us, has there been a world situation remotely resembling the present; how then should the old institutions hold up? The new world is the work of science (including technology), and it is science which will dominate it.'

That, the letter-writer assures the Kaiser, meant German science. Only the Germans were sufficiently permeated by science to organize the earth. To be sure, the English seemed to dominate the globe at the moment, 'by muscle, sinew, and will,' but this epoch of domination by sheer power was past. And English science was too atomized, too unsystematic, too *'happy-go-lucky,'*[1] for the great world task. The writer seasons his whole letter to the English-speaking Kaiser with English expressions. With obsequious flattery he compares the rise of German culture with English intellectual decadence, and even quotes an English authority on the subject: *'To my mind,'* the English chemist Dewar had recently declared at a scientific congress, *'the really appalling thing is not that the Germans have seized this or the other industry, it is that Germany possesses a national weapon of precision which must give her an enormous initial advantage in any and every contest depending upon disciplined and methodized intellect.'* Yes, the letter-writer goes on, Dewar is right, and this must be Germany's aim: to become a 'nation acting according to plan, a scientifically drilled nation.'

The writer lacked the intellectual integrity which made Nietzsche cry out openly for slavery, but he meant the same thing; against his will the word slips out after all, and he is not embarrassed to call it the consequence of higher education: 'True organic subordination — not slavery — requires a higher education than the English system demands or even allows. The Englishman does his best work alone, while the German does his best in community. Germany can only wrest the leadership from Anglo-Americanism by pursuing a totally different method and acting as a cohesive unit, disciplined and methodized as our good Dewar correctly says. Germany — of this I am firmly convinced — can dominate the whole globe in part by direct political methods, in part indirectly through language, culture, techniques.'

This was not written by a native German, but by Houston Stewart Chamberlain, born an Englishman, for the first twenty-five years of his life a virtual Frenchman; in the end a German. Natural scientist and philosopher, he exerted a decisive influence on two

---

[1] The words in italics are English in original.

generations of German intellectuals. He was the intellectual adviser, indeed the mentor of Wilhelm II.

Chamberlain was born in Portsmouth in 1855, the son of a British naval captain, later admiral. His uncle, Sir Neville Chamberlain, the field marshal, died a lonely, embittered man after carrying on a vain fight against the Boer War. Houston Stewart Chamberlain was brought up by relatives in France, and French was the language of his youth and education. At the age of twenty-seven, he accomplished the astonishing feat of acquiring a new nationality as a relatively mature man. For several decades he remained a British subject — but he became a German in language, mind, and soul. He lived first in Dresden, later in Vienna, finally in Bayreuth. Wagner's music and philosophy had drawn him to Germany; he married one of Wagner's daughters. The three greatest poets of humanity, he declared, were Homer, Shakespeare, and Wagner, but Wagner was the greatest.

Chamberlain was one of the most astonishing talents in the history of the German mind, a mine of knowledge and profound ideas. He combined sensitivity, gentleness, and elegance with a great intellectual stubbornness. A conflict between intellectual toughness and an almost pathological human softness was the weak side of his nature. Excessive politeness, an almost mincing caution in his personal relations, point to a profound uncertainty, for which his strange career accounts only too well. He addressed every run-of-the-mill German officer in tones of gushing obsequiousness. He treated Wilhelm II's generals and court flunkies with a respect which he thought he owed to living history. The correspondence which he carried on with Wilhelm II for over a quarter of a century abounds in well-nigh unequaled expressions of flattery.

In 1897, Chamberlain published his chief work, *Die Grundlagen des 19. Jahrhunderts* (The Foundations of the Nineteenth Century), which quickly made him world famous. Wilhelm II wrote inviting him to the court, and thus began a friendship which was to endure until Chamberlain's death in 1926. 'It was God who sent your book to the German people and you personally to me,' wrote the Kaiser, and Chamberlain replied that he had hung Wilhelm's picture in his study opposite a Christ by Leonardo, and that during his work he walked back and forth between the countenance of the Saviour and that of the Kaiser.

Chamberlain denied that he was Nietzsche's successor, but nonetheless he was. From Richard Wagner he took over the doctrine of race, but he totally rejected the master's theory of decay and degeneration, rather holding, with Nietzsche, that a higher race could and must be bred. But while the German had doubted his own nation, the Englishman placed the Germans above everyone else in the world, and agreed with Wagner that they were destined 'to ennoble mankind'; though first, to be sure, 'mankind must be made sufficiently German in feeling and thought to be able to assimilate this ennobling influence.'

As a pearl forms about a tiny irritant, a grain of sand or the splinter of a shell, a nation forms around an historic irritant; around a spiritual event which is strong enough to give the entire population the feeling of a homogeneous and equal spiritual participation. Thus the British nation arose in the struggle for freedom of conscience, the French in the struggle for the moral perfection of man. Thus the German nation arose through faith in the omnipotence of education, which later degenerated into a belief in the omnipotence of technology. And since the intellect, as Chamberlain puts it, 'leaves nothing to chance,' it does not leave the birth of a nation to chance, to the historical grain of sand; but, as pearls can be grown by means of artificial irritants, the intellect artificially creates the nation, and manufactures a people as an instrument of its domination.

Race is made by man — this is Chamberlain's key to the secrets of history. 'A noble race does not fall from heaven, it becomes noble little by little, like fruit trees, and this process of development can begin anew at any moment, as soon as a geographico-historical accident or (as in the case of the Jews) a *fixed plan* creates the conditions.' A fixed plan allegedly created the Jewish race, and a fixed plan must create the great, intellectual, organizing, and ruling race of the future. Chamberlain said that he had learned the essential facts about race, like Charles Darwin, 'in the horse stable and on the chicken farm.'

Four phenomena are needed to produce Chamberlain's race.

First, good material must be available. 'And if someone asks where this material comes from, I must reply that I don't know.'

Second, the firmest, most powerful material, material endowed with definite desired characteristics, must be sought out systematically over a period of generations, and in this artificial selection you must not be sentimental. 'The exposure of sickly children,' says Chamberlain, 'was one of the most beneficent laws of the Greeks, Romans, and Teutons.' Nietzsche wanted to slaughter millions to the same end.

Third, this good material must for generations be kept pure by inbreeding; that is, by 'producing offspring exclusively in the narrower tribal circle, avoiding all admixture of foreign blood.'

Here we seem to have arrived at the 'pure race' of song and story. Have we really? Chamberlain ridicules the legendary 'pure race.' It is a 'mystical concept,' an 'airy phantasm.' Inbreeding, the safeguarding of the blood against outside influences, is, to be sure, a necessary stage in the process of race breeding, but it is a late stage. This safeguarding preserves the race, keeps it rigid and fresh, once it has been created; but the race does not receive its original vital spark in cool purity, but in a mobile mixture of foreign saps and qualities — for this, in Chamberlain's view, is the fourth and deepest secret of all race-making: 'The genesis of extraordinary races is invariably preceded by a blood mixture.' As an example, Chamberlain cites the particularly gifted Germanic tribes of Franks and Saxons, mixtures of Germanic and Slavic blood; and, as the finest example, he considers a nation arisen in the last three hundred years from blood even more mixed; the Prussians.

And when by this fourfold process — discovery of good material, natural selection, mixture, and finally inbreeding — a new race has arisen, what have we then? Then a noble new type of man has been born, who, throughout the globe, may sense, seek, and find kindred beings of equal nobility, with like or similar gods, legends, and longings. This kinship is not necessarily of blood, but merely of 'affinity'; the kindred race may be of like type and similar genesis — but without blood connection. The type is decisive, not the blood.

For always, and everywhere on earth, we find qualities typical of a like race, even where a blood relationship is unproved and perhaps improbable. Thus, everywhere on earth there is a generically similar type of the noble and most gifted: 'Is this family of men united by blood ties, is it unified? I do not know, and I do not care; no relationship creates a closer bond than elective affinity.' So speaks an Englishman who grew up as half a Frenchman and became a German.

Chamberlain designates this highest type by the old and much-used term 'Aryan.' To the question what this is, he gives a startling answer: 'What is an Aryan? One must know nothing of ethnography to venture a definite answer to this question.' It is absurd to speak of an Aryan blood community: 'The peoples we have learned to combine under the name of Aryan vary greatly from one another; they show the most varied cranial structure, and different colors of skin, eyes, and hair; and supposing there had been a common Indo-European mother race, what argument can we offer against the constantly accumulating evidence to the effect that other, totally unrelated, types have from time immemorial been represented in our present so-called Aryan nations? At most we might call individuals, but never a whole people, Aryan. Linguistic relationship offers no compelling proof of like blood.'

Chamberlain considers race relationship higher and more profound than blood relationship; it is a relationship of souls, based on affinities, on similarity of character and manner of thought, despite variation in physical characteristics: 'In this sense the Indo-European Aryans unquestionably constitute a family.' And: 'The Germanic peoples belong to that group of most gifted people which we are accustomed to designate as Aryans.' The true Aryan type is not frequent in the so-called Aryan nations, and the task is to make it frequent and dominant: 'Even if it were proved that in the past there never was an Aryan race, we want there to be one in the future.'

Let there be an intellectual brotherhood of the most gifted and strong-willed; let there be an order of Supermen, distributed throughout the earth, permeating and leading the so-called Germanic nations and through them dominating the whole earth.

'Physically and spiritually, the Aryans stand out among all men; hence they are by right the lords of the world.'

This was just what the German intellectuals, who had once created the German people without being able to give it a state, and who now had a state to whom they could give no people, had to be told. The Kaiser was firmly convinced that God in person had sent him this Englishman. In 1902, he wrote Chamberlain that according to his generals 'nearly all the young officers in the Guard Corps study and discuss *The Foundations of the Nineteenth Century.*' The officers of the Guard Corps were the leaders and demigods of the Kaiser's régime.

What Chamberlain wrote was a very bold self-portrait of an important trend in German opinion; but it was not a reflection of basic German thought. Just as this book chooses Hegel as an example of the political philosophy of the early nineteenth century, so Chamberlain, at the end of the century, stands for a series of political thinkers — Treitschke, Lagarde, Langbehn, Bernhardi; finally, and most significant, Oswald Spengler. Hegel, like Chamberlain, had founded or led a new school of political philosophy, but not (contrary to popular belief) the only, nor indeed the dominant, school. Through the entire nineteenth century the spiritual leader of German thought was not Hegel, but Friedrich Schiller, a humanist if there ever was one, and a believer in the nobility of mankind. Between 1900 and 1914 the most successful political books were Berta von Suttner's radical and pacifistic *Down Arms!* and the autobiography of the Socialist leader, August Bebel, a book hostile to militarism. True, the 'Pan-German' movement had found its strongest support among the intellectuals and among the big business men, but Heinrich Class, their leader through thirty years, called his life-work an 'upstream' struggle.

For the nation as a whole was averse to taking the bold and dizzy path to Aryan world domination, and no one knew this better than the Kaiser. Chamberlain, to whom the restlessly speech-making, traveling, telegraphing monarch opened his heart, so often bleeding from bitter wounds, knew it too. He wrote the Kaiser that public opinion was made by idiots or malicious traitors, and the Kaiser replied, in some embarrassment, that the two of them, he and Chamberlain, would continue to stand loyally together in common struggle for the good cause: 'You wield your pen, I my tongue. I strike my broadsword and say: "In spite of hell and high water!"'

Wilhelm was unable to crush the open opposition, and the opposition was admittedly unable to break Wilhelm; but the Kaiser's personal authority suffered a severe blow in 1908 when a majority of the Reichstag, annoyed by the calamitous interference of the monarch in foreign affairs, censured him publicly; the Reichs Chancellor had to promise that in the future the Kaiser would keep himself more in the background. In 1912, the German people elected a Reichstag with an uncontested 'anti-Prussian,' anti-militarism majority, and a third of this Reichstag actually consisted of Social Democrats. When, in 1913, in the Alsatian border city of Zabern, an excited colonel arrested some civilian participants in an anti-militarism demonstration, and had them thrown into jail, all Germany roused itself in a rebellious mood, and with a vote of 293 to 54 the Reichstag voiced its disapproval of the conduct of the government.

It was partly because of this internal opposition that imperial Germany's foreign policy did not yield to the lust for conquest, as Chamberlain expected. Between 1900 and 1912, when England conquered South Africa through military force, when France took Morocco and Italy Tripoli, Germany made no such acquisitions. It had withdrawn in Morocco before France, in Persia before England and Russia. Toward the turn of the century Germany had refused a Franco-Russian offer to unite against England who was then involved in the South-African Boer War. Then, when Russia and France concluded a pact directed against Germany, the latter, in 1904 and 1905, allowed the tempting opportunity of waging a lightning invasion of France to slip away, although Russia was at that time hard pressed by internal revolution and the defeat by Japan. Even the First World War did not begin as a German war of conquest; the deeper guilt began when, after Bismarck's retirement, Wilhelm entrusted Germany's destiny exclusively to the army. The generals of this army decided in 1914 that Germany, in the face of the Russian mobilization, must now immediately be victorious on all fronts or there would not be any chance of standing up against the superiority of the combined powers of France and Russia.

After the outbreak of the First World War, Chamberlain tried to create a world program for the German intellectual. The German monarchy, he taught, should direct Germany as an engineer directs a factory. 'The monarchy represents an age-old German heritage; what is new — rising in our midst but an unconscious process — is a second political principle of the German future: the indubitable mission of Germany to organize all political life scientifically. . . . By "scientific organization" I mean application of those scientific principles which in Germany have led to such unprecedented results in the fields of technology, research, and, to a great extent, in administration as well; furthermore, I include the most meticulous precision in directing the available means toward the aims to be achieved, and the application of forces in such a way as to obtain the maximum results with a minimum expenditure, thus multiplying the forces at our disposal a hundredfold; besides, division of labor, whereby every man does the work he understands and for which he is suited by nature — all this presupposes practical systematization; that is to say, planned co-ordination of all the parts of every productive unit.'

'Productive unit!' Here we have the future state called by its proper name. Its member is the technically thinking man, to whom the world appears as a task that can and must be solved.

The man of this type lives in order to work. 'If I were dictator of the world,' one of the better-paid priests of the idol of mass labor prophetically cried, 'I would shoot all idlers at sight.' This type of engineer-tyrant is by no means limited to Germany; the above-quoted sentence was uttered by a Dutchman, knighted by the King of England for his services to the empire: the oil magnate, Sir Henri Deterding.

Chamberlain's 'scientific' world plan for Germany is based on the idea that there can be no world domination through mere power, as there is no domination of any sort through mere power — as far as power means compulsion. No, this coming German world domination must be 'the realm of *homo sapiens* . . . an entirely new type of power, resting on intellectual and moral foundations: on a high average development of purely intellectual faculties, on thorough scientific knowledge, on the integration of individuals into the frame of scientific methods.'

Seriously questioned, Chamberlain would have said that he had learned from the great masters of world domination, from the Jewish prophets Ezekiel, Ezra, and Nehemiah, who created, as he says, by order of the Persian king the race-conscious Jewish people. To penetrate the other nations, to devour them from within by virtue of superior intellect, bred in the course of generations; to make themselves the dominant intelligence in foreign nations, and thus make the world Jewish — this, according to Chamberlain, is the aim of the Jews. Later, Hitler was to reveal this supposed Jewish secret to the people in passionate and gruesome pictures: how Isaac Kohn inveigled the workers and Moses Kohn the capitalists into following Jewish leadership; how the demonic brothers incited the two classes against one another until they sank exhausted into the Jewish net; how the Jewish intelligentsia won control of the economic system, the press, art — this, according to the forged *Protocols,* Chamberlain, and Hitler, is the true road to world domination, allegedly discovered by the Jewish intelligentsia. And hence it must become the road of the German intellectual.

> If up to now the Germans abroad, because of the political weakness of their mother country, had not given up their language and special character, this penetration of the thinking, creating, organizing — predominantly German — element in all countries of the world would be clear for all eyes to see. If from now on they remain closely bound to Germany, consciously, openly, and proudly German — then the world conquest will mature with astonishing rapidity. To mention but one example — Why should Germany have to conquer Australia? How would this conquest be begun? How would it be executed? But once even ten per cent of the inhabitants of that continent are conscious Germans, they will constitute nine tenths of the intelligence and education, and consequently provide the guiding mind.

How threadbare and pale beside this are our present conceptions of the 'fifth column'! Chamberlain writes Australia, because the vigilant military censorship forbade the intended 'South America' or plain 'America.'

Inspired by the mania of perfection, he foresaw a perfect Germany that would create a perfect world:

'Once Germany has achieved the power,' Chamberlain prophesied, 'and we may confidently expect her to achieve it — she must immediately begin to carry out a scientific policy of genius. Augustus undertook a systematic transformation of the world, and Germany must do the same. . . . Equipped with offensive and defensive weapons, organized as firmly and flawlessly as the Army, superior to all in art, science, technology, industry, commerce, finance, in every field, in short; teacher, helmsman, and pioneer of the world, every man at his post, every man giving his utmost for the holy cause — thus Germany, emanating efficiency, will conquer the world by inner superiority.'

For this program of world domination the Emperor decorated his friend (who had become a naturalized German) with the Iron Cross, Germany's most popular war medal. But just as Chamberlain was not really a German, so Wilhelm was not really the master of Germany. On July 25, 1917, at the height of Germany's military successes, when Russia seemed to be liquidated, and when in France the commander-in-chief Pétain advised a negotiated peace, the Reichstag voted, 212 to 126, for a peace of 'understanding and conciliation'; it wanted 'no enforced cessions of territory,' no 'political, economic or financial oppression.' True, the Pan-Germans, Chamberlain among them, attempted to form, in protest, a movement for a 'good' or 'strong' peace, a peace of conquest. This group, calling itself the Fatherland Party, enjoyed the support of the all-powerful Ludendorff and a large number of followers, but it remained, all the same, a minority that did not reflect popular feeling. Its most remarkable effect on history was probably the founding of a small subdivision in Munich which tried to recruit followers among the workers — without any success at that time. This committee called itself the 'Free Workers' Committee for a Good Peace.' Its leader was Anton Drexler. It was the original cell of the later German Workers' Party, which in turn was to become the National Socialist Movement.

When in September, 1918, the World War was driving toward a German military defeat, Ludendorff strongly advocated the formation of a democratic German government to conclude peace. He pressed the Kaiser to hurry; the Kaiser, irritated, shouted back,

'I am no magician!' Then the defeated general himself was forced out and the Kaiser said to him sadly that he would now have to build up a new Reich with the help of the Social Democrats. All changes took place behind the strange human façade of an old general who had been pensioned off even before the war, Field Marshal Paul von Beneckendorff and Hindenburg. Two weeks after Ludendorff's fall, Hindenburg advised his own Kaiser to abdicate and flee to Holland; in his person the army overthrew the monarchy in order to preserve itself. Hindenburg did this prudently, more by agreeing with nods and murmurs of assent to what others said. He allowed Groener, Ludendorff's successor, to say to his Kaiser on November 9, 1918: 'The army will march home under its leaders and commanding generals, quietly and in order. It will not do this under Your Majesty's command, for it no longer stands behind Your Majesty.' Thus the generals first brought democracy to Germany and overthrew their emperor. Both were done under pressure of events, particularly because Woodrow Wilson demanded it in the name of the Allies, and even more in pale fear before the force of the people which was no longer to be held in check. Ludendorff firmly maintained on the day of his downfall that 'I believe all to be lost, and expect Bolshevism to come to us.' Two weeks later, the head of the Social-Democratic Party, Friedrich Ebert, became President of the now republican German Reich.

This was the downfall of the German 'Kaiserreich,' the historic moment of the German revolution. It was also the beginning of the officers' counter-revolution. In a purely military sense the war was not completely lost as yet; as statements made by the Allied generals show. But the military leaders of Germany preferred to lose the war and even to overthrow their emperor in order to save the army and beat down the revolution.

But the army could not be saved, at least not for the moment. The soldiers, disgusted, threw their guns away and went home. It is true that finally this hurt the new republic even more than the old army. For when the government tried to organize troops to defend the young republic against the counter-revolution, it found that it had scarcely enough soldiers among its own supporters to do so, and its very existence was threatened by dislike of the workers for everything military.

At this moment, a young officer in Hindenburg's headquarters had a decisive idea; a sudden inspiration of historical significance. The army had fallen to pieces, but great groups of unemployed soldiers had been left behind. Although the majority of them were opposed to war, still there was a minority ready for anything. If only a small army of volunteers could be organized, this force, for lack of armed resistance, would soon become master of the country. This was the idea of Captain Kurt von Schleicher, aide of Hindenburg and Groener. Hindenburg at first would have nothing to do with such a troop of mercenaries and bandits, but Schleicher, who was in private conversation a man of winning eloquence, was able to persuade him. This was the origin of the German 'Free Corps,' the 'murderers' army,' of which later the new German army was to consist. The outward pretext for the forming of this army was the communistic revolts in several different parts of the Reich. The first one was in January, 1919, when there was a rebellion in Berlin that for a time looked dangerous. Even the Allies for a short time tacitly agreed with this revival of the German army. For with them, too, there was fear of Communism. The German Free Corps fought with Allied approval in the first months of 1919 in the former Russian-Baltic provinces, Lithuania and Latvia, against the Bolsheviks. During this time the English fleet was fighting the Bolsheviks in near-by Estonia; Allied troops, the British and American, had occupied large parts of Siberia; they had landed in Murmansk and Archangelsk in the North. Groener asserted April 24, 1919, in the Reich cabinet that Germany could put an end to the Soviet régime if an Allied army, in conjunction with the German troops from the west, would march into Soviet Russia. Some of the soldiers of this German Free Corps were soldiers of fortune of a very peculiar sort. They expected to receive from the new governments of Latvia and Estonia a reward of land on which they could settle as farmers. When they were not supported in this by the German government, they tore the German cockades from their caps and sewed on the cagle of the tsar.

Those were the early germs of development which later proved to be fateful. But in the broad German masses at this time — in the last days of 1918 and the early days of 1919 — a new and glowing hope had arisen, part of that strange millennial belief in the coming of a great and bright future which had seized almost the whole world after the dark four years of butchery. A national parliament gave Germany a democratic constitution, called 'the freest constitution in the world,' which it assuredly was on paper. There was the famous promise of a peace that would 'make the world safe for democracy' and realize the highest goal of the European nations, the right of self-determination.

And then this German democracy seeped away: not immediately in externals and institutions, but in the hearts of men. The German masses had expected a better world from democracy, better at least than the war; the development was rather for the worse. The Allied blockade against starving Germany went on, war conditions went on; finally, there was a peace which did not really end the war, but intentionally left important questions unsettled. Of this Treaty of Versailles three things can be said with certainty: it burdened Germany — and only Germany — with a war guilt, whose onesidedness has not been confirmed by historical research; it subjected Germany (badly bled, but materially almost intact) to a morally defensible, but economically senseless and unfulfillable, indemnity; and though granting the right of self-determination to many peoples, refused it to Germany. But the chief sin of this peace was its lack of democracy. The democratic framers of this treaty had not understood that democracy, national in its beginnings, was moving toward world scope. They might have learned from Chamberlain, from the Wise Men of Zion, from Wagner and Nietzsche, in short, from the Antichrist, that the time had come to organize the world as a whole because, as Chamberlain had put it twenty years before, 'the planet had become small and round.' They should have tried to create the beginnings of a world democracy which would give nations the feeling that they were masters and not playthings of their destiny; that they could mold their own policies instead of being mere victims of their politicians. Instead of this, they dissected the world, Europe and Asia at least, into innumerable, ostensibly democratic national sectors, actually infected with the germs of national hatred and violence. With the current means and concepts of their time, the men of Versailles could have attempted to build up a world democracy. They could have tried to create a world parliament elected by the nations, or rather by the people in the nations — for a moment, in 1919, there was some talk of this in Paris. Instead, they called a conference of diplomats, to which they gave the absurd, because inwardly untrue, name 'League of Nations.'

The consequence was an increasing doubt of democracy. World organization was inevitable and urgently needed, and there was a growing readiness to accept it at the hands of anyone who was ready to undertake it even by violence. Democracy did not act in its hour; and so the Antichrist acted. When the dream of peace had vanished, a skeptical Germany began slipping toward the same abyss of despair as in 1849.

And so, disillusionment and despair gave birth to the moral chaos, in which an army of murderers could seize authority. At this time Chamberlain, who had fallen sick and silent after the war, privately uttered the hope that from the bands of volunteers on the Russian frontier a young, unknown leader might arise, who would clean out democracy.

An unknown young leader from the frontier! When he actually came, he came from the Austrian, not the Russian, frontier; and by meeting him Chamberlain definitely became a key figure of world history. In October, 1923, Hitler went to Bayreuth where Chamberlain lived as son-in-law of the late 'master of all masters.' Hitler first delivered a public speech and was then received at Wahnfried, home of the Wagner family. There he met the aged 'mistress of Bayreuth,' Cosima Wagner; Siegfried Wagner, the weak son and heir, composer, director, laborious preserver of the great musical tradition; Winifred, his English-born wife; and finally a paralyzed old man in a wheel-chair, with spent eyes in the face of a child: Chamberlain. Hitler felt that he was among kindred spirits; he was happy and at ease. He put on a big show and spoke at length. Chamberlain was carried away. The next day, the half-dying man, by a supreme effort of the will, dictated a letter to Hitler, telling him that this meeting was his strongest experience since 1914, when his illness had overtaken him; since then he had never slept so well as that night, and he found it miraculous that Hitler, the awakener of souls, should have possessed the power to bestow on him so soothing a sleep. 'My faith in the Germans has never wavered for a moment, but my hope, I must own, had sunk to a low ebb. At one stroke you have transformed the state of my soul.' One more who had succumbed to the thundering, hypnotic voice!

Hitler had come to Wahnfried in the company of two men. One was a little-known anti-Semitic poet and journalist of Czech origin, a fulsome admirer of Wagner; his name was Josef Czerny, and, in order to have a German pseudonym, he called himself Josef Stolzing, after the Wagnerian figure. The other was Alfred Rosenberg, the Russo-German and prophet of the Wise Men of Zion. It appears that it was he who had acquainted Hitler with Chamberlain's ideas, and since Hitler was too impatient for steady reading, had underlined the most important and useful sentences in the thick tomes. Rosenberg regarded himself as Chamberlain's disciple and successor, and as executant of his spiritual legacy. After Chamberlain's death in 1926, the Russo-German wrote a biography of the Anglo-German, published an anthology of his writings, and himself wrote a book the very title of which was intended to indicate that it was a continuation of Chamberlain's chief work: *The Myth of the Twentieth Century*.

Among the guests at Wahnfried, Hitler met Count Richard du Moulin-Eckart of French émigré stock, the biographer of Cosima Wagner; he met Count Manfred Gravina, an Italian, who married one of Wagner's daughters; he met the wife of Chamberlain's publisher, Elsa Bruckmann, née Rumanian Princess Cantacuzene. This Rumanian princess soon became one of Hitler's most ardent supporters — like an American woman from the same circle, the widow of the publisher Hanfstängl.

Chamberlain had developed the doctrine of the elective affinity of Aryans, extending beyond nations. The phrases and the gestures are stubbornly German; but in reality an international type, dimly foreseen by Heine and Nietzsche, was in process of formation. To the Austrian Hitler, Chamberlain wrote: 'I always wonder whether the lack of political instinct, for which the Germans are so often reproached, is not a symptom of a far profounder gift for state-building. The organizational talent of the Germans is in any case unexcelled, and their scientific capacities unequaled; it is on this that I have built my hope. . . .'

Now perhaps we can better understand the deep meaning of seemingly simple words. To this end we have taken a long excursion through the history of the European nations and the German mind. In the world of today we see this history reflected, intensified as in a concave mirror. We see Adolf Hitler as the belated anachronistic German answer to Napoleon. We see him cursed in advance by the Richard Wagner he so venerates, as an imitator of Napoleon, a man of violence, a beast of prey. We see in him a man regarding himself as business manager of the world spirit, which can do no wrong, because to Napoleonic greatness every wrong is permissible. We see him as Thor, the thunder-god, raising his giant hammer and smashing the talisman of our culture, the cross. We see him rise up out of the teeming, nameless 'intelligent herd mass,' writing a book of 'power philosophy'; see the student rejected by the Vienna Academy of Art, growing to be an 'artist tyrant.' We see him, with subtle science, building a human machine such as the world has never known, and, at an early date, drawing up plans according to which the entire globe will become his machine. We see him as the Antichrist with the banal mustache, gathering round him the uprooted intellectuals among his own people and among many foreign peoples; a type of men willing to go to any length in order that the machine may 'work': willing to command and also to obey, to trample and to be trampled, to kill and even, if they must, to die.

We see Adolf Hitler surrounded by half-Englishmen, half-Americans, half-Frenchmen, half-Italians, half-Czechs, half-Rumanians, and all of them also half-Germans; and we hear him utter his wolf-cry, expecting the howling wolves from everywhere to answer him: 'Aryans and anti-Semites of all nations, unite!'

Chapter XI

THE AGE OF GOLD

FOR THE FIRST TIME SINCE THE WAR THE GERMAN people were happy. Again there was work for all; there was money for those who knew how to make it; there was enough food; for those with the sweet tooth there was whipped cream — a sign of prosperity that appeared very late in the German post-war world. Again there were silk stockings and even pure silk dresses; women began to use lipstick; the first radios croaked; even people who were not immeasurably wealthy began to buy automobiles; more people began to travel in the little airplanes permitted by the Versailles Treaty — and negotiations for larger ones were proceeding in Paris. Passport regulations, travel restrictions, closed borders vanished; it was as though a cloak of mist were removed from Germany. The world opened up like an immeasurable blue sea full of golden islands. Again all water and land routes led into the infinite; again each man was free to go out and search for his horn of plenty. American financiers went to Germany looking for factories willing to borrow good American dollars from them. German scholars again appeared at foreign scientific congresses. French students went to Germany and invited their German comrades to youth congresses and festivals at Paris or Geneva. A Zeppelin flew from Germany to America; a German car won the first prize at a big automobile race in Italy; a German of Jewish descent won the world chess championship.

This was the great year of recovery, 1925. Everything was to be as before. Back to 1914 was the unuttered command. The bitter

Peace of Versailles had established that the war had been a German crime; now, everywhere in the world, the kind and comforting view was advanced that the war had been a common mistake.
The world wanted the soft, caressing air, the freedom, comfort,
and abundance of peace. For one side to dominate the other — as
five violent and crisis-ridden post-war years had shown — cost
money in spite of apparent reparations and tribute payments; why
not live together in peace, and make money from one another as
before? Capital and labor as before, heavy and light industry as
before, exports and imports as before, confidential conversations
between diplomats, and alliances as before, national self-seeking as
before. The great occasion to give the world new unity had been
missed in Versailles; no one had thought of it seriously. A world
parliament, a radical union of peoples from below, common education, an intermingling of the youth of all great nations — what a
tremendous task that would have been! But the world wanted to
have it easy; it made things comfortable for itself; the post-war
hatred that had endured five years suddenly burst and flew away,
and the vanquished profited as well as the victor. The world strove
to shake off the burden of victory, and Germany, too, felt a fresher
air. The number of unemployed sank to half a million; that was
almost better than normal.

And so gaiety! Great public festivals! An end to the old mourn-
ing which had lain over Germany since the war and had grown
deeper and darker since the French incursion into the Ruhr! No
more sour police regulations against public dancing! The first carnival after the outbreak of the war, the great mass festival 'with all
bars down,' was held in 1925. In the Bürgerbräu Keller where
Hitler had fired at the ceiling, and in dozens of other halls, night
after night thousands danced in masks and costumes. In a city
with less than seven hundred thousand inhabitants, from fifty to
one hundred thousand people would go for a week without sleeping in
their beds. A wild masked throng in theatrically bedizened vehicles
moved with shouts and music through the city, past the Feldherrn
Halle, across the Odeonsplatz — almost the same route Hitler's
death march had taken in 1923. A man in a grotesque disguise was
addressed by an acquaintance in the crowd: 'Why, you were here

in 1923, but dressed differently — you had a Swastika and a gun then, you loafer!' The man thus addressed removed his scarlet cardboard nose for a moment, fastened his artificial mustache more securely, and said with embarrassment: 'Well, in those days we were crazy.'

In 1925, Mardi Gras, the high point of the carnival, fell on February 24, the anniversary of the day on which Hitler in 1920 had made his first public speech. Released from his comfortable arrest two months before, Hitler had again found himself free, but alone and little noticed, in semi-obscurity. Now, with his playful belief in symbols and numbers, he would have liked to raise his thundering voice again on a twenty-fourth of February. And it had to be a Mardi Gras! On this day Hitler wouldn't have found a hundred people wanting to hear him talk on Germany's defeat, Germany's disgrace, or Germany's future. He would have found no hall, no free wall space for his posters, no trumpeter to greet his entry into the hall with the old familiar heart-lifting fanfare. Germany, Bavaria, even Munich, had almost forgotten him — as they had forgotten the war.

Within a year after his defeats and false prophecies the prisoner of Landsberg had become an embarrassment to his friends, and a laughing-stock for the masses, in so far as anyone mentioned him at all. The movement had fallen apart; the leaders reviled one another to the amusement of the public; there was scarcely one whom the others did not accuse of stupidity, cowardice, financial irregularities, or an unsavory private life. They fought for a share in sudden fame, for the approval of the masses, for frequent mention in the newspapers; and most of all they fought over money. This was one of the main reasons why they suddenly participated in parliamentary elections, although the imprisoned leader loathed parliaments. For a member of parliament received a monthly remuneration of four hundred to eight hundred marks — by German concepts a considerable sum, and at that epoch of beginning stabilization positively gigantic. In the various parliamentary elections, under the aura of Hitler's great speeches before the bar of justice, they registered at first considerable successes; later, their successes rapidly diminished and turned to bitter defeats. In two elections in 1924, the number of their seats in the Reichstag fell from thirty-two to fourteen, and most of these fourteen soon ran away to other parties. Both the successes which he had not expected, and the defeats which he could not prevent, depressed Hitler deeply.

People of ability and importance instinctively avoided the fallen figure, which again vanished into the mass of the unknown. A Royal Bavarian infantry captain, for instance, could not very well be expected to worship this man like a god, to set him above his King Rupprecht or his General Ludendorff — particularly if the captain himself had actually created the man. In grave disappointment Ernst Röhm parted with Hitler. Röhm was one of the four or five who addressed Hitler as 'Du,' and, to the leader's own secret relief, dared to treat him like a common man. For this very reason, Röhm resented his friend's megalomania which, since his *débâcle*, had become intolerable even in his own inner circle.

Against the terrible feeling of defeat, Hitler armed himself with an inner arrogance which stopped at no human relation. During his imprisonment he led a more comfortable existence than ever before, but he claimed — and ended up by believing it himself — to have been languishing in a dungeon; he dreamed himself into the rôle of a saint, suffering in chains for Germany; he was the hero for whose freedom Germany was waiting; he was the German people itself, humiliated and misunderstood, yet destined and secretly marked by Fate for inconceivable future greatness, a laughing-stock to the masses and the mighty, a miracle and consolation to the faithful and the seeing.

Röhm was loyal, but for him Adolf, in the Munich dialect 'Ade,' nevertheless remained a man. When he went to see him during his imprisonment, he found him each time more demoralized and lacking in decision. From the heights of a theatrical, brilliant activity, Hitler had relapsed into inert lurking and listening; he waited for voices, inspiration, opportunities, let himself drift, allowed his party to fall apart, friendships to break. In the end it was impossible for him to speak objectively to anyone on political questions, needs of the movement, present or future tasks, because he interpreted any statement of fact as a criticism. When there were difficulties, or when successes were achieved, when in the beginning, despite his arrest, the movement went forward, or when later, though marching in his name, it disintegrated and almost vanished — if the least mention of all this was made, he viewed it as a disrespectful carping at his person or his nimbus. In Röhm's opinion, he could only stand the 'flatterers and Byzantines' who 'unscrupulously crowded around,' exploiting his vanity, feeding him on illusions and 'venturing no word of contradiction.' Röhm decided, as he says in his autobiography, 'to speak openly to his friend as a loyal comrade.' His words were so open, such sharp insults were uttered by both that Röhm leaped to his feet and left. He wrote a letter to Hitler begging for the resumption of their old personal friendship, but Hitler did not answer. Another letter and again no answer. This was in the middle of April, 1925. Thus the real creator of Adolf Hitler parted with his creature who had grown too great and thought himself even greater.

Others also vanished. Göring, a high-living beggar in his exile, traveled through Italy and then Sweden, where his wife's well-to-do family, horrified at the dope addict's dissolute behavior, treated him coolly and for a time positively dropped him. Ernst Hanfstängl, a merry friend in merry days, gave up politics and devoted himself to his late father's art business, spending much time in America; Hitler still was his debtor for thousands of dollars; Hanfstängl had sold his claim to Christian Weber, one of Hitler's minor henchmen — but Hitler was not worth ten dollars at that time. Dietrich Eckart, long a sick man from too much eating and especially drinking, had died in the last days of 1923.

That Hitler was free and allowed to speak again he owed partly to a remnant of loyal complicity in high places, and partly to the depth of his fall, his apparent insignificance and harmlessness. Franz Gürtner had put through Hitler's release contrary to the law and against the resistance of his state's attorneys; and he had persuaded the Bavarian cabinet to legalize the forbidden National Socialist Party. In return, Hitler had to make humiliating concessions. He had to promise to break with Ludendorff. The general had involved himself in a public fight with the Catholic Church, had openly declared the Pope to be an enemy of Germany, as dangerous as the Jews and Free Masons — and Bavaria was an overwhelmingly Catholic state, governed by Catholic priests and

Catholic organizations. Parting with Ludendorff was easier for Hitler than the world imagined; he hated the Quartermaster General since he had put him to shame at the Feldherrn Halle by his example of physical courage. The hate grew deeper when, at the trial, Ludendorff showed no inclination toward going to prison for an unsuccessful *putsch* which Hitler had started and lost without asking him. Since then there had been jealousy and hatred on both sides. Hitler was too cautious to make any public expression of this; but Julius Streicher, one of his few supporters to remain loyal, wrote Ludendorff insulting letters recommending modesty to the general, since Hitler had reawakened the German people while Ludendorff had at best lost the World War.

The well-nigh forgotten World War which a well-nigh forgotten revolution had ended! For another revolution, a bold march into the future, the masses lacked strength and curiosity; and when Hitler again organized his 'band of freedom, seeking light,' only the strangest human scum rallied to his banners. A dozen more or less dubious characters — that was all that had remained loyal of his great staff of leaders.

The most important was Julius Streicher, for he had money. As editor of scandal sheets, as a speaker at scandal meetings, he had assembled, by blackmail and other methods of similar refinement, a fighting fund with which, for practical purposes, the movement stood or fell. A man of equal ability and unscrupulousness was a certain Hermann Esser; years before, Hitler had said — and admitted the utterance in court — that he knew Esser was a scoundrel, and used him only as long as he could not get along without him. During Hitler's imprisonment, these two had clung to him most faithfully because, with their unsavory reputations, they found no one else who wanted their slimy loyalty. Not without some justice Streicher accused the so-called 'fine people' in the movement, the officers and men of academic education, of secretly despising Hitler for his lack of higher education; Esser, who at times had been supported by his numerous mistresses, threatened his opponents with revelations in the 'Jewish' press. These two had outshouted each other in praise of Hitler's greatness, uniqueness, and authority; both had maintained the crumbling Hitler legend with the energy of the possessed. To the question: Who are you? — they had answered: We are nothing, but Hitler is everything! Now the best elements urged Hitler to break with these unsavory fellows; Pöhner, the former police commissioner and protector of the murderers, demanded that Hitler get rid of these two 'dunghills'; Ludendorff demanded the same; also Rosenberg and Anton Drexler, the founder of the party. Hitler, however, stubborn and insulted, clung faithfully to the two questionable characters, and on the telephone yelled at Drexler to go to the devil, at which the original founder left the National Socialist Party. But more obscure figures gathered around Hitler. For some time the photographer, Heinrich Hoffmann, belonged to the inner circle; a good bit of Hitler's popularity resulted from Hoffmann's photographs. Then there was the horse-dealer, Christian Weber, to whom Hitler owed a thousand dollars; and finally his publisher and business manager, Max Amann, in whose hands his own material existence rested. In order to assure the support of these men, who were useful and able in their way, he calmly threw overboard his most respected followers whose names would only have obscured his own.

Yet through it all, Alfred Rosenberg remained true to him. He was joined by Wilhelm Frick, Pöhner's former assistant, who had now gone into politics completely, and had become a deputy in the Reichstag. The most important of the new figures was Gregor Strasser, a druggist. He had not been prominent before 1923, but during Hitler's imprisonment he revealed himself to be a great organizer, an indefatigable speaker, a powerful personality, and Hitler's equal in self-reliance. It was a circle of unknown men. To the unswervingly loyal Rudolf Hess, Hitler said: 'I shall need seven years before the movement is on top again.'

It was not his task, he wrote in embarrassed apology, 'to attempt to improve or even unify the human material at my disposal.' His task was not to educate these men, for human nature could not be changed in the individual, only the type could be changed in the course of centuries; 'ideal universal men' were not to be found; consequently he did not look for men 'ideally suited to my idea.'

No, he purposely sought men of small stature with whom he

could easily deal; men whom he could impress even when he was in the humblest circumstances, who would take anything from him; who were literally willing to be beaten, and remained loyal because they could not find easier or more abundant bread any-where else. He consciously gathered little men around him — and this quite literally; for it is noteworthy that the intimate circle of Hitler's old guard, the Streichers, Amanns, Hoffmanns, Webers, Berchtolds, were physically puny, some of them dwarf-like.

To his little men peering up at the summit of the social pyramid that seemed so hopelessly distant, Hitler said consolingly that this summit would some day come down of its own accord: 'Believe me, this time will come. The illusory foundation of our economic life will again vanish beneath our feet and then perhaps people will be able to understand our words better than now.'

This he said to four thousand people who assembled on Febru-ary 27, 1925, inside and outside of the Bürgerbräu Keller. Carnival was past, the faithful were on the spot. They had come from all Bavaria, and there were four thousand of them — no more.

Be simple, be primitive, be brutal! — that was the command which in many different versions Hitler kept hammering into his four thousand for two hours. Let them not rely on reason, but rather trust in their emotion: 'Reason can treacherously deceive a man, emotion is sure and never leaves him.' Nowhere in the present day has politics been conducted with so much calculating intelligence as by Hitler; but it was a cardinal rule of this intelli-gence to bring the masses into a condition in which they were con-scious of a goal, but uncritical. Go to the masses! he cried to his discharged lieutenants, professors, and bank clerks. Only among the masses will you find idealism and spirit of struggle, and that is because they possess little material or spiritual goods: 'For posses-sions, whether of a spiritual or a material nature, will always para-lyze the desire for struggle.' Therefore, go to the masses; however, do not beg from them, but beat your fanaticism into them accord-ing to the methods which for five years you learned as armed bohemians; do not forget: 'The key to the heart of the people is not "if you please," but power.' In this the masses are like women: 'It is not for nothing that you see so many women here in this hall.

. . . In the woman emotion dominates and rightly tells her that the future of our children is at stake. . . . Our adversaries may talk as much as they like about our hysterical women. In former days woman brought Christianity to the countries. In the end she will also lead our movement to lasting victory.'

And again: Be simple! Be simple above all in the formulation of your aims. Do not set up three, four, or five aims at once — this was a side blow at Ludendorff, who had unnecessarily involved himself in a struggle with the Catholic Church. Yes, the Church is an enemy; in his heart Hitler knows this perfectly well, but he reserves this enemy for later. First look at people and then look at the mass: 'Every individual has certain views, certain abilities, a certain temperament, a certain character; every individual particularly loves certain things and dislikes certain others. It is, therefore, very hard to set up a common goal for ten thousand people. But it is even harder to set up a goal for these ten thousand, which consists of sixteen or twenty individual aims.' Again Hitler takes the enemy as a model. He describes the tactics of the Allies in the World War. Did they cry: We are fighting first against Germany, second against Austria, third against Bulgaria, and fourth against Turkey, and so on, and so on? No: they had concentrated their whole hatred and propaganda on one thing, yes, on one person: German militarism and the German Kaiser: 'Whether they fought in Mesopotamia or in Russia, in France, in Serbia, or elsewhere, it was all the same: against the Kaiser and against militarism. Thus they brought twenty-six states to the front against Germany, and every Englishman felt that he could not be wrong if twenty-six nations fought with him against the one.' In Germany it had been just the opposite — fatally so: 'In our country the little man wondered: Can we be right if twenty-six stand against us? Can all twenty-six be wrong, and we alone right?'

No, the more aims were set up, the more the confidence or faith in the individual sinks. 'And if you have twenty aims that are supposed to be fought for, perhaps only five people will remain who are in agreement with all twenty.'

With this speech Hitler gave birth to his theory that in propaganda the same thing must be repeated indefatigably. Later he said that this was the same in politics as in the business field, in advertising a soap or a toothpaste. Actually it was entirely different in politics. What Hitler wanted was power, and the struggle for power demands an endlessly shifting adaptation to shifting circumstances. But when he was discharged from prison, these were the circumstances: He was impotent, a political nonentity, dependent on the good humor of the Bavarian government; and for that reason he had to avoid any suspicion of ever wanting to harm this government. Therefore, he cried: The fight of his party was not against the government, not against the bourgeois parties, not against the police, but only against a single enemy, which he would best have liked the government to choose as an enemy, too. And again this enemy had to serve as a model:

'To make a struggle intelligible to the broad masses, it must always be carried on against two things: against a person and against a cause.

'Against whom did England fight? Against the German Kaiser as a person, and against militarism as his cause.

'Against whom do the Jews fight with their Marxist power? Against the bourgeoisie as a person and against capitalism as its cause.

'Against whom, therefore, must our movement fight? Against the Jew as a person and Marxism as its cause.'

And against nothing else! Sharpest concentration! And so Hitler was perfectly serious and sincere when he cried that it was necessary 'to choose only one enemy, so that everyone can see that he alone is guilty.' He was as sincere as a general who attacks the enemy from the front, but has a second troop lying in ambush; for that is the nature of war. 'Especially in a people like the German people,' Hitler thundered, 'it is absolutely necessary for psychological reasons to point to only one enemy, to march against one enemy. . . .' Suddenly he lowered his voice and grinned, some of the listeners laughed, for they guessed what was coming. In an easy-going tone Hitler said: 'By one enemy, if necessary, many can be meant.'

On pacified, contented Germany he wanted to force enemies and redeemers; enemies of which she was not aware, and redeemers whom she laughed at if she saw them at all — so poor, insignificant, and slimy was the impression they made. The disorganized, reduced National Socialist band had lost the savior's and prophet's pride of their early days when they were a legend to themselves and felt the protecting wings of the Reichswehr over them. Now they were oppressed by the consciousness of defeat, of having failed at an hour when the stars were favorable as they never again would be.

New pride had to be injected into this demoralized band behind their beer mugs in the Bürgerbräu Keller. And if people call you fools — and if this state doesn't want to hear any more about you — if you don't get ahead in your jobs — if you go bankrupt in your businesses and aren't taken seriously in society, it is because this post-war world doesn't know how to distinguish between high and low, between noble and common. Men are unequal, but you are the higher type, and that is what the world does not admit.

It is no malicious legend that the leadership and nucleus of National Socialism in the years from 1925 to 1930 consisted for the most part of failures; of men who became National Socialist functionaries because they found nothing better; of the figures Lieutenant Brückner described, who joined in 1923 because they hoped to become something and stayed on in desperation because they had not become anything; of men whose professional career (according to their own literal statements in the handbook of the German Reichstag) ran more or less as follows: 'About two years each in agriculture, big banks, glass industry, and textile trade,' or, 'clerk, buyer, traveling salesman, assistant gymnastics teachers, manager, director of a home' — how many bankruptcies or dismissals are hidden among these shifting careers? Or, student, merchant, again student, again merchant, then so-called private secretary (in reality on relief), then owner of a tiny poultry farm — this is the career of Heinrich Himmler, later chief of the secret police. Or, transport flier, then so-called student, then storm-troop leader, then for years completely without occupation, frequent visitor at pawnshops, for a time inmate of a nerve sanitarium, later parachute manufacturer and representative for aeroplane motors, deep in debt, for years snowed under by complaints over unredeemed notes — this is the civil career of Hermann Göring. Or, finally, student at a secondary school, leaves the school because of laziness before an examination, three times rejected at two academies, successively occasional worker, suitcase carrier, beggar, painter of picture postcards, poster painter, several times inmate of a men's lodging-house, later without profession, supported by friends — this typical failure's career is the civil life of Adolf Hitler.

And now in the Bürgerbräu Keller, this failure speaks words of consolation and encouragement to those like him, telling them not to despise themselves, for in reality they are better than the others. You are Aryans. You are the pure blood; that is more than possessions or rank; it is the highest, and this highest is just what the Jew wants to take away from you and destroy because he has already taken away and destroyed everything else. For the Jew is the type suited to the normal world of today, with its equalization which kills the personality; he is the type who makes the mass dominant in order to kill the outstanding individual; for the outstanding individual might offer resistance to Jewish world domination.

In order to kill the people's instincts of defense, the Jew poisons the pure Aryan blood. If, says Hitler, he could take his audience out of the Bürgerbräu Keller for a moment, and carry them away — as on a magic carpet — he would take them to Berlin and give them a look at the Friedrich Strasse, the center of night life in the capital: 'There you would see Jewish youths and more Jewish youths with German girls in their arms. Bear in mind that thousands and thousands of our blood are destroyed in this way every night, and children and children's children are lost to us.' Hitler spoke as plainly as is possible in a public speech. The German nation could shake off all its miseries, nullify its reparations obligations, eliminate its ruling political parties — yes, 'we can break the peace treaty . . . but once the blood is poisoned it can no longer be changed. It remains and multiplies and presses us lower from year to year. If today you are surprised that our people is inwardly so torn, remember this: out of the torn German people speaks its torn blood.' Applause from a thoughtful audience. It was clear that anyone whose own feeling prompted him to defend himself against this division and blood-poisoning must have good, un-spoiled blood; by becoming a National Socialist he proved it. He proved — even if he were ten times a dwarf with a squashed face like Max Amann or a bald, grinning faun like Julius Streicher — that he belonged to the higher type, which, according to Houston Stewart Chamberlain, was to arise only in the future. 'Everything beautiful,' Hitler went on, 'which we see around us today is only the creation of the Aryan, his spirit and industry; only the bad things are the heritage of the Hebrew.'

Aryans of all nations, unite! Into what immeasurable distance this aim had been removed! For the moment Hitler could be glad that the Aryans united in the Bürgerbräu Keller. The squabbling must end, he cried. Anyone who didn't like this could stay away — most had stayed away, anyway — and no one should try to impose any conditions on him, Hitler. By 'conditions' he meant the de-mand of his more respectable old friends that he drop the unsavory Hermann Esser or the repulsive fellow, Julius Streicher: 'I lead the movement, and no one gives me any conditions.' But if any-one should do so, here was the answer: 'Friend, just wait and see what conditions I'll give you.' He wasn't going to take any orders as long as he personally bore the responsibility — 'and I bear all the responsibility for everything that happens in this movement.' At the end of a year he would give the party an accounting; if by then he had done his work badly, 'I'll give my office back into your hands.' (Cries of Never!) Well, he himself didn't think so. He believed in the Swastika banner; he himself had designed it, he him-self had been first to carry it, and only wished 'that some day, when Father Time strikes me down, it may be my winding sheet. . . . Either the enemy will pass over our corpses or we over his.'

Four thousand were happy, exalted, consoled; again they felt a force that drove them on, a stream that bore them. The despised band again felt something like pride; this was the secret of this unusual speech coming after a year of silence. Up front, right under the platform, sat ill-tempered sub-leaders, resolved not to give Esser and Streicher their hand, doubting whether Hitler still had his old power; some, after personal experiences, were convinced that he had suffered a mental collapse in Landsberg. But now Hitler had burst forth from the cloud of silence like a lightning flash and had mightily kindled the demoralized souls of the four thousand; stormy applause rained down. Suddenly Streicher, Esser, and Frick stood on the platform; also Hitler's old companion, Gottfried Feder, the 'breaker of interest-slavery'; and in addition, two sub-leaders by the names of Dinter and Buttmann. Only two hours before, the six had been furiously fighting one another, had justly called one another men without honor, swindlers, pornographers. Now they all shook hands, and swore to forget all hostility, to follow the leader, to be faithful comrades; Streicher stammered with emotion that Hitler's return to politics was a 'gift of God.' None of the six except Frick ever rose to a leading position; they have been practically forgotten even among National Socialists; half-childish, mentally deranged, weak natures. But at that time they were the best Hitler had.

Next day Hitler, half-sleepy, and drunk with success, sat in the living-room of a little house in a snow-covered suburb of Munich. It was the house of Frau Carola Hofmann, an old lady who for years had been rather bashfully mothering and caring for him, sometimes stuffing him full of cakes and sweets like a child; he called her his 'little mother.' Into this comfortable atmosphere — a faithful reflection of the mild new German conditions — burst a terrible message. Hitler had again been forbidden to speak in Bavaria. Why had he spoken of the 'several enemies' which could be understood under the one? Why had he spoken of passing over the corpses of the enemy? In such a case even Gürtner could no longer help him.

The dissolution of parties, the prohibition of public speeches — these were strangely violent measures of the state in defense of free-dom. 'The freest constitution in the world' did not officially pro-vide or allow for such brutal intervention of police power. But Hitler and his like had for years filled the country with violence, murder, and destruction, and the state had not found the strength to suppress them with the cold majesty of law; and now, having un-justly spared them, the state could no longer defend itself except by injustice. Where Hitler began to speak, murder could be expected as a result. Hitler forced the state to stretch the laws in a rather arbitrary way — this in itself was a success. When he attacked, a few drops of his own poisonous spirit dripped on the enemy and infected him. In all points of his career, in the most insignificant and the most important situations, this was his most dangerous power, though unfortunately least understood: that he lured or forced his opponent to imitate him, to use similar methods and even adopt the qualities which he really wanted to combat in Hitler.

What sort of ragged company was this that the state was getting so incensed about! In Berlin there was an office clerk who in the evening after working hours assembled a few half-drunken figures, bordering closely on the underworld, in a gloomy beer hall and read them obscene or bloodthirsty stories about the Jews from ill-printed little pamphlets; this in the pompous jaw-breaking style was called 'Gau Berlin-Brandenburg of the National Socialist German Workers' Party,' and the clerk was the *Gauleiter*. It was the same in Cologne where an industrial chemist by the name of Doctor Robert Ley carried on the same work, and also in Breslau; the high-sounding title of *Gauleiter* might fall to an elderly eccentric who raised bees in a tiny provincial city on the Elbe, to a bankrupted landowner in Pomerania, a discharged school-teacher in Hanover. Or a pensioned major who, unable to live on his half-pay or to find any other suitable occupation, made knapsack and bicycle his home: a political vagabond, he rode from village to village, speaking ardently of Adolf Hitler. They nicknamed him the 'knapsack major.' Wherever he went, he found a few like-minded eccentrics to support him, found a bed for the night and a breakfast in the morning. These semi-madmen wandered about the country, seeking and finding half-mad supporters. Again the first tiny cells of a movement formed. A spirit deprived of all restraint and fear looked behind the revolving wheels and the striking pistons and sensed the profound helplessness and inertia of the society which had received so thorough a technical organization, sensed that it could be dominated.

For the state of the world was such that the fools and misfits were profoundly right while the intelligent and normal were fatally mistaken. This world in its main traits had returned to the normalcy of the days before 1914, and this precisely was its profound ailment. The intellectual and political leaders of the epoch endeavored to re-create what had been, to rebuild pre-war conditions. No really new idea enlivened this period of reconstruction; the only attempt of the sort, the League of Nations, degenerated into a conference of diplomats. With all their own inertia, the people for the most part felt these things more sensitively than their leaders; and the echo which the National Socialist vagabonds found arose from this feeling. Hitler's speeches from this period are particularly needful of detailed criticism; his prophecies, in part sharply confuted by events, attest a faulty knowledge of his subject; but he did recognize, and mercilessly and effectively describe, the inadequacy and folly of the attempts to reconstruct the world that had been shattered by the war. 'All this,' he shouted, pointing to the glittering rottenness roundabout, 'must and will collapse'—this was his simple and cheap message of calamity, and it proved correct.

He recognized decay wherever he met it; for it belonged to his own nature. All his life Hitler never had conducted a household, never had a budget; for him money is something you give away or borrow, but never earn; in his youth, his receipts were tiny, in his maturity they were immense; but he never established any relation between them and his work, for he worked, not to earn money, but to secure his public position, to win the applause and admiration—shared, to be sure, with a glass of beer—of his audience. What Hitler understands and what fills him with enthusiasm is the heartlessly overflowing power of nature, creating superabundance of life and at the same time superabundance of death, which 'only lets live the strongest and best and lets the rotten and sickly die,' in order to preserve a type in a few specimens. He was likewise convinced by the boundless capacity for production of the modern technology, by the boundless fertility of human invention, by the alchemy of technical processes, transforming stones into bread. In politics he uses and squanders the superabundance of vital force and also deathly force furnished by nature or artifice. For in his opinion life in its mass exists to be sacrificed for the attainment of a purpose superior to the individual life; multitudes of individuals must fall in order that the type remain. By frugality and limitation economics strives to preserve the individual, and Hitler's deepest reproach against it is 'that economy, to be sure, nourishes a man, but cannot fill him with enthusiasm for dying.'

Hitler's hatred of economy arises from the depths of his soul; but there were practical reasons why he so publicly and furiously proclaimed it. 'I myself most solemnly confess: I regret that German industry does not support us.' He reproached the German economic leaders, saying 'that these men who were so big support the Marxists out of cowardice' — he was referring to the collaboration between industrials and trade-unionists first begun by Hugo Stinnes — 'while they don't even know their German national comrades.' The German 'national comrades' were Hitler's *gauleiters,* who dreamed of envelopes containing five hundred marks 'for political purposes.' 'I would take every penny and every million without strings to it from a German,' Hitler assures us; yes, he would not refuse 'to accept ten millions from a German.' But contrary to a widespread legend, this was out of the question from 1925 to 1929 — even later. The German economy did not raise up Hitler. He is no creature of money; to be sure, he did approach big capital — though as a blackmailer, not as a lackey. But in that springtime of self-confidence, there was nothing to be had from capital by blackmail.

These were the years of high living in the world, when all limits fell, when money again bought everything, when a bank account again meant freedom, a safe-deposit box security, and a packet of stocks domination. These were the years of blessed optimism, when Calvin Coolidge was President of the United States, when the magic of prosperity seemed to deprive problems of their weight, and when the poverty which unquestionably still existed was explained by critics as the mere consequence of capitalist greed. It was the time when capitalist prosperity seemed so unquestioned that Russia-led Communism regarded as its closest and most intimate enemy, not the bourgeoisie, but moderate Socialism. 'Fascism and Social Democracy are twin brothers, Social Democracy is only a wing of Fascism' — thus spoke Josef Stalin in 1924. It was about the time when the Bank of France was able to overthrow a democratic government under Edouard Herriot; when in England a Socialist government under James Ramsay MacDonald after some months in power was swept away for five years by a Conservative landslide (1924). It was exactly at the same time when in Germany the Social Democrats in two elections suffered a remarkable defeat; when for four years the moderate non-socialist parties governed unmolested, and business launched the slogan: 'An end to politics, on with reconstruction!'

Peace positively forced itself on the world, irresistibly taking form despite obstacles and difficulties. The style of the peace councils remains memorable. They were great social events, political drama festivals with the most famous performers, on the most beautiful stages in the world, before the eyes of a glittering, elegant, good-humored public, representing the power and the wealth of the earth — and never perhaps have international festivals been so impressively propagandized. These diplomatic festivals usually took place on some lake in southern Switzerland; in a land where man by centuries of toil had stamped his civilization, like a fine gold plate, on a raw, terrifying nature. At the foot of the high mountains, tamed with hundreds of roads, railroad lines, passes, tunnels, electrical works, and grand hotels, the statesmen of the epoch tried to master the yet unmastered problem of human society, just as Nature was here mastered, channelized, and walled about. They went strolling in fresh green parks, looked out upon a flawless fragment of blue lake, set like a jewel amid the green; they saw gardens, paths, bathing establishments, stone steps, all designed to facilitate the passage from friendly land to friendly water; across the lake, gleaming in the sun, they saw a paradise full of little castles, forests, hills, gently piled one upon the other. In the presence of all this natural and man-made beauty and abundance, it was hard not to be optimistic, not to believe in peace.

Here Aristide Briand, the French Foreign Minister, tragically searching for peace, cried from the platform of the League of Nations: 'En arrière les canons, en arrière les fusils!' — in front of a public of hard-boiled politicians and newspapermen, some of whom had tears in their eyes. Here his German colleague, Gustav Stresemann, formerly a rather run-of-the-mill German patriot, praised the 'great world architect' according to whose plan the peoples should live in peace; he himself so permeated and transformed by the idea of peace that his closest friends did not recognize him any more, while his old opponents began by doubting him, then stared with amazement, finally cheered him. And here the third man in the trio, Sir Austen Chamberlain, head of the British Foreign Office, worked as a successful mediator between Germany and France, feeling, as he later said, that there must be an end to 'the bickering and pin-pricking which Germany had no doubt suffered ever since the war.'

In the little city of Locarno, on Lago Maggiore in southern Switzerland, a treaty was concluded in the fall of 1925 which can be called a second, improved, though still incomplete, peace treaty. Germany again voluntarily declared that, with regard to her western boundary on France and Belgium, she recognized the results of the war as irrevocable. Irrevocably Germany renounced Alsace-Lorraine whose population at heart really did not belong to her. Irrevocably she again renounced the small strips of territory which Belgium had acquired in the peace treaty. With regard to her western frontier, she irrevocably accepted the Peace of Versailles. But France also irrevocably declared that she definitely recognized the German frontiers; that she would make no attempt to annex any more German territory — a somewhat ironic promise when every morning the French flag was hoisted over the German cities of the Rhine; when the white and black troops of France still marched through their streets and, depending on how you interpreted the Peace of Versailles, would continue to do so until 1935 or perhaps much longer — in Clemenceau's view, forever. But perhaps the French would some day leave the Rhineland after all. And for this reason the Treaty of Locarno again expressly stated the provision of the Peace of Versailles that Germany should never send troops into her own Rhineland and never build fortifications there for the defense of her own border. At any time a French army then could descend on this vulnerable German artery close by the border, and if Germany should ever make a suspicious move, with one blow cut off her life stream. Clauses justifying this could always be dug up in the League Covenant; if the worst came to the worst, they could be found in the Peace of Versailles itself.

The *cordon sanitaire* of French bayonets on the Rhine continued for years to give Hitler occasion for mordant and popular attacks on German foreign policy; gave him occasion to make the peace hated and ridiculous. By 1928, a Czech newspaper took him seriously enough to call him a disturber of world peace; he proudly replied: 'Yes, we want to be a danger for this peace [stormy applause]. As far as in our power, we shall see to it that disorder arises, that there is no quiet in the world as long as this quiet means Germany's death.'

It was important to France as well as to Germany to have a stronger party on her side, protecting each against the other. For years France had continued to set her hopes in the security pact which had vanished in Versailles, preferably a general pact in which all had to protect all. But England was not ready to defend all Europe against all Europe. She was not even ready to enter into a onesided defensive treaty with France; she was not willing to enter into a policy directed against Germany. In Locarno she condescended only to promise that she would come to the help of any country to whose disadvantage the Treaty of Locarno was broken: she would help France against an 'unprovoked' German attack, but Germany as well against an unprovoked French attack. Fascist Italy which wished, by sharing European responsibility, to win recognition as a 'great power,' proudly promised the same, although it did not get any advantage of its own out of the treaty. In the laconic language of Locarno: Germany, France, Belgium, England, and Italy promised to guarantee 'the maintenance of the territorial *status quo* resulting from the frontiers between Germany and Belgium and between Germany and France and the inviolability of the said frontiers as fixed by or in pursuance of the treaty of peace signed at Versailles on June 28, 1919.' France, Germany, and Belgium promised each other 'that they will in no case attack or invade each other or resort to war against each other.'

It was up to England and Italy to see to it that the pact was faithfully kept by both sides. It was expressly stated that they would have to come to the help of the attacked party (for practical purposes France) even if they were convinced 'that by reason . . . of the assembly of armed forces in the demilitarized zone immediate action is necessary.' This meant for all practical purposes: If France should ever evacuate the Rhineland; if Germany, after inner changes that were not yet foreseeable, should again have an army deserving the name; and if she should dare to send a part of this army into her recovered western province — then Germany was breaking the Treaty of Locarno, and England and Italy had 'immediately to come to the help' of France. But — what was 'help'?

This was prudently left undefined, and thus for practical purposes the help remained a vague word on paper. France expected an English blockade fleet on the German North Sea coast, an English army in the Channel ports, English air squadrons over the Rhine. But neither Sir Austen Chamberlain nor his legal adviser, Sir Cecil Hurst, meant anything so thundering and irresistible by their 'help.' They thought of sharp, diplomatic notes, a shaming condemnation of the aggressor by international conferences, at most the calling-in of credits, the severance of commercial or even diplomatic relations. England, dreaming away in her island, with her eyes turned toward five continents and seven oceans, could not make up her mind to see the absolute focus of current history and her own fate in these three hundred miles along the Rhine. Yet in this European isthmus of nations where France and Germany touched through a relatively narrow breach in the wall of little neutral states, the fate of mankind was being decided. Forty million Frenchmen then (1925) faced sixty-six million Germans — could the future of the remaining twenty-four hundred million inhabitants of the globe depend on these one hundred and six millions? It did; but observers outside of the Continent simply could not grasp the fact.

Even less could the world realize that its fate, for example, should depend on the existence and prosperity of Poland and Czechoslovakia — these countries no bigger than pin-points, scarcely visible amid the oceans and continents? These small and medium states in the East owed their immediate origin to the war against Germany and the Peace of Versailles had expressly thrust them into the flank of Germany like thorns. But left to themselves, Poland and Czechoslovakia clung rather helplessly to the feet of the German giant, who was slowly awakening from the paralysis of defeat and beginning to move again. At the same time a new life was beginning to stir menacingly in the outwardly still mightier giant of the East, the Soviet Union.

In 1920, Polish armies had advanced as far as Kiev in the Ukraine, were driven back to Warsaw and then advanced again. Pressed by the same enemies, defeated Germany and torn Russia had approached one another and finally concluded their treaty of Rapallo; Wladimir Maiakovsky, the poet laureate of the Soviet Union, had dreamed of the day when the German and the Russian proletarian would grasp each other's hand and Poland 'will be nothing but the little drop of sweat that remains when strong men shake hands.'

In the West the French military still had the German giant firmly by the throat. As long as Marshal Foch's army, then the first in the world, was deep in Germany, the German might was paralyzed; and the political leadership of Poland as of Czechoslovakia had founded the welfare of their states upon Germany's paralysis and weakness, upon the strength and help of France.

But was France strong? She herself constantly appealed to England's aid; in her fear she had even contented herself with the highly ambiguous promises of Locarno. Could this power, herself needful of help, be expected to help others? The truth which shines through the fragile psychology of all these alliances was this: France by no means counted on giving aid, but wanted to receive aid from others; the others, however, made exactly the same calculation, but the other way around. Each wanted help, but none wanted to help — this was fully proved when a serious situation arose.

This self-deceptive playing with the danger again took the form of solemn promises at Locarno. France promised. Again she guaranteed the security of her allies in the East; and precisely because the import of the entire Locarno system was that France should no longer guarantee the security of the small states in the East. This at least was England's wish. She expressly withheld support from the renewed promises of France. But France, nevertheless, promised aid to Poland as well as Czechoslovakia, if necessary without the agreement of the League of Nations.

And Germany? She had recognized her western frontier in the expression 'the maintenance of the territorial *status quo*'; but in the

Treaty of Locarno there is no corresponding phrase which refers to the East, and this missing phrase one day would prove as fateful to Poland as the other seven words seemed comforting for France. Germany finally renounced Alsace-Lorraine, but she did not renounce the Polish Corridor or Upper Silesia — limiting all her promises to the assurance that anyway she would not use force.

England had not demanded that she renounce these things. Even at Versailles, England had fought against the establishment of Poland, against her excessive territory, against the Polish Corridor, and against giving Upper Silesia to Poland. Lloyd George had contemptuously called Poland 'a state for a season.' He had been defeated by Woodrow Wilson and Clemenceau; but English statesmen had not ceased to regard Poland as a hotbed, a useless source of dangers and wars, a disturber of the peace which only lured Germany to ally herself with Soviet Russia. Too weak even as a protective wall against Russian Bolshevism, Poland by her provocative geographic situation prevented Germany from adopting a clear anti-Russian and hence anti-Communist policy; by her very existence she represented a constant menace of future war and was not worth it — this roughly describes the English attitude toward Poland.

And what if Germany or Russia or both should attack Poland? French aid was promised. Yes, but in this way France robbed herself of English support and would have to attend to Germany alone. For England promised her support to the French in Locarno only if France were first attacked by Germany; but if the French came to the help of the Poles, it would be the French themselves who attacked Germany. Then, according to the letter of the treaty, Germany could even appeal to English aid. But what counted even more than the wording of the treaty was its purpose and this was clear: England wanted to protect neither Poland nor Czechoslovakia; to the best of her ability, she would also prevent France from helping them.

Poland herself had the feeling that despite all the fine promises of France she had been sacrificed at Locarno. In the Warsaw parliament, sharp words fell. After the Treaty of Locarno, Poland began to move away from democracy, first in domestic, then in foreign politics. Seven months after Locarno, Joseph Pilsudski, Marshal of Poland and national hero, overthrew the rule of the democratic parties. Like Mussolini in his beginnings, Pilsudski continued to rule formally with parliament; formally he was most of the time only Minister of War; actually he was dictator, expanding his power from year to year. A piece of the modern world began to die in Poland — as in so many other countries: the world of national democracy, the epoch of the liberal national uprising. An ideal was extinguished which had shone for a century: the association of national freedom with the immortal human rights of the American and French revolutions. The political leaders who had brought the Polish state to life with the help of French and American democracy vanished, some in exile, some in prison, a few by murder. Henceforth the army ruled. 'Army,' here as always, means a circle of officers; it has been called a régime of 'colonels' — in victorious, expanding Poland it was the same human type which in Germany was embodied by retired or active captains and majors. In Germany after the World War the army had disintegrated into an armed party of freebooters; in Poland it had arisen in the war out of an armed party of freebooters. In Germany the officers had become politicians; in Poland, the politicians had become officers; Pilsudski, the marshal and hero of this troop, did not start out as a military man, but as a Socialist agitator — in one word: in 1926 armed bohemia had come to power in Poland.

In spite of its limitations and shortcomings Locarno was a remarkable success for Stresemann's foreign policy; another step on Germany's way back to the rank of a great power; it prepared her entry into the League of Nations. Meanwhile, Hitler's business — not a very thankful one — was to convince the masses that they were doing badly while actually they were getting along fairly well: 'That the development is downward in a straight line,' was no very impressive prophecy at a moment when the speaker himself had to admit that 'business is temporarily reviving.' Again, as in the early days of 1923, he flayed the 'spineless masses eaten with decay'; their rule, the rule of the majority, he declared, 'could only open the door to stupidity and cowardice; it must lead with mathematical certainty to the dissolution of the entire foundation of our force and strength.'

And then the hardest blow fell: the 'decay' went so far as to hoist the national banner.

In spring, 1925, Friedrich Ebert, the Social Democratic President of Germany, died. As candidates for his successor the parties of the Right put forward Paul von Beneckendorff and Hindenburg, the old field marshal, the supposed general-in-chief in the World War. This living monument of the 'heroic lie' had for some time after the war acted as a shield and a tool for stronger schemers — not without finding its own advantage in it. After the German Army had gone astray in the last days of 1918, a group of generals and other officers had wandered through Germany, settled first in the western German city of Kassel, then in Kolberg on the Baltic. This wandering band of officers was the German General Staff, hence the soul of the army and in those days for all intents and purposes the army itself. Everywhere they dragged their venerable field marshal with them like a totem; it was then that Kurt von Schleicher had his idea of the 'Free Corps.' In June, 1919, when President Ebert telephoned Hindenburg to inquire whether he, the responsible leader of the largely disbanded army, considered resistance against the hard peace terms of Versailles to be possible, the marshal silently left the room, pretending a physical need, and his chief of staff, Groener, had to tell Ebert that resistance was hopeless; afterward Hindenburg came back into the room and said to Groener: 'Now you have taken this responsibility, too, upon yourself.' When the war seemed lost in the military sense, Hindenburg, on Ludendorff's advice, had hastily requested an armistice because he did not know whether the front could still hold another day; a year and a half later, Hindenburg, evidently instructed by others, launched the slogan that the German front had been 'knifed from behind' by treason. Running for President, he let his election propaganda men promise that he would restore the fortunes destroyed by inflation; afterward there was no further mention of this.

Why Hindenburg? Because he was a general, because he represented the army, the war, or the Kaiser? Very few people in Germany would have tolerated the Kaiser or even one of his sons. Very few voted for Ludendorff, the real World War chief, when he ran in the first elections. Essentially Hindenburg was elected precisely because he had not been chief in the lost war and because he had not staked life and death on his Kaiser. When Hitler crawled like an invisible insect about the feet of the gigantic artificial figure and cried, unheard, that Hindenburg should be elected because 'in him our people's will for liberty is coupled with the righteousness and honesty of the greatest models in our history,' the masses instinctively knew better. They sensed that this square mustached face with its cold eyes represented much more the mediocrity than the greatness of German history; they knew almost with certainty that the warrior's brain they had admired was not behind it; that the first great victories were not Hindenburg's accomplishment; but also they knew that he had not been to blame for the last defeats. He had sworn an oath to the Kaiser, but then served the republic; the legend of loyalty that clung to him was based only on the fact that he remained stolid and untouched as a block of concrete while everyone around him fell or fled.

In 1925, when he was elected President, a new segment of history began for the German Army. But in the sentiment of the German voter it was not militarism that triumphed, but bourgeoisism, law and order. It was basically the same bourgeois need of security that in England brought Stanley Baldwin, in France Raymond Poincaré, to the helm, and that throve in the United States under Calvin Coolidge; this same spirit favored Mussolini in Italy, Pilsudski in Poland, and General Primo de Rivera, then dictator of Spain. All the same it was a minority that elected Hindenburg. He got 14,600,-000 votes; his democratic opponent, 13,700,000; the candidate of the Communists about 2,000,000; Hindenburg would have been defeated if these two million had not been diverted from the democratic bloc. But for the Communists, democracy remained the main enemy; and above all the democratic party of the workers, the Social Democracy.

It was a prosperous time. Germany was making a mighty domestic effort, overhauling her whole industry from top to bottom. The Germans studied American production methods, introduced the conveyor belt, thus appreciably increasing their productive power. The German chemical industry, which had always been especially efficient, had already, during the World War, produced large quantities of nitrogen by a newly discovered process; now a way was found to transform coal into gasoline; methods were studied for manufacturing artificial rubber, for making textiles out of plant fibers and a metal substitute out of milk. Steel production, which in 1920 had amounted to 8,500,000 tons, rose in 1927 to 16,300,000; iron production in the same period rose from 6,300,000 to 13,100,000 tons; in the same period English steel production remained static at 9,000,000 tons, that of iron actually fell from 8,000,000 to 7,200,000 tons.

In the years from 1924 to 1928 German industry was rebuilt with much energy and genius. That remarkable machine was created from which post-republican Germany was able to draw so much military strength. The rest of the world helped with large loans; certainly not from altruism, but because Germany paid abnormally high interest; German municipal loans, some of which were floated in foreign markets, paid as high as eight per cent. At all events, Germany was in large part restored through foreign capital. At the end of 1927, Germany's long-term indebtedness again mounted to 5,500,000,000 marks, and the short-term foreign indebtedness was not much lower. But in 'reparations' she had to pay an annual sum which in 1928 rose to 2,500,000,000 marks and was expected to go on indefinitely. It was an interesting circle: American money poured into Germany, Germany paid reparations, chiefly to France, but also to England; France and England paid their war debts to America.

'Credulous optimism has befogged hundreds of thousands, in fact, millions of our people,' cried Hitler, rather desperately. He said this in August, 1927, in Nuremberg to twenty thousand supporters — the most he could gather in one place at that time. This, to be sure, was five times as many as in February, 1925; nevertheless, this first of the so-called 'Nuremberg Party Days' offered no sign of strength. He, therefore, devoted much time to ridiculing the 'army of optimists,' who speak of German successes and 'build on the future with a light-mindedness that is positively indecent.' He admitted that the sight of the discontented National Socialists 'may seem strange and unbelievable to the army of optimists.' And he wanted to seem strange to this confident, German crowd; like

Röhm at an earlier day, he said contemptuously: 'What we face today is Marxist masses of humanity, not German people' — the twenty thousand, according to report, 'applauded loudly.'

And yet there was no reason to despair. He only had to look beyond the border; there he, as well as everybody, could see what was coming for Germany. For even before the world knew the name of Hitler, dictatorship covered a larger area than democracy on the map of Europe. In 1926, the dictatorship of a party apparatus ruled in Russia and was moving rapidly toward the dictatorship of a single man; Lithuania and Poland were governed by dictatorships; it was a matter of taste whether to call the systems prevailing in Hungary, Yugoslavia, Bulgaria, and Greece oligarchy or dictatorship — it certainly was not democracy; a dictator modernized Turkey; a dictator held Spain in questionable peace and order; the darling and white-haired boy among all these dictators ruled clamorously over Italy, admired and publicly praised even by the democrats of other countries, by Sir Austen Chamberlain and Winston Churchill.

This was the state of affairs eight years after the war which had been fought to make the world safe for democracy. But in the mid-twenties the leading men of all democracies saw the most important problem in making the world safe for construction, economy, and capital; and for this greater stability of political conditions, a mild or even drastic restriction of democracy often seemed expedient, at times indispensable. The economic leaders who took the leadership from the politicians were no democratic doctrinaires, especially where internal conditions in foreign countries were involved.

In those years Alfred Rosenberg liked to show in the *Völkischer Beobachter* that Mussolini was dependent on Jewish finance capital, particularly the Jewish finance capital of America — he believed that American banking was in Jewish hands. Julius Streicher called the Italian dictator simply a Jewish hireling, apparently expressing Hitler's thought. It is certain that international finance in that period and for a long time to come was overwhelmingly friendly to dictatorship. But what probably most of the present and future dictators really thought was expressed by Rosenberg as early as 1927 at the first Party Day in Nuremberg: 'The gold currency of the Jewish world state must be overthrown. This would be the strongest blow against Wall Street which would then have waged the World War for nothing.' Against Wall Street and against Bolshevism, intrinsically the same thing — with somewhat modified terminology Rosenberg repeated what Houston Stewart Chamberlain had written to Wilhelm II at the beginning of the century: that Germany must defend herself 'against drowning in the waves of a Yankified Anglo-Saxondom and a Tartarized Slavdom.' And as he had learned it from Chamberlain, Rosenberg passed it on to the S.A. men in Nuremberg: 'In the treasure vaults of Wall Street lies the blood of twelve million men of the white race coined into gold. There is no freedom for Europe before this world state and its financial power are broken for good.'

Chapter XII

'FEW FLAMES BURN

IN GERMANY'

IN THESE SOFT YEARS, EVEN HITLER SUCCUMBED TO the temptations of the age. In public he remained the prophet of doom; but in his private life he could not help enjoying the blessings of what seemed to be a time of peace and ease.

He lived in a little house on the 'Obersalzberg,' above the market village of Berchtesgaden; to some extent a hide-out from which he could escape at any time into near-by Austria if the German police should again be on his heels. Since his Vienna days he had feared the police like any tramp. He now strove passionately for what Nature had denied him: an orderly domestic life. If he publicly swore that he meant to observe the laws strictly, he meant it more seriously than friend or foe suspected. At the Feldherrn Halle, he had learned his lesson. The restless spirit still hungered for power, but the unassuming mortal had a need for peace and quiet. He wanted to achieve power in a quiet way, without risk or personal danger. He no longer wanted to fight and play for high stakes; he wanted to 'grow organically and with mathematical certainty' into power — even if it took ten years! 'Perhaps we are only forerunners,' he sometimes said comfortably. 'Twenty or even a hundred years may pass before the National Socialist idea is victorious; those who believe in the ideal today may die: what is a man in the development of a people, of mankind?'

He wanted to live in orderly, legal circumstances. With Franz Gürtner, the Minister of Justice, his eternal protector, he devised a trick to obtain permission to speak again in public. Hitler solemnly declared to the Bavarian government that he would never again make a *putsch*. How many times had he promised this? But this time he was serious and honest. Gürtner put his permission to speak through the Bavarian cabinet in 1926, while in Prussia the Social Democratic government did not allow him to appear in public until 1929, with the result that — on Prussian territory — he could speak only under the not very iron fist of the French occupation authorities in the Rhineland, who probably thought that an opponent of the Berlin government in any case had to be treated nicely. .

Furthermore, Hitler wanted to become a German citizen and not have to tremble forever at the thought of deportation. Although he had publicly sworn that he would never beg for a citizenship that should have been his for his deeds on the battlefield, he let his friend, Wilhelm Frick, the former deputy of the police president, make secret inquiries with the Bavarian government in 1929. But this was too much even for Gürtner's influence. The Bavarian government coldly refused.

Hitler now established a kind of family. It was not he himself who rented the mountain villa of 'Wachenfeld' on the Obersalzberg, but his half-sister, Angela Raubal. The half-buried, strange family history began to revive. For twelve years his people had heard nothing of him. In 1922, on a visit to Austria he had seen his sisters again. Angela was widowed. Now in 1925, she came to Berchtesgaden, rented the villa, and kept house for her brother. With her came her seventeen-year-old daughter, also named Angela; a pretty, almost too blooming creature, with an immense crown of blond hair, a beauty inclining even then to the stately side, cheerful and apparently unneurotic.

And so he dwelt in his border hide-out, still half a fugitive from the police; always in fear of the unknown murderer in the big cities. When he appeared in Munich, he moved through the streets armed with a heavy dog whip, always prepared to strike. But what tormented him most was fear of material poverty. The question of his personal existence occupied him far more than before. Though in other things he still understood nothing about money, he had at least learned that it meant independence. And in those years on the magic mountain it dawned on him, a man in his late thirties, that private life could also have its glamour. With Angela, his niece, Geli for short, he rode through the countryside from time to time, showing the blond child how 'Uncle Alf' could bewitch the masses and scare his lieutenants out of their wits; he commanded and raged before her eyes, he was kind or grim, and felt as happy as a romantic tribune of the people in a bad play.

The lieutenants, most of whom led frugal lives, were irritated; most of all, they resented his money-making. In 1926 he told *Gauleiter* Munder in Württemberg that Mussolini had invited him to call on him in Italy. 'Go at once!' was Munder's advice. 'No,' was the Führer's answer; 'to impress Mussolini I would have to arrive with at least three automobiles — I just haven't got them yet.' There was always ample pomp around him, and it was one of his master accomplishments that he was able to conceal his own comfortable person in a gray legend of frugality and even asceticism. On the lieutenants, of course, he could put nothing over. They openly accused him of drawing too much money from the party. This was at a provincial Party Day in Stuttgart in 1925. What, he — he drew too much money? Could anyone deny that he never took a penny of the thousands of marks that his big meetings brought in? True, this money actually went to the party, but not to the *gaus;* inexorably it went to the central office in Munich where Hitler's party treasurer, Franz Xaver Schwarz, took it from the *gauleiters* with an iron fist.

But Hitler himself had another way of earning money; he wrote newspaper articles which, in the opinion of everyone excepting himself, were among the worst products of German journalism, and could not be compared to his speeches — precisely because they were essentially speeches written down. And for these articles he demanded gigantic fees of the party's miserable provincial dailies and weeklies. 'Yes, indeed,' he said when called to account, 'I accept payment for these articles and good payment; after all, I am not the employee of our enterprise, I am its founder and leader.' This, too, for Munder's benefit, but the discontented *gauleiter* refused to be gagged. He ventured to hint that it might be better if Hitler were not always accompanied by the blond creature who did not fit into the modest social circumstances of the National Socialist province. This was too much for Hitler. Were they going to forbid him his private life? Was Munder drawing an innocent young girl into the debate? Attacking a defenseless woman? If this *gauleiter* was such a petty bourgeois, he was useless; with fine morals and family feeling you do not build up a National Socialist movement. The quarrel went on for years; finally Munder was dismissed (1928).

The beauty of life, independence, money! That was the deepest reason why Hitler sat on his magic mountain, left the party more or less to its vicissitudes, and piled up the pages of a thick manuscript. In 1922, he had sat down to write a work to be entitled *A Reckoning*. What he meant was a reckoning with his own friends, the lukewarm and the three-quarters warm, the apparent allies and bitter rivals. Dietrich Eckart had already written a book about him. It was called *Bolshevism from Moses to Lenin;* Hitler, introduced as a speaker, explains how Judah tried to conquer the world; first with the help of the Ten Commandments; then (this was only hinted rather shamefacedly) by Christianity; finally through Marxism and Bolshevism; for Hitler and Eckart had no doubt that Lenin was a Jew. Then Gottfried Feder, the 'breaker of interest-slavery,' had written a book about the party aims and arrogated to himself the right to proclaim and interpret the basic doctrine of National Socialism as the highest intellectual arbiter; he had not even bothered himself about the sacred party program of the twenty-five points, but based his book on a draft program which he himself had written in the old days. He had declared the diabolical omnipotence of banking capital, Judah's world domination through loan interest, to be the key to world history. Alfred Rosenberg, embittered over so much dry economics, had thereupon himself written a book about the aims of the party, holding strictly to the twenty-five points; following his teacher Chamberlain, he laid far more emphasis on race in world history, the inequality of human types, the superiority of the Germanic. But in one thing the rivals had been tacitly agreed: there must be an intellectual authority which would definitely fix the party's aims; and Hitler, the great orator and strategist, was not this intellectual authority.

Thus he, too, had to write something and that was how he began his book, *A Reckoning*. The underlying thought of the first chapter arose unconsciously and characteristically: Hitler described his own youth. He saw it as a hard struggle for self-assertion and self-education. In his account he became a symbol of the socially and politically oppressed German masses; he himself was a victim of German fragmentation, a victim of the racial conquest of Germany by inferior peoples, particularly the Jews. In his person he had borne Germany's suffering — as he saw it. A metaphysical line runs through the book, not always easy to find amid all the vulgar vilification and barren, long-winded meditations; here a man seeks for God and discovers himself. This is exactly what had happened to Soloviev's Antichrist; he too, like Hitler, had written in his thirty-third year, a book in which he claimed to be the Savior.

For the book tried to give an answer to the question of the meaning of life, and that is its significance; this is far more important than the particular political remarks, which for the most part have been taken too seriously. The actual content of the confused book is that young Hitler thanked God on his knees for the World War; that he declared success to be the highest criterion of right and wrong; that he regarded the pitiless extermination of the weak as the premise of all culture; that he demanded the immersion of the individual in the nation; and that finally the nation, in turn, like a thinning mist, is sucked up by the radiance of the individual genius shining over all things.

He wrote a good part of the work in the fortress of Landsberg, dictating it at first to his friend, Emil Maurice, later to Rudolf Hess. Hess did more than take dictation. He was then twenty-seven, a man of flawless manners. His admiration for Hitler filled his whole person and, like an expert secretary, he tried to make everything as easy as possible for the author; when Hitler's flow of thoughts clogged or his store of knowledge was wanting, Hess was rich in helpful suggestions. Having enjoyed a fair academic education, Hess had a mature contempt for bloated school learning; he found it right and proper that his leader — who far surpassed him in sheer intelligence — had not stuffed his own head too full; he also found it right and proper that Hitler should avail himself of his friend's knowledge where it suited him and leave it unused where it did not suit him.

At Munich University there was then a former German general who, before the World War, had spent some time in Tokyo on a diplomatic mission; he had become a professor and lectured on a new science which he called geo-politics. This professor and retired general, Karl Haushofer, was the teacher and friend of Rudolf Hess; he was an occasional guest at Landsberg, and Hitler and Hess were certainly stimulated by their conversations with him; Hitler's 'space as a factor of power,' is Haushofer's expression. But this does not mean that Haushofer was 'Hitler's guiding brain' as he has sometimes been called. The essential parts of the book do not deal with foreign policy or military geography, but with race, political education, the building of a spiritual force at home. Hitler always insisted on the predominance of domestic politics over foreign policy; holding that the former determined the latter.

Hence far too much has been read into the so-called foreign policy chapters of the book. No statesman is in a position to indicate ten years in advance what he is going to do later; on the pathless fields of politics one cannot proceed by schedule like an engineer. The whole work is essentially a loud argument with the author's closest friends and associates, with the moderate nationalist parties, the so-called bourgeoisie, and with his own party friends, Feder, Röhm, Gregor Strasser.

Hitler's strongest hold on his party in these times was the owner-ship of the party's paper, the *Völkischer Beobachter*. But the paper did not make money. Max Amann, in a practical sense the most important of his collaborators, was now business manager of the *Völkischer Beobachter*, paid his editorial workers starvation wages, gave them prodigious amounts of work to do, and had furious arguments with Alfred Rosenberg. The two threw scissors and inkwells at each other's head. The paper must be sensational, Amann demanded; it must politically educate our members, said Rosenberg, whom God had not created to be a newspaperman. 'I spit on the members; business comes first,' Amann cried back; and he said the same thing to his leader, Hitler. Now and then Hitler, sick of working and eager for companionship, would appear in Munich; he would rage through the shabby party office above the *Beobachter's* printshop, keeping the employees away from their work with endless speeches. Max Amann, none too respectfully, would drive him back to Berchtesgaden, for 'the book has to come out in the fall, or else the booksellers will cancel their orders.'

And so here he was back in Berchtesgaden, writing, or dictating at the typewriter either to Hess, or to his niece, Geli. Of course, it was impossible that the book should be what Amann wanted: a history of the unsuccessful *putsch* of 1923. Hitler lacked the narrative gift to tell the story; but even if he had wanted to, he could not have spoken openly for fear of the Bavarian government and even more of the Reichswehr. Thus the book contained no sensational revelations. Publisher and public were both disappointed; but to Hitler even less than to most men was it given to speak of himself with critical honesty.

In course of writing, the book had grown beyond the original plan of the 'reckoning.' Hitler next wanted to call it 'Four and a Half Years of Struggle Against Lies, Stupidity, and Cowardice.' From this ponderous phrase Amann gleaned a short, striking title: *Mein Kampf* ('My Struggle').

The first volume was published in June, 1925. It cost twelve marks (approximately three dollars), double the normal German book price. Amann claimed to have sold twenty-three thousand copies in the first year, but this is an extremely doubtful boast. Even Hitler's best friends said: Yes, he is an amazing speaker, probably a great leader, perhaps even a political genius — but it's a pity that he had to write this stupid book. *Mein Kampf* does not effectively argue Hitler's cause, because the author does not dare to express his innermost thought: that he himself is the greatest figure in history. The keynote of the book is the noisy style which signifies: Be silent, you others, I alone am right; disappear, I am the only one who matters. Trifles are said two or three times, adjectives preferably doubled. A man is 'honorable *and* upright,' an outlook is 'national *and* patriotic.' In the first edition the first volume is written almost in dialect, and the spelling is by no means above reproach. Endless heaps of substantives are intended to cover over the jargon of the Vienna lodging-house. Hitler uses few verbs, for he seldom says what happens; he always tries to create an image with his own luminous figure striding through columns of majestic substantives. He has enriched the German language with a dozen of the most hideous foreign words (hideous especially because they are not really at home in any language of the world). But even this terrifying style is not his own creation; it is borrowed from Richard Wagner's prose writings; both authors take to elaborate bombast because they fear to betray or commit themselves by a simple word. The author speaks even when he thinks nothing at all; one of the most priceless examples of empty babbling is the beginning of the tenth chapter of the first volume. In the whole book hardly a single actual fact is related tangibly and credibly. Houston Stewart Chamberlain had once said: 'The frivolity with which such an artist-spirit treats facts is inspired in him by the certainty that he will penetrate to a higher truth regardless from what premises he starts; therefore he takes the best that he can assimilate.' With Richard Wagner in mind, Chamberlain foreshadowed a whole school which falsifies facts and calls the result higher truth.

Mein Kampf did little to establish Hitler's intellectual authority in his party; in fact the party sailed along almost rudderless during nineteen-twenty-five and twenty-six. The Führer wrote his book, worked for his newspapers, issued leading articles, occasionally spoke at meetings; but in these years another man grew to be the real leader: Gregor Strasser. He was the ideal type of armed intellectual; a former wartime officer, though no professional soldier, but an enthusiast, almost a gourmet in matters of civil war; at the same time an idealist. He owned a drugstore in Landshut, Bavaria, which he sold in 1924 to devote himself entirely to the business of National Socialist leadership; his aim was to push Hitler aside and replace him. A big, heavy man; in contrast to Hitler, an unusually monolithic type, in whom everything, gestures as well as voice, was energetic; he was ponderously loyal to his plans once they were formed, while Hitler was devious and unstable; insensitive to light winds, unable to foresee storms. For a time borne high by the wave, he missed the moment for the leap which might have assured him a place in history. Like Hitler in his early years, he was inspired by an almost boyish pleasure in political activity and work among the masses. Lacking Hitler's oratorical gift, he possessed something just as rare: the power to move an audience by his very personality. His career provides one more example of the trifles which sometimes determine historical destiny. As deputy in the German Reichstag, Strasser enjoyed parliamentary immunity and free travel on the German railways. In contrast to Hitler he could travel for nothing and insult people with impunity. It was a big thing to be able to call your opponent a traitor to the nation and a thief in the bargain — and to do so, today here, tomorrow more than six hundred miles away, without a penny's traveling expenses — and without fear of the courts. At that time the radio was virtually unavailable for political speeches, since in Germany it belonged exclusively to the state. Free travel and free slander — Strasser had a big headstart over his Führer.

This bon vivant, a lover of struggle and of girls, alcohol, cards and sports as well, now reached for the leadership of the party; he founded so-called 'party *gaus*,' that is provincial groups, had *gauleiters* elected who, he hoped, would be personally devoted to him, and worked out a program which he intended to force on the party. He had a helper in a volatile young man, little suited to the clique of freebooters, but fitting in perfectly with the bohemians. It is hard to classify this young man, for he was actually nothing — not even a former lieutenant or ensign, not even a corporal. Nature had given him a crippled foot; though seventeen at the outbreak of the World War, he had not been taken into the army. He had studied literature and philosophy at six universities, had lived on a scholarship from the Catholic 'Albertus Magnus Society,' and had later written film scripts which were never accepted; he had offered a 'culture-Bolshevistic' publishing house in Berlin a novel which had been rejected; according to his own story, he had secretly fought the army of occupation in his native Rhenish city during the Ruhr War — but most of his later comrades did not believe this. Now, despite his six universities, he was nothing at all; that is, he was an 'editor' of a National Socialist weekly. His name was Paul Joseph Goebbels.

A second aide of Strasser's was his brother Otto; better educated, less a man of action and speech, more of a writer; if possible, more ambitious and conscious of his aim than Gregor, whom he drove on.

The Strassers and Goebbels now founded a Strasser party in the Hitler party. Its program was anti-capitalistic, even nihilistic. Germany must be built up in a socialist 'corporate form'; everything opposed to this goal would be shattered in a great cataclysm; and it was the aim of the National Socialists to hasten this cataclysm. What Gregor Strasser meant by the cataclysm was an alliance of Germany with Bolshevik Russia, with Gandhi's rebellious India, with the anti-British Soviet-supported revolutionary movement of China, with the Kuomintang under the leadership of Chiang Kai-shek. In short, with all the forces of destruction against democracy; with the 'young,' in part colored, peoples of the East against the declining West; with Bolshevism against capitalism; with — as Houston Stewart Chamberlain would have put it — the Tartarized Slavs against Wall Street, with world doom against Versailles.

'The class struggle, like all things, has its two sides,' said Goebbels publicly, and among friends he insisted that the National Socialist Party must above all be socialist and proletarian. He wrote an open letter to a Communist opponent, assuring him that Communism was really the same thing as National Socialism: 'You and I are fighting one another, but we are not really enemies. Our forces are split up and we never reach our goal.'

Strasser and Goebbels believed in 1925 that the party belonged to the proletariat; Hitler intended that the party should capture the proletariat and hold it in check; especially that fifty per cent of the proletariat which 'glorify theft, call high treason a duty, regard courageous defense of the fatherland as an idiocy, call religion opium for the people.' They actually are enemies within: 'Fifty per cent have no other wish but to smash the state; they consciously feel themselves to be advance guards of a foreign state' — and rightly so; for 'we must not forget that our nation is racially composed of the most varied elements; the slogan "Proletarians of all countries, unite!" is a demonstration of the will of men who do possess a certain kinship with analogous nations of a lower cultural level.'

In 1926, Hitler promised the employers — as he had in 1920: 'We stand for the maintenance of private property. . . . We shall protect free enterprise as the most expedient, or rather the sole possible, economic order.' At the same time Strasser and Goebbels wanted to put an end to the free economy. On November 22, 1925, the two of them called their North German *gauleiters* to the city of Hanover and proclaimed their program, and one of those assembled, Bernhard Rust, a school-teacher (later Minister of Education), cried out that they would take no more orders from the 'Pope' in Munich. Gottfried Feder came to supervise the meeting at Hitler's behest; Goebbels demanded the ejection of 'this idiot' from the hall. Of all the North Germans only one came out openly for Hitler: Doctor Robert Ley, the chemist from Cologne.

So far Gregor Strasser, with the help of his railroad pass, had made progress in his fight for the party leadership. Hitler countered in the same style. On February 14, 1926, he summoned the *gauleiters* to the South German city of Bamberg. Those who now came were mostly South Germans, leaders of older *gaus* who had not been personally appointed by Strasser; the journey was too long and above all too costly for the North Germans.

A great word battle ensued between Hitler and Strasser. The issues were the workers, socialism or free economy, the alliance with Soviet Russia, the concept of revolution: Shall we create chaos, or shall we 'legally' worm our way to power? We are against the old bourgeois world — in this Hitler and Strasser were agreed. But what does this mean in a serious situation? And things were getting serious. A mighty popular movement was at that time rolling through all Germany, far more powerful than National Socialism; it aimed at preventing the former German princes from retaining a good part of their so-called private property, which in some cases amounted to hundreds of millions and was private only in name, being actually state property appropriated in former times. A plebiscite was ordered; it was a popular moral uprising, and Gregor Strasser declared: As National Socialists we belong to this popular uprising. . . .

At that time Hitler received each month a sum of fifteen hundred marks from the divorced Duchess Eduard von Sachsen-Anhalt.

The noble lady had been divorced from the former ruling duke; but she still received from the large ducal estate a comparatively small allowance of two thousand marks monthly. Hitler had been able to persuade the none too intelligent woman to send him regularly three quarters of this income; he had convinced her that when he came to power he would make her a duchess again. She was not his only noble patron; the former Duke of Sachsen-Koburg-Gotha, a half Englishman, was another. Hitler was also fighting for his own money when he fought for the money of the princes. As always when nothing better occurred to him, he said: the movement against the princes was a Jewish swindle.

The entire propertied classes took the part of the princes, foremost among them the propertied Jews; rabbis publicly came out for the nobles, and the majority of the German Jews doubtless proved Goebbels right in saying that '... the Jewish question is more complicated than people think.' The plebiscite became for many a struggle for or against private property. Dr. Hjalmar Schacht, considered by many the restorer of the German currency, who owed his position as president of the Reichsbank to his membership in the Democratic Party, now made use of the excellent opportunity to resign with much noise from this party, because it had not come out energetically enough for the sanctity of the princes' property. Meanwhile, in Bamberg Hitler declared that the plebiscite was an attack of the 'subhuman' against the élite and this must be true even if — as Hitler did not hesitate to admit — quite a few of the princes were not very much 'élite.'

Suddenly Goebbels stood up and stammered with emotion: yes, he saw that he had been wrong. The Führer in his address had disclosed fundamentally new paths. He must be followed; this was no Damascus. Strasser did not follow, but his best supporter had left him; he was clearly beaten. When the session was ended, the former captain, Franz Felix Pfeffer von Salomon, at that time supreme leader of the storm troops, came up to Goebbels and said: 'Listen, I am no Socialist, but what you did today was an unspeakable betrayal of your friends!' Goebbels had gone over to the princes' money. To the two Strassers he declared, publicly and in writing, that they were 'revolutionaries of the big mouth.' He bade them 'study, and trust' the Führer. Above all, they must realize 'that he is more than you and I, that he is an instrument of the Divine Will which shapes history in the maelstrom of new creative joy.'

When Goebbels issued this statement, he was twenty-nine years old, no longer a child. Hitler had brought him to Munich, thence to Berchtesgaden. Goebbels was introduced to Hitler's 'family'; he met Hess and Rosenberg; he was unable to win Amann, who declared him to be the 'Mephisto of the party'; but he did make friends with Schwarz, the party treasurer. In Goebbels, Hitler had found a man who could listen for days to his endless speeches; the arduously cultivated fire of enthusiasm in his eyes never abated. 'A man who burns like a flame,' said Hitler to others, though the act was piled on so thick that it should not have escaped him.

Goebbels was a man who could control his nervous tension as well as Hitler, if not better. In certain externals they were similar. Both came from poor families, both had made a failure of their start in life. But Goebbels was by far the more worldly; he knew how to adapt and incline himself to circumstances amid which Hitler would simply have given up. Hitler felt a certain community of fate, and Goebbels conscientiously developed it. The younger man copied the older in manner, speech, ideas, even hobbies, partly because there was no better example of the political career, and partly because it unconsciously warmed the heart of the party leader and filled him with confidence in his young admirer. Actually Goebbels learned much from Hitler: through him he achieved full certainty that this was an era of decay in which a minority that knew what it wanted could confidently reach for the highest power, provided it found no means too evil, and shunned no lie, betrayal, or act of violence. In their Munich and Berchtesgaden conversations of February, 1926, the strange teacher must have shown a wild contagious conviction — perhaps he had never found so willing and unquestioning a disciple; this was even better than Hess.

'Dear, honored Adolf Hitler,' wrote Goebbels to his leader after these conversations, 'I have learned so much from you. In a com-

radely way you have shown me ways so fundamentally new. . . .'
Goebbels suggested to Hitler that the party needed a new 'general
staff,' of course with himself on it: 'The men are available. Just
call them. Or rather, summon them one after another just as in
your eyes they seem to deserve it. . . . Then a day may come on
which everything smashes, when the mob around you fumes and
grumbles and roars: Crucify him! Then we shall stand like iron,
and shout and sing: Hosanna!' A comparison with the Savior
was practically *de rigueur* in a letter to the party leader.

With his well-directed flattery, his affected ardor, Goebbels successfully penetrated the circle of little men among whom Hitler
felt privately at ease — all of them physically small. He also was a
dwarf; the 'scheming dwarf' as the betrayed Gregor Strasser called
him from now on. He had Jewish blood, the Strasser clique said,
and a proof of it was his club foot; for men thus 'marked' by nature
were always of mixed race. One of this circle, Erich Koch, many
years later president of East Prussia, attempted to prove this in a
newspaper article. He compared Goebbels with Talleyrand, the
club-footed French statesman who had betrayed Napoleon. Like
him, he asserted, Goebbels was a man of 'racially conditioned mental
and physical disharmony.' Among the National Socialist thugs
and murderers, Goebbels was like a boasting cripple in the stands at
a football game, loudest of all in cheering the players. Goebbels,
wrote Koch, knew how 'to dazzle, to inflate himself, to circulate
false rumors, ruthlessly to exploit the devotion of others, to squeeze
them like a lemon and throw them away, to appropriate the services
of others for himself.' He was 'an expert in the arts of slander, intrigue, and falsehood.' Assuredly this young dwarf had an uncanny
knowledge of the weaknesses of humanity and knew how to exploit
them, because he knew better than other men what weakness is.
'Men like him,' Koch concluded, were 'intelligent but boundlessly
ambitious and unfeeling egoists, who up to now have done nothing
but harm to the people.'

Essentially Koch's criticism applied just as well to Hitler himself;
for in Hitler's self-pitying nature there is something of the dwarfish-
ness characteristic of Goebbels. True that Goebbels coldly copied his
Führer, learning his tricks of public speaking, poster-writing, theat-

rically staged meetings, intentional tardiness, rehearsed choruses of storm troops. But the basis of what he learned was inherent in both men: an intelligence cultivated to avenge their physical handicap against the normal world. There stood Goebbels on the speaker's platform, wearing a gray suit resembling a worn uniform; the audience looked at the club foot and thought with emotion: look, a brave soldier from the World War, torn by enemy bullets.

In Goebbels's break with Strasser, Hitler had smashed a dangerous party clique and gone a good way toward cementing his domination of the movement. Now he assembled the Munich members of his party in May, 1926, and had them vote a by-law which was intended to break the Strasser Party in the North for good. According to this by-law the actual 'bearer' of the movement was henceforth only the 'National Socialist German Workers' Association' in Munich. Only this small Munich group had any say in the party. It chose its own leadership which was at the same time the leadership of the whole party. The German association laws made it necessary to have the chairman formally elected by the members; but this was a pure formality as Hitler stated amid general merriment. The first chairman appointed or dismissed all the other important party leaders at his pleasure; above all, he henceforth had the right to appoint or dismiss the *gauleiters*. From now on 'nothing is done in the movement without my knowledge and approval. Nay, more: nothing is done without my desire.'

To prevent any schoolmaster or editor in the North from again creating disorder on pretext that the party program was not good enough, it was decided in Munich that the program of twenty-five points — about which Hitler had long ceased to concern himself — was immutable.

Thus, step by step, the party became Hitler's property. This tenacious but ultimately successful struggle is reflected in the genesis of *Mein Kampf*. In 1926, Hitler completed the second volume. The manuscript of this second volume and the printed edition of the first were again carefully read by Josef Czerny, the man who three years previous had accompanied Hitler to Bayreuth. He studied the text for grammatical mistakes, smoothed out the worst of them, corrected the spelling, introduced page-headings. A basic change was made only in one point. Concerning the party structure Hitler had written in the first edition: 'The first chairman of a local group is elected, but then he becomes its responsible leader. . . . The same principle applies to the next higher organization, the district, county or *gau*. The first chairman is always elected, but then vested with unlimited power and authority. And the same, finally, applies to the leadership of the party as a whole. The chairman is elected, but then he is exclusive leader of the movement.'

But in the following edition the passage runs: 'The first chairman of a local group is appointed by the next higher leader, he is the responsible leader of a local group. . . . The same principle applies to the next higher organization, the district, county or *gau*. The leader is always appointed from above and at the same time vested with unlimited power and authority. Only the leader of the whole party, because of the association laws, is elected in a general membership meeting. But then he is exclusive leader of the movement.'

And thus, after seven years of existence, the National Socialist Party ceased to be a democratic party. Its founders had preached and practiced violence, intolerance, and hatred; but they had not desired to bow to a dictator. Their program had declared that the future Germany must be governed by a central 'parliament.' The strongest personalities had withdrawn from the movement, unwilling to recognize Hitler's dictatorship (Ludendorff, Röhm); others had openly rebelled against this dictatorship (Strasser, Goebbels), or accepted it with embittered silence (Rosenberg, Feder). On purpose Hitler had sowed hostility among his followers and now finally harvested power.

But he had not harvested money. One of the best providers, despite princes and princesses, still remained Streicher in Nuremberg with his large following and sometimes more than murky sources. Streicher boasted that one of his most reliable contributors was a wealthy party comrade whose wife was his, Streicher's, mistress. But then young Hermann Esser, a great lady's man, claimed that he, in his own personal way, had found a more direct access to this wealth, and that he had done so with the full knowledge of Hitler. A bitter feud ensued between Streicher and Esser, formerly close pals. Hitler, extremely embarrassed by Esser's revelations, took Streicher's side and forbade Esser to call him *Du* in the future. But to silence the dangerous fellow he had to make him editor of the party's new illustrated paper, which had just been founded by Max Amann and Heinrich Hoffmann, the photographer. These two businesslike dwarfs bet their shirts on the future of the movement, for it was clear that only a large following could make the paper profitable. Hitler for a long time made his living from this magazine, which first appeared monthly, then bi-weekly, finally weekly; to every issue he contributed an editorial which, in this by no means amusing sheet, was certainly the dullest spot.

Goebbels, too, obtained his thirty pieces of silver for his betrayal of Strasser. In 1926, Hitler appointed him *gauleiter* for Berlin, 'responsible to me alone.' It was no sinecure. A certain Kurt Daluege had been S.A. leader in Berlin up to this time and had maintained his authority by having recalcitrant storm troopers beaten up at night by a so-called 'rolling commando.' In his indignation Strasser had thrown a few of the thugs out of the party, but the party members did not obey and took the expelled men back in defiance of Strasser. Strasser declared that the leader of the expelled men, a certain Heinz alias Hauenstein, was a police spy — the National Socialists knew what to expect of one another. Despite everything, Hauenstein remained in the party. Hitler in despair disbanded the whole Berlin organization, suspended Daluege indefinitely, and told Goebbels to start out from scratch in God's name.

At the same time Erich Koch accused *Gauleiter* Karl Kaufmann in Essen of embezzling party funds; an examining commission confirmed the accusation and furthermore found Kaufmann guilty of committing adultery with the wife of a party comrade; of untruthfully boasting that he had fought at the front in the war; of having worn medals that had never been conferred on him; of 'twice breaking his word of honor. . . .'

How could it have been otherwise? These were the most depraved elements remaining of the old murderers' army. They called themselves fighters for truth and enlightenment; actually they even concealed their own names. The S.A., for instance, denied that they were a 'storm section' (*Sturm Abteilung*), pretending to be merely a 'security section' (*Sicherheits Abteilung*); the initials S.A. stood for both. They boasted of their old Prussian discipline, but disobeyed their leader to his face. Edmund Heines, a choice example of the armed bohemian and political murderer, was the leader of these malcontents in Munich; and, what really made him dangerous, led them in the name of Röhm, who stood aside. Heines was a born ruffian, tall and broad as a barn door, yet as agile as a greyhound; his mighty form was graced by a repulsively girlish face. He would sit with Röhm and other friends in the Bratwurst-glöckl, a tavern in the inner city; the host, a certain Zentner, also an S.A. man, was one of the group. They accused Hitler of letting the S.A. go to ruin, not training it in sufficiently military style, giving the soldiers in it unworthy jobs to do. With a heavy heart, Hitler had to intervene — with a heavy heart, because he regretted the loss of a single man; but his personal authority came first. At the end of May, 1927, he called the Munich S.A. together in the 'Hirsch-bräu-Keller' beer hall; the public was strictly excluded. Hitler shouted at the crushed assemblage: 'The clique from the Brat-wurstglöckl are all fairies: Heines, Röhm, Zentner, and the rest. Am I expected to take accusations from such people!'

A serious matter, worse than a scandal. The perversion was widespread in the secret murderers' army of the post-war period, and its devotees denied that it was a perversion. They were proud, regarded themselves as 'different from the others,' meaning better. They boasted about their superiority in more or less the same terms which Plato had coined in his *Banquet*:

> They [the homosexuals] are the best among the boys and young men because they are the most valiant of them. This is strikingly demonstrated by the fact that, after growing up, they — and they alone — are fit for ruling the state.

Röhm said that the misfortune of the present age was domination by women; he praised the epochs that had been dominated by figures like Alexander the Great, Caesar, Charles XII of Sweden, Prince Eugene of Savoy, and Frederick the Great — five great warriors and five homosexuals. Alfred Bäumler, the National Socialist philosopher, whom his comrades in 1933 at once made a professor at the University of Berlin, wrote a whole book about the 'heroic young man': 'Everywhere the relation between man and man is degenerating,' he lamented . . . 'there is no place where man stands beside man, where men come together, the young with the young or the young with their elders, for no other purpose than because it must be so . . . The modern world is a world without friendship . . .' With the pervert's arrogance, he went on: 'The contest for a woman has the peculiarity that both contestants are always defeated, for the victor like the vanquished loses his time. Weak natures . . . are ruined in erotic relationships . . .' And then he gave expression to the idea whereon this whole group based their special pride: 'The friendship relation has a connection with the state, the erotic relation has not . . . Because the German is essentially a warlike nature, because he is a man, because he is born for friendship — democracy, which, in its ultimate consequence, leads to the right of women to judge over men, can never thrive in Germany.'

Here we intend no moral judgment. Yet assuredly the pressure of public censure has distorted more characters, weakened more moral resistance, created more dishonesty toward oneself and others among modern homosexuals than among other people. Lieutenant Rossbach's troop, roaring, brawling, carousing, smashing windows, shedding blood, and nevertheless seeking the light of freedom, was especially proud to be 'different from the others.' Heines had belonged to it before joining Hitler; then Rossbach and Heines had formed a center with Röhm; it led the S.A. while Hitler was under arrest. According to his own indications, Röhm was perverted by the other two. In 1924, his suitcase and papers were stolen from him in the lowest Berlin surroundings, and thus his private life became known to the police. After his break with Hitler, he was destitute; he peddled books, and for a long time lived as a guest of wealthy homosexual friends. In Berlin for a time he frequented the homosexual dregs; he admitted that he had moved in circles 'where the good citizen blushes and shudders.'

Hitler had erroneously been counted among these men. But he

unscrupulously used the forces of perversion, just as he used murder and lies. A heart-broken father from the little town of Uffen-
heim in Franconia whose son had been perverted by Heines in the
S.A., complained to him; he replied that the young men must take
care of themselves, the S.A. was no kindergarten. A delegation led
by Count Ernst zu Reventlow, an elderly party comrade, brought
him a message from Ludendorff: the general viewed the activities
of the homosexuals in the S.A. with great misgivings. Hitler told
Reventlow to tell General Ludendorff that all this was a matter
of total indifference to him, Hitler; his actual words were unprintable. When in May, 1927, he finally threw Heines out of the
party, it was not for his loose morals, but because Heines had called
his Führer a dishrag and was stirring up the S.A. against him.

He might have thrown half of the S.A. after him. While Röhm
peddled his books or sat around with his friends, the S.A. was led
by a man who at heart was no National Socialist at all, Captain
Pfeffer von Salomon. He used his power like a hired captain in
the Renaissance; he had exacted the condition that Hitler should
have no right to interfere. Pfeffer knew that he could not, on Sundays and Saturday afternoons, make a serviceable military troop out
of these students, white-collar workers, and sons of peasants. But
the S.A. could be a preparatory school for the army; as many S.A.
men as possible should enter the Reichswehr and flood it with rebellion. Hitler trembled at the slightest thought of illegality; they
would deport him at once, of that he was certain. Pfeffer ordered
the S.A. to engage in military maneuvers; Hitler issued counter-
orders. Pfeffer's orders were not valid, he declared, unless counter-
signed by him, Hitler. Violent scenes ensued; masklike and immobile behind his pince-nez, Pfeffer listened to Hitler's violent outbreaks. Afterward he said to others, 'you can't take orders from
this slovenly, terrified Austrian!' It was impossible to make those
S.A. captains understand that the purpose of the S.A. was expressly
not military. They held to a statement Hitler once had made himself: that 'An army cannot be trained and taught the highest self-
respect unless the function of its existence is preparation for warfare. There are no armies for the preservation of peace, but only
for the victorious waging of war.'

In the eyes of these former lieutenants and captains, the storm troops were a piece of the future army 'waging a victorious war.' They must be ready to slip into uniform at once and shoulder arms when the Reichswehr called them. The S.A. leaders had changed their views about Seeckt's army. Rossbach, for example, who had previously been so skeptical, said: 'The Reichswehr in a superhuman struggle of infinite perseverance has step by step achieved an inner elevation, as we old soldiers today can perceive with seeing eyes.' Consequently, the old soldiers must forget their old rancor and revise their faulty judgments. Pfeffer desired nothing more and would have liked best to hand over the whole S.A. to the Reichswehr, calculating that he himself would then become a general, and Hitler, if necessary, could go to the devil. He led the S.A. back to the drill grounds of the Reichswehr and trained them to bear arms; it was beginning to be a repetition of 1923, which Hitler recalled with horror. That must not happen again. The Reichswehr must not be allowed to take 'his' S.A. out of his hands, and perhaps look on smiling while the bourgeois state's attorney prosecuted Hitler for illegal military drilling and the Socialist Minister of the Interior ordered the foreigner deported. He forbade his troop any connection with the Reichswehr, on grounds amounting to high treason: 'The National Socialist, and first and foremost the S.A. man, has no call to stir so much as a finger for the present state, which has no understanding of our outlook and can only perpetuate the misfortune of our people. . . . The coming Reich for which we are struggling alone obligates us to stake our persons.'

The Reichswehr Ministry on the other side forbade the army to accept National Socialists as soldiers, and even forbade the arsenals and other supply establishments to employ National Socialist workers, 'since this party has set itself the aim of overthrowing the constitutional state form of the German Reich' (1927).

Rebuffed by the Reichswehr, uncertain of his own troop, deserted by his old friends, surrounded by unreliable new ones, Hitler stood like a modest dwarf beneath the wall of his great plans. Even in his personal relations with the leading circles of reaction and counter-revolution he lacked the right introduction; Goebbels in Berlin, despite his firm will to live in that world where life is not dull, was not the right man. But then Hitler had an unexpected stroke of luck: Göring came back. Hitler never had a better contact man than this old friend of the former German crown prince. During Göring's exile his old friend Prince Philipp of Hesse had married the Princess Mafalda, daughter of the king of Italy; thus Göring was introduced to the Italian court, and his own person became the strongest cornerstone in the beginning of personal relations between Mussolini and Hitler. This Italian introduction may not have meant much so long as Göring was living in poverty in Sweden, broken down by morphine, at times in a sanatorium, and declared by the courts unable to bring up his adopted son. But Göring became a great help to Hitler when, in 1927, the German parties of the Right, supported by the Communists, put through a political amnesty and he returned home.

Göring brought with him a Swedish invention, the Tornblad parachute; with his friend Wilhelm Körner, like him a former war aviator, he manufactured under the Swedish patent in Germany. Other old friends, fliers and administrators in Germany's modest commercial aviation, had to buy the product. One of these friends was Erhard Milch, technical director of the Lufthansa, a monopolistic concern, half controlled by the state. Milch was the son of a Jewish father and bore a Jewish name, but that did not disturb Göring. Milch was an excellent flier and organizer, a staunch patriot — hence an armed intellectual of the best class; besides, he was a helpful friend to Göring. Like other large enterprises, the Lufthansa had a slush fund, from which men with political influence were bribed in a refined way. With a straight face the company representatives would approach them for technical advice and even pay for so-called affidavits, while in reality expecting them to use their influence with the authorities.

Göring, too, delivered his affidavits, and in his case the corruption was twofold; for everyone knew that he had far too little influence to earn his money honestly — that is, through successful conniving. To be sure, Hitler had sent him to the Reichstag with eleven other National Socialists in May, 1928, but the twelve lonely Brown Shirts were helpless and almost ignored. Göring's old friend, the former German crown prince, had written him a letter congratulating him on his election with the cynical remark that, thanks to his physical strength, he would surely make his way as a representative of the people. Goebbels had once said that the National Socialists needed no more than twenty men in parliament; ten would have to be experts at shouting interruptions, ten expert boxers. However, there were not even twenty, but only twelve, and Göring, despite his furious speeches demanding that the Reichstag vote the Lufthansa more funds, achieved nothing. He could not very well say publicly that the money was to be used for the secret preparation of the future German air armament; he could only hint that German aviation had a great patriotic task to fulfill; if challenged, he could not have denied that this and other patriotic tasks enabled certain people to earn a lot of money. One of these people was Camillo Castiglioni, an Italian Jew from Trieste; by a bold financial *coup* this Castiglioni had gained possession of a factory in which one of the best German aviation motors was manufactured, the Bavarian Motor Works near Munich. Unprejudiced, he employed Göring as his representative; he generously paid him advances and when Göring proved unable to earn back the advances, Castiglioni silently canceled the debt.

Göring must have made money in these affairs — but it was never sufficient. He spent it in the gay world; his sick wife meanwhile lived in Sweden with her mother. In his small bachelor apartment in the Badische Strasse in Berlin, he turned night into day, both in work and pleasure; in this resembling the insomniac Hitler. There sat Göring, preferably by candlelight; on the wall before him a picture of Napoleon; behind him, over his head, a medieval headsman's sword which he regarded as a special ornament. His work was often devoted to the constantly arising problem of how to pay the next note that was due, how to avoid the pawnshop. He was deeply in debt.

His political task also required hard work. The friend of the German and Italian princes, frequenting good society as an equal among equals, had to represent the still half-nameless Reichswehr spy; he had to raise the party of Julius Streicher and Hermann Esser from notorious insignificance to notorious greatness. The resistance in Germany's leading social strata was strong. There were plenty of people who would have agreed to dictatorship, to a sharp policy against France, even to a little war against Poland; but when the dictatorship of Hitler, the 'Bohemian corporal' as Hindenburg later called him, was suggested, the answer was laughter at best. No, no leadership of the nation by the disinherited, uprooted — and unsuccessful! There were other formations, organized and armed along the same lines as the National Socialist S.A.; above all the Stahlhelm, an organization of several hundred thousand members, with a nucleus of some hundred thousand former soldiers; well-disciplined, prepared for civil war, and, in case of a small frontier war, serviceable as a reserve army. It was on the 'green' Stahlhelm and not on the brown S.A. that the leading classes pinned their hopes when things again began to look like civil war in Germany.

While Göring was seeking approval for his party in his circles, Goebbels was noisily making the party known, and himself even more. He thought up tricks that would have occurred to no one else. He made his S.A. men wear white bandages colored with a red liquid round their heads; thus they appeared as 'heroes' who had bled for their party; their club-footed doctor, looking like a wounded World War lieutenant, marched at their head. To the *Völkischer Beobachter* Goebbels sent articles, apparently written by others, in reality by himself, reporting Doctor Goebbels's amazing deeds of heroism, always in the third person. One article related that Doctor Goebbels, riding in a motor-car with comrades, suddenly sensed with vibrant nerves that an unknown danger was threatening: 'Suddenly Goebbels stood up from his seat. Halt, Comrade Chauffeur, halt! The car stops. What's the matter, doctor? — I don't know, but we're in danger. We reach for our guns and jump out. Nothing to be seen or heard. All four tires are hard and firm. But holla, what is that! On the left hind wheel four nuts are missing. Four nuts out of five. Diabolical treachery. Traces of clumsy violence tell the rest. That is how the Jews and their servants fight.' The loudest noise came from a nature essentially timid. For Goebbels has admitted that, alone among strangers, he preferred not to be recognized as a Nationalist Socialist: 'I travel without party insignia; I seldom feel the expediency or necessity of getting mixed up in political discussions.' When Hitler spoke in public he had to grow up from a human nonentity to monumental size; Goebbels, too, had to overcome his natural timidity before he could become incisive and unforgettable.

Between his most talented pupil and Hitler there arose a spiritual intimacy which permitted Hitler to use Goebbels as a thinking tool; in 1928, he appointed him party propaganda leader, and that he has remained ever since. The younger man did not become an echo and a complement for Hitler like Hess, but a perfectly functioning executive organ; Goebbels avidly seized on the slogans thrown out by his leader, and developed an artistry in giving form to Hitler's original ideas. It can be shown that Goebbels copied many of his ideas and phrases from Hitler; his life's aim was to be Hitler's mouthpiece. Hitler had given his party the swastika flag; in 1932, Goebbels had millions of swastikas cut out of paper and strewn on the streets — this characterizes the collaboration between the two.

Hitler distributed his creatures throughout the party, systematically set rivals beside his rivals, fomented quarrels among his lieutenants over whom he remained the unassailable leader — such was the work of party building up to 1930. The endless quarrels among his faithful enabled him to build a new organ of his authority into the party apparatus. To deal with the internal accusations of all sorts and keep public justice away from the many shady members of his élite band, he established in 1926 a party court, the so-called *Untersuchungs- und Schlichtungs-Ausschuss* (Committee for Examination and Adjustment), popularly known by the unbeautiful abbreviation: Uschla. The Uschla in a sense is the secret moral strong-box of the party, in which the National Socialists keep their best and strongest possession, their cynicism, safe from the world. Its first leader was a former general by the name of Heinemann; he took his job too seriously, failing to understand the real purpose of the institution, and had to be dismissed. His successor was Major Walter Buch, a discharged Reichswehr officer who had not been conspicuous in the party up till then; his assistants were Ulrich Graf, the loyal henchman wounded at the Feldherrn Halle, and the lawyer Hans Frank, a human instrument blindly devoted to

Hitler. The Uschla pursued a simple and brutal method. Offenses against party discipline, disobedience to a leader or lack of respect toward the Führer, were examined and punished, in grave cases with what these men feared as much as death: expulsion from the party. Transgressions of a different sort, slander, even criminal offenses, in so far as they were not directed against the leadership, were on principle ignored, unless they had become known or threatened to become known outside the party. It was a party precept that one comrade must simply not believe accusations of this sort against another comrade. 'Always believe the party comrade and never the enemy!' said Hitler in 1931 in a New Year's proclamation, 'and raise this faith to a mighty conviction, not only of the right of the individual, but of the right of the party, and beyond that of the right of our people in this world.'

If a party member was proved guilty of private immorality, dishonest business conduct, exploitation of employees, Buch had a standing formula: 'Well, what of it?' One S.A. leader was a bigamist, another a gambler and drunkard, a third a homosexual, a fourth discharged from his position for robbing the cash register: Well, what of it? The party had no use for 'moral frills.'

The Uschla expressed Hitler's unlimited power in the party — like a provisional symbol which slowly was becoming a reality. In order to secure his absolute domination over the party, Hitler had half-destroyed it, letting Röhm go, dismissing Drexler, throwing Heines out. But that he had the clearer plans and the firmer will in the long run, now was proved by success. The old deserters came back; not quite beaten, not without making conditions — but they came back.

Röhm came again. The ghost of the secret army of murderers had to rise from its grave to bring this about. In a common proclamation for the murderers' army they made their peace. The immediate cause of the *rapprochement* was Edmund Heines, whom Hitler, as an open insult to Röhm, had thrown out of the party. In 1928, Heines was brought to trial for a murder he had committed eight years previous as a member of the murderers' army. 'Heines,' runs the court sentence, 'thrust his pistol into Schmidt's [the victim's] face and fired twice.' The sentence was as characteristic as the crime: only five years in prison. At the end of a year and a half, the condemned man was freed by a new amnesty. But the murderers' army had expected more: complete acquittal with honors. They were suddenly united in angry protest. General Franz von Epp demonstratively joined the party of the man whom five years before he had accused of breaking his word of honor. He did not withdraw the accusation, but merely stated that his old grudge 'had quickly passed off'; in return, Hitler offered him a seat in the Reichstag. Röhm appeared on the platform of a party meeting with his closest friends, the homosexuals so often castigated by Hitler, and cried out that the sentence of his friend Heines was 'an attack of formal justice on the soldier's right to self-defense.'

Röhm returned to Hitler with great plans. While the party still looked threadbare and hopeless from without, he assured friends that Hitler would become Reich Chancellor and that he, Röhm, would build up Hitler's army. He resumed his work in the same broad, systematic style as in 1920 and 1923. Ostensibly quite outside the party, he formed an officers' club, which officially had neither political nor professional aims; but was devoted merely to the theoretical study of military questions and bore the non-committal title of *Wehrpolitische Vereinigung* (League for Combat Policy). This private military academy had local groups in the garrison cities of Bavaria. Röhm traveled around the country, found his old comrades in all the garrisons, some of them in high posts, and, as 'Adolf Hitler's envoy,' revealed to them the future that Hitler had conceived for the German army and its officers. The *Wehrpolitische Vereinigung* conducted itself like the general staff of a future army. The importance of this contact cannot be overestimated; and Hitler, who felt perfectly at home again with Röhm, hoped the old friend would now take over the leadership of the S.A.

It seems that a purely external reason unhinged this plan. Röhm suddenly disappeared. A quarrel with his former friend, Lieutenant Neunzert, seems to have been one of the main reasons. Neunzert threatened revelations, and Röhm suddenly found it advisable to put an ocean between himself and Europe. The Bolivian Army, led and trained by a German general named Kundt, was seeking German officers, and Röhm, the discharged German captain, was engaged with the rank of Bolivian lieutenant-colonel. Röhm seems to have done a good job as a military adviser. He wrote his German friends letters full of bitter complaints that there was so little understanding for homosexuality in the country; yet he cynically promised 'to spread culture.'

Hitler temporarily abandoned hope of regaining control of the S.A. He did what he had done in 1923: he split the organization and drew out the reliable sections, bringing them closer to himself. In 1923, before his *putsch*, he had set up within the S.A. a troop swearing personal loyalty to him, the 'Hitler shock troop,' led by an old friend named Josef Berchtold. When the S.A. virtually fell apart in 1925, after the break with Röhm, a new band of the most reliable men with a similar-sounding name was formed to take its place, again under Berchtold. Instead of *Sturm Abteilung* (S.A.) it was called *Schutz Staffel* (defense corps), abbreviated as S.S. Instead of the brown S.A. shirt, these men wore a black Fascist uniform. Berchtold did not understand the spirit of his task; he did not have the heart to draw his troop out of the party mass. For the idea of a chosen band insulted the broad section of members which was still permeated by the democratic mood of the old founders — Berchtold himself among them. 'The party expects you all to come,' said the founding proclamation of the S.A. in 1921. Now, in 1926 Hitler said that 'a small band of the best and most determined is far more valuable than a large mass of camp-followers'; therefore 'the numerical strength is closely restricted.' And thus it remained. The motley S.A. troops under Pfeffer's leadership carried on their half-independent existence; many of them had no further regard for Hitler than a half-contemptuous admiration for his boom-boom oratory; the new S.S. troop represented only a few black dots amid the brown mass. At first everything was intentionally made hard for them. They had to wear a relatively expensive uniform, cut according to regulation, and this black splendor, including the belt with the motto devised by Hitler, 'My honor is loyalty,' on the buckle, had to be paid for out of the men's own pockets. For the S.S. men must learn to make sacrifices for their convictions. The result was that poor party members seldom joined the S.S. The Black band did not expand until about 1929, when the party began to attract broader sections of the population and wealthy men rushed to its banners. To them it was a point of honor to make the sacrifice of the expensive S.S. uniform, and thus the Black troop became a reservoir for the more prosperous members. There could not be much objection to this, for Hitler said that economic prosperity was often a sign of greater ability and hence better race; and better race was just what the S.S. was intended to embody.

Hitler gave the S.S. the 'blood banner' to keep. This was a flag that had been carried on November 9 at the Feldherrn Halle, and had become a fetish of the movement. When Hitler, whom his men in that period nicknamed the 'Manitou,' consecrated a new flag, the blood banner had to be brought forth. Manitou grasped one of its corners, at the same time holding the new flag; he let the spirit flow from flag to flag through his person, as he pronounced his words of consecration.

Berchtold was not only S.S. leader, but also an editor of the *Völkischer Beobachter,* letting himself be bullied into the most humiliating services by the efficient and violent Amann. Consequently, Berchtold had to instruct his troop 'to recruit readers and advertisers for the *Völkischer Beobachter.'* Finally, forced with the choice of leading the Black élite or earning his modest living on the party paper, he preferred to earn a living. The S.S. was then led for a time by a certain Erhard Heiden, a stool-pigeon of the worst sort. Not until 1929 did Hitler find the right man, an old friend of Röhm's and later collaborator with Gregor Strasser; an eccentric who made his living from a poultry farm in the village of Waldtrudering near Munich. He had studied to be an agronomist, but in his free time concerned himself with genealogy. This man was Heinrich Himmler.

The post-war generation now begins to assume prominence in the party. Himmler was the first party leader who had been too young to serve in the World War. Born in Munich in 1900, he grew up in Landshut, where Gregor Strasser later lived. He attended the *gymnasium,* and like all German gymnasiasts of that day was given an opportunity to become an officer. He spent the last year of the World War as an ensign (aspirant to the officer's career) in a Bavarian regiment, but never reached the front. Defeat and revolution put an end to his dream of becoming an officer, and a dull, gray life began. Himmler chose a simple and practical course of study. He wanted to become a farmer but with an academic title; from 1919 to 1922, he studied agriculture at the *Technische Hochschule* in Munich, and, on passing the easiest of all academic examinations, won a diploma for agronomy. Off and on, he was active with Röhm in the secret murderers' army and stood beside him on November 9, 1923, when he delivered the Munich District Military Command to General von Epp. After the *putsch* he led a hard life; for a time he served as private secretary to Gregor Strasser, succeeding Goebbels. In 1928, he made himself independent in a modest way by acquiring a poultry farm in Waldtrudering.

Himmler is an excellent example of what a task can make of a man. He had a task of the first order to solve, and the task made him; to a nature mediocre at best it gave a weightiness which the apparatus that grew up around him helped him to bear. Men who combine the gift of creation or leadership with deep insight or independent judgment are always rare; in the National Socialist Movement they can be counted on the fingers; Himmler in any case is not one of them. His great qualities, infrequent in his milieu, are industry, precision, thoroughness. It is a quality inherent in a body of men working for a common purpose that great results can be achieved by the men who are not great. A preponderance of strong personalities can even force a split, and only through the addition of average qualities can an efficient machine be built up. Himmler is the living, actual proof of Hitler's thesis, 'that the strength of a political party lies, not in having single adherents of outstanding intelligence, but in disciplined obedience. A company of two hundred men of equal capabilities would in the long run be more difficult to discipline than a group in which one hundred and ninety are less capable and ten are of greater abilities.'

In the National Socialist machine Himmler is a wire activated by the electric current, connecting important parts. He looks like the caricature of a sadistic school-teacher, and this caricature conceals the man like a mask. If one takes away the pince-nez and uniform, there is revealed, under a narrow forehead, a look of curious objectivity. Apart from pose and calling, he gives the impression of a certain courtesy — even modesty. But this objectivity is of that frightful sort that can look unmoved on the most grisly of horrors. A demonic will to power has been attributed to him; in truth he, more than any other of the first rank of his party, has been guided by devotion to the cause, and compared to others he might be considered a model of personal selflessness. He is married, his private life is unassuming. He loves flowers and birds, yet this offers no contradiction to his political rôle; personally he is almost without demands. More than anyone else in this circle, he feels that he is only a part of the whole embodied in the person of his supreme leader; his passion for race and race-building arises from a deep contempt of the individual, including his own. He has found classic formulas for the creed of the armed intellectual — that the state is all, the individual nothing. He takes the doctrine of 'you are nothing, your people are everything,' more seriously than almost anyone else in the movement, and for that reason Hitler took this man more seriously than many others who were more intelligent.

Himmler understood with his heart when his Führer demanded that the party must become the racial élite of Germany, the party of the ruling minority. But by the party was meant Hitler's party which grew out of the unbridled National Socialist mass and raised itself above the mass; Himmler saw his own S.S. as the motive force of this special party. 'We are not more intelligent than two thousand years ago,' he said to his men in 1931. 'The military history of antiquity, the history of the Prussian Army two or three hundred years ago — again and again we see that wars are waged with men, but that every leader surrounds himself with an organization of men of special quality when things are at their worst and hardest; that is the guard. There has always been a guard; the Persians, the Greeks, Caesar, Old Fritz,[1] Napoleon, all had a guard, and so on up to the World War; and the guard of the new Germany will be the S.S. The guard is an élite of especially chosen men.'

[1] Frederick II, the Great.

Chosen average men in positions of mastery. That is the meaning of the S.S., which represents the model of National Socialist education. These men are not — and are not supposed to be — great individuals, but 'good material' for the fabrication of a race, as Chamberlain put it. Therefore, their 'honor is loyalty'; that is, obedience toward the few who really rule and lead. 'Few flames burn in Germany,' Goebbels once said of these top personalities, naturally counting himself among them; 'the rest are only illumined by their glow' — he wrote these words of contempt in his diary after returning from a meeting of party officials (1932), where he had seen the good material assembled.

The S.S. was stamped forever by the reason for its founding: Hitler's need to control an undisciplined party by founding a new party. The National Socialist despises his fellow-Germans, the S.A. man the other National Socialists, the S.S. man the S.A. men. His task is to supervise and spy on the whole party for his leader. The first service code of the S.S. lists among its tasks, protection of the Führer, a promotion of understanding within the ranks; information service. The last two terms mean espionage within and outside the party.

In 1930, Hitler surprised a circle of his friends by asking them if they had read the just-published autobiography of Leon Trotzky, the great Jewish leader of the Russian Revolution, and what they thought of it. As might have been expected, the answer was: 'Yes . . . loathsome book . . . memoirs of Satan. . . .' To which Hitler replied: 'Loathsome? Brilliant! I have learned a great deal from it, and so can you.' Himmler, however, remarked that he had not only read Trotzky but studied all available literature about the political police in Russia, the Tsarist Ochrana, the Bolshevist Cheka and G.P.U.; and he believed that if such a task should ever fall to his lot, he could perform it better than the Russians.

With this in mind he drilled his troop, imbued it with his Führer's arrogance and contempt of humanity, thus arming its men with the moral force to massacre their own people as well as foreigners, and to regard this as absolutely necessary. At a time when the party still meant nothing, Himmler's service regulations ordered that once a month at least the men must attend a confidential local party meeting; at these meetings they must not smoke nor leave the room like common mortals, and above all never take part in the discussion; for 'the nobility keeps silence.' The good material does not discuss, but only obeys and commands, 'in responsibility upward, in command downward,' as Hitler put it. The finest and most venomous flower of his contempt for humanity is the contempt of their own person that is expected of the good material: not only ruthless struggle to the death, but, in case of grave failure, suicide.

Chapter XIII

'THE UPROOTED AND

DISINHERITED'

DEATH IS THE FINAL GOAL OF THE SCIENTIFI-cally drilled nation. The task of the leaders becomes easy when the followers are ready to die.

This was the philosophical issue about which Germany's military leaders endlessly pondered after their lost war. No doubt, Hitler, too, in his way, belonged to these leaders, although the professionals in those days would not have admitted it; and in creating his élite formations he tried to solve the puzzle in a practical way. But the answer he found in doing so did not satisfy the men who, for the time being, still felt responsible for what might happen to Germany in the next war.

'To what success,' wrote General Hans von Seeckt, referring to World War I, 'did this general mobilization, this giant mustering of armies lead?' Seeckt, the creator of the new Reichswehr, spoke here of the twenty million-odd men who had lain in the trenches all over Europe, a third of whom had never returned, and another third of whom, crippled, with health impaired for life, embittered, never readapted themselves to peace and home. Despite all their exertions, Seeckt went on, 'the war did not end for the Allies with complete annihilation of the enemy on the battlefield. . . . Is the victor pleased with his success? Do the results of the war stand in any proportion to the sacrifices in national strength?' This is the profoundest question that a military leader can ask himself; and Seeckt gave the answer by again asking: 'If warlike settlements are inevitable, must whole nations forever fall upon one another? The soldier must ask himself whether these giant armies can still be led in the sense of decisive strategy and whether every war between these masses is not doomed to paralysis.'

A German general doubting the sense of war! It had taken a terrible defeat to teach him, but in any case he had learned. In 1928, when Seeckt wrote, it had long become glaringly clear that the victory had neither strengthened nor enriched the victors — aside perhaps from the small nations; victorious France had actually been defeated by a loss of blood that could not be made good, and was weaker than before. For years the victor world had inwardly forgotten about its victory. Hitler, by contrast, sought unceasingly to refresh his people's memory of the defeat; sought to convince the German masses, living happily and at peace, of the necessity, nay the beauty, of war: 'Struggle is the father of all things, as with the individual, also with the fate of nations. Only the stronger can raise himself above the weaker by struggle, and everyone who succumbs in this ever-changing struggle, has gotten his due from nature.'

A remarkable dialogue between the former corporal and the former general. Hitler regarded his speeches partly as answers to the articles which Seeckt published at the same time. The general admitted that he did not believe in eternal peace; especially when he thought of the great wars in which 'a people sets out to devour another with a better, easier life.' Also he saw no reliable protection against 'the wars that arise from great spiritual movements.' But this type of war between people and people, though perhaps as inevitable as a natural cataclysm, had at all events shown its questionable nature in the World War; and it was certain that the mere contest of arms 'between army and army' could be avoided. Here Seeckt saw 'a possibility of reducing the probability of war.' It must, as he put it, be possible to take the road at whose beginning stands the sign, 'To eternal peace, distance unknown,' and reach at least a little village with a sign over its tavern door saying, 'Limitation of armaments.'

Contemptuously Hitler replied: 'This nation of sixty-two millions must advance its claims to the globe. . . . Germany will not be saved by men who fall a victim to universal world love, but by those who direct universal hatred to themselves.' Seeckt, the specialist, regarded the people's war of millions as a useless bloody drama of the past: 'Perhaps the principle of the mass army, of national mobilization, is already on the wane; the *fureur du nombre* is at an end. The mass becomes immobile. It cannot maneuver, hence cannot win; it can only crush.' But Hitler: 'The basic idea of National Socialism, in its striving to create a strong race, is that an entire people must enter the lists and fight for its life. If it succumbs, that is right. The earth is not for cowardly peoples!' And: 'The earth is our football; in this game we do not for a moment renounce staking our whole people.' In Seeckt's eyes the World War confuted itself; Hitler by contrast: 'For the National Socialists the World War has not ended. We have not disarmed. As soldiers we do not weep and complain, we do not rack our brains whether we may not have done the enemy an injustice.' Seeckt uttered the obvious, 'Precisely the soldier will greet all efforts to lessen the possibilities of war,' and Hitler replied with the cannibalistic wisdom which he held to be obvious, 'All the nations which have surrendered to peace have not only ceased to dominate the world, but have slowly rotted.' Seeckt, following the doctrine of Clausewitz, the German philosopher of war, declared peace to be the aim of every war, but Hitler knew better: 'There is no differentiation between war and peace. There is always struggle.'

These were not clever speeches. With his strident battle-cry Hitler did not sweep millions off their feet; he only expressed the sentiment of his group of uprooted men who in 1928 were still a small circle around their little-regarded Führer. Himself uprooted, he screamed out his nostalgia for war, his lost home: 'I was a dispatch carrier at Arras,' he related, 'in the night when the roaring twenty-one-centimeter cannons suddenly began to speak and illumine the horizon with lightnings. Then I had the ecstatic feeling: Here stands Germany, that is our language — over there they know this language and hide from it!' He was speaking to two thousand people, and the reports tell of 'stormy, continuous applause.' On the night before the German Reichstag elections of 1928, Hitler promised five thousand listeners: 'If Fate should give us the power, we shall use it to cleanse the nation of its enemies and we hope that God gives us strength to march to the ultimate destiny on this earth. It will not be spared us. . . . We shall grow into a mighty army of termites, before the final hour comes. . . .' The 'ultimate destiny,' the 'hour': these, of course, are the war, and 'we hope' for its coming. The national elections of May 20, 1928, following this speech, brought Hitler twelve seats out of six hundred in parliament — it was a grave defeat.

Despite such disappointments the war speeches served a purpose. They were addressed to a type of man who, like Hitler, found his fatherland in war; to this type Hitler promised a new home — a home with boots, spurs, gold epaulets, and three hundred marks a month. He wanted this kind of men because they possessed what he called the 'sense of struggle.' The type is found in all classes, including the working class; he must only be freed of his class conceptions, his faith in economics and work ('through work and industry a people has never grown free, only through hatred'). Let the Social Democrats preach the love of peace to the German masses. Perhaps they will have success for a time, 'until suddenly a plain ordinary military band comes by; then the man awakens from his dream state, suddenly he begins to feel like a member of the nation that is marching, and he joins in. All our people need is this one example — one, two, three, we are on the march. [Thunderous cries of *"Heil!"*] . . . There was one place in Germany in which there was no class division. That was the front-line company. There no one ever heard of a bourgeois and a proletarian platoon; there was just the company and that was the end of it. And there has to be a way of creating this unity at home too. . . .' Therefore, we must wage war at home: 'If I want to weld the people into unity, I must first form a new front, facing a common enemy. Then each man will know that we must be one, because this enemy is the enemy of us all.' To that end we wage meeting-hall battles and war on the open highway — assemble the human type which no longer believes in work ('by work we shall never get the Frenchmen out of the country'); which does not believe in equality

('equality and freedom cannot exist side by side, democracy is the eternal conspiracy of twerps against the outstanding head'); which does not believe in justice ('justice is what benefits my people, injustice what harms my people').

In September, 1928, Hitler assembled his sub-leaders in Munich for a working session. The future of the movement did not look very hopeful. The elections had brought failure. At the end of the session, Hitler rose to the platform and declared that to him it seemed necessary 'to strengthen the individual party comrades' confidence in the victory of the movement.' This victory, he continued, must come with mathematical certainty. And for this he found a reason which lifted the hearts of the small, rather depressed band:

> It does not require much courage to do silent service in an existing organization. It requires more courage to fight against an existing political régime. As soon as a man engages in offensive opposition to an existing régime, he will have to summon up more courage than the man who defends it. The movement requires more courage than naked tenacity. Attack attracts the personalities which possess more courage. Thus a condition containing danger within itself becomes a magnet for men who seek danger. A program with radical ideas will attract radical men, a program with a cowardly tendency will attract cowardly men. And then there is the reaction of the existing order. Furthermore, the resistance of the masses sifts even this small number once again. What remains is a minority of determined, hard men. It is this process which alone makes history explicable: the fact that certain revolutions, emanating from very few men and giving the world a new face, have actually taken place. And now, finally, comes the active resistance of the existing state. All parties, public opinion, take a position against us. But therein lies the unconditional, I might say the mathematical, reason for the future success of our movement. As long as we are the radical movement, as long as public opinion shuns us, as long as the existing factors of the state oppose us — we shall continue to assemble the most valuable human material around us, even at times when, as they say, all factors of human reason argue against it!

A noteworthy theory of the *coup d'état,* not devised at the writing desk, but gathered entirely from experience. If the party's propaganda for long years hardly kindled a flame, if it netted plenty of beatings and defeats, the leader of the beaten men consoled himself with the thought that such bitter trials would separate 'the nation's new nobility from nature's mass production.'

It will always remain one of Hitler's strongest gifts that he knew how to learn from his enemy: 'Let us glance at the development of Marxism in Germany!' he cried out a year later at the second of the Nuremberg Party Days. 'Wherever a revolt takes place, it is always against weakness and never against strength. Marxism created a community of force-filled men. . . . Where force, determination, boldness, ruthlessness — where these qualities are harnessed to the service of a bad cause, they can overthrow the state. The presupposition is a demand which itself in turn demands force of the individual. . . . For the individual is eager to prove his strength, quite regardless where he is placed. That is why great movements in world history have been able to conquer despite apparently insuperable obstacles, despite economic interests, despite the pressure of public opinion, even despite reason if it is feebly represented.'

That is the secret. 'Therein lies the future of our movement,' he cries out, confident of victory, 'that slowly, imperturbably, by this process we assemble the historic minority which in Germany perhaps will constitute six to eight hundred thousand men. If you have these men united as the membership of a movement, you have created the center of gravity of the state. If I regard our development up to now, I note the following: First, our program passes as radical, and weak men are afraid to come to us because of the radicalism of our ideas. Second, the régime oppresses us with all the means at its disposal, for it sees the danger inherent in the fact that the human material assembling with us is the best that Germany possesses. As long as this continues, and only the more courageous espouse our cause, we are on the right track and are marching toward victory with an iron firmness. . . .'

A confident prophecy, yet heavy with anxious foreboding. For Hitler continued: 'If the great mass were to join us with cries of hurrah, we should be in a sad state. That is why we distinguish between members and supporters. The supporters are the entire German people, the members six to eight hundred thousand. That is the number which alone is worth anything. All the others only come along when we line up in march columns. This principle of selection, which takes place through eternal struggle, is the guaranty of the future success of our movement. First we shall draw their valuable men from all the national parties, and finally from the international [Marxist] ones as well. What then remains is the crowd; not persons but numbers that hand in a ballot. That is the great mass. . . .'

In 1929, when he held the second Nuremberg Party Day, Hitler had already assembled a tenth of his historical minority. Sixty thousand of the elect marched in columns. A foreigner, bewitched by the stiff arms and thundering boots, said to Hitler: How wonderful; it seems as though all these sixty thousand men had the same face. This remark was more accurate than the foreign guest suspected, for the same column passed the spot three or four times to indicate a greater mass. Even so there was deep truth in the words; the same uniform, the same cap, the same step, the same cry, the same song, the same simple thought, end by making almost identical men. 'That is the great thing about our movement . . . that these men have outwardly become almost a unit, that actually these members are uniform not only in ideas, but that even the facial expression is almost the same. Look at these laughing eyes, this fanatical enthusiasm, and you will discover how in these faces the same expression has formed, how a hundred thousand men in a movement become a single type.'

The type for whom the World War was not over. Staring into a bloody distance, Hitler continued: 'Today when I saw these boys passing by me, suddenly I thought: how would it be if two more years passed and these boys were to don our old steel helmets, if they were volunteer regiments at Ypres again — the same face, the same expression, the same life in these men? We saw heads of boys in which was already imprinted the proud man to be, which the people needs as a leader if it is not to be destroyed. That is what this movement wants.' (Loud applause.)

The dream of a future hecatomb of Ypres was exactly what scared a man like Seeckt; but the professional soldier would not have understood that the real purpose of a coming mass war was the opportunity it gave for selecting a minority of rulers or leaders. As a matter of fact only from this minority itself could an understanding be expected. The really important thing was that this minority was not to be found in Germany alone; the whole war philosophy was based on this.

The idea of a German-Italian front against France appeared in both countries immediately after the World War; the same political forces appeared too: in Germany the secret murderers' army of the Free Corps, in Italy the much opener murderers' army of the *Arditi* under Gabriele d'Annunzio and the Fascisti under Benito Mussolini. In 1919, Houston Stewart Chamberlain wrote to his Italian brother-in-law, Count Manfred Gravina: 'It is my opinion that Italy and Germany, in consequence of their geographical position as well as the nature of their population, are destined to be friends, and I believe that Germany has greater interest in seeing Italy great and strong than in the contrary. France, on the other hand, will never be your true friend, and never has been in the past: she hates you as a neighbor and rival and has always deceived you; hence it is in no way to your interest to see Germany weakened, let alone destroyed.'

True, between Germany and Italy lay independent Austria, and Mussolini declared in 1925 that Italy could never tolerate the *Anschluss,* since it would destroy all Italy's World War gains. Then there were the two hundred and thirty thousand Germans in the South Tyrol annexed by Italy; but Hitler stated: 'If today Satan came and offered himself to me as an ally against France, I would give him my hand. . . . It was a happy day for me when I heard that Mussolini meant to renew the old Roman Empire. For that meant that some day Italy will have to march against France.' The struggle for a Roman Empire (for practical purposes North Africa) was in Hitler's eyes a struggle of races. 'Italy needs Africa in order to settle her surplus population; France needs Africa in order to supplement her own population from there.'

To this vanishing French national force, maintaining a shaky security by a net of artificial and unreliable alliances, the overflowing German national forces must be counterposed in all Europe by bloodshed if necessary. Hitler demands 'different slogans for the

Germans in foreign countries. In Czechoslovakia: Germans, revolt against the state. It is an auxiliary troop of France. In South Tyrol: Germans, comply with the state. You are the bridge between Germany and Italy; train your sentiments for the great mission that is yours. Not your destiny is the primary matter, but the destiny of a great people which you must serve.'

The day of the young faces, the day of a new Ypres will come soon: When the German youth, 'driven by the boyish instincts that make them search for new forces, embodying in themselves ninety-nine per cent of the best Aryan blood, led upward to the leadership of the German people' — when this youth gets its great day, 'the world will see with admiration that the German people, even externally, will assume those traits of character again which justify us in saying that our history is the world's history.' Then the leadership of Fascism will no longer be in Italy, but in National Socialist Germany, and a new reality will rise up beside which even the reality of the most realistic alliance pales: the reality of the inner German revolution.

'Then reality will keep step with this iron revolutionary process, then the hour will come in which world history will again be weighed to see whether the weights have not changed. Then France will be set into one side of the scale, while the new Germany steps into the other, and by the force of her own worth she will lower the tray. Our prayer to the Lord is only this: Lord, we do not ask you to help us, only watch to see that the weighing is done fairly, and the sword is our weight.' (1928.)

There was hardly a doubt that the German weight would be the heavier one. In March, 1928, France reduced military service to one year, lower than it had ever been before. Then the country began to build that supposedly impregnable defensive line, named after André Maginot, Minister of War. A war-weary nation wanted to shut itself off securely from war. But in March, 1929, an unnamed French general wrote in a Swiss newspaper:

Demagogic madness has led us to the absurd conception of defensive war. During the World War we had to promise parliament never again to take the offensive. As far as results, that is,

losses are concerned, there is no difference between attack and
defense. In defending Verdun, we lost just as many men as the
Germans attacking us. But the Germans had a chance of winning
the war by taking Verdun, while our only chance was not to lose
it. . . . Hence: offensive, offensive, and again offensive! Defensive
must in no case be regarded as the basic tactic. The best it can
accomplish is to cause the adversary loss of time until the moment
when we are enabled to attack. . . . With a handful of soldiers,
with a few cannon and barracks, with an army such as we shall
have in five years, split, disorganized, badly trained, with mediocre
cadres, nothing can be accomplished. We are doomed to destruction. An undisciplined troop either lets itself be killed or flees.
Our new army . . . will flee, it will be defeated by anybody. . . .

Hitler's learned friend, General and Professor Karl Haushofer,
had developed a new type of military science based on a division of
the world into great land and sea masses. Previously the power
dominating the sea had dominated the world; today, however,
Haushofer, himself a pupil of Rudolf Kjellen, the Swedish geographer, taught that this condition had been reversed. Immediately
after the World War he had been of the opinion that the great
battle fleets would gradually be transformed into 'scrap iron' by
growing swarms of U-boats and airplanes. Both planes and sub-
marines depended for their power on land bases from which they
could not stay away for any protracted period. But that is not the
chief reason for the rising importance of the mainland in world
politics. Through the development of the continental trade economy, the great inner spaces have become 'less dependent on the
coast'; in modern world politics, domination of the production
centers is decisive, no longer domination of the trade routes.

Haushofer took for granted the decline of the British Empire,
based on English domination of trade routes; all territorial relations, based only on trade and especially maritime relations, would
soon be broken. This would first happen in Asia with its great
land blocks of China and Russia, and Japan would not necessarily
be the winner in the 'Eurasian space catastrophe.' For Japan is also
a power based on sea lanes; but today we stand, as Haushofer puts
it, 'at the great turning-point in the favorable position of the island

empires.' Against the coming catastrophe he saw but one help, the early union of continental Europe. As late as 1932 he could conceive of this, though reluctantly, only under the leadership of French democracy, with at least the approval of the British: 'Either democracy and pacifism create a sort of United States of Europe by 1950 at the latest, or the Eurasian space catastrophe will inevitably occur — probably in the form of a retrogressive small-spaced dismemberment even of the so-called colonial powers.' The great land mass, not control of the sea, is today the aim of high politics.

Hitler adopted as much of this doctrine as was possible for a student of Houston Stewart Chamberlain. For the really decisive factor in all politics remains man, and not numbers but quality. He said:

> Our space is absurdly small, for a plane can cross our German territory in barely four hours. That is no longer a land surface bearing a protection in itself, as is the case with Russia whose land surface alone represents a power, a coefficient of security. . . . Sixty-two and a half million people, four hundred and thirty-six thousand square kilometers of land surface! This land surface does not suffice by far to nourish our population. . . . German foreign policy, therefore, is concerned not only with liquidating the Versailles Treaty. For then the condition of August, 1914, would be restored, which means that basically the life-possibility of the nation would not be assured. . . . In barely a hundred years there will be two hundred and fifty million Germans living on this continent. . . . It is clear that the more a nation grows in numbers, the more its soil is bound some day to become too narrow; that such a nation must some day either succumb to this restriction of its soil and collapse, or that it will burst this restriction and acquire new soil somewhere.

Hitler tried to make one of the most important phenomena of recent history clear to a simple-minded audience: that new, large-space powers were forging ahead of the old-style great powers. With a native area of only 94,000 square miles, and a white population of barely 70,000,000, England dominated a quarter of the inhabited earth, approximately 500,000,000 people; France with a motherland embracing 212,000 square miles, but a population of only 40,000,000 whites, governed an empire of 4,600,000 square miles and almost 70,000,000 people. These space-systems are confronted by the new great space-blocks, which seem to be developing their full force only today: the United States, the Soviet Union, and perhaps China. Why they did not enter world history with full force until today can be explained by Haushofer's theory that sea transport loses its dominant rôle only in the present era. Hitler's sermon on space meant that at this crossroads of history Germany must not choose the false road and attempt the conquest of an old-style colonial empire on the English or French pattern. Germany must become another land-block.

But for the moment she was nothing but a land-based island, so to speak; a small territory swimming amidst other territories. Germany did not feed herself from her own soil; like England, but without the overseas resources of that country, she exported industrial products, buying raw materials and foodstuffs in return. Thus she was, too, a country relying on trade lanes. 'I protest against the German people working as the industrial coolie of the world,' said Hitler, grossly exaggerating, 'while other peoples live on its sweat, some of them with an excess of land and soil. Who gave the Russians their land and soil?'

The land and soil of the Russians . . . ! That was what he wanted for Germany: 'We shall take the soil — on the strength of a natural right — in places where it is not tilled as we shall till it. . . . The earth belongs to him who tills it industriously. Nations which are lazy, which are incompetent, which are stupid, have no right to possess soil of the earth that they cannot make useful, while at the same time other nations starve through lack of soil. It is criminal to ask an intelligent people to limit its children in order that a lazy and stupid people next door can literally abuse a gigantic surface of the earth.'

Hitler viewed Russia with desire and contempt. Russia, to him, was an empty space full of people who do not count, and one day will be an easy prey; but Germany must be on her guard against a much stronger power — the second great land-space of the white race. America is for Hitler an object of terror. America, to his mind, mustered every hostile power against Europe; in America space and race joined forces against the Old World. Hitler's view of

America has developed with the years and has grown more serious.
The land of 'Jewish domination, stock-exchange dictatorship, and
the crassest capitalism' has become, in his eyes, a land of magnificent
national planning; a land with an alarming headstart over Germany on the road to the mechanized nation. America sucks the
whole world dry; she can do this because she possesses the space
which Europe, and particularly Germany, lacks. 'Every emigration,' says Hitler sadly, 'will lead to a loss of energetic, bold men.
The coward never leaves his home. The little proletarian must
have self-confidence when he says: Now I'm going to Argentina.
That is Vikingism, a voyage of the Argonauts that is not sung, but
which should be sung, as the most terrible catastrophe that has
struck our nation. It accumulated through the decades and centuries and gave a new continent a highly valuable human content.
We came face to face with it in 1918 on the Western Front.'

Respect for the American menace, fear of American strength,
and envy of American space — all this is, for Hitler, an entirely
new conception of America; it has developed slowly, in conflict
with his original idea of American 'barbarism.' He describes the
American menace in the same admiring tone which, at times, he
adopts for Communism, and again the enemy becomes his model.
The creeping American menace has transformed itself into a
stormy catastrophe for all Europe and particularly for Germany,
since the United States has begun to subject its immigrants to a
strict physical examination, rejecting the sick and defective. Germany, says Hitler, could do no better than imitate the catastrophe.

Emigration to America [he says] has been brought into a form
constructively dangerous for us, in so far as the human material
which we deliver to America is not picked out by poverty alone.
No, the receiver himself picks out this material and examines it
to see if it is suitable for his own racial aims. . . . The natural
process of selection has become an artificial one. The American
Union strictly prescribes how a man must be constituted if he is
to be admitted. What our bourgeois democracy does not want to
understand is there prescribed by law. Health, a certain stature, are
demanded; no one may have hereditary taints, etc. From a multi-
tude of men, they seek the most highly valued individuals. This

process must bring about a shift of forces between America and Europe. Our official science acts as if this were a statistical experiment. But it is a power problem for the American Union and an infinite danger for old Europe. Not in the number of the population lies the worth or worthlessness of the whole mass, but in the qualities of the individual; not the sum value is decisive, but the specific value. If you want to mobilize Europe against this danger, you will not do it by a mingling of valuable and inferior, but only under the leadership of a state which acts consciously according to racial laws.

Since Hitler, when he speaks of force, value, and higher culture, really means murder and homicide, if possible on a mass basis, he adds nonchalantly: 'If Germany should get a million children each year and eliminate seven to eight hundred thousand of the weakest, in the end the result would be an increase of power.' Seven to eight hundred thousand murders a year — that is what he means by 'in accordance with racial laws'; he was in deadly earnest and found the omission of these murders criminal: 'The clearest racial state of history, Sparta, carried out these racial laws systematically. In our country the opposite is done systematically. By our modern humanitarian drivel, we strive to preserve the weak at the expense of the healthy. . . . We slowly cultivate the weak and kill the strong.' And the whole far-reaching import of these speeches on power and race is summed up in one sentence: 'It does not cost more blood to win the land that we need for bread than is now removed from life and suppressed by artificial reduction of birth.'

The opportunity to spend blood for land he saw approaching in the shape of a war in which at least England, perhaps all Europe, allied with Japan, would march against the American menace. This American war would give Germany an opportunity for decisive action.

At the beginning of 1930, the Washington Naval Conference convened again, this time in London, attended by the five first naval powers. Its purpose might have been called cheap world domination, or rather, distribution of world domination at low cost. All the armament and disarmament conferences have the aim of upholding the existing distribution of military power, while sparing excessive costs. At the conference of 1921 the United States had been recognized by Great Britain as a sea power with equal rights, 'Rule Britannia' was a thing of the past. America, whose real strength consists in her land-block, had now the maritime strength of England, whose power depended entirely on her sea lanes. This was the outcome of the World War, and it is understandable that in England bitter doubts should arise as to the sense and utility of such a war.

The rising sea power of Japan was not granted parity with the two others. The formula for the naval strengths of the five sea powers, United States, England, Japan, France, and Italy was set at 5, 5, 3, 1.75, 1.75. Practically speaking, this resulted in Japanese parity, for the Japanese Navy, for any predictable period, was occupied only in the western half of the Pacific, the American on at least two oceans, and the British on all seven.

This quiet argument among the great powers over the destinies of the earth was drowned out by the shrill bickering of France and Italy over a relatively small strip of the globe: the Mediterranean, the ancient cradle of human civilization and navigation. The British Navy dominated the western exit to the Mediterranean with the mighty rock fortress of Gibraltar; she dominated the eastern exit, the Suez Canal; and although financially France owned fifty-two per cent of the canal, British troops, stationed in Egypt and the canal zone since the eighties, proved to the economic age by their tranquil presence that military, not financial, domination is decisive. But up to 1925 Italian wrath was directed primarily against the nearer France, more envied as her superiority was not felt to be so great. France laid claim to a stronger fleet than Italy; Italy insisted on her parity, granted in 1921 at Washington. It was Germany which profited from this quarrel. France insisted that the 'pocket battleships' which Germany was permitted to build by the Versailles Treaty (to use them in the Baltic against Soviet Russia) should be limited to twenty-one-centimeter guns; Italy obtained permission for Germany to retain the original twenty-eight-centimeter guns.

Did this presage the coming Italian-French war? Hitler thought so; and it was plain that Italy was courting Germany with little

favors. Hitler also believed that the British-American war was silently developing. As early as *Mein Kampf,* he had predicted that England would join with Japan against the United States: England
'grasps avidly at the yellow fist and clings to an alliance which,
racially conceived, is perhaps indefensible, but politically offers the
sole possibility of strengthening the British world position against
the rising American continent.'

The English-American world war will bring Germany's hour,
Hitler declared now in January, 1930.

> All Europe is moving toward a hard fate if American expan-
> sionist economic activity is not stopped somewhere and some time.
> But the British Empire will be struck hardest of all by this devel-
> opment. . . . And here begins the British attempt to put a stop to
> so-called 'armament' by means of agreements, not because they
> think they can avoid a future conflict with America, in this way,
> but because they think the preservation of the present ratio be-
> tween the two fleets is more favorable for England than a boundless
> armament race, in which England might lose her breath sooner
> than the American Union. . . . Regardless how the naval conference
> turns out, the actual causes of the British-American controversy
> will not be touched by it, for they lie far deeper and can neither
> be treated nor far less settled at the conference table.

The coming war between England and America! Hitler has
seldom referred to this possibility, but up to 1930 he looked upon it
as a certainty, and his foreign policy, however much it changed in
other things, always has been based on this tacit premise. In the
above-quoted article he continues:

> We Germans have no reason to desire even in the slightest that
> events of any kind whatsoever will preserve a 'world peace' whose
> sole result, as recent events show, is to make possible, to encourage
> in fact the most horrible plundering and exploitation of our people.
> . . . Germany can harbor only the single ardent desire, that over
> every conference the spirit of misfortune should reign, that discord
> should arise from it, and that finally in blood and fire there should
> be an end to a world peace which otherwise will be the end of our
> people! And for the more distant future we might hope that in
> this struggle an opportunity arise for Germany to play a part in
> world-historical events.

Germany needs a new war and fortunately war, according to Hitler, is the normal condition on this earth.

> The struggle will begin again, the stronger, more forceful, will remain and will press down the weaker. The whole period of years before the World War was not normal; for actually the earth knows of hardly any state of peace lasting from forty to fifty years.

At one and the same time Hitler desired to plunge the world into a new war and to be innocent of the war; his propaganda strays between two equally beautiful ideals or lies:

> We National Socialists welcome this development with all our hearts quite regardless of whether Germany is in a position to take any active part or not. For: 1. For us Germans it is true good fortune if the world again comes to power-political conflicts. . . . Through the new conflict now developing, Germany will be acquitted of guilt in the World War. . . . It will be seen that Germany was no more the instigator of the World War than she will be the instigator of the coming struggle, but that the nations are lashed into these mighty catastrophes by entirely different forces. 2. We believe that in such a period of general unrest, of tensions and power-political decisions, there are more possibilities for loosening the present servitude under which our people is sighing and pining than in a period of peace. . . . As long as peace prevails, Germany has nothing at all to hope for, and only when this world is thrown again into disorder can it be possible for a gifted German government to recognize German interests and, where possible, secure advantages for the German people in these conflicts.

The world's unrest increased; more and more people questioned the hastily improvised peace of 1919. With his sensitive ear for the enemy's weakness, Hitler had sensed at an early date that the world of Versailles was slipping apart, but he had not always correctly interpreted the particular symptoms. In the mid-twenties an undersecretary in the British foreign office had supported German reactionary leagues with funds whose origin was not clear, because in his opinion they were Europe's best protection against Bolshevism; the deal came not completely to light, but for other, less savory reasons the diplomat had to go. Yet at the same time Hitler found it insane to expect help from England. As late as 1927 he thought it 'an error on the part of our government to suppose that England, which has fought us for thirty years, should today take our part.' Three years later, in May, 1930, at a general meeting of his party in Munich, he expressed a new insight: 'The formation of the world powers which once oppressed us no longer seems indissoluble, and already shows the most serious breaches. For many years I have been fighting for a connection with Italy. In the future England, too, will be France's foe [she will also be the adversary of America, but Hitler could not very well tell his assembled lieutenants that Germany should prepare for a new war against America] . . . and after a certain time seek new support in Europe. A time will come when a new triple alliance: England, Germany, Italy, will form. With it will come our hour for the German Reich and people.' The 'hour,' as always, means war.

Two dictatorships and a democracy would form a triple alliance! But Hitler doubted that England was a democracy; in any event, he was convinced that the England which won the World War under Lloyd George had been a dictatorship. Aryans and anti-Semites of all countries, unite! 'Today we are mobilizing a great people,' he said in December, 1928, 'and even today we can see how, though under different banners, the same spirit is beginning to stir in the most different nations, how it presses forward, seeking the form that seems suited to the particular peoples, how everywhere the same spirit fights, how everywhere this spirit creates the same forms to carry through the struggle against the carriers of poison throughout the world. . . .'

That England belonged to this Aryan world was a favorite idea of Alfred Rosenberg, ambassador of the Wise Men of Zion. For five years full of privations, Rosenberg had written the *Völkischer Beobachter* almost single-handed; with the energy of the possessed, he had gathered anti-Semitic material on all sides and written a thick book; in addition he had found time to devise a sort of theory of foreign politics for his party. Since 1928 he held a seat in the Reichstag, where he made speeches on foreign policy, sharply attacking the views of his party associate, Gregor Strasser. While Strasser wanted to incite all the colored peoples — Chinese, Indians, Persians, Egyptians — against the City of London, Rosenberg re-

garded the English capitalists, in so far as they were not Jews, as
the born Aryan rulers of colored 'sub-humanity.' With these rulers,
the German master-men must systematically and peaceably share
Aryan world domination, each in the corner allotted to him by Fate.
'England, Germany, Italy,' wrote Rosenberg in July, 1930, 'stand as
though back to back. The stronger they become, the more dependent they are on one another. England's task is the protection
of the white race in Africa and West Asia; Germany's task is to
safeguard Germanic Europe against the chaotic Mongolian flood
and to hold down France, which has already become an advance
guard of Africa. (Take a look at the French colonial army and
bear in mind that even now a Negro represents the French Government in the Geneva League of Nations.) Italy as a growing nation
has a claim to Corsica, Tunis, Dalmatia, in order to prevent the
destruction of Europe by French Negro armies. None of the three
states can solve the task of destiny alone. . . .' In the *Völkischer
Beobachter,* Rosenberg ran pictures of the Viceroy of India and
Mahatma Gandhi with his thick lips and protruding ears. And the
question was, whether a race-conscious National Socialist could
doubt for a moment on which side he belonged?

Aryan Europe! Hitler looked confidently around the modest
offices he had rented beside the studio of his friend, Heinrich Hoffmann, the photographer, in Schelling Strasse. When his glance fell
on the wall map, he could say: Half of this Europe already belongs to dictatorship, and the section that is still free in the heart
of the continent will be bent to dictatorship by me.

Chapter XIV

FIRST TRIUMPH

IN THE SPRING OF 1928, GUSTAV STRESEMANN, THE
Foreign Minister, went to Munich to deliver an election speech in
the same Bürgerbräu Keller where Hitler had fired at the ceiling.
For the first time Hitler had a leader of the German Reich within
personal reach. Five hundred of his élite led by Hermann Esser
invaded the meeting, taking the seats near the platform. During
the dark days of the Ruhr War, Stresemann had once spoken of
seeing 'a small silver stripe on the horizon.' The five hundred had
fastened glittering strips of stanniol paper to their hair, to their buttonholes, some even to the seats of their pants; they cried out in
chorus: 'Where is the silver stripe, Herr Stresemann?' Stresemann
managed to shout down the five hundred with brutal oratory. At
their wits' end they suddenly stood up and began to sing the
national anthem: *Deutschland über Alles*. The audience rose to
their feet, also singing, and the gentlemen on the platform stood up,
too. Stresemann's party associates, a former general, a lawyer, a
manufacturer, a banker, joined obediently in the singing, for it was
the national hymn and they were patriots. Though the wild scene
served no other purpose than to break up the meeting, to silence
their party's leader, to make the German Foreign Minister ridiculous in the eyes of the world — nevertheless they sang. Stresemann paled and clutched the speaker's desk; that same night he
had a new attack of a malignant kidney complaint, and was constantly ill after that. But in the same elections Hitler was badly
beaten; in the Reichstag his party got only twelve of around six

hundred seats. It was his worst enemies, the Social-Democrats, who won these elections.

Hitler could stir up the crowds, but he was as yet unable to get their votes. Sober reasoning made it clear to the masses that the country must be on the right path since it stabilized its currency, got the French out of the Ruhr, and finally entered the League of Nations with a permanent seat — that is, the full rights of a great power (September, 1926). Nevertheless, there was an inarticulate feeling that in this structure of successes there might be a rotten spot, and their very contact with the artificial and formal international apparatus served only to remind the people of the frustrated hopes of 1919. What a magnificent world it might have been, managed and run by a great world administration, directly and vitally connected with the masses of all civilized nations by direct suffrage! But when by the Peace of Versailles the individual citizen, taxpayer, and voter found himself again locked within the borders of his national state; when he became aware of the great incongruity, that, with the increasing complexity of international relations, events on the other side of the globe directly affected his own destiny while he himself by his vote could not influence the whole globe, but only his narrow national state — when this basic limitation, rendering national democracy useless as a guide to world destiny, came to the consciousness of the individual, it was the end of the democratic passion which had enriched the nineteenth century, and for a brief moment in 1919 kindled a light even in Germany.

Meanwhile, starting in the fall of 1928, Communism began its attempt to build Soviet Russia into a socialist model state. Through unspeakable sufferings, through famine, through the death of whole sections of the population, through the misery of whole regions, Josef Stalin, the dictator, drove his first Five-Year Plan forward. Along with brutal energy and love of personal power, Stalin possessed a gift which perhaps recalls Hitler's best quality: a worldly experienced eye for the limits of human strength. He saw possibilities where others despaired; and where fanatics stormed blindly forward, he sensed limits. He called his system 'socialism in one country,' indicating that he meant to socialize without waiting for general world revolution. The privations of the consumers, the exploitation of the workers, made the Soviet Union appear gray and poor beside most capitalist countries. Some observers spoke of state capitalism. Actually, in the year 1928, the armed intellectual definitely took power in Russia. The chief aim became almost at once the creation of a great war machine.

On the other side of the globe, prices on the New York Stock Exchange crashed in October, 1929. It was the beginning of that crisis which, within a few months, spread to all continents: the depression of 1929-1933. The age characterized by Henry Ford when he said that 'anything which is economically right is also morally right' was drawing to an end. In Russia and the United States two tremors of the same crisis occurred. With satisfaction the Russians beheld one more of the capitalist crises predicted by Marxism; with fear American capitalists saw the approaching socialist doom; meanwhile both countries moved toward a new social form.

Between the two upheavals, Germany sought her way. She was the first European country to feel the full impact of the crisis. This crisis was brought to Germany neither by the Peace of Versailles nor by the policy of *rapprochement* with her former war enemies. The economic burdens of the Versailles Peace did not weigh more heavily on Germany than on the other countries, for their pressure practically was intercepted by the golden shower of foreign capital that up to 1928 incessantly filled the vacuums of German economics. It would be too simple to say that German reparations were paid with borrowed foreign capital; on the contrary, the entire system of borrowing and high interest payments put a heavy additional burden on the German economy. But it was the time when in many countries the burdens and mortgages were not felt, at least by the working masses in the cities, because economic progress made up for them. In Germany improvement and cheapening of production made the situation appear sounder than it was. From 1926 wages, which had been sharply cut down by the stabilization of 1924, began to rise, not seldom pushed up by successful strikes, always a certain sign of at least seeming prosperity. But the most remarkable gain the working masses made in the German Republic was the broadening and strengthening of the system of social insurances; every wage-earner was automatically insured against illness, accidents, to some extent even against the dangers of old age. The most important of these public insurances was that against unemployment which in normal times actually would have given the working man a wonderful feeling of security. But somebody had to pay for this progress. The cost of social insurance embittered the employers even more than the question of wages. Between them and the trade unions a hostility grew up after 1926 that hardly had existed before 1924; they launched the slogan that the 'state socialism' of the Weimar Republic must be broken. But an even heavier burden was heaped on the shoulders of German economy when the state, which after the stabilization had dismissed a great number of civil servants, now reversed its policy and raised salaries considerably (1927).

Hjalmar Schacht, president of the Reichsbank, traveled through the country, making speeches full of threats: the Germans were not saving enough; it was intolerable that German women should have a new hat every year. The athletic fields, swimming pools, parks, public buildings, being built in the German cities were also intolerable. Parker Gilbert — agent for reparations payments, the 'American slaveholder, the taskmaster of Wall Street,' as Hitler called him — made the same complaint. 'What if new foreign loans should cease to come in, with which to pay the greater part of our foreign indebtedness as we have done up to now?' Schacht warned in 1927. 'Our products would have to be sold abroad at dumping prices, workers and employers would have to make the greatest sacrifices. . . . I do not see the future calmly.' Hitler read this and prophesied triumphantly: If ever Parker Gilbert's employers in Wall Street should withdraw their money from Germany, the whole fine edifice of German economy would explode. How, exactly, would this come about? Hitler could imagine but one thing: there would be a new inflation; no, it was already at hand; he thought he saw a 'creeping inflation' — a grave error in detail, but not an unsound judgment on the whole.

The influence of America on European development is one of the many features of the general complex that transformed all prosperity into world prosperity and every crisis into a world crisis; but each rise and fall made the extent of American leadership clear. America had given Europe, and particularly Germany, more than money. The renewal of German productive technique after 1924 was based on an American idea, the assembly line; it so affected all life in Germany that the words *laufendes Band* (assembly line) have found all sorts of figurative uses in the German language. Since her discovery four hundred and fifty years ago, America has never ceased to live in the European imagination as a fairy tale turned reality, as a proof that the seemingly impossible is possible; first as the land of unlimited wealth, then of unlimited natural wonders, then of unlimited liberty, and finally of unlimited technical possibilities. As a technical model, the United States has played an immeasurable part in the building of two states alien to it: the Soviet Union and National Socialist Germany. The American engineers who built Russian factories and German 'study commissions' bore the American idea across the ocean, and the magic of 'America' became more potent throughout Europe than that of any other country, even of France or Italy with their ancient civilizations; even of the Soviet Union.

But this technical leadership of America in turn helped to create a situation that finally upset all gains made before. Almost everywhere on the globe the era after the First World War was filled with an effort to build, to create, to produce — an effort that looked noble and enterprising, but in its final effect was as destructive as it seemed creative. Countries which had hitherto produced chiefly raw materials and agrarian products began to develop manufactures at least for their own use; states which had not existed until then tried to start industries of their own that had not existed until then either. Some entered the world market as new competitors, underbidding everyone in sight, partly with the help of starvation wages — Japan, for instance. But of all new competitors by far the strongest in force and capacities was America. The gradual rise in American customs duties gave the world market a sign that a new industrial country was entering into sharper and sharper competition with the old production centers. The Fordney-McCumber Tariff Act of 1922 showed that America intended to protect her production, based on high wages, against the cheap, foreign goods; the Hawley-Smoot Tariff Act, signed in June, 1930, by President Hoover, was even more drastic; some duties were increased by fifty to one hundred per cent, creating semi-panic in the world market; within eighteen months twenty-five countries responded with sharp counter-measures.

This was the outcome of the age of national liberty and unlimited sovereignty; the universal right of self-determination had led to a senseless piling-up of forces and material. Everybody a producer, nobody a buyer — this ideal goal was not completely reached, but all the same, the international exchange of goods and services between 1928 and 1935 lost half of its volume and almost two thirds of its value, due to the inevitable decline in prices on a crowded world market (from 67 to 26 billion dollars).

Because everybody tried to produce everything, there seemed to be overproduction. The world was becoming glutted with capital and consumers' goods — in so far as one may speak of glut in a world which objectively is always suffering from shortage. Raw-material prices crashed, and everywhere in the world it became difficult for farmers to cover their costs.

When the dream of gold began to burst, the farmers all over the world were the first to feel it. The agrarian crisis in most countries hit a class which during and after the war had been on top of the economic situation, dealing, as it did, with the most coveted goods. But probably in no country had this class profited from the situation as in Germany. In the frightful time of vanishing fortunes (1923) they had been the most contented class, for the inflation had wiped out their debts without hurting their estates. Now the only class which had not suffered from inflation was the first to suffer from stabilization. After 1924, German landowners, grown overconfident, began to assume new debts on their property. These became more and more oppressive as it became apparent that their products could often not compete with the world market in quality, and never, despite high tariffs, in price. Misery began to spread among the farmers; many went bankrupt and were driven from their estates. They answered with open rebellion; refused to pay interest and taxes; gathered into armed bands and threw bombs into tax offices. The freebooters, the former army lieutenants, who had been unemployed since the beer-hall *putsch,* found a congenial occupation in organizing these peasant bands. A new opportunity for the National Socialist leaders to split over an issue; Strasser hailed the bomb-throwings as the beginning of the great catastrophe in which the Weimar Republic would perish; but Hitler, always afraid of police and public prosecutor, forbade his followers to have any share in the attacks.

All the same, the moment had come for him to alter his unalterable program once again. For Germany was faced by something new: by an uprising of peasants and big landowners against cities and industry; and nowhere in German politics was this new development so well recognized and exploited as by the National Socialists.

In the beginning of his movement (1919-1923) and in his 'immutable' program, Hitler had not considered the peasants at all; the hungry city dwellers who filled his meetings up to 1923 even hated them. One point in the 'unalterable' program advocated 'expropriation of the soil without indemnity for community purposes.' In 1928, Hitler withdrew this threat to the landowners: 'Since the N.S.D.A.P. stands on the basis of private property,' it planned only 'to expropriate, if necessary, land which was acquired in an unjust way or which is not administered according to the needs of the popular welfare. This is chiefly directed against the Jewish speculators.' With this shift in program began the systematic, arduous recruiting of a section of the population which envied the metropolitan masses, blaming them for their own misfortunes. The discovery of the peasants was a master-stroke of National Socialist propaganda. The Communists, rigidly following the Marxist principle of class struggle, tried to incite the small peasants against the large landholders. In this they followed the Russian example of Lenin, which, like so many of the Communist International's methods, proved totally unsuitable for export. In Germany they met with no success, because the big landowners and the peasants had the same interest: higher prices; as long as sweat and toil on the field did not bring them there could be no 'hunger for land' among the poorer peasants.

The National Socialists had a far better understanding of the agrarian struggle. Convinced that by propaganda he could make his city supporters swallow anything, Hitler tried to set himself at the head of the peasant uprising against the cities. In a great agrarian program promulgated in March, 1930, he proclaimed that the 'country people were the chief bearers of hereditary racial health, the people's fountain of youth, and the backbone of our military power.' His conclusion was that 'the preservation of an efficient peasant class in numerical proportion to the total population constitutes a pillar of National Socialist policy.'

He discovered this pillar when the debt-ridden, mortgaged, tax-crushed, bomb-throwing peasants began to fill his meetings — not before. He appointed to his staff a new man, an agricultural expert, R. Walter Darré, who, though new in the movement, had achieved a powerful influence over Hitler. Another of the many 'Germans abroad,' Darré was born in 1895 at Belgrano in the Argentine. He was an agrarian specialist with academic training. The agriculture ministries of the Reich and of Prussia had sent him to observe foreign farming methods in Latvia and Estonia, where for centuries, under the government of the Russian tsars, a German upper class had dominated the peasantry. It may be presumed that Darré, although a learned specialist, did not concern himself only with the Latvian egg production. At all events, he sent reports on the conditions among the Latvian and Estonian Germans to the Deutsche Akademie in Munich; this was an institute founded by Karl Haushofer for research on the culture of the Germans abroad; for a time Rudolf Hess had worked at the institute as Haushofer's assistant. For a German raised abroad and hence imbued with the arrogant conception of the *Herrenvolk,* these Baltic countries were a good school; here the past glory and the present misery of the *Herrenvolk* could be studied day in and day out in the newspapers. The learned agronomist built a theory on the basis of his observations, and when in 1929 he came into conflict with his superiors and was forced to leave the service, he returned to the vicinity of Wiesbaden on the Rhine and there wrote a book: *The Peasantry as the Life Source of the Nordic Race.* Rudolf Hess brought him to the National Socialist Party; Darré made so strong an impression on Hitler that he at once commissioned him to draw up a peasant program. Darré proved himself a brilliant, convincing propagandist. The program begins:

> Today we pay for our food imports chiefly with borrowed foreign funds. Thus the German people is led deeper and deeper into the debt slavery of the international high finance that gives us credit. If the present state of affairs continues, international high finance will expropriate the German people more and more. By blocking credit and hence the import of foodstuffs, in other words, by hanging the bread-basket higher, it can compel the German proletariat to work for starvation wages in its service, or to let themselves be shipped off to foreign colonies as working slaves. Liberation from this slavery is possible only if the German people can sustain itself mainly from its own soil. To increase the productivity of domestic agriculture has therefore become a vital question for the German people.

Therefore taxes on agriculture must be reduced — this was an easy promise and the peasant voter would not normally have had much faith in it; but Darré found a persuasive National Socialist basis for it. Taxes, he declared, were so high only 'because the Jewish world power which actually governs German parliamentary democracy desires the destruction of German agriculture, since the German people, and especially the working class, is entirely dependent on it.' Since, moreover, German agriculture 'suffers from the competition of foreign agriculture producing under more favorable conditions, protective duties must be increased.' The program contained a section directed for practical purposes against a part of the large landholdings of the Prussian junkers, though the junkers as such are not attacked, but actually encouraged with the words: 'Large-scale agriculture also fulfills its special, necessary tasks.' But: 'A large number of small and medium farms are above all important from the standpoint of population policy.' To preserve and sustain these small and medium farms, and, particularly in the German East, to prevent them from being sucked up by mechanized, factory-like giant farms, is one of the most important points in the program: 'In future, soil can be acquired only by him who means to farm it himself.'

Germany was one of the most heavily taxed nations of the world. Even very small wage-earners had to pay an income tax, but about four fifths of the German farmers were exempt. If this disease spread through the whole economic body — and this seemed inevitable — how could Germany be expected to fulfill her obligations? The problem was no longer if and how the Versailles Treaty would work, but whether it was worth while to defend this treaty against the mounting world crisis.

What would become of American investments if Germany were to break down under the burden of reparations, as Schacht prophesied? The French argued that if 'guilty' Germany stopped payments, then France, the innocent victim, would be condemned to pay for having been attacked, for she still had to pay back her American war loans. Therefore, it was impossible to do away completely with German reparations, but a new conference, held in the spring of 1929 in Paris and presided over by Owen D. Young, somewhat relieved the burden, which had gone up to two and a half billion marks (about $600,000,000) annually. Now it was stipulated that during fifty-nine years (until 1988) Germany should pay an annual average sum of 1,700,000,000 marks. This was still a heavy burden, especially since the safeguards which had protected German currency under the Dawes plan now were taken away, although, on the other hand, the supervision by Parker Gilbert was also ended. But the 'realists' who believed that such a system of political payments could be established for almost three generations proved to be naïve dreamers.

German industry still found the weight too heavy, but Schacht, Germany's chief delegate in Paris, defended his work against criticism at home, although only half-heartedly. Stresemann, too, defended it. He was already gravely ill, and died in October, 1929.

He did not live to see his greatest triumph. For Germany accepted the new 'Young Plan' of reparations only under the condition that the French evacuated the Rhineland; and, pressed by America and England, France gave in and promised to evacuate every inch of German soil, except the small Saar territory at the Lorraine border, the fate of which was to be settled by a plebiscite in 1935. On June 30, 1930, the last French troops left the Rhineland. Germany was still burdened with the obligation imposed by the Treaties of Versailles and Locarno never to send troops into the liberated Rhineland or build fortifications; the Reichswehr was still limited to a hundred thousand men, without aviation or heavy guns. But aside from the small Saar territory, German soil was free. France had withdrawn behind her own borders.

But this political triumph of the Weimar Republic was immediately overshadowed by the mounting economic and financial crisis. In 1928 America had exported over a billion dollars, in 1929, it was only $221,000,000. What Schacht and Hitler had prophesied began to happen; the golden stream which had flown over Germany dried up. German communities, which had leaned heavily on foreign loans, fell into difficulties; the Reich's Treasury itself did, and the pressure of the too hastily augmented salaries of the civil servants began to be felt. Wages had gone up, but so had unemployment. The critics of the government, Schacht among them, asked that the costs of administration — that is, salaries — should be cut down; the employers and their advocates, again Schacht among them, wanted a cut in wages and in the cost of social insurances. They argued that the slowing down of foreign capital import made the burdens of the Young Plan too heavy, and Schacht finally joined them in condemning his own work. In February, 1930, he resigned as president of the Reichsbank.

The opening attack of big business on the economic structure of the Weimar Republic gave Hitler his first great chance; it was a split between two forces which hitherto had both been against him. To be sure, he had finally found supporters among the industrialists, but the most important of them, big as they were, nevertheless were not typical of German industry as a whole.

One was Fritz Thyssen, son of a powerful industry-builder of the Kaiser's day, a Catholic and convinced nationalist; during the Ruhr War he had faced a French military court. Thyssen was the prototype of the National Socialist money-man, an adept at eight-figure bankruptcies. He was the chief shareholder in the most powerful German steel trust, the Vereinigte Stahlwerke; from its very beginning, the Vereinigte Stahlwerke had watered its stock. A shaky structure, its shares constantly dragged down prices in the

German Bourse, and helped psychologically to intensify the economic crisis. The steel trust gambled heavily on the coming Third Reich, a state whose gigantic armaments program would require immense quantities of steel and steel products. Thyssen financed Hitler just as confidently as the foolish duchess who hoped to recover her lost throne.

Even more important was a second contributor. Again history went its secret and personal ways. Among Hitler's followers there was a young journalist who had studied economics and philosophy in Munich. He had worked in the Ruhr where the 'big men' were at home; then he returned to Munich and became business editor of a 'bourgeois' newspaper, but secretly he remained a National Socialist. His name was Doctor Otto Dietrich. In Essen he had married the daughter of a certain Reismann-Grone who owned the *Rheinisch-Westfälische Zeitung*. This journal was the mouthpiece and political bulletin of German heavy industry, and Reismann-Grone was one of the political advisers of these men, most of whom knew little of politics and were sometimes even aware of the fact. Two of their most important organizations, the Bergbauliche Verein (Mining Association) and the Verband der Nordwestdeutschen Eisen-Industrie (Association of the Northwest German Iron Industry), had raised a political slush fund, the so-called 'Ruhr treasury'; this Ruhr treasury was administered by an old man, the industrialist, Emil Kirdorf, who by his gift of organization had assured Ruhr coal a high price in the German market and a place in the world market. Before the World War Kirdorf had been hated and feared by the German workers as a ruthless employer; he was an intense nationalist, a pan-German, and even a bitter critic of the Kaiser, whom he found too weak and mild. Otto Dietrich, with the help of his father-in-law, succeeded (1927) in interesting Kirdorf in Hitler. In the summer of 1929, the eighty-two-year-old man went to Nuremberg to have a look at the third National Socialist Party Day. On his return he wrote Hitler the following letter, which in content and form says much regarding the relation between Hitler and his billionaire backer:

> *Dear Herr Hitler*: On our return home my wife and I are eager to express our thanks to you for asking us to attend the con-

vention of your party held between August 2 and 4, and for the elevating impressions we obtained there. Our intention was to express this thanks to you at the end of the session and for that reason we were in the Deutscher Hof, where, unfortunately, we awaited you in vain, since without doubt your time was taken up with the brutal attacks of the Communists on your faithful party members and with concern for the protection of the latter. . . . We shall never forget how overwhelmed we were in attending the memorial celebration for the World War dead and the dedication of the banners in the Luitpold Grove, at the sight of your troops marching by on the Hauptmarkt, of thousands and thousands of your supporters, their eyes bright with enthusiasm, who hung on your lips and cheered you. The sight of the endless crowd, cheering you and stretching out their hands to you at the end of the parade, was positively overwhelming. At this moment I, who am filled with despair by the degeneration of our masses and the failure of our bourgeois circles toward the future of Germany, suddenly realized why you believe and trust unflinchingly in the fulfillment of the task you have set yourself, and, conscious of your goal, continue on your way, regardless how many sacrifices it may demand of you and your supporters. Any man who in these days, dominated by a brutal destruction of the patriotic qualities, could gather together and chain to himself such a troop of national-minded racial comrades, ready for every sacrifice, is entitled to nourish this confidence. You may be proud of the honors and homages done you; there is hardly a crowned head who receives their equal. My wife and I are happy to have been able to witness them. . . .

A strangely respectful tone for a coal king and financial backer. Kirdorf did not hide the fact that Hitler's program contained some points he did not like — presumably he was referring chiefly to state seizure of the big industrial concerns, a point which had long since been tacitly abandoned. But this practical doubt was nothing against the old man's personal emotion and enthusiasm. To be sure, he was hardened in his contempt of the world and men, and even the Nuremberg Party Day did not wholly convince him that anything could prevent Germany's decay. With mingled doubt and emotion he concludes his letter in words that recall Richard Wagner's summons to 'go down like gods':

Anyone who was privileged to attend this session will, even though he may doubt or decisively reject particular points in your party program, nevertheless recognize the importance of your movement for the rehabilitation of our German fatherland and wish it success. With this wish, which we utter from a full heart, there rises in me even a small hope that it may be realized. Even if my doubts in the future of the German people cannot be entirely dispelled, since my observation, extending years back into the Bismarckian golden age of Germany and further, has shown that the German bourgeoisie are nationally speaking at a low level such as can be found in no other country, yet I have taken with me from the Nuremberg Congress the consoling certainty that numerous circles will sacrifice themselves to prevent the doom of Germanism from being accomplished in the dishonorable, undignified way I previously feared. With true German greetings from my wife and self; in friendship, Your Kirdorf.

But even with Kirdorf's admiration and Thyssen's help alone Hitler would not have gone very far; between the lines of Kirdorf's letter it can be read that he himself saw in Hitler more a rallying point for the forces of German youth, a source of enthusiasm, but not the man whom he would trust with running Germany. The man on whom the reactionary section of German industry at this time relied was Doctor Alfred Hugenberg, a self-made man, who had amassed a fortune by combining politics and business. Exploiting his financial power, he had made himself leader of the German National Party, up to 1930 numerically the strongest party of the German counter-revolution. Hugenberg and his circle sought to force German rejection of the Young Plan by one of these democratic weapons the Weimar constitution had handed over to its own enemies: a plebiscite.

A gold-driven propaganda wave now rolled over the land, and on its crest rode the most capable propagandist of the time, on whose collaboration the financial backers of the campaign had insisted: Adolf Hitler. But despite Hitler, the plebiscite was a failure, bringing only 5,800,000 votes; it was less than a half of the number which, four years previous, had voted against the princes. Hindenburg, after some hesitation, signed the law accepting the Young Plan.

For Hitler it was, nevertheless, a splendid piece of business. He had filled his treasury; and Hugenberg, who owned Germany's greatest newspaper and film organization, had for the moment been obliged to put this power at his disposal. For the first time since 1924, the thundering voice of the unknown was heard in the great political arena. Hitler had found a friend on whose back he could climb — whose head, by way of gratitude, he was later to trample. Hugenberg announced the alliance to the public, declaring that the Nationalist parties had united for life and death; Hitler said dryly that the alliance was only temporary, and that later, 'in the free play of forces, the clearest and boldest German movement would fight through to final victory.' One of his sub-leaders characterized the alliance by saying that the Führer would know how to hoodwink Hugenberg.

Why had the plebiscite been a failure? Because the people had felt that this was not the real issue. Young Plan, reparations, Treaty of Versailles — these worries of yesterday began to be engulfed by the much bigger monster, the world crisis. At first the victors had tried to break Germany. When this failed to improve their own position they had then shared their own prosperity with Germany, but still under the fiction of victor and defeated. Now victor and defeated alike were overwhelmed by the greater common enemy, the depression. Abroad, many people still saw in the crisis nothing but an unfortunate accident. But many Germans saw in it a millennial event, the definite proof that something was rotten in this kind of state and society. While the Social Democratic chancellor, Hermann Müller, carried to power by the elections of 1928, defended high wages and social insurances against the attacks of the employers, the anti-democratic forces grew ever stronger. No particular foreign or domestic issue was responsible, the simple fact was that democracy more and more seemed unable to 'work.'

The strongest of these forces had been, up to 1929, the Stahlhelm (Steel Helmet), a union of former soldiers, well organized on semi-military lines, practically an outgrowth of several of the former 'free corps.' The Stahlhelm, boasting of a *coup d'état* rather than actually planning one, was confronted by a similar gigantic troop, consisting mostly of trade-union workers, the loyal Reichsbanner Schwarz-Rot-Gold. These private armies marched through the German streets on Sundays with brass bands and held maneuvers in the country. From 1925 to 1930, they faced one another in a state of armed peace like the armies and navies of the world powers; they tried to frighten one another by their existence and generally avoided open clashes. This changed at once when the true uprooted and disinherited, the National Socialists and Communists, entered the field. In 1930, there began a continuous series of street fights, with thousands of dead and wounded on both sides. The Communists organized as 'Red Front Fighters' or 'Anti-Fascists,' sometimes effectively trained by Russian instructors. Their slogan was: 'Strike the Fascists wherever you find them!' But even earlier, in ornate German, spiced with wrongly used foreign words, Goebbels had cried: 'Dominance of the street gives claim to the state; we must mount the barricades!'

At this time, when the authority of parliament began to decline, a strange new experiment started: the Reichswehr tried to regenerate parliament and democracy.

The Reichswehr as a political force was embodied in three persons: Hindenburg, Marshal, President, and Supreme Commander; Wilhelm Groener, his old chief of staff in 1918-19, with whom he had dethroned the emperor; and who now was Minister of the Reichswehr; and the former captain, now General Kurt von Schleicher, deviser of the Free Corps, now Groener's most important aide and political adviser. Schleicher, who, for an officer, was on extremely good terms with parliament and even the parliamentary leaders of the Left, in the beginning of 1930 conceived the idea that a new form of government must be found; a government which would be able to force its will upon the representatives of the people, but by their own consent. The man whom he wanted to appoint as Chancellor was Doctor Heinrich Brüning, at that time one of the leaders of the Catholic Center Party. Brüning was a former officer; but he was also an able politician and speaker, familiar with the ways of administration and parliament, and a man of an unselfish character. Schleicher's attention had been drawn to him when Brüning began to criticize the high cost of public administration and warn against the dangers of the Young Plan.

The opportunity for Brüning's appointment came when Hermann Müller lost his majority in the Reichstag. His was a coalition government based on half a dozen parliamentary parties, some among them representing capital and industry, others the workers. In a dispute over a government contribution of seventy million marks to the unemployment insurance fund, the party of the industrialists withdrew its votes from the government which then no longer had a majority. Chancellor Müller asked President Hindenburg for his support; he desired him to invoke his constitutional emergency powers (as a rule too widely construed) and impose the cabinet's measures over the head of the parliament; in other words, a bit of dictatorship. This was the expected cue. Hindenburg solemnly asked the Reichswehr if it would be advisable to govern against the parliament; the Reichswehr, namely Groener, and even more Schleicher, said 'No.' Schleicher told Hindenburg that there was another candidate who would be able to gain a majority in the reluctant parliament. Thereupon Hindenburg refused Müller his emergency powers; Müller tendered his resignation (March, 1930); and, according to plan, Brüning was appointed Chancellor.

He began his career by denouncing the methods by which Germany hitherto had been governed, accused the Reichstag of not living up to its task, and told the representatives that they must find a way to make the Reichstag 'work,' or else the parliamentary system would dig its own grave. The centuries-old complaint about German disunity came to life again in this bitter denouncement of party strife. Brüning was by no means the first to accuse the political parties of helping to disrupt the 'communion of the people (Volksgemeinschaft)'; by him, however, in a decisive hour, the question was definitely put before the nation: was democracy able to 'work' in Germany?

It did not seem so.

Brüning, also unable to govern with parliament, had to ask Hindenburg to dissolve the Reichstag (July, 1930) in the hope that the election would bring a reliable majority. Seldom has a political speculation been so cruelly disappointed.

It is always the greatest triumph for an opposition when a government becomes its own opposition, attacks its own system, adopts the criticism of its adversary. This happened in Germany in 1930.

Hitler cried out: 'Eight months ago I stood in the Zirkus Krone in Munich and declared to the masses: If what we predict does not happen; if what our opponents proclaim does happen — you can chase me off the platform, you can strike me dead. And now a short time has passed, and we face an unprecedented collapse. Now I ask you: who was right? [Cries: "Hitler was right, Hitler!"]' (Speech on July 25, at Nuremberg.)

What had he been right about? His judgment of the Versailles Peace, he himself would have said. But the Versailles Peace was already in tatters. True, when the treaty punished the German Republic for the sins of the defeated empire, when Woodrow Wilson, despite all his weaknesses the greatest prophetic figure of the age, let himself be pressed to the wall in Paris — then that vacuum was created in which the armed bohemian would thrive; but the treaty did not create the armed bohemian. At the time when this peace most stifled Germany, Hitler's *putsch* shattered against the resistance of the German masses and institutions (1923); but when the treaty had been smashed by its own impracticability, Hitler came to power (1932). It is therefore a legend to call him a creature of the Versailles Treaty. Hitler himself has sometimes denied 'that the peace treaty is the cause of our misfortune. . . . The Peace of Versailles is itself only a consequence of the inner spiritual confusion that is slowly overcoming us.'

In 1923, money in Germany had lost its old majesty. Now, in 1930, work lost its value; three million men could no longer sell their labor and more millions expected to lose their jobs in the near future. This new death of all values struck, not only the proletarian, but also the capitalist; small shareholders, in Thyssen's Steel Trust, for example, whose stock fell to a third of its original value; holders of German municipal bonds; landlords trembling for their rents; mortgage-holders trembling for their interest payments. Property no longer had its old meaning; large holdings maintained themselves, even increased; small property slipped away. The big capitalists had always dominated the stock companies through a minority of shares. In the period of rationalization they had enriched themselves at the expense of the small shareholders by keeping dividends down, enlarging the plant with the savings, and voting themselves increased profits in the enlarged industry. The basic difference between large and small property became clear to the small shareholders when their holdings were wiped out by the stock-exchange crash, while the big men bought up the depreciated values. Every small enterprise suffered under the pressure of large-scale industry. The department stores stifled the small shop; the small tavern-keepers became mere slaves of the breweries; the small business could get no bank credit, while the large industry obtained it with ease. Thus, a class which, for a century, had tenaciously defended private property in all social struggles developed a hatred against large-scale property, blending with the old hatred of the propertyless proletarian. An 'anti-capitalist' longing had awakened in the German people, said Gregor Strasser in the Reichstag.

The Wise Men of Zion in their day gave a masterly picture of a similar state of decay; they showed the helplessness of a type of government which preaches democracy, but can help itself only by dictatorship; and how the political pirate exploits this period of decay: 'We shall arm all parties, set up state authority as a target for every ambition, and turn the states into arenas for uprisings. Just a little more patience and the uprisings and collapses will be universal. Untiring babblers will turn the sessions of parliaments and cabinets into bouts of oratory. Insolent journalists will each day attack the representatives of the government. The misuse of power will finally shake the pillars of the state and prepare their collapse.'

The crisis had made the masses aware that they were cut off from the springs and levers of their own fate. The state had become their destiny more than ever before, and at the same time it had become more invisible and nameless; a body of rulers almost unknown to the people, which decided on the basis of unknown principles whether the people should eat or go hungry. While the state lay hidden in the yellow twilight of the Reichstag, the Brown gangs appeared in the streets crying: 'Germany, awaken!' They marched with flags and music, and great crowds followed them to their mass meetings. There a sprightly little orator with a club foot declared, 'Today no one knows who rules Germany, for the supposedly ruling bourgeois parties baptize themselves with new names each year, but with all their baptism they have remained in reality circumcised.' When the laughter had died down, he continued, 'Parties cannot save Germany, but only a man — the unknown soldier of the World War.'

The great day had dawned for the uprooted, unbalanced men who had no other occupation than addressing the masses in smoky beer halls; who had lost their normal livelihood, sold their businesses, given up their jobs; who bore no responsibility in public life and felt responsible for nothing. They had become more than a type; they were a marching, blackjack-swinging machine. 'If today in Germany a question arises,' said Hitler, 'I never have to speak with my editor-in-chief, my collaborators or my *gauleiters,* for to-morrow this question will be answered in the same way by dozens of party speakers. Philosophy as the granite foundation of thought forces them to the same conclusions' — the inevitable conclusion that the Jews are to blame for everything.

How profoundly the state of mind of the German people had changed by 1930 can be seen in the sharp curve described by the barometer of National Socialist propaganda. All the sage plans for coming to power as a minority were forgotten. Resistance to parliament suddenly ceased. The contemptuous speeches about the broad mass of zeros died down. Instead, the party's election proclamation ran: 'We shall overthrow the present parliamentary régime of the destroyers of our people in a legal way with legal means, through the soundness of our idea. . . .'

In 1930, the great political vision of the Wise Men of Zion was fulfilled in Germany. 'We know,' said Hitler on July 27, 1930, to the party leaders assembled in Munich, 'that no election can finally decide the fate of the nation. It is not parliamentary majorities that decide the fate of nations — they can destroy nations. But we know that in these elections democracy must be destroyed with the weapons of democracy.'

Formerly he had hoped to subdue the German people with the help of the Reichswehr; the fact was that the Reichswehr, led by Wilhelm Groener, did not accept National Socialists in its ranks. But Hitler now saw his great democratic star rising in the political sky, and he began to speculate on the idea that his Brown Shirts with the help of the German people could subdue the Reichswehr. This he proved to himself and his audience with impressive, though none too accurate figures:

'Herr Groener can do what he likes. We do not need a *putsch*. Herr Groener need only reckon: In 1919 we were seven men; in 1920, sixty-four; in 1921, three thousand; in 1922, seven thousand; in 1923, thirty thousand.' Then came the moment when he could joyfully announce: 'In 1925 we were again one man. In 1926, seventeen thousand; in 1927, over forty thousand; in 1928, over sixty thousand; in 1929, over a hundred and twenty thousand; today (March, 1930), we are over two hundred thousand. Herr Groener, in two years we will be five hundred and six hundred thousand. And a time will come when a radiant Brown majority will enter the Reichstag, and then, Herr Groener: at Philippi we shall meet again!'

For years Hitler himself had not understood that democracy must be conquered by democracy; small wonder that some of his more or less faithful never understood it. They grumbled, demanded continuation of the revolutionary course. Hitler threw the chief complainants summarily out of the party, Otto Strasser at their head. Strasser and his supporters had long opposed the party's 'legal' course; when the conflict grew serious, most of his friends, as usually happens in such cases, left him in the lurch, including his elder brother Gregor, who felt himself exposed and drawn into undesired adventures by the undisciplined Otto. 'I have sold my drugstore,' said Gregor; 'and put all my money into the party. I am now dependent on my Reichstag mandate; if Hitler takes away my mandate, it's all over.' In an open letter Hitler called Otto Strasser a 'parlor Bolshevik'; his adherents were 'doctrinaire fools, uprooted literati, political boy scouts.' 'We founded the party,' he went on, 'and anyone who doesn't like the essential content of the movement as laid down by me should not enter the movement or should get out of it.' Then he commanded his faithful Goebbels to throw Otto Strasser and his supporters 'ruthlessly and without exception out of the party' (July 4, 1930), which Goebbels did with the greatest pleasure. Otto Strasser's supporters were but few; he claimed, to be sure, that he was the true National Socialist, that Hitler had betrayed National Socialism, and he attempted to set up his own National Socialist Party. But the attempt failed, his party remained a splinter group; Otto Strasser's daily degenerated into a weekly while Goebbels was able to develop his weekly *Angriff* (Attack) into a daily.

More serious was a rebellion of the Berlin S.A. shortly before the elections. These faithful were primarily concerned about money; they complained that they had not been put forward as Reichstag candidates, with the prospect of a monthly salary amounting to six to eight hundred marks. For the first time, Himmler's Black S.S. attacked the Brown S.A., but were so badly beaten that they had to phone the police for help. Hitler rushed to Berlin, drove from beer hall to beer hall, and even burst into tears to melt the hardened hearts of his Brown Shirts. As a weightier argument he poured forth money, subjecting the whole party to a 'special tax' for the S.A. He put the blame for the misunderstanding between himself and 'his' S.A. on bad leaders, who had forced themselves between him and his faithful. Never had there been so glowing an opportunity to win over the Brown Shirts. Pfeffer was deposed and Hitler personally assumed supreme command of his private army, assuming Pfeffer's title: Oberster S.A. Führer (Supreme S.A. leader), abbreviated as 'Osaf.'

The new supreme S.A. leader now showed the shaken bourgeois parties, especially the party of Hugenberg, what it meant to be allied with him. True, Hitler's propaganda seemed directed against the Communists, against the Social Democrats, and finally against Brüning's Center Party. But even the most sensational, brutal, well-directed propaganda had astonishingly little effect against these solid political institutions, and the figures show that the adherents of Social Democracy and the Center stood firmly by their parties. But in the crisis of 1930, the nationalist groups, especially Hugenberg's German Nationals, wedged in between democratic and National Socialist parties, became chaff, and this chaff flew to Hitler.

The shift that occurred in 1930 was no hysterical crash as in 1923. The new crisis approached slowly like an inexorable doom, gripping the souls of men almost before their outward circumstances. It is not hard to find parallels between the rising economic distress and the increase in Hitler's adherents. In autumn, 1929, when Hitler was emerging from the years of defeat and preparing the 'popular decision' against the Young Plan, a German miner earned an average of 602 marks in a quarter of a year (third quarter, 1929). Hitler was still of little importance. A year later, the miner's wage had gone down to 548 marks, and Hitler achieved his first great electoral success; one more year and the miner's pay had dwindled to 497 marks, and Hitler's vote increased. We shall see that Hitler's strength began to fall off as soon as wages started to rise a little.

Some observers maintain that Hitler's successes were, in part at least, due to the enormous financial aid given him by German and foreign capital. Actually the funds were attracted by success, rather than the other way around. There is also a widespread theory that the petty bourgeoisie, ruined by 'monopoly capital,' 'dispossessed' and reduced to a proletarian condition they themselves did not understand, created the pseudo-revolutionary solution of fascism. It is true that this class fought a desperate struggle against its doom; but the class was already vanishing, while other allegiances and lines of demarcation were developing.

In 1930, 4,600,000 new German voters went to the polls; most of these were young people, a new mass in the life of the nation. With these young people came a new human type: the man who could not and did not want to be counted among any definite social class. This youth had not lost its class like the lieutenants of 1919; it had never had a class. Those born in 1910 and later came of age at a time when work was rare, when the crisis had thrown millions out on the streets; the youngest, in particular, found virtually no jobs. The young man, beginning his adult life without work and remaining unemployed for years, became perhaps the most heartbreaking of social types. Between fourteen and seventeen he may have learned a trade, or he may have studied until twenty-two if his parents had the means; in both cases there was great possibility that he would then begin to vegetate without work or hope, or, if he was employed, that his wages would be less than he needed to live. These young people had frequently grown up in families which had fallen from one catastrophe into another; the father had often been killed in the war, the mother found herself unable to support the children and had no authority over them. From such families the youth could get no view of life, no traditional class conceptions. The best that this youth could derive from its situation was a radical will to get ahead, which in many turned into criminality, in most into a demand for new group loyalties, often into both. In a song that became very popular after 1930, this generation boasted of being 'shameless to the testicles,' and 'even if the shopkeepers and cynics laugh at us, our sun does not go down'; this song, it goes without saying, was taken over by the S.A.

These young people of 1930 contributed a great mass inclined to fuse with the human type we have encountered since 1919 in the murderers' army. It would be absolutely false to say that they brought with them the bulk of German youth, but surely an appreciable proportion. At all events, it is here, in the cynicism of this youth, and not in the rage of the 'dispossessed petty bourgeois,' that we must seek the origin of the human type which later buried their fellow men alive in stone coffins, struck out their eyes, shot them down by the score. Material misery doubtless helped to release this barbarism; but since such barbarism is frequent in history, though comparatively rare in the last hundred years, it can scarcely be derived from the social structure of the last century; and no one will seriously try to explain the philosophy and behavior of an S.S. man by the fact that the S.S. man is a baker or stationer. The whole popular concept of class is an intellectual left-over from a period when men were confined to distinct occupations or groups all their lives and often for generations on end.

The type which came to the fore in 1930 was rapidly departing from the old class concepts. He was led by the declassed of *all* classes, the armed bohemians. The worn-out occupational and class concepts had concealed the decisive phenomenon, a new human type, which now revealed himself in a brown or a black shirt, with pistol, club, and torture chamber: the armed intellectual. This total disregard of humanity is born not from bloodthirstiness, but from cold calculation — for the vilest horrors of this age have been perpetrated out of cold intellectual calculation and not out of bestial cruelty.

In this era of general failure, in which the state became all-powerful and yet accomplished nothing except to increase unemployment, to halve property holdings, to destroy livelihoods to no purpose — the ideal state of the intellectuals was the state based, as Hitler put it, 'on accomplishment, on energy.'

In the technological sphere, the war damage had been repaired and Germany's technical apparatus was actually better than before the war. But the social apparatus was deficient, the state proved unable to administer the new technology. The intellectual generation of 1930 no longer recognized and accepted this incapacity on the part of the state. That is the great development that was taking place in Germany. It was natural that unknown, new men should be active in bringing it about; that it should be the unknown man from the Viennese lodging-house, this Nothing in human form, drawing all the problems and passions of the day into himself by the suction of an empty personality — this was a profound tragedy for Germany, and not only for Germany. It could be foreseen and was foreseen that the great achievements of the nineteenth century would some day have to be utilized more systematically and distributed more justly; the time for this was ripe when the working class, through an arduous process of education, began to develop into a position of intellectual leadership. But the fact that this process of transformation was introduced by a World War with its consequences, that the armed human scum of five destructive years were first to take possession of the new possibilities, blinded many people to the great aspects of our era. This was almost inevitable. Great progress begins with abuses; robbers and swindlers have often been the pioneers of civilization.

Men sought new faith, some sought new gods. Anyone traveling through Germany in August and September of 1930, with open eyes, saw the landslide coming. But to the capital and the Reich government, to Schleicher, to Brüning, to Hindenburg, it came as an unexpected blow when, on the evening of September 14, it turned out that Hitler had obtained a sixth of the German vote, 6,400,000, or a hundred and seven seats in the Reichstag. Alarmists spread the rumor that a march of the S.A. on Berlin was to be expected at any hour. Stocks fell sharply in New York. American and other foreign creditors began to call in short-term loans from

Germany. Hitler was creating the catastrophe which he had so
often prophesied.

In Rome, however, the organ of the Fascist Party wrote that Germany was experiencing 'a stormy national rebirth'; Hitler was 'a
herald and organizer who shook men's souls.' The young people of
today, the paper declared, 'had no further use for the principles of
the past century, calling themselves liberalism, democracy, and
socialism.' Mussolini's paper, *Il Popolo d'Italia,* was not entirely
enthusiastic; it accused the French of responsibility for Hitler: their
brutal insistence on the peace treaties, the reinforcement of the
gigantic French military machine, the hopeless defeat of the Left
parties in France — all this had weakened the position of the Left
in Germany.

The loudest cry of joy over Hitler's victory came from England.
Lord Rothermere, publisher of England's biggest newspaper, the
Daily Mail, went to Munich and spoke with Hitler, who was ex-
ceedingly gracious to the brother of the late 'Jew Northcliffe.' The
Englishman was convinced that he had found Europe's man of
destiny. He wrote an article which appeared simultaneously in the
Daily Mail and the *Völkischer Beobachter.* It runs in part (re-
translated from the German):

> If we examine more closely the shift of political power to the
> National Socialists, we find that it has all sorts of political advan-
> tages. For one thing, it erects a reinforced wall against Bolshevism.
> It eliminates the grave danger that the Soviet campaign against
> European civilization would advance to Germany and thus achieve
> an impregnable position in the strategic center of Europe. . . . If
> the young Germany of the National Socialists had not worked
> with so much energy, there was a great likelihood that the cause
> of communism would make important progress and that this party
> would even have become the strongest party. . . . Enlightened
> opinion in England and France should therefore give the National
> Socialists full recognition for the services which they have per-
> formed in Western Europe. Under Hitler's supervision, German
> youth is actually organized against the corruption of Communism.
> I pursued the same purpose in founding the United Empire Party
> in England. . . . It would be the best thing for the welfare of
> Western civilization if Germany were to have a government, im-

bued with the same healthy principles by which Mussolini in the last eight years has renewed Italy. And I see no need for Great Britain and France to maintain an unfriendly attitude toward the efforts of the National Socialists in the field of foreign affairs. Their complaint that Germany, alone among the Great Powers, is disarmed, has just grounds. In Part Five of the Versailles Pact, the Allies obligate themselves to gradual disarmament. The disarmament of Germany was intended only as a prelude to a general renunciation of military power. While the German armed forces have been limited to a hundred thousand men and a few ships for coastal defense, Germany's neighbors have steadily increased their armaments. To subject a solid mass of more than seventy million patriotic and extremely able men and women in the real center of Europe to such a lasting sense of bitter injustice, is like opening the gascock in a sealed room. Sooner or later there must be an explosion. In their own interests the Allied Powers should open the tightly sealed windows behind which German rancor is gathering. . . .

On October 23 of the same year, Mussolini addressed the assembled leadership of the Fascist Party in the Palazzo Venezia in Rome. He referred to the statement once attributed to him that fascism was not an 'article of export.' Such words, he declared, were 'too banal' for him; they betrayed the style of the commercial press and were therefore not by him: *'La frase que il fascismo non e merce d'esportazione, non e mia,'* though this very phrase may be found in Volume VI of his collected writings and speeches. Well, at any rate, he would now correct it. Today, he declared, fascism was 'the order of the day in all countries'; in detail, to be sure, it was Italian, but in its ideas, doctrine, realization, it was universal; it could, therefore, be foreseen that in the future all Europe would solve the problem of the modern state in a fascist sense; it would be a Europe with institutions inspired by the theory and practice of fascism; it would be *'una Europa fascista.'*

Chapter XV

'THE UNHAPPIEST OF
ALL MEN'

BY 1929, ADOLF HITLER WAS LEADING A COMFORT-
able life. In 1928 he had left his worst private worries behind
him. In one of the most attractive and expensive thoroughfares of
Munich, the Outer Prinz Regenten Strasse, he rented a nine-room
apartment which he shared with the two Angelas, his sister and
niece. He allowed himself this luxury after the contributions of
Emil Kirdorf had enabled him to give the party a new and magnificent home — the Barlow Palace, a spacious old patrician man-
sion in the Brienner Strasse. For the first time in his life the unsuccessful artist-prince could abandon himself to his passion for
building and designing; with the architect Troost, and Speer his
helper, he introduced new intermediary floors and walls into his
'Brown House,' transformed great halls into moderate-sized rooms.
He showed a gift for creating an impression of size with limited
space.

The need for size followed him everywhere like a magnified
shadow dwarfing his personal stature. Having read that Mussolini had his desk at the far end of a gigantic hall, and compelled
his callers to undertake a long, painful march across the endless
floor, he designed his own study in the same proportions. The
difference was only that Hitler often impressed visitors as a shy,
embarrassed creature, cowering unhappily behind his gigantic desk.

Even while his circumstances remained humble, he had great plans. One of his favorite amusements was designing building projects, mighty paper monuments to his own gigantic figure. At a time when his party was still sorely in need of money, he went about among rich people, collecting money for an opera house which he wanted to donate to the city of Munich. One of his early friends and backers was Admiral Schröder, who in the First World War had led a corps of marines fighting in Flanders and liked to hear himself called the 'lion of Flanders.' With Schröder, Hitler planned nothing less than to erect a monument to the Flanders marines in the inland city of Munich. These plans for theaters and monuments were among the many fanciful eccentricities from which his friend Hess had to dissuade him with patient arguments. Hitler knew that his boundless imagination sometimes prompted him irresistibly to follies, and he expected Hess to protect him against himself at uncontrolled moments. When the party proved slow to recover its strength and his political rôle remained negligible for years, he had to create a substitute to comfort him with at least a semblance of greatness. Hitler's whole career was designed according to a principle which carried him high and far, which in the most impossible and difficult situations sometimes opened up to him escapes which ordinary men would not have found; but which sometimes, without a firm brake, might have smashed him to bits. This life principle may be designated as 'flight into greatness.' Big things are easy. The masses, with a sound instinct, had sensed this by observing public life; and it was Hitler's decisive realization. Greatness is the way out of the difficulties, defeats, insignificance of his private life; to be a great man makes it easier to be a small individual. His gigantic historical figure extended far beyond himself, a monument to the unsolved problems of his human existence.

Goebbels drew Der Führer's portrait as Hitler wanted to be seen, but indicated between the lines how he really saw him. In 1932, the National Socialist propaganda chief published a diary, allegedly kept in the period before his party came to power; in it, he seemingly pours out his heart, depicting his Führer as a superman: '. . . He alone was never mistaken. He was always right. . . . Amazing how great the Führer is in his simplicity [read: human nonentity] and how simple in his greatness. . . . In the fact of greatness he is above us all. . . . Der Führer is always like a star over us. . . .' A star of the cabarets. For Hitler liked to move in the spots where life was amusing; preferably in places where he could eat a great deal of cake to the tune of waltzes and marches. Men who were present on many of these occasions later spoke of the 'impossible women' he usually took with him. In 1932, when a decision affecting the life and death of the party had to be made (whether or not Hitler should run for the Reich presidency), he hesitated for almost four weeks while Germany waited with bated breath. Unable to make up his mind, he sent for Goebbels to confer with him in Munich. Goebbels arrived, but Hitler spent his afternoons in the studio of his friend Troost, the architect, looking over plans for his future gigantic buildings. At night the program, according to Goebbels's notes, was as follows: First night, Gärtner-Theater, operetta, *The Fledermaus*; second night, movies, Greta Garbo; third night: another operetta, *The Merry Widow*. That was how he passed the momentous weeks; when the month had gone by and he had finally made his decision, Goebbels heaved a sigh: 'He is and remains our Führer after all' — for he had doubted it.

When the whole party apparatus was busy with preparations for one of the Party Days, the Führer vanished for a few days; in his seclusion he spent his time designing a plaque for the party comrades in Nuremberg to wear in their buttonholes. He himself designed the banners, standards, arm-bands, decorative buttons, newspaper layouts, and later the house façades, stadiums, posters for big meetings, usually aided by men like Troost and Speer. Rarely has anything uglier been conceived than the official party insignia designed in 1922, a lead disk about the size of a twenty-five-cent piece, ornamented with a red ring, a white field, and a black swastika. In these designs he attempted to realize the unfulfilled artist's dream of his youth. And all of them were lines in the giant figure which was his picture of himself. In choosing the title of Führer, he chose an image for himself, the image of Napoleon. The columns which adorn his blueprint palaces and monuments were designed for a new Napoleon. Napoleonic was the eagle between whose claws he placed the swastika; Napoleonic the Latin ornaments on the S.A.

standards, the antique inscriptions, and even the studied simplicity of his personal uniform.

The image of the great man always hovers like a model and catchword before his inner eye. He always tries to act as in his opinion the image would act. His action is nevertheless basically his own; but it remains a histrionic gesture, an imitation of a thought-out model, and this accounts for the monumental, unnatural quality of his most effective moments. When the unimpressive, stooping figure draws itself to its full height and unexpectedly spews flame like an archangel, it is as though his hands and feet had been bound with invisible cords to the hands and feet of a model. To observers this bond with a hidden image sometimes became almost palpable. Suddenly, in the midst of a conversation, Hitler's face grows tense as with an inner vision; these are the moments in which the humanly repulsive falls away from him and the unfathomable is intensified until it becomes truly terrible. His eyes peer into the distance, as though he were reading or gazing at something which no one else sees; and if the observer follows the direction of his gaze, sometimes, it has been claimed, Rudolf Hess can be seen in the far corner, with his eyes glued to his Führer, apparently speaking to him with closed lips. It may be that the strange atmosphere of such scenes confused the observer, making him see more than was there. But it is certain that in the decisive years of his career Hitler used his younger friend as a necessary complement to his own personality; as a stage director or spiritual ballet master who helped him shape his own powerful but formless and uncertain nature into whatever image he momentarily wanted.

When preparing a speech, he declaimed large sections of it to his friend Hess; he practiced gestures and facial expressions at the mirror. He practiced other things too. There was an important visitor to be received; the reception was previously rehearsed with Hess. Hess had to meet the stranger in advance, take a good look at him and report. Then there would be an interview like the following:

Hitler: Fire away, Hess! Can he be used or not? — *Hess:* He can be used. But he's the silent type. — *Hitler (suspiciously):* Critical? — *Hess:* No, embarrassed. Would be terribly glad to admire, but he's embarrassed. — *Hitler:* They are all prepared. For ten years they have heard of me, for the last year they have heard of nothing else but me. What does he expect? — *Hess:* Authority, of course. You can speak at length. Your will is unshakable. You give laws to the age. — *Hitler:* Then I'll speak with the firm voice, without yelling? — *Hess:* Of course.

Hitler utters a few sentences. Hess, the human tuning-fork listens: '. . . No, not like that, quiet — no passion, commanding. You want nothing of him. It is Destiny that speaks. . . .' At length the adviser falls silent. Hitler is in the swing and speaks evenly for several minutes, with the 'firm voice': ' . . . It is indulging in a self-deception as harmful in the long run as it is catastrophic in its effects, to believe that a movement such as the one led by me can for all eternity be held down by the night-sticks of Messrs. Severing and Grzesinski. I warn you against regarding us as a movement comparable to the usual party formations. We are Germany's destiny and her future, regardless whether people think they have to question us on this point or that point in our program. We are restoring to the nation a faith and a will, and by concentrating all our strength on action, revolutionary action if you will, we are gathering in our ranks every member of the German people who still has energy and capacity for life. . . .' And so on. After six or seven minutes he breaks off, already somewhat moved by his own words. 'Good, now I think we have it,' he concludes. Then the time and place of the reception are set.

He has conceived a picture of himself, and in all his philosophizing and politicizing he is constantly mixing colors for this picture. When he assured his bankrupts that their failure in civil life was really a proof that they were an élite — he meant himself, seen in the picture of the superman misunderstood by the people: 'There is nothing great in the world that does not owe its origin to the creative ability of an individual man.' The human mass, reflecting rank, exuberant, undirected life, must be shaped, it must be given meaning and purpose: 'Genius is not in the majority, but always in the single individual. The Napoleonic era did not give Napoleon his name, Napoleon imprinted it on the era. . . . People talk of woods, meadows, fields, mines, buildings, and believe that these are our national wealth. The national wealth of a people is its great men.' He wants to become the Napoleon of this era; in other words, this era is his era, it belongs to him, he can do with it what he likes, '. . . and for this there is only one justification: genius, and nothing else.'

Flight into the great image has from early youth been this man's answer to all life's enmity; that was why he wanted to become an artist when his father tried to break him into a normal respectable man; he wanted to shine and be admired — 'as two lovers, far removed from one another, look up to the stars with the feeling: in this moment our thoughts meet — the great spirits of a people are the uniting stars which hold men together.' That was he, a prince and star in the realm of art; or rather, that was what he would have become, if, as we know, he had not lacked both talent and energy. But, as he will always feel, that was what he would have become if his alleged poverty, the social arrogance of the age, the resistance of a world hostile to him and all its sentiments, had not kept him down. Art is the struggle of the great man against the resistance of the dull world, the ultimate subjection of the ordinary to the creative spirit . . . 'until the artistic genius reveals itself so brilliantly that all of them fall, overpowered, to their knees.' In such phrases, he betrays what he expects from art: triumph. Art — that is the career of Richard Wagner, from the defeat of the Paris performance of *Tannhäuser* to the erection of the spiritual empire in Bayreuth; art is the last word in the *Meistersingers,* when the man of the world and the patron falls to his knees before the master.

On trips and walks he would suddenly run ahead, dragging his companions to some church or cloister, where he would surprise them with a lecture: gaze and see how the old master builders made a room out of walls. There he stood, his whole form an abrupt line, his gloves clasped in his uplifted hand. Can't you see, he cried, that the old window-makers knew that a window determined not only the façade but also the space within? Can't you see how that accounts for the magnificent stained-glass windows? It was not to be denied: when he asked if they did not see, nearly everyone saw; at times he could really make people see what he wanted. From time to time he was possessed by a true passion for instructing the men of his *entourage*. It became an established practice that at least once a year he subjected his staff of leaders to a course in art; as a rule at the Party Days. From this developed the custom of his so-called 'art speeches'; infinitely long-winded lectures, which inspired secret jokes in men who otherwise admired him. In their content they are perhaps the most questionable, in form beyond a doubt the weakest of his speeches; and yet it is these speeches in which the orator expressed his profoundest, if most useless, thoughts. For here he speaks of himself, trying to attain clarity concerning his own nature. Here he speaks of his relation to art, his power and gifts in this field, in which, outwardly at least, he doubtless failed in his youth; and the sense of the whole speech is finally a stubborn, though inwardly uncertain: *'Anch' io son pittore.'* (I too am a painter.)

For it is art which distinguishes the noble men from the common herd; and his division, as Hitler learned from Houston S. Chamberlain, is no accident; it is here that the races divide. Therefore, in every people, including the Germans, there is the sub-human who merely eats and drinks, and the Aryan yearning for higher culture:

> It is just as natural that a part of the human species should attain the fulfillment of their life tasks in the satisfaction of the lowest needs as it would be unnatural if the races chosen by Providence for higher things should, contrary to the admonishing voice of their conscience, yes, the burning compulsion of their being, desire to retrogress to this most primitive life conception or even, which is the same thing, let themselves be coerced into it. . . . Discord entered among those nations in which two racial ingredients, different in nature, wanted to live and express themselves side by side. The man who requires nothing but eating and drinking for the satisfaction and fulfillment of his life, has never possessed understanding for the man who would rather stint on his daily bread in order to still the thirst of his soul and the hunger of his spirit. But the lack of inner understanding in those who have been born to this, the eternal incomprehension of their heart and soul, must at least be transformed into deferential respect by conscious education. . . .

Here, after twenty-three years, the misunderstood artist-prince spits his contempt into the faces of his companions in misery in the Vienna lodging-house; of Hanisch, for example, who sold postcards and brought in sausages, while the young idealist read three newspapers at once and pondered the deepest questions in the world. Hitler delivered this speech on the necessity of keeping the 'sub-human' in deferential respect in September, 1933, when he was already dictator; and scarcely anything else characterizes the man and his cause as much as the intrusion of such brutality into a discussion on art. Art must be brutal. The 'races chosen for higher things' must finally realize — this is the heartfelt wish of the unrecognized artist-prince — that art is not a matter for any 'absurd international humanitarianism,' but their own privilege, to be defended against the sub-humans: 'Art cannot be divided from blood. It is the expression of the psychic sentiments of a people.'

Every race has its ideal of beauty, and we Aryans have ours; yes, by this ideal of beauty we recognize ourselves; it is the surest sign of our invisible order, which has existed everywhere, yet nowhere: 'The ideal of beauty of the ancient peoples will be eternal as long as men of the same nature, because of the same origin, inhabit the earth. . . . Every politically heroic people seeks in its art the bridge to a no less heroic past. The Greeks and Romans, then, become so close to the Germans because they must all seek their roots in one and the same basic race, and hence the immortal achievements of the old peoples exert again and again their attractive effect on their racially related descendants.'

He was working on a manuscript, in which he wanted to draw the portrait of the artist genius who molds his people. He discussed the work for whole nights with Alfred Rosenberg, who had studied to be an engineer and architect, and like himself had never done any creative work in the field. Some of the conclusions arrived at in these conversations were put down in another book which Rosenberg was writing at the same time. While Hitler, with his endless brooding, never finished his work, Rosenberg in 1928 wrote 'Finis' to his own. He entitled the book with a slogan which, as he probably failed to suspect, was put into circulation by Georges Sorel, the French socialist, syndicalist, and friend of Bolsheviks.

Sorel had applied the term of 'myth' to the great conceptions which result in the birth of political movements. Rosenberg called his book: *The Myth of the Twentieth Century*. He gave Hitler the thick manuscript, for it contained some rather daring passages which Rosenberg, thinking of the party's reputation, did not want to publish without Hitler's approval. Hitler took the pages home and put them on his bed-table, where Rosenberg when he called saw them lying untouched. This went on for a year; then the author grew impatient and asked to have his manuscript back. Hitler gave it to him and said: 'I feel sure that it's all right.'

The party publishing house put it out in 1930, and it turned out to be 'all right' in a very strange way. To be sure, the book contained reflections on art and race no different from what Hitler would have written. Rosenberg defended the theory — not original with him — that the 'Nordic' race came from a vanished continent to the north of Europe and consequently had taken important characteristics, memories, and spiritual qualities from an Arctic or semi-Arctic environment; it was a race of blue water and gleaming ice. But the ambassador of the Wise Men of Zion, the German purified from his mixed Russian-German milieu, was wildly intolerant toward all elements which he viewed as non-German. To these belonged Russian 'Tartardom' and, to an even greater extent, the Semites. With Gobineau and Wagner, he regarded the force of Semitism as far broader and more dangerous than its modern Jewish representatives. In this view the whole Mediterranean region and the Latin races are permeated with Semitism, and Rosenberg, basing himself on the researches of an insane scholar named Albert Grünwedel, took special pains to demonstrate the Semitic origin of the ancient Etruscans, who subsequently imbued all the Latin peoples with a Semitic essence.

But the deepest and most widespread poison, the most dangerous product of the Semitic-Latin spirit, is Christianity, at least the Christianity of the Catholic Church. Rosenberg hinted that the Catholic clergy was in a spiritual sense a continuation of the old Etruscan priesthood, concerning which he told the most hideous tales; he called the Pope the Roman medicine man, church history a series of atrocities, swindles, and forgeries. Though all this came from Houston Stewart Chamberlain, who had violently insisted that he was a Christian; though Rosenberg still approved a 'positive' Christianity — that is, a Christianity removed from all tradition — he brought the party a reputation for godlessness. The National Socialists were violently attacked, Catholic bishops forbade holy rites over the graves of party members, and all this might have been avoided if in the course of a year Hitler had taken a look into Rosenberg's manuscript. But he took the consequences on himself. Rosenberg wrote him a letter in which he offered to give up his position as editor-in-chief of the *Völkischer Beobachter,* even to resign from the party; Hitler wrote diagonally across the letter: 'Doesn't enter my head. You stay!' His own manuscript on the interrelations between art and race, however, did not see the light; he thought it better not to make enemies in this field too.

Hence we possess no written and developed definition of the beautiful by Hitler — since definition has never been his strong point, it is perhaps no great loss. In his speeches he occasionally attempted a clarification of beauty as 'functionalism fulfilled with crystal clarity.' The phrase has an empty sound; it is intended to convey, for example, that the form of the Greek roof, which he felt to be perfect, is explained by the vital needs of all Aryan or Nordic peoples, who in the rainy, snowy regions of the cold and temperate zones needed the slanting roof. This accounts for Hitler's furious fight against cube-shaped houses, or towers with flat roofs; the fight against the flat sun roof was conducted with almost religious ardor, for this roof was 'Oriental, Semitic,' and absolutely 'un-German.' Hitler declared everything which ran counter to his penchant for simplification and massiveness to be a product of foreign, hence hostile, race will; particularly the whole 'artistic and cultural stammering of the Cubists, Futurists, and Dadaists.' For him, all searching after new, unaccustomed forms is only a sign of the decay of the Aryan forces among modern peoples, who were no longer strong enough to feel the value of traditional classical forms.

'What we experience today,' he said in January, 1928, 'is the capitulation of the intellectual bourgeoisie to insolent Jewish composers, poetasters, painters, who set miserable trash in front of our people and have brought things to such a pass that for sheer cowardice the people no longer dare to say: that doesn't suit us, away with this garbage. No, against their better knowledge and conviction the so-called intellectuals in our nation accept as beautiful something set before them by those people, which they themselves must automatically feel to be ugly. That is a sign of our universal decay, a cowardice that can be thrown to the ground with one slogan: you are a philistine. . . . These are indications of the decay of taste and hence the racial decomposition of our people. . . .' The good people of this nation, said Hitler, went timidly and sheepishly to operas and concerts, where 'there is an echo of dissonances. . . . The people do not want that in the least, but no one dares to stay away. The wretched sound is an insult to their ears; they look around: beside them sits a blasé young chap or an old bounder who begins to applaud and looks impudently around, and the others, instead of giving the young chap' — cry in the audience, 'a licking' — '. . . begin to wonder in all earnestness whether they haven't heard something profound after all, and finally they begin to clap, too, though they hadn't the slightest desire to clap. . . .'

According to Hitler, we had adapted our daily lives to forms which were profoundly alien to us and which we also felt to be alien; but National Socialism would give the German people courage to repulse the alien: 'The things that we cannot understand because they are alien to us, we do not need to understand,' he cried loudly and with furious gestures: 'Nor do we want to understand them.' According to report, there was stormy applause at this spot. It is as though the politician in him were jealous of the artist — or perhaps the unsuccessful artist-prince was jealous of his more successful colleagues. Do we really need art? 'Minds who give birth to something new are infinitely rare,' he declares. 'It is only a very few great men on earth who really bless the nations by new achievements in the field of art. More than that is not necessary . . . for what an artist devises in a month, a people often needs thirty years to understand. . . . We need to produce no new art. If we accomplish nothing better, let us concentrate on what we already have, on what is immortal. . . .' This he said in the year 1928, and to this renunciation of original creation, unlike his many other promises and assurances, he has remained faithful. When in 1933 he commanded the German people to take the 'ancient peoples' ideal of beauty' as a model, he justified this by saying: 'Since it is better to imitate something good than to produce something new and bad, the predominantly intuitive creations of these peoples can today fulfill their educational and leading mission as a style raised above doubt.'

Here art loses itself in politics, where, as a matter of principle, everything serves as a means to an end. The end is permanence and greatness: 'There is nothing in all the cultural monuments,' says Hitler, 'that does not owe its existence to a political intention. Rome and Hellas — no cultural state has arisen except through political hope and the will to obtain monuments in harmony with it, monuments to the unification of peoples, to celebrate the outstanding might of the central political power. . . . I could not imagine the victory of our philosophy of life, otherwise than embodied in monuments which outlast the times.' And 'Art and politics belong together as nothing else on earth belongs together.'

Hitler dreams of his own giant monument in the future. 'When a people is extinguished and men are silent, the stones will speak' — of the great deceased, in whom his own people stamped its 'highest values.' 'Everything that I say and do belongs to history,' he said at a time when the great red posters with his name attracted at most a thousand people to a beer hall. For basically everything that he said or did was calculated only to imprint his infinitely enlarged image on the present, to multiply himself in his creation, and to disappear as a man behind his legend.

He made the masses see what they did not see, and not to see what they did see. The masses, yes — but what about individuals, particularly those around him? They still had before them this face that looked like an advertisement for a shaving lotion; this emptiness with the avid, frightened eyes; this sometimes slinking, sometimes hopping, never naturally moving form with its narrow shoulders; this whole impersonal appearance, in which for want of other distinguishing features the ridiculously correct suit most caught the eye. They were forced to hear this know-it-all, equipped with all the semi-education of his age, talking constantly of things he did not understand; they had to swallow the miserable

German, the defective logic, the tasteless humor and false pathos which he brought forth at the dinner table as at the mass meeting; they had to suffer the bad manners, and some could not dispel the feeling that he was even physically unclean — this was not true, but water and soap avail nothing against a slovenly nature. How did the armed intellectuals come to submit to the leadership of this raving dervish? For when success brought masses to the party, men rose to the leadership who far excelled Hitler in practical ability, education, and character. It can be understood how the phenomenon subjected the masses; his hypnotic effect on certain individuals must be accepted as a fact; but by what human means did Hitler handle the men around him?

The answer is that he did not handle them successfully. These men never ceased to laugh at him or to become enraged against him — and, in between, reluctantly to admire his amazing political success. He was not on terms of true friendship with any, not even with Hess who was seemingly so close to him. No one addressed him by his first name or by the intimate 'du'; those who had done so in earlier years had long since given up the practice. Companions in struggle for twenty years addressed him as 'Mein Führer,' to which he returned: 'Herr Reichsmarschall,' 'Herr Minister,' or 'Herr Reichsschatzmeister' (Reich Treasurer); at best, 'My dear party comrade.'

The phenomenon's name is 'Mein Führer'; whenever his men so address him, they presumably have the feeling of coming into contact with history. Among themselves, however, these subordinates were never so solemn. Then they were aware that above all they were participants in a wild venture, the maddest speculation in history, which was bound to pay off prodigiously if successful; and coldly businesslike, they called and still call the head of their firm the 'boss.' But they also had their disparaging nicknames. These realists, thugs and businessmen, had known their 'Manitou' intimately for years, and no one could pass off any forged gigantic portrait on them. They saw his weakness, nearly all of which could be reduced to a phenomenal untruthfulness, which all his collaborators complained of. For most of his faults, otherwise humanly understandable, became ugly only because he falsified them into virtues. His big lies constitute the content of his book; but he deceived his co-workers even in small personal matters. In 1926, with tears in his eyes, he assured a journalist to whom he owed money that he had no funds at all, not even for his most urgent needs; the next day he started on a pleasure trip to Bayreuth in an automobile. When the journalist complained, Hitler screamed at him: how could such an incompetent good-for-nothing even dare to open his mouth? And a few days later, when the unfortunate, who really was none too competent at his profession, committed a grave blunder — the stenographic copy of a speech delivered by Hitler was lost — the Manitou fell on his slave and gave him two resounding slaps in the face. Later, more apologies and tears. To the outside world it was staunchly maintained that Hitler was always the best friend and comrade of his co-workers; that they came to him with all their troubles; that he had helped many — it was one of the lies which Hitler's staff had come to take for granted. The remarkable part of it was the pathos with which he lied; whenever possible, he attached an oath or at least a word of honor to the lie. With trembling passion in his voice, he swore in court that he had never made an attempt to obtain money from Henry Ford (February 5, 1930); the man who could have had him sent to prison for perjury by producing a document, and might thus have spared the world its encounter with Hitler, unfortunately kept silent.

What got on the nerves of his co-workers perhaps even more than his alternate whining and brutality was his indecision. Yet, tongue in cheek, they systematically built up the myth of Der Führer's determination. True, to this lie there was an almost philosophical sense. The party calls itself a 'political army,' carrying out the orders of a general; everywhere it must arouse the impression of military precision and rapidity. This is the basis of the magic which it emanates. The truth, however, is that politics cannot be conducted with an uninterrupted series of lightning decisions. In this deceptive field, what really counts is one of Hitler's strongest gifts: the ability to wait, to keep an eye open for possibilities, to watch events pass and patiently look on as, frequently, one difficulty is canceled out by another. Politics is the opposite of what today is understood by 'total action'; it is an intrinsic part of the political art to leave most things undone, trusting that they will take care of themselves; in the decisive moment, however, to act ruthlessly — and what the layman calls political determination is the gift — a rare one, to be sure — of knowing when the decisive moment has come; of understanding where action in this moment will lead. Hitler's impatient staff and sub-leaders expected him to act like an armed intellectual; instead, and this is what made him their superior and leader, he acted like an armed bohemian. The best of them were prepared to sacrifice everything for the party machine; he and his most trusted cronies were determined if necessary to smash the machine to bits for his own person: '. . . It would be better,' he wrote in controversy with rebellious subordinates, 'that there should be no National Socialist movement at all than a movement of in-discipline and disobedience.' For he is a politician to his last fiber — that is, a man for whom everything is a means to an end; and the whole universe, from God down to the cheese-mite, including all love and all hate, including man and beast and the elements, is only raw material for power.

Most of the S.A. leaders did not fully realize that they had a politician for a leader and must incline to his political will. For many of them, the Leader myth was a lie, serviceable perhaps within limits. Hitler's ability to chain masses with the power of the word aroused in some a rather disparaging admiration; he talked so much, they said, that he never got around to action. Aware that this doubting and mocking S.A. must be subjected once and for all, he had recourse to the one old-timer for whom he was still *'Ade,'* the bosom friend: Ernst Röhm, lieutenant-colonel in the Bolivian army. Röhm's position in Bolivia had been made difficult by a rev-olution in which Kundt had involved himself; a telegram was sent from Munich to La Paz, and by the end of 1930 the man who had created the National Socialist Party was back in Germany. Again Hitler had beside him the man who knew him too well for any pretenses on either side. Röhm clearly understood that his task was to build up Hitler as 'Der Führer.' To a collaborator endowed with such talents, ironic clearsightedness, and at the same time good-will, Hitler had to allow the greatest liberties, despite Röhm's faults and his own misgivings. He was obliged to look on while Röhm with cold calculation built up in the eyes of the S.A. an idol of the Führer in which he himself obviously did not believe.

Many of the lower S.A. leaders, however, openly and disrespectfully opposed him. Röhm provided pretexts for opposition by filling the S.A. leadership with his homosexual creatures, Captains von Petersdorff and Röhrbein, Count Ernst Helldorf, an adventurer and military profiteer of the worst sort. The beloved Heines was given command of the S.A. in Silesia. Pfeffer's staff of leaders felt their position endangered and tried to make Hitler remove Röhm. Actually this was an insurrection against Hitler himself; the rebels admitted as much by attacking the 'legal' course of the party, demanding riots and civil war. It was all very well for his horse-dealers and butchers in Munich to gape at '*Ade*,' to stretch out their arms and shout '*Heil, mein Führer!*'; even to greet one another with the strange cry of '*Heil Hitler!*' The Prussian officers in the North, though admitting that all this was adroit magic for the people, became contemptuous and rebellious when they themselves were expected to join in the magic with a straight face. At all times this has been the attitude of men who knew the magic at close quarters, or before it had become magic. Even historical figures, today universally regarded as 'great,' had the same difficulty in their day:

> ' . . . Ye gods! It doth amaze me
> A man of such a feeble temper should
> So get the start of the majestic world
> And bear the palm alone . . .
> Poor man! I know he would not be a wolf
> But that he sees the Romans are but sheep:
> He were no lion, were not Romans hind.'

Thus speaks Cassius in Shakespeare, and he is speaking of the 'greatest' of them all: of Caesar. For a time in 1931 Goebbels spoke thus of Hitler. Along with the Berlin S.A. leaders he grew embittered at Röhm's really repulsive 'men's harem,' and in secret conversations Hitler was not spared. In speaking publicly of Hitler, Goebbels laid on the flattery so thick that the suspicion arose that he was making fun of his Führer; in private conversations, he simply made fun, without flattery. In his diary he called him the 'great man above us all' and a 'star'; but in the Berlin squabbles of 1931 he cried out, with an irritation that was perhaps affected, that he too was sick of taking orders from the 'vain operetta queen' in Munich.

This he said to the former police captain Walter Stennes, who led the discontented S.A. in North and East Germany. For a time, perhaps, Goebbels meant this seriously. With him one could never be certain. In any case, he later disclosed these conversations and particularly Stennes's answers to Hitler, and it is possible that he only attacked the Führer in the first place to win the confidence of the guileless S.A. captain. It is certain that Stennes, no more than Otto Strasser, wanted to depose Hitler, but Hitler's principle was that criminals must be punished before they commit their crime. Again Goebbels had to carry out the expulsion, but this time the task put him in a cold sweat. Stennes and his followers did not give up as easily as Strasser. A sort of *putsch* developed, consisting of brawls between the 'politicians' and the military-minded rank-and-file; local headquarters were occupied by the 'rebels.' Stennes later boasted of having personally beaten Goebbels to a pulp. In any case the Berlin *gauleiter* fled to Munich and there sought protection. Always, when he betrayed his former friends, he attached himself with especial warmth to the previous common enemy; in this case to Röhm, with whom he now formed the closest bond. With Röhm and Heines, he helped to cement the rule of the homosexuals over the S.A. A month later, Hitler himself had to write a letter of praise and thanks to the depraved murderer Heines, because Röhm demanded it; the disciplining of the S.A., he wrote to the man whom he had formerly thrown out of the party, 'remains . . . above all, dear Heines, your achievement and that of your staff' — read: men's harem. He praised Heines 'for your services which have been above all praise.' And: 'Today I feel a special need to thank you most heartily for this and to express my full appreciation.' Thus did Hitler praise one half of his uprooted desperadoes, while, in an open statement, he covered the other, mutinous half with ignominy: 'Freebooters . . . clique of mutinous officers . . . traitors without honor . . . rabble . . . men without character. . . . From the very beginning of his activity in the N.S.D.A.P. Herr Stennes never moved a hand without a bill and a receipt. . . .'

This was what came out when he spoke of his best men without embellishment. They had had the insolence not to take him seriously; in bitter complaint, the Führer, who had thought himself capable of debating with retired colonels in officers' clubs on tank technique, bellowed forth his sense of injury: 'I was not a child of well-to-do parents. I was not educated at universities, but was drawn through the hardest school of life, through poverty and misery. The superficial world never asks what a man has learned, and least of all what his real abilities are; as a rule, unfortunately, it asks only for his diplomas. They never noticed that I had learned more than tens of thousands of our intellectuals; they only saw that my diplomas were lacking. And I was not an officer but a common soldier. . . .'

No school diplomas! That was his whole misfortune — or so at least he told himself. In reality it was the qualities of the man, the lack of integrated personality, which made this extraordinary historical phenomenon a lightweight in the human sense, and through all the terrors of his career surrounded it with an air of absurdity. Hitler was already the man of the hour in Germany, very probably the man of tomorrow, and in the eyes of many the man of destiny; and still the most able men of his *entourage* refused to take him seriously — except as a demagogue. Could this be merely the philistinism of mediocre talents unable to appreciate genius? What people noticed about Hitler was not the madness of his actions; even the most hostile observer soon saw that behind the first deceptive cloud of noise and excitement there was an amazing certainty and purposiveness in his movements. But what always surprised men who spoke with Hitler face to face was the poverty of his arguments and explanations, particularly in private conversations, where it was not brilliance or wit that mattered, but thinking. When it was soberly explained to him that Germany's one to two billion marks in annual reparations were assuredly a heavy burden, but could hardly be responsible for the crisis, he answered in all seriousness that with the rapidity of currency circulation one billion marks left in Germany would provide the country with seven or eight times as much in wages and salaries. Whether he was predicting the second German inflation — which never occurred — or the coming British-American War, or — each year anew — the imminent collapse of Soviet Russia; whether he was flaying the 'Jewish' banking system of the United States, reviling his future friend Lord Rothermere as a Jew, or venturing the prophecy that France would never evacuate the Rhineland — he was always conspicuous for his hostility to hard facts, his fear of checkable details; and he has still to make a speech adducing names, places, dates, or literal quotations in any factual controversy. Occasionally, in the responsible post of Chancellor, he has sensed this deficiency and attempted to prove a point with heaps of figures, mostly referring to the economic successes of his régime. Anyone with even the slightest statistical experience can observe that Hitler does not understand his own algebra, and certainly never studied his own figures. The lack of demonstrable reality in nearly all his utterances permits us to characterize the unquestionable intellectual power which carried him so far and so high as a stream in which all substance is pulverized.

No, he will not founder on the cliffs of reality. Something which may be called instinct will almost always indicate to him the facts which he can calmly neglect, spring over, disregard, without disturbing his course. But should he ever encounter a state of affairs over which it is impossible to glide with lifted oars, should a really obstructing problem ever appear in his path, he will adapt himself to this unexpected resistance with such a power of self-transformation that his closest friends will hardly recognize him. This happened, for example, in 1930, when he suddenly developed an enthusiasm for legality and democracy in Germany, and in 1933, when he became a peace enthusiast in world affairs.

Hitler's indifference to facts which he does not regard as vitally important explains his strange relation to books. He does not allow them to instruct him, but only to confirm his opinions. He has given us his ideas on how books should be read: Do not read too much, for that will only give you useless ballast; this kind of learning only removes you from the world. Feeling, however, enables the expert reader 'to perceive at once everything which in his opinion is fit to be permanently retained as expedient or generally worth knowing.' The material read 'is meaningfully fitted into the picture, which is somehow always present in advance, and which the mind has created with regard to this or that matter.'

The purpose of books is to say yes. As a young man, according to his own story, he began to read the 'main documents' of Marxism. Let us suppose he was referring to Karl Marx's monumental *Capital*: 'If I arrived at my goal more rapidly than I myself may at first have dared to think, it was solely due to my newly acquired, though at that time not yet very profound, knowledge of the Jewish question. It alone enabled me to draw a practical comparison between reality and the theoretical boasting of the founding fathers of Social Democracy, since it had taught me to understand the language of the Jewish people, who talk to hide, or at least to veil, their thoughts, and whose real aim is therefore not to be found in the lines, but slumbers well hidden between them.'

In other words, after reading a few dozen pages at most, he closed the thick volume forever. But there is a grave suspicion that he treated other books, more important for him, in the same way. He virtually never quotes a single word from a classic author. Once he cited a few sentences from Clausewitz, the military theoretician, but these were often printed in cheap little pamphlets. Over a period of twenty years he only once has recourse to the authority of Germany's greatest author, Goethe, and then only to quote an anti-Semitic passage in which Goethe rejects mixed marriage between Christians and Jews — it seems certain that this treasure was gleaned from some anti-Semitic tract, and not from the original. 'You would be astonished,' said a man who knew him well, 'to see Adolf Hitler's library. Whole walls full of the most beautiful books. And all of them unread.' He could not force himself to look at Rosenberg's important and dangerous manuscript; he released the bomb, sight unseen, hoping that nothing would go wrong.

Years later, a Polish journalist, by way of testing his learning, asked him frankly: 'What great minds of the past have exerted a decisive influence on Your Excellency in an intellectual sense?' Hitler replied: 'It is hard to list the number of those minds in the past which have furnished fertilizing contributions to every great idea. Our whole body of views arises in overwhelming part from

the results of the intellectual work of the past, and in smaller part
on the basis of our own discoveries. The decisive factor is only to
organize the intellectual heritage handed down by the great minds of
former times in a sensible, expedient way, and to draw the resulting logical consequences from them. For of what avail is all
knowledge if we do not possess the courage to make use of it? By
drawing the practical political consequences from a huge sum of
intellectual and scientific ideas and insights, we have overcome an
inertia that had grown totally sterile, and given to our national life
a new and, as I am convinced, decisive impetus.'

What an answer! He has learned neither from the living nor the
dead. Here he laid himself bare, a rambling barbarian soul, without
bond or loyalty, burdened with no intellectual possessions, obligated to no one; a child of nature who would be quite capable of
frying a chop over a Stradivarius violin, and boasting that he had
sensibly and expediently organized a spiritual heritage.

That is his intellectual armament. But he had a wisdom all his
own. When he related horror stories about the Wise Men of Zion,
a skeptical henchman might protest: 'Adolf, you can't tell people
such stuff!' Then he would smilingly reply: 'You can tell people
anything!' And the skeptic was suddenly seized with the terrible
suspicion, subjecting the whole world to doubt: perhaps he is
wiser than all of us! Hitler's deepest wisdom consists in his conviction, gathered from the world sense of the modern intellectual,
that everything is possible, that all problems are capable of solution,
and that — and this is the most important — the big things are the
easiest; but this cannot be reasoned out, it can only be demonstrated.

In great questions and conflicts, every attempt at proof or deduction soon leads to ultimate beliefs beyond the realm of the
demonstrable — to basic conceptions regarding the world and
man; and Hitler cannot afford to speak publicly of his basic conceptions. They arise from a deep contempt of human nature and
run sharply counter to the comforting self-confidence which he then
was trying to instill in the masses. When he calls upon them to
demonstrate their noble breed and heroic nature by staking their
health and their life, he means essentially: for you rabble are worthy
of nothing better; and this attitude would come out in the end if

he were to pursue his conclusions, statements, exhortations, and commands, step by step, back to their sources and grounds. Actually he has never concealed his contempt of mankind, though always giving those present to understand that he was not referring to them. But he cannot very well reveal and name the chief source of his contempt for humanity: his own person. The true source of his belief in human vileness is self-observation. He is so ashamed of his humanity because, as an historical phenomenon, beguiled by his own star, he expects superhuman things of himself. In the contemplation of human affairs, all logic ultimately leads back to the human individual; a logical analysis of National Socialist politics would have to end with an analysis of Hitler's person; hence Hitler's unconscious resistance to logic and factual truth.

It is not unusual that a man should wish to cut a figure different from his real person; all public activity consists in compressing one's own personality into certain qualities and effects, omitting and repressing other aspects of one's nature; to a smaller extent, this phenomenon occurs even in private relations between man and man, and this line of falsehood in human relations partly accounts for the pessimistic conception of man as a sinner and miscreant. Hitler's special trait is his concentration on greatness. This is the source of his power. When suddenly this man, who has been awkwardly standing around, now and then muttering a remark that by no means dominates the conversation, is seized with determination and begins to speak, filling the room with his voice, suppressing interruptions or contradictions by his domineering manner, spreading cold shivers among those present by the savagery of his declarations, lifting every subject of conversation into the light of history, and interpreting it so that even trifles have their origin in greatness; then the listener is filled with awe and feels that a new phenomenon has entered the room. This thundering demon was not there before; this is not the same timid man with the contracted shoulders. He is capable of this transformation in a personal interview and facing an audience of half a million. The magic power of this image of greatness emanating from human nullity greatly appealed to the German people after the World War, when this people, oppressed by their own nullity, longed for greatness; but a far deeper and more decisive explanation of Hitler's effect is the soul state of modern man, who, in his pettiness, loneliness, and lack of faith, longs for community, conviction, and greatness. Here he sees greatness emerging from a creature who as a man is smaller than you or I — that is what made Hitler an experience for millions.

This sharp division of his personality — colorless on the one hand, dazzling on the other — does not mean, however, that two men dwell in one. Hitler is no split personality; the two sides of his nature belong entirely together and condition one another, like the two weights of a centrifugal top. This contrast between greatness and nonentity, as it presents itself in Hitler, is the product of education and growth through a life almost unique in the whole of history; anyone who tries to judge Hitler solely on the basis of mad or inadequate utterances and actions of former times forgets that power in itself is instructive and that only the dullest of minds fail to learn from the possession of responsibility and influence. With the years the two poles of his personality became purer and more pronounced. His nature was sensitive, quick to react; now it would rush to one side, now to the other, thus creating an impression of great instability and adaptability. Perhaps the medical man will discover hysterical symptoms in this; at all events, the layman, including the present author, will speak readily of hysteria; for the sake of clarity it should be stated that the fixation of this hysteria is on the contradiction between greatness and nonentity. Max von Gruber, the specialist, observing him in the course of a passionate action lasting several hours, found the facial expression of the man 'madly agitated,' and, at the end, the characteristic 'expression of gratified self-esteem.' Another specialist, though not of the first rank, who observed him systematically over a considerable period, categorically denied any pathological tendency. This was Doctor Brinsteiner, a prison physician who saw him in Landsberg in 1924; he was 'firmly convinced that Hitler was always master of himself and his will and not pathologically affected in his mental activity.' Brinsteiner did observe a 'passing pathological depression which appeared in Hitler for a short time after the *putsch*,' but drew from it 'no inference of a pathological tendency in Hitler.' Brinsteiner, as can be seen from his report, was filled with enthusiasm by Hitler; but as a physician he is doubtless right. Mental unreliability is not a disease; Brinsteiner attempted to analyze this mentality, driven back and forth by his own emotions and the reaction of public opinion, and came closest to the truth: 'This way of thinking and acting, partly aroused by suggestion and auto-suggestion, cannot always stand up against subsequent unprejudiced criticism, but it is not for that reason necessarily pathological.'

Yet whatever the mental state, the emotional abnormality of this nature darting restlessly back and forth between somnolence and frenzy cannot be overlooked. No normal man strives for world domination; and a normal man would hardly lead Adolf Hitler's private life. Capable of great physical and mental exertions, he is almost pathologically disinclined to regular work; a magician does not work, and greatness is not achieved by ordered activity. Perhaps it is basically his disinclination for regular activity that makes him sleepless. He is nocturnal in his habits; when possible, he forces his staff to confer with him at night, and it is at night that he prefers to make his decisions. One night Goebbels arrived in Berlin dead tired after two days of work and a journey by plane. 'At two in the morning,' the propaganda chief writes, 'he was still sitting fresh as a daisy in the midst of his work, alone at his home; he made me lecture him for almost two hours about the construction of the Reich super-highway'; strange work which was suddenly interrupted by two hours of chatting — for a lecture on this subject by Goebbels, who was certainly no specialist, cannot be regarded as anything more. 'Every night till six or seven in the morning, you could see the light shining from his windows. Der Führer was dictating his great speeches . . .' again a report by Goebbels, this time referring to a visit in Berchtesgaden.

Later, when Goebbels administered the German film industry, he forced actresses to sign contracts agreeing to keep Hitler company occasionally at night; under perfectly respectable circumstances, to be sure, at the big all-night parties which he often gave. Goebbels also did real pandering if it could procure or reinforce Der Führer's favor; and all the while he informed the world how frugally Der Führer lived — shunning drink, tobacco, meat, pomp, and festivities, renouncing the joys of family life. It is true that Hitler does not smoke or drink, but he does consume immense quantities of sweets; as though he had remained a child in matters of taste and pleasure. He indulges in every pleasure that might appeal to a child; he goes out driving when the mood takes him; abandons all duties and spends half the day at the movies whenever he happens to feel like it; he can never get his fill of light music and operettas — nor of Wagner's sweet poison, for that matter. According to Goebbels, he has attended *The Meistersingers* more than a hundred times. It was probably Wagner's sermon which finally induced him to give up meat-eating, which did not greatly appeal to his taste to begin with. One of the greatest childhood pleasures, staying up late at night, became in time an ingrained habit; even as a young man, even as a soldier, he had difficulty finding sleep, which is one of the strongest elements of human routine and hence in violent opposition to Hitler's undisciplined character. He lies awake whole nights, pondering problems, turning them over and over hundreds of times; from this sleepless pondering, often after weeks of silence and aloofness, arise those so-called lightning decisions which surprise those blessed with better sleep. And then he speaks of his inspiration or intuition! The only element of truth in this is that he usually follows the dictates of his mood, seldom forcing himself to act against the voice of his inclination. This is not lack of energy; he can endure the most astounding physical and emotional exertions with the insensibility of a Simeon Stylites. But even when — as occurs from time to time — he works restlessly, it is with the restlessness of a playing child.

And so, though he is the real source of energy in his cause and his enterprise, his incalculability is a serious obstacle to regular business. Things must be done and the responsibility for getting them done lies on the shoulders of such men as Goebbels; for Hitler only does the things that he happens to feel like doing. He does them with the greatest expenditure of force, but often he cannot find the extra ounce of strength to do what is uncomfortable, to decide what is doubtful, to make a difficult decision; for at the bottom of his heart he trusts that a difficulty will be canceled out by a second difficulty. When a member of his staff presses him for some unpleasant decision, he often escapes by embarking on a speech about art and race, until an adjutant comes in to announce that the car is waiting. He can then abandon himself to the pleasant experience of being driven, which presents a certain aspect of activity. These pleasure trips are 'tours of inspection.' They frequently end among crowds shouting with enthusiasm, young girls presenting flowers, children who let themselves be caressed — they end in triumph, which he can never get enough of; one more experience of greatness.

And then he may escape into total obscurity; as though seeking the illusion of being dead. For many years he was in the habit of disappearing on Christmas Eve, leaving even his family, his sister and nieces to their own resources. It is said that he regularly spent this most solemn night of the German year in the stable of the Munich Reichswehr Barracks, for a few hours recapturing the Christmas mood of his soldier days; this cannot be checked, but his disappearances have been confirmed by several sources.

He is a restless and indefatigable consumer of men, provided they are served up in the proper way, compliant and giving the desired answers. Goebbels, who had learned this conduct so well, had to let himself be questioned well into the dawn about irrelevant things. With questions Hitler replaced reading, he used people instead of books; he knew what he wanted and would coax from obedient men the desired answers, which could not have been obtained from silent, stubborn books. By his questions he endeavored not only to learn, but to influence and mold the people he questioned. A young diplomat from the German Embassy in Paris, London, or Washington happens to be in Berlin and is invited to one of Hitler's banquets; Der Führer draws him into a long and strange conversation: 'From the Arc de Triomphe, as you know,' says Hitler, 'twelve streets run in all directions. In which streets are there gardens in front of the houses, in which streets not?' The answer is by no means perfect. Next Hitler wants to know in which streets there are shops, in which purely residential buildings. Some are definitely residential streets for rich people — which ones? What sort of people frequent the shops in the other streets? The answers are all unsatisfactory, and the dismayed attaché gets the friendly advice to pay more attention to such things in the future, as they are important. He supposes that Hitler is possessed by a frenzy for municipal building and gewgaws. Perhaps it does not dawn on him until years later that Hitler was questioning him on military matters.

The consumption of human beings in large quantities is Hitler's real private pleasure. A penchant for using and abusing people made Hitler the archetype of politician who uses men only as a means to an end, whether the end be business, war, or even what he calls love. From this cruel, ultimately useless wallowing in human material, unsatisfactory both for himself and others, he gathers again and again the plaintive conviction that he is the unhappiest of all men. And assuredly he is unhappy, for what torments him and causes him to torment others is in the last analysis his fear of men, acquired in his youth and never overcome. He cannot meet his fellow man naturally, on an equal level; he can only do him violence, or himself suffer violence — and here we have touched his secret wound, from which probably most of his inadequacies arise. This is the source of his concealment, his vagueness; his nature is always faced with the terroristic command: do not betray yourself. It was this part of his nature that taught him his profound contempt of men; and this is his secret that must not be betrayed. Hence the vagueness of presentation in his speeches, hence his avoidance of facts and arguments. It is the same fear of providing a window into himself that makes him so careful to keep any specimen of his handwriting away from the public. With this — obviously unconscious — resistance, he shelters and protects a nature which feels that, exposed to the light of public scrutiny, it must wither in shame. It is the same resistance which makes him try to appear so abnormally virtuous in his relations with women. In this connection many false conjectures have been circulated.

For a time he was accused of homosexual tendencies; such accusations, in view of his friendship with Röhm and the composition of the S.A., were natural but false. However, we can sense that here, too, in his convulsive, exaggerated way, he is hiding something. Here we shall deal with this subject only as much as is necessary to cast a little more light on the contradiction between the private individual and the public picture.

It has been observed that, having attained power, he frequently commuted the death penalty to imprisonment for murder inspired by erotic motives. Exponents of the psycho-analytical school have diagnosed a 'castration complex,' a pathological fear of losing his virility. His strange, furious discourse against syphilis in *Mein Kampf* might support such a theory. A more reliable indication is the fact that both in his speeches and writings he likes to linger on the presentation of killing, especially the death penalty. Hanisch relates that young Hitler once told him of a visit he had made with his father to the courthouse in the Upper Austrian town of Ried; his father showed him all sorts of instruments of murder which the police had taken away from brawling peasants or real criminals — revolvers, knives, blackjacks; and Hitler owned that the sight of all these implements of murder had put him in high spirits. In his early speeches he liked to describe how the National Socialists, after their victory, would hang the lamp-posts full of their adversaries; the heads of their enemies would roll. And, in general, beheading is one of his favorite ideas. In the early years of his movement he had 'promissory notes' printed to serve as receipts for a loan floated by the *Völkischer Beobachter,* redeemable after the victory of the movement. These notes were designed by Adolf Hitler himself. The note was a rectangle the size of a dollar bill, and was intended to look like a bank-note. The text, framed in a maze of swastikas, obligated the N.S.D.A.P. to pay back ten marks. The left quarter of the note was taken up by a little picture — and what a picture! A young man with an open shirt and a head covering not clearly recognizable (though the mustache was lacking, the grave, threatening face had the features of an idealized self-portrait) held by the right hand a sword dripping with blood; the left hand grasped the curls of a severed female head. Head and sword seemed to lie on the page of a newspaper, perhaps the *Völkischer Beobachter*. In the background a banner with the swastika; beneath the picture in Gothic letters: 'Warriors of truth, behead the lie!' A warrior of truth might have been expected to pierce the lie, to face it in battle, to struggle against its embrace — the artist Hitler, however, dreamed of beheading a defenseless woman.

Is this, then, the true picture? A Bluebeard, a murderer of

woman, who must exercise the greatest self-control to avoid committing a crime, or at least to avoid creating a scandal? His psychology has been interpreted in this way, and inventive informants have even told stories to this effect with full details. The truth is that in private relations as well as in public life he much too easily falls into a seeming brutality which does not exactly indicate strength, and which makes no distinction between man and woman. But he is not in the least ashamed of this brutality; he is proud of it. He publicly declares that the woman longs for domination by man, and hints that this is his own insight gathered from a wealth of experience. With these utterances he adds a harsh and jarring splotch of color to the public picture which he has made of himself, and which he himself admires and worships. Behind it is concealed the realm of his most private experience: Hitler feels that his inner life is a humiliating, embarrassing contradiction to his public image; he feels that this contradiction fills his whole life with untruth. He longs for humiliation — but no one must know this.

In his most intimate private life he is not a sadist, but the contrary. Here it is not intended to describe his various experiences, with names and addresses; but there is one case worth reporting because it really sheds some light on the human figure behind the gigantic image, and because it plunged Hitler the man into a real catastrophe and may perhaps be called *the* tragedy of his private life.

One day his parental relations to his niece Geli ceased to be parental. Geli was a beauty on the majestic side, with an abundance of blond hair, simple in her thoughts and emotions, fascinating to many men, well aware of her electric effect and delighting in it. She looked forward to a brilliant career as a singer, and expected 'Uncle Alf' to make things easy for her. She, her mother, and a less conspicuous younger sister, named Friedli, lived with Hitler in his mountain house at Berchtesgaden, and after 1929 often shared his Munich dwelling. Her uncle's affection, which in the end assumed the most serious form, seems like an echo of the many marriages among relatives in Hitler's ancestry.

At the beginning of 1929, Hitler wrote the young girl a letter couched in the most unmistakable terms. It was a letter in which the uncle and lover gave himself completely away; it expressed feelings which could be expected from a man with masochistic-coprophil inclinations, bordering on what Havelock Ellis calls 'undinism.' (Who wishes to do so may find some samples in this author's *Psychology of Sex,* 1936 edition, vol. III, pp. 56/57 and 60/61.) The letter probably would have been repulsive to Geli if she had received it. But she never did. Hitler left the letter lying around, and it fell into the hands of his landlady's son, a certain Doctor Rudolph; perhaps this was one of the reasons for Hitler's change of lodgings. The letter was in no way suited for publication; it was bound to debase Hitler and make him ridiculous in the eyes of anyone who might see it. For some reason Hitler seems to have feared that it was Rudolph's intention to make it public.

With the help of a remarkable human instrument, Hitler was saved from disgrace. In Munich lived a dwarf-like eccentric named J. F. M. Rehse, who for years collected so-called political documents with an almost pathological ardor. Rehse, the son of an officer, was a photographer by profession, but he had given up his trade and lived only for his collector's frenzy. In his extremely modest quarters he collected all the official decrees, political posters and leaflets he could lay hands on; at night he crept to the public billboards, tore down posters, and took them home. In the course of the years he had collected such a mass of paper that the floor of his apartment was beginning to buckle. Rehse was the type of person who was bound to become a National Socialist as soon as he first heard about it, and so he was among Hitler's early acquaintances. He was friend and partner of a strange fellow of a very different sort, but equally a close acquaintance and almost friend of Hitler: Father Bernhard Stempfle. This Stempfle belonged to the Catholic order of Saint Jerome; by profession he was an anti-Semitic journalist, a political conspirator — all in all, an armed bohemian in priest's robes.

Rehse and Stempfle now were approached by Franz Xaver Schwarz, the party treasurer, who asked them to buy Hitler's letter from Rudolph on the pretext that they must have such a precious document for their collection. They seemed to have scented the opportunity: in return they demanded that Hitler assume financial responsibility for the collection. The deal was concluded, Hitler and Schwarz acquired the collection for the party and employed Rehse and Stempfle as curators. This was in April, 1929; the National Socialist Party was still insignificant, it was sorely in need of money, and when highly deserving party comrades of the old guard came to the offices of the *Völkischer Beobachter,* begging for ten marks in payment for an article they had contributed, Rosenberg was perfectly capable of kicking them downstairs. While the editors of his paper were still running about ragged and threadbare, Hitler spent good money, ostensibly for a collection of dusty old posters. He went so far as to boast that National Socialism had saved a valuable cultural undertaking. His most devoted followers shook their heads at this new whim; even the best-informed did not suspect its true motives.

Stempfle, who was wonderfully gifted for haggling and intriguing, then bought the letter from Rudolph — under exactly what conditions is not known. The sum of money does not seem to have been small. Presumably Schwarz advanced it from the party treasury in order to save Der Führer's reputation; in any case it was he who provided the money. The letter probably did not go through Rehse's hands, and in this he may have been fortunate. Stempfle gave it to Schwarz and he to Hitler. It is perhaps this service that later made Schwarz one of the most powerful, though publicly obscure, figures of the Third Reich.

Relations between Hitler and his niece became troubled as time went on; the incident of the lost and recovered letter perhaps contributed to the final catastrophe. For a time, at least, the strange lover seems to have grown rather repugnant to the young girl. But surely Hitler's almost pathological inconstancy had something to do with this. Hitler thought himself entitled to extend his affections on all sides; and all the stories which he assiduously spread about his unworldliness and aloofness had their basis in the fact that he knew no constancy or fidelity in any human relationship. Nature gave him the faculties and instincts of a great egoist and devourer of people, but denied him the hardness which might have enabled him to bear such a lot without pain. His loveless core is covered over with a thick foam of sentimentality and self-pity; he demands pity of his victims. He not only expected his women friends to tolerate competitors; he also claimed the right to have several families at once. His sister and nieces had to look on while he made himself at home in the family of Richard Wagner's son, Siegfried Wagner, in Bayreuth — after Siegfried's death, to be sure (1930). Here he spent most of his time, and rumors went about that he intended to marry Frau Winifred Wagner, Siegfried's widow; he regarded and treated the children of the family almost as his own. And this was by no means the only case of inconstancy of which Geli could complain. When she protested, her uncle lost all the devoted chivalry with which he treated the ladies in his good hours; he fumed and cursed like a truck-driver and locked the beloved child up in the house. She made other friendships, for example with Emil Maurice, the man to whom Hitler had dictated the beginning of *Mein Kampf;* by profession a clock-maker, by nature an armed bohemian of the lowest order. In the end, she made up her mind to end her whole life with Hitler, and go to Vienna.

Hitler resisted violently. During this quarrel Geli in her despair seems to have told outsiders about her relations with her uncle and about the dangerous letter. Hitler was beside himself; he felt he had been betrayed as a man. Geli was determined to leave for Vienna where a friend was awaiting her. Her uncle forbade her. One day he went to Hamburg; as he was setting out, she asked his permission for the last time to leave Munich. She called down to him from a window in the house on the Prinz Regenten Strasse, 'Then you won't let me go to Vienna?' And Hitler, from his car, called up, 'No!' According to the testimony of neighbors, she was not especially dejected. In a tone of indifference she announced that next day she was going to Berchtesgaden to see her mother, who was living in the mountain house on the Obersalzberg. She went about the apartment with a little box bearing a dead canary, bedded in cotton; she sang to herself and wept a little and said she meant to bury poor dead 'Hansi' near the house on the Obersalzberg. She began a letter to a friend in Linz — an everyday letter without special content. That was her last known act. Next morning she was found shot to death. It was September 18, 1931. Geli Raubal was twenty-three years of age.

After a thorough investigation, the state's attorney declared her a suicide. The coroner's report said the bullet had entered the chest below the left shoulder and penetrated vertically to the heart, a probable direction in case of suicide. In Vienna where she had grown up, Geli Raubal was buried in the Central Cemetery. A Catholic priest who was a friend of the family blessed her remains. As a rule the Catholic Church does not do this in the case of suicides; but it admits of one exception — where there is a likelihood that the suicide occurred in a state of mental confusion. It was a terrible blow to Hitler. Gregor Strasser later claimed that for two days he didn't let him out of his sight, fearing that he might do himself harm. The Austrian government granted Hitler special permission for a trip to Vienna. A week after Geli's death, he spent an evening at her grave, shedding many tears.

How and why had Geli Raubal died? Was it suicide? Was it murder? In either case, what was the reason? To a close friend her mother later hinted at murder, or else suicide under compulsion or strong suggestion. She did not accuse Hitler; on the contrary, she said she was sure that Adolf was determined to marry Geli. She mentioned another name: Himmler.

Himmler's part in the matter can only be presumed. The mentality of this man and his entire circle justifies the most hideous speculations. Conceivably he thought it his duty to free his Führer from a dangerous woman. But the circumstances do not point very clearly in this direction. Corrupt as the Bavarian administration of justice may have been under the leadership of Franz Gürtner — it would at that time scarcely have hushed up a murder, even though it did its best to keep the matter quiet on the ground that suicide was a private affair.

Yet there is no satisfactory explanation for suicide. An outbreak of hysterical rage? Close friends insisted that the merry, robust girl had never shown any such propensities. If we are to believe the assertions and hints of her mother, we might piece together a gruesome scene, compatible with the spiritual twilight of this milieu. We can see Himmler, calling at a late hour; explaining to Geli that she had betrayed the man who was her guardian, her lover, and her Führer in one. According to National Socialist conceptions, there was only one way of making good such a betrayal. To be sure, she was a woman, but at the same time, in a special and eminent way, she was a member of a kind of aristocratic order with strange concepts of honor. We may ask what Himmler hoped to gain by the inevitable scandal; but a worse scandal was to be feared if Geli went to Vienna and began to talk, ultimately to the press. But again: these are pure conjectures, though they do possess a certain inner plausibility.

At all events, Geli Raubal died under strange circumstances. As for Adolf Hitler, life here played a cruel trick on an idol unfit to be a man. The story as it is related here was told by Stempfle to a friend who had already learned a great deal from Geli herself. And probably Stempfle talked to other people, too; perhaps in retaliation because Hitler ignored him after coming to power. One thing is certain: on June 30, 1934, when Hitler settled accounts with hundreds of enemies and former friends by mass murder, Pater Bernhard Stempfle was killed by three shots in the heart in the Forest of Harlaching near Munich, by a murder gang led by Emil Maurice.

Chapter XVI

'ADOLPHE LÉGALITÉ'

UP TO 1930 THE MASSIVE SUCCESS OF ADOLF HITLER could be understood only with a constant eye to an epoch hiding from its doom. After 1930 the epoch struggling with doom can no longer be understood except with a constant eye to Adolf Hitler.

The world crisis was driving toward the point where it awaited Hitler — or some other demon who was ready to trample beneath iron feet the generation awakening from its dream of money and abundance. Dictatorship had established itself firmly at many points on the globe; the Bolshevist and Fascist designs were completed; the souls were prepared. A meaning had to be given to a world that had grown meaningless; if this could be done in no other way, then by force. The poor people of the whole world were stirred to their very depth by a deeply symbolical news report from South America: the fire-boxes of locomotives were to be adapted for burning coffee instead of coal. Very well, then, have a pleasant journey with your coffee that we can no longer pay for; farewell, all you other foreign pleasures and comforts! Keep them. We can no longer buy them, for you no longer buy our coal, but use coffee for fuel; you don't even buy our locomotives any more! Said Hjalmar Schacht: 'We must do like Frederick the Great in the eighteenth century — base ourselves firmly upon the home economy and take from our home soil what can in any way be taken; and for a generation we must live frugally, save and work.' And by so doing, the youthful extremists added, we shall utterly smash this declining world.

An unknown young man by the name of Friedrich Zimmermann, who for two years mystified the German public with his pen-name of Ferdinand Fried, published a book in which he declared that what was actually declining was the 'West,' as Oswald Spengler had predicted. Geographically speaking, the West was 'the territories bounding the North Atlantic and grouped around the three financial and commercial centers, New York, London, and Paris.' 'Here' — in the 'West' — 'the daring of the capitalist, which is the true Viking spirit, begins to flag. The tribute of debts' — Fried meant the German reparations and at the same time the debts of the Allies to America — 'can no longer be physically assimilated; the West is like an old man who can no longer take nourishment. But with the coldness and hardness of old age it insists on the collection of interest. It is in an attitude of defense against a world in revolt. It can maintain itself only by chaining the rest of the world together in a complicated and subtle system — unfathomable to the average eye — which is called world economy; in reality the world is chained by world economy to the interest-exacting West. But this world can no longer be held together, it is crumbling apart, and as a result the West itself is beginning slowly to disintegrate. . . . Protective tariffs give rise to national autarchies; immense spaces' — Fried had in mind Soviet Russia — 'are disengaging themselves entirely from world economy, perhaps to join with other spaces; state planning and state intervention become state capitalism or state socialism, in a word, state economy. . . .'

Ten years before, John Maynard Keynes in England, one of the keenest students of capitalism, had predicted the great twilight of the gods in his own way: 'The bluff is discovered,' he wrote; 'the laboring classes may be no longer willing to forego so largely, and the capitalist classes, no longer confident of the future, may seek to enjoy more fully their liberties of consumption so long as they last, and thus precipitate the hour of their confiscation.' Keynes had written a book with the title: *The End of Laisser-Aller;* Fried's book was entitled *The End of Capitalism,* and was for years the greatest success among political books in Germany.

The young German intellectuals saw the capitalists of their own country failing in their tasks. The German employers made their aimless, unsuccessful, and heartless attack on the poor people; Brüning decreased wages by violent decrees, supposedly lowered prices too, but not enough — and despite all the efforts and sacrifices of those who were still employed, more and more workers were discharged. From 1930 to 1932, according to the official estimate, the number of unemployed rose from three millions to over six millions, actually to far more than seven millions; and since German industry had a tendency to keep its workers even in hard times, this unemployment figure showed a graver economic distress than would have been the case in other countries.

There stood the wonderful smelting furnaces of Fritz Thyssen and his like, capable of producing twice as much steel as England, now useless, cold and still. Kirdorf's precious coal lay in great heaps around the mines and found no buyers; while the unemployed miners spent the winter in unheated rooms, at times banding together to break through the fence and seize as much fuel as they could carry. In the summer of 1930, gas broke through the walls of the Wenceslaus Mine near Waldenburg in Silesia, and three hundred miners were asphyxiated; rows of corpses were found with raised faces; they had died trying to snatch a last breath of air above the layer of gas. The mine had been a death trap; it should have been closed long before, and now the authorities did officially close it. Three thousand miners were unemployed, and in the collapsing economy found no other work. They banded together and petitioned; for three years they sent memoranda to the ministry, sent delegations to Berlin, addressed proclamations to the German people: they wanted their death mine reopened; it was better to live in constant fear of death than to suffer the constant hunger of their families.

In the woods around Berlin tent colonies sprang up; here lived unemployed who could not pay their rent in town. Straight streets ran through the camps; the residents shared such tasks as removal of garbage; there were community kitchens. Discipline and order prevailed. But in the fields around Berlin the peasants posted guards with loaded rifles; for large troops of starving men came from the city, flung themselves on the potato fields, and carried the potatoes away in sacks — this in broad daylight, while the traffic rolled by on the roads. Often the guards with their rifles were powerless against the famished and desperate marauders. Young men, who had seen the last remnants of property dwindle away in their families and had never learned the meaning of work, wandered through the countryside in bands, literally singing with hunger; the residential sections were full of the terrible singing of poor people, who had never dreamed that they would some day be singing for bread. It was still good times for the unemployed when they could crowd in long, gray, shabby lines on the pavement outside the so-called employment offices; they presented a little booklet at a window, and a grumbling official pasted in a stamp certifying that they had presented themselves and had vainly asked for work. This entitled them to an unemployment benefit, which might amount to as much as seventy marks in a month. When the gray, shabby army swelled beyond measure, they were allowed to come only twice a week; but after thirteen weeks of unemployment a person was transferred into another class, where the benefits were much smaller and actually were based on a kind of state charity. Originally what he received had been an insurance benefit; he had paid for it in good times by a compulsory deduction from his wages. Little by little, it became a gift from the state.

Everyone expected help from the state in his distress; when the economy collapsed, the state became the symbol of security, sustenance, productivity. Unable to collect their rents, landlords could no longer pay interest on their mortgages; a quarry-owner in the Rhineland took to living in his quarry, because no building was going on; barbers were starving because their customers could not afford to be shaved; a stationer lost his customers to a new one-price store; a drygoods shop was crushed by a near-by department store. The state had to help, raise a subsidy fund, and was besieged with pleas to pass a law against department stores and one-price stores, which it finally did. As in 1923, millions of personal failures and collapses gave rise again to a feeling of the state's omnipotence and divinity. It was a feeling that fluctuated between confidence and fear; the optimist, according to a widespread joke, predicted: Next winter we'll all go begging. The pessimist inquired: From whom?

The industrialists were afraid to produce, because production was bound to bring loss at a time when the masses whom they did not employ had no money with which to purchase. The sight of this worthless wealth breathed a spectral life into men's doubts about the existing society. So the employer lost money if he put men to work; well, then, let him lose money. Production just had to be given a push; in this time of universal want there could be no lack of use for whatever was produced. This production might not be so carefully calculated as before; it might cost more; the state could stretch its credit, increase the circulation of money — this could be called inflation, but it would fill stomachs. German labor leaders seized on the new gospel of American employers: the capitalist economy, they said, would find markets and prosper if it paid higher wages to more workers, thus giving them purchasing power — though Karl Marx had taught that a capitalist economy throve precisely by paying the workers as little as possible. The German Socialists who demanded the increase of mass purchasing power actually did admit their desertion from Marxism indirectly, by saying that at the moment they did not want to destroy capitalism, but to be the doctor at its sickbed; thus, far better than the founders of Marxism, they saw the true sense of the class struggle, which is waged to win a larger share in capitalism for the proletariat.

Brüning and his advisers, however, were stricken with panic by the specter of a new inflation, and were prepared to accept any other, equally catastrophic, destruction of the economy, provided only that the Reichsmark remained the Reichsmark. Thus Germany was governed against the masses, who did not inwardly accept the crisis, who had 'discovered' the bluff. As Gregor Strasser expressed it in the Reichstag, they expected the state 'to be able to restore an honest living for work honestly performed'; they expected this state to exert a power it did not possess, and so the time was ripe for a new state.

This was the profoundest reason why the majority of the Reichstag no longer followed any government. Brüning was conducting a business which presumably ran counter to his own nature. The solemn, embittered man, who let no one, least of all the people, see the thoughts hidden behind his spectacles, must sometimes have shuddered inwardly at his own attempts to preserve the economic age. He had started on this course half unawares, followed only by a small group of his closest co-workers, and by them with hesitation. He had to promulgate his laws in opposition to parliament, as presidential decrees. To be sure, the largest democratic party of the Reich, the Social Democratic Party, felt constrained not to overthrow him; for Brüning seemed the last defense against Hitler. But in this hopeless attempt Social Democracy used itself up, without in the end averting the catastrophe. While half Europe was already under the domination of dictatorship, Brüning called himself Germany's 'last parliamentarian chancellor.'

The German collapse, which tore down the authority of the laws, raised up the authority of violence in its stead. A new Reichswehr dictatorship seemed to be arising, similar to the one which, simply, inconspicuously, inexorably, had for a short time been exerted by Seeckt in 1923. People should not be so afraid of this hobgoblin of dictatorship, said the retired general, who had defeated Hitler. He had gone into politics, and had even permitted Stresemann's party to elect him to the Reichstag. No one was thinking of bloody tyranny, he insisted; dictatorship was only the 'natural reverse side of democracy and parliamentarianism in the event that the forces in this parliament cannot agree; but it must be limited to emergency.' What the Reichswehr really wanted was a functioning but obedient democracy. When the democracies had won the World War, the generals found it timely that Germany should have a try at this victorious state form. When Seeckt spoke of dictatorship, he meant that the Reichswehr must force the disintegrating parliament to perform its political function; and the foreign policy of Germany, said the general, who had learnt that even victorious war not always pays, should be 'reconciliation, peace, co-operation.'

Against the Reichswehr, if things grew serious, there could be no resistance; on this friend and foe were agreed. It was all very well for the political parties, sensing the new conditions, to arm their private armies with pistols and infernal machines, and have them march and swagger; but once force began to speak, only the machine guns and artillery of the army would be heard. To be sure, there was a second armed force that was not to be despised: the police of the various states, especially Prussia, which disposed of some fifty thousand men with military training; and this Prussian police was, according to the law, entirely, though in reality only partially, in the hands of that group of trade-union secretaries, government officials, and parliamentarians which constituted the leadership of the Social Democrats and governed Prussia. But against a determined Reichswehr there could be no reliance on this troop.

But what was the Reichswehr determined to do, and to what lengths would it go — this was the question. 'Generals!' cried Hitler to the leaders of the Reichswehr in one of his speeches, 'with a hundred thousand men you cannot wage a foreign war, but you can give the state a new form. It lies partly in the hands of the army which tendency will be victorious in Germany; Marxism or ourselves.' The Reichswehr's answer was that National Socialism began 'to show Russian character,' as one of its spokesmen put it.

As a matter of fact, the Nazis began to undermine and to destroy the state from inside; especially to destroy the loyalty of its servants, armed and unarmed. They had their helpers, most of them carefully concealed in the ministries and other government offices; they gathered information about the inner movements and decisions of the state and accumulated their treasure of state secrets in a party office which was headed by a man at that time almost unknown to the outside world: Rudolf Hess, the 'private secretary.' A minister wrote a decree that National Socialist meetings must be watched by the secret police; the National Socialist *gauleiter* in a provincial city knew this even before the police president, and informed the members of the secret police, for they too were secret National Socialists. One of the most popular ministers, in private life rather a good, harmless soul, had a mistress — she actually was a National Socialist spy. To be sure, this minister also had his spies among the National Socialists, but it can be said that the results were disappointing. A spying state against a spying political party — public opinion already took this feature of the silent civil war as a matter of course. Probably by far the most efficient spy system had been built up by Schleicher; he spied on his own superiors, on the ministers of the Reich, on Brüning himself, and tapped their telephone wires. One day Brüning, sitting with a visitor in his studio in the chancellery, suddenly sprang up, ran to the door, ran through the

founded, the leader had to report his organization to a higher S.A. leader, and had to be confirmed by him — and thereupon the S.A. was stronger by four to twelve men. In honor of the founder, the squad bore his name for all time. Three to six squads formed a 'troop,' two to three troops a 'storm'; the storm, embracing seventy to a hundred and twenty men, was and is the actual marching and fighting cell of the Brown Army. Up to 1930, scant squads and troops had maintained themselves with difficulty in many places; in the crisis they rapidly grew to be storms, the storms grew into 'standards' (a thousand to three thousand men) — and so on up to the 'brigade' and the 'group' (later *Obergruppe* or 'superior group'), which counted up to a hundred thousand men. By January, 1931, the S.A. included approximately one hundred thousand men. Exactly a year later, Hitler claimed over three hundred thousand, while the party membership stood at eight hundred thousand. Another year later, shortly before Hitler came to power, Röhm mustered some eight hundred thousand storm troopers in his eight *Obergruppen*.

Was this already the workers' army which the Reichswehr once had desired? The truth was that the Reichswehr — its leadership — had not always stuck to the original concept of Ludendorff, its lost supreme captain, or of Röhm, its own rebellious spirit, or of Hitler, its outgrown former tool. 'The era of mass armies is over,' Seeckt had said; 'the future will bring small, highly efficient armies which are suited to carrying out quick and decisive operations'; it would be 'the aim of a modern strategy to bring about a decision with mobile, expert, and maneuverable forces, before any masses can be set in motion'; this small army of the future would not 'let the numerically superior but qualitatively inferior mass deploy its forces, but above all will prevent it from forming solid material fronts'; and a mass army in the old sense 'is therefore cannon fodder in the worst sense, when confronted by a small number of trained technicians. . . . Therefore the modern small army must consist of long-term professional soldiers; as far as possible of volunteers.' The rest of the nation has to serve on the home front and constantly to produce the most modern equipment; for the secret of good armament was not to have large, probably obsolete stocks of arms at the time of the declaration of war, but to dispose of an industry which could quickly manufacture the most up-to-date arms in large quantities.

This conception of the small, superior élite army far above the rest of the nation was anathema to Hitler's military advisers. In the *Wehrpolitische Vereinigung* former Colonel Konstantin Hierl had delivered vehement diatribes against Seeckt, and one day Hitler himself, to the astonishment of all present, had given a lecture full of military wisdom; had denied that the next war would be decided by clouds of gas, armored planes, or endless swarms of tanks; no, it would be decided finally by the single man 'who was prepared to die for his cause.' He had complained that the professional soldiers still did not realize what this meant; and just this was why they were unable to understand what the S.A. was for: 'to inspire the men with an idea for which they could die'; and this single man was nothing but 'the whole mass of our people.'

This was the double talk of propaganda adapted to circumstances; for when Hitler spoke to his inner circle he admonished them to consider themselves as the élite, high above the masses; but when he talked with the generals he himself spoke for the masses.

Without a doubt the fight for men sharpened more and more to a fight for the workers, for the mighty human mass which would have the final say about the destiny of the modern labor state. The Communists tried to build up a shock army in the big factories. On the day of the great revolutionary reckoning, this shock army would take over the factories, halt work, and seize the machines, electric plants, and waterworks as strategic pledges; from the conquered factories they would send the masses into the streets, and occupy first the suburbs of the big cities, then the centers of political power. That is how civil war is waged. The great factories are the heart of capitalist society, as Marx and Engels have taught, and this heart lies in the open hand of the workers, who, in the words of the *Communist Manifesto* of 1847, have a world to gain, but nothing to lose but their chains. The workers — this is the central idea of this whole philosophy of the revolution — need only become conscious of their power. In this they were obstructed by only one force, of this the Communists were convinced, and this force was

the Social Democratic Party with its unions. The Social Democrats — the Communists insisted in dead earnest even as the National Socialist wave was engulfing them — were the chief enemy
of the workers. Therefore, the main attack of the Communists was
directed, not against the National Socialists or, as they put it, the
Fascists, but against the Social Democrats — the 'Social Fascists.'

To be sure, the Social Democrats and the unions had no revolutionary aim and hence no plan for the civil war that was obviously
approaching. And even if there had been a plan, up to 1932 they
had no suitable organization. The unions were not organized by
factories but by trades; hence a rapid mobilization of the masses
was impossible. But the pusillanimity of the Social Democrats
merely reflected the condition of the working masses themselves.
The worker who still had a job did have something to lose, Marx
and Engels notwithstanding. In this period of hopelessness his job
meant all the world to him. The best way to safeguard it was to
keep his nose to the grindstone, to say nothing and hear nothing.
Six or eight millions were standing outside waiting for this job;
and all that awaited the dismissed proletarian was a place in the
endless gray lines at the employment offices. If one day the sirens
announced a general strike, could he be expected to stand up and
leave the little piece of world which he had so painstakingly defended with his silence and renunciation? Robbed more and more
of the most elementary comforts, cut off more and more by increasing poverty from the culture to which he had been so attached,
he exhausted himself morally in a merciless struggle for existence;
unwittingly he himself was a fragment of the declining economic
age which in Hitler's phrase 'filled no one with enthusiasm to die.'

The National Socialists, on the other hand, preached death at
every hour to their S.A. These desperate men were not all heroes
either. 'When you are scared,' Röhm used to say, 'always remember
that the others are just as scared as you are!' And Hitler taught
them not to be soft, for the soldiers in the field had borne a thousand
times greater hardships. But civil war is not won by heroes; it is lost
by vacillating weaklings — and the secret is to frighten these cowards in any way possible. For this purpose the S.A. was the right
tool. Precisely because the National Socialists for the present were

unable to gain power over the factories and those workers who were still employed, the Brown Storm battalions were able to gather in that human type which was most usable, most supple, a type ready for all extremes: the bohemian of the proletariat, the unemployed. In normal times these would have been chaff, living at the edge of society; but now, if they were not the strongest, they were the most determined tenth of the nation. This tenth really had nothing to lose, often not even ideals. A part of these men believed neither in God nor in human rights nor in the classless society, and almost with pride Hitler declared: 'If this process of moral disintegration lasts much longer, the nation will fall apart and only egoism will be left. . . . That is why we have in our ranks hundreds of thousands whose life would have no sense and purpose if National Socialism had not given them a sense and purpose [several minutes of applause]. . . . You are nothing, your nation is everything!'

The sense and purpose of life for tens if not hundreds of thousands was to sit day after day in the 'storm centers' which the National Socialists had strewn all over the country. The storm centers were their headquarters, for the most part back rooms of beer halls. Both proprietor and customers had sworn loyalty to Adolf Hitler, for beer-hall proprietors have at all times been the faithful voice of the people. There sat the unemployed in their coarse brown breeches and discolored yellow shirts for many hours of the day over their half-empty beer mugs; at mealtimes they were fed for a few pfennigs from a great iron kettle that simmered in the laundry room; their uniform, often the only suit they possessed, had been sold to them by the 'field ordnance department' of the S.A. on credit. Every day — later twice a week — they spent several hours at their 'employment office' and with the money received from the state they paid the ordnance department for their uniforms and meals. Thus, Hitler's private army maintained itself as a sum of innumerable little groups defending themselves in common against cold and hunger, financed by the state they were planning to overthrow.

But when the whistle blew in the back room of the beer hall; when the squad leader cried, 'Attention!' then these men rotting in inactivity sprang up, formed ranks, and stood at attention while a man in high boots and armed with a horsewhip shouted: 'Everyone listen! . . . In the name of the Führer, the chief of staff has ordered . . .' And they marched off. For wherever they might be marching, it could only be better. Suddenly one of them had a pistol in his hand, he hardly knew how it had got there; rushing through a house door with a dozen others, he found himself in a strange room, he didn't know where; the pistol went off, a man lay groaning on the floor, he didn't know who. This is no fiction, but an account of the notorious murder in the village of Potempa in 1932. One December night in Berlin boxes in which something seemed to be moving were pressed into the hands of a few dozen of these men; they were led into a movie house in the center of the city; suddenly a whistle shrilled in the darkness, they stood up, shouted, opened their boxes, and hundreds of white mice ran through the theater. Women jumped up on chairs and railings, a snake wound its way through one of the aisles. Outside, uproarious shouts answered the noise within; thousands who had been standing there in silence suddenly began to yell. Joseph Goebbels stood in an automobile, saluting and shouting. With a thousand raised hands the crowd shouted its reply. This went on for several nights, then the government capitulated and did what Goebbels had been aiming at with his white mice and snakes: it distorted the laws to prohibit the picture that was running in the movie house. It was an American anti-war picture, written by a German and eagerly awaited by millions of other Germans, a picture revealing war in all its misery and horror: *All Quiet on the Western Front,* adapted from Remarque's best-selling novel.

Could these rowdies be expected to inspire the officers with confidence that the gray revolutionary horror of 1918 would not be repeated? On October 14, 1930, the hundred and seven National Socialists in parliament, at the behest of Strasser, Feder, and Frick, introduced a bill to limit the interest rates to four per cent; furthermore, 'the entire property of the bank and stock exchange princes . . . must be expropriated without indemnification for the welfare of the German people as a whole'; the same should be done with the property of all eastern Jews, of all 'persons of foreign race' in general, and 'the large banks must be taken over by the state without delay.' Strasser, Feder, and Frick had for years put forward this suggestion at every new session of the Reichstag, and no one had paid much attention to the little group. But now a hundred and seven deputies, a sixth of parliament, were demanding the expropriation of the banks, and the bourgeois public, Hitler's financial backers among them, was shocked: that was Bolshevism!

So these were the aims of the mouse and snake heroes, the libertarian bands, the Brown People's Army! Goebbels had been speaking of it for years — '. . . certainly we fight with Marxist methods, only we will do it better than the Marxists' — but who had listened? For a long time it had been one of his favorite images to say that the National Socialists would one day 'mount the barricades.' He had been looking for a poet and musician to provide a revolutionary song, 'whose chords would ring out on the barricades of freedom.' At length he found his poet of the barricades. It was the son of a Protestant military chaplain named Wessel, a student, National Socialist, and storm trooper. This young Horst Wessel was the exact mixture of ruffian and idealist that constitutes the armed bohemian. As a student, he suddenly broke with his family and student connections, to lead the life which in his opinion was suitable for a young savior of the lost national soul; he lived in a slum section of Berlin with a girl who had formerly been a prostitute. It was an exaggeration to call this minister's son a pimp, but it is true that he lived, fought, and finally died surrounded by pimps. He was the leader of the S.A. in his neighborhood, a militant and extremely successful leader. A gang, doubtless instigated by Communists and later hidden by Communists for a time, forced their way into his room in February, 1930, and killed him. After his death, Goebbels blew up this somewhat shady hero into a National Socialist legend; after all, he had died for the party. Horst Wessel had left behind him a marching song, three stanzas not unskillfully pieced together from the party's most familiar slogans; he had borrowed the melody from various existing tunes. The rather melancholy, unpretentious piece became the party's official song; later the 'Horst Wessel Song' became a second national anthem. Two of the lines in the last stanza ran: 'For the last time the rifle is loaded . . . Soon Hitler banners will wave over the barricades. . . .'

With horror the generals and their officers saw the day approaching when the army's machine guns would be the last bulwark against the people — an army in ferment against a people in ferment! Hitler impressed it upon them as often as he could: 'Take away from the present state the machine gun, take away the cannon, the hand-grenade, the police, take away the Reichswehr, and leave the present state to the love of its citizens — and you will see what remains of it!'

Many officers would doubtless have been ashamed to fire on their own people again — even if this people had marched under the Red banner. They had expected the republican state to save them at least from this. What Hitler wanted to say was: Not the republic, only I can save you. Therefore he took all possible pains to persuade the generals not to judge his party by the mice and snakes. The verses about rifle and barricades were removed from the 'Horst Wessel Song' — presumably by the author himself. The text now ran: '. . . For the last time the call to arms rings out . . . Soon the Hitler banners will fly over all the streets. . . .' And Hitler would do more than that to prove that he planned no attack on the discipline of the army. In one case, for example, the Reichswehr leaders proceeded sharply against their enemies and detractors among the lieutenants; Hitler utilized the occasion to dissociate himself from these enemies and detractors. Scheringer, the lieutenant and secret National Socialist, was arrested with two of his comrades on the drill-ground; from prison he wrote his memorable article. Asked if he were a National Socialist, he admitted that he was. Hence, the prosecution continued, he belonged to a treasonable party that wanted to overthrow the government by violence. Scheringer was defended by Doctor Hans Frank of Munich, a personal friend of Hitler's and almost slavishly devoted to him; Frank was a young man of the post-war generation. At the trial he insisted that his party did not want to overthrow the government by violence; to prove this, Hitler, who led the party as a dictator, was ready to take oath in court. Frank obtained permission for Hitler to appear as a witness, and Der Führer delivered his oath without hesitation: 'If we have two or three more elections, the National Socialist Movement will have the majority in the Reichstag and will then make the National Socialist revolution. . . .' When the judge asked him: 'Only in a constitutional way?' he replied sharply: 'Absolutely!' The judge could not believe that he really thought he could achieve power without recourse to violence, but Hitler swore that he did think so. Then, the judge asked, once he had achieved power by 'strictly legal' means, would he not use force against those who had been defeated and weakened? On this point he would not express himself at first. Actually Hitler had made the most blood-curdling threats in his speeches; and if Seeckt had promised that the dictatorship of the army would not be a bloody tyranny, Hitler had promised that *his* dictatorship would be bloody. 'Either our heads or the heads of the others will roll,' he had predicted years before. The judge reminded him of this, and Hitler answered slowly and solemnly, savoring all the horror of his favorite fantasy, and calculating its effect on millions of men: 'When the National Socialist Movement is victorious in its struggle, there will be a National Socialist court of justice; November, 1918, will be expiated, and heads will roll too.' For the constitution, said Hitler to the judge, does not prescribe the goal, but only the road to it; it was the road of the Wise Men of Zion: via the strictest democracy to the most unbridled tyranny. 'We are traveling the road prescribed in the constitution,' said Hitler at a meeting, 'toward the goals prescribed by us' — toward beheadings, shootings, mutilations. One of Hitler's most gifted co-workers, the journalist Johann von Leers, described the scene in Leipzig a year later with enthusiasm: '. . . when Hitler uttered the wonderful words that sprang from the hearts of all of us, the lofty promise of expiation: then heads will roll!' Scarcely any other of his utterances ever so stirred up the mud that filled the souls of his men.

Just the same, he had sworn that he would not mount the barricades with guns, that he would not march, not shoot, not storm, the enemy positions; to his contemporaries it seemed as though Hitler had sworn that he was not Hitler. Actually he had with his oath shown himself to be what he was: a destroyer of democracy through democracy. To be sure, he did not really hope to obtain a majority of the German people and hence of parliament. It was enough for him to lead the strongest minority, to perpetuate the paralysis of democracy, to destroy the democratic dream of the Reichswehr, to force the generals into dictatorship even against their will, and not out of embarrassment and as a temporary measure, but with joy and for good. But the generals should have no need to tremble at the thought of another collapse of the army as in 1918, of a 'Russian' program, or of a 'Bolshevist' Third Reich. And his financial backers, too, his Kirdorfs and Thyssens, should be put at ease — although Hitler probably was more afraid of the generals. He coldly ordered his deputies to withdraw their bill for expropriation of the bank and stock exchange princes. This they did in a silent rage. Thereupon the Communists indulged in the joke of reintroducing the bill in the exact National Socialist wording. Hitler commanded his followers to vote against their own bill, and they did so. Laughter in parliament and all over the country. Hitler saw that every time his party grew he had to conquer it afresh, break it and smooth the edges. These deputies, often unknown to him personally, still took the program seriously; many honestly regarded themselves as a kind of socialist.

The whole National Socialist fraction was withdrawn from the Reichstag to keep them from committing any further mischief; publicly the National Socialists declared that they were boycotting parliament (February, 1931). In fact, Hitler once again broke and tamed his own party, and he did not intend to stop at his parliament members. Röhm, after his return from Bolivia at the end of 1930, called at the Reichswehr Ministry; declared that Hitler meant his legality seriously and would prove it; unreliable S.A. leaders who planned acts of violence would be removed. Röhm found a friend and supporter at the Reichswehr Ministry in the person of an old comrade from Bavaria, Lieutenant-Colonel Franz Halder, who, many years later, became chief of the German general staff. On his visits to the ministry, Röhm had to become reconciled with many other officers whom for years he had reviled as cowards, weaklings, toadies, and slaves; his success in conciliating them speaks well for his self-control and diplomacy.

The chief of these despised officers was Kurt von Schleicher, then a major general, a short time later a lieutenant general. Schleicher most certainly was an army man, but he deserved to some extent the name the National Socialists gave him: 'office general.' To be sure, he was an officer by profession, but he was a politician if there ever was one. In 1900 he had entered the Third Foot Guards as lieutenant; in this regiment, one of the most exclusive of the old Prussian army, he had become the comrade and friend of another young lieutenant, Oskar von Hindenburg, son of the later marshal and president. At thirty-one he became captain and entered the general staff; some years later, during the war, he became — still captain — one of Hindenburg's close collaborators; and as friend of the old man's son he became the old man's own younger friend. A similar, even closer, friendship connected him with Groener, who spoke of him as his 'adopted son.' Through all these personal relations shines one of Schleicher's strongest talents — his ability to win the hearts of people. It almost seems as if the man's name (Schleicher: crawler, intrigant) had shaped his personality and career. Not that Schleicher was a timid or gentle nature; he loved life and power and showed it. But he pursued his lofty ambitions by means that seemed consciously adapted to his name, utilization of personal relations, extreme suppleness and amiability in conversation, persistent good humor. He was always ready with some affable assurance, but not always to back up his words. His bearing was self-reliant, but never seemed unpleasant; he was so amiable people forgot that he looked like a Caesar. But even his most congenial manners could not conceal his lack of scruples in the choice of his means.

During the war, in Hindenburg's headquarters it had been Schleicher's task to supervise German politics and at the same time to spy on Germany's allies; to some extent he had been the political brains of Ludendorff's short-lived war dictatorship. The career of Schleicher was one of those living threads which connected the political struggles of the old imperial army with the fate of the Weimar Republic; for years he had been the political brains of the Reichswehr Ministry as so-called 'Chief of the Minister's Office' — an all-powerful position which Schleicher in 1928 had secured for himself by an extremely skillful deal with the unsuspecting Reichstag. He had his share in the overthrow of Seeckt; the former chief's doctrine that the army ought to remain powerful and small was not necessarily his.

Röhm made a splendid impression on this powerful man, and won his confidence; to ingratiate himself, he even told Schleicher all sorts of amusing stories about Hitler's life and career; their general import was that Hitler, with all his eccentricities, was not really so bad. Schleicher, instructed by Röhm, was able to convince his chief Groener that Hitler was actually a rock amid the German chaos, a bulwark against the radical masses; even if, personally, he was perhaps unstable and none too strong, politically he was an anchor to the party of the Uprooted and Disinherited. The result of these conversations was a gentleman's agreement: on January, 1931, Röhm announced his inauguration as chief of the S.A. staff, and on January 2, Schleicher decreed that, since it was still by no means certain the National Socialists were really enemies of the constitution, National Socialist workers until further notice should no longer be dismissed from the arsenals and powder factories of the Reichswehr. In February, Hitler in turn issued a proclamation to the S.A. ordering them to refrain from street fights — 'I understand your distress and your rage,' he said, 'but you must not bear arms.'

Mass discontent seethed among the extremists of Right and Left in the S.A. These men were by no means all noble warriors yearning to risk their necks; no, for them legality or revolution was a question of existence. Without street fights they would one day be superfluous, and they would probably be superfluous if their Führer was serious in using democracy as his chief weapon. They knew that Röhm had promised the Reichswehr Ministry to dismiss the most dangerous among them. It is possible that someone in the Reichswehr Ministry had passed this on to them in order to create unrest among the Brown bands; anyhow they knew that Röhm was selling them out. Hitler threw out these elements, after accusing them of planning an uprising. This was the Stennes crisis. 'I am your Führer, and not elected or hired by you, not sought out by you and appointed by majority vote,' cried Hitler to the discontented storm troopers. 'No, I am your Führer on the strength of my work! . . . And if all of you were to leave me, I should go on alone!'

Even before the court had sentenced Wilhelm Scheringer to imprisonment, the first doubts had come to him. He had visited Hitler in Munich; with enthusiasm Der Führer had dragged him around the new party palace and subjected him to one of his art speeches; when Scheringer wanted to speak of politics, Hitler had replied that the young lieutenant should believe and obey. Back in Berlin, Scheringer had complained to Goebbels of his experience with Hitler; he had asked the Berlin *gauleiter* whether the party still seriously intended to break down interest slavery? Goebbels replied: a breakdown only could occur to him who had to read 'Feder's nonsense,' and when Scheringer argued that all this stood in the unalterable twenty-five-point program, Goebbels cried in despair: 'I wish to God we had never heard of those miserable twenty-five points.'

That was the party's way with its most sacred principles! Even if the lieutenants were no more loyal to principle, many of them must have felt the same as the young officers of 1923, who had declared: 'It's all the same to us who marches; we'll march along!' (Meaning: and if Hitler doesn't, we march with somebody else.) But what if they had principles and believed in National Socialism? In both cases, the practical result was perhaps the same. Scheringer sat in his prison cell and thought things over; the result of his thinking was that in March, 1931, Hans Kippenberger, a Communist deputy, stood up in the Reichstag and read a letter from Scheringer. In it the imprisoned lieutenant renounced Hitler and declared himself a Communist: 'Only by smashing capitalism in alliance with the Soviet Union can we be freed,' he wrote. Goebbels wired Scheringer asking if he had really made such a declaration. Scheringer wired back: 'Hitler betrayed revolution declaration authentic reprint Scheringer.'

A German lieutenant, nationalist, and warrior for freedom saw the sole remaining salvation in Communism; high S.A. leaders were stirring up rebellion against Hitler — was that the picture among the National Socialist masses? Groener went around preaching to his fellow ministers that the hour demands we support Hitler against the other National Socialist leaders; he is a prudent man who will obey the laws because he has every reason for doing so. Röhm had convinced Schleicher that Hitler desired nothing but freedom for propaganda; provided this were given him, he could easily be held in check, if for no other reason, because he lived in constant fear of being deported if he broke the laws. 'I have sworn legality,' Hitler often said, 'and Herr Stennes will not make a perjurer of me,' and the eternal fear of the Vienna vagabond trembled in his words.

And so the men in the government let Röhm persuade them that Hitler was more harmless than he looked, and not quite right in the head to boot. Brüning talked with Hitler, and afterward each had the feeling that he could swallow up the other. The gloomy, silent chancellor, a patriot as impassioned as Hitler, but shy and fearing his limitations, made a profound impression on the volatile Führer, and realized it; at times, perhaps, he thought he could lead Hitler. A formal understanding on the course to be taken was not possible, though Brüning himself had given Hitler the catchword that things could no longer go on as they were.

Thus Hitler wormed his way into the state system and the calculations and almost the confidence of those he intended to destroy — just by playing the good boy. Amazing how comparatively easy this was. He never won the confidence of the popular majority — never as long as there were free elections in Germany; but the men of the ruling caste, whether they secretly admired or only just tolerated or openly detested him, began to take him for granted as an indispensable and very big cog in the machine. It was not only cold reasoning that led Hitler on this promising and successful path; he followed some instinct of his nature that forbade him to take unnecessary risks. With this strategy he was already one step ahead of events. The world was in a state of revolutionary disintegration that had its repercussions from the vast spaces of the 'declining west' to the petty misery of bankrupt German communities. In the midst of this general decline there had to be the rainbow of a new order, based on force and firmness; a promise to the bewildered millions who did not — as Stennes imagined — long for more disorder, but for peace at home and abroad. To be sure, chaos was for Hitler a 'necessity of fate,' or there would be no general longing for what he wanted to stand for; but certainly in his own private desire for personal safety he was a genuine interpreter of this longing. It was a desire for greatness and safety at the same time.

In Germany there were eighteen parliaments to be elected, not to speak of municipal bodies, and at every election the sworn enemies of democracy descended on public opinion in the name of democracy. These were the armed bohemians sent into the parliaments by the National Socialist voters. Goebbels called them P.o.F. and P.o.I.; Possessors of Free Tickets — that is, of the right to use the railroads free of charge — and Possessors of Immunity — that is, of the right to lie with impunity. By now the National Socialists were winning an occasional cabinet post in the smaller provinces. For more than a year Frick was a minister in Thuringia (1930-31); and when Frick finally, by a parliament intrigue, was forced out of his post, Hitler considered this as the biggest defeat he had suffered since the Feldherrn Halle.

Frick had tried to render his leader a service which might have been more important than a victorious election. He wanted to make Hitler a German (to be exact, a Thuringian) citizen by appointing him as civil servant of his little administration, and so he appointed him constable in the small town of Hildburghausen.

Two years before becoming dictator, Hitler became what his father had been. With joyous solemnity, Frick gave him the certificate of appointment as a surprise, just before a big meeting in the city of Gera (July, 1930). At first Hitler did not know whether to be thankful or angry, but finally decided that the elevation to the rank of small-town constable was altogether too ridiculous to make up for the advantages of being a citizen now. Better think it over, said Frick with annoyance; after all, it's not so easy to smuggle yourself into German citizenship. Hitler thought it over for fifteen minutes, then spoke again with Frick and muttered vaguely: better give the certificate back. Frick's feelings were hurt. He told Hitler in no uncertain terms what he was throwing away. Changing his mind again, Hitler obediently put the certificate in his pocket. He made speeches to his Thuringian S.A. men, wearing the document over his heart; then he returned to Munich, a regularly appointed constable of Hildburghausen. When the story came out and aroused widespread laughter, Hitler maintained that he had quietly destroyed the certificate long since, and had never become what his father had been for forty years and had wished his son to become too: a policeman in a small town.

Chapter XVII

'NOW I HAVE THEM IN

MY POCKET!'

HITLER WAS ON HIS WAY TO BECOMING THE MAN of the hour. This did not necessarily mean that it would be the hour of this man. Decay and disintegration of society certainly created an atmosphere in which Hitler could thrive; however, a thorough process of adaptation was required. He had to pay the price for power, and this price always consists — among other things — of principles which have to be sacrificed.

Up to 1930, the coming man of destiny had appealed to an uprooted, disinherited, and small minority of desperate men, and had promised them the 'coming great divine judgment,' the 'great hour for Empire and Nation' — war against France. Now he was appealing to the masses for whom the enemy was not France but poverty; who did not want war but jobs. And so war speeches had to stop. His article in January, which expressed the hope that world peace would 'go down in blood and fire,' was about the last utterance of this style. From now on his slogan in his struggle for Germany was 'democracy'; in his struggle for Europe it was something even more surprising: peace.

Peace between armed intellectuals. For Hitler made his peace offer in an exchange of open letters with a French writer who had been a Socialist and now was kind of a Fascist, Gustave Hervé. It was Hervé who opened the conversation in October, 1930.

Hervé asked whether, if France should cancel the German reparations in case the United States should cancel the French War debts; if France should give Germany's colonies back, permit German rearmament and *Anschluss* of Austria, favor the restoration of the Polish Corridor, etc., would Hitler then be ready to come to an understanding with France and conclude a military alliance?

Hitler made this surprising answer: 'I think I can assure you that there is no one in Germany who will not with all his heart approve any honest attempt at an improvement of relations between Germany and France. My own feelings force me to take the same attitude. . . . The German people has the solemn intention of living in peace and friendship with all civilized nations and powers. . . . And I regard the maintenance of peace in Europe as especially desirable and at the same time secured, if France and Germany, on the basis of an equal sharing of natural human rights, arrive at a real inner understanding. . . . The young Germany, that is led by me and that finds its expression in the National Socialist Movement, has only the most heartfelt desire for an understanding with other European nations.'

On October 26, 1930, the *Völkischer Beobachter* published this statement of its editor. The date is worth remembering. On this day Hitler began his peace propaganda which continued uninterrupted for almost ten years. Inexplicable and incredible, it moved men by this very fact, but also by an undeniable breath of passion. With the same passion Hitler had said the exact opposite; had for ten years attacked the German government for its willingness to conclude an understanding with France: 'The sword is our balance [he had cried] . . . the language of cannon is our language!' And now, when Hervé, in the style of the best *Realpolitik,* proposed that Germany should have equal military rights and as large an army as France, Hitler, the orator of blood and fire, crushed the Frenchman with the hyper-pacifistic answer: 'If this intention is really present in France, it strikes me as less important for Germany to arm than for France to disarm. France has it in her power to carry out at any time the disarmament that was solemnly promised Germany in the treaties, to free all Europe of a nightmare and set everyone's mind at rest.'

Half a year before this discussion with the Frenchman, Hitler had declared to the judge at a trial in Munich: 'In political life there are no principles of foreign policy. The programmatical principle of our party is its position on the racial problem, on pacifism and internationalism. Foreign policy is only a means to an end. In matters of foreign policy I shall not permit myself to be bound' — meaning, by programs, oaths, or treaties.

Hervé's somewhat irritated reply was to the effect that there must be both a French army and a German army, and an alliance between them, because they had to defend Europe against Bolshevism — how could just Hitler forget that? This reminded Hitler that he was not debating with a Frenchman only, but with a kind of French National Socialist. He was speaking to the 'Aryans and anti-Semites' of France; and so he told them that National Socialism was not only a German movement, but a world movement as well; he lured them with a world plan: 'In my opinion the European cabinets in their present make-up cannot think seriously even of a purely defensive war with Soviet Russia. The present-day states have equipped their armies and their soldiers for war with every conceivable weapon — grenades, machine guns, flame-throwers, tanks, airplanes, gas — and they are also familiar with all the weapons of defense against these arms. But only a single state has armed and immunized its people spiritually against Bolshevism: Italy. The other European states possess neither political offensive arms nor political gas-masks against Soviet propaganda! The question of overcoming Bolshevism is a question of fascizing the European states. The present European states contaminated with Marxism cannot oppose any enduring resistance to the disruptive work of this world plague.'

Fascization of the European states! That was just what his new friend Rothermere was aiming at when, in September, 1930, he prophesied that Germany 'would draw not only the three million Germans in Czechoslovakia along with the three million Hungarians in Czechoslovakia and Rumania, but perhaps also the Hungarian people into its sphere of influence. As a result of such a development, Czechoslovakia, which has so gravely offended against the peace treaty (by the repression of national minorities as

well as by her total rejection of disarmament), could be put out
of existence overnight. . . . This great national combination under
German leadership, which I see forming step by step as the new
face of Europe in the immediate future, would be a bulwark against
Bolshevism. . . .' Hitler concluded his correspondence with Hervé
by saying that 'to my deepest regret, I must reject any offer of
German rearmament and a German-French military alliance.' His
reason was that the German-French alliance would prevent the formation of a fascist world front and lead to new wars. He, Hitler,
wanted peace — peace among Fascists.

The Central European bulwark which Rothermere foresaw was
indeed on its way. On March 19, 1931, Germany concluded a customs union with the little republic of Austria, the 'brother land,'
which had been forbidden to join with Germany by the victors of
1919. Austria, a country without any appreciable resources, a country where even the peasants starved on their stony mountainsides,
was even more deeply shaken by the crisis than Germany; the
political parties were even more radical, the contradictions more
violent. Cut off from its economic resources by the disintegration
of the Hapsburg monarchy in 1919, the country was living solely
on its spiritual forces which were bleeding it to death; solidly German in nationality and strongly conscious of it, it was torn ideo-
logically into two main groups: the faithful Catholic population,
for the most part peasants and middle class, and the strongly anti-
clerical Socialist working class. The armed intellectuals and bohemians had also put in an appearance, and had mobilized many
bourgeois and peasants; the workers had likewise mobilized. A
starving Austria, bristling with arms, was on the brink of civil war.

The customs union was an emergency act. An exhausted Austria
entered into an economic union with an exhausted Germany. An
enlarged economic area was created, an even larger one was
planned, for all the Danubian countries to the southeast of Austria
(Hungary, Yugoslavia, Rumania) lived in large part from the sale
of their agrarian products to Germany. Germany and Austria
offered to take them into their new economic *grossraum*. It was
Brüning's first attempt at a 'great policy of liberation.'

It is understandable that the leading men of Czechoslovakia became agitated. Was this the beginning of Lord Rothermere's new *Mitteleuropa,* built upon the ruins of the Czechoslovakian state? It is nevertheless tragic that in 1931 the small country could find no better answer to an act arising from the right of self-determination than a sharp protest. France, fearing everything that made Germany stronger, likewise protested. Italy wavered for a moment, but then decided against Germany. All three powers, France, Czechoslovakia, and Italy, issued their protest, for practical purposes a command: the customs union must be dissolved at once, for it was nothing other than a disguised *Anschluss* of Austria to Germany. The world was solemnly called to judge; the issue was put before the Hague World Court. Dino Grandi, Italian ambassador in London and the real director of Fascist diplomacy, said cynically to Doctor Julius Curtius, the German Foreign Minister, that, regardless of the World Court's decision, Italy would never permit the customs union.

Italy was right, said Hitler, and Brüning was wrong: for 'it is simply inconceivable to carry through a measure in foreign affairs if at home there are no forces to fight for it consistently and perseveringly or if they are left entirely unused. . . .' Brüning's failure confirmed his oft-expressed theory 'that it is not foreign policy which decides the course of a nation; it is first and foremost the nation itself, in its organization and education that prescribes its own course within the surrounding world.' To the German public, smarting under this last of the great diplomatic humiliations at the hands of the victors of Versailles, Hitler said dryly: 'Not Versailles is the cause of the catastrophe. Your parties are the cause.'

The hardest blow against the customs union was financial pressure brought by France; short-term loans to Austria were called off, and this helped to bring the little country to her knees. The slow economic decline turned into a crash. The Oesterreichische Creditanstalt, Austria's largest bank, controlled by the Viennese branch of the Rothschild family, collapsed in May, 1931, and this crash may be considered the beginning of the second period of the European economic crisis; in its darkness and despair comparable to the German inflation. Collapse of German banks was imminent, and collapse in other countries was bound to follow. Europe (with the exception of conspicuously stable France, little touched by the events outside her borders) was threatened with a sudden standstill of even the most indispensable economic functions, and only a miracle could save it.

The miracle seemed to come from America. On June 20, 1931, President Hoover called on the European states to declare a one-year moratorium on *all* intergovernmental debts, and America for her part agreed to declare a moratorium on her own demands. This might have been called the fulfillment of Ferdinand Fried's prophecy: that the creditors had become unable to accept and digest their dues. It meant the almost certain end of German reparations, for few people believed that they would be resumed after a year's breathing spell, since it was equally improbable that America's splendid capital investments in Europe would be resumed on the same scale. France, by shattering Austria's economy, had helped to bring about a situation which forcibly put an end to Germany's reparations. For two weeks the French government resisted the American proposal, but on July 6, Hoover announced the acceptance of his moratorium by all the important creditor governments. It seemed a miraculous last-minute rescue.

But for the German banks the miracle came too late. On July 13, 1931, the Darmstädter und Nationalbank, one of Germany's largest, stopped payments. The government was forced to intervene. Ten years later, it seems like a legend of long forgotten days that the insolvency of even a great bank should immediately have become a national catastrophe; since then we have seen the state master crises of this sort; we have seen the crises themselves pale before more serious problems. But the Brüning government found no means of preventing bank crashes; it proclaimed a bank holiday, other houses followed the example of the Darmstädter und Nationalbank, several were put under state control for a long time to come, the flow of money halted, salaries and wages were not paid at all or only in driblets. A domestic German moratorium helped temporarily, and German public opinion, overwrought and filled with a sense of doom, largely adopted the popular interpretation that this was the final downfall of capitalism.

But Hitler gave the following official explanation in his news-

papers: 'Never in my life have I been as well disposed and inwardly contented as in these days' — the darkest for the German
economy. 'For in these days hard reality has opened the eyes of
millions of Germans to the unprecedented swindles, lies, and be-
trayals of the Marxist deceivers of the people. In these days,' says
Hitler, highly pleased to have won a bet through the misery of his
people, 'great masses have seen, perhaps for the first time, who was
right: the Young Plan swindlers, or the men of the Young Plan
popular protest. In these days, therefore' — when once again hundreds of thousands thought they had lost their small savings, when
millions failed to receive their wages and salaries — 'I have rightly
felt happy and content, while conversely fear and consternation
have crawled up the necks of the party and newspaper swindlers of
the Young Front.'

That is Hitler. The house must burn for the sake of this flame.
When Hoover proclaimed his moratorium, it looked for a moment
as though the doom would itself be doomed in the last minute as
in 1923. And now Fate sent him this bank crisis. The state declared itself incapable of mastering the financial catastrophe, which
it could have mastered. Hjalmar Schacht demanded 'salvation from
this system.' 'If the word democracy has any meaning at all,' said
Schacht in the National Socialist jargon which he had opportun-
istically assumed, 'it means the subordination of the individual, employer as well as worker, to the great demands of the common welfare.'

In this summer of distress the anti-democratic forces rallied in a
truly demoniac lust of destruction. To bring about the downfall
of the power that was still most dangerous to them, the Social
Democratic Prussian government with its police and administrative
apparatus, the Rightist organizations again engineered one of their
noisy and for the most part unsuccessful plebiscites. Their supposedly bitterest enemies, the Communists, marched with them.
The disinherited of the Left called on their supporters to vote with
the disinherited of the Right and thus overthrow the Prussian government; in this they were faithful to their belief that not the
National Socialists but the Social Democrats were the 'main enemy.'

In the Prussian plebiscite, the Communists were privileged to join with the house of Hohenzollern. Prince August Wilhelm, a son of the former Kaiser, had become a member of the National Socialist Party and an S.A. man. When police dispersed a National Socialist crowd in the city of Königsberg, using their clubs, it happened that the prince was in the crowd; proudly he wrote to his father about this absolutely new experience, and Wilhelm answered from his Dutch exile: 'You may be proud that you were permitted to become a martyr of this great people's movement.' But princes and Communists together were unable to arouse enough people against the Prussian government; the plebiscite gave them only 9,800,000 votes, or 36 per cent (August 9, 1931).

This was certainly no time for princes. When Brüning cautiously sounded Hindenburg out on the subject of appointing a grandson of the former emperor as regent in Germany, the man who had dethroned Wilhelm II balked, this time acting the all too loyal servant. The only legal emperor, Hindenburg said, or rather the only legal king of Prussia, was the man in comfortable Dutch exile; to appoint one of his grandsons would be against tradition and legitimacy.

No king could give Germany bread, and it was bread that almost literally began to be lacking. Foreign markets were glutted and could no longer absorb the German exports to pay for raw materials. Even German capitalists had begun to withdraw funds from the collapsing economy. Brüning decreed stern laws forbidding the flight of capital, and raised the discount rate of the Reichsbank, for practical purposes the minimum rate for capital interest, to 15 per cent. Loan capital became as rare as butter in wartime. Again Germany sought the aid of foreign capital.

In this misery Germany had to decide between two possible foreign policies: either leaning on England — and this was advocated by Hitler — or looking for help in an understanding with France. France had a new premier who had started a policy of buying or bribing a number of eastern and southeastern states — Austria among them — with loans, to bind them more firmly to the French line. He was also willing to buy Germany with a loan, provided she would renounce for ten years any revision of her international treaties. This French premier, who wanted to purchase

a ten years' peace and French semi-hegemony over Europe with
cold cash, was Pierre Laval. He was the first French premier to pay
a visit to Berlin, a bold, unusual step; he came at the end of
September with his foreign minister, the aged and declining Aristide Briand. Deep in thought, Briand stood at Stresemann's grave,
his lion's head bowed and sad. But Brüning declined the French
offer, stuck to his British policy; and under British leadership Germany's foreign short-loan creditors concluded in September a so-
called standstill agreement — a veiled half-bankruptcy which for the
time being kept the fleeing foreign capital in Germany.

Between England and France — between parliament and dictatorship — between the Left and the Right — between the workers'
parties and the National Socialists, Brüning had a difficult path
which his own followers made even more difficult. In the Prussian
diet sat Franz von Papen, a representative almost unknown to the
great public. He was the scion of an impoverished family of
Catholic nobles from western Germany; despite the 'von' he was
hardly a junker, for the Papens were in business. Papen was something different from a junker. He was a professional officer, and
before entering political life, served for twenty-two years in the
Prussian army with moderate success. Born in 1879, he entered
the Fifth Regiment of Uhlans in 1896 as an ensign; in 1913, he
became a captain in the general staff. Lieutenant Kurt von
Schleicher, three years younger than himself, was sent to the general staff at the same time. Here the two men met, but soon their
ways parted. In 1905, Papen had met Martha von Boch, daughter
of a family of industrialists in the Saar. The von Bochs had intermarried with aristocratic families in Luxemburg, Belgium, and
France — and in this connection aristocracy frequently meant heavy
industry. Papen was advancing too slowly in the army; his fortune
and connections directed him to the diplomatic field. At the outbreak of the World War, he was military attaché in the German
Embassy in Washington. In the midst of peace he organized acts
of sabotage in the American armaments industry and was recalled
at the insistence of Secretary of State Lansing. Exposed and hence
useless as a diplomat, he returned to the army, and fought in sub-
altern posts in France and Palestine. When the English stormed

Jerusalem, Major von Papen is said to have saved himself at the
last moment, awakened from sleep by a subordinate young Lieutenant Joachim Ribbentrop.

After the war, Papen attempted without success to return to the
diplomatic service. His dream was to become ambassador to Luxemburg. From headquarters in the tiny neutral country, where
the great international iron and steel cartels of Europe had their
business offices, he meant to intervene in high European politics.
He believed he had the talents and other requirements for bringing
about a Franco-German understanding, based on the leading men
of both countries; for he was convinced, as he later expressed it,
'that the man of good race and inner qualities is more highly suited
to bear responsibility than the average man. We must recover the
habit of looking up to men who amount to something by their
mind and character; who are masters because they can serve. . . .'
To lead Europe through such an international master-class was the
aim of the German 'Herrenklub,' which Papen had helped to found
— the word 'Herr' meant gentleman with an overtone of 'Master.'
One of Papen's French friends was Paul Reynaud, who later won
tragic fame as premier. In Luxemburg, Emil Mayrisch, one of the
foremost iron magnates of the Continent, founded a committee for
German-French understanding, to which Papen belonged. One of
Papen's publicist friends went so far as to maintain that his aims in
foreign policy 'were not really German but occidental'; Papen tried
to do what hardly another German statesman dared: to reach an
understanding with as bitter an enemy of Germany as Raymond
Poincaré. For he believed in what French fascist doctrine called
'le pays réel': the all-importance of a superior leader class, beside
which democracy was only a pretentious sham. He hoped to arrive
at an agreement with this leading stratum of France on conditions
such as Gustave Hervé later proposed to Hitler: revision of the
Versailles Treaty, return of the Polish Corridor to Germany, German rearmament, German-French military alliance against Russia,
the overthrow of Bolshevism.

Such an armed understanding between Germany and France was
possible only if democracy were overthrown in both countries. For
years Papen had believed that the Third Republic in France would

be superseded by something like the future Pétain régime. He trusted that the Catholic Church would reconquer France spiritually and politically. In Germany, the Catholic Church was less strong, but it did have a strong direct influence on parliamentary politics. And so the uhlan and saboteur joined the Center Party. Under the pressure of the Catholic working masses the party had moved steadily toward democracy. A lonely voice, Papen had vainly tried to buck the current. His fellow parliamentarians found him irritating or absurd. Now in October, 1931, he raised his voice again; he told Brüning not to pretend that he was still governing democratically; he was already a dictator and that was good; but why conceal it? 'The concealed dictatorship of the Chancellor must strip off its parliamentary trimmings. The Chancellor should and must direct a national cabinet, a government, a dictatorship on a national foundation.' With a sense of insult, Brüning replied that he had no intention of parting from his parliamentary base. But Papen went on preaching that the strength of Germany lay with the National Socialists, and that it was Brüning's duty 'to forge these glowing masses before they overflow with hostility; above all, this youth, still undisciplined, to be sure, but valuable material, must be fitted into the state, and by education won for the state.'

The man who had invented the Brüning government thought along not quite identical but similar lines. After a year and a half of disappointments, General von Schleicher had become convinced that the popular base of a strong government could no longer be found where Brüning, half reluctantly, had so far found it: with the democratic parties of the Reichstag. Schleicher had studied the National Socialists through personal contacts and his private spies. By the fall of 1931 — this can be discerned from his policy — his decision was made. The German government must detach itself from the Left parties; the strength of the National Socialists must no longer be wasted in mere opposition. Reichswehr wanted the people, here they were. The Chancellor himself confided to his visitor, Laval, that in one year the National Socialists would sit in the government.

A few days after the German bank crash, Brüning had a conversation with Hermann Göring; he tried to persuade Göring to

influence his party to moderate its attacks on the government; otherwise Germany would be ruined. Formally Göring may have given
a sharp answer; but events ran their course. Catholic bishops had
excluded National Socialists from worship because Rosenberg's
utterances compelled them to regard the party as anti-Christian;
the whole Catholic press carried on an impassioned fight against
the party and its dubious 'positive Christianity.' But the Catholic
Church, which had already reached an understanding with Italian
Fascism (1929), could not ignore the fact that National Socialism
officially combated Bolshevism and actually embodied strong anti-
Bolshevist forces. In August, 1931, Göring went to Rome and was
received by Cardinal Pacelli, the Pope's secretary of state (the future
Pope Pius XII); he attempted to dispel the Vatican's poor opinion
of National Socialism.

But these conversations and attempts at understanding were not
aimed at a dictatorship such as Papen demanded; the aim was the
creation of a new popular majority, and Hitler himself had pointed
the way when he swore his oath to legality and the constitution.
Here a cleavage arose between himself and the bourgeois-national
groups; between the National Socialists and the German Nationalists under Alfred Hugenberg. Hugenberg, like Papen, desired the
dictatorship of a leader-class independent of the people, of a group
too small to be called even a minority. However, it was a half-dicta-
torial government, but one based on a majority and confirmed by
parliament, which the other great opportunist in this political game,
General von Schleicher, desired. To this end he obtained for Hitler
an interview with Hindenburg.

The two men were seeing one another for the first time. Hitler
was agitated and embarrassed and seems to have feared the meeting
with the dull old man. He was afraid to go without someone who
was sure of his nerves. Röhm would have been the right man; he,
after all, was responsible for the close connection with the Reichswehr, thus indirectly for the invitation itself. But Hindenburg had
a personal revulsion against the homosexual adventurer, and Göring
could not bear the idea that Hitler should appear before the field
marshal with anyone but him. Göring was in Sweden at the death-
bed of his wife, whose long illness was drawing to an end. Hitler

wired him impetuously; the meeting with Hindenburg seemed to both of them a turning-point in history. The dying woman herself is said to have urged her husband to go. Göring left her, met Hitler in Berlin, and went with him to Hindenburg.

What was said at the meeting is still unknown. Probably Hitler spent some time on his favorite theme, that only National Socialism could save the country — all Europe, in fact — from Bolshevism. It is certain that he complained of how patriots — that is, himself and his party — were being persecuted, and presumably in his agitation he threatened that under such circumstances no spirited resistance could be expected of the German people if tomorrow the Poles should overrun the eastern border. At all events, the meeting was a failure. Schleicher later related that the old gentleman had been disappointed and had said that he would not make this 'Bohemian corporal' chancellor, but 'at most general postmaster.' Hindenburg seems to have had the impression that Hitler was no real German. As for Göring, he never again saw his wife alive.

It was a dismal time in Hitler's personal life. Geli Raubal, his beloved niece, had died three weeks before. Hitler does not seem to have been in full possession of his faculties at this time; he drifted along and let himself be pushed into decisions which he himself held to be mistaken, such as a new alliance with Hugenberg and the Stahlhelm. On October 11, one day after the talk with Hindenburg, a solemn foundation of a so-called 'national front' was laid in the little spa of Harzburg, with many brown and green uniforms. Hitler felt like a prisoner; he was so disgruntled and agitated that he could scarcely speak, and he refused to eat at the same table with Hugenberg and the Stahlhelm leaders, Franz Seldte and Theodor Duesterberg. In his speech he flung a few attacks at Brüning and demanded 'that the power and responsibility be put into the hands of the national opposition'; but went no further than to reject 'governments which are formed without us or against us.' On the other hand, he did not shrink from saying that as long as Brüning governed against them, the National Socialists would not defend the national boundaries: 'From now on, a system which persecutes us cannot count on our help or protection in times of need, or even of mortal peril.'

But now Brüning himself let this system fall. He was making a sort of palace revolution against himself and his closest friends; he threw out of his cabinet some ministers who belonged to the Left, among them Doctor Joseph Wirth, the former Chancellor. Groener, the Reichswehr Minister, took over the Ministry of the Interior; this meant that Schleicher had his way. From now on, with planned inactivity, the Reich government looked on as Hitler strengthened his private army and sent it swarming into every town and village. The half-forgotten General Ludendorff, grown bitterly hostile both to Hitler and Hindenburg, wrote in an angry newspaper article that Germany 'had become a country occupied by the S.A.' To dissatisfied associates like Prussian State Secretary Abegg, Schleicher declared that it was utterly impossible to suppress the National Socialists or dissolve the S.A. The S.A., Abegg replied, was Hitler's private army, and where in the world was a private citizen allowed to maintain an army? Then Schleicher said: 'We simply cannot forbid the S.A., for we are no longer strong enough; if we attempt it, we shall be swept away!'

In November, 1931, a set of careful and bloodthirsty plans for an uprising were found in one of the South German National Socialist headquarters, on the Hessian estate of Boxheim. They had a suspiciously Communist air about them: the S.A. would assume state power, suspend all private enterprises, confiscate all revenues, take away the products of the peasants, feed the population in public kitchens; and anyone resisting, said nearly every paragraph, 'will be shot . . . will be punished by death . . . will be shot. . . .' Hitler, without whose knowledge presumably nothing could be done in the party, declared indignantly that he had known nothing of these plans, but he did not question their authenticity. Yet in private conversation he was able to convince Schleicher that he did not favor such radicalism and that his person constituted a sort of dam against the revolutionary flood that was rising in the National Socialist Movement.

These conversations, which took place in November and December, 1931, must have made a strong impression on Schleicher; also on Groener, to whom Schleicher passed them on; even on Brüning himself. Groener began to reproach high Prussian police officials for spying on the National Socialist Party, and secretly or even openly supporting Hitler's personal enemies; for example, the renegade Stennes, who marched around certain quarters of Berlin with a kind of S.A. of his own. 'I hear you give Stennes money,' said Groener to Abegg, the Prussian State Secretary. Abegg replied that unfortunately he could not do that, as he had no money; but he felt that Stennes should be supported. Groener: 'That is absolutely wrong. Stennes is working against Hitler!' Abegg was speechless, but Groener continued: Hitler was the man of legality, he had sworn to respect the constitution. 'He must be supported against the others, who are all wild men.' The 'others' were Hitler's lieutenants, concerning whom Groener was prepared to believe all evil; only Hitler, he thought, was trustworthy. In consternation Abegg asked if the minister believed a word of what Hitler said. Did he believe that Hitler would keep his oath? Groener repeated: 'He will definitely keep it. He is a man of legality. We must do nothing against him. We must support him!' Then he intimated that this was also Brüning's opinion.

These soldiers in government had an idea that only Hitler could realize: a democratic dictatorship. What he actually desired, said Brüning on October 13, 1931, in the Reichstag, was 'a government of those parties which are responsible and prepared for responsibility,' and to such an idea he himself would gladly cede his post; but an 'agreement between the parties which are necessary for such a government is unfortunately out of the question in Germany.' In other words, democracy has destroyed itself. In leading a powerful unpopular government, based solely on the authority of the Reichs President, Brüning thought perhaps that he was doing the will of Hindenburg and Schleicher; but he should have known what these two really wanted better than they knew it themselves: and that was a popular government. But Brüning believed that he was making himself more respected by making himself 'more independent' of the Reichstag parties, his own Catholic Center Party included. Now he felt in an even stronger position to carry on a sovereign foreign policy and to solve the problem of reparations, which had defied friendly negotiations, by a violent coup.

It was the right hour. The world — with the exception of France

— was sick of reparations; Hoover's moratorium had actually ended them. The structure of international political debts was tottering; the world economy was beginning to dissolve into great separate blocks; gold, the international standard of value, the universal medium of exchange, was losing its dominant position. The world of 1924 was really collapsing, and in 1931 this was again recognized by one of the great world powers: England.

In 1929, the Labour Party had returned to power. It was the second MacDonald government, socialist in name. In 1931, under the pressure of the crisis, which also in England took the form of a financial stringency, James Ramsay MacDonald and a few of his comrades split away from the majority of the Labour Party. Mac-Donald founded a group of his own which he called the National Labour Party, and formed a coalition with his opponents, the Conservative Party (the Liberals had lost their former importance with the fall of Lloyd George in 1922). This coalition took the decisive step that had been an object of impassioned controversy for years: it detached the English pound from the gold standard. With far greater caution and incomparably firmer control, this was basically the same thing that brought chaos and ruin to Germany in 1920-23; a thing which the German government frantically feared. A pound was now no longer a pound; its value fell from $4.89 to $3.49, thus giving a strong impetus to British exports. The stringent economy measures of the new government temporarily plunged the country into unrest; there were riots in London and other cities, in one place even a mutiny in the navy; but the government stood firm, dissolved Parliament, and in the elections of October 27, 1931, the country approved the new policy by giving a majority of almost five hundred seats to the government coalition, or, to all intents and purposes, the Conservative Party. Hitler, already dreaming of the day when, like Napoleon III, he would order elections and plebiscites in his country, said of MacDonald's electoral accomplishment: 'The MacDonald government clearly demonstrated to the whole world the national urge for self-preservation. This was not only fair, but also logical from the standpoint of democracy' — of the democracy which, as Hitler hoped, would destroy itself.

After these elections the MacDonald cabinet ruled for five years.

It was actually a Conservative government. The National Labour Party remained without importance, and Stanley Baldwin became once more the actual leader. From now on the English currency was a paper currency, the value of which did not depend on the free play of exchange, on the basis of gold, but on the will of the government. The currencies of the Scandinavian countries followed the drop in the pound. In February, 1932, the MacDonald government introduced a new tariff, which meant the end of British free trade; for a certain quantity of home-grown wheat the English farmer was guaranteed a price of one dollar a bushel. This new policy of the mother country, directed toward a closed economy, drew the whole empire after it; the Empire Conference of Ottawa led in July and August, 1932, to a series of agreements by which the various parts of the empire granted each other preferential tariffs.

The conference aimed at making the British world empire really British. Hitherto England had carried on more trade with other countries than with its dominions and colonies. Now this was to cease in the main; in the following years trade between mother country and colonies assumed first place; a great 'Buy British' campaign was launched throughout the empire. Thus a step had been taken toward British Empire autarchy; this autarchy was an answer to the new protective tariff policy of the United States, but it was also an answer to the commercial expansion of Japan, which, with the help of her wretched wages and the misery of her peasants and workers, flooded the world market with articles so cheap as to defy competition. The Ottawa decisions, which, in 1932, were ratified by the British Parliament, affected almost eight per cent of the United States export trade, about twenty per cent of the Argentine trade, and approximately sixty per cent of the Danish; they strongly affected Russia and Japan, and to a lesser degree Germany.

In the British developments Hitler and Rosenberg believed they detected the beginning of that spirit 'which is everywhere creating the same forms, though under different banners.' Hitler could not regard Ramsay MacDonald and Stanley Baldwin as the Aryans and anti-Semites with whom he wanted to ally himself; but in December, 1931, when Alfred Rosenberg went to London and became celebrated as 'one of the best dressed Germans,' he spoke to English questioners almost as to friends. 'I admire the calm and assurance with which the English nation is combating its difficulties,' he said. 'This nation has no nerves and in this it is setting the world an example.' Germany, he said, expected the support of England in her demands both for the cancellation of reparations and an international adjustment of armaments. England, he declared, has a strong sense of justice. Besides, he had distinctly perceived 'that England herself is beginning to feel the pressure of the present situation. . . . The economic and political pressure from Paris is becoming intolerable.' Unfortunately, Rosenberg went on, there were people in England who advised Germany to reach an understanding with France under any circumstances; but there was also another British opinion, 'which says that it is now time for England as well as the rest of us, to offer resistance.'

It was on this section of British public opinion that Germany must rely, said Hitler in his speeches and in open letters to Brüning; she must direct her policies toward this England; and Italy, even America, would stand by Germany's side. In December, 1931, he received the visit of supporters from the Sudetenland, members of a minority grouplet of that German minority of which Hitler had said that Germany must constantly incite them to rebellion against the Czechoslovak state, not because they had a right to independence as Germans, but because Czechoslovakia was allied with France. He made them a speech telling them to be of good cheer: National Socialism would soon come to power in Germany and then it would take them under its powerful wing. The world situation, he said, already looked promising enough: 'In England at present a significant shift in public opinion is taking place. France with her military and financial policy is making herself responsible for all the world's wrongs' — he meant, because she would not cut her armaments or cancel German reparations. 'In America and Italy, as well,' Hitler continued, 'the anti-French tendency is growing from day to day, yes, we might even say from hour to hour. The untenable position of the world market literally forces the other states into a defensive front against the former beneficiary of the present state of affairs, and that is France.' But by this, he hastily added, he did not mean war. For, he declared, 'a war of European states among themselves would be as good as opening the door to Bolshevism.'

By October, 1931, a German observer, who, in his official capacity, saw much of foreign countries, felt justified in saying that 'Germany has become the great fashion; everywhere in the world everything German is the last word in *chic*.' But while Germany saw her territories freed from foreign troops, while reparations vanished and further diplomatic progress was in the offing, internal conditions deteriorated more and more, economic life destroyed itself, parliament fell a prey to its own disunity, and the misery of the people increased. At the end of 1930, while Germany still bore the burden of reparations, while there were three million unemployed and the German miner earned 562 marks in a quarter, Hitler sent a New Year's message to his followers, full of rather questionable encouragement: 'After twelve months more, the road to German freedom will be open!' Toward the close of 1931, reparations had been lifted from Germany's shoulders, but the number of unemployed had risen to almost eight million, the miner earned only 473 marks a quarter, and Hitler promised his followers that this would be the year of final decision: 'Let us march into this new year as fighters, in order that we may leave it as victors!'

It is profoundly characteristic of this segment of European history that it contained too many victories, too many concessions, and no real peace. As before 1914, they were wrested by one nation from another, or dearly sold by one nation to another. The fetters of Versailles binding Germany rotted and fell one by one; the German people correctly sensed that this did not mean more peace but more power; concessions are not made to us because we have become more trustworthy, but because the world's ability to cling to Versailles is dwindling.

On September 18, 1931, a mysterious explosion occurred on the Manchurian railway near Mukden, which legally was still Chinese territory. The Kwantung Army advanced and 'avenged Japan's honor,' occupied the Manchurian cities, and the Chinese central government in Nanking, weakened by Communist disorders at home, could offer no military resistance, but had to content itself with a boycott which reduced Japanese imports to China to one sixth. Thereupon the Japanese landed in Shanghai at the end of January, 1932, drove out the Chinese army and destroyed the Chapei Quarter. On February 18, 1932, an 'independent' empire of Manchukuo, consisting of three raped Chinese provinces, was proclaimed in Manchuria. China protested to the League of Nations, of which Japan was still a member; the League sent a commission to Asia, led by an English statesman, the Earl of Lytton.

Was it for this that 'the war to end wars' had been fought? The Japanese assault on China profoundly stirred everyone who had previously believed in the peace of Geneva. At such a time, it attracted little attention when Brüning declared in an interview (January 9, 1932) that 'Germany's position makes the continuation of political payments impossible'; and that these payments would inevitably lead the rest of the world 'to catastrophe.' In Asia, a great nation had been cut to pieces because it was unarmed and torn by internal conflicts. This was exactly the situation in Germany, said Hitler, and he was not the only one to say so.

And let nobody believe, he went on, that this German weakness would be turned into strength by the Disarmament Conference, which, after endless preparations, finally was going to meet at Geneva, Switzerland, in February, 1932. No conference would make Germany strong again, but only the nation's own firm will. The official German line was that the aim of the Disarmament Conference must be to bring about the disarmament of the great nations, as it was promised in the Versailles Treaty, which explicitly had stated that Germany's disarmament should only be a first step toward general disarmament. Hitler asked mockingly if anybody was so naïve as to hope that this promise would be kept; the answer was that to insist on her right was Germany's biggest asset in international politics.

Groener handed the cabinet a memorandum stating that now, after thirteen years of unilateral disarmament, Germany must finally insist on equality of armaments. The world was spending seventy per cent more on armaments than in 1914; this at least was the estimate of President Hoover in a speech to the International Chamber of Commerce (May 4, 1931). Three days after Brüning had declared that he would pay no more reparations, Soviet Russia issued a public statement, placing herself on the side of Germany in the disarmament question: peace, she declared, depended on general disarmament, and disarmament 'requires the unqualified admission of the principle of complete equality of states to each participator in the conference [of disarmament], whether a great or a small power.'

In all this clamoring for equality by disarmament a silent threat was hidden. If Germany could not reach equality by general disarmament, then there was only one way left: equality by German rearmament.

Amid the blackest domestic misery, Germany was struggling to become a respected power in the crumbling council of nations. Brüning accepted Hitler's line, that foreign success must be based on unity and strength at home, and invited Hitler to reach an understanding with the government. Groener wrote his memorandum on Germany's equality of armaments in the first days of January, shortly before Brüning announced the definite end of reparations. Germany took a deep breath, and tried to gather strength. Hitler paced the floor of the editorial offices of the *Völkischer Beobachter* in Munich; with him were Hess, Rosenberg, and Wilhelm Weiss, one of the editors. A telegram was brought to Hitler. It was signed Groener and requested his presence at a conference in Berlin. Hitler hastily read the wire, thrust the paper under the nose of all those present, and uttered a purr of triumph like a contented beast of prey. By turns, he brought his face close to Hess's, Rosenberg's, and Weiss's, stared in their eyes, with little cries of, 'Hey . . . hey . . . hey . . .' — as if he wanted to say: 'You see? You see? . . . Here we are, at last.' Then he brought down his fist on the telegram and cried: 'Now I have them in my pocket! They have recognized me as a partner in their negotiations.'

Chapter XVIII

DEFEAT

ON JANUARY 6, HITLER CONFERRED WITH GROENER, the following day with Brüning. Two years ago he had been an almost unknown figure. Now the future of the Reich was to be shaped by these conferences. The outward pretext for the meetings was that President von Hindenburg's seven-year term was due to elapse in May, 1932. A new president had to be elected. The most powerful political figure next to Hindenburg was already Hitler, but an electoral battle around the person of Hitler was bound to release violent inner conflicts, and inner conflicts could be fatal for Germany at the moment when she was fighting for recognition as a great power. Groener and Brüning had not been mistaken in thinking that Hitler would understand the situation. As always in such conferences, he was not quite sure of his own position. Both men hinted that he would doubtless come to power in the not too distant future; they hoped he would realize that until then Brüning could obtain more easily than he himself those foreign concessions without which Hitler could not hope to govern. What Brüning wanted of Hitler was his support in a kind of peaceful *coup d'état*. The presidential elections would simply be suppressed. The Reichstag could theoretically prolong the present President's term as long as it liked without elections; it could suspend the entire constitution, provided that two thirds of its members were present, and that two thirds of those present decided for the suspension. Hitler could give Brüning this majority, for the Chancellor thought he could count on most of the other parties. Hitler made counter-proposals: first elect a new Reichstag — for he calculated correctly that in the meantime the number of his followers had considerably increased; but then, why not simply re-elect Hindenburg by virtually unanimous popular vote, without an opponent except the inevitable Communist? 'Democracy,' as he later put it in an open letter to Brüning, 'espouses the view that all state power issues from the people and hence all the representatives of the state power are only mandatories of the popular will. No domestic and foreign arguments against new elections can ever be a license to infringe upon the constitution. . . .' Incited by Goebbels and Röhm he wrote, over Brüning's head, a letter to Hindenburg, telling him that Brüning was planning to make the President infringe on the constitution; against this Hitler felt obliged to warn him; but he was willing to work with Hindenburg in the coming elections if Hindenburg previously stated that he disapproved Brüning's unconstitutional proposal. 'Then Brüning is done for,' said Hitler to Goebbels; and to Hindenburg's secretary of state, Doctor Otto Meissner, he said: yes, he, Hitler, would agree to nothing, unless Brüning were dismissed first.

From this moment on, Hindenburg entered Hitler's life, and Hitler entered the life of the old man. It was an encounter between two men made great by history and created for one another, and the encounter was not only political but personal as well. When the two were face to face, the corners of their mouths seemed to show something like the grin of Titans who see through one another and contemptuously conceal the fact. Up to his last breath, Hindenburg treated the Bohemian corporal, the former Reichswehr spy, with ungrateful contempt; he gave him no credit for his really great achievements and regarded him neither as a personal nor political equal, but brushed him off like dust from his fingers. Hitler in turn saw through the foxlike, self-seeking old man behind the colossal legend, and in his intimate circle complained bitterly that Fate should have given him no more worthy adversary. The square head, the bushy mustache, the close-cropped hair, the lurking eyes — Hitler must have been terrified at the close resemblance between the old marshal and Alois Hitler, the customs official. From some of the Bohemian corporal's words and gestures, we almost sense that in Hindenburg he hated, and at the same time feared, something like a father. His struggle against his own father ended almost murderously by death; a struggle at the same time against the state, tradition, law, and common sense seemed to revive in his relation to Hindenburg. And ultimately it had a similar end.

Now he informed this menacing, fatherly figure that he, Hitler, was ready to honor him as his marshal, his president (read: his father); but that Hindenburg must make him chancellor. For that is what he meant by the dismissal of Brüning. We seem to hear old Alois Hitler: painter? — no, never as long as I live! Several times Hindenburg said almost the same words: Hitler — chancellor? Never, as long as I live; and certainly not by these indelicate, blackmailing methods. Moreover, in a talk with Hugenberg, the questionable ally, who made up for his dwindling political importance by a provocative, overbearing attitude, Hitler in rage had claimed the Reichswehr Ministry for himself — they were already dividing the future power over Brüning's political corpse. Hugenberg had seen to it that this should come to Hindenburg's ears. The Reichswehr spy wanted to become Reichswehr Minister! Almost any concession might have been wrung from Hindenburg — but the Reichswehr never; to prevent that was almost a religious duty. Immediately (January 12) he sent word to Hitler that the dismissal of Brüning was out of the question.

For Hitler there followed nights more sleepless than usual, a time of covert watching and waiting. He listened to a thousand counsels and could not make up his mind to follow any of them. Goebbels reckoned that if Hitler should declare that he himself were running for president, Hindenburg might retreat to avoid the clash. On January 19, Goebbels wrote in his diary: 'Discussed the question of the presidency with Der Führer. No decision has yet been reached. I am pleading strongly for his own candidacy. By now nothing else is seriously possible.' But two weeks later he was no further advanced. 'Der Führer's decision,' Goebbels noted on January 31, 'will be made on Wednesday. It can no longer remain in doubt.' On February 2, Goebbels wrote: 'Der Führer is deciding to run himself,' but a week later, on February 9, he is obliged to admit: 'Der Führer is back in Berlin. New debate on the presidential elections. Everything is still in the air.' That was Hitler's force of decision, and in order to dispel unpleasant thoughts, he engaged in his favorite sport, pistol practice; Der Führer was 'an absolutely dead shot,' wrote Goebbels admiringly in his diary.

Then again Hitler spent long hours in Munich at the house of Architect Troost, who had to draw plans 'for a grandiose alteration of the national capital.' 'Der Führer has his plans all finished,' Goebbels reports; 'he speaks, acts and feels as if we already had power. This gives a magnificent self-assurance to everyone about him.' Only in the most immediate problem, the question of the presidential elections, none of his self-assurance was discernible. To be sure, on February 12, after 'computing all the figures again with Der Führer,' Goebbels felt justified in saying: 'At last the decision has been made!' But he was very much mistaken; only on February 15 was any decision reached, and it was Hindenburg who reached it; although it was probably Groener who put this decision through. Hindenburg publicly announced his candidacy, remarking that no one should accuse him of leaving his post in critical times. Could Hitler dare to announce his candidacy in opposition to the old man? He did not dare. Again Goebbels found his Führer undecided. On February 18, after a conversation with him, he wrote half in despair and half in contempt: 'We must have the courage to live dangerously!' On the following day — for the how-manyeth time? — he was able to declare: 'The decision has been made,' but two days later, on February 21, he was sitting with Hitler and some Italian Fascists in the Hotel Kaiserhof, discussing 'questions of plutocracy and anti-Semitism,' and on the question which ostensibly had already been decided, Goebbels could only sigh despairingly: 'The eternal waiting is almost demoralizing.' Three weeks after the decision had been 'made' for the first time!

On the next day it really was made. At a meeting in the Berlin Sportpalast, Goebbels declared: 'Our Führer is going to be Reichs President!' — a propaganda confident of victory could not consider the possibility that he might not be elected. The audience cheered as a matter of course, and when Goebbels came home, Hitler called on the phone and asked if they had cheered. Goebbels was able to reassure him, and suddenly Hitler was in a good mood; he wanted to spend a merry evening and drove to Goebbels's house.

Goebbels, then newly married, lived in one of the outlying sections in the west of Berlin. His wife, née Magda Ritschel, was born in the city of Duisburg, not far from Goebbels's own birthplace in Rheydt. Her mother's husband had been a Herr Friedländer, so that the future Frau Goebbels had a Jewish foster-father. Magda Goebbels's first husband had been the industrialist, Günther Quandt, by whom she had a son; Goebbels, then an unknown young man, had been engaged by the family as a tutor, a divorce had followed, and Magda Quandt for some time had lived with Goebbels as his secretary. In 1931 they married, without the blessing of the Catholic Church to which they both belonged.

In this household Hitler had established a third family; beside his own Munich family, half destroyed by Geli's death; and that of the late Siegfried Wagner in Bayreuth. On his visits to Berlin, he often appeared at the Goebbels', almost always accompanied by Wilhelm Brückner, that tall, broad-shouldered silent ruffian, who had led his storm troops in 1923, had left the S.A. with Röhm, and in 1930 had returned with Röhm. Often Hitler also brought Otto Dietrich, his 'press chief'; another often present was Ernst Hanfstaengl, the Harvard student, who had likewise reappeared in 1930, and, with his excellent English and effervescent manner, was used by Hitler as spokesman for the foreign press. When Hanfstaengl wanted to cheer his leader, he sat down at the piano and played his so-called 'musical portraits,' and Hitler nearly laughed himself to death when Hanfstaengl hammered out a portrait of the pompous and corpulent Göring, or played soft runs to portray Himmler moving noiselessly across the carpet.

And so Hitler appeared in his third family after Goebbels had sworn to him on the telephone that the masses had cheered. After four weeks of anxious hesitation, his own decision had finally carried him away like a gust of wind, and in this moment he probably believed again in his superhuman force of decision. 'He is happy that the proclamation of his candidacy made such a good impression,' wrote Goebbels in his diary. '. . . Der Führer told us long stories of his war days. Then he is very great and moving. When he left, there was an almost solemn mood among the few of us.'

They had a right to be solemn. Since the Feldherrn Halle in 1923, they had not gambled for such high stakes, and Hitler knew perfectly well why he had hesitated. Against his better judgment he suddenly found himself engaged in a bitter struggle with that Herr President, without whose permission the revolution could not take place; or rather against the three or four officers in the Reichswehr Ministry who guided Hindenburg's will. But Schleicher could not so easily be diverted from his aim — as his friend Franz von Papen had formulated it — : to 'forge these glowing masses,' to 'put each man in his proper place and educate the valuable material'; at least not by the irritating accident of a passing election campaign. In tones overflowing with righteousness, Groener, at Schleicher's behest, declared to the surprised Reichstag: 'The repeated declarations of the National Socialist leader and his profession of legality show that he is endeavoring to exclude illegal elements from his party. And the Reich Court has expressly established this fact. These facts have decided me no longer to deny the honorable right of national defense to the members of the N.S.D.A.P. . . .' (February 24, 1932). A magnanimous gesture! In spite of the bitter struggle, Schleicher, believing himself to be immensely shrewd, took all pretext for complaint away from Hitler. If anyone had made a mistake, it was, in his opinion, Brüning, who had dragged Hindenburg into this fight.

It was a three-cornered battle; not only a struggle between Hindenburg and Hitler. Both had to fight against a third party — the party which for decades had wielded the strongest political influence in Germany, especially in Prussia.

Hindenburg had fought heroically to make his own life as comfortable as possible; even before the World War, he had demanded a higher pension on the ground that a head injury limited his ability to work. He had never striven for the unusual; but when at an advanced age it fell in his lap, he installed himself comfortably in his undeserved greatness. He enjoyed the advantages of a lofty position, and basked, none too appreciatively, in the blind love of an unsuspecting people. In 1925, when he was elected President for the first time, he haggled over his salary like a good business man, and secured almost double what the Social Democrat Friedrich

Ebert had dared to accept. Thus a professional officer without personal means concluded his career most successfully. While he was serving as President in Berlin, Herr Elard von Oldenburg-Januschau, a junker in the province of East Prussia, discovered that an estate which had once belonged to the Beneckendorff and Hindenburg family was for sale. He made it clear to various other junkers what it would mean if the Chief of State were to become one of them. They collected money among themselves and a few industrialists, and for Hindenburg's eightieth birthday, on October 2, 1927, the Stahlhelm presented its honorary president with the estate and castle of Neudeck. As a precaution, Hindenburg's son Oskar was entered in the property register as owner; thus, if Hindenburg died in the near future, the state would receive no inheritance tax.

And so Hindenburg was a junker again, after a lifetime as a salaried professional soldier. He became a member of the class which was literally the most unproductive in Germany. For most of these Prussian junkers lived in a barren region, extending from the banks of the Elbe in Central Germany to the eastern borders of the Reich. The soil is full of gravel and clay, its chief products rye and potatoes. The land cannot support a population of small farmers; only large-scale farming, with large unpopulated areas planted to rye, potatoes, and beets, can hope to maintain itself. The farms are agricultural factories with poorly housed and poorly fed personnel; at harvest time, itinerant workers are brought in, either unemployed from the cities or impoverished country proletarians from near-by Poland. The holdings of the junkers are in the main no giant estates, but farms of seven to twelve hundred acres. Within his own petty realm such a landowner is really a lord. Down to the twentieth century he enjoyed a kind of jurisdiction over his 'subjects.' He decided who should marry whom, and when universal suffrage was introduced, he told his subjects whom to vote for. By 1930, to be sure, the power of the junkers was much weakened by the political progress of Germany; but the memory of it was not yet dead, the big estates were still there, and when the lord drove across the fields in his carriage, the workers still doffed their caps and cried: 'Good day, Herr Oberleutnant!' — for the junkers liked to be addressed by their former military titles.

When these landowners maintained that agriculture could thrive on their poor soil only in the form of large estates, the truth was that even in this form it could not thrive. The rye of eastern Germany could not compete on the world market with that of Canada or the Argentine; spirits, the most important product of their potatoes, was produced in such great quantity that it could not be sold. 'It's not a nice thing to say,' one of them declared, 'but if the German people would only drink more!' And things grew worse than ever when the landlords tried to improve their estates. Let your estates run down, Oldenburg-Januschau had been advising them since 1924 when Germany's period of post-war prosperity began. Instead of that, many borrowed large sums of money from the banks and burdened their poor holdings with costly farm buildings and stills. With a great expenditure, usually not of their own money, they tried to squeeze from the poor soil yields that it simply could not give. From the purely business point of view, it would have been sensible to turn large parts of the East German soil into pasture, or even better, forest, as was done in the Scotch Highlands at the end of the eighteenth century. The large Prussian landholdings were saved by the Prussian army, and not only because many officers came of junker families. The army was interested in maintaining the large East German estates, because it regarded them as necessary for war. Even if the rye and potatoes cost too much to produce, even if people did not like the taste of the black bread — these coarse and expensive foodstuffs were nevertheless a great food reserve in the event of a war in which Germany would be a besieged fortress. 'That nation is doomed to decay whose agriculture decays,' said Field Marshal Helmut von Moltke, the founder of the Prussian General Staff. The rye production of the East German junkers was protected and artificially kept alive by means of high tariffs on foreign grain. The junkers themselves thought the state was only doing its duty, and that inadequately. They threatened the German Kaiser that they would obstruct the building of the German fleet in parliament if their tariffs were not approved. Few classes have been so adept at manipulating the state for their personal interests. Otto von Bismarck, who was one of them, frankly admitted: 'A state that takes my property is no longer my fatherland.' And half a century later, Alfred Rosenberg said with admiration: 'Those are the words of a *Herr*.'

How many of them were there actually? German statistics, usually so thorough, and well able to compute the amount of potatoes, beets, and needles produced in a year, never counted the German junkers; that is, the number of East German landowners and the extent of their property was never officially revealed. But in private researches Johannes Conrad, an economist writing in the eighteen-eighties, counted 11,015 large landowners; together they owned 16,433 estates; 113 of them owned from 12,000 to 25,000 acres; 46 over 25,000 acres; the largest landowner was doubtless the Hohenzollern family, with 415,000 acres.

Now this class entered Hitler's life, and his struggle for power in Germany was in no small measure a struggle with them and a victory over them. At first the junkers were full of distrust. National Socialist masses in the eastern plains often struggled bitterly with the landowning aristocracy; for it was the Uprooted and Disinherited, the day laborers and hired hands, who began to fill the ranks of the S.A. in the country. The National Socialists inspired them with a self-confidence they had never before known. Hitler solemnly promised the large landowners to protect property; but when R. W. Darré or Gregor Strasser spoke to the masses, they said pretty much the opposite. Gottfried Feder, the breaker of interest slavery, who still regarded himself as the spiritual founder of National Socialism, proclaimed that after its victory his party would create a belt of small peasants in the East, 'with farm beside farm'; in other words, that he would smash many of the large, heavily indebted and unprofitable estates.

Since 1929, the Reich had thrown large sums of money into the distressed agriculture of East Germany. Taxes had been remitted, there had been cash gifts; but above all, the state intervened when a landowner had overburdened his property with debt and could no longer pay the interest — in other words, when he went bankrupt. Then a financing establishment set up by the state assumed the debt, paid the creditors, and frequently became the creditor — which in practice often meant that the money was lost for good. In 1930-31, over two hundred and eighty million marks were given to Eastern agriculture and vanished like a drop of water in a giant sponge; in March, 1931, it was decided to pour in another nine hundred million marks in the course of the following years. And that was not all, for in the warehouses of the Reich there lay about a billion marks' worth of unsalable potato spirits, which the state had purchased from the big potato producers with the taxpayers' money.

This was the *Osthilfe* (Eastern aid). It cannot be said that the small group of junkers received most of this money; it is even true that per acre the small owners received higher sums than the big ones. It was the single cases of feudal favoritism that stirred up public opinion. Cases came to light such as that of Herr von Q., who had squandered his whole fortune in light company and then applied for *Osthilfe;* the official to whom he applied turned down his request, but his superior, himself a baron, decided that the debts which von Q. had incurred on gambling and women must be paid from the taxpayers' money in order to preserve his estate, 'since it has belonged to the family for several hundred years.' The family of the former Kaiser, one of the wealthiest men of Germany, took their share; old Oldenburg-Januschau used the sum, with which he was supposed to bolster up his three insolvent estates, in order to buy a fourth; when the scandal came to light, he wrote indignantly in the German press that everyone else had done the same, and his article began with the words:

> 'The aged pelican said: "Be fair,
> You folks, now let me have my share." '

But the problem of the German East and its junkers was something bigger and more serious than this scandal. That such a group with its petrified class consciousness should still exist, tearing and tugging at the political body: this was the real problem. For it was actually the last remaining group in Germany with an exclusive class consciousness. For years it had been steadily losing political power; its economic straits were growing worse and worse, and now it was struggling desperately against extinction. At first Brüning had believed it unjust to let the big Eastern landowners suffer more than their share from the world crisis; for that reason

he had let them have the *Osthilfe*. Gradually he became convinced
that there was something fundamentally rotten. He and his cabinet
developed plans for a solution: those large estates which were overwhelmed with debt and economically untenable should be fore-
closed by the state, divided and settled with peasants; it was hoped
that the peasant with his tenacity and frugality would be able to
maintain himself where the large landholder had failed. The big
landowners spoke of 'agrarian Bolshevism' or 'Bolshevism' pure and
simple, and began to put pressure on Hindenburg, the highest landowner of the Reich, to remove Brüning.

But in the presidential election Brüning and Hindenburg seemed
inseparable. And so the junker class could not vote for the first
junker of the Reich, in spite of Oldenburg-Januschau, in spite of
the estate of Neudeck. The great virtue of loyalty turned strange
somersaults in this election. The junkers left the field marshal in
the lurch, but did not go over to Hitler. Hitler's comrade of many
pacts, Hugenberg, worried that his comrade might win, knifed him
by setting up a candidate of his own. This was the former Lieutenant-Colonel Theodor Duesterberg, the second president of the
Stahlhelm of which Hindenburg was honorary president — comrade against comrade, president against honorary president! Enraged, the National Socialists struck back at Duesterberg with a
deadly weapon: they discovered that the unfortunate candidate's
great-grandfather had been Abraham Selig Duesterberg, a Jew.
Duesterberg answered that he was deeply shaken by this revelation.
He swore on his honor that he had known nothing of his Jewish
origin, but that he would let no revelations drive him out of the
political struggle. The junkers also refused to be frightened by
revelations. Incensed against Brüning, doubting Hindenburg, and
thoroughly opposed to Hitler, they voted for Duesterberg; most of
the princes of the House of Hohenzollern, for instance, were among
his supporters.

Hitler's adversaries might well have fought back with the reply
that only yesterday he himself had not been a German. To make
his candidacy possible at all, National Socialist-controlled government of the little 'country' of Braunschweig, in all haste, had made
him an attaché at the legation which the country, in accordance

with antediluvian custom, maintained in Berlin. By becoming an official, Hitler automatically became a subject of Braunschweig, hence a citizen of the German Reich; a living symbol of Austria's 'Home to the Reich' sentiments; a foreign-born German fighting to become President. The new citizen traveled day and night and spoke to crowds of sometimes a hundred thousand. Many people were puzzled by the fact that millions followed him, although almost the whole big press was grimly against him. Brüning carried on a similar campaign for Hindenburg; the old man himself spoke only a few sentences of which a recording was made to be played over the radio. The record made a robust impression with its gruff words: 'Anyone who doesn't want to vote for me doesn't have to.'

A large part of German capital financed Hindenburg's election campaign and thus refuted the legend that German capital, acting as a body, has brought Hitler to power. The three most important German industrialists — Carl Friedrich von Siemens, who controlled the electric power industry; Carl Duisberg and Carl Bosch, leaders of the chemical industry — belonged to the Hindenburg Committee, not to mention the bankers who came out almost unanimously for the Marshal-President.

The organizer of the Hindenburg Committee was a young politician, extremely talented and ambitious, but up to that time relatively unknown: this was Günther Gereke, Reichstag deputy, officer, jurist, and landowner. Gereke put aside a part of the money collected by the Committee, and later, when summoned into court, refused to say what had become of it. It is improbable that he used it for private purposes, but there is reason to believe that Oskar von Hindenburg used the money for purposes which, to put it mildly, had little to do with the political functions of the Hindenburg Committee.

Yet Hindenburg was not *the* candidate of German capital; a considerable part of Germany's political funds were at the disposal of Hugenberg and Duesterberg, and Hitler had his Kirdorfs and Thyssens, who had not abandoned him. The powers of German finance created no united front in this campaign. But one group of citizens was solidly behind Hindenburg, and these were the partisans of democracy. Since the beginning of the year, these elements had formed a new organization with an unprecedented propagandist appeal. The old 'Black, Red, and Gold Reichsbanner,' the fighting organization of the Social Democrats and the trade unions, had been reorganized under a new leadership. The new organization was called the 'Iron Front'; it tried to emulate the Communist principle of organizing the workers in the larger factories into self-contained combat groups; and it began to make preparations for a serious civil war. The idea was to win a firm grip on some of the big, strategically important factories, and by threatening nationwide sabotage to cut the nerves and sinews of any political *coup* before it started.

This front bore the actual burden of Hindenburg's election campaign. But even if the democratic masses rallied to Hindenburg, the candidate himself was no democrat — as has often been the case with the leading figures of democracy, and not only in Germany. Since labor leaders and capitalists were both for Hindenburg, Hitler might well have cried out: There you have it, Isaac and Moses Cohn, the capitalist and the labor leader arm in arm, a pair of brothers wanting the same thing. True, for some time he had been moderating this tone — association with big industrialists and bankers had doubtless taught him caution. But in the provinces his speakers made no bones about calling Hindenburg the candidate of the Jews. The Communists, in turn, required no great flight of the imagination to represent Social Democratic support of the Kaiser's field marshal as a 'betrayal of the workers.' As seven years before, they chose Ernst Thaelmann, their party chairman, as their candidate.

Hitler set himself up as the candidate of the workers and the masses in opposition to Hindenburg. He described conditions in a sentence that was effective and not untrue: 'Things have come to such a pass that two workingmen must feed one unemployed.' When asked by what right he set himself above all the authorities, specialists, ministers, and excellencies, Hitler declared: 'With the right of a man who comes of the nameless mass that is the people,' and Groener may again have scented Bolshevism. In an open letter to Hindenburg, Hitler complained about persecution by the police: 'Even you, Herr Reichs President, cannot set aside the article of the constitution which provides for free elections.' It was hard to uphold the strategic line that this was no fight against the venerable field marshal, but against Brüning and his group. 'Old man,' said Hitler, embarrassed and not quite tactfully, 'we honor you too much to suffer that those whom we want to destroy should use you as a front. We are sorry, but you must step aside, for they want to fight, and so do we. . . .' Most of the upper class were at a loss in this election fight, and many decided for Duesterberg; but Fritz Thyssen, the heavy industrialist, declared: 'I am voting for Adolf Hitler, because I know him well and am firmly convinced that he is the only man who can and will rescue Germany from ruin and disintegration.'

And all blows were permitted! Röhm put his S.A. and S.S. in readiness; he ordered them to gather in their private barracks; flying commandoes stood ready to seize the arsenals of the Reichswehr. A ring of National Socialist troops was thrown around Berlin; the families of the leading National Socialists left the capital. Then Röhm called on Schleicher like a good boy and informed him that he had taken a few precautionary measures; nothing of importance. But Reichswehr agents brought in different reports, and Groener began to quarrel with Schleicher, saying that this was beginning to look dangerous. The minister no longer followed his adviser without question as before. When Schleicher refused to recognize the danger of an insurrection of the S.A., Groener wrote a letter to Carl Severing, Prussia's Social Democratic Minister of the Interior, calling on him to act; he wrote another open letter to Hitler, demanding that he publish his 'positive aims,' and 'thus destroy the grave anxiety of millions of Germans . . . over the dangers of a Bolshevist development.' Severing's police raided National Socialist headquarters, and obtained a copy of Röhm's order. Severing also found strategic maps and complete revolutionary battle plans. And near the Polish border a very strange thing was found: orders of local S.A. leaders, stating that in case of a sudden Polish attack on Germany the S.A. should not take part in the defense. This was what Hitler had several times threatened in his speeches and afterward represented as harmless. It was high treason.

But the German voters showed with determination that they would not tolerate Hitler's *coup*. Hindenburg's campaign office had announced that he would receive 18,000,000 votes. Goebbels had retorted that on the day after elections the '1' would have to be crossed off this figure. Hitler, more cautious and worried, admitted in a speech that regardless how the elections turned out, the fight would go on. As it happened, Hindenburg obtained 18,600,000 votes, Hitler only 11,300,000; the 2,500,000 of the upper class who supported the great-grandson of Abraham Selig Duesterberg found themselves hopelessly lost on the battlefield of democracy. The Communists garnered nearly five million votes for Thaelmann, two and a half times as many as seven years before.

The victor's name was Hindenburg, but it was democracy that had really been victorious. Hindenburg's support consisted of the solid Social Democratic block of eight to nine million voters; some six million Catholic voters, who followed Brüning; and the greater part of the moderate liberal bourgeoisie. The figures clearly showed that only a small fraction of the conservative, reactionary, military-minded population had followed the old magnetism of Hindenburg's name. Goebbels was beside himself; he dashed to the telephone and asked Hitler in Munich whether the useless election battle should not be abandoned. It is possible, though not certain, that he asked whether the S.A. should not march and correct the election results by a *coup d'état*. Hitler rapidly countered the danger of unauthorized eruptions by the desperate announcement that he would continue the electoral struggle. This meant: I forbid violence; we remain legal.

For when all the figures were computed, it turned out that Hindenburg had not achieved an absolute majority. A second election was required by law, and in the very night of his defeat, Hitler dictated to Otto Dietrich, his press agent, a proclamation to show his disappointed and frightened followers that they had really won a great victory. 'From seven men we have grown to almost eleven and a half million,' he said. In difficult circumstances he always found consolation in recollecting the party's meager beginnings. Since 1930, he went on, they had gained five million votes. As Duesterberg's votes 'rightly' belonged to them, they really had

13,800,000, and needed only 'to snatch two and a half millions from the enemy's front' — with such juggling he tried to persuade his followers that a hard task was really easy.

He changed his methods fundamentally. In the first campaign he had attacked his enemies; in the second he spoke of himself. In the first he had painted the misery of Germany — 'the whole people up to the ears in debt, trembling from month to month that their checks will be protested, the municipalities ruined, whole cities facing collapse, the nation and the states without money. Small countries scoff at Germany and large ones despise us. Since the destruction of Carthage no important people has been treated like the German people' — now he described the brilliant, miraculous future that would be embodied in himself. He became the great apparition descending on Germany from Heaven — and that literally. He hired a large Junkers plane and flew from city to city. Three, four, sometimes five times a day Hitler spoke to crowds of ten thousand and over; millions saw him, and while sometimes he was so hoarse that he could scarcely emit a croak, he continued to depict a picture of boundless future happiness: 'In the Third Reich, every German girl will find a husband!'

In this second campaign, Hitler was able to win over the class that really belonged to Hindenburg. The Kaiser's eldest son, former Crown Prince Friedrich Wilhelm, who led a merry life on his estates in Silesia, in the theaters, bars and sport stadiums of the capital, had quietly voted for Duesterberg in the first election. In the second, in order to break publicly with Hindenburg, he said: 'Since I regard it as absolutely necessary for the national front to close its ranks, I shall vote for Adolf Hitler.'

One representative of this class, Hans Grimm, author of a widely read novel about Germany's 'Lebensraum,' declared that he would vote rather for Hitler's cause than for the 'coarse and demagogic' Hitler himself, because Hitler's 'new national movement has become — and this is the greatest thing that can happen to a man — more than he is'; therefore, and because there was no other choice, his, Grimm's, vote for Hitler was meant, 'not for the National Socialist Movement, not even for Hitler's person, but for a new Germany.'

Poor fatherland. You must entrust yourself to the wolves unless you want to go to the dogs. And it did not even help. At the second election, Hitler, though increasing his vote to 13,400,000, was again defeated by Hindenburg with 19,300,000. In the decisive hour Thaelmann was abandoned by many; his vote fell to approximately 3,500,000.

One thing was clear after these elections: the large majority of Germans were opposed to National Socialism. But nothing else was clear. It was plain what the country was against, but not what it was for. Nevertheless, the elections surely gave the government a moral sanction to stamp out the smouldering flame of National Socialist civil war after so much hesitation. Groener was embittered; for many months he had believed firmly in Hitler's legality, he had even told him so publicly — and then suddenly the S.A. had drawn its ring around Berlin and armed for an attack on the arsenals of the Reichswehr.

But Schleicher had entirely different plans for the S.A. and not only for the S.A. In his conversations with Röhm a plan had matured by which both men had involved themselves in a treasonable plot, one against the state, the other against his party. The plan was to separate not only the S.A. but the other combat leagues from their parties by a sudden blow and put them under the jurisdiction of the state. At once Germany would have a 'militia' numbering millions, with Schleicher as their general. If the general suddenly felt that his chief, Groener, was in his way, Röhm had almost the same feeling toward Adolf Hitler. Röhm had become more and more open and confiding toward Schleicher; he had played Hitler into Schleicher's hands by telling him a number of unrepeatable stories about his Führer; in conversation with third parties, Schleicher boasted of knowing the most gruesome details.

Röhm was convinced that Germany was approaching a period of pure military rule; and not only Germany. In every country, he thought, there was a nucleus of soldierly men with an inner bond between them. It was immaterial under what party banners they had previously marched. For the parties were associations of shopkeepers; they had grown out of bourgeois interests and bourgeois experience; they pursued the aims of a peaceful world that seemed to be doomed, and consequently they were obsolete. This might be equally true of the National Socialist Party organization, to which Hitler had firmly welded the S.A. Now the party had again been defeated in an election, and perhaps Hitler's course would turn out to be wrong. Then it would be the hour of the S.A. Civil war was hanging over the country. If Röhm had known Nietzsche better, he might have recognized his own dreams in the philosopher's prophecy of rising European nihilism.

The unusual step which Röhm now took was probably taken with the knowledge, even the wish, of Schleicher. Röhm opened negotiations with the 'Iron Front.' Among its leaders there was a man who had once worked closely with Röhm, and who, like Röhm, might have called himself one of the inventors of Adolf Hitler. This was Karl Mayr, a former major in the Reichswehr. He had been a captain in that information section of the Munich Reichswehr which had sent out Hitler as its civilian employee, first to spy on the inner enemy, then to speak to the people in the streets and squares. Mayr, a true genius in the department that military men euphemistically call 'information service,' had a few years later broken with the Reichswehr and all his political friends. He had gone over to Social Democracy, had helped to build up the Reichsbanner, perhaps in the conviction that this was the right way to create a people's army. When a new leadership transformed the Reichsbanner into the 'Iron Front,' Mayr vanished from the central leadership, but continued in his own way to work in the ranks. Röhm now turned to this old comrade. Was there no way, he asked, of bringing the S.A. and the Iron Front together, of getting rid of the useless political windbags and 'making the soldier master of Germany'?

Röhm was shrewd enough not to keep the conversation secret from Hitler. The interview took place in Mayr's apartment, and with all the trappings of a spy movie; behind a curtain sat a lady taking shorthand notes. Mayr asked Röhm what grounds he had for thinking that he could detach the S.A. from the party. Röhm replied that he knew he had powerful and dangerous enemies in the party; Mayr's comment on this was: Would you like me to tell you the name of your future murderers? At that time Röhm's wild homosexual life had become fully public; there was great bitterness in the ranks against this leader who brought shame to the organization; Hitler had defiantly covered Röhm. 'Captain Röhm,' he said, 'remains my chief of staff, now and after the elections, despite all slanders.' The underground hostility to him was all the bitterer. A few months later, a Munich court actually did sentence two obscure National Socialists, Horn and Danzeisen, to short jail terms for having talked of murdering the chief of staff; but the court believed them when they said that it had been mere talk.

The conversation between Röhm and Mayr seems likewise to have gone no farther than talk, because Mayr had lost his influence on the Iron Front.

But the fact remains that Röhm was willing to subordinate the S.A. to the state. Groener, however, wanted no part of this and insisted that the army of civil war must be destroyed; Schleicher clung to his opinion that this was impossible, Groener threatened to resign, and put through a unanimous cabinet resolution; Hindenburg gave his consent. Three days after his re-election, the S.A. and S.S. and their subsidiary organizations were dissolved. For, said the government proclamation signed by Groener: 'No Reich government can tolerate an attempt by any party to form a state within the state and create for itself an armed force. . . .' Hindenburg was not fully convinced until Groener told him about the treasonable orders to the S.A. in Pomerania.

Neither Hitler nor his followers dared to resist for so much as a moment. First they had been beaten by the voters, now they were crushed by the army. Was Adolphe Légalité on the right way? Would democracy really destroy itself? And if so, would National Socialism still live to see the day? The movement grew and grew, but it did not become more powerful, only more needful of power. 'You know, I am one of Germany's biggest business executives,' Hitler used to say humorously, when he met with industrialists. For the S.A. in the form of its 'ordnance department' had become a great department store with large stocks of clothing, uniforms, boots. The annual turnover in these goods was estimated at seventy million marks in 1932. In addition, the party had its own insurance against homicide and disability, which paid out a few hundred marks to the survivors of S.A. men shot down in battle for Adolf Hitler. The funds for all this had to be raised among the party masses; no millionaire or any group of millionaires was rich enough to do more than cover an occasional deficit for such a giant enterprise. There was indeed a deficit which mounted dangerously; its source was the brown shirts and breeches which the S.A. men bought from the ordnance department and took a long time in paying for. The longer Hitler struggled for power, the more the burden of debt grew; he would not forever be able to find the money to feed his unemployed S.A. men. 'When you have power,' wrote Goebbels-Machiavelli in his diary, 'you can get money enough. But then you no longer need it. If you haven't got power, you need money, but then you don't get it.' The fight for state power became a fight for the state treasury.

Chapter XIX

HINDENBURG'S STICK

THE SPIRITUAL FOUNDER OF THE MODERN CATHO-
lic Church, Pope Leo XIII, said in his encyclical, *Libertas Humana*
(1888): 'It is quite unlawful to demand, to defend, or to grant unconditional freedom of thought, of speech, of writing, of worship.'
Some years earlier he had dealt with certain philosophers who 'say
that all power comes from the people . . . but from these, Catholics
dissent, affirming that the right to rule is from God.'

The Church was not, as many radicals believed, the defender of
present-day society, for in his most famous encyclical, *Rerum No-
varum,* Leo XIII sharply attacked the economic age: 'A small number of very rich people are in a position to subject the mass of the
poor to a yoke that is little better than slavery . . .' Altogether:
'On the other hand, the socialists . . . are endeavoring to destroy
private property. But private property is the natural right of every
man.'

The spirit of the age is truly mirrored in these ecclesiastical documents. With the *Communist Manifesto* and, in their particular
way, the *Protocols,* they are among the most potent documents of
our times. What they reflected was not so much the imprint of existing things as the shadow of coming ones. Deeply human and
Christian as they were, there was an overtone, inaudible at the
time, which was to be re-echoed decades later, in many phrases of
Hitler.

That successor of Leo who made peace with fascism in 1929,
Pope Pius XI, published in 1931 another encyclical, *Quadragesimo*

Anno (the title means that it came forty years after *Rerum No-varum*). Here the Church attacked sharply the system of monopoly capitalism, that 'immense concentration, not only of capital, but also of power and economic might in the hands of individuals'; it attacked also the 'imperialism of international finance capital,' which feels at home 'wherever there is booty to be had'; and said, 'the just ordering of economic life cannot be entrusted to free competition.' To be sure, communism was 'godless and unjust,' and even moderate 'socialism . . . remains incompatible with the doctrine of the Catholic Church.' Hitler would have said: 'Down with Marxism and the international dictatorship of the stock exchange!'

Quadragesimo Anno went on to say that the 'corporate state' created by Mussolini in Italy was an economic effort of quite a different sort. It subordinated economics to politics, but protected property by putting it in its place. 'A moment's reflection,' said the Pope, 'permits us to recognize the advantages of this order: peaceful co-operation of the classes, repression of socialist organizations and efforts, regulatory influence of a special administrative apparatus.' True, the Pope continued, some feared that the state was regulating too much, that an excessive bureaucracy would arise; to counter these dangers, Pope Pius XI asked the 'co-operation of all well-meaning people.'

In the age of parliamentarian democracy the Church had tried, more out of necessity than of desire, to exert a direct influence on this system of power. Thus, the Center Party in Germany had grown up. The Center was a secular makeshift and concession to the era of parliaments; a democratic mobilization of the Church's voting millions against the hostile forces of crown and army; a mustering of the Church's strength in a predominantly Protestant world. When labor became a great movement it had a sharply distinct Catholic sector; but nevertheless, 'We are workers, and all workers are our comrades,' said Giesberts, one of the Catholic labor leaders, as though he had never heard of *Rerum Novarum*. But there were other forces too. All 'patriotic, Christian, popular, and truly social-thinking circles of all strata, especially the intellectuals,' should band together, said Heinrich Brüning, then an unknown young Catholic politician, in 1920. 'In this point, especially, I set my hopes on the young intelligentsia, in whom I know that the spirit of 1914 is not yet extinguished.'

In the spring of 1932, a new archbishop had to be appointed in Freiburg im Breisgau, a city of southern Germany. For a hundred years this dignitary had been chosen by the archdiocese of Freiburg and merely confirmed in Rome. But the Holy See suddenly broke with the old custom and appointed a man whom the Freiburg diocese did not want. This archbishop, Doctor Mathias Groeber, made a speech to the clergy of his diocese, in which he said that the Church must gradually assume a more conciliatory and more 'prudent' attitude toward National Socialism; it must, as the archbishop put it, 'put on the brakes.'

This was the changing, shifting ground on which Brüning desperately strove to keep his feet; eventually this man who, in 1918, as an army officer, had attempted to stop the German revolution, fought almost against himself. Adolf Hitler sensed a certain affinity between himself and the silent chancellor and expressed his feelings by an unalterable attitude of deep personal respect.

Behind the scenes the Reichswehr also felt the shifting of the ground. To put it bluntly: the Brüning experiment had failed; parliament had not been conquered; the popular will was not captured. To Schleicher's surprisingly narrow reasoning, the problem presented itself in oversimplified form: Was there another man who, like Brüning, would have the confidence of the Center, and, unlike Brüning, the confidence of the National Socialists, too? Who could deliver to the Reichswehr a 'functioning Reichstag'? Schleicher hit on his old pal, Franz von Papen, the major of Uhlans, the diplomatic spy, the son-in-law of heavy industry — and the Catholic nobleman. For months he built up this new tool. In Schleicher's seemingly shrewd, actually superficial judgment, Papen, with his smiling worldliness, seemed a great leader and diplomat. 'In most things there must be a certain frivolity,' he said. 'People sometimes say that Herr von Papen is frivolous. But that is what we need.' Both men belonged to the Herrenklub, and Papen's political ideas can be regarded as a genuine product of this spiritual atmosphere; but it is only a legend that Heinrich von Gleichen, the secretary of the club, or Count Bodo von Alven-

sleben, its president, pulled the political wires in Germany in 1932
— much as they may have desired to do so.

To Schleicher this shrewd, wealthy, distinguished man, with the
highest connections, apparently in good odor in Rome, was 'the
Center,' just as Schleicher himself was 'the Reichswehr,' or Hitler
was 'National Socialism' — for it was one of the weaknesses of this
intriguer that he consistently confused personalities with forces.
Papen may have persuaded him that he really was the Center, because he had bought one of the Center's leading newspapers with
his wife's money. Schleicher, on the other hand, had persuaded
himself that he could win the National Socialists — and there it
would be: the strong, 'authoritarian' government, based on a majority in parliament. This new form of government thought up by
Schleicher was to be called 'the President's Government.' The President should appoint as ministers men of his own — that is, Schleicher's — choice, and these men should make the laws; but the parliament would have to confirm, or at least tolerate, them. This
strange type of government hung legally by the fragile thread of a
single article of the constitution intended only for emergency; actually it could govern only as long as parliament itself refused to
govern. Former Captain von Schleicher had gone a long way since
1918, when he had conceived his master plan of the Free Corps;
time had passed by, and the nature of things had driven him — as
this type is inevitably driven — to the plan of the Wise Men of
Zion: dictatorship through democracy.

On April 22, Schleicher had a conversation with Röhm and
Count Helldorf, Röhm's friend, who led the S.A. in Berlin.
Schleicher told the two National Socialists that he disapproved the
dissolution of the S.A., but apparently the conversation had no result. Next day, Goebbels wrote in his diary that Schleicher 'has his
ideas about National Socialism. But of course he cannot understand us!'

That was on April 22. On April 24, the masses of the Uprooted
and Disinherited of all Germany arose and helped Schleicher's
understanding along. On this day, elections were held for many
state diets. It was still these eighteen separate states, grown out of
the innumerable large and petty principalities, that controlled the

body of the German administrative apparatus, and the police as well. Prussia, by far the most important state, for years governed firmly and reliably by democratic parties, among them Brüning's Catholic friends, had thus far, despite occasional conflicts, been a reliable support of the 'last parliamentary chancellor.'

The elections shattered this Prussian support. The National Socialists won a hundred and sixty-two seats in the Prussian diet, the Communists fifty-six; together, they had two hundred and eighteen seats, a clear majority. That decided it: the Prussian parliament was against the Prussian government. In other words, the last parliamentary majority in Germany on which Brüning had been able to rely to a certain degree was no longer in existence.

From this moment on, personal intrigue dominated the political game. All the real forces had so enmeshed and paralyzed each other that a few accidental figures, enjoying irresponsible freedom in influential positions, seemed to make history. That was the outward appearance, but the truth behind it was that in two bitter, dark years the Brüning experiment had not brought the people to the Reichswehr, and therefore the Reichswehr began a new experiment.

On April 26, Röhm and Helldorf again called on Schleicher. This time the conversation was far more hopeful; the Berlin S.A. leader reported to his *gauleiter,* who wrote in his diary: 'Count Helldorf has been to see Schleicher. Schleicher wants to change his course.' Two days later, on April 28, Hitler himself spoke with Schleicher; Goebbels contents himself with saying: 'The conversation turned out well.'

In this conversation, as later events show, Hitler must have informed Schleicher that for the present he did not want to take power. He was satisfied if Brüning fell and the S.A. were again allowed to function. And so he would create no difficulties for a new government picked by Schleicher.

Hindenburg in those weeks must have seen himself as a tragic figure. He had been triumphantly elected President — by more or less the same people who in 1918 had created the republic! And when he looked out at his junker's estate in Neudeck, he must have been pained by the thought that most of his neighbors had rejected him, although they said their rejection was not directed toward his person, but toward Brüning.

On May 8, in Schleicher's home, Hitler met Oscar von Hindenburg, the President's son, and State Secretary Otto Meissner, his adviser. These figures, little known or entirely unknown to the general public, now concluded an agreement for the salvation of parliamentary democracy with the best known, most voiced and photographed demagogue of the day. In order that Hitler might help to provide a 'functioning Reichstag,' the present Reichstag must be dissolved and new elections held — which lay within the sphere of the Reichs President's power. Then the National Socialists would return with twice their strength; but in order that they might fully develop their strength, the stirring tramp of the Brown S.A. must once more be heard in the streets. Hitler again had an opportunity to make it clear to doubting minds that the S.A. was no army for civil war, but a propagandist organization for the election campaign. The salvation of parliamentarian democracy demanded that the S.A. must again enjoy freedom — this was the gist of the pact of May 8. For Hitler promised at the same time to 'tolerate' the cabinet which the President would appoint after Brüning's fall — this meant not to attack it, hence actually to support it.

Brüning seemed to have at least one strong personal support against this intrigue, and that was Wilhelm Groener, Minister of the Reichswehr and the Interior, the general who, with Hindenburg, had overthrown the Kaiser and approved the acceptance of the Peace of Versailles. But now Groener was rendered ridiculous and abhorrent to the old man. At the age of sixty-two, the Reichswehr Minister had married, and five months after his marriage a son was born; Schleicher told Hindenburg that in the ministry the hasty baby was known as 'Nurmi' after the Finnish runner. Hindenburg replied that the affair was a scandal which in earlier days would not have been tolerated in a noncommissioned officer. Defiantly, Groener exhibited his pride and joy in a baby carriage; he let himself be photographed and permitted the picture to appear in the press. Meanwhile, Schleicher telephoned the higher officers of the Reichswehr and asked them what they thought of it; he more

or less put the answer into their mouths: they thought that **Groener**
had become 'unsuitable' as their minister.

On top of this, a political intrigue was heaped.' The 'Iron Front'
had elected Hindenburg. Material was collected to prove that the
'Iron Front' was arming for civil war just as much as the S.A., and
this material was laid before Hindenburg with the implication that
the prohibition of the S.A., upon which Groener had insisted so
strongly, was at the very least one-sided and unjust. To top it all,
the Chief Reich Attorney (*Oberreichsanwalt*) found that Hitler's
orders to his Pomeranian S.A., juridically speaking, were not
exactly high treason. Hindenburg had the feeling that Groener had
deceived him, or at least advised him badly on this point; he wrote
him a sharp, insulting letter and had it published.

Groener's distress affected him physically. When Göring reviled
him in the Reichstag for his prohibition of the S.A., and Goebbels
helped with poisonous cries, both intimating that they were well
informed about certain confidential occurrences in the government,
Groener's voice failed him. In the midst of his speech he stood for
a time open-mouthed, unable to utter a word. When at last he sank
back exhausted, Schleicher, his 'adopted son,' appeared beside him
and said amiably that the army thought his resignation indicated.
Groener still hoped that Hindenburg, whose legend he had in
large part created and certainly done much to preserve, would keep
him out of gratitude; but Groener's own prophecy was cruelly
fulfilled: 'One thing you can rely on,' he had said, 'is the old gentleman's disloyalty.' Two days later, on May 12, he resigned.

Brüning, sensing that a heavy attack against himself was in
progress, still believed that great political forces would carry him
through these apparently petty intrigues. President Hoover in
America, the MacDonald government in England, were pressing
for an end to the German reparations that were disorganizing world
economy. Brüning saw a great success close at hand. A day before
Groener's resignation he cried out to the invisible intriguers in the
Reichstag: 'Don't think you can stop me now, a hundred yards before the goal!' Then he went to Geneva to a meeting of the League
of Nations Council, to obtain the consent of England and France
for the end of reparations.

But Hitler was proved right: it was home affairs that decided. Domestic intrigue even managed to knife Brüning's foreign policy in the back. Schleicher was on terms of friendship with André François-Poncet, the French ambassador in Berlin. He told him that there was no sense in France continuing to negotiate with Brüning; for soon there would be another government, more friendly to France. The consequence was that Brüning waited in vain for French Premier Tardieu in Geneva; Tardieu pretended illness, and the German Chancellor did not bring back the end of reparations, as he had hoped. This was a situation that could not last; but meanwhile the mass drama and intrigues rolled on at home.

The Prussian diet was preparing to overthrow the democratic Braun government; the Communists gave the signal. On May 25, they entered a motion that the diet should give the Prussian government a vote of no-confidence. If the Communists had wanted to put Hitler in power, they could have acted no differently. Actually they did want to put Hitler in power. They staunchly believed that they were the born heirs of fascism; that they would speedily overthrow fascism if it took power, but that it must first take power. Rosa Luxemburg had regarded military dictatorship as the necessary preliminary to the dictatorship of the proletariat, and in 1923 Stalin had written in a letter to his comrades, Zinoviev and Bukharin: 'It is more advantageous for us that the Fascists [in Germany] should strike first: that will rally the whole working class to the Communists!' For that reason, Stalin thought, the German Communists must be 'restrained, not encouraged.' It was the firm conviction of all Communist leaders, including Leon Trotzky living as an exile on a Turkish island near Constantinople, that the united front of the working class would conquer Germany. But Trotzky demanded that the Communists create a united front through a pact with the Social Democrats, while the Communists under Stalin's leadership clung to the view that the Social Democrats must be smashed before fascism could effectively be combated, and for that reason fascism must come to power.

In the Reichstag on October 13, 1931, Brüning warned the German capitalists of the menacing united front of the workers, and urged them not to provoke the working class too far. The worker, he said, understood the need for sacrifices; but it was not possible to 'teach him this understanding if from the very start it is associated with conceptions and slogans which must inevitably drive the German working class into a united front.' Brüning had warned capital not to go too far; the Communists understood: not to establish open fascism, for, in Stalin's words, 'fascism is a fighting organization of the bourgeoisie.' The following day the Communist speaker, Remmele, stood up in the Reichstag and put the following interpretation on Brüning's remark: 'Herr Brüning has spoken very clearly: if once the Fascists are in power, the united front of anti-fascism will come into being and will sweep everything before it [stormy applause from the Communist benches]. . . . Who will strike whom? This question is already decided [applause from the Communists]. The only remaining question is: At what time shall we overthrow the bourgeoisie? . . . The Fascists do not frighten us. They will be finished even quicker than any other government [cries of 'Right!' from the Communists].' So thought the party which led the Uprooted and Disinherited of the Left. Their leaders and many of their followers were convinced (as Trotzky reproachfully said) '. . . that the task of struggle against fascism is a task of the second order; that it can wait; that it will solve itself; that fascism is essentially already in power; that Hitler will bring nothing new; that Hitler does not have to be feared; that Hitler will only break a path for the Communists.'

It did not disturb the Communists that this path was strewn with Communist corpses. When, in the Prussian diet, they entered the motion that was to overthrow the Prussian government, their deputy, Wilhelm Pieck, made a violent speech against the National Socialists, whom he called a party of murderers. The National Socialists jumped up, flung themselves on the numerically inferior Communists, thrashed them out of the hall, and sang the Horst Wessel song on the scene of their victory. There were pools of blood on the floor, and Hitler danced with joy when Goebbels told him the story on the telephone. Der Führer could not hear details enough of the smashed skulls and knocked-out teeth. When the two met three days later, 'I had to tell him the whole story in epic length, and he rubbed his hands with pleasure.' But incapable of learning from blows, the Communists stuck to their motion which was calculated only to bring their assailants to power.

This bloody scene in the Prussian diet took place on May 25. On the twenty-sixth, Meissner called on Hindenburg in Neudeck and reported to him that if he wished he could have a cabinet which the majority of the Reichstag would support; constitutional without any doubt or artifice. Yet no cabinet of party politicians, but of men whom he could trust and with some of whom he was personally acquainted.

On the twenty-eighth, Hindenburg was back in Berlin; on the twenty-ninth, a Sunday, Brüning was ordered to appear before him. The Chancellor knew that an intrigue against him was in progress; he did not know that it was already complete, that his fate had been decided. He wanted to demand that Hindenburg put a stop to the intrigues until he, Brüning, had forced the cancellation of reparations. Instead, it was Hindenburg who did the demanding. The old man had written what he planned to say in inch-high letters on several slips of paper. He read them one after another through his spectacles. 'I am informed,' he said to Brüning, 'that you have ministers with Bolshevist plans in your cabinet. That cannot go on!' Brüning tried to discuss and explain, but Hindenburg could not be distracted from his slips of paper. He said that he had to defend his name and his honor. And his last sentence was: 'I request you to give me no more emergency decrees to sign!'

In other words: If you can make laws with the Reichstag, good; you won't make any more in my name. This meant dismissal, though the word was not uttered. But Brüning wanted a clear statement. Next day he returned to see Hindenburg. Before the conversation was well started, a noise was heard in the courtyard of the palace, cries of command, clicking heels: the guard was being changed. Impelled by curiosity, the old soldier stepped to the window, turning his back on Brüning whom he had seemingly forgotten. After a while he remembered his chancellor and asked whether Brüning might want to stay on as foreign minister in a new government. Brüning replied that he too had his name and honor to preserve, and left the room.

Meanwhile, Oskar von Hindenburg notified Göring that his

father was expecting the 'Bohemian corporal' at four in the afternoon. Hitler had remained hidden in the country, to avoid arousing Brüning's suspicions by his presence in Berlin. In the afternoon he called on the Reichs President with Göring. Hindenburg informed him that he had appointed von Papen as chancellor. Was it true that Hitler would support the Papen cabinet? Hitler said yes.

And now Papen attempted to form his democratic parliamentarian government. It was the time to show whether he was able to bring his Catholic friends to join forces with the National Socialists. On the day after Brüning's fall, Hindenburg received Doctor Kaas, the leader of the Center. The ground of German politics indeed had shifted. Kaas said: Yes, the National Socialists must now enter the government; he demanded a 'total solution,' the 'entry of the opposition into the government, with full responsibility, and, in particular, the National Socialists must take their share of responsibility fully and openly.' In the government — this was the idea — the National Socialists would be tamed and exhausted; the dust of day-to-day work would settle on their glamour; it would be necessary to pass hard, exacting, unpopular laws, and the names of Hitler, Strasser, Goebbels, instead of Brüning and Stegerwald, would stand under these laws; Hitler had promised wonders; he should be forced to break his promises. These parliamentarians, in the past two years, had learned by hard blows what an ungrateful business power could be; they imagined that by power Hitler might, like Brüning, be broken.

But open power, connected with open responsibility, was not to be heaped on Hitler by the construction of the new Papen government; the National Socialists were to have influence and power secretly, and Papen was to help keep it secret, only exposing himself and possibly his friends. In the eyes of these friends — the men of the Center — Papen was an idiot and a betrayer at the same time. The next day, May 31, Papen debated and struggled all afternoon with Kaas, Brüning, and other leaders of his own party for their agreement and aid; it was refused with sharp words. Kaas intimidated Papen so much that he promised to abandon his attempt to constitute a government. He had failed to win his own party and hence had no majority in parliament; by the afternoon of May 31, Schleicher's master plan had failed.

But when the weak-kneed Papen appeared before Hindenburg the next day, he again let himself be intimidated. For the sake of his own prestige, the old man could no longer retreat. He roughly commanded Papen as a soldier to form a cabinet. In mad haste the ministers were sought out, some by telegram; all of them former officers whom the Field Marshal more or less ordered to their posts. Some, indeed, could not have been induced in any other way. There was Konstantin von Neurath, ambassador to London, who became Foreign Minister; Wilhelm Baron von Gayl, one of the economic leaders of the junkers in the province of East Prussia, a frequent guest in the Hindenburg household. Schleicher became Reichswehr Minister; for finances there was an outstanding specialist, Count von Schwerin-Krosigk, despite his name no junker but an official. But it was hard to overlook that the seven leading men of the cabinet were all nobles. For justice, however, Schleicher had found a commoner from the Bavarian South; this new Minister of Justice was the same Franz Gürtner, who had been unable to find the patriotic murderers; who had freed Hitler from prison long before the end of his term, who had made it possible for him to speak in public, and who finally had failed to throw full light on the death of Geli Raubal.

On June 2, Papen was Chancellor. On the third, the last remnant of parliamentarian democracy voluntarily abdicated before the new *coup*: the Prussian diet, with two hundred and fifty-three votes, the National Socialists in the lead, adopted the Communist motion to give the Braun government a vote of no-confidence.

Now Papen and Schleicher attempted to forge and educate the National Socialists. The Reichstag was dissolved; thus far Hitler had had his way. But when he expected the prohibition of the S.A. to be lifted, Papen demanded that Hitler first give a clear, written promise to support him even after elections. Hitler wanted to put nothing in writing, but finally let himself be persuaded. On the estate of Severin in Mecklenburg, belonging to Goebbels's brother-in-law, Walter Granzow, Hitler dictated a memorandum. Meanwhile, Schleicher was waiting for him on a near-by estate near the little city of Fürstenberg. Hitler dictated in haste and was not sure whether what he had written was the right thing. He gave the

memorandum to Goebbels and Göring to look through and meanwhile went to see Schleicher. The memorandum, which apparently
displeased Hitler's critical lieutenants, never reached Schleicher;
but in the meantime Hitler had let himself be ensnared by the general, even without any exchange of documents. Schleicher promised
that the S.A. would soon be permitted to function and that a National Socialist would become Premier of Prussia. According to the
secret plan of the Papen government, this meant 'tying Hitler to responsibility,' without giving him any real power; Hitler did not
notice the trap, but said, beaming, to Schleicher that a tablet should
be erected on the wall of the house with the words: 'Here there
took place that memorable conference between Adolf Hitler and
General Kurt von Schleicher, by which . . .' When he returned
and reported, Goebbels was beside himself, and no doubt thought:
he must never be allowed to attend conferences alone; it was the
same way before the presidential elections — this can be read quite
clearly between the lines of his diary. The Prussian deputies, Kube
and Kerrl, were summoned, and Hitler was enlightened, no doubt
as gently as possible; thereupon he hastily departed, and two days
later his representatives, Göring and Kube, innocently told Papen
and Schleicher that they could agree to nothing definite, for their
Führer was absent and unfortunately ('Thank God,' wrote Goebbels in his diary) could not be reached.

Papen grew distrustful and hesitated to lift the prohibition of
the S.A.; both sides began to accuse each other of broken promises.
Hitler thundered at Göring, Goebbels, and Strasser over the telephone, ordered them to see Schleicher and Minister of the Interior
von Gayl, but the longed-for three-line notice in the newspapers did
not appear — and two weeks had passed since Hitler's handshake
with Hindenburg. One night Goebbels assembled fifty S.A. men in
his office. They put on their brown shirts, their brown breeches,
their high boots, and then the fifty of them marched straight
through the city, went into the cafés. Not a policeman ventured
to arrest them, and the fifty felt like bold law-breakers, great revolutionaries. It did not occur to these warriors that with their millions
they could seize the right of the streets without any question; that
they could flood the whole country with their brown columns re-

gardless of prohibitions; no, first the President had to give his permission.

It finally came on June 15. Now this new type of democracy could run its course unrestrained. On July 31, six weeks hence, the people were to express their opinion at the polls. In giant swarms, the S.A. appeared again in the streets, to hammer the right opinion into them. Hitler was drunk with enthusiasm for elections and the people; the former despiser of parliament and the masses was unrecognizable. 'I do not know,' he said, 'whether these Reichstag elections will be the last. I hope not. I hope that the time will never come when our leaders say to themselves: now we shall rest!'

On June 26, he gathered his S.A. leaders in the village of Schoenau, near Berchtesgaden, and gave them a severe lecture. They must not believe that they were at their goal. Power must be won every day anew; that was what the National Socialist Party had been built for; and that was what made it stronger than the 'government of the barons,' which felt secure in the possession of machine guns and lacked the intelligence to see that seven noble ministers are an insult to an impoverished people. Papen declared freely that he governed on the strength of authority and not by the will of the people. 'A strong government,' he said, 'does not need to prescribe the convictions and inner life of the people'; at any rate, it pays no attention to these convictions.

Hitler told his S.A. leaders in Schoenau that these unpopular masters would soon come into conflict with the Reichswehr. For the Reichswehr wanted the people, and the S.A. was the military-minded German people. Conditions in Germany were not the same as in Italy, said Hitler. A dualism, such as existed between the Italian army and the Fascist militia, was fundamentally impossible in Germany, for one thing because in Italy the militia to a certain degree had to replace an obsolete officers' corps, while in Germany the army had a first-class officers' corps. The tasks of the S.A. would always lie in the field of domestic politics, not in military matters; for this the Reichswehr was thankful to the S.A., and the S.A. should in turn be thankful to the Reichswehr for leaving it a free hand in the shaping of German conditions. The S.A. leaders listened to Hitler with consternation; without enthusiasm

Röhm thanked 'Der Führer for his explanation and assured him of the loyalty that was a matter of course in view of the military training of the S.A.'

The Brown People's Army had long ceased to be the élite of which Hitler had once dreamed and had become a loosely knit mass. More solid, more military, but numerically inferior, the Stahlhelm marched out on Sunday to secret maneuvers. With these reserves in the rear, Germany now began to demand a stronger army at the Geneva Disarmament Conference which, since February, had been sitting in Geneva. Germany still concealed its demand beneath the ambiguous words 'equal rights,' and cited the Versailles Treaty with its broken promise of general disarmament. In Papen's earlier plans this projected German army had appeared as a western army against Bolshevism, in alliance with the French army. Papen had in mind a great conciliation with France, a total solution of all controversial questions; but once again home politics had spoken and destroyed these hopes — if they had ever been founded. In France, the elections to the Chamber in May, 1932, returned the Left to the helm, and again Edouard Herriot, the democrat and freemason, was premier. Herriot, who for years had been cultivating a *rapprochement* between France and the Soviet government, offered determined resistance to Germany's 'equal rights,' and also refused to draw a line beneath the chapter of German reparations.

It was clear, to be sure, that Germany would pay no more reparations, and thus, on July 8, 1932, the peace beside the Swiss lakes was enriched by one more treaty. In the city of Lausanne, the victor powers of Versailles concluded an agreement with Germany which for practical purposes put an end to reparations. But Papen in private complained that Herriot, the man of the Left, had not wished to give the 'cabinet of barons' a full success; in this attitude, according to Papen, he had been reinforced by one of his advisers, the Socialist Grumbach; international Marxism had showed its hand. And that was why Herriot had not consented to revoke Article 231 of the Peace Treaty which placed the war guilt on Germany; that was why the reparations had not been canceled in principle. Meanwhile, however, they were reduced to three billion marks, a sum which, considerable as it was, seemed insignificant beside the previous astronomic figure; and even this sum was not payable at once, but only when circumstances should permit — and circumstances never did permit. This was Papen's 'failure of Lausanne,' as Hitler called it, declaring the final payment of three billions to be 'intolerable.' In near-by Geneva the Disarmament Conference was dragging along almost without hope; there was no prospect that France would consent to 'equal rights' for Germany.

And this was no wonder, Hitler carped, for France knew that this government did not have the people behind it any more than had previous governments. To Hitler, Papen's contempt of the people was almost a personal insult; for the people, he felt, was himself. This was not even true. Certainly he was not the people of the big coal and iron districts in the west of Germany. Here the National Socialists encountered a passionate hostility and comforted themselves that this hostility was limited to the Communists. Actually it was shared by workers of all tendencies, by Social Democrats, and even the Center. Goebbels describes a trip through these cities in July, 1932:

> *July* 12. We force our way through the howling mob in Düsseldorf and Elberfeld. A wild trip. We had no idea that things would get so serious. In all our innocence we drive into Hagen in an open car and wearing our uniforms. The streets are black with people. All of them mob and Communist rabble. They close off the road, so that we can go neither forward nor back. . . . We cut our way through the middle of the pack. Each of us has his pistol in his hand and is determined, if the worst comes to the worst, to sell his life as dearly as possible. . . . The meeting place is on a hill, framed by a forest of beeches in the background. The Communists have ingeniously set fire to this forest, so that it is almost impossible to carry on the meeting. Nevertheless, we make our speeches. . . . On our departure we are followed by a bombardment of stones. We manage to leave the city by detours. . . .
>
> *July* 13. . . . The experience in Hagen has made us more circumspect. Now we travel in disguise. Constantly we pass lurking groups of Communists. We can hardly get into Dortmund. We have to take a side-street to keep from falling into the hands of the Communists who have occupied all the other entrances. . . .
>
> *July* 14. . . . A trip to the Ruhr involves mortal peril. We take a

strange car, because our own with its Berlin number is known and people have descriptions of it everywhere. In Elberfeld the Red press has called the mob into the streets. The approaches to the stadium are blocked off completely. It is only because they take us for a harmless passenger car that we get through. . . . After a speech we change into a new car. Again the mob has occupied the streets. But it is dark and so we get through.

July 15. . . . I must leave my own native city like a criminal, pursued by curses, abuse, vilification, stoned, and spat upon. . . .

The National Socialists were a mighty mass, but a still mightier mass stood against them. Actually this mass was itself disintegrating, and had mortally wounded itself when the Communists overthrew the Prussian government.

This government, despite its downfall, was still governing, because the Prussian parliament could agree on no other cabinet; for the Communists and National Socialists together could overthrow the state power, but together they could not establish any state power. Papen, who personally did not have even a tenth of the votes in the Reichstag behind him, now declared himself unwilling to tolerate a Prussian government which still commanded over four tenths of the votes. Braun, the Social Democratic Premier of Prussia, himself lost heart and wanted to resign; and when his Social Democratic comrades would not permit this, he took a vacation and sat at home sulking, letting his colleagues govern by themselves. These colleagues, led by Carl Severing, the white-haired Social Democratic Minister of the Interior, told themselves that, though they represented a minority, it was still the only minority capable of governing; and so their right to power was not much inferior to that of Hindenburg, who had been President for seven years after being elected by a minority.

When Hindenburg looked out of his window, he saw the broad dark gray façade of the building in which the overthrown Prussian government was still calmly governing. Hostility now reigned between the two palaces. Half consciously, Hindenburg regarded himself as the deputy of his 'most gracious Kaiser,' who had been head of state before him and was now sitting in Holland; but the Kaiser had at the same time been his 'most gracious king and lord'

— that is, King of Prussia — and this part of his heritage was now administered by the enemy in the gray palace. The conflict between Prussia and the Reich was intolerable to Hindenburg. In this he was entirely at one with Papen, but Schleicher's mind was not made up so quickly. What Papen wanted was to suspend the Prussian government by force; and this was his first great disappointment to Schleicher. For the Reichswehr Minister had invented Papen in order to avoid the necessity of governing by force; his wish was that in Prussia the National Socialists and the Center should form a majority government in good democratic style. For the moment this had failed, but after the Reichstag elections of July 31, it would doubtless succeed; for the Center would not continue forever to uphold the present Prussian government.

To be sure, this government would at once have ceased to be a minority government if the Communists became reasonable; if they gave up the idea that Hitler must come to power. Wilhelm Abegg, the Prussian state secretary, attempted on his own responsibility to bring the Communists to their senses. He invited two Communist Reichstag deputies, Torgler and Kasper, to see him and tried to persuade them to give up their sabotage in Prussia. The Communists did not say yes and they did not say no.

But Abegg did not suspect how shaky the ground beneath his feet had already become. Since the fall of Brüning, an intangible but ubiquitous and corrosive conviction that Hitler would soon come to power had penetrated every pore of the public consciousness. The most convinced were to be found in the great silent army of men who are seldom openly convinced of anything, but who always adjust their business, their career, and, in this epoch of race war, even their love, to the forthcoming political events. Business connections were broken, friendships severed, men and women broke off their engagements to Jews. Many found it timely to wear the swastika in their buttonhole, for when the first booty was distributed, you had to be an 'old fighter'; long party membership would be rewarded with employment, advancement, and loans from public funds. And so now the opportunists stepped forward with loud cries. But the party disapproved their sudden loudness and preferred to use these shady characters in the shade. Occasionally such proclamations as this appeared in the National Socialist press:

> Halt! Before you leave your present party, convinced of the truth of the National Socialist idea, reflect if you cannot be more useful to the National Socialist Movement by remaining a member where you are and informing us about all the occurrences and intentions of your present party comrades! . . . Your work will be valued as highly as the sacrifices of every party comrade and S.A. man who does his duty!

One of those who did their duty thus silently was sitting at the table as Abegg conferred with Torgler and Kasper. This was Councillor (*Regierungsrat*) Werner Diels; Abegg had unsuspectingly called him in as a witness, and he took down a protocol of the conversation. Treason could not have been performed more comfortably; Diels took his protocol to Papen and reported that the Prussian government was allying itself with Bolshevism!

This forced Schleicher's hand; reluctantly he permitted the Reichswehr to march. On the morning of July 20, 1932, Papen asked the Prussian cabinet ministers to call at the Chancellery. He told them that a state of military emergency had been proclaimed in Prussia; General von Rundstedt, commander of the Berlin division, had been given full power. The ministers, said Papen, should regard themselves as deposed. He, Papen, as 'Reich Commissioner,' would assume power in Prussia and set other commissioners over the ministries. It was a short conversation without much argument and counter-argument; on his way out, Severing said philosophically that in this hour world history was in the making. The ministers returned to their offices; when Severing was back at his desk, he received a telephone call from a certain Bracht, mayor of Essen; Bracht declared that he was Severing's successor and would present himself at twelve o'clock.

This was the gravest political upheaval that Germany had experienced in thirteen years; superficially, it occurred as a sequence of depressingly tragi-comic scenes without greatness. It was the leadership of the Social Democratic Party which determined the form and course of this upheaval. These men decided to accept the blow and offer no resistance.

The Communists thought differently. They proclaimed a general strike to support a government which they themselves had overthrown two weeks before. Nowhere did anyone follow their call, and this historic fact contains the profoundest reason for the otherwise incomprehensible decision of the Social Democratic leaders. The condition of the German working class had changed since March, 1920, when in a similar situation they won their strike against the military *putsch*. Six to eight million unemployed were waiting outside the factory gates; the workers' leaders believed that they could not expect a general stoppage, a solid outpouring from the factories that would crush all opposition.

Rundstedt had orders to arrest the Social Democratic leaders at the first sign of resistance; later, Reichswehr officers boasted that they would not have shrunk back from mass shootings. But it is improbable that the Reichswehr would have risked a blood-bath; it would have been the opposite of what they had longed for since 1919. If there had been an uprising, its leadership could have been moved to the Rhineland, which, in accordance with the treaties of Versailles and Locarno, the Reichswehr could not enter. It is possible that the South German states and their governments would have joined the Prussian government; for these states, with their largely Catholic population, were embittered by the fall of Brüning, distrusted the Prussian junkers and military camarilla. The South and West of the Reich were beginning to show resistance to the hegemony of the North and East; again there was talk of the frontier drawn by the river Main, which divided Germany, historically and temperamentally, into North and South, much as the Mason-Dixon line divides the United States.

But resistance along these lines required preparation, and there had been little preparation. The 'Iron Front' was still in the building and it was not ready to strike. Side by side with the Reichswehr, the S.A. and the Stahlhelm would at once have marched out in great swarms and almost entirely dominated the great plains of northern and eastern Germany. Against them, the Prussian police presented no reliable force, particularly in the smaller towns. But in this struggle the Social Democratic leaders may have feared their friends, the Communists, even more than their enemies. It was the admitted and openly expressed aim of the Communists, not to save the German Republic, but to smash Social Democracy. The participation of the Communists in this struggle would have driven considerable neutral sections of the population to the side of the Reichswehr; particularly the Catholics, despite all their bitterness against Papen and Hindenburg.

And so there was no struggle. When Bracht appeared in Severing's office at noon, Severing declared that he was 'ceding only to force,' meaning that he ceded. The two men had known each other well for years and had worked closely together. They entered into conversation and agreed that the exercise of 'force' should take place at eight that night. At eight o'clock, Bracht returned, accompanied by Police President Melcher, whom he had brought with him from Essen, and two police officers. Melcher, a good-natured fellow, wanted to shake hands with Severing; Severing held his hand behind his back and Bracht again informed him that he was deposed. Severing repeated that he was ceding only to force, and passed through a door into his adjacent private home. Similar scenes occurred with other high officials of the Prussian government. There was little seriousness about the form of this capitulation; but the objective grounds for it were serious; the expected result — to prevent a fusion between the Reichswehr and the National Socialists — was for a time achieved, but in the end was lost. Resistance might not have altered the outward course of history; but the fact that in this moment between life and death the Social Democratic movement showed only prudence and no strength was its undoing.

Thus ended the short-lived Weimar Republic. Because of its failures in power politics, it has generally been judged adversely. But this is not entirely fair. The reconstruction of defeated Germany after the war was a significant achievement. The period saw considerable accomplishments in literature, the arts, especially architecture, and these achievements were filled with the spirit of the republic. It is hard to decide whether to count it as a weakness or a virtue of this republic, that it allowed a freedom of speech and of the press which endangered its dignity and security and was often shamelessly abused. In any case, under the Weimar Republic, the

German masses developed a new sense of their own worth, a new self-reliance.

Papen's *coup* brought him no luck. From the first day of his government, his own Center Party, aside, perhaps, from a few church dignitaries and Catholic nobles, was bitterly hostile to him. For the Catholic masses Papen was a renegade, the representative of a 'paper-thin upper crust' which 'looks at the people with a cold, domineering eye.' By his Prussian stroke he made enemies of both people and leadership in the South German states, and in Bavaria key men began to make speeches to the effect that if Papen should dare to send them a Reichs Commissioner, they would arrest him at the border. They should be made to realize in Berlin, said Councillor Schaeffer, one of the leaders of the Bavarian People's Party, 'that at the time when the Cathedral of Bamberg was being built in the south of Germany, the Prussians in the region of Berlin were still climbing around on trees.' The Bavarian ministers, led by Prime Minister Heinrich Held, a Catholic, fighting with his unreliable parliament much as Braun and Severing had fought with theirs, declared that they would cede not even to force. Hitler cried that the unity of the Reich was menaced, and that not Papen, but 'the National Socialist Movement has the great and responsible task of becoming the preserver of Reich unity.' Goebbels said that Papen was shattering the Reich by his clumsiness; therefore: 'Out with Papen and Gayl! Adolf Hitler to power!'

With the breaking of the Social Democrats in Prussia and the settlement of the reparations in Lausanne, Papen had already over-reached himself — and this was only the beginning! His ultimate goal was to put an end to the rule of sterile masses; the great day of the enlightened minority was dawning everywhere in the 'Abendland'! The collaboration with Soviet Russia was definitely dropped; the policy of secretly fabricating guns and ammunition, of building forbidden military planes and training pilots with the help of the Red Army, was abandoned; the so-called Berlin Treaty of Friendship (1926), modeled on the old Rapallo Treaty, was not renewed when it expired in 1931. But the democratic Herriot government in France, firmly clinging to the idea of collective security against the German threat and therefore eager for an understanding with

Soviet Russia, was no partner to Papen's 'occidental' ideas and therefore unable to admit the necessity for a stronger German army. The Disarmament Conference, assembled in Geneva since February, 1932, adjourned on July 23, without acceding to Germany's claim to 'equality'; the United States, England, and even Italy took the French side.

In a remarkably short time Papen had succeeded in making an enemy of the working class, weakening the unity of the Reich, and now this diplomatic fiasco! Five days before elections, Schleicher stepped up to the microphone and apologized to the German people for the government he had invented — this was the veiled meaning of his speech. 'I am no friend of military dictatorship,' he affirmed. 'I regard the dictatorial government of the armed forces in Germany as absolutely impossible. . . . The government,' he said, audibly carping at Papen, 'must be supported by a strong popular sentiment. . .' In between he announced that Germany, whatever Geneva might decide, would do what was necessary for her defense, 'revamping, not enlarging,' the Reichswehr. What embittered him most, said he, was the talk about a 'plot of junkers and generals' in Germany, for 'the Reichswehr is not a force to protect any classes or interested persons, and no more does it want to protect any obsolete economic forms or untenable property relations.'

This challenge to capitalism and feudalism sounded strange in the mouth of the leader of the Reichswehr; it was widely quoted, debated, interpreted. But it hardly penetrated the ear of the masses which was filled with the roaring noise of Hitler's gray Junkers plane. More than ever these masses regarded the flying voice of thunder as the secret ruling power. Papen seemed not more than a proxy; he sat half invisible in his chancellery; his weak, strained voice over the radio made people think of a little man standing on tiptoes. What they saw were the bands of the S.A. men, protected by the police, and the Junkers plane descending from the clouds.

And yet — these intimidated masses did not give Hitler a majority in the elections of July 31. The Social Democrats lost a little, but the Communists regained more, almost doubling their strength; and the Catholic Center with its working masses remained unscarred. True, the old middle-of-the-road bourgeois parties which had formerly been so strong, among them the party of the late Gustav Stresemann, vanished almost entirely. Hugenberg's German Nationalists, who alone supported the cabinet of the barons, had hardly a trickle of the people behind them — unless the two and a half million voters who sent forty German Nationalist deputies to the Reichstag could be called 'people.' The fragments of the shattered bourgeois parties now piled up like a mountain beneath Hitler's feet. But the mountain was neither firm nor high enough. Hitler occupied a large sector of parliament, with two hundred and thirty out of a total of six hundred and seven members; no one was stronger than he. But he was far from being stronger than all together. The elections had the same monotonous outcome that had been repeated for years: the majority was *against* Hitler, but it was *for* nothing at all.

'Der Führer is faced with grave decisions,' wrote Goebbels in his diary two days after the apparently overwhelming victory. 'Should he proceed legally? With the Center? . . .' For the Center alone could give him the majority he lacked. By the Tegernsee, in a charming mountain region south of Munich, Hitler and his henchmen held anxious deliberations on the consequences of their dangerously incomplete victory. 'Der Führer is deliberating with us,' Goebbels reports, 'but' — and this is the way he is doing things — 'he has come to no final conclusion. The situation must first ripen. At any rate, the party must not shrink back from grave decisions. Something must happen.'

Only one thing must happen: Hitler had to be definitely victorious. In the eyes of the German people, he was committed to swift, complete success, otherwise it would be the end of him. 'In Berlin we have lost a little due to the Red campaign of lies,' wrote Goebbels in his diary on the night of the elections. 'Inference: we must take power!' And if the National Socialists did not take power within a reasonable time, they could speak to the hearts of the enormous audiences and be allegedly a thousand times in the right against an allegedly unjust government — there would be no further purpose in voting for them. Hitler had trained his electorate in cynicism; now came the cynical answer.

The S.A. men whetted their long knives — and this almost literally. Hitler and his sub-leaders had openly assured the Brown People's Army that on the day of their seizure of power they would 'clean the streets' (Strasser); that they would 'reckon with their enemies, an eye for an eye and a tooth for a tooth' (Röhm); a few thousand Marxists 'would meet their doom' (Frick). Many had again hoped for a decisive election victory, had expected election day to be the day of the knife. In Königsberg the S.A. threw bombs into a Social Democratic newspaper building on election day, and a raging Brown-shirted band shot down two Communists in the street. Goebbels wrote in his diary: 'This is the only means of bringing the Reds to reason; nothing else impresses them any more.'

To invent, to stir up and then to shoot down the 'red peril' was the simple secret of power for him who sets out to become dictator by democracy; as Louis Bonaparte, later Napoleon III, had shown eighty years before. After becoming President of the French Republic by 'outwardly legal means' (as Scheubner Richter later put it), he had secured the favor of the generals, telling them that they 'were the hope and salvation of menaced society'; he had placed his creatures in the key positions of power; accused his opponents of arming to occupy the police and administration buildings. When the Chamber rejected a law he had proposed, he declared it dissolved on December 2, 1851 — and this was exactly Hitler's plan: 'If the Reichstag rejects an enabling law demanded by Der Führer, it will be sent home,' writes Goebbels. In order that he might prove that he was saving his country from a great danger, Louis Bonaparte had sent thirty thousand soldiers through the capital, had them fire on the people — and now local revolts did flare up in a few departments. The dictator proclaimed that this was 'Communist revolution,' declared a state of emergency, had some twenty-seven thousand people arrested, ten thousand deported to Africa, a few hundred to Cayenne, and had others interned or banished. Then he staged a plebiscite; of 8.12 million voters, 7.48 confirmed him as president — dictator — for ten years. The Wise Men of Zion had this *coup* in mind when they said that the people admires great acts of villainy.

On August 5, Hitler went to Berlin, talked with Schleicher, demanded to be made Chancellor and also Premier of Prussia. He boasted that he would be able to wrestle a majority from the Reichstag, 'like Mussolini in 1922.' This was exactly what Schleicher wanted, and he seems to have answered: If Hitler could gain a majority, nobody could and would prevent him from governing. Hitler, who, when excited, never was a good listener, believed that Schleicher had promised to 'make' him Chancellor; well satisfied, he returned to Munich, and Goebbel's diary, not for the first time, shows a suspicion that his Führer again might have been duped.

The party was in a fever of anticipation. Röhm ordered a state of alarm for the S.A., stationed strong troops in the headquarters so that hundreds of thousands could be mobilized within an hour. 'The whole party,' Goebbels reports, 'has prepared itself to take power. The S.A. men are leaving their places of work in order to make themselves ready.' And the other great and small functionaries of the party 'are preparing for the great hour' — the great hour of mass murder. 'If things go well,' sighed Goebbels in his diary, 'everything is in order. But if things go badly' — that is, if Hitler does not become Chancellor and there is no blood-bath — 'there will be a terrible setback.'

The smell of revolution was in the air. Almost hourly, news reached Berlin of new murders committed by National Socialists, particularly in the eastern parts of the Reich; and the opposing side, the 'Iron Front' and the Communists, also shed blood. The Reich government declared martial law; providing summary justice and the death penalty even for lesser acts of violence. That was at noon of August 9. In the night of the same day, in the village of Potempa in Upper Silesia, five National Socialists armed with revolvers entered the house of a Communist miner by the name of Konrad Pietrzuch; the whole family — Pietrzuch, his mother, and his brother — were in bed; the five pulled Pietrzuch out of bed, threw him to the floor, and, before the eyes of his mother and brother, beat him and trampled him for half an hour; the heel of a boot fractured his larynx, and he died.

Hitler was back in his house a few hundred yards above Berchtesgaden; he was in good spirits and thought himself near his goal. Then — on August 9 — Strasser and Frick came for a visit and dispelled his illusions. Schleicher had expected a parliamentary government of or with Hitler; now he found himself faced with the specter of a bloody *coup d'état*. Even good friends suddenly became wary. Industry did not want to put economic life at the mercy of such men as Gregor Strasser or Gottfried Feder, who, marching at the head of small property owners incited to revolution, wanted to hurl a bomb at large-scale wealth. Feder announced that the coming Hitler government would create a new form of treasury bills, to be given as credit to innumerable small business men, enabling them to re-employ hundreds of thousands and millions of workers. Would this be inflation? Yes! said Walter Funk, one of the many experts who for the past year or two had advised Hitler; an experienced and well-known finance writer, collaborator of Hjalmar Schacht, and, in Hitler's own eyes, a guaranty that big business would treat him as an equal. Funk, too, arrived on the Obersalzberg with a message from Schacht: important people were so upset by Feder's plans that these threatened to become a serious obstacle on Hitler's road to power.

On August 11, Chaos, in the form of a long column of automobiles, again left Berchtesgaden for Berlin. On the shore of the Chiemsee, with a view of the Alps and a majestic castle that had belonged to the 'mad' King of Bavaria, the company paused at an inn for rest. Hitler sat with Strasser, Frick, Goebbels, and others, and for the last time they calculated the chances. Should they govern with the Center? This seemed a good threat against Hindenburg if he was not ready to appoint Hitler dictator with full powers. But the truth was that seriously they could have done nothing with the Center. This moderate party would not consent to the long adjournment of the Reichstag, and even less to the projected blood-bath. The blood-bath had gradually become the main point in Hitler's plans. Eating a big omelet, he declared to his henchmen: 'If we are not given an opportunity to settle accounts with Marxism, it is perfectly useless for us to take power.'

Most of the sub-leaders then went on to Berlin by train. Hitler followed slowly by car. Announcing his Führer, Röhm, on August 12, went to see Schleicher and Papen. He spoke calmly, as man to man, inquiring as to their intentions. Had Hitler misunderstood?

Who was going to be Chancellor? Perhaps Hitler had misunderstood; Röhm was reminded that his Führer had given his word of honor at least to 'tolerate' the Papen government.

Late at night Hitler arrived; he lodged at Goebbels's summer villa near the village of Caputh, and conferred with Goebbels, Röhm, and Göring. A strategic plan followed for two years was slipping through their fingers. They were now the strongest party, but not strong enough for their own devious brand of democracy aiming at dictatorship. Now the question was: Could they resist the temptations of a brilliant defeat? Schleicher, eager to build up a synthetic popularity for Papen, who cared little for popularity, offered the National Socialists high offices, apparent key positions: the vice-chancellorship, the premiership of Prussia, provincial presidencies and mayoralties; this would take care of thousands of careerists with the swastika over or under their lapels. Did the party have the moral strength to continue an uncertain struggle for full victory? Was it not better to accept the bribe: a piece of power, a share in the offices and state salaries, some access to the state treasury, some relief from the nightmare of an indebtedness running to twelve millions?

'All evening,' Goebbels relates, 'Der Führer has been striding up and down the room and the terrace outside. A visible conflict is going on inside him. The decision which must be made tomorrow has immense implications. It is being pondered carefully from all sides. . . . ' In situations of this sort, Hitler had demonstrated greatness of will — this should not be denied. He has often been mistaken in his appraisal of circumstances; he has ventured the falsest interpretations and the most frivolous prophecies; at times he has acted with astonishing lack of judgment; but in August, 1932, he knew exactly how much he could risk — and yet he risked more. The situation, he often repeated in those days, was not yet ripe; blows and failures had not yet sufficiently taught the opposing side — the state power, the Reichswehr, the President — that their edifice was bound to collapse without National Socialist aid. Nine years before, Hitler had proclaimed that the decisive struggle between Swastika and Soviet Star would bring him to power; this would be his great hour. It almost literally cost him his head that he was unwilling to waste this hour in bargaining for fragments of power; but in the end the risk brought him his great triumph.

On the morning of August 13, Hitler, Röhm, and Frick went to see Schleicher. A wild argument broke out, and was continued in the presence of Papen; insulted and enraged, scarcely letting the others say a word or listening when they did speak, Hitler loudly explained why he insisted on full power and a free hand. He had given the same reasons, almost with the same words, to the Munich court in 1924: The great thing for him was not to become minister — so he said — but to break Marxism. In his long, deafening outburst he made ample use of such words as 'mow down,' 'Saint Bartholomew's Night'; for three days 'the S.A. must have freedom of the streets.' He is reported to have declared that he counted on five thousand dead.

Hitler's outburst seems to have made a terrible impression on Papen and Schleicher; Schleicher said later that he doubted Hitler's sanity. Perhaps Hitler expected to set the minds of Papen and Schleicher at rest when he said that what he was proposing was far from a National Socialist dictatorship. He desired neither the Reichswehr nor the foreign ministry; he desired 'only as much power as Mussolini took in his *coup d'état* of 1922.' Mussolini had had non-Fascists in his cabinet; but Papen and Schleicher, who had not studied the history of *coups d'état* as thoroughly as had Hitler, misunderstood; they believed that he wanted to govern alone and without them — and basically they were right.

It was the will of Hindenburg, and even more of Schleicher, to create a government which would at least be tolerated by the Reichstag. Since Hitler had made no attempt to 'bring' them the Reichstag, they could offer him no more than the post of Vice-Chancellor in the Papen cabinet, the Prussian Ministry of the Interior and similar posts; nothing was asked in return except that he keep his promise and help to give the Papen government a majority which would have to be completed with help from other sides.

Bursting with rage and disappointment, Hitler drove to Goebbels's Berlin home with Röhm and Frick, and there he gave his nerves free play. His failure to obtain power had not been a complete surprise to him; but that they should have lured him to a conference and humiliated him by such absurd offers — that was too much. And the cruel events of that day were not yet ended. Thoughtlessly Hitler, six weeks before, had given Hindenburg his word to support Papen. Now the old man insisted that Hitler appear before him. The telephone rang; Frick answered; Papen's aide, State Secretary Erwin Planck, asked him to tell Herr Hitler that the President expected him at four in the afternoon. Frick shouted back, what would be the use of it? The decision, he shouted in an accusing tone, had already been made — he meant, 'by your side.' Planck answered that no decision had been made — he meant probably that Hindenburg refused to accept officially Hitler's going back on his promise as long as he had not heard it from him himself, and in his own words. Hitler came, escorted by Röhm and Frick. Hindenburg had a horror of Röhm and little sympathy for Hitler; he received the three standing, leaning on his cane; a man of eighty-five, he forced himself to undergo this discomfort in order to make the quarter of an hour as painful as possible for his visitors under the coldly staring eyes of the onlookers: Oskar von Hindenburg, Meissner, Papen, and Schleicher.

Hindenburg began the conversation abruptly: 'Herr Hitler, I have only one question to address to you: Are you prepared to offer me your collaboration in the Papen cabinet?' Hitler was so humiliated that he could scarcely speak; he muttered that he had already named his terms to Papen and Schleicher. Hindenburg, rather pleased that things were as he had imagined: 'So you want the whole power?' Hitler, almost in a whisper: Only as much as Mussolini . . . Hindenburg, too, misunderstood about Mussolini, but was right, nevertheless: That, he said triumphantly, meant the whole power. The official communiqué on the interview continues that Hindenburg 'definitely rejected Herr Hitler's demands, stating that his conscience and his duties to the fatherland could not permit him to give the entire governing power exclusively to the National Socialist Movement, which wished to make one-sided use of it.' If the fight must continue, Hindenburg went on, he would request Herr Hitler at least to conduct it chivalrously. Then the blow fell, the sharp blame for not keeping his word: Hindenburg, said the communiqué, 'regretted that Herr Hitler did not see himself in a position to support a national government appointed with the confidence of the Herr Reichs President, as he had agreed to do, before the Reichstag elections.' Large parts of the German public had felt for months that Hindenburg himself had broken faith with Brüning; the exiled Kaiser in his Dutch exile likewise felt deceived and forsaken by his field marshal. The marshal himself has been convinced since August 13, 1932, that Hitler was not a man of his word.

The whole interview had taken less than ten minutes.

Hitler's almost unerring feeling for the significance of great events in his life was expressed in the emotion with which he received Hindenburg's rebuff. The defeat in the presidential elections did not break him; the ten minutes' talk with Hindenburg did. Before the eyes of the German people, he had mounted the steps of the President's palace, the steps to power; before the eyes of the people, he had slunk down them. He had thirteen million votes behind him, and he was helpless against an old man who had to lean on a stick and was no longer able to concentrate his thoughts for more than a few minutes. But these few minutes had been enough to stop a so-called national revolution which by its own definition was impossible without 'the permission of the President.'

Chapter XX

THE RACE WITH

CATASTROPHE

'GREAT HOPELESSNESS REIGNS AMONG THE PARTY comrades. The S.A. is desperate,' wrote Goebbels in his diary the next day. Hitler's failure struck the Uprooted and Disinherited personally, in their most private sensibilities. It meant no state power, no state treasury, no state jobs. For the numerous administrators of party homes, the S.A. kitchens, the uniform factories, it meant creditors in terror of losing their money, rude reminders, expired notes; for the party as a whole, with all its subsidiary organizations, it meant the menace of a bankruptcy to the amount of twelve millions; for thousands of employees it meant starvation sooner or later.

For some it meant the executioner's axe. A special court sentenced the five murderers of Potempa to death, in strict accordance with the law. Hitler sent the five who had trampled a man to death before the eyes of his own mother a telegram beginning with the words: 'My comrades! In the face of this most hideous blood sentence, I feel myself bound with you in unlimited loyalty . . .' The five murderers, he said, had his picture hanging in their cells; how then could he forsake them? 'In our movement, comradeship does not cease when someone makes a mistake.' Moreover, the murdered man had been a Communist and a Pole, hence an enemy of Germany, and 'anyone who struggles, lives, fights, and, if need be, dies for Germany, has all the right on his side; and anyone who turns against Germany has no rights.'

Hitler had landed in one of those situations where every gun goes off backward, where bombs explode in the hands of the thrower, and the trapper steps into his own traps. He got a sharp answer from Papen: Hitler, the Chancellor cried, did not have 'the right to regard the minority in Germany that follows his banner as alone representing the German nation, and to treat all other national comrades as free game.' He continued: 'I shall, if necessary, force recognition of the equal justice that is the right of all German citizens. I am firmly resolved to stamp out the smouldering flame of civil war.' Papen could say that because the flame began to lack fuel.

If it is true that prosperity and depression follow each other in a nine-year cycle, then the time for prosperity had come again. The bottom of the depression had been hit in the summer and early fall of 1923; in late fall the recovery had begun; in vain Hitler had tried at that time to save the chaos which he had helped to create. And now again, in the fall of 1932 there were the first signs of recovery; reports that in some industries there were more orders and more work to do; and these signs appeared exactly after the first signs of Hitler's forthcoming decline. The burden of international political debts had practically vanished; it had become clear that there would be no war or warlike attempts to save the tottering structure of the Versailles Treaty; Germany in particular was confident that the specter of reparations was definitely gone.

Papen, with all his faults a man of courage, seized the first opportunity with a bold hand. Unafraid of unpopularity, he slapped the masses in the face because he firmly believed that this was the only means to help them. To clear the streets of the unemployed, hopeless, lawless, and classless youth, an allegedly 'voluntary' labor service was created, mostly with the help of the Stahlhelm, but neither S.A. nor 'Iron Front' were completely rejected. About 280,000 young men found work, although under hard conditions; for little more remuneration than military board and lodging, they built roads, drained swamps, straightened rivers. Then Papen did what Brüning had been afraid to do: he tried to encourage private enterprise by an artificial state credit, not intimidated by the whispering about 'inflation.' A state 'tax certificate' was devised, which could be used for the payment of future taxes; such certificates, to a total value of seven hundred million marks, were distributed — as a loan — to concerns that engaged new workers, and an additional eight hundred million marks were kept in reserve. For every worker hired, the employer received four hundred marks in the form of tax certificates, and in this way Papen hoped to employ a million and three quarters workers. Finally Papen, with a light heart, dared to do something which no man in his place before or after him did, at least not in this harsh and one-sided way: he permitted every employer who hired unemployed workers, to reduce, as a reward, the wages stipulated in the union contracts and hitherto sanctioned by a state law.

This 'experiment Papen' was jubilantly hailed by the employers and their political representatives: Hugenberg's German Nationalists; it was grimly rejected by almost everybody else, by the trade unions and the political parties of the workers, Social Democrats and Communists; by the Center with its big workers' following; by the National Socialists who would have condemned anything that came from Papen; and finally — and this was decisive — by the Reichswehr, which had struggled during twelve years for the workingman's sympathy. The result was an estrangement between Papen and Schleicher.

But there was one friend who stuck to Papen: old Hindenburg himself. In his eyes Papen was the first chancellor who, for many years, in a difficult situation dared to act and did not lose precious time by thinking things over too thoroughly; this appealed to Hindenburg's soldierly mentality. In his way Papen was more of a soldier than Schleicher, the intriguer and diplomatist with his brilliant skill who sometimes saw difficulties which did not exist at all, only because he found his pleasure in overcoming them by ruse and scheming. His undeniable successes had taken Hindenburg in for a long time; he admired the way the younger man led and fooled the parliamentarians, and got from them what he wanted for the army without allowing them to stick their noses too deep into the Reichswehr business. But the soldier Schleicher had got caught in his own web of intrigues, and through the meshes he had slowly lost sight of the real world and of the whims and wishes of that still powerful old man whom, through many years, he had flattered, pleased and cajoled with seemingly unending success. The old man, firm in his few ideas but fickle in his personal likes and dislikes, slowly began to be annoyed with Schleicher and occasionally went so far as to say that it would not do him any harm if he were to take over again the command of a division in the provinces in order not to forget what a soldier had to look like.

Around this family tragedy between Germany's military men spun the wheel of the greater fate which in these days seemed to swing Hitler downward — perhaps definitely. Outwitted by the junkers, forsaken by heavy industry, not supported even by the Reichswehr in the decisive moment, Hitler had retained hope only in what, in his own judgment, was the most unreliable power of all: the people. 'I am writing an editorial with sharp attacks on the upper crust,' wrote Goebbels on September 4 in his diary. 'If we want to keep the party intact, we must again appeal to the primitive mass instincts' — to the instincts of the 'stupid, lazy, cowardly.' And so Hitler's speeches during the next weeks and months were filled with remarks such as: 'Who is against us? Only a little group of old junkers.' And: 'We have long expected that when things were very bad with the Jews, they would find a few run-down aristocrats to help them.' But 'These old excellencies will not get us down!' Yes, he meant Hindenburg. 'My great adversary, Reichs President von Hindenburg,' he said at a meeting, 'is eighty-five years old today. I am forty-three and feel in the best of health. And nothing will happen to me, for I feel clearly what great tasks Providence has in store for me. By the time I am eighty-five years old, Hindenburg will have been dead a long while.' He meant Hindenburg again, when he said that the revolution of 1918 had come to success only because 'at the head of the nation there were only old men, impotent statesmen, overweening leaders, raised in class arrogance.' He said what most of his armed intellectuals thought; for Röhm, too, meant Hindenburg when he wrote in the *Völkischer Beobachter*: 'The system that was ingloriously overthrown on November 9, 1918, capitulated without manliness in a decisive hour. The soldier who was fighting at the fronts will not forget that this system was not worthy of his sacrifices. With this world, with this society, with this mentality, nothing binds us any longer. It is the object of our hatred and contempt.' And Hitler added: 'I can only say that if in November, 1918, I had had only one army corps under me, the revolution would not have succeeded.'

If, in his few conferences with Hindenburg, he had been able to make this point clear to the old man, perhaps he would not be in the tight spot he was now. True, the field marshal might have understood that National Socialism had the one great aim of making a second November, 1918, impossible; but it was beyond the old man's understanding why mass meetings were necessary for this purpose. And the 'Bohemian corporal' and old Reichswehr spy just was not the type from which Hindenburg would take a lecture. Now Hitler had among his followers some other old generals and colonels who perhaps might be able to do what he was not. They were banded together in a committee for the sole purpose of influencing a dozen generals and colonels in the Reichswehr staff; their leader, Franz von Epp, the man who in bygone times had helped to 'invent' Hitler, was assigned to influence Hindenburg himself. This 'Military-Political Bureau' (*Wehrpolitisches Amt*) was going to make the old generals understand why there had to be a National Socialist Movement: to win 'spiritual domination over the people . . .; to penetrate,' as the program of the new bureau put it, 'the soul of the proletariat'; as a matter of fact, 'only the National Socialist S.A. has succeeded in drawing valuable fighter material from these circles.'

Meanwhile, let nobody fool himself that this new army would be had just for the asking. What was the use that Schleicher clamored in public: 'Germany will do what is necessary for her national defense, whatever happens' — and, 'We shall no longer stand for being treated as a second-class nation'? But it was, in Hitler's opinion, even worse that Papen still chased after his dream of a Franco-German occidental front, a Franco-German understanding that would give Germany her much-coveted army. No wonder that Mussolini became angry and shouted his anger in the face of

Göring, who, at that time, was continuously shuttling between Berlin, Berchtesgaden, and Rome; no wonder that the Italian dictator publicly warned Germany not to demand her right to rearm. Hitler took up this cue. Had not Papen been so foolish even to demand more ships in Geneva — old-fashioned, half-obsolete battleships, good for nothing but to stir up bad feelings in England? Did Papen honestly not realize that the Disarmament Conference was bound to be a failure and that 'the sole concern of German diplomacy must be to make it plain that the blame for the failure of disarmament lay clearly and exclusively with France? . . . This would inevitably have isolated France. But under no circumstances should we have come before the world, or even this conference, with a rearmament program of our own.' For, after all, Germany's rearmament is inevitable; but 'it will not take place in Lausanne or Geneva, but in Germany . . . and it will not lead to an international ratification unless it represents an accomplished fact.' With this sentence, published in an open letter to Papen on October 21, 1932, Hitler announced his policy of 'accomplished facts' which afterward was going to shatter definitely the peace from the lake shores of Switzerland.

But while Hitler reviled Papen because he gambled Germany's best chances away, many of his own faithful accused him of doing the same with the chances of the party. Losses were to be expected in the next elections. Hundreds of Uprooted and Disinherited, who, for a brief period, had been deputies, would again have to go out in search of an uncertain living; and the twelve-million-mark bankruptcy seemed almost inevitable.

As far as is known, the majority of the National Socialist functionaries held this view in the autumn of 1932, and doubted in the wisdom of their Führer. Hitler was supported by Goebbels and Göring. Both were essentially his creatures, picked by him and elevated to leadership, not slowly risen from the ranks; consequently neither had any large personal following among the party masses. The sentiments of these party masses were best known to the man who, as business manager and organizer, had his hands on the sensitive levers of the party machine, who was responsible for it from its *gauleiters* down to its office boys, who gave the orders and could see how they were obeyed — Gregor Strasser. He was joined by Wilhelm Frick, the former Munich police official. Frick had organized National Socialist cells in state and municipal offices; he had covered the state with a network of spies, who now began to doubt if they were serving the party which would soon be in power.

Strasser upheld the interests of the party against Hitler, and to a certain degree the party had its way. Negotiations were taken up with the Center. Hitler was ready for the most humiliating coalition. 'I report to the leader by telephone; he agrees to everything,' Goebbels writes. Hitler met Brüning, who seems to have listened in courteous silence; Hitler felt that Brüning had been 'very compliant.' Perhaps Brüning felt the same. The leaders of the Center, believing that this might be the time to tame the National Socialists and to 'burden' them with responsibility, agreed that they, as the strongest party, might appoint the president of the Reichstag, as custom decreed. Perhaps they expected Hitler to suggest Strasser, but he appointed Göring. For the first time the public attention was drawn to this man, who up till then had stood somewhat in the shade. On August 30 he was elected, over the opposition of the Social Democrats and Communists.

From now on Hitler had his Berlin headquarters in the gilded, red-plush palace opposite the Reichstag that Göring as president was entitled to occupy. Here he invited, ten days later, Kaas, Brüning, Stegerwald, and other leaders of the Center and tried to talk them into a coalition government, with himself as Chancellor, governing with the help of a far-reaching 'enabling law,' free from the control of the parliament for at least one year. Goebbels claims: 'The gentlemen of the Center, who had never seen him before, are, it is clear, quite overcome by his personality.' In reality they went away with the impression that, even if a National Socialist ever could be Chancellor, Hitler personally could not.

For the first time he had tried to find a majority, and he had failed, largely on account of his senseless demands and his terrifying behavior. But one thing remained certain: there could be no majority against him — not in this Reichstag. But what if Hindenburg dissolved the Reichstag; and supposing the new one were

also refractory, what if he dissolved it, too; and then again? Which
would break first: the state or the National Socialist Party? Hitler
and Papen threatened one another with endless overthrows and
endless dissolutions of the Reichstag, and amid these mutual threats
the Reichstag met on September 12. On the morning of this day,
Hindenburg gave his Chancellor a crumpled slip of paper, on which
it was noted in Meissner's handwriting, invoking article 25 of the
constitution, 'I dissolve the Reichstag,' because of the danger that
the Reichstag would suspend Papen's economic decrees. Under-
neath stood Hindenburg's name; in his haste Meissner had written
the wrong date, and then corrected it.

Goebbels had prepared and discussed with Hitler a long speech
attacking Papen; Papen brought with him a statement of the government which he planned to read; but things turned out differently. A Communist stood up and demanded an immediate vote
of no-confidence in the government. If there were no opposition,
the vote would have to be taken immediately. The 230 well-salaried
members in brown shirts were stunned. Fate ran faster than they
had expected; they had been representatives now for six weeks —
and this was probably the end! Frick, amidst laughter, rose, and
obtained a half-hour adjournment. Meanwhile, Hitler — no representative himself — sat across the street in Göring's gilded palace.
The National Socialists rushed across to their Leader and reported
to him. Hitler had been undecided for weeks, but now the decision
came to him in the shape of a dramatic picture. Here was an opportunity for a legal master stroke, at least a great scene which would
make an impression on the entire country. Papen must fall, before
he had a chance to speak and declare the Reichstag dissolved.
Papen saw more or less what was in the offing; in haste he sent to
the Chancellery for the crumpled slip of paper with Hindenburg's
signature; meanwhile Hitler gave Göring — one of the few of his
people he really trusted — his instructions. The house reconvened.
The deputies had no sooner taken their places than Göring, as
president of the chamber, announced a vote on the Communist
motion of no-confidence. Papen, taken by surprise, arose to speak.
Göring ignored him. The voting had begun, he said later, and as
long as it lasted nobody could be allowed to speak. Papen ad-

vanced a few steps; pale and agitated, he set Hindenburg's note on
the table in front of Göring; there was a shuffling of chairs, the
other ministers arose, and the whole cabinet, with Papen at its
head, left the hall. Göring did not so much as look; he proceeded
calmly with his act, and the entire Reichstag, stupefied, angry, or
amused, obediently voted, not knowing that legally it no longer
existed. Five hundred and thirteen votes of nearly all parties were
cast against Papen, only thirty-two for him. Germany had gone on
record against Hindenburg's Chancellor; but Hindenburg, by dissolving the parliament, demanded that Germany reconsider her
vote.

'The Leader is beside himself with joy,' wrote Goebbels. 'Again
he has made a clear, unmistakable decision.' The party did not
share this joy; Strasser and Frick, angry and desperate, predicted
a grave defeat. 'Money is very hard to raise at the moment,' Goebbels reported; no one would give money for an evidently lost cause.
For a moment it seemed as though there might be no more Reichstag. Papen wanted to postpone the elections indefinitely; to force
a new constitution on the country from above; to create a second
parliament in the style of the English Upper House and eliminate
equal suffrage by giving every head of a family two votes, and
three to every family head who had served in the war — but this
was prevented by Schleicher. Nevertheless, the elections were set
for November 6, the latest date allowed by the constitution; by
that time, Papen hoped, his economic laws would have poured forth
their blessings on the German people.

On the day after the dissolution, Hitler assembled his deputies
and gave out the election slogan: 'Against reaction!' His hope was
that the people would rise up for him against the 'Barons.' He
knew the people, he declared in his election speeches, and the people
knew him; 'but five months ago nobody knew Herr von Papen.
. . . I am a child of the people and shall remain one. . . . I am fully
aware that especially the workers in the National Socialist Movement are blindly devoted to it. I shall never betray them and will
never break with the people.'

The 'people' nailed him to his word. A few days before the elections, the Communists paralyzed traffic in Berlin by drawing the

bus and subway employees into a strike; the Brown Shirts joined in the strike in order not to lose votes to the Communists, and Goebbels treated Berlin to a wild revolutionary drama. He dressed some S.A. men as workers and put them to work on street-car tracks; other sham workers stood near-by, reviling them as 'scabs' and threatening them; the police appeared and drove the threateners away. The 'scabs' ripped up the rails under protection of the police who were convinced that the work had been ordered by the transit company. The unions disapproved the hopeless strike; Goebbels cried that the Social Democrats were betraying the workers — just as the Communists had been saying for thirteen years. Bourgeois supporters of the party, especially in the country, took fright; in their election speeches the German Nationalists warned against 'Brown Bolshevism.' At a cabinet session, Schleicher said that if these two radical streams should ever flow together in earnest and turn against the state, the Reichswehr would not be strong enough to resist them.

But the stream was falling. In the elections of July 30, the National Socialists and Communists together had won three hundred and nineteen mandates. When the votes were counted on November 6, they obtained only two hundred and ninety-seven. But of these two hundred and ninety-seven, the Communists alone had a hundred. Alarm spread through Germany. Communism had reached the level at which the National Socialists had first terrified the world in 1930.

But what moved the public even more profoundly was that in these elections Hitler for the first time had been defeated, as all the prophets had predicted. He alone had forced himself to be optimistic, predicted a 'great psychological success.' Now the defeat was at hand. More than two million votes had been lost, thirty-three deputies did not return to the Reichstag; the National Socialist fraction was reduced from 230 to 197.

'A somber mood prevails in the *Gau* of Berlin,' was Goebbels's entry on November 6. 'There is widespread despair among the voters.' The old Strasser party rose up in every corner; Frick, Gottfried Feder, Deputies Kube, Kaufmann, Erich Koch, demanded a policy of concessions; Gregor Strasser publicly stated that Hitler must abandon any idea of the chancellorship.

This was now a foregone conclusion; the National Socialists could not expect more than a 'share' in a future government, as Strasser stated. He bitterly pointed out to his Leader that before the elections the National Socialists in the Reichstag might have formed a majority with the Center; now this possibility was ended, the two parties together were less than half of parliament; Hitler's unfortunate passion for overthrowing governments was responsible. But with the Communists they still had a majority, Hitler replied; no one can govern against us. And that, said Strasser in despair, is what Hitler called 'saving Germany!' 'A growing willingness to compromise,' wrote Goebbels in his diary. True, in public Hitler went on threatening the 'enemy' with 'annihilation'; secretly he admitted that for the moment he had to give in and that one or several of his lieutenants would have to accept the second-rate posts which were offered: vice-chancellorship, government in Prussia, etc. The only question was: Who should be the bearer of the white flag? The party wanted Strasser; just on account of this, Hitler wanted Göring. The rivalry between Strasser and Göring overshadowed for the next two months all other developments in the party; it was a natural rule of the game that the sultan preferred the weaker, therefore, less dangerous figure.

But the opposite side, too, was divided. Schleicher demanded that, whatever happened, Papen must patch together a majority in the new Reichstag. But Papen was profoundly convinced that the days of majorities were over; in this view he was upheld by the only party that supported him in the Reichstag, Hugenberg's German Nationalists, who in the last elections had increased their microscopic strength to fifty votes, and, in a different way, by the Social Democrats who refused so much as to talk to him. The majority which he despised answered by boycott. When Papen tried to straighten out past differences by a conciliatory letter to Hitler, the 'son of the people' answered in a letter full of scorn in which he admitted between the lines that he actually had broken his word that he had given Hindenburg; an oral conversation with the Chancellor was, he wrote, useless.

Hitler hardly expected dramatic consequences from his letter. His lieutenants, all unsuspecting, were far from Berlin. Göring

and Rosenberg had gone to Italy to attend a 'European Congress' of
the Roman Academy of Sciences. At a banquet on November 17,
Göring had the seat of honor beside Mussolini. He was still at
table when word reached him that Papen had resigned.

Pushed by Schleicher, rebuffed by all parties, Papen had performed a master stroke to prove that there was no majority. In accordance with strictly parliamentary procedure, the Leader of the
party that was still strongest was summoned to tell to the President
how he would go about forming a new government. It is strange
that every time Hitler was called to see Hindenburg, Göring was
in foreign parts. On the morning of the eighteenth, Göring saw
Mussolini, and assured him that the Fascist century was about to
begin in Germany. An Italian government plane rushed him to
Venice, where a German machine was awaiting him; in the record
time of six hours he was in Berlin. The next morning he went to
see Meissner, negotiated a worthy form of reception for his Leader,
and when Hitler called on Hindenburg at noon, he was given a
chair and was permitted to speak for a whole hour. This time he
succeeded in arousing the old man's interest, though he could not
convince Hindenburg that the rearmament policy of Papen and
Schleicher was false at this moment; the facts rather argued that it
was correct, for four days after the Reichstag elections, on November 10, Sir John Simon, the British Secretary of Foreign Affairs, had
declared in the House of Commons that England recognized in
principle the German claim to equal military rights. Hindenburg
was greatly pleased and told Hitler that whoever governed, he,
Hindenburg, would choose his Reichswehr Minister and his Foreign Minister, and he himself would determine the policy of these
departments.

Hitler requested that the actual negotiations should take place in
writing. At a second conference on the twenty-first, the two men
sat face to face and read manuscripts. Hindenburg: 'You know that
I favor the idea of a presidial cabinet. By a presidial cabinet I mean
a cabinet that is not led by a party leader, but by a man standing
above parties, and that this man is a person enjoying my special
confidence.' This sounded as if the man enjoying Hindenburg's
special confidence should govern against parliament, but it was

store on a minority grouplet like the German Nationalists, for stubbornly overlooking the will of all big parties to reach a parliamentary understanding with the government. He asked Theodor Leipart, chairman of the Social Democratic trade unions, to call on him. Leipart, a tight-lipped, elderly man with a small pointed beard like many Socialist officials of the elder European generation, came with Wilhelm Eggert, a younger co-worker. Schleicher inquired into their grievances, and both spoke of Papen's attack on the wage contracts, of the recently introduced high tariffs on foodstuffs. Schleicher replied that he, too, disapproved of wage-cuts, regarded the rise in food prices as unfortunate, and held that too much money had been given away to the big landowners. He assured Rudolf Breitscheid, leader of the Social Democrats in the Reichstag, that he desired a functioning parliament. But if the Reichstag were not capable of functioning; if it must be dissolved; and if the Reich government should put off elections indefinitely, then, Schleicher inquired amiably: Would 'the Social Democrats mount the barricades?' Breitscheid answered cautiously: He would not commit himself to the barricades, but the entire working class would act against such a breach of the constitution with all the legal means at their disposal. Schleicher saw nothing very formidable in legal means; from all these conversations he gained the impression that with friendly treatment the parties would listen to reason; even the Social Democrats, even the National Socialists. They would quietly permit individuals among their leaders to enter the cabinet, and for the present would not overthrow the government.

But since Papen definitely was not willing to look for a majority, but instead planned to force upon the country a new, half-feudal constitution, Schleicher, using his authority as leader of the Reichswehr, overthrew him by a palace revolution. At a cabinet session on the morning of December 2, approximately half the ministers declared that they would resign unless Papen himself resigned. Very reluctantly Hindenburg let his favorite go; asked him to remain his private adviser; both agreed that now Schleicher himself must take the responsibility of the chancellorship, since only he, in Papen's skeptically intended words, 'would relax the tension and

avoid a conflict with the Reichstag.' Schleicher would have preferred to govern by a straw man, but Hindenburg and Papen
forced him into the open and explicitly commissioned him to form
a government which would have the Reichstag's confidence. Schleicher was quite unaware of it, but by this act his fate was sealed.

Whom of the National Socialists would he ask to enter his cabinet? For the policy he had in mind it could only be Strasser.
Schleicher made him, in a confidential talk on December 3, the
best offer which the National Socialists in their situation could expect. Strasser was to enter the government as Vice-Chancellor. At
the same time he was to become Premier of Prussia, not appointed
from above by force, but regularly elected by the votes of the
National Socialists and the Center in the Prussian diet. If Strasser
wished, he could administer Schleicher's great re-employment project; the 'voluntary labor service' would be in his hands; he could put
the S.A. in charge of the labor service and burden the state treasury
with its expenses and debts. To be sure, he would have had to find
a basis of understanding with the Social Democratic unions. Strasser
thought well of Theodor Leipart, and the understanding was conceivable.

'We are agreed,' wrote Theodor Leipart at the end of 1932 in a
message to the trade-union functionaries, 'that the ultimate aim of
the working class is the realization of socialism. But you know that
the trade unions were established in order to improve the situation
of the working class in the framework of the present economic
order.' He told a French press correspondent that Schleicher was
really trying to relax the tension with the unions, in order to remove their resistance to his government; hence Schleicher should
not be reproached for his past. If his rearmament speeches had inflamed public opinion in France, said Leipart, the only possible
reply was that Schleicher's demand for equality had only expressed
the view of all Germans.

'Betrayer of the workers!' the Communists shouted back. In a
party proclamation of their own, the Communists, in an effort to
take the wind out of the sails of the Nazis, had declared that the
'fetters of Versailles' must fall. The official Social Democrats, in
turn, condemned Leipart and forced him to make retractions.

Schleicher's government, said a party proclamation of December 5, was a 'one-sided government representing that capitalist economic system the failure of which has become more apparent from day to day.' No statement could have been more ill-advised. But 'only on the basis of this line,' said Breitscheid, 'can we attempt with any hope of success to revive the democratic will of the working masses that have succumbed to all the talk of dictatorship [on the part of Communists].' But the unions, representing a far larger, less political mass than the party, took no part in the opposition. Seventy years before, Ferdinand Lassalle, the founder of the German labor movement, had explained in a correspondence with Bismarck 'that the working class is instinctively inclined toward dictatorship if it can only be convinced that it is exercised in its interests.' Now nearly all the leaders of the trade unions believed, secretly or even openly, that Schleicher's 'dictatorship' would be exercised in the interests of the workers. Schleicher 'has turned successfully back to the people,' said Jakob Kaiser, one of the leaders of the Catholic workers in the Rhineland; 'the assault of reaction has been defeated,' and 'a wave of calm, conciliatory expectancy lies over the working class.' An article in the Social Democratic press, inspired by the trade-union leadership, demanded: 'Allow Schleicher to work! Even an adjournment of the Reichstag . . . no longer frightens us.' And Leipart, despite all the anger of the Social Democratic leaders, stuck to his opinion: 'The one and only thing that we need now is a productive policy, resolute action to improve the situation of the German workers.' 'Schleicher,' he said, 'is attempting to fulfill a part of our demands. This government will not bring us socialism, we are well aware of that. But can we, in this situation, reject the government's call to help in the task of providing employment?'

Gregor Strasser believed that the hour for his great positive contribution to Germany had come. In case Hitler did not comply, Schleicher said he would see to it that the big industrialists gave Hitler no more money. In those days Strasser may well have had the feeling that he had unexpectedly become the Leader of Germany, for he seemed on the point of becoming the leader of the German working class.

On December 3, when Schleicher and Strasser agreed on their plan, new elections in Thuringia had taken place. The result had been a new National Socialist defeat. The party lost up to forty per cent of its votes; this was no longer a slip, it was a crash. To save the party, desperate measures were in order. Hitler sent Göring to Schleicher with instructions to discuss the possibilities of appointing a National Socialist premier in Prussia; but this premier, he insisted, must be Göring and not Strasser. Schleicher had an easy answer: the Center declared that it would approve and vote for Strasser as Prussian premier, but not Göring.

A sordid comedy — this mutual betrayal of the National Socialist leaders! Strasser conspired with Schleicher against Hitler, Hitler with Schleicher against Strasser. But more and more, the unexpressed sentiment in the party was gathering behind Strasser. In vain, Hitler attempted at a meeting on December 5 to inspire his Reichstag deputies with courage. It was not true, he told them, that the party had suffered a defeat in Thuringia — all of them knew that it was only too true. Never, he said, had a great movement achieved victory by taking the road of compromise. The closer the show-down approached, the greater the sacrifices; 'only one thing is decisive: who in this struggle is capable of the last effort, who can put the last battalion in the field.' For the deputies who knew that they themselves would be the sacrifice at the next elections, this was no consolation. 'God save us from having to go through with the next election campaign,' Goebbels had recently written in his diary. On December 6, he noted: 'The situation in the Reich is catastrophic.'

On December 7, Hitler and Strasser met in the Kaiserhof; their conversation ended with mutual threats, reproaches, and accusations of betrayal. Hitler accused Strasser of trying to cheat him out of the chancellorship, and even the party leadership — of trying to split the party. Strasser replied that he had wanted to save the party, but Hitler had disloyally stabbed him in the back. Perhaps he did not say everything he had in his heart; after the conference, he sat down in his room in the Hotel Excelsior across from the Anhalt Station, and wrote Hitler a letter overflowing with the anger that had been gathering within him for years. The letter took up differences that went back to 1925, the beginning of Strasser's collaboration with Hitler; Goebbels was not spared, while Röhm was covered with vilification. Strange was the reproach that Hitler, in order to come to power, was consciously playing with the German catastrophe: for years Strasser had done nothing else. In conclusion, Strasser resigned from the party leadership. This letter reached Hitler the next day, December 8.

It was a 'bombshell' as Goebbels put it. In the Kaiserhof, Hitler met with Frick, Göring, Goebbels, Hess, Doctor Robert Ley, the *gauleiter* of Cologne; Wilhelm Kube, deputy in the Prussian diet. For weeks they had felt their party tottering; and now this blow! Many regarded Strasser as the man who might have saved the party and thought Hitler had prevented him out of injured vanity. Frick openly said as much. Though no great thinker, he was a man of independent mind. Now he rebuked Hitler in the presence of his lieutenants. Strasser, he declared, might be right about many things, and though his letter was a calamity, it was one that could be repaired; Hitler must make his peace with Strasser. Hitler gave in and permitted Frick to drive about Berlin looking for Strasser.

But that morning Strasser had left the Hotel Excelsior; he had checked his suitcase at the Anhalt Station and had vanished. With a friend by the name of Moritz, he sat in a wine room, drinking and cursing Hitler. In Italy the sun was shining, he cried out boisterously, and that was where he was going — with his wife and children. In unprintable terms he predicted that within a month Hitler would come to him crawling.

Meanwhile, Hitler, Göring, and Goebbels racked their brains. Where and with whom was Strasser intriguing now? Was he working out plans with Schleicher? It seemed a bad sign that his friend Frick should be unable to find him. Restless and unnerved, Hitler went to Goebbels's home; here, as Goebbels writes, everyone was 'very depressed, especially because there is now a danger that the whole party will fall apart and all our work will be in vain.'

By this time Strasser had called for his suitcase and had started for his home in Munich. But the bomb rolled on, and where it struck, it burst. While Hitler was sitting with Goebbels in irresolute gloom, an energetic man made vain attempt to save the party on his own responsibility. This was Doctor Robert Ley. He sat with other National Socialist deputies in the Kaiserhof and tried to convince them that Hitler was right while Strasser was in the wrong; he telephoned to the provinces and inquired about the mood. Finally he reached Hitler on the telephone and told him that 'the situation is becoming more acute from hour to hour.' He implored him to come out of his hiding-place since he alone could save something. Meanwhile, a letter arrived from Gottfried Feder resigning his offices and asking for a vacation; he boasted that by his propaganda he had won millions of supporters to the party, but that since Hitler obviously meant to break off this anti-capitalist propaganda and dissolve Feder's economic bureau, millions would drift away in addition to the millions who already had gone.

Hitler now awakened from his lethargy and decided to destroy the mutineers before they could strike. Late that night he went back to the Kaiserhof and dictated a decree, deposing the party leadership. Strasser's state within the state was smashed, the whole machine ready to take power was broken to pieces; it was of no use, anyway, said Hitler, for in the next months the party need concern itself only with one thing, with holding the vanishing voters; all the project-makers in the Brown House would do better to go out into the villages and speak to the people. Ley was set at the head of the organization; his title of 'staff leader' made it clear that he was merely supposed to be Hitler's helper. A 'Central Commission' was set over the party, with the function of supervising the policy of the movement in the provincial diets, to determine such matters as strike policy; the chairman of this mighty new party committee was a man almost unknown in the movement, the Leader's personal friend and private secretary, Rudolf Hess.

But the question remained: Should the party, at the risk of cracking, continue in its struggle against the government? Should it continue to demand the chancellorship for Hitler? Did the mass of party functionaries possess the moral strength to persevere in desperate opposition, if going over to Strasser offered a prospect of becoming ministers, provincial presidents, mayors, superintendents of welfare offices, sergeants in the labor service, or nightwatchmen in some municipal gas works? Hitler knew that his loyal followers in the brown uniform were running by the dozen to government offices and 'Jewish newspapers' to sell so-called party secrets for a few marks.

'The Leader,' writes Goebbels, 'is taking long strides up and down the hotel room. You can see by his face that a great struggle is going on inside him. He is embittered and deeply wounded by this disloyalty. Once he stops still and says only: If the party falls apart, I'll put an end to it all in three minutes with a pistol.'

Finally Hitler reached a decision. By morning it was apparent that he would fight, and 'throw the whole party into the struggle.' Before the opposing side could gather strength for an ultimatum, it would be crushed by a previous ultimatum. A declaration was drawn up, sharply condemning Strasser, full of praise and declarations of loyalty to Hitler. On the following day the sub-leaders would have to sign this statement.

The great surprise of the next day, December 9, was Strasser's unexpected disappearance. Now it was the turn of Strasser's friends to be dismayed; they were abandoned and had no idea what to do. The statement condemning Strasser was submitted to them, and nearly all of them signed it. Gottfried Feder, one of Hitler's few remaining intimate friends, refused: 'Either you sign or you'll be kicked out of the party,' cried Hitler. Feder signed. In the afternoon Hitler assembled his deputies and *gauleiters* in Göring's palace; he spoke with tears in his voice, related how Strasser had always rebelled against him and for years had contested his authority as Leader; but this last betrayal! 'Never would I have believed that of Strasser!' he cried, laid his head on the table and sobbed. Many of those present began to weep with him. The tears ran down Göring's cheeks, and Goebbels brandished a big white handkerchief; from a modest place in the background Julius Streicher, who for years had been humiliated by Strasser, cried: 'Maddening that Strasser could do this to our Leader!' On the evening after this success, Hitler 'looked quite happy and exalted again.' The demonstration of faith, as Goebbels put it, had 'encouraged and strengthened the indomitable man.'

It was decided that Hitler should travel around the country and have confidential talks with the functionaries and S.A. men. Göring, Ley, and Goebbels would do the same. They set out; their reception was not always friendly. 'A heavy depression prevails in the organization,' wrote Goebbels in his diary. 'The sentiment among the party membership is still divided,' he finds on December 10. 'It costs us no end of effort to keep the S.A. and the party administration on a clear course [December 15] . . .' Occasionally he reports that he has been successful in 'lifting up' the mood of a meeting; but this was not always the case. On December 17, Hitler addressed his functionaries in Halle. Only his will counted in the party, he shouted; then he bade each one of them give him his hand and swear loyalty. While those in the front rows were giving him their hands, fighting broke out in the back of the room; men were knocked down, rebellious S.A. and S.S. men shouted that the comedy should be stopped. In these speeches, Hitler did not strike a very convincing tone: 'Perhaps our enemies did give us a numerical setback in the last Reichstag elections, but next year we shall pay them back with interest and compound interest. . . .' In three months the catastrophe would be at hand: 'I think that in March we shall again face these gentry in open battle. By then we shall have created the necessary conditions and the guaranty that our blade will be sharp.'

But at first this timorous hope in the misfortune of the fatherland was bitterly disappointed. Hitler's prophecies, that without him no German government could accomplish anything in foreign affairs, again turned out to be false. After the MacDonald cabinet in England had decided for Germany's right to equality in armaments, Paul-Boncour, now French Foreign Minister, made it plain that France would break with England under no circumstances and that no German-English front must arise. The result was a great moral success for the Schleicher government. On December 6, the Disarmament Conference reconvened in Geneva. Again Germany was represented. On December 11, Germany, Italy, France, England, and the United States agreed 'that one of the principles that should guide the conference on disarmament should be to grant Germany and the other powers, disarmed by treaty, equality of rights in a system that would provide security for all nations, and that the principle should itself be embodied in a convention containing the conclusions of the Disarmament Conference.' True, this was only a declaration of principle; the statement also stipulated that France must receive some guaranties of security, to compensate her and relieve her fears. For Germany the declaration represented no material gain like the evacuation of the Rhineland in 1930, the cancellation of reparations in 1932; wherein the equality should consist, and how soon it should be realized, was not said. But for the world that takes principles seriously, this was the most brilliant satisfaction that Germany had received since 1919. The victors of Versailles had given the Reichswehr general what they had denied the democratic ministers of the German Republic.

At home, too, Schleicher began his government with an almost effortless success. Papen had been overthrown at once by his Reichstag; but no one dared or desired to overthrow Schleicher. The German Nationalists expected him to provide a powerful dictatorship; the Center hoped that he would restore parliamentarianism; the Social Democrats did not wish to do anything that might halt the disintegration of the National Socialists; hence none of them wanted to overthrow Schleicher. Not even the National Socialists. 'Whatever happens, no elections — we need a breathing spell!' wrote Goebbels in his diary. The Reichstag made an important decision: Papen's wage-cutting decree must be suspended. Schleicher was delighted, and of his own accord withdrew all Papen's other attacks on the wage laws. Then the Reichstag adjourned without demanding a program of the government, without any expression of confidence or no-confidence. The parliament voluntarily gave Schleicher a free hand. Meanwhile, with cautiously chosen words, the leading representative of German industry declared that the depression was slowly vanishing; Doctor Krupp von Bohlen und Halbach, chairman of the Reich Association of German Industry, said on December 14 at a session of the leading committee of the organization: ' . . . The world economic situation, in the money market and above all the raw-material market, shows signs of an improvement; the low point seems definitely past.'

The chaos was lifting; slowly, but at many points. Desperately Hitler tried, in secret negotiations, to save what he could. Göring again and again had his talks with Schleicher about Prussia; no result. True, behind the curtain of these political conversations, the door to Hindenburg's private study had opened to Göring. The questions that the old marshal wished to discuss with the former air force captain were not strictly political. He was curious to know how much benefit could be expected of the S.A. in case Germany should build up a large army; or rather, as Schleicher planned it, a 'militia' around the nucleus of the professional Reichswehr. Werner von Blomberg, a general little known to the public, worked out plans for this militia; served as an expert adviser to the German delegation at the Disarmament Conference in Geneva; personally kept Hindenburg informed of developments. In Berlin, Göring, Blomberg, Franz von Epp, in the presence or at least with the knowledge of Hindenburg, discussed the dividing lines between army and S.A., and later events indicate that an understanding was achieved. Röhm had no share in these talks.

But this was far from an understanding concerning the political leadership of the Reich. The nation had a deep desire for peace at home — and Schleicher seemed to bring the peace. This was the darkest Christmas Hitler had had in years. In Italy, Roberto Farinacci, former general secretary of the Fascist Party, leader of the radical, anti-Semitic tendency in the Fascist Movement, wrote in his newspaper, *Regime Fascista,* that Hitler was on the down grade; that he had played his cards wrong, as was only understandable, for the National Socialists despite their claims were no revolutionaries, but peaceful citizens who had missed every favorable moment for striking.

The entries in Goebbels's diary at this time read like a confirmation of the Italian judgment. Goebbels, an outwardly excitable but inwardly cold temperament, dramatizes the feelings of the party masses at this period; he was doubtless a good observer and a good actor. From December 8 to December 23, he writes: 'All of us are in a very depressed mood. We are so sore inside that we desire nothing more fervently than to flee for a few weeks from the whole mess. . . . It is high time for us to come to power. If we succeed in keeping the movement together, we will also succeed in saving the situation. . . . We must muster all our strength to put the organization on its feet again. . . . There is a great deal of wrangling and dissension in the party. . . . We must cut salaries in the *Gau,* or else we won't get by financially. . . .' And one day before Christmas: 'The most terrible loneliness is descending on me like dark hopelessness.'

Chapter XXI

CHANCELLOR AT LAST

ON NEW YEAR'S DAY, HINDENBURG RECEIVED Schleicher and his ministers and expressed his pleasure that 'the gravest hardships are overcome and the upward path is now open to us.'

The waters had stopped rising; they will fall, said the economists. We cannot wait, answered the politician. We must consider the mood of the masses, said Schleicher: to combat their distress, 'dikes must be built into economic life, even if they are not a hundred per cent in agreement with the laws of economic reason.' He said this in a kind of 'fireside chat' over the radio on December 15, 1932. 'My heretical view is that I am a supporter neither of capitalism nor of socialism. For me concepts like private economy or planned economy have lost their terrors.' He even had no respect for the holy property of the big landowners in the East; 'settlement of peasants,' said he, 'must proceed more rapidly than before'; on about eight hundred thousand acres of land he wanted to build twenty-five thousand small and medium farms, and these figures 'could be increased considerably.'

The old 'isms' were no longer valid. Hindenburg's youthful friend, Guenther Gereke, as 'commissar for re-employment,' started a big program of public works with no less than one billion marks. Stop! cried Krupp grimly, that is inflation! 'No government acting this way could escape the moral responsibility if the present beginnings of an improvement should be destroyed by a wave of distrust.' Industry finally forced Schleicher to abandon his program for spending a billion, and for the present only half a billion was allotted for re-employment.

While the laws of economic reason were bringing about slow and hesitant upswinging, the elements played a strange trick on the German economy: a mild winter and an abundant harvest. The mild winter was a hard blow to coal-mining, a branch of industry which had long been struggling against a sick domestic market. Doctor Paul Silverberg, chairman of the Rhenish Board of Industry and Commerce, himself a coal man, spoke at the beginning of January with great confidence of the economic revival in the Rhineland: ' . . . Indubitably a better mood and increased confidence have made their appearance. More and more voices in industry and economic life are speaking of increasing employment and a growing market. . . . The iron industry can register an improvement; the domestic market is reviving somewhat and the foreign market is also becoming steadier. The same is true of the machine and textile industries. . . .' There was only one dark spot in the picture: the coal business, said Silverberg, 'in consequence of the mild winter, has not kept step.'

At the same time German agriculture groaned beneath the weight of a mammoth harvest such as Germany had not witnessed for decades. A mockery of Fate in this winter of starvation! A surplus of grain, of potatoes, even of meat, milk and butter — and on the other side, unemployed people without money, insufficient demand, crashing prices. For half a century Germany's military leaders had been insisting that the country must be in a position to feed itself like a 'besieged fortress,' without imports. Now Germany's peasants and big landowners had achieved this historic feat for the first time, and they were pale with fear. 'After decades of bitter struggle,' said Baron von Braun, the Minister of Food Supply, 'German agriculture has succeeded in meeting its own breadstuff requirements, an idea which formerly would have been regarded as utterly Utopian. Likewise in meat production, increases have been achieved which would formerly have been considered impossible.' To a country with more than its share of starvation, the minister spoke of this blessing as of some devastating enemy army that must be defeated by all possible means: grain production, he said, must be limited, in order to obtain 'healthy prices'; by the purchase of one hundred and ten thousand tons of potato flakes, by a law ordering the mixture of potato spirits with gasoline, and by similar measures, 'the assault of the record potato harvest may have been repelled at least in part.'

The coal miners complained because Germany was not freezing, and nearly the whole farming population felt embittered and hopeless because there was too much to eat. Schleicher does not seem to have fathomed the full seriousness of this discontent. It came as a great surprise to him when a spark from abroad caused the whole rebellious mixture to explode.

The decisions of Ottawa were beginning to inflame Europe. The new Empire tariffs forced Danish butter out of England; desperate Danish producers now threw their butter on the German market at dumping prices, and in December, 1932, German butter prices quickly fell to a new and unexpected low. In the last years German agriculture had stepped up its butter production; and so Germany now suffered from a surplus of butter in addition to grain and potatoes. This caused the profoundest hardship to German agriculture, for it largely affected small and medium farms. The Schleicher government was unwilling to bar Danish butter, for fear of driving the Danes to counter-measures against German industrial exports. Instead, it thought up a remarkable way of relieving the distress of the butter producers. It persuaded margarine producers to mix fifteen thousand tons of the finest Danish butter with their product each year. The butter producers were not at all pleased with this secret improvement of margarine, for they feared that margarine would become so good that consumers would cease to buy any butter at all. They loudly demanded that Schleicher should bar Danish butter from Germany as Papen had planned to do; and when Schleicher refused, the butter producers gave the danger signal to the whole of agriculture by declaring that Schleicher was hostile to farming interests. Toward the end of the year the League for the Defense of Peasant Interests (*Interessenverband der Bauern*) in Württemberg declared in 'boundless indignation' that agriculture, the most important occupational group, was being sacrificed to a 'more than senseless export fanaticism'; the league threatened that 'despair and hopelessness will drive the peasants to measures of self-help which run counter to the needs of people and state.' This incendiary cry did not come from big landowners, but from small peasants, and similar voices, proclaiming 'the sharpest struggle against the Reich government,' were heard from the dairy farmers in West and North Germany.

For a moment it looked as if Schleicher would be overthrown as a result of the butter controversy, magnified and exploited by the National Socialists. With the support of considerable numbers of middle and small peasants, they had won a share in the leadership of the *Reichslandbund,* the leading German farm organization. Two of the four leading officers were National Socialists, Vice-President Werner Willikens and Director von Sybel. Under their pressure, the *Reichslandbund* decided to present Hindenburg publicly with a demand for Schleicher's dismissal; against the will of the president, Count Eberhard Kalckreuth, a memorandum was drawn up, stating that the misery of agriculture, especially in the field of peasant processing (butter, cheese), had, 'with the toleration of the present government,' assumed dimensions 'which would not have been thought possible even under a purely Marxist régime,' and that 'agriculture was being plundered for the benefit of the almighty moneybag interests of the international-minded export industry and its henchmen.' The memorandum demanded a foreign trade war and measures to relieve agriculture of its interest and debt payments. Foreclosures of bankrupt farms must be stopped — this demand was raised especially by the large East Prussian landowners. There already was an 'anti-foreclosure law,' but the landowners wanted it strengthened and extended.

With this paper in hand, the four leaders of the *Landbund,* Sybel and Willikens in the lead, called on Hindenburg on January 11. Hindenburg was always accessible to complaints on the part of agriculture. He sent for Schleicher and instructed him to give the agricultural problem further study. Schleicher was prepared to look into the matter. Hindenburg left the room, Sybel gave Schleicher the paper with its violent attacks. Schleicher, who as a soldier did not take strong words very seriously, said comfortably: 'But, children, you can't say such things'; then he promised relief, better protection for the dairy farmers and stronger measures against foreclosures.

He apparently thought that he had talked the farmers out of their political attack. But they had previously given their statement to the press, and it was published. Now Schleicher answered sharply that the government would do what was necessary for the protection of agriculture, but it would have no further dealings with the leaders of the *Reichslandbund*. Hindenburg also declared that if he had known in advance of the *Landbund's* rude public attack, he would not have received its leaders. Schleicher informed the German public how the decisions of Ottawa had shaken the German butter market, and added that the small peasants were much harder hit than the big landowners. He satisfied Hindenburg by submitting to him an order for the strengthening of the anti-foreclosure laws; a few days later, Hindenburg wrote the *Landbund* that he hoped 'my order extending and broadening the anti-foreclosure laws will serve to pacify agricultural interests.'

While Schleicher with cautious steps had to find his way between these sometimes petty snares of world economics and domestic politics, his most dangerous enemy seemed in swift decay. The National Socialist movement, seen from outside and probably even more from inside, was evidently in full physical and moral disintegration. In the city of Kassel the S.A. had mutinied because it had come to light that their leaders had embezzled and sold food donated by peasants for starving storm troopers; the S.A. men did not mutiny against the embezzlement, however, but because the leadership had been forced to discipline the culprit; for leaders and rank-and-file were both involved in the embezzlement. The guilty leader issued an indignant statement to the effect that S.A. men had informed 'party officials (meaning the *gauleiter* of the Kassel district) outside the S.A.' of the events; they should take note 'that the affairs of the S.A. are absolutely no concern of outsiders,' and anyone who shot off his mouth again would be thrown out. They really did have something to keep secret, for the S.A. leader, in order to cover up the embezzlement, had arranged for subordinates to break into his office and stage a faked burglary.

In the Westphalian town of Volmarstein, the police discovered that the S.A. Home was the headquarters of a band of thieves who committed burglaries all over the region; on one occasion Adolf Hitler's storm troopers had arranged a hold-up with a store cashier. And in several other localities the police discovered that the S.A. barracks were positive robbers' dens, in which stolen goods were stored. In Regensburg in Bavaria, Mairhofer, the National Social-ist *gauleiter,* was sentenced to a month in prison for defrauding the unemployment relief office; Hitler publicly thanked the convicted swindler 'for his self-sacrificing activity in the party'; he was forced to depose him, but promised to 'appoint him to another post in which he could be useful to the movement.' In Dresden, S.A. man Hentsch was murdered in the woods; a National Socialist deputy fled abroad; and it was whispered in the party that other recent killings ascribed to the 'Marxists' could be explained in the same way. The top S.A. leadership maintained, in a secret order of December 8, that the troop was full of Communist stool-pigeons who aimed to provoke the S.A. to perpetrating blood-baths — in other words, whether provoked by Communists or not, blood-baths were in preparation. The German Nationalists were convinced more strongly than ever that this undisciplined, disintegrating troop was what they had always described as Bolshevism.

Were these the noblest and best of the nation, the cream of self-sacrifice and will-power? Challenged, Hitler sometimes answered: 'With us the criminals are better cared for than with the Com-munists'; it was absurd, he said, to expect force to be respectable; it was the mission of National Socialism to transform the dark pas-sions of the masses into strength for the nation; if National Social-ism were destroyed, this force would not be destroyed with it, but would turn against the nation in the form of sub-human criminals and Communists, which were the same thing.

Meanwhile, Strasser had returned from Italy. He sent word to Hitler through Mutschmann, *gauleiter* of Saxony, that he would enter into the Reich government; that he was ready for a recon-ciliation, but only on condition that he become general secretary of the party with virtually unlimited powers. On January 3, he re-sumed his conversations with Schleicher; on the fourth, he was received for the first time by Hindenburg, who listened to him patiently for several hours, though he himself did not say much and may not have been very convinced by the man and his plans.

'We shall not enter into any more negotiations until we have won,' wrote Goebbels about this time in his diary. In the tiny state of Lippe-Detmold in Northwest Germany, a new diet was to be elected on January 15. Hitler decided to fight for Lippe as though it were Germany, at any price to squeeze a success out of this little state. Baron von Oeynhausen, a supporter, granted him the use of an isolated castle in the midst of a lake as headquarters. Hitler traveled around the few square miles of Lippe for ten days, spoke in villages to audiences of a few hundred peasants at most — he who for years had been addressing tens of thousands. This condescension on the part of the famous figure of the time greatly flattered the peasants of Lippe, though, of course, it was a questionable expenditure of Hitler's popularity, like cutting down a forest for the sake of a bird's nest. In this election, the whole vanishing strength of the movement, its remnant of respect and terror, was staked on a fight for ninety thousand votes.

The ultimate aim of all these struggles was only to seem strong for a moment, in order to obtain a better peace. There was one member of Hitler's political family, little noticed then, who never wearied of describing to anyone willing to listen the quietness, gentleness, moderation, legality of a future National Socialist government. The radicalism ascribed to the movement had long been discarded, he maintained; the movement did not give free rein to its radical elements, but held them in check; he pointed out that the Leader had virtually stopped mentioning the Jewish question in his speeches; for practical purposes, the movement had outgrown the anti-Semitism of its early days. And a number of Jewish businessmen were impressed to hear this from Hitler's associate and translator, Joachim Ribbentrop, by adoption von Ribbentrop.

Ribbentrop, former officer, since the war a good friend of Papen, since 1931 a supporter of Hitler, for whom he often translated English newspaper articles, was made by nature and conviction to be the messenger of peace between the two. Why Papen desired this peace is not the riddle which sensationalists have tried to solve by such explanations as envy of Schleicher, desire to avenge himself on the man who had overthrown him, uncontrollable lust for power. By the dark winter of 1932, the primitive delight in power of most German politicians had long since turned to terror. That is why the Social Democratic leaders, resigned and weary, had allowed themselves to be forced out of their positions of power in Prussia with an indifference which would have been unthinkable five years before; Groener had abandoned his post full of disgust; Brüning had tragically accepted the fact that one day he would have to cede his place to Hitler. The misery of the nation, the disintegration of society, destroyed the confidence and energy of most men; cynicism, herald of all world twilights, had a greater share in the political commissions and omissions of the day than any calculation or lust for power.

Unofficially, Papen, the dismissed Chancellor, remained Hindenburg's adviser. The old man requested him to remain near him; and so Papen, though a private citizen, still retained his former official residence in the Chancellery. It so happened that in the winter of 1932-33 alterations were being made in Hindenburg's adjacent palace; and so the old man moved into the Chancellery for a time. Hindenburg and Papen lived door by door; with Oskar von Hindenburg and Meissner they formed a sort of family. One of their chief topics of conversation must have been: What shall we do with the National Socialists? After all, we wanted to educate them, not destroy them. Aren't we missing our opportunity?

Over and over again the idea that National Socialism was rich in demonic force, but poor in brains, beguiled this upper-class type into the arrogant experiment of 'curbing' and 'sifting.' The question was only what should be sifted out and what retained. Formerly Groener had argued with Abegg whether Hitler or Stennes was better. Now that Schleicher wanted to draw Strasser's 'sensible' National Socialists to his side, the question arose whether they were really the 'sensible' ones? It had not yet been proved that Strasser could bring important parts of his party with him; but supposing he could, what kind of men were they? In the National Socialist program it was stated that the trusts must be socialized; Gottfried Feder wanted to abolish capital interest, or reduce it to a minimum, to flood Germany with inflation money; and it was Strasser and his immediate following, his 'economic department' just dissolved by Hitler, that had forced 'socialistic' economic projects on the party. And now these people came and offered Schleicher their collaboration!

'Thank God, we're rid of the radicals . . . the party has become more realistic.' With these words the party's secret propaganda had been trying for some weeks to make the best of the Strasser catastrophe. There was no more talk of revolution against the barons. Only a short time before, Hitler had rudely refused even to speak to Papen. Now Ribbentrop was able to tell Papen that Hitler was extremely eager for an exchange of opinions. False ideas about National Socialist aims must be dispelled. At this moment Papen may well have felt that he had succeeded, that his policy of education had been effective; Hitler was about to let himself be disciplined.

On January 4, 1933, the two men met in Cologne at the house of Baron Kurt von Schroeder, a National Socialist financier, part owner of a banking house with a large share of Jewish capital. Schroeder was one of the bankers of West German heavy industry, with a powerful influence in the distribution of its political slush funds. Göring, who had been on the outs with Papen since the clash in the Reichstag, was absent; tact forbade the presence of Goebbels, the mortal enemy of the barons. Ribbentrop did not seem important enough to attend. On such occasions Hitler chose his escort with extreme care, as though to say: These are the men with whom I shall rule when the time comes. This time he chose Rudolf Hess and Heinrich Himmler, silent men endowed with impressive self-control; but his most important companion was a man totally unknown to the public, the manufacturer Wilhelm Keppler. For some time Hitler had been consulting him in order to avoid the old economic boners in his speeches. Keppler could explain with authority and suitable technical phraseology that it was a gross error to identify the party with every line in the program of the twenty-five points. After all, it was now not Feder, the author of the economic program, who advised the Leader, but he, Keppler; along with Strasser's other planners, the breaker of interest slavery had been shelved. A year earlier, Hitler had spent two hours in

Düsseldorf vainly trying to convince the heavy industrialists of his harmlessness; now he found a simple formulation: as Chancellor he would take full charge of the political sphere, but as for economic affairs, gentlemen — with a glance at Schroeder — that is your province.

The conversation took place at a luncheon. No minutes were kept, and probably there will never be full agreement regarding its substance and results. Even when the talks ended, an hour and a half later, the conclusions were hardly clear, especially as Hitler seldom remembered after such exchanges exactly what he himself, not to mention the others, had said. But one thing is certain: Papen did not — as has been claimed — promise that Hitler would now become Chancellor; he was in no position to do so, nor would he have wished to. The basis of the whole conversation was that Hitler was intensely eager for a compromise and was seeking a face-saving formula for the concessions he was willing to make. The pivotal question was whether Hitler, after all the bitter disappointments he had suffered, was now willing to support a cabinet other than his own. Even earlier, Hitler had been prepared to let Göring accept the premiership of Prussia or even the Reich vice-chancellorship. Though murders were still taking place in the party, Hitler had renounced the blood-bath which he had demanded in August. As late as November, he had been unwilling to let Hindenburg reserve all decisions in foreign and military affairs. Now, in case there should be a chance for him to become Chancellor, he conceded even this point. In any event, the government which he expected to support would probably carry through German rearmament, perhaps with that insane bluntness and lack of diplomacy which Hitler condemned. If this rearmament should bring about grave decisions regarding the fate of the private combat leagues, the supreme S.A. Leader would surely have his word. Therefore, let Hindenburg have his Reichswehr Minister, a general, a specialist, a good friend; if he were also a good friend of Hitler, all concerned could be satisfied. Hitler mentioned the dismissed general, Joachim von Stuelpnagel, until 1930 one of the Reichswehr's 'office generals,' and a bitter enemy of Schleicher. As part owner and editor of the *Berliner Börsenzeitung,* Stuelpnagel was the friend and employer of Hitler's other economic adviser, Walther Funk, disciple of Schacht. The *Börsenzeitung,* founded to serve German stock-exchange interests, had become a mouthpiece of the Reichswehr; it had conducted the press campaign which had overthrown first Groener and then Brüning. If Stuelpnagel became Reichswehr Minister, Hitler would not demand the chancellorship for the present; he would create no difficulties for a Papen government.

Probably Hitler's most important move in Cologne was to come out for a hands-off industry policy. For in those weeks the struggle between state leadership and private initiative was one of the great subjects of German politics. Hitler sat across the table from Papen and repeated what he had said in hundreds of speeches: that of course the creative personality must have free play in the economic sphere as elsewhere; that of course it had to serve the common welfare. A pathetic utterance — its substance, stated in simple terms, was approximately: Let them make plenty of money, then they'll do what we say.

If Hitler got no definite promises at this meeting, he did obtain an important piece of information. Papen told him that Schleicher possessed no signed order for dissolution of the Reichstag, such as he had possessed. For the Schleicher government had been appointed for the express purpose of bringing about a reconciliation with the Reichstag where Papen had failed. If it could save itself only by dissolving the parliament, it had failed in its aim. Hitler had not been quite clear about the parliamentary nature of the Schleicher government; now he was informed.

The Cologne conversation probably saved Hitler from bankruptcy. A consortium of heavy industrialists was formed for the purpose of putting National Socialist finances in order. The most important member of this group was Otto Wolff, an industrial leader who up till then had been close to the moderate parties and whose shift made a strong impression on the business world; Fritz Thyssen was also a member. The sum raised to cover the most pressing obligations cannot have been small; 'finances have also improved very suddenly,' noted Goebbels with satisfaction on January 17.

All the same, the Cologne meeting did not immediately halt the decline of the National Socialist Party; it did not bring the political compromise that was so sorely needed. Schleicher had got wind of the meeting and accused Papen of acting behind his back. Papen replied that, on the contrary, he had been trying to do him a service, that Hitler was now ready for an understanding. But when Papen came out with the suggestion of making Stuelpnagel Reichswehr Minister, Schleicher flatly refused.

And so, from the purely political point of view, Hitler had merely gained the meager knowledge that he could, if he pleased, overthrow Schleicher with the help of the Communists, though the result apparently would be a new Papen government. Meanwhile, the undisciplined party was continuing to crumble away beneath his feet. In the Bavarian province of Franconia, nearly the whole S.A. mutinied, with its group leader Stegmann at its head. The mutineers accused *Gauleiter* Streicher of embezzling funds due to the S.A. leadership, and revealed interesting particulars of Streicher's private life, from his 'nude culture' to his friendships with ex-convicts. Röhm was obliged to return in haste from Capri, where he was spending platonic vacation days with his friend Count Wolf Helldorf. With the help of the new funds, the most dangerous breaches were hastily mended, a number of Stegmann's subordinates were bribed and bought back, and the golden rain that began to fall after the middle of January soon soothed rebellious spirits throughout the country. Whether the calm would last if the party did not soon come to power was uncertain. The speedy fall of Schleicher remained a question of life and death for Hitler.

It still looked as if the National Socialists would scarcely survive the blow of Strasser's entrance into the cabinet. Hitler, Goebbels, and the National Socialist deputy Kerrl were gathered in their castle in the state of Lippe; on January 13, Göring arrived with the terrifying news that Strasser was soon to enter the cabinet; 'only a great success in the Lippe campaign can save us from this dangerous situation,' wrote Goebbels in his diary.

Suddenly another, almost equally dangerous enemy, attacked them in the rear: Hugenberg. The leader of the German Nationalist Party, owner of the largest German newspaper and film trust, was in financial difficulties and wanted to save himself by reaching an understanding with Schleicher and entering his government. This would have strengthened Schleicher immeasurably. Hugenberg wished to become Minister of Economics and Agriculture; he had a plan, the main elements of which were the cessation of payments on Germany's private debts, reduction of interest on agricultural debts, drastic reduction of food imports, increased farm prices. On January 13, he was received by Schleicher, on the fourteenth, by Hindenburg himself. He informed both men that he was determined to enter the cabinet, but that he must be guaranteed a period of years to carry out his plans; Schleicher must persuade the Reichstag to adjourn for at least six months; otherwise he must dissolve it, preferably without setting immediate elections.

On January 15, Schleicher received a visitor from Austria, Kurt von Schuschnigg, then Minister of Justice. As Schuschnigg later related, Schleicher was 'amazingly optimistic about the German situation.' Hitler was finished, said Schleicher to his guest. 'I remember the exact words he used in this connection,' wrote Schuschnigg. 'He said he was engaged in building up a cross-connection through the trade-union movements and hoped in this way to find a new and practicable political platform which would provide a peaceful and healthy development; Hitler was no longer a problem, the question was solved, his movement presented no political danger, it was yesterday's concern. He added — I cannot vouch for the exact wording, but this is the sense — that an attempt at a possible collaboration (with Hitler) had come under discussion, but that the National Socialists had demanded the Reichswehr Ministry, apparently aware that he could not let them have it.' Schuschnigg was surprised; he had not thought political conditions in Germany so stable. But in the afternoon he spoke with Doctor Schreiber, a prelate and leader of the Center Party. 'Here, too, I found surprising economic and political optimism, which made the strongest impression on me.'

But on the same January 15, the elections were held in Lippe, the forest was cut down, the bird's nest seized. Indeed, the National Socialists failed to reach their high-water mark of July, 1932, but they had apparently recovered from the November low, with a rise of approximately 17 per cent (38,000 as against 33,000). True, other parties without much effort had obtained even comparatively greater gains. Stresemann's former party gained 20 per cent and the small democratic party 60 per cent. The Social Democrats, 15 per cent (29,700 as against 25,000). Moreover, this sample of 90,000 voters could not really be called a barometer for the rest of Germany. Yet for Hitler's state of mind it was vital. He had shown that he still knew how to win, and he was able to reckon that Strasser's departure had made no further inroads on the party's strength. 'There can no longer be any question of compromise,' Goebbels suddenly blared forth, hinting at the extent of the concessions Hitler had still been prepared to make in his Cologne conversation with Papen. Strasser 'is sinking back into the nothingness from which he came,' and 'there can be no more mercy. The Leader above all!' Hitler, looking back at the past, began to admit that perhaps he had not done everything correctly; and even so, things had turned out all right. 'I, too,' he said with modesty at a meeting of his functionaries in the Berlin Sportpalast after the elections in Lippe, 'can go wrong and make mistakes. But what counts is, who makes the most mistakes?' The opposing side, he declared, had made the greatest mistake by trying to smash the National Socialist Party.

When Hitler said this, he already knew that Schleicher's plans had been frustrated. The two days, from January 15 to January 17, had changed much. He had not been able to give his government a broad base. 'Never with Hugenberg!' his most loyal followers — the Center — had cried. This was the answer when Schleicher inquired of Prelate Kaas whether Adam Stegerwald, the Catholic labor leader, would not enter his cabinet. Schleicher had expected too many miracles of his diplomacy. His eternal hesitations and conferences, his evasion of any definite decision, finally brought even Strasser to despair. He asked Hitler for a meeting, wanting to find his way back. Göring informed him that Hitler no longer wished to see him.

Slowly, almost invisibly, the weight shifted. Hitler had threatened that with the help of the Communists he would make it impossible for the government to maintain parliamentary rule. Now

he put his threat into effect. Schleicher had publicly and truthfully
declared that Germany was freed from reparations. Thereupon
Alfred Rosenberg drew up a statement, which was submitted on
January 20 to the Reichstag's committee on foreign affairs, where
it was passed by the united majority of National Socialists and
Communists: The committee on foreign affairs declared that Germany was not free; that she was subjected to excessive interest payments; that the Lausanne accord had not been ratified by the
foreign powers; and 'for all these reasons the committee on foreign
affairs [that is, the National Socialist-Communist majority] is of the
opinion that the Chancellor's above-mentioned remarks may give
rise to false ideas at home and abroad, and have therefore not benefited German interests.'

The game which the National Socialists played with the Communists in the last months of their fight for power will always be
remembered as a masterpiece of political strategy. They systematically shattered the political order of Germany by fighting in the
streets with the Communists and collaborating with them in parliament. In the Reichstag they destroyed the basis of all government,
on the streets they destroyed the peace. After their electoral victory
in Lippe, they did everything in their power to arouse and provoke
the Communist menace. They sent the S.A. more systematically
than before into the workers' neighborhoods, the centers of Communist power; they provoked street brawls, ending the lull that had
followed the murder of Potempa, and publicly mourned their dead
as victims of 'Communist murder agitation.' And they did all this
with a party machine which constantly was on the point of falling
apart. Certainly they lacked neither courage nor resourcefulness.

Goebbels tried to prove that the decline of the National Socialist
Party would be the greatest misfortune for middle-class Germany.
'We came,' he said at the beginning of January, 'with twelve million people. If we lost these people, they would be lost to the nation;
they would go over to Bolshevism.' Even Schleicher voiced these
sentiments; through Hans Zehrer, one of his press spokesmen, he
declared that the National Socialist Party must not be allowed to
disintegrate, for if it did, Germany would have ten million Communists the next day.

In order to convince these worried souls that there really was a Communist menace, which only National Socialism could avert, the Berlin S.A. was assembled in the heart of a Communist neighborhood. A gathering of some ten thousand storm troopers in the Bülowplatz, facing the broad façade of the Karl Liebknecht House, Communist Party headquarters, was announced for Sunday, January 22. Near-by lay the Luisenstadt Cemetery where Horst Wessel was buried. The Communists ordered a countermarch at the same hour; the most violent street battle since 1923 seemed inevitable. A responsible government could have done only one thing: forbid both demonstrations. Schleicher, as usual too clever for his own good, reckoned that an impartial measure, striking both sides equally, would put both into a common rage against the government. Perhaps in the hope of maneuvering the two apart, he prohibited only the Communist demonstration, and promised to protect the National Socialists with all possible police measures. It was Schleicher's last important act. Escorted and fenced around by police, the S.A. 'conquered' 'Red Berlin' as the workers so proudly called it. Goebbels, who organized this dress rehearsal for the 'revolution with the Herr President's permission,' describes the scene:

> ... Everywhere armored cars and machine guns. The police have occupied the windows and roofs across the street and are waiting to see what will happen. Outside, in front of the Karl Liebknecht House, stands the S.A., and in the side streets the Commune is fuming in impotent rage. The S.A. is marching. It has victoriously conquered this Red domain. The Bülowplatz is ours. The Communist Party has suffered a terrible defeat. . . . This day is a proud, heroic victory for the S.A.

Surrounded by a heavily armed police cordon, protected by armored cars and machine guns — that was their heroic victory. But when they became a government party, such victories would really begin; armed with the state power, they would frighten the 'Commune' back into its dark streets and win over large masses of workers. With this almost effortless victory of the Bülowplatz, they must have made an impression on the Reichswehr leadership — whoever this leadership was.

Among Hitler's fanatical adherents was Ludwig Müller, the Protestant chaplain of the East Prussian Reichswehr, assigned to the
First Military Command in Königsberg. In 1930, Müller persuaded his commander to attend a mass meeting at which Hitler
was to speak. It was the time of hysterical frontier tension with the
Poles, when Hitler was hailed as a 'German margrave' and prayers
were addressed to him. This faith seems to have touched General
Werner von Blomberg. He was a gifted, cultivated officer, very
soldierly in appearance, though nicknamed the 'rubber lion' because
of his gentle manner. Blomberg was bowled over by Hitler at their
first meeting, and frankly admitted it; he soon virtually became an
instrument of the thundering voice. Shortly after this fateful meeting, he was sent abroad to study military progress in the United
States. The public seems to have taken little notice of his visit; some
day perhaps it will be known how much of his American observation Blomberg worked into the German military machine. In 1932,
at any rate, he was one of the directors of German army policy,
the third after Schleicher and Hammerstein; and he was Germany's military expert at the Geneva Disarmament Conference.
German bourgeois ministers were surprised when this Reichswehr
leader advised them to read *Mein Kampf,* and even quoted passages.
A colder nature was Blomberg's chief of staff, Colonel Walter von
Reichenau; perhaps less of an admirer of Hitler, but in his thinking and manner of life a true National Socialist officer, who broke
with the Prussian tradition by making personal friends of the men
under him. Blomberg and Reichenau were among those supporters
of National Socialism who, like Ribbentrop, assured their Jewish
friends that things would not be so bad; when they did get so bad,
Reichenau said that Hitler had brought Germany so much good
that a patriotic German Jew must regard himself as 'fallen on the
field of honor.'

This type of officer considered it the duty and right of National
Socialism to bring the army 'spiritual domination over the people.'
It became the creed of Blomberg, Reichenau, and many others that
the Reichswehr must withdraw again from politics. Schleicher, they
believed, had led it on a false path. Schleicher 'had ceased to be a
soldier,' Reichenau later declared; he was 'a born conspirator and

a sad proof of the fact that in politics officers can so easily lose the qualities of their profession.'

History now played one of its bitterest jokes. It forced the Prussian general, Kurt von Schleicher, to decide whether to govern democratically — that is, with the National Socialists, the party of violence and mass murder — or whether to smash the party of violence and mass murder; but to do that, he would first have to smash or at least paralyze parliament. It was perhaps Hugenberg who was most determined to bar the National Socialists from real power; for he wanted to exclude the people itself from power. On January 21, Hugenberg accused Schleicher, the 'social General' of letting Germany slip into Bolshevist mass rule; above all in agriculture, the Chancellor was 'permitting conflicts between big and small to arise.' The color of this rural Bolshevism which the big landowners were so fond of invoking was Brown, and its true name was National Socialism. The decisive accusation was that Schleicher wanted to govern with parliament; but Germany, said Hugenberg, could 'be saved only by a strong state leadership.' He meant by his own dictatorship; but he would have been satisfied if he himself, perhaps under the chancellorship of Papen, could be dictator over the economic life, including agriculture; for economic life, he believed, was the national destiny.

The Bolshevist uprising of the small against the great, which Hugenberg feared, was actually in progress; its scene was parliament; its mover, National Socialism. The budget committee of the Reichstag was investigating the use and misuse of the Eastern Aid funds; it aimed to discover which of the junkers had enriched themselves on the taxpayers' money. With National Socialist votes the budget committee resolved, on January 25, that the Reich court of accounts should conduct a thorough investigation of the Eastern Aid scandal and issue a detailed report on its findings; with National Socialist votes it was decided that the government should also render a complete report showing which estates over two hundred and fifty acres in size had received state support. With National Socialist votes the committee demanded an investigation of whether the gentlemen, for the most part nobles, had really used their 'loans to relieve indebtedness'; and whether they could not have paid their debts from private resources: 'The name of the recipient, his private fortune, the amount of his indebtedness and assets at different times, his private income, the amount of the loan to relieve indebtedness, and the amount transferred by the recipient to his creditors shall all be itemized. . . .' The whole Reichstag raged against the big land-owners, with the National Socialists in the lead, sure of having the people behind them; only the German Nationalists, a lost grouplet, voted against the resolution.

The big landowner of Neudeck, who filled the post of Reichs President, very probably regarded these decisions of the budget committee as bitter proof that Schleicher had failed to curb the Reichstag. There had been no 'relaxation of tension.' The immediate issue was East Prussian landed property, for which Hindenburg surely had stronger feelings than for West German coal mines or the shipping interests of Hamburg and Bremen. But if Hindenburg was perturbed, because the big landowners were menaced, then he certainly was even more perturbed because his government no longer had the Reichstag in hand.

Even Schleicher for a moment lost his lighthearted confidence and considered a desperate plan, which had been recommended to him by Hugenberg and Papen as well as to Hindenburg: to dissolve the Reichstag and then to declare a state of emergency precluding elections; meanwhile to form a strong and popular cabinet. This would have been unconstitutional, a *coup d'état;* but Hindenburg's overstrained authority might still have sanctioned it. Now the very men, who up till then had been Schleicher's most faithful friends, stayed his hand; the day after the decisions of the budget committee, Kaas, the leader of the Center, went to Schleicher and gave him a sharp warning. Schleicher replied that there was no cause for alarm; that he was contemplating no state of emergency; that it was only Hugenberg and Papen who were trying to force him to take the dangerous path of open dictatorship against the people. At the time he said this, it may have been true. On the same day Kaas wrote Schleicher a pathetic letter, probably prearranged by the two of them; he sent a copy to Hindenburg and then made the letter public. He threatened revolution in the streets if the Reichstag were forcibly dismissed: 'Illegality from above will unleash illegality below. . . . ' When Kaas wrote this, he knew that the National Socialists would inevitably come to power by way of the Reichstag; but it seemed to him that the only salvation from 'illegality' and all the horrors inherent in the word was for the inevitable to come about through the Reichstag and the constitutionally expressed will of the people.

The crisis between the cabinet and the Reichstag meant a crisis between the Chancellor and the President. In so far as personal feelings play a part, Hindenburg surely had held a silent grudge against the once esteemed general ever since Schleicher had forced him to dismiss Papen; but since Schleicher had undertaken to bring the parliament around, to put an end to the eternal state of emergency, to relieve Hindenburg of responsibility for the constant emergency decrees, he had hopefully let him try. The success in the disarmament question and the upward trend of business conditions had even improved the old man's humor, and led him to shield Schleicher against the fury of the landowners. But the whole relationship presupposed that Schleicher would succeed in controlling parliament.

Up to the last days of January, 1933, Hindenburg was determined not to appoint Hitler Chancellor. In Goebbels's diary, depression and exaltation alternate with monotonous regularity. 'Schleicher is doing badly,' he is 'tottering, but doesn't know it himself'; on the other hand, 'we must not be too optimistic,' 'great difficulties still lie in our path,' 'we must not cheer too soon.' Hugenberg's response to Hitler's plans for the chancellorship was still a determined 'No, no, never!'—and his assent was necessary for a majority. Papen contented himself with pointing to Hindenburg's insuperable resistance. On January 26, Göring and Frick had a conversation with Hugenberg and conceded that a solution might perhaps be found, with Papen as Chancellor. Hitler traveled back and forth between Berlin and the provinces, making speeches that were none too confident; as late as January 23, he said that if he went into the government, there must be 'fair play, in which we give the others our strength and they give us the corresponding power in return,' and if they were unwilling to do this, 'I would rather wait another three months.'

The party's downward course was by no means ended. This was apparent even among a section of the population where National Socialism was believed to be most firmly entrenched: the students. In the elections to the student committees of various universities, the National Socialists lost many votes and mandates; as late as January 25, they lost approximately a tenth of their votes at the South German university of Tübingen. Hindenburg remained unfriendly, and Hitler was apparently willing to do anything, provided only that Schleicher should fall. 'The Leader maintains an attitude of waiting,' wrote Goebbels on January 27. 'There is still a possibility that Papen will be reappointed.' He hastily added that this would be 'a hopeless, short-term affair'; but essentially, he says elsewhere, only one thing was important: the Reichstag must not be dissolved before the National Socialists had won power because (he implied) that would bring a new defeat.

On the twenty-seventh, the Reichstag's council of elders — a kind of rules committee — decided that parliament should convene on the last day of the month. No party was very eager for this meeting, but it was hard to avoid the decision. Only Schleicher could have asked for an adjournment, but he suddenly decided that this was the time to put the fear of God into parliament; to let them convene and then calmly tell them that they were dissolved if they did not do his bidding.

And so Schleicher had come to the point where Papen had left off; his policy of conciliation with parliament had failed. True, he did not admit this. His government, he maintained, even if it did not at the moment have a majority in the Reichstag, enjoyed the confidence of large sections of the people, for he confused party and trade-union leaders with the people. And he would have regarded the return of Papen, especially with Hugenberg in his cabinet, as a catastrophe more ruinous even than a Hitler government, for Hitler at least represented the masses, while Papen and Hugenberg would 'have only a tenth of the people behind them.' Kaas had just threatened him with 'illegality from below.' Schleicher and his friends vehemently refused to send out the Reichswehr to defend an unpopular government against the people. On the twenty-seventh, Schleicher met with his associates in the Reichswehr

Ministry and discussed the dangers of a new Papen government. They appear to have speculated on means of breaking Papen's influence on Hindenburg. It has been claimed that a suggestion was put forward of taking Papen and Hugenberg into protective custody in order to separate them from Hindenburg. According to another rumor, they thought of sending troops into Berlin from Potsdam. If this suggestion was ever made, it can scarcely have been more than idle day-dreaming, but it is said that a young officer attending the conference was horrified and reported the remark to Oskar von Hindenburg.

On the next day, January 28, Schleicher called on Hindenburg as Brüning had done eight months before. The overthrower of chancellors was himself falling. He told the President that the Reichstag was to meet in three days and demanded the power of dissolution. According to the official report, Schleicher said 'that the present Reich government, in accordance with its character of presidial government, would be in a position to defend its program and its opinions in the Reichstag only if the Herr Reichs President put an order of dissolution at its disposal.' Schleicher called his government a presidial government in order to make it clear to Hindenburg that this was his own government. But this was untrue; from the beginning, Schleicher's government was oriented toward parliament, and Hindenburg logically answered that 'in the situation prevailing at the present time, he could not accede to this proposal.'

The conversation could not be friendly. Schleicher told Hindenburg that if he could not dissolve the Reichstag he could not prevent a discussion of the Eastern Aid and the attendant scandals. Hindenburg is said to have replied: It is sad that you are not in a position, without such an order, to prevent a debate in which Prussia's oldest historical families would be covered with mud. This was the origin of the legend that Schleicher threatened Hindenburg with disclosure of the Eastern Aid scandal, and that Hindenburg hastily dropped his general and called Hitler to power, in order that Hitler should hush up the scandal (after his deputies had just voted for its exposure!). The truth is almost the exact opposite. Schleicher demanded dictatorial powers in order to repress the debate on the Eastern Aid, and Hindenburg demanded that he do this without dictatorship. The old man did not act in fear but in anger. Hitler did not force his hand; Hindenburg broke Schleicher's attempt to do just this. The true interpretation of the episode is simply that the fickle old man felt the weight of Schleicher's domination and shook it off when it became just a fraction of an ounce too much.

The old President seems to have referred in harsh terms to the conversation in the Reichswehr Ministry and the plans for arresting Papen and Hugenberg. According to Schleicher's own version, he answered fearlessly that most of the rumors were nonsense, but that he did indeed regard it as his duty to do his utmost to prevent a return of Papen to the government. For such a government meant civil war, and neither the Reichswehr nor the police was morally equal to a civil war. In a statement which he himself gave to the press, he declared that 'not a single word is true' of all the assertions about a march of the Reichswehr on Berlin and the arrest of Hugenberg and Papen; these were 'absolutely senseless and malicious inventions and slanders.' However, 'Herr von Schleicher considered it his urgent duty as Chancellor still in office and as leader of the German armed forces, to describe to the President the dangers which, in his opinion, were inherent in the plan, still much discussed in public, of reappointing former Chancellor von Papen. Herr von Schleicher regarded such a cabinet, based on a tenth of the German people, as a challenge to the other nine tenths of the German people; in view of the complications and political struggles which, in his opinion, were inevitable, such a challenge would have led to demoralization in the Reichswehr and the police. In this situation, he declared it was the right and duty of the Chancellor and Reichswehr Minister in office to prevent such a development to the best of his ability.'

With a stubbornness bordering on mutiny, these Reichswehr officers were determined to prevent a new Papen cabinet. Through misunderstandings, this, too, gave rise to a legend that Schleicher wanted, by a *coup d'état,* to prevent Hitler from taking power. According to his own account, which, perhaps with slight shifts of emphasis, is not unworthy of credence, he desired the exact opposite. The above-quoted statement continues: 'In the same connection Herr von Schleicher gave his opinion that collaboration with the National Socialist Party on the basis of a parliamentary majority would be the best solution.'

Parliament . . . majority . . . and therefore Hitler! It was Hitler's own plan, and for years it had also been Schleicher's plan. There was nothing improbable or surprising about it. For Hitler, the plan meant dictatorship by way of parliament, after the example of Napoleon III and the counsels of the Wise Men of Zion; for Schleicher, the curbing of the National Socialists by way of parliament, as, so often in the history of parliamentarianism, radical parties had been curbed by the necessity of forming a majority. When Hindenburg brusquely dismissed Schleicher, he, too, hoped that Hitler was now curbed; he had some reason to believe that this time Hitler would not refuse Chancellor von Papen his support, at least for the moment. It was Schleicher who, representing himself as the spokesman of the Reichswehr, opposed the Papen project and forced the old man reluctantly toward Hitler. There were three possibilities, he said, of solving the government crisis. The third and last was a presidial cabinet with full powers to dissolve the Reichstag, and thereby bend the Reichstag to its will — this Hindenburg had just refused him. But after the unfortunate experience of the past, the Papen experiment must on no account be repeated. Therefore, Schleicher, according to his own story, considered these two possibilities: '1. A government with a parliamentary majority which probably could be established only under the leadership of Adolf Hitler. 2. The formation of a minority government based on a strong popular tendency; this likewise could be achieved only under the leadership of Adolf Hitler, but with the support of the Right groups. This would have a chance of success only if the President were to abandon his resistance to entrusting Adolf Hitler with the chancellorship.'

Hindenburg was still resisting the appointment of Hitler; Schleicher now urged him to consent. Schleicher was a man whose political acts always had an *arrière-pensée*; if Goebbels is to be believed, he had sent Hitler a warning, two days earlier, not to accept an appointment. Up to the last moment, perhaps, he played a double game; but whether knowingly or not, when he recommended to the President a majority government under Hitler's leadership, he was recommending exactly what he had been preparing consciously, and sometimes unconsciously, for two years.

Hindenburg received the same advice from the most responsible and probably most influential of his advisers, State Secretary Otto Meissner. Meissner's chief aim was to free the old man from the oppressive burden of his own terrifying political position, to relieve him from the position of a dictator governing against the Reichstag. The Center was willing to give a Hitler government its vote, if this government were prepared to rule by strictly parliamentary means. The German Nationalists, it is true, demanded that the Reichstag be sent home for a long period. Would it not be possible to adjourn the Reichstag for a limited time in strict accordance with the constitution and in this way satisfy both sides?

Oh yes, this was possible, said Hitler. In his person, in his movement, the principle of democracy and the principle of leadership fused into a unit; he was the man to satisfy both sides, to adjourn the Reichstag in accordance with the constitution.

Two days before Schleicher's fall, Hitler might have accepted a Papen cabinet. Now, after his adversary had fallen, he was unbending. 'A compromise solution is now out of the question,' writes Goebbels on January 28, after discussing the situation with Hitler; but 'we are all still very skeptical and are not cheering too soon.' Negotiations went on for two days. The German Nationalists put up the hardest struggle against Hitler's chancellorship; they fought for a Papen government that would be tougher than Papen himself; in this the party of landed property and heavy industry doubtless did what the interests it represented desired. It fought against the Schleicher-Meissner formula of a majority government under Hitler's leadership; it fought against a participation of the Center in the new government. In their fight against the Center, they also had Papen on their side; meanwhile, not only Meissner demanded participation of the Center; Hitler also desired it, to avoid being entirely at the mercy of the German Nationalists. The Stahlhelm, under its leaders Franz Seldte and Theodor Duesterberg, also forced its way into these negotiations; the two asserted that they were present by the will of Hindenburg, for Hindenburg was honorary president of the Stahlhelm, and actually did want the Stahlhelm to have a share in the government. But the Stahlhelm itself was not clear about its own desires, its leadership was not united; Duesterberg supported Hugenberg, Seldte supported Hitler; and it became apparent that these half-dozen dictators could no more find a common aim than the six hundred deputies in the Reichstag.

No power can be won without a sacrifice of principles; and Hitler, who looked to power as his salvation, abjured many things that had seemed to him absolutely indispensable a few months before. After he had reluctantly renounced massacres and rolling heads, and only too readily renounced inflation and socialization, he became Chancellor by declaring his readiness not only to be a strictly parliamentary chancellor, but also to tolerate continuous interference on the part of Hindenburg and to submit to every conceivable restriction. Of ten ministers only three were to be National Socialists. These three were himself as Chancellor, his friend Frick as Minister of the Interior, and Göring as head of a newly established Ministry of Aviation. There was no mention of Goebbels, much less of Röhm. At the same time the Prussian government posts, which gave more practical state power than those of the Reich, were distributed. This was the 'commissar' method of distributing posts that had prevailed in the largest state of the Reich since Papen's *coup d'état*. Göring became Prussian Minister of the Interior, and that could mean power, for the police is power. But Göring's superior, also appointed by the Reich, was Papen. In this government, Papen turned up wherever there was a key position to fill. He also became Vice-Chancellor in the Reich cabinet, and Hindenburg exacted the condition that Hitler should never appear before him alone, but always accompanied by Papen; for the old man wished to speak only with him.

Konstantin von Neurath, Hindenburg's personal adviser, remained in charge of foreign policy. A general regarded by Hindenburg as trustworthy obtained the Reichswehr Ministry. This was a general who for some time had come forward as an opponent of Schleicher, having attacked him for forcing the Reichswehr into politics. Was no one aware of the relations between Werner von Blomberg, the new minister, and Hitler? Was no one aware that Colonel von Reichenau, whom Blomberg brought with him as the new chief of ministry, was widely known to be a National Socialist? The German press in those days took scarcely any interest in the person of the new Reichswehr Minister, but used up much space and time in pointing out that Hugenberg was the real new dictator of Germany. For by stubborn negotiation the German Nationalist leader had attained his goal: he had become Minister for Economics and Agriculture. The cabinet, he felt sure, would force the Reichstag to grant it one year in which to work undisturbed. He, Hugenberg, would remold the economy and save the country. Not even Labor was accorded to the National Socialists; Franz Seldte, the Stahlhelm leader, became Minister of Labor. Hitler was no dictator; he had sworn that he would not 'use his power one-sidedly'; and even if he wanted to break his oath, he was apparently in no position to do so.

Meissner and Papen probably thought they had accomplished a master stroke. As Chancellor, Hitler now bore the responsibility for German policy, and since he would achieve no greater miracles than anyone else, his supporters would be disillusioned in time and turn back to the reliable old parties; the heavy burden of responsibility would reduce Hitler as a public figure to normal proportions. For the present he brought the government strong support in parliament; and yet this cabinet was so cleverly constructed that Hitler could do no real damage and could no longer become a dangerous power; he would be a powerless chancellor and hence a broken party leader.

This was the cabinet that had been recommended to Hindenburg by Papen and Meissner. Up to the last minute, the old man seems to have resisted. At noon of January 30, when Hitler drove over to Hindenburg's palace with his new ministers, his friends remained behind in the Kaiserhof, anxious and uncertain. 'Our hearts are torn back and forth between doubt, hope, joy, and discouragement,' writes Goebbels. 'We have been disappointed too often for us to believe wholeheartedly in the great miracle.'

To a large part of the public, Hitler's appointment did indeed seem a miracle, and many believed that only another miracle, and a very unsavory one, could account for it. One story was that Hitler had promised Hindenburg to restore the monarchy; if ever he made such a promise, he needed only seven weeks to retract it in an official statement. It was further maintained that Meissner and Oskar von Hindenburg had been blackmailed with threats to expose some shady stock speculations with a Jewish banker in which they had made improper use of their inside political information. It seems to be true that Oskar and Meissner, as the result of losses they had suffered in such a speculation, were indebted to the banker for about a million marks; it is said that the banker kept the account of this business, called 'sub-account B,' not in his office, but in a safe in his house. The safe one night was broken into by unknown burglars, and 'sub-account B' disappeared; some days later, the banker got the 'friendly advice' to leave Germany as soon as possible. So far the story seems true, but people who knew Schleicher well would rather believe that he himself engineered the burglary in order to get a hold on his unreliable friends, Oskar and Meissner; then, too, he was probably much better informed about their shady deals than a National Socialist outsider.

But even if Hitler got 'sub-account B,' Oskar and Meissner could hardly be in danger, for they knew at least as many unsavory stories about Hitler, Göring, Goebbels, Röhm. It was also known to Hitler that when Neudeck was given to Hindenburg, the state had been cheated out of the inheritance tax; it was known to him that the chief of state had received another four hundred and fifty thousand marks through private collections in order that he would require no Eastern Aid. Unpleasant as these facts were, they could not be used for blackmail, for they were known, not only to the National Socialists, but to the public as well; General Erich Ludendorff, for years a bitter enemy of Hindenburg, had told the whole story, including the tax swindle, in a widely read weekly. Later, when Hitler was in power, he did not hesitate to use one or another of these scandals to intimidate Oskar von Hindenburg; but an understanding of the National Socialist seizure of power is not advanced by these mystery stories. Hitler came to power because he seemed the only man who could restore to Germany a parliamentary government, such as Hindenburg had demanded in August and even more in November.

Röhm stood at a window in the Kaiserhof and looked across at the Chancellery through binoculars; for when Hitler came out, his face would show how things had gone. Suddenly Hitler was in the room. 'He says nothing, and all of us say nothing. But his eyes are full of tears.' It was a day full of ceremonies and pageantry; at noon, Hindenburg administered the oath of office; at night twenty-five thousand S.A. men marched past the Chancellery with torches, and the National Socialists of Berlin marched with them.

Hindenburg stood at the window, beating time with his crooked stick to the old military marches that resounded from below. A few yards away, Hitler stood at an open window, laughing, dancing, gesticulating with childish joy, now and then bowing to someone.

Hugenberg and Papen could not have organized any such torch-light parade in six hours. Here for the first time in many months the 'ruling powers' again saw a part of the 'people' before them, and perhaps they thought that 'public opinion' was marching down there in the glow of the torches. The torch-bearers in turn believed that their Leader had now become a ruling power and they with him; the Leader himself knew better. 'We shall still have to carry on a very intensive struggle,' writes Goebbels on February 1. 'The situation in the country is not yet clear enough for us to speak of an absolute consolidation of our position.' We have been called because we are the people — are we? The will of the people is still expressed in ballots and in parliament; the task set us by Hindenburg is still to relieve the tension between the executive and parliament; to win over the block of votes we need for a majority. Practically speaking, this meant an understanding with the Center, which, in secret, was exceedingly willing for an understanding.

For a moment Hitler was probably serious about this understanding. The Center was even to be offered a cabinet post; one ministry had been left free for the purpose, and, strangely enough, it was Franz Gürtner, Hitler's old protector, whose portfolio was intended for a man of the Center. Public and private assurances were meanwhile given that the National Socialists would commit no act of violence, no breach of the constitution; to the question whether the S.A. would not assume the powers of a state police force, Minister of the Interior Frick replied in a press conference of January 30: '. . . The integration of the S.A. with the state played no part in the formation of the cabinet, and there are no existing plans to integrate the S.A. with the Prussian police.' Hitler announced in his press that the Reichstag would meet on February 7, when he would issue the government's statement and demand the necessary powers.

In order to assure himself of these powers, he lectured Kaas for two hours on the morning of January 31. He told him that all he wanted was the Center's consent to a law enabling the government to work for one year 'without the vicissitudes of parliamentary obstruction,' for this was the 'last and only constitutional possibility of meeting the danger of ruin to our people and our Reich.' Kaas wanted a clear promise from Hitler that he would hold strictly to the constitution, and, though Hitler spoke for two hours, he gave no clear answer. It was agreed that the Center Party should repeat its questions in writing. This was done on the same day; Kaas asked the new government for 'Guaranties . . . that its measures would remain within the limits of the constitution'; binding assurances that no unconstitutional measures would be taken 'on the basis of a so-called state of emergency.' An express promise was also demanded that the rights of the workers would not be impaired; this meant that Hugenberg would not be given the power to smash the trade unions. Every question meant: We don't trust you, but say something satisfactory and you shall have a satisfactory answer. It was Hugenberg who, up till then, had used all his power to prevent new elections; now it was primarily Hugenberg, with his great plan for the salvation of German economic life by his own economic dictatorship, whom the Center wanted to stop. All Kaas's demands — renunciation of emergency laws, settlement of peasants in the East, increase of exports — were directed against Hugenberg's known plans, not against Hitler's unknown and actually unformulated and uncertain aims. Now Hitler could tell his minister of economics that there was only one way to shake off the yoke of the Center: dissolution of the Reichstag and new elections.

For months Hitler had lost election after election — in spite of

Lippe. But if he dissolved the Reichstag now, he had everything in his favor that he had lacked since August: the magic of triumph, the irresistibility of power. 'Now it is easy to carry on the fight,' writes Goebbels. 'For we can call on all the state's means. The radio and the press are at our disposal. We shall furnish a masterpiece of agitation. And this time of course [of course!] there is no lack of money.'

Hugenberg resisted stubbornly, for he had experience enough to suspect that Hitler alone would be the victor in this election, and that everyone else would be defeated. What he needed, he insisted, was a strong government, no parliament! Send the Reichstag home — yes. Elect a new one — no! Hitler replied that this was in sharp contradiction to the injunction of strict constitutionalism which the field marshal and President had given the new government. If the National Socialists should gain an absolute majority — Hitler was asked — would they not form a cabinet to suit themselves and throw out all the other ministers? In reply, Hitler gave his word of honor 'that, regardless of the results of the coming elections, all the ministers active in the present cabinet would remain.' A tactician of uncanny adroitness, he forced his will on his startled cabinet with arguments and words of honor. Hugenberg gave in. The following morning Hitler and Papen called on Hindenburg and bade him dissolve the Reichstag. The situation had changed since Schleicher; Schleicher had been unable to hope and promise that he would have a majority in a new Reichstag. Hitler could make such a promise, and hence the dissolution of the Reichstag was no longer an act of violence against parliament, but a hand outstretched to the people, a questioning of public opinion. Once again Hindenburg signed a paper in which he declared the Reichstag dissolved, 'since the formation of a working majority has proved impossible.' In an unctuous letter, Hitler explained to Kaas why he had preferred not to answer his questions: Such an answer, he wrote, would have served a purpose only if it had been clear on principle that the Center was prepared to give the government a year in which to work. A discussion of the questions put by Kaas would only 'lead to bitterness as sterile as it is to me undesirable.' And Hitler did not abandon hope of still reaching an understanding with the Center: 'I venture to hope even today that, if not at once, then in a future that is perhaps not too far distant, it will be possible to broaden our front for the elimination of the menacing domestic dangers within our nation.' Kaas replied indignantly: It was not true that the formation of a majority in the Reichstag had proved impossible; if he had received a satisfactory answer 'only in essential questions, . . . the Center Party, in accordance with its political principles, . . . in awareness of the gravity of the hour, in selfless objectivity, would have been prepared to help the government with its work.'

Now Gürtner became Minister of Justice after all. Elections were set for March 5, 1933. The final struggle for the people began.

Chapter XXII

THE REICHSTAG FIRE

ON JANUARY 31, GOEBBELS WROTE IN HIS DIARY:

> In a conference with the Leader we establish the directives for the struggle against the Red terror. For the present we shall dispense with direct counter-measures. The Bolshevist attempt at revolution must first flare up. At the proper moment we shall then strike.

Thus began the quest for a Communist uprising, the great secret of every counter-revolution. Revolution always needs legal justification, it must claim to re-establish broken laws. To endure, an act of violence requires the consent of the victims. Hence revolution, in its formulated aims, is always directed against the illegal abuse of state authority by the government, and even when it overthrows institutions that are decades or centuries old, it does so, at the very least, in the name of a 'natural' law, if it has no positive, written law at hand. But even in the most extreme cases, legitimacy is almost always preserved in some form, perhaps by invoking the authority of a parliament created for this purpose. Even the Bolshevik Revolution of 1917 in Russia attacked the state in defense of a higher authority, conceived as legitimate, the authority of the councils of workers and soldiers. Conversely, the counter-revolution regularly attacks the menace to legitimate authority by the governed. In the classical case of European counter-revolution, Louis Bonaparte and the party of the 'Mountain' clashed under these conflicting battle-cries; an even more classical and venerable example is found in the sixteenth chapter of the Book of Numbers. When the sons of Korah rose up against the authority of Moses and Aaron, they accused them of arrogating to themselves a special holiness, while according to the law all Israel was equally holy; Moses, however, called the rebels — who desired nothing more than democratic worship — 'godless,' thus stigmatizing them in the public consciousness with a terrible name which even today has not lost its power. A mysterious fire broke out — allegedly falling from heaven. There followed ostracism and political murder, falsified by an unscrupulous propaganda on the part of the victors; Moses' government communiqué maintained, in the style of the time, that the earth had opened up and swallowed the rebels, and, by this wonder, 'ye shall know that the Lord hath sent me to do these works.'

It was not easy for the National Socialists to find a new Korah. As early as January 30, to be sure, the Communists called a general strike, but no one took the strike order seriously, not even the Communists themselves, who wanted only to 'unmask' the cowardice and inactivity of their Social Democratic competitors.

There were other, more serious possibilities of resistance in the Reich. The leadership of the Social Democratic Party had gone to Munich, where the Bavarian government, sharply hostile to the new National Socialist government in the Reich, carried on its business and hurled threats at the national capital; other South German states showed a disquieting resistance to Berlin. The demarcation line of this zone of resistance ran from east to west, along the Main River, turned north near Frankfort and ran down the Rhine, dividing the West as well as the South from the rest of the Reich. In the West, the population was Catholic, largely proletarian, and overwhelmingly opposed to National Socialism. These were the people who, by Goebbels's own account, had driven him with curses from his native city. And this was the district barred to the Reichswehr, by the Treaty of Locarno, where armed resistance of the Iron Front would not have been hopeless.

The National Socialist leadership waited eagerly for something to flare up somewhere. Papen and Hugenberg were worried enough to acquiesce to the first important limitation on the freedom of elections. Schleicher had had an emergency decree for such purposes in his drawer; now Hitler pulled it out and gave it the high-sounding title, 'For the protection of the German people.' Hindenburg signed it. The authorities obtained the right to forbid open-air meetings and the wearing of party uniforms. This meant opposition meetings and opposition uniforms. Newspapers could be suppressed for insulting leading state officials — an unfriendly word against Hitler sufficed. All this a few weeks before an election — when the Reich constitution still guaranteed freedom of speech and of the press. 'I explicitly stress that, as a matter of principle, freedom of criticism will not be diminished,' said Hitler to a press delegation that called on him at the Chancellery. 'I am opposed to any gagging of the press.' Meanwhile, Göring suppressed the leading organ of Social Democracy twice in succession, and both times the Reich court nullified the suppression; the same was repeated with innumerable other papers in the states. The National Socialists made masterful use of the red, pink, or black (Catholic-clerical) danger to paralyze their partners in the government. In their blind self-assurance these partners believed that they had the power firmly in hand and that they alone benefited from any increase in the power of the executive.

But the attempted revolution, whether Bolshevist, Social Democratic, reactionary, or separatist, did not flare up. In the middle of February a meeting of Social Democratic Party and trade-union leaders was held in Munich. One of the trade-union representatives reported that preparations had been made to sabotage the whole West German industrial region. Mines could be flooded, railroad traffic could be halted, and many factories incapacitated for a long time to come. But it was clear that such desperate measures could serve only as a threat. Once carried out, they lost their terror and could be of little use in the actual fight. 'Comrades, I ask you,' said the trade-union leader, 'who among you will assume responsibility for these things?' Responsibility was not assumed. It was not necessary, said the leaders, for Hitler's government would succumb to its own weakness. 'For everyone who understands the signs of the times, the contradictions in this cabinet yawn fathoms deep,' said Peter Grassmann, after Leipart the most influential leader of the

Social Democratic trade unions, in a speech on February 12. 'Messrs. Hugenberg and Papen have scarcely mentioned the name of their Leader in the cabinet. Here there are gaping contradictions which promise victory for our struggle' — he meant the struggle by means of ballots. And he was not the only one to deceive himself. Adam Stegerwald, the leader of the Catholic workers, proclaimed in his newspaper: 'Hitler will be the prisoner of Hugenberg, Papen, and the big agricultural interests.' Ten days after Hitler had become Chancellor, a widely read liberal publicist wrote:

> We shall find that in important matters the practical influence of the three Hitlerians in this cabinet ends exactly where their colleagues in the cabinet want it to end. They have less than thirty per cent of the votes in this cabinet. And as for independent action, the Ministry of the Interior is so hemmed in by its own character, the Chancellor so hemmed in by special regulations, that they, too, will hardly be in a position to do anything but what the feudal camp allows them. Even clearer is the distribution of posts in Prussia. There are no longer any independent ministers there, the 'commissar ministers' are employees of the commissar whose will they have to carry out. The commissariat, however, has been taken away from the Chancellor [Hitler] and transferred to the Vice-Chancellor [Papen]. Minister of the Interior Göring and Minister of Education Rust are mere officials subordinate to Herr von Papen.
>
> And so the first thing to be noted is that for the present the 'national union' means the least possible freedom of action for the new partners [National Socialists] and a maximum of influence for the old, entrenched interests.

It was neither the first nor the last time that the belief in the weakness of National Socialism fatally misled its adversaries.

The National Socialists, on the contrary, worked in the belief that their enemies were incredibly strong. The specter of Rhenish secession enabled them to win their first position of power. Since the Reichswehr could not enter the Rhineland, a substitute army had to be created. Blomberg agreed and Papen could venture no opposition when Göring at one stroke deposed the police presidents, first throughout the Rhineland, then elsewhere, and replaced them by S.A. leaders, or, occasionally, by former officers who were his personal friends. The police in the Rhineland was subjected to a military type of organization, under Police President Stieler von Heydkamp. Despite Frick's promises to the German public, the S.S. and S.A. were only waiting for the day on which they themselves would be the police. In order to prepare for this day, Göring had brought a helper with him into the ministry, a man who bore the high-sounding title of *S.S. Obergruppenführer* (chief group leader), the same type of obscure ruffian who in 1925 had thrown the *gau* of Berlin into mutiny and confusion: Kurt Daluege.

Within a few days, several hundred leading officials of the Prussian state changed their posts. Then the S.A. began to march. They were still a mere private army and not yet police, but they were encouraged by the knowledge that their Leader was in the Chancellery and had given them 'freedom of the streets,' sanctioned by the seal of state. They invaded the taverns where the Communists and Social Democrats held their meetings; even the official police reports showed that such clashes regularly took place in the vicinity of 'Marxist' headquarters — a clear indication of who attacked whom.

In their enthusiasm the S.A. men even went so far as to break up meetings of bourgeois parties; once they prevented Brüning from speaking, on another occasion they knocked down ex-Minister Stegerwald. Hitler was embarrassed. These, he said, were 'provocative elements,' out to promote disorder 'under the cloak of the party.' In truth, it was his own party, which at some points was striking too soon and going too far. 'The enemy,' cried Hitler in a plea to the S.A., 'which must be downed on March 5 is Marxism' — meaning that other enemies would come later. 'Our entire propaganda and this whole election campaign must be concentrated on Marxism.' Election campaign, as distinguished from propaganda, meant bloody street brawls; for the period from January 30 to March 5, the German papers report fifty-one murders of anti-Nazis, while the National Socialists set the number of their own victims at eighteen. This murderous swarming of the S.A. through Germany is comparable to the march of Louis Bonaparte's guards down the boulevards of Paris; and though the result was still no 'flaring up' of the Bolshevist revolution, Göring and Daluege made the most of the murders.

On February 17, Göring issued an order to all police authorities, stating 'that the police must under all circumstances avoid so much as an appearance of hostility toward the S.A. and the Stahlhelm'; on the contrary, the police must with all its strength support this private army of the government 'in every activity for national aims.' This meant that the police should help the S.A. in its attacks on political opponents, give them the freedom of the streets, and come to their rescue if they were getting beaten. Göring also made it clear that the police 'must oppose with the sharpest means the activities of organizations hostile to the state.' The mass of police officers were not National Socialists; they were none too enthusiastic over this order. Göring intimidated his subordinates by dire threats and compelled them to commit acts of bloodshed to which many of them were surely opposed: 'Police officers who make use of firearms in the exercise of their duties will, regardless of the consequences of this use of firearms, benefit by my protection; those, however, who, through misplaced leniency, fail in their duty will face disciplinary consequences. . . . Every officer must always bear in mind that failure to take a measure is a graver offense than mistakes made in exercise of the measure.' This order for ruthless firing on the non-National Socialist people was the first unmistakable blow of the 'outwardly legal' counter-revolution. These blows were calculated with extreme skill; always hard enough that the enemy should feel them; never so hard that the weapon was in danger of breaking.

It is still unknown what decisions were reached in the conversations held in those days between Hitler, Göring, and von Blomberg, the new Reichswehr Minister. But it is here that Germany's future course must have been decided. The wish, formulated again and again by Seeckt, Groener, Schleicher, that the Reichswehr should not be drawn into bloody street battles, may have dispelled all other considerations in Blomberg's mind; the danger in the Rhineland surely made an impression on the Reichswehr Minister. In any event, he consented to the arming of the S.A.

This was the decisive revolutionary act of the National Socialists. The storm troops became police; they themselves became the Herr President, by whose permission the revolution would be made.

On February 22, Göring, as Prussian Minister of the Interior, shamelessly forgetting what Frick as Reich Minister of the Interior had promised two weeks before, issued the following decree, a model for the *coup d'état* cloaking itself in legality:

> The demands made on the existing police force, which cannot be adequately increased at the present juncture, are often beyond its power; by the present necessity of utilizing them outside of their places of service, police officers are often removed from their proper field of activity at inopportune times. In consequence, the voluntary support of suitable helpers to be used as auxiliary police officers in case of emergency can no longer be dispensed with.

Some fifty thousand men were mobilized in this way in Prussia. A fifth of them belonged to the Stahlhelm; some twenty-five thousand came from the S.A., the remaining fifteen thousand from Himmler's black-shirted S.S. They served in their own uniforms and wore white arm-bands inscribed with 'auxiliary police.' This auxiliary police went around with rubber truncheons and pistols in their belts, traveled free of charge on the street-cars and buses; with pistols in their belts, they marched into restaurants and cafés. Fingering their weapons, they sold the frightened guests photographs of Hitler, Göring, or Goebbels at exorbitant prices. At side tables terrified waiters served the auxiliary police their meals. From the police treasury each auxiliary policeman drew three marks daily. Thus, the first fifty thousand of the Uprooted and Disinherited were scantily provided for.

The army of the *coup d'état* stood ready, at least in Prussia. But in the South, distrust and resistance grew. In Bavaria, plans were forged to proclaim Prince Rupprecht regent, or even king. At the same time a similar group was active in Prussia; it is not clear whether Hitler, by ambiguous talk or significant silence, encouraged these people to hope that he was really their friend. He could point to Prince August Wilhelm, who called him 'my Leader.' But his profound, heartfelt hostility toward princes could escape only the most superficial observers. To the Bavarian king-makers he cried out that their plan 'would be broken and smashed by the Bavarians themselves,' for the Bavarian people wanted nothing to do with these things of the past. Blomberg went to Munich and made a speech to the Munich Reichswehr garrison, 'which stands watch in the south of the Reich.' He assured them that the 'armed forces are stretched over the Reich like a steel claw,' and it did not matter 'which tribe the individual soldier belongs to'; for when he entered the armed forces, 'he has obligated himself without reservation, by oath and by will, to the entire German fatherland.' As for the National Socialists and their S.A., Blomberg stated without false caution 'that we [the Reichswehr] are and shall remain the armed might of Germany.' When he said this, he knew that the S.A. was armed; he also knew that Röhm had been working for months to make his private army the 'Brown People's Army' in the hands of the state. But Blomberg trusted in Hitler's word, and perhaps it sufficed him that the Brown auxiliary policemen were forbidden by law to take their pistols home with them. In any case, he called on the Reichswehr to regard the S.A. as their friends: 'Behind us and beside us stand many millions of determined men, disarmed, to be sure, but as determined as we are to live and to fight for the fatherland. Let us seal our alliance with them with the cry: Our beloved fatherland, the proud German Reich — Hurrah!'

With these words the Reichswehr put its stamp of approval on the acts of the S.A. — present and future. It was becoming clear that the Hitler régime was more than an experiment, that its power was considerably greater than the 'less than thirty per cent of voting power in the cabinet'; for the will to power cannot be measured in percentages, and no will in Germany approached Hitler's, either for determination or breadth of aim. Next to his movement, it was the Communists who had the greatest historical ambition; but the Communists clung stubbornly to their strange, mysterious conception of history. On February 23, Max Brauer, Social Democratic mayor of Altona, met Ernst Torgler, chairman of the Communist Reichstag fraction, in Berlin. Pointing out that 'it is five minutes to twelve,' he asked Torgler whether the Communists would not at least give up their fight against the Social Democrats and conclude a united front alliance. Torgler answered: 'It doesn't enter our heads. The Nazis must take power. Then in

four weeks the whole working class will be united under the leadership of the Communist Party.' Brauer thought Torgler must be
suffering from the strain. But a few days later, he met Soviet Ambassador Chinchook in Hamburg. Brauer asked the same question
and received the same answer: 'No, they [the National Socialists]
must come to power now, and then at last the old fight will come to
an end. In four weeks the Communists will have the leadership of
the whole working class.' No disappointment could destroy this
faith. A German Communist leader by the name of Heckert, who
fled to Russia a few weeks later, publicly declared before the executive committee of the Communist International that the German
events had confirmed Comrade Stalin's predictions, and that Social
Democracy and Fascism were twin brothers. In a resolution of
April 1, 1933, the International stated that the open Fascist dictatorship in Germany had freed the masses from the influence of Social
Democracy and thus 'accelerated the tempo of the evolution of Germany toward proletariat revolution.'

The Communists were prepared for illegal struggle; they had
maintained an illegal machine for years under the parliamentary
governments. They were convinced that they would come through
the brief period of Hitler's dictatorship relatively unharmed, while
the Social Democrats, softened by democracy, would succumb to
the unaccustomed climate. The calculations of the conservatives
and the Bolsheviks were startlingly similar. Generals, junkers, big
capital, and Communists were convinced alike that it was the
generals, the junkers, and big capital who really had state power;
all were agreed that Hitler as Chancellor would inevitably disap-
point the masses and lose his supporters. The National Socialists
were full of contempt for this unrealistic view; Hitler declared
publicly that he had set elections because a government cannot rule
in the long run unless it has the people behind it; because 'there
can be no resurrection of the nation without the might of the
workers'; true, for these reasons, he wished the German people to
decide for him — but 'not because I lack the determination to settle
with the spoilers of the nation without an election. . . . On the
contrary, their lordships' — he meant the generals, junkers, and
capitalists — 'can be convinced: on the fifth of March, so help me

God, Germany will no longer be in the hands of her spoilers.'
Meaning: regardless of how the elections turn out. For, as he said in
another speech: 'It is now for the German people themselves to decide. If the German people abandon us in this hour, that must not
deter us. We shall go the way that is necessary if Germany is not
to perish.'

The terror became more and more blatant, scorning to conceal
itself; yet it did not lure the counter-terror from its hiding-places.
The Social Democrats, demonstrably, intended no illegal action on
a large scale; nor can any such plan be deduced from the acts of the
Communists during this period. Hitler was alone in publicly claim-
ing the right to make a *coup d'état;* he alone was supported in this
claim by a section of public opinion; and this because he alone,
amid the fury of this last impassioned struggle for freedom and
power in Germany, believed himself able and willing to give
society a new shape. In his first government proclamation he promised to solve the economic crisis 'with two great four-year plans.'
'Within four years,' he promised, 'the German peasant must be
saved from pauperization; within four years unemployment must
be ended once and for all.' Four years was the legal term of the
new Reichstag, and by now he was determined to demand of the
Reichstag four years of dictatorial powers instead of one: 'German
people, give us four years' time, then pass judgment on us!'

The vastness of his plans, now that he was in possession of state
power to carry them out, made a profound impression on the
voters, though he did not reveal details and doubtless had not
formulated any. Germany, he said, had 'become dismal and sad;
our people have nearly forgotten happiness and laughter, as in
Soviet Russia; and where people have laughed, it has been the
laughter of despair.' Here he spoke the plain truth; and it was the
official statistics that he summed up in the sentence: 'Of twenty-
three million potential wage-earners, eight to nine millions are condemned to unemployment.' He would promise no one that things
could be better in a few days, weeks, or months; no, he would
need four years; it would mean hard work for all — 'let no one believe that freedom, happiness, and life will suddenly come as a
gift from Heaven,' for nothing whatever comes as a gift: 'We never

believe in outside help, never in help that lies outside of our own strength, outside of our own people.' Therefore, he would make no cheap promises, and the first point on his program was: 'We shall not lie and deceive.' He saw no reason to explain the details of his plans to the disrupters; by their very questions about his program, they had shown that they understood nothing: 'For all programs are vain; the decisive thing is the human will, sound vision, manly courage, sincerity of faith, the inner will — these are the decisive things [uproarious applause].'

A great will indubitably flowed through these speeches, a powerful magnetism gripped many who heard him. They promised no paradise — though some simple souls may have understood 'paradise'; what Hitler really promised was that he would attack great problems with the big methods of a man who respects history. 'I have resolved to undertake the greatest task in German history; I am willing and determined to solve this task.' To this end he was prepared to shake the nation to its foundations, to break and remix souls; for this great task demanded great men, and 'therefore we shall break with all the products of a rotten democracy, for great things can come only from the power of the individual personality, and everything that is worth preserving must be entrusted once more to the power of the individual personality.'

What Hitler promised was not that the hard times would end, but that they would acquire a meaning; the German nation should learn to look on itself as a task that could be solved; it should learn once more that action can help, and that 'it is better to make a mistake than to do nothing.' This accounts for the attraction of his propaganda; even in the horrors and injustice, a dulled and demoralized public could sense the will to action. It is in the times of the greatest disappointments and fears that injustice is approved because it is a force, and (as the Wise Men of Zion said) the vilest deeds of statesmen are most admired.

Many a newspaper reader and radio listener was moved to tears when the Leader renounced his salary as Chancellor; a thing that meant little to the author of *Mein Kampf*, for since 1930 the sales of his book had mounted sharply. When he was informed that he could not legally give up his salary, he had it transferred to a fund for war invalids. But this was not yet the great symbolic deed that bathed his figure in the aura of irresistibility. The tempo should not be stepped up too much, wrote Goebbels in his diary on February 25, 'for up to the last day it must be possible to intensify it.'

The great act, which would give content to Hitler's speeches, had been considered for over a decade. The 'fight to the finish between Swastika and Soviet Star' must appear to the people in the garish light of an 'attempted Bolshevist revolution.' 'Then you will see that the Lord hath sent me to do these works.' When the revolution refused to flare up, Göring's police and auxiliary police set out in search of the flame. On February 24 they invaded the Karl Liebknecht House. The building had been quietly evacuated long before by the Communist Party leadership. But in the cellar lay piles of pamphlets; and the mere existence of a cellar led the S.A. to speak of 'catacombs.'

The German press was full of stories about catacombs and underground passages. Otherwise there were no exciting revelations in the official reports. True, in the night of February 25, a trifling fire was discovered beneath the roof of the rambling 'Castle' in the center of Berlin, the former residence of the Hohenzollerns, now used for government offices. The blaze was extinguished at once; there were indications of incendiarism, but nothing was made public. Regardless who had set it, there was not enough fire to talk about.

Meanwhile, the material from the Karl Liebknecht House was carefully studied — though it seems to have consisted only of pamphlets. But three days later, Göring made breath-taking disclosures, though he remained vague about the evidence. The Communists, it seemed, were planning to fire government buildings, castles, museums, and vital factories all over Germany. A sensational fire was to be the 'signal for bloody revolution and civil war.' At four in the afternoon, on the day after the fire, general looting was to begin in Berlin. (Report of the official Prussian Press Service, February 28, 1933.) According to one of Göring's reports, hostages were to be arrested and food poisoned in restaurants. All this was discovered by Göring and Daluege in the papers they had found in the Karl Liebknecht House on February 24 — or so they said later.

In the first three days after February 24, the German public learned nothing of these terrors. But the Reich government and the National Socialist leaders must have been waiting with feverish anxiety for the bloody revolution, the fire and the looting. It therefore seems strange that Goebbels's diary says nothing about all the tension. On the evening of February 24, when the horrible discoveries were made in the Karl Liebknecht House, he notes: 'Glorious weather, snow and sun. Leave the night train after a good sleep and return refreshed to work. In the evening I deliver my attack on the Social Democrats in the Sportpalast. . . .' Not a word about the Communists!

February 25: 'Everyone is concentrating on the election campaign' — not on defense against the Communist threats. 'If we win it, everything else will take care of itself.' That night there had been the fire in the Berlin Castle. Goebbels passes over this event as though no attempted Bolshevist revolution had been imminent.

February 26: 'Sunday. Vacation from my Ego. Reading, writing, and music at home. At night we hear *Götterdämerung* in the Municipal Opera and are overcome by the eternal genius of Wagner. Now we have strength again for a whole week's work.' All this when he must have known from the evidence found in the Karl Liebknecht House that the Communists were about to launch their orgy of arson and murder.

Count Helldorf, leader of the Berlin-Brandenburg group of the S.A., was similarly unconcerned. Helldorf wielded the greatest National Socialist power in Berlin. He must have been thoroughly familiar with the disclosures about the imminent Communist revolution. That did not prevent him from making the rounds of the Berlin taverns on the night of February 27 with his friend and associate, Sixt von Arnim. In a wineroom near the Nollendorfplatz, they heard that the Reichstag was burning. Now this must be the expected 'signal' for a Bolshevist revolution.

Strange to say, Helldorf did not rush post-haste to the Reichstag. On the contrary, he, who was responsible for the safety of the Leader and the Nazi Movement in Berlin, told his deputy, Sixt von

Arnim, that he was tired and was going to bed — Helldorf himself related all this later as a witness in court. He instructed Sixt to go to the Reichstag and see what was going on, and report to him if there was anything serious.

At the same time, Hitler was eating dinner in Goebbels's house. Were they anxiously conferring about the Communist blow that hung over their heads? Oh, no — 'we play music and tell stories. . . . Suddenly a phone call from Doctor Hanfstaengl: the Reichstag is burning. I think he is making wild jokes, and refuse to tell the Leader anything about it.'

It was no wild joke. The flames were rising over the Reichstag's cupola; the inside was completely gutted and the building a ruin. The police arrested a single suspect at the scene: Marinus van der Lubbe, twenty-four-year-old mason and vagabond, a Dutch subject who had previously belonged to the Communist organization in Holland, an asocial type of Left radical tendencies and definitely unbalanced. At once the official bureaus flooded the public with announcements that later had to be retracted: van der Lubbe had carried a Communist Party book on his person; he had confessed to relations with the Social Democrats. Hitler and Goebbels drove to the scene of the fire with a large escort; to an English newspaper correspondent Hitler said that this was the incendiary torch of Communism, and that the fist of National Socialism would now descend heavily upon it.

The next day Göring, through the official Prussian Press Service, reported the plans for a Communist uprising. To the assembled cabinet he made a speech in which he claimed 'that Torgler, the Communist deputy, had conversed with van der Lubbe for several hours in the Reichstag building.' Of this, said Göring, 'we have unexceptionable proof.' The 'unexceptionable proof' was the observation of three National Socialists, later rejected as false by the court. Göring also spoke of men with torches, and, according to an official report, he said that these men had escaped through an underground passage which led from the Reichstag to the palace of the Reichstag president — that is, Göring's own palace, filled from top to bottom with S.A. men.

On the morning after the fire, Ernst Torgler, chairman of the

Communist Reichstag fraction, went to the police; he declared that
the accusations against the Communists, and especially against him
personally, were ridiculous and that he would refute them. He
stated that he did not know van der Lubbe, had never seen him, and
consequently had not made incendiary arrangements with him.
Torgler was immediately arrested. The police also arrested Georgi
Dimitroff, a Bulgarian, of whom they knew only that he was a
prominent Bulgarian Communist. Not until more than a year later
did it come out that this Dimitroff was the leader of the Central
European section of the Communist International. Two other
Bulgarian Communists, Popoff and Taneff, were also arrested.

As days went on, Göring's stories about the terrible Communist
plans became wilder and wilder. He said that he would publish
the material 'in the very near future.' Former Chancellor Brüning
replied in a speech that this was good, and he only hoped that the
material would soon be published. To which Hitler replied in a
public speech of March 3: 'Herr Brüning may set his mind at rest.
We shall publish the material.'

It was never published. If the public had then known anything
about Helldorf's strange behavior on the night of the fire, further
questions might have been asked. The leader of the armed might
of the National Socialists in Berlin knew — if the statements about
the documents from the Karl Liebknecht House are to be believed
— that a Communist uprising was imminent. He knew that a fire
was to be the 'signal.' He knew that two days previous an attempt
at incendiarism had been discovered in the Berlin Castle. But
when he heard that the Reichstag was burning, he did not go and
look; he did not summon his S.A. to battle; he went to bed. His
was the kind of implausible behavior that occurs only when a man
is building up an alibi. And scarcely less remarkable was it that
Hitler and Goebbels should have been playing music with Communist incendiary murder staring them in the face.

Months later the world was still waiting for the documents that
Göring had promised to 'submit to the public in the very near
future.' His police had many months' time in which to search for
proofs of the attempted Communist revolution, and there were no
earthly limits set to its investigation. For many months the Reich

Court investigated the fire and studied the evidence. Göring's documents were no part of it; they were not mentioned in court. In its verdict, to be sure, the Reich Court said that it believed the Reichstag to have been set on fire by Communists, but the court admitted that it had no proofs of this: 'This can' — *can!* — 'have been an act only of Left radical elements, who probably' — *probably!* — 'promised themselves an opportunity for overthrowing the government and the constitution, and seizing power.' Then the court did a strange thing: it acquitted the two Communist leaders, Torgler and Dimitroff, and their Communist comrades, Popoff and Taneff. Only the apathetic, evidently insane van der Lubbe, who admitted that he knew none of the four others, but stubbornly insisted on his guilt, was condemned to death, hastily executed, hastily cremated.

Today it is as good as proved that the Reichstag fire was not the Communist crime which the National Socialists made of it. It is not quite so clear who really did set the fire and how. For the work of a single individual, the preparations were too extensive. It may be assumed that the incendiaries were close to the National Socialists, but their identity and methods have remained unknown. The world was duped with all sorts of 'documents,' a number of them presumably manufactured by the National Socialists themselves, to create confusion. Supposed confessions of the incendiaries were offered for sale, and the forgeries were not always very competent. The irrefutable document in the case, however, is that which was not produced: Göring's material from the Karl Liebknecht House.

Whether a troop of S.A. men passed into the Reichstag through the underground passage from Göring's palace; or whether a band of National Socialist deputies went about sprinkling benches, cushions, and carpets with inflammable liquids, is still uncertain. At all events, the fire would be the signal for a Saint Bartholomew, for that 'night of the long knife' which Hitler had at first been obliged to renounce. Now the cabinet, the Reichswehr, the President, would allow him to break his promise. He wanted — as Göring later publicly admitted — to hang van der Lubbe in front of the Reichstag immediately and without trial, in order that the people should see how sub-humans are exterminated; he wanted the same

fate to strike five thousand bearers of the 'Asiatic plague' throughout the country in a single night. At the scene of the fire, Hitler
issued the command, and auxiliary police (S.A. and Stahlhelm)
swarmed out, occupied public buildings, railroad stations, district
halls, gas works. For a whole day the Reich cabinet wrangled over
Hitler's projected blood-bath, and the National Socialists did not
entirely have their own way. Hugenberg, and for a time Papen,
wanted an immediate Reichswehr dictatorship: a state of military
emergency, a régime of the commanding generals, mass arrests, suppression of political propaganda on all sides; and above all, indefinite postponement of the Reichstag elections. None of these
proposals was approved by Reichswehr Minister von Blomberg.
Was it not the purpose of Hitler's cabinet to spare the Reichswehr
the need for military dictatorship? Hadn't the Reichswehr formed
its alliance with the 'millions of determined men' in order to extri-
cate itself from politics? The aims of the conservatives and the
generals were tragically at variance, and the ultimate result of this
conflict was the Third Reich as we know it today.

The power was thrust at the Reichswehr, which thrust it back,
and the armed bohemians seized it. Hitler and his people did have
to accept certain restrictions: van der Lubbe would not be hanged
outside the Reichstag; Germany's highest court was to investigate
the mysterious fire; Göring must offer better proof for his allega-
tions against the Communists; no mass blood-bath would be sanctioned. These were the obstacles which this cabinet could place in
the path of what the furious Chancellor called the salvation of
Germany. Still thinking that they were the true masters of the
government and well pleased that they had checked the National
Socialists to some extent, the ministers decided to assume a dictatorship of their own until after the elections. Hindenburg signed an
emergency decree, 'For the Protection of People and State.' It suspended the most important property rights and personal guarantees
in the Reich constitution, and proclaimed: 'Therefore restrictions on
personal freedom, on the right of free speech, including freedom of
the press, freedom of association and meeting; infringements on the
secrecy of the mails, telegraphs, and telephones; orders of house
search and confiscation; as well as restrictions on the rights of

private property, even beyond the legal limits, are permissible.' And there follow threats of heavy penalties, with the death sentence for relatively light offenses.

From now on the police was almost uncontested master over the German people. In Prussia, by far the largest state, this included the auxiliary police, the National Socialist private army. Göring, the Minister of Police, could issue any command he pleased, and could be sure that the S.A. would carry everything out; actually it carried out far more than its minister could order. By truckloads the storm troopers thundered through cities and villages, broke into houses, arrested their enemies at dawn; dragged them out of bed into S.A. barracks where hideous scenes were enacted in the ensuing weeks and months. If the victims were not beaten to death and concealed in the woods or thrown into ponds and rivers, they were usually found in a condition which an official, who has remained unknown, described in a report to the police press bureau of the city of Bochum on April 6: 'A Communist who had fled was found and brought to the police. Since he was in no condition for being taken into custody, he was transported to a hospital. His body shows a number of wounds resulting from blows. He was found to be intermittently unconscious and without pulse. At present there is danger of death. The circumstances under which the injuries occurred have thus far been impossible to determine, as he is still in no condition to be questioned.'

At first one was lucky to be arrested on the strength of Göring's big blacklist. These men were sent to ordinary police prisons and as a rule were not beaten. But terrible was the fate of those which the S.A. arrested for their own 'pleasure.' Göring made use of his power to destroy the leadership and propaganda of the two workers' parties. He imprisoned all the Communist deputies he could lay hands on and a few Social Democratic deputies. The whole Communist press was suppressed indefinitely; and the several hundred Social Democratic papers suspended for two weeks. This was a week before the elections. From then on there were virtually no Social Democratic meetings, while Communist meetings were officially suppressed.

To destroy Communism, the Nazis had to smash democracy.

Nevertheless, elections were to be held. A people which had been deprived of all liberties should voluntarily say yes to all this. Sefton Delmer, correspondent of the London *Daily Express,* asked Hitler whether the present suspension of personal freedom in Germany would become permanent. Hitler replied: 'No! When the Communist danger is eliminated, the normal order of things will return. Our laws were too liberal to enable me to dispose of this underworld suitably and quickly enough. But I myself desire only too urgently that the normal situation shall be restored as soon as possible. But first we must put an end to Communism.'

There remained only one party of any size that was neither the declared enemy of the government nor explicitly associated with it. This was the Center. On the day after the Reichstag fire, it met to consider a course of action. Crime was openly ruling Germany; none of these men believed that the Communists had set the fire. Kaas, however, put through a resolution that for the present the Center should 'hold its peace,' and not openly accuse the government of incendiarism and falsehood. A few words of veiled though unmistakable doubt, publicly uttered by Brüning, were all that the Center Party said about the Reichstag fire.

Before the ashes of the Reichstag building were cold, the air waves were alive with National Socialist voices blaring forth details about the murderous, incendiary plans of the Communists, that had been frustrated just in time; S.A. men rushed about in trucks, drunken with victory and roaring threats at the people; in the cellars of the S.A. barracks, woolen blankets stifled the cries of victims. In a public speech Göring cried: 'My measures will not be weakened by juridical scruples or bureaucracy. My work is not to administer justice, but only to destroy and exterminate.' This was the mood governing the elections. Outside the polls, giant posters screamed: 'Your vote for Adolf Hitler!' or, 'Stamp out Communism! Crush Social Democracy!' Other placards, here and there, advocated a so-called 'Black, White, and Red Fighting Front.' This, for practical purposes, was the old German Nationalist Party, led by Hugenberg, Papen, and Franz Seldte of the Stahlhelm. Of other parties the voter saw and heard next to nothing; the Social Democrats made no speeches and issued no literature. In many smaller localities, the polls were manned only by National Socialists; occasionally the secret ballot was discarded and voting took place publicly; and after the secrecy of the mails and of telephone conversations had been suspended, many people ceased to believe in the secret ballot even where it was still observed.

This was the political condition which the voter was called upon to judge. Confused by an overpowering propaganda; stifling beneath the crumbling ruins of a disintegrating state; grown distrustful of his own ability to shape a democratic world; moved by the will to greatness apparent in the speeches and acts of the new men; face to face with tangible injustice, yet hour after hour lectured by his government on the necessity for hard measures to avert the Communist blood-bath; and, on top of all this, intimidated by threats — the German voter gave his verdict on March 5, 1933. With 56.1 per cent of all the votes cast, he rejected National Socialism and its methods.

Under the normal conditions prevailing in earlier elections, this would have been a great victory for Hitler. His party, which had been on a steep down grade since November 6, 1932, had mightily recovered, obtaining 17,200,000 votes, four million more than at its previous peak; this was 43.9 per cent of all votes cast, and National Socialism showed itself by far the strongest united mass-power in Germany. But greater, nevertheless, remained the multi-colored mass which, with all its contradictions, was absolutely united in one point, its opposition to National Socialism. It cast 20,400,000 votes against Hitler's 17,200,000.

Of this opposing mass, 7,100,000 belonged to the Social Democrats; 4,800,000 to the Communists, a fifth of whose former voters had been frightened away in these elections; 4,400,000 fell to the Catholic Center, a million to the related Bavarian People's Party; and, decisively, 3,100,000 to the Red, White, and Black Fighting Front. The people who voted for this last group wanted a conservative counter-revolutionary government, perhaps a dictatorship; in no event did they want Hitler and Göring, and some, without inner enthusiasm voted for Hugenberg and Papen in the belief that these were the only men who might still be able to do something against Hitler and Göring.

With the votes of the Black, White, and Red Fighting Front, the Hitler government had a bare majority of a little over fifty-one per cent in the Reichstag. In itself it was a feeble majority, lacking the constitutional power to undertake profound changes in the form of government. With Hugenberg and Papen, Hitler could just fulfill Hindenburg's order to bring him a democratic majority in the Reichstag; but this was no majority sufficient to sanction dictatorship — which meant change of the constitution.

If only the figures were taken into account, Hugenberg and Papen could have cheated Hitler of his success; but if the political conditions were considered, they could not. On the day after the elections, Papen expressed the thanks and admiration of the cabinet to the Chancellor. There was already ample ground to distrust the assurances given by Hitler when the government had been formed; but both partners would have been lost if they had separated. As Hitler had said during the election campaign, 'Against National Socialism there are only negative majorities in Germany'; this state of affairs, under which German politics had suffered for two years, had not changed: the majority did not want Hitler, but it wanted nothing else; there was no united will to confront the united will of the National Socialists.

Consequently, the S.A. met slight resistance when on March 6 it began to flood the main streets, to invade public buildings, even to occupy factories and business houses. Göring, Papen's 'subordinate,' wired his own subordinates in the provinces not to resist the encroachments of the S.A.; above all, they must do nothing to prevent the S.A. from raising the swastika flag on public buildings. The best that Papen could obtain from his 'subordinate' was that he also tolerated the hoisting of the old reactionary black, white, and red flag; the Stahlhelm, panting along wearily in the wake of the S.A., was permitted to go looking for empty flagpoles on which to raise its black, white, and red rags — 'the typical battle-followers,' wrote Goebbels, 'who are always to be found when the danger is past.' And so the revolution by permission of the Herr President fluttered from the flagpoles of Prussia. The 'best of the nation' lost all restraint; they broke into private homes, dragged political enemies away, shot them, beat them to death or unconsciousness;

occasionally looted Jewish shops; 'borrowed' private cars, expropriated Jewish firms, to which they appointed so-called 'commissar
managers'; for the most part this was done according to individual
whim and no comprehensive plan. The regularity and uniformity
of procedure arose from the lust for loot and pillage which for
years had been nourished in these masses. Since the regular authorities had no legal basis for action against the arrested leaders of
the Left parties, the S.A. established its own prisons, which it called
'concentration camps'; at first these were unoccupied factories or
warehouses. The S.A. had learned the simplest rule of police repression: that the will of an imprisoned mass must first be broken by
the most loathsome cruelty. Every arrest consequently began with
a severe beating, and life in a concentration camp, particularly in
times of overcrowding, was for most prisoners a monotonous series
of kicks and blows; a coat improperly buttoned, a spot on one's
clothing, a wrinkled bedcovering, inevitably meant a blow from the
inspecting officer. Years of incitement from above had taught the
S.A. a bestial lust for torture and murder; many who may have been
good-natured human beings when they began their service in the
concentration camps were gradually turned into torturers and murderers by the routine.

Trade-union leaders went to Papen and reported the excesses, submitting proofs and statements by witnesses. Papen threw up his arms
and cried that he simply could not believe such things. But he need
only have read the newspapers with a little care. Many of the
murders could not be kept secret; the official reports of the Brown
auxiliary police then stated with cynical regularity that the victim
had been 'shot while trying to escape.' It became a favorite practice
to hurl the victims from high windows, because this could easily be
represented as suicide. An English newspaper wrote: 'The habit of
jumping out of the window in an unguarded moment has cost
many political prisoners in Germany their lives in the past weeks.'

Franz von Papen must have known these things. But after
March 5 those forces gathered around the person and the legend of
Hindenburg could no longer part company with Hitler. For after
the defeat of Communism, another danger, which had hovered over
Germany for some time, assumed serious forms: South German

separatism. If anyone could prevent the open rebellion of these states against the unity of the Reich, it was the S.A. For Hitler's government had been created just to keep the Reichswehr out of politics, to avoid using the troops in civil strife.

Since 1871, it had been a truism of German politics that the Bavarian people at heart wanted nothing to do with the 'Lutheran' and 'Prussian' German Reich; the Bavarian royalist projects of 1933 were still based upon this belief. Like all historical truths, this, too, had died one day, and most observers were slow to notice the fact: after the World War a new generation had grown up in Bavaria, loyal at heart to the Reich, rejecting Bavarian separatism, and year after year obtaining stronger and stronger majorities in the elections. The three groups of National Socialists, Social Democrats, and Communists were agreed on nothing but this one point: that the great majority of the Bavarian people were absolutely devoted to the Reich. It was one of Hitler's greatest political achievements to have recognized this truth more clearly than his opponents, and to have acted on this knowledge.

Again the telegraph was put to work, this time by Frick, Reich Minister of the Interior. He wired to Baden, Württemberg, Saxony, appointed the *gauleiters* or S.A. leaders as Reich police commissars; these police commissars put the white arm-bands of the auxiliary police on their S.A. men; with strict legality they occupied government buildings, herded the ministers into their new concentration camps, often with the usual brutality. Separatism was not to be feared in these states, but Hitler could not leave their administrative apparatus to themselves. In Bavaria, on the other hand, an attempt was in progress that really might have endangered the edifice of the Reich. Circles supporting the Held régime considered placing Prince Rupprecht at the head of the state, not as king, but under the title of 'general state commissar,' once borne by the ill-starred Gustav von Kahr. This was to occur on March 11.

The Held government, like the Braun-Severing government in Prussia before it, no longer had a majority in parliament; here again the opposing majority was incapable of forming a government of its own; here, too, German democracy had slowly destroyed itself through the growth of the radical parties; and thus, if Hitler destroyed Bavarian separatism, he could invoke the democratic popular will with more right than ever before. Papen could not very well object to Hitler's intervening in Bavaria as he himself had intervened in Prussia; but, whereas on July 20, 1932, the Reichswehr had marched in Berlin, in Munich it was the S.A. that marched. Hitler had the good fortune to have a relatively popular man in Bavaria, Franz von Epp, the Catholic general. On March 8, the Bavarian National Socialists demanded that the government appoint Epp as general state commissar. The government refused. On March 9, the storm columns of the S.A. marched through the streets by the tens of thousands; the swastika banner was raised on public buildings. Held indignantly wired Papen in Berlin, and Papen wired back that the Reich government had no intention of interfering in Bavaria.

It is strange how little the old routine politicians on both sides understood the hour. The Bavarian government was fully reassured by Papen's reply and was confident that after the S.A. men had marched around for a whole day, they would get tired and disband. A few leading men of the Bavarian People's Party sat in a back room of a big beer hall and deliberated; a friendly journalist called one of them, Party Secretary Doctor Pfeiffer, on the telephone, and asked him if he knew what had happened. Frick, the Reich Minister of the Interior, had wired Epp, entrusting him with the supreme police power in Bavaria on the strength of the emergency decree 'For the Protection of People and State.' Epp, with a few S.A. men, had gone to the government building on the Promenadenplatz. The building was empty and silent. He had brought along Ernst Röhm and Hermann Esser, who had suddenly risen out of oblivion; Deputy Wagner of the state diet, and Hitler's attorney, Doctor Hans Frank. On the evening of March 9, 1933, this group began to govern. This is what Doctor Pfeiffer was told by his journalist friend. Pfeiffer replied: 'Don't make silly jokes!' So unexpected and incomprehensible to most people were the series of events that subsequently became known as the 'National Socialist Revolution.'

But they were to become acquainted with it that same night. The S.A. dragged Minister of the Interior Stützel and Finance

Minister Schaeffer out of their beds and beat them to a pulp. Prince Rupprecht, who had nearly been proclaimed regent, rapidly set out for Greece. On March 10, Hitler in Berlin issued a joyous proclamation to his party comrades: 'A gigantic upheaval has taken place in Germany,' he said. This was the 'national revolution.' From this day on, the National Socialists, throughout the country, called their enterprise a revolution.

The looting of Jewish shops, the theft of automobiles, the violent expropriation of businesses and houses; the torture and murder of political enemies had swollen to an orgy of mass terror; once again the melancholy lesson of history was confirmed, that nothing turns people so rapidly into beasts as a great cause. And yet, humanity rebelled against this hideous form of greatness; people who had voted National Socialist, even on March 5, grumbled; the *Deutsche Allgemeine Zeitung,* a newspaper close to industry, had courage to protest. In his proclamation, Hitler wrung his hands and asked for an end of the atrocities; delicately, he referred to the misdeeds of his men as 'molestation of individual persons, obstruction of autos, and interference with business life'; this, he said, must stop. On March 12, he flew victoriously to Munich, alighted from the plane and made a little speech: 'Years ago I here took up the struggle, the first part of which may now be considered as ended. A coordination (*Gleichschaltung*) of political life, such as we have never before experienced, has been completed.'

One people, one state, one machine, one stream — that is what Hitler meant by his engineer's term; society can be guided; we have discovered this, and that is why we have our hand on the controls. Only seven days before, the German people had examined its conscience in the solitude of the election booth, and its majority had rejected Hitler; but this solitude was at an end when the S.A. filled the streets and shouted up at the windows: 'Flags out!' The people were now drawn into the 'streets and squares,' by the ruse of pageantry, but also by the violence of fists knocking on doors and voices speaking through the keyhole: 'Everyone out to hear the Leader's speech.'

The omnipresence of society, which embraces the individual in every state form, began to grow noisy. Hitler liked to maintain that his state was the best democracy; 'an ennobled form of democracy,' as Goebbels some months later declared to newspapermen at the meeting of the League of Nations; only that we do not 'obscure the will of the people streaming upward or render it infertile by parliamentary intercalations.' There was more truth in this lie than the speakers themselves believed. For it is not the force of armies, police, judges, but the so-called 'will of the people,' that almost imperceptibly, but most effectively, tyrannizes the will of the individual; caught in the popular will or the social mood, the individual is carried upward by the mounting flood or drawn down by the receding wave — this is human nature and cannot be entirely prevented by the most excellent state. But it was to the credit of the liberal state that it did make room for the individual conscience amid the maelstrom of the mass; that it did force upon him a freedom of choice, which he himself was far from always desiring.

The new democracy, ennobled by flags, drums, and concentration camps, now quickly put an end to this liberal freedom which elevates its citizens by education. Set in motion through no effort of their own, that section of the people which had hitherto resisted now began to forget its remnant of personal conscience; it no longer obeyed its own judgment, but the great super-mind which led the march columns and thought for all. The soul of the individual was broken apart by the disintegration of the popular will, and National Socialist propaganda skillfully exploited the lack of logic in human desires. Even those who were most violently opposed to National Socialism could not deny its reality; and this reality was a mighty attraction. The bitterest hatred against Hitler could not deny the grandeur of the mass drama that was breaking over the nation — no political conviction could banish from the world the eternal march rhythm of the Horst Wessel song. The power of accomplished facts called forth reluctant admiration; the worship of bigness, even when it is hostile, degenerated, in the Germany of 1933, into an ugly fanaticism and servility. Napoleon, the century-old nightmare of foreign grandeur, had appeared among the Germans; now he belonged to them, as though created and achieved by their longing; Fate, which had denied them victory in 1918, now belatedly gave them, if not victory, a victory celebration.

'It is no victory, for the enemies were lacking,' Oswald Spengler grumbled. 'This seizure of power . . . it is with misgiving that I see it celebrated each day with so much noise. It would be better to save that for a day of real and definitive successes, that is, in the foreign field. There are no others.' A profound lack of comprehension for the truth that 'internal politics is decisive.' The masses knew better than the philosopher. Victors as well as vanquished felt that the great task was the molding of their state, not a victory over the world. Whatever the secret intentions of the leading clique, the masses on both sides of the domestic fighting front felt that here was a new attempt to solve the problem of modern society, though some might call the new solution heroic, the others barbaric. Hence the abolition of party boundaries and state boundaries. The same people who regarded the victory of the National Socialists as a catastrophe, often a personal one, welcomed the firmer union of Bavaria with the Reich; the idea of co-ordination presented the twofold aspect of subjection and greatness. Even the groups that had been thrown into the discard felt their effacement to be an historic necessity. A few weeks later, when Prince Rupprecht returned from Greece, Epp called on him, introducing himself as the new 'Reich governor in Bavaria,' and politely asking His Majesty for his commands. He wore the brown shirt of the S.A.; the prince, who knew that the likelihood of his becoming king was past, muttered with ill humor: 'What kind of a shirt have you got on? Bavarian generals never used to wear such shirts.' There was wounded pride in these words of the dying era to the new age, but no protest.

Even Hindenburg admitted that National Socialism had saved Bavaria for the Reich, and strengthened national unity. His violent but effective method of winning the resisting states for the new régime procured Hitler a kind of reluctant respect with the President; on March 12, the field marshal, the old Prussian and servant of the Kaiser, put his signature to a decree to the effect that 'from tomorrow until the final establishment of the Reich colors, the black, white, and red flag and the swastika flag are to be hoisted together.' The constitutional colors remained black, red, and gold, but the constitution was forgotten. The new flags, said the decree, signed by Hindenburg but written by Hitler, 'combine the glorious past of the German Reich and the mighty rebirth of the German nation.' Hindenburg had consented to the use of the swastika flag throughout Germany — with one exception. On military buildings and naval ships, the Reich battle-flag was retained without the swastika.

At this time men, who had hitherto regarded themselves as powerful, began to fear the new masters. Doctor Hans Luther, president of the Reichsbank, had boasted only a few days before that he would not relinquish his post; but on the sixteenth Hitler sent for him. Luther resigned on the spot and permitted himself to be sent as ambassador to Washington, where he served the new régime with enthusiasm. The Reichsbank was the key position and commanding post of the German economic system; to this highest post of the dying economic age, Hitler appointed Doctor Hjalmar Schacht, who had resigned from it only three years before and since then had been Hitler's prophet among the financiers and industrialists.

Hugenberg was still in charge of economics and agriculture; von Neurath of foreign affairs, Blomberg of the Reichswehr; Papen remained Vice-Chancellor. Since January 30, nothing had changed in the cabinet personnel; Hitler's 'thirty per cent of voting power' had not been increased by a single per cent; and yet the relations of power had been completely revolutionized. This was possible because Hitler and his henchmen understood the secret of the modern state, which Hugenberg or Blomberg did not even suspect: the secret that the power of this state does not rest on administration and dead machinery, but on the persuasion and education of people. Again and again, various moments in history have produced this 'educational state,' which, because it conceives man as a living unit and not merely as a bundle of independent interests, has also been called the total state. The new state machine, which in the first months of 1933 was built up in Germany under the cloak of the old constitutional state, arose, with all its cruelty toward individuals, far more through suggestion than violence; the S.A. did not defeat its adversaries, but took them prisoner without a struggle; and Hitler's great personal achievement was to persuade the masses that he was already master and that resistance would serve no purpose.

This state — which dominated men by fear and hope; which did not entrench itself in citadels of power, but permeated the whole people; which did not bind itself by laws, but commanded and altered its commands according to circumstance — had its models in history. Plutarch tells us that Lycurgus, the Spartan lawgiver, purposely issued no written laws; 'for he believed that the most important and excellent decrees, aimed at the happiness and virtue of the state, persist firm and immutable only if they have been deeply imprinted upon the character of the citizens by education, because in the free will they have a bond which is stronger than any compulsion. . . . On the other hand, he held it advisable not to restrict, by prescribed formulae and immutable customs, all the trifling concerns which relate to trade and commerce and which are continuously changed this way and that, but to leave them to the judgment of wise and prudent men. . . .' It was into such an 'educational state' that Hitler wished gradually to remold the old 'legislative state.' He took his first measure in this direction on March 14, when he created, through his cabinet, a 'Ministry for Popular Enlightenment and Propaganda,' and entrusted it to the most willing and capable of his pupils, who until then had implemented his propagandist inspirations in the party: Doctor Joseph Goebbels.

Goebbels had been an unsuccessful novelist, an unsuccessful dramatist, and an unsuccessful film writer — all this side by side with his activity as an extremely successful political speaker. He was possessed by the idea that all success in these fields is merely a question of publicity; he was convinced, far more seriously than Hitler, that ideas, desires, standards, could be forced on a nation from above. The municipal theaters of Germany suddenly began to produce his plays; his novel *Michael* suddenly found a mass public, and only because he was the minister. This was the beginning of an artificial intellectual tornado, in which the driest leaves flew highest. Writers whom no one had wanted to read marched, with the swastika in their buttonholes, up to terrified publishers and forced them to print large editions; incompetence loudly protested that it had been repressed only because of its patriotic opinions; at his crowded banquets, Hitler suddenly found himself sitting beside actresses, no longer exactly in their prime, who whispered to him how they had been kept down by the old Jewish theater clique; players of second- or third-rate rôles suddenly turned up at rehearsals and announced that in the name of the Leader they were assuming the direction of this theater, which from now on should serve the true German intellectual effort; and the drama critic of the National Socialist newspaper was on the spot with a play from the days of Frederick the Great, or, if he was a little more modern, with a so-called front-line drama from the World War; if he was a real genius, the product might be entitled *S.A. Man Kruse, a Life of Struggle for Nation and Leader;* Jewish publishers of big democratic newspapers began to ask a local reporter for his political advice, because he was reputed to be a member of an S.A. group in his free time.

If ever the bankrupts and intellectually underprivileged have had a period of greatness, it was in the spring of 1933, in the realms of literature, theater, press, and film in Germany; the wild determination of thousands of shipwrecked, untalented careerists to make something of themselves on this great occasion, merely by proclaiming their political faith, gave the so-called National Socialist Revolution a powerful impetus, absolutely genuine in the human sense, an impetus arising from the most primitive instincts of greed. With the skill of a true general, Goebbels hurled this army of incompetent opportunists and job-hunters against the large and small key positions of German intellectual life, and took them by storm. The radio, which in principle had always been an instrument of the government in Germany, but for reasons of objectivity had scarcely been used for political struggle by former governments, was immediately taken in hand by Goebbels, and men of doubtful reputation even by National Socialist standards were appointed heads of the big stations; for these shady characters, owing to their lack of other accomplishments, were at least reliable.

These new lords and masters, suddenly raised to the light from obscurity and personal nonentity, looked important in their silver-braided uniforms and helped to spread a mood of sudden bliss. The unexpected had suddenly come to pass, nothing had become something; wonders were still possible. That the man whom his own party comrade Rosenberg had kicked through the doorway when he came begging for ten marks had suddenly become Minister of the Interior and omnipotent master in Bavaria seemed like the confirmation of some Messianic prophecy. For years millions had thought that everything must be changed; for thousands the change had now come to pass.

Under Goebbels's direction, the parvenus now staged a great victory celebration; the outward occasion was the convening of the newly elected Reichstag. As the scene, Goebbels had chosen the grave of Frederick the Great, that Prussian King whom the National Socialists rather unaccountably proclaimed as the first German socialist. The Garnisonkirche (garrison church) in Potsdam near Berlin, where the Prussian Kings lie buried, is looked upon by a limited number of people in Germany as a national shrine, somewhat comparable to Independence Hall in Philadelphia, or, even more, to the Invalides in Paris. For the Prussian officers' corps, above all, this place is endowed with a sentimental aura; to the German public the city of Weimar, with its memories of the great German poets, is far dearer; it is with good reason that the German Republic was founded in Weimar. And now, as a calculated gesture, Weimar was to be replaced by Potsdam.

On March 21, the members of the Reichstag met in the Garnisonkirche, but the Left parties were not invited. Prior to the act of state, the members of the government and the Reichstag had attended services at various churches. Hitler and Goebbels were conspicuous by their absence. 'In the morning I go to the Luisenstadt Cemetery with the Leader,' writes Goebbels. 'We do not attend the services, but stand at the graves of our fallen comrades.'

Then a glittering procession poured into the Garnisonkirche. Hindenburg read a short speech, in which he maintained that the people had 'with a clear majority shown its support of this government appointed by my confidence' — meaning that everything is in the best democratic order, but this applies only to the present government, mind you, not to a purely National Socialist régime. 'Thereby,' Hindenburg continued, 'the people have given the government a constitutional basis for its work.' Hitler, in one of his most bombastic speeches, promised that the new government would 'restore the primacy of politics,' which may have been intended to mean that politics was more important than the constitution. Then Hindenburg, for whose benefit the whole show was probably put on, arose with difficulty from his place and descended into the crypt; those assembled could peer through the open door and watch him as he stood deep in thought at the tomb of Frederick the Great. The ceremony was accompanied by the tramping, singing, and shouting of the S.A. and the Stahlhelm. After the scene at the tomb, the assemblage drove back to Berlin; at the Kroll Opera House, near the Reichstag, the new parliament met for its first business session, again chose Göring as president, and resolved to hear Hitler's government statement two days later, on March 23. It was already a rump parliament. Of the Communists, most of whom were imprisoned, none, of course, had appeared; more than twenty Social Democrats were absent, most of them under arrest or in flight.

From this Reichstag the government demanded dictatorial powers. The idea of one year had long since been shelved; the parliament was to go into retirement for four years, ceding the right of legislation to the government. The sole restriction on the government's power was that it could not modify or abolish the Reichstag or the Reichsrat — the semi-parliamentary body representing the individual German states. The President, now that there was again a legislative majority in the Reichstag, automatically receded into the background; this was expressly confirmed and underlined when he was deprived of his right — a mere formality under normal conditions — to sign laws. The government itself fought bitterly over this dictatorship law; in the cabinet session of March 20, it was not unanimously accepted. Later, this ennabling law was several times extended, but historically the first draft has remained the foundation of the National Socialist Reich. Its most important provisions were:

> Article 1. Laws can be passed, not only by the procedure provided in the constitution, but also by the Reich government. . . .
> Article 2. The laws decreed by the Reich government can deviate from the Reich constitution in so far as they do not apply to the

institutions of the Reichstag and the Reichsrat. Article 3. The
laws decreed by the Reich government are drawn up by the Chancellor and reported in the Reichstag's law journal. . . . Article 4.
Treaties of the Reich with foreign states, which relate to subjects
of Reich legislation, do not, for the duration of the validity of this
law, require the consent of the bodies participating in the legislation. . . . Article 5. This law . . . expires on April 1, 1937; it
furthermore expires if the present Reich government is replaced by
another.

The present Reich government was the one in which, according
to Hitler's word of honor, all the ministers appointed on January
30 should keep their places indefinitely; Hugenberg later maintained that if a minister should resign for political reasons, those
who remained would no longer be the 'present Reich government.'

Passage of the law constitutionally required a two-thirds majority
of the Reichstag, or, rather, two thirds of the deputies must be
present, two thirds of those present must vote for the law. A sufficiently large group of deputies, who under the pressure of terror
might not indeed have dared openly to oppose the law, could, by
remaining absent, have reduced the attendance figure to less than
the required two thirds; since 81 Communists had been forcibly
removed, the 120 Social Democrats and approximately 15 members
of the Center would have sufficed — and there was assuredly
enough secret rage among the Center to activate 15 men. The 73
men of the Center and the associated 19 of the Bavarian People's
Party had it in their power to deny Hitler's government the legal
basis for dictatorship, either by an open vote or by remaining
absent. Hitler believed it necessary to lure the Center by threats and
promises. He told Kaas that all parties which consented to the dictatorship law would be united in a working committee, and thus
in a sense constitute a reduced and refined parliament, to which
the government would be responsible for its acts. He even promised to confirm his promise in writing. Kaas waited in vain for the
letter. The Reichstag met on March 23. Kaas approached the government bench and asked about the letter. Hitler answered amiably
that it was written and in the hands of Minister of the Interior
Frick who had to countersign it. Kaas went to Frick and asked

him about the letter. Frick replied that it was in his portfolio and that he would attend to it at the first possible opportunity. This was the last that Kaas heard of the letter. He may only have been pretending to believe that it existed at all.

False witness and simulated confidence ushered in the new era. Those who had expected the old times back again were quickly and bitterly disappointed. After the day at Potsdam many had thought that the national revolution was on its way back to the Prussian monarchy, to imperial Germany. In vain had Hitler repeated over and over again for ten years that the past would not return, that the wheel of history could not be set back, and that this was good, for the past had been bad and rotten — who had noted the exact content of his speeches? The rumor went about that he would soon make place for the Hohenzollerns; that he had even promised as much to Hindenburg. In his government statement, Hitler destroyed this fantasy: 'In view of the distress now prevailing among the people, the national government regards the question of a monarchist restoration as undiscussible. It would view any attempt at an independent solution of this problem in the individual "countries" as an attack on the unity of the Reich.' This was the first of many statements of similar nature by the Chancellor.

No, his dictatorship was the end itself; not the means to an end. But he promised to wield this dictatorship with moderation: 'The government intends to make no more use of the powers given it than is necessary for the execution of vital measures . . . the existence of the states will not be abolished, the rights of the Church will not be narrowed, its relation to the state will not be changed.' The speech contained many another phrase smacking of moderation and conciliation: 'The national government regards the two religious denominations as important factors for the preservation of our people.' It was the compliment of an atheist who admits the usefulness of Christianity. Even to the Jews he promised 'objective justice,' a term ambiguous to say the least. As it proceeded, the speech grew sharper — not in tone, which remained calm, but in content, which became monstrous. Hitler left no doubt in the minds of the Reichstag that the old legal state, with its equality of all before the law, was dead: 'Theoretical equality before the law cannot lead us to tolerate those who despise the law as a matter of principle; we cannot surrender the nation to these people' — if here, as so often, he cloaked a grim announcement in a phrase of artificial banality, in the next sentence he became quite frank: 'Equality before the law will be granted to all those who stand behind the nation and do not deny the government their support.' But those who deny the government their support have, as Hitler had stated earlier, 'no rights whatever.' Then came the conclusion, for the sake of which the whole speech was made: 'The government offers the parties an opportunity for a peaceful German development and for the future conciliation that can grow out of it. But it is equally determined and ready to take up any challenge of rejection and resistance. Now, gentlemen, you yourselves may make your decision: will it be peace or war?'

War was Hitler's last word, his eternal war against the other half of the people. In the galleries, in the corridors between the deputies' benches, stood S.S. and S.A. men with pistols at their belts. Göring, in his president's chair, looked out over the hall through binoculars as though prepared at any moment to command: 'Fire!' Otto Wels, leader of the Social Democrats, explained why his party would vote against the dictatorship law; it was a clear speech of rejection, but between Göring's binoculars and the pistols of the S.A., Wels no longer dared to say what was happening in the country and how the masses really felt. The S.A. had ceased to limit its acts of violence to Communists and Socialists; already they were invading courthouses, dragging out Jewish lawyers and thrashing them through the streets. Protests had been raised abroad; refugees had reported some of the atrocities; Hitler roared at Wels that the Social Democratic International was helping to spread these lies — he actually called them lies. Kaas explained why the Center, despite all its misgivings, would vote for the government's dictatorial powers. He recalled Hitler's promises, and all the National Socialists applauded. A few small splinter parties made dejected speeches for the affirmative. And then the mutilated Reichstag submitted, avoiding war. The attitude of the Center was decisive; with 441 against 94 Social Democrats the law was passed. The National Socialist fraction jumped up and sang the Horst Wessel song.

Chapter *XXIII*

COUP D'ÉTAT BY

INSTALLMENTS

FROM THE AFTERNOON OF MARCH 23, 1933, HITLER was dictator, created by democracy and appointed by parliament, although he was still bound to his cabinet. But he could boast of being independent of Hindenburg now, and he allowed scarcely a minute to pass before showing it. As the deputies were leaving, two detectives went up to the government bench and arrested Günther Gereke, who was still Reich Commissar for Re-Employment. Hitler arranged to have Hindenburg's favorite prosecuted in connection with the vanished funds of the Hindenburg Committee, most probably with the intention of showing publicly that these funds had remained in the hands of Oskar von Hindenburg. The case was tried before two courts; Gereke was sent to prison for years, but refused to say what had become of the money, darkly intimating that he was shielding high-placed persons; and that some day people would be grateful to him. So the terror penetrated to the very midst of the cabinet. Hitler declared, with dignity: If we are radical toward the masses, we must be radical toward ourselves.

The movement was bursting bulwarks which even on January 30 seemed built for all eternity; the *coup d'état* of the Wise Men of Zion was assuming the traits of a real revolution. The armed intellectual no longer followed only the commands of his leaders, now in power; he drove them before him and forcibly seized the posts to which he thought himself entitled. The intellectual proletariat awoke from its hopelessness. Here was a class which could give impetus to a revolution. They streamed out of the overcrowded universities, took the jobs or created new ones for themselves. For years Germany had been suffering from a surplus of men with academic training. At the German universities there were some hundred and forty thousand students. It had been reliably calculated that there were roughly three hundred and thirty thousand positions in Germany for persons of academic training, and since the professional worker remained active for an average of thirty-three years, approximately ten thousand such positions became free each year. Setting the average duration of study at five years, this meant that of a hundred and forty thousand students only fifty thousand had a prospect of employment, while nearly twice that number, or ninety thousand, were without hope. At the end of 1932, some fifty thousand of those graduated from the universities actually were unable to find work. The great moment had now come for this intellectual mass. At the head of S.A. squads, young National Socialist lawyers thrashed their Jewish colleagues out of the courtrooms; at the head of brown-shirted student groups, young National Socialist instructors drove Jewish professors out of the universities. Behind them pressed those hopeless masses of the so-called middle class, who thought that the great hour of vengeance against monopoly was at hand. They, too, were led by intellectuals. Only recently Doctor Theodor Adrian von Renteln, leader of the National Socialist students, had also been appointed leader of the National Socialist middle-class movement. This National Socialist middle class now began to storm the department stores, occasionally trying to close them by force, while National Socialist intellectuals appeared in the offices of the big Jewish newspapers, and declared on their own responsibility that they were now taking over the whole enterprise as commissars of the national revolution. Clever businessmen were sometimes able to bribe these revolutionaries with a well-paid job, and carry on under their protection. But often things were not so peaceful; louder and louder grew the complaints that despite Hitler's 'objective justice' Jews had been mishandled and sometimes beaten to death.

This was something stronger than system. Hardly anything could have been worse for the young National Socialist régime than a premature anti-Semitic economic revolution. But no more than Lenin in 1917 was able to forbid the Russian peasants to seize the land was Hitler able to curb a human type that demanded economic security and had learned that this was his right at the expense of an inferior and hostile race.

Was this a pogrom, an anti-Semitic blood-bath? In a conversation with a foreign journalist, Hitler maintained that less than twenty persons had lost their lives in the 'national awakening.' This was doubtless a conscious falsehood. A careful compilation from official reports in German newspapers shows that in the time from January 31 to August 23, 1933, at least a hundred and sixty opponents of the National Socialists were killed, either in street clashes, 'shot while trying to escape,' 'jumping out of the window in an unguarded moment,' or 'hanging themselves in prison.' The figure one hundred and sixty represents those admitted by the National Socialists; the true figure must be considerably higher, for it has been proved that many murders were not reported in the press. These atrocities caused widespread indignation abroad. The foreign newspaper reader may well have imagined at times that Germany was swimming in a sea of blood. Spontaneous protests arose; most effectively in the United States, where in some sections an effective boycott against German goods was organized.

There was an attempt at a world protest against something which, it was felt, might become an attempted world pogrom; for the S.A. man who killed a Jew in Germany felt, vaguely at least, that he was killing a fragment of world Jewry. But the mass of National Socialist atrocities in the spring of 1933 was directed, not against Jews, but against political foes; most of the Jews murdered or tortured were Communists or Socialists. Social Democrats and Communists, it is true, had a worse time of it if they were Jews; in the concentration camps they were segregated and treated with special harshness. But primarily the blow was directed against 'Marxism,' the socialist and democratic Left; in the National Socialist formulation, the political weapon of Jewry must be broken, not yet Jewry itself. But though it was primarily the political foe and not the Jewish race which fell a victim to the bestial cruelty of the S.A., it was the persecution of the Jews that produced the strongest reaction abroad.

The National Socialists declared that here again the influence of Jewish world power was at work. The true reason lay deeper. Up till this time, foreign countries, as well as the German public, had been lulled by the National Socialists in the comfortable faith that 'things would not be so bad'; that the anti-Jewish agitation was not meant so seriously; that the breaking of interest slavery was not meant seriously; that the war speeches were not meant seriously. Now it turned out that this was a lie. The anti-Semitic agitation *was* meant seriously — perhaps the war speeches as well. The persecution of political enemies — bestial as it was — was still part of the political struggle; but the attack on the Jews was an assault on a peaceful group. The ambassadors of foreign powers uttered polite warnings; Hugenberg and Papen apparently tried to restrain Hitler; Hjalmar Schacht spoke with his habitual bluntness; it was fortunate for Hitler that he had so devoted a personal admirer in Reichswehr Minister von Blomberg. Hitler had to find a way out, and what a way he found!

On March 26, Goebbels wrote in his diary:

In the night I go to Berchtesgaden, whither the Leader has summoned me. Up there in the mountain solitude he has pondered the whole matter fully and has come to a decision. We shall make headway against the foreign lie only if we get our hands on its originators or at least beneficiaries, those Jews living in Germany who have thus far remained unmolested. We must, therefore, proceed to a large-scale boycott of all Jewish business in Germany. Perhaps the foreign Jews will think better of the matter when their racial comrades in Germany begin to get it in the neck.

This was a sudden, unexpected attack on the Jewish world power, at first not foreseen by Hitler himself; at the same time a test of the existence of such a Jewish world power. Presumably Goebbels believed in it no more in 1933 than in 1925; this is implied by his carefully chosen words about 'originators or at least beneficiaries.' But Hitler, in the depth of his feeling, if not of his intelligence, was

surely convinced of the Jewish world conspiracy; and if he anni-
hilated the Jews in Germany, he would, in his opinion, not be
harming innocent persons. By a mass mobilization of S.A. cor-
dons, the party was in a position to stop the business of all Jewish
shops, in this way destroying their owners economically without
the use of extreme violence. It was a senseless plan, and it was from
Schacht that Hitler had to learn that the economic destruction of
the Jews would create an economic vacuum which would inevitably suck in large numbers of Germans; Schacht even threatened
to resign. If Goebbels is to be believed, the fear was even expressed
in the cabinet that the Jewish question might bring war. Unquestionably Hitler, in his mountain solitude, had thought out an impracticable scheme; for the first time since he had been Chancellor,
he had gone out of his way to invite difficulties, to lose sympathies,
to make unnecessary enemies.

What Hitler might have been if he had not alienated the Jews!
This was more than the half-humorous sigh of lukewarm reactionaries, who would have liked to join him. Mussolini threatened
Göring, who had come for a visit, that the anti-Jewish agitation
might cost Germany the friendship of Italy, for Italy could not expose herself to a struggle either with the spook of world Jewry or
with the reality of Jewish influence in international economic life.
And, subsequently, Göring, more than any other National Socialist
leader, soft-pedaled the Jewish question. The most vociferous anti-
Semite was Julius Streicher of Nuremberg, *gauleiter* of Franconia,
whose pornographic lunacy had strengthened many in the belief
that the anti-Semitism of the Nazis could not be serious. To the
consternation even of many National Socialists, it was now announced that Streicher would direct the boycott. There were few
who still remembered Hitler's early speeches, in which he set forth
how the Jew, consciously and for political motives, poisoned the
Aryan peoples sexually, degraded their sense of honor and emotional
life, and subjugated them morally by desecrating their women.
But it was known that for Streicher the 'racial question' was nothing
other than a struggle between Aryan and Jewish men for domination of the feminine sex; that he seldom spoke of anything else in
his agitation; that his illustrated newspaper, *Der Stürmer,* was the

soul of indecency; that he himself ecstatically wallowed in filth and made libertinism his religion. Now that he had come to power in Nuremberg, he went so far as to clip the hair of girls who had been friendly with Jews and publicly exhibit the couples in amusement parks; in his domain, Jewish prisoners were forced to eat grass which had previously been befouled; in a public speech, he boasted of having personally thrashed a defenseless prisoner. With all this, Streicher spoke and acted aloud what Hitler secretly thought and desired; his *Stürmer,* Streicher claimed, was the only newspaper which the Leader read from cover to cover, including the rather detailed drawings of Christian girls being raped by Hebrew voluptuaries; with his concentration on the pornographic aspects of racism, Streicher was the embodiment of Hitler's subconscious. This grimacing faun was now raised from his semi-obscurity and shown to the world as the face of National Socialism.

It was the true face, and herein lay the strength of this policy, for in general no strong policy can be carried out secretly in the long run. This was the appearance of a world type which meant to carry on a world struggle, to unite the 'Aryans of all countries.' It was the premature beginning of a long-term propaganda: the Jews have attacked us, we are only defending ourselves; the Jews incite the world against Germany — Germany doesn't want to harm the world in any way; it is they who desire the struggle, not we; peaceful peoples are the tools and the victims — against our will. The various excuses were lies, but as to the great aim, there could be no deception: it was spiritual world conquest. Here and there an inept thrust might fail; but a powerful policy does not conquer by individual thrusts, but by persistent pursuit of its aim and constant — though not always successful — adaptation to circumstances. In fourteen years of political struggle, Hitler had made many mistakes and false steps, but through errors and failures he had nevertheless become a force attracting greater and greater successes. Prematurely driven by circumstance, he now initiated a new and powerful policy with a small failure.

To destroy the German Jews economically at one stroke soon proved impossible. The most benevolent supporters, the best foreign friends, gave warning. The United German Societies in New York cabled to Hitler, 'in conjunction with local German Jews of German and American citizenship,' declaring that they themselves 'protested strongly against the anti-German agitation in America,' but, with a view to warding off attacks, requested a 'statement on the future legal, political, and economic situation of the Jews in Germany.' At Hitler's behest an official in the Chancellery wired back: 'Chancellor Hitler thanks you for your co-operation in the struggle against Jewish agitation. German Jews, like all other subjects, will be treated according to their attitude toward the national government. Defensive action of the National Socialist Party is necessitated by the challenging behavior of German Jews abroad.' German Jews at home sent numerous messages abroad, requesting cessation of the boycott; Cyrus Adler, president of the Jewish Agency and the American Jewish Committee, cabled to Berlin that no responsible Jewish body in America had inspired the boycott, and that he and his friends were doing everything in their power to oppose the agitation.

This might already be called a result, even before the struggle had begun. The Jewish world power did not show itself very powerful; if Hitler was not yet strong enough to carry out his boycott, he was strong enough to intimidate and divide the enemy by a mere threat. Hastily this straw was seized. Hitler was able to maintain that the 'world Jew' had already capitulated; for the present, therefore, he could temporarily abandon a plan that was temporarily impracticable, and postpone the economic annihilation of the Jews. To be sure, a demonstration boycott was organized for April 1, as a kind of party holiday. S.A. men stood outside Jewish shops and barred admission, though occasionally a rebellious public broke through. Hitler and his followers forcibly persuaded themselves that they had won a victory and silenced world Jewry; 'the foreign atrocity propaganda has abated perceptibly,' wrote Goebbels in his diary. The events soon contradicted him; but he was fully aware that National Socialism was fighting for the world and not only for Germany; and that this struggle would last a long time. 'We are faced,' he wrote on April 2, clearly quoting Hitler, 'with a spiritual campaign of conquest, which must be carried through in the whole world exactly as we have carried it through in Germany.

In the end, the world will learn to understand us.' The Jews, he said, would do well to keep silent about their persecution in Germany. 'For the more they speak of it, the more acute becomes the Jewish question, and once the world begins to concern itself with this question, it will always be solved to the detriment of the Jews.'

Through these words shines the truth that National Socialism does not find the question of Jewish world domination ready-made, but creates it. National Socialist Germany suddenly cast this question upon the world, probably sooner than originally intended; but from then on systematically, not only by means of speeches, but by a conspicuous act: stringent anti-Semitic legislation. It was legally established that the Jews were not citizens with equal rights; in unofficial speeches it was stated that they were not human. Or, as Goebbels had said in a pamphlet, *The Nazi-Sozi,* in 1932, 'Certainly, the Jew is also a man, but the flea is also an animal,' and the other animals do not harbor and cultivate the flea, but exterminate it; as Walter Buch, chairman of Hitler's highest party court, expressed it some years later: 'The Jew is not a human being, he is a manifestation of decay.' In most of the countries of central and western Europe, the Jews were profoundly fused with the rest of the population; in some places they were scarcely distinguishable. The Jews in the German city of Worms on the Rhine boasted that they had been living there longer than the Germanic population; their cemetery showed tombstones from the fourth century A.D. In the beginning of the sixteenth century, when the Jews of Regensburg on the Danube were threatened with annihilation because their ancestors had crucified Christ, they replied: it could not have been the ancestors of the Regensburg Jews, for they had been living in Regensburg even before the crucifixion. Not even the anti-Semites denied that the Jews played a large part in the economic rise of Germany in the nineteenth century; Richard Wagner regarded the creation of the economic age as the sin of the modern Jews. It was a Jew, Walter Rathenau, who at the beginning of the First World War, created the essentials of German economic mobilization; it was the same Jew who, toward the end of the war, made a profound impression on the German youth with his prophecy that the economic age was drawing to an end.

The attack of the National Socialists was not directed against the Jews in economic life. Here it became apparent that a new day really had dawned. The economic was no longer dominant, and the Jew in economic life no longer seemed dangerous; the new state, which subjected economic life, was able for many years to use the German Jews in its economy and to draw profit from them. How new the times were was to be learned with bitterness by the German middle class, which critics, still thinking in terms of the economic age, have declared to be the force behind National Socialism. This middle class might have had the most grounds for anti-Semitic feeling; for years the small independent shop had been carrying on a hard fight against department stores and one-price shops which in Germany belonged predominantly to Jewish capital. Point 16 of the party program even declared that these department stores would be broken up and their space rented to small-business men; representatives of small business were already going around the department stores, looking over the places they thought of renting. Seldom has a party so bitterly disappointed its own supporters as National Socialism these small-business men; on July 7, Rudolf Hess stated that the party leadership regarded 'active measures with the aim of abolishing department stores and enterprises resembling department stores as not indicated for the present,' and he therefore forbade 'any actions against department stores and enterprises resembling department stores.' The Jewish department stores continued to thrive for years.

It was not the Jewish businessman, but the Jewish intellectual, who was excluded from German society in 1933, first from government administration and the practice of the law, later from other intellectual professions. Frick submitted statistics to the Reich cabinet showing that the great majority of Berlin lawyers, and in some courts even the majority of the judges, were Jews; he cited Jewish utterances to the effect that the Jews themselves ought not to favor so high a proportion. There had been resistance to the destruction of the Jewish masses by the boycott, but reduction of the Jewish share in the state proved a plan of great popularity, against which good will and sense of justice availed nothing. Jewish officials had entered some branches predominantly through the influence of the Left parties; and in order to show that these Jews were party favorites of Marxism, bacilli of Jewish world revolution, and hence the born enemies of the ruling intellectual, the first anti-Semitic law issued by the Hitler government, through Frick on April 7, 1933, was called the 'Law for the restoration of the professional civil service.' Its key sentence was: 'Officials of non-Aryan origin are to be retired.'

Similar laws followed in quick succession. Jews were no longer allowed to teach at universities; were not admitted to the judiciary; were not allowed to practice law or serve as physicians for insurance companies; their attendance at schools of all types was limited to 1.5 per cent. At Hindenburg's insistence, those who had served as soldiers during the war or had fought in the Free Corps of the counter-revolution — for there were some — were exempted from these harsh measures. In later years even these Jews had no Hindenburg to protect them.

Some time later, other special laws drove the Jews out of journalism, literature, and theater; they were forbidden to write for newspapers, books written by them might not be published; Jewish painters were forbidden to paint. In short, the Jews were rapidly excluded from all spheres of intellectual and artistic life; for these, after all, were the key positions of the 'educational state.' Wilhelm Furtwängler, the non-Jewish conductor, opposed Goebbels in an open letter, demanding 'that men like Bruno Walter, Otto Klemperer, Max Reinhardt, etc., must continue in the future to express themselves in Germany'; for 'in the last analysis I recognize but one dividing line: that between good and bad art.' Goebbels replied that Furtwängler was very much mistaken, 'Art in the absolute sense, as known under liberal democracy, must not be'; art and intellect — and this is his meaning — are only instruments of domination; he, Goebbels, for example, was also an artist, whose task it was 'to mold the firm and well-shapen image of the nation from the raw material of the mass.'

This molding proceeded with great thoroughness, and the slightest and subtlest traces of the combated influences were burned out of the masses. For the first time the German public was made aware that one could be a Jew without wanting to be or perhaps even knowing it. For the first time the National Socialists succeeded in teaching the whole world what they meant by the concept of race. Hitherto, the couplet, 'What you believe is no disgrace, The swinishness is in the race,' had been a mere Nazi joke, understood by few. Now it became bitter earnest. On April 12, Frick handed down a definition in which 'non-Aryan' meant far more than Jewish: 'Anyone is considered non-Aryan who is descended from non-Aryan, and in particular Jewish parents or grandparents. It suffices for one parent or one grandparent to be non-Aryan.'

One 'Jewish grandmother' made the subject a 'non-Aryan,' treated exactly like a Jew, at least with regard to employment in the civil service. The grandmother did not even have to be Jewish; she became a curse to her grandchildren even if she was a Christian, but non-Aryan; that is, descended from Jews. This was a blow to the Duesterberg type, particularly widespread among Germany's upper crust. And, indeed, the whole anti-Semitic legislation was a weapon in the struggle between different leader groups.

Hitler himself stated that the main thing was to drive the Jews out of the intellectual professions and to create an intellectual upper class free of Jews. On April 6, in an address to a delegation of physicians, he declared: 'Germany's claim to an intellectual leadership of her own race must be satisfied by a swift eradication of the majority of Jewish intellectuals from the cultural and intellectual life of Germany. The admission of too large a percentage of foreigners in proportion to the whole of the nation might be interpreted as recognition of the intellectual superiority of other races, and this must absolutely be rejected.' As an individual, the armed intellectual got rid of competition; as a class, he founded a new system of domination; competition was replaced by command.

Up till now the object of this command had been the seventeen millions who had voluntarily subordinated themselves to Hitler by giving him their vote. But the true goal was the twenty millions who were still opposed to him; for they included the working class. To gain control of this group, trained to handle the technical apparatus, seemed at this point more important to the National Socialist leadership than to occupy additional posts of command; for if you had the workers you had the state — provided only that you were a little more conscious of your aims than the weary and unenterprising trade-union leaders. In many localities the S.A. had already forced their way into trade-union headquarters; beatings had occurred. No trade-union leader called for determined resistance, and there is every reason to suppose that the leaders knew what could and what could not be expected of their followers. The education of the working masses in the ideals of the economic age was now making itself felt. The worker, taught for decades that the only thing he had to fight for was his material interests, was bound to ask himself whether these interests would be better served by resistance to the new order or by participation in it.

Just as the German generals discovered in 1918 that under certain circumstances democracy was the stronger state form for military purposes and hence could be a means of future victories, the German proletariat, trained to regard democracy as a means of achieving material aims, did not regard it as an ideal in itself; it was now willing to exchange the worn-out implement for a new one, as Ferdinand Lassalle had predicted. The founder of the National Socialist Shop Cell Organization (N.S.B.O.), a certain Reinhold Muchow, proclaimed that the workers would be the leading estate in the new Reich. Johannes Engel, another leader of the N.S.B.O., speaking in April at the Berlin Sportpalast, cried out to the employers: 'You are only servants. We do not recognize the employer as an employer. Without the people, you are a heap of dung [uproarious applause].' Göring was present at the meeting; he stepped forward and added: '. . . not only has German National Socialism been victorious, but German socialism as well.' Of course, it was well known that the National Socialists held words cheap, and Hitler's remarks about the low cultural level of the working masses could not be entirely forgotten. But this state needed the workers anyhow and would be prepared to pay for them. The cold-blooded realism of the masses contributed at least as much as any surge of enthusiasm to the success of co-ordination (*Gleichschaltung*) in the spring of 1933. Even the Communists, who had originally conceived things differently, began to give out the watchword: Go into the National Socialist organizations and bore from within; turn them into revolutionary cells. A national law of April 5 gave employers the power to discharge an employee 'on suspicion of hostility to the state' — in other words, to fire Social Democrats and Communists; the real decision rested with the National Socialist 'shop cell.' The workers began to join the shop cells by droves.

Under the Weimar Republic the German factories and mines were political battlefields, and the political life of the masses was reflected more strongly in them than in the unpopular apparatus of the public elections. In the revolution of 1918-19, factory councils had arisen, which later became permanent and official under the name of 'workshop councils.' Intended by their Socialist founders as a democratic instrument for the expropriation of the 'capitalists,' for the removal or subjection of owners or managers, in practice these councils often became an instrument for leading the masses; shrewd and up-to-date employers were often able to use them as an instrument of control over their workers. Others, to be sure, complained that they were no longer 'master in their own house'; on the other hand, the trade unions sometimes found that the councils obstructed their own influence on the workers. In the big industries, the elections to these councils often represented important political decisions. On April 7, such a decision occurred in the mines of the Ruhr. The National Socialists had proclaimed that no Social Democrat elected to the industrial council would be permitted to hold office; the workers understood, and the National Socialist shop cells, with 30.8 per cent of the votes cast, for the first time overshadowed the Social Democratic unions.

The mass flight of the workers threw the trade unions into a crisis. The workers still belonged to them formally, but many stopped paying their dues, creating financial difficulties for the unions. The embarrassed leaders insisted that they really had nothing to do with politics; as early as March 21, Leipart and his colleagues published a statement that Social Democracy and the trade unions had different and separate functions; that the trade unions would not reject state control; and, apparently in the belief that capitalism had conquered with National Socialism, the statement added: 'The trade unions declare themselves ready to form a working organization with the employers' — the employers whom Engel, two weeks later, was to call a heap of dung.

For years no Social Democratic trade-unionist had said, 'We no longer recognize the employers as employers'; on the contrary, the recognition of the classes as classes, each in its place and struggling for this place, had become the philosophy of the trade-union movement. No such sharp words had been spoken at the May Day celebration which Hitler, exactly ten years before, had wanted to break up by force. It was a startling example of propaganda as an art of adaptation, when Goebbels, immediately after the acceptance of the enabling law by the Reichstag, put forward a motion in the cabinet that May First should be declared a national holiday. In the Weimar Republic, which they themselves had established, the German workers had not been able to put through such a measure; now Hitler gave them their holiday, at which ten years before he had wanted to shoot them down 'like mad dogs.'

In these ten years the National Socialists had grown and learned. The 'anti-capitalist' intellectuals, appointed by Gregor Strasser, still led the shop cells. A group of them, with a certain Brucker at their head, met with Leipart and Grassman at the beginning of April, and summoned them to resign immediately from their posts of leadership of the trade unions and thus avert the collapse of the unions; for — according to the minutes of the conference — 'we as National Socialists have no interest in that. On the contrary, we want to create a unified trade union.' Leipart insisted that he was speaking to them as a German, and as a German he must demand an end to the maltreatment of labor leaders and withdrawal of the S.A. from the trade-union headquarters: 'For you have the intention of smashing the trade unions!' All National Socialists in one voice: 'No, we do not. It is Hugenberg who wants that!' Leipart went on to say that if the National Socialists, especially Göring, had not committed so many acts of violence, 'the attitude of the trade unions toward this government would be the same as toward any previous government.' But he could not, said he, be a traitor.

Brucker repeated that the National Socialists had no desire to harm the trade unions themselves: 'Adolf Hitler himself has demanded that the trade unions must not be destroyed. . . Every worker must be organized.' When Leipart asked Brucker if he had been commissioned by Hitler to negotiate, the National Socialist gave an answer characteristic of Hitler's reptile-like leadership: 'We have no direct commission, but the Leader expects us to handle everything in the sense of the new state idea.' Consequently, the negotiations could lead to no practical result, but they were historically significant in that they confronted the new type of intellectual fighting to win the workers with the old class-conscious labor leaders. Brucker said: 'We do not recognize that trade-union leaders must come from the unions and from the same trade as the workers. The chairman of a trade union can, for example, be a doctor. Wage negotiations with employers will not exist in future. Wage contracts: no! Wage schedules: yes! In future the state will regulate wages and prices.' Whereupon Leipart, struggling to make himself understood: 'Do you know how things looked fifty years ago? Do you know that the workers slaved for fourteen hours a day; that they had no vacation and hardly a Sunday off? Do you know that their wages were bad; that they lodged in miserable huts; and were totally excluded from cultural benefits? Then we came and raised the workers up to their present position.' Grassman spoke up: 'The working-class leader must come of the same social class as the worker if he wants to be understood. We have the same upbringing and feel the same pressure. Even if the workers beef at their leader off and on, they know that he is their man. . . .' The National Socialist Fikenscher: 'In our shop cells all active persons have equal rights and equal obligations: the editor, the engineer, and the doctor, side by side with the worker. . . .' Eggert, a trade-unionist: 'In our trade unions we speak our own language which permits us to think and feel with the worker. If you try to approach the worker from outside, you'll never be able to get inside him. The stock of skilled workers will always stand behind us!'

This was a desperate self-deception. The skilled worker stood where his interests called him; for decades the trade-union leaders had been training him to do just that; but now his interests instructed him better than his leaders. Whether the employers would really be a 'heap of dung' may not yet have been decided; but it had been decided that the National Socialist shop cell could drive any resister from his place of work. Meanwhile, Hitler received reports that the trade unions were on the brink of financial collapse because so many members had ceased to pay their dues. The demoralized organization was scarcely in a position to withstand an act of violence, but perhaps only an act of violence could save the unions and force the members to go on paying their dues.

What Hitler decided was an act of violence against a section of his own party; he decided to crush the remnants of Strasser's once powerful apparatus. Not the leaders of the N.S.B.O., the Bruckers and Muchows, should infiltrate and buy their way into the unions; representatives of the new party leadership created in 1932 should seize the trade unions and at the same time sweep aside the N.S.B.O. The leader of the undertaking was to be Robert Ley, who had always hated Strasser and idolized Hitler. One of Hitler's most faithful satraps, he was leader of the party's 'political organization,' meaning its whole non-political apparatus. On April 17, Goebbels, too, received his directives from the Leader on the Obersalzberg: 'We shall mold May First into a grandiose demonstration of the German popular will. On May 2, the trade-union headquarters will be occupied. Co-ordination also in this field. There may be a fuss for a few days, but then they will belong to us. . . . Once the trade unions are in our hands, the other parties and organizations will be unable to survive. . . . It is too late to turn back. Now things must take their course. In a year all Germany will be in our hands.'

Hitler's optimism and self-confidence rose by leaps and bounds; in the cabinet he demanded an end to voting: he as chairman would simply make all decisions; and how often decisions had been made before they were even presented to the cabinet! The conservatives were still at their posts of command, but the ground was receding from under their feet; throughout the country the S.A. was in power, but when Papen crossed the Wilhelmstrasse from the Chancellery to the Prussian Ministry of State, he was still ostensibly Vice-Chancellor, Premier of Prussia, the President's confidential adviser, the man without whom the Chancellor could not say a word to the old Chief of State. On these few square yards of asphalt, in these few offices, Papen still seemed a powerful man; Hitler was his ward and Göring his 'subordinate.' On April 7, a law was

passed puting an end to this lie; by this law the *de facto* rule of the
S.A. over Germany was given legal force. So-called Reich *statt-halters* (governors) were appointed over the states. Hitler kept his
promise to preserve the states intact, but his *statthalters* now ap-pointed the ministers and high officials and decreed the laws; more-over, all eighteen of them were National Socialists, mostly party
gauleiters, wherever *gau* and provincial boundaries more or less co-incided. In Prussia the governor was the Chancellor himself, and
Hindenburg could not complain, for by this act the Reich and
Prussia were 'indissolubly bound together,' as he had always de-manded. Papen, Göring's 'superior,' had suddenly become Hitler's
'subordinate,' and even this questionable glory lasted only four
days. On April 11, Hitler appointed Göring Premier of Prussia
in Papen's place, and also made over to him his prerogatives as
governor of Prussia. Papen was now only Vice-Chancellor of the
Reich, actually a figure without competency and hence without
power; the only thing he could do — which seldom helped him —
was to complain to Hindenburg.

What a metamorphosis in seventy days, from January 30 to
April 11! Aside from the sudden exclusion of Gereke, no changes
had occurred in the personnel of the Reich cabinet; and yet it was
no longer even true that the cabinet contained only thirty per cent
of National Socialists. The authors of this calculation had not
realized that the magic of Hitler's propaganda would not halt be-fore the members of his cabinet. Increasingly impressed by the
fabulous successes of his Chancellor, Franz Seldte, Stahlhelm leader
and Reich Minister of Labor, became a National Socialist at heart;
and the same process occurred in thousands and millions of people
all over the country. The National Socialists were always victorious;
therefore, it seemed to many, they were always right. After the
dubious success of the Jewish boycott, May 1 gave promise of being
an uncontested triumph; on April 19, even Leipart, after hesita-tion and evasions, called on all his trade-union members to 'partici-pate everywhere in the celebration inspired by the government.'

Events had gone beyond Hitler's own prophecies of three years
before. The great masses were 'joining in with shouts of Hurrah';
at this moment, Hitler had predicted, National Socialism would be

'lost.' But the exact opposite proved to be true; by the pressure of the great masses, National Socialism, to cite another of Hitler's formulas, had won the compliance of the Reichswehr and of a section of industry; and now the hurrahs of the millions forced the Herr President's consent to the further progress of the revolution. 'The revolution in the country will be continued' — this was the content of a three-hour, confidential speech which Hitler made to his S.A. leaders and *gauleiters* on April 22 in Munich. Röhm coined the slogan that there must be a 'second revolution,' this time, not against the Left, but against the Right; in his diary, Goebbels agreed with him. On April 18, he maintained that this second revolution was being discussed 'everywhere among the people'; in reality, he said, this only meant that the first one was not yet ended. 'Now we shall soon have to settle with the reaction. The revolution must nowhere call a halt.'

The 'reaction' was well aware of this. Theodor Duesterberg, second in command of the Stahlhelm, publicly complained that the fury of the S.A. against political opponents was destroying the 'national community'; he quietly permitted Social Democrats and members of the Iron Front to join the Stahlhelm, in order to build up a mass force for the day of the great reckoning under the protection of the black, white, and red flag, under the protection of Hindenburg, when Hitler should have 'shot his bolt' — in the fall at latest, said these optimists, for Hitler was a 'madman.'

Meanwhile Franz Seldte, his brother-in-arms, with the childish joy of the novice, buried himself in his work as Minister of Labor, and in all innocence actually thought his post gave him the leadership of German labor, hence the key to all political power; just as the far shrewder Hugenberg did in his Ministry of Economics. Many Stahlhelm men began to regard Seldte as a traitor out of stupidity; and many thought that something more than stupidity played a part.

A human drama became intertwined with the political drama. Duesterberg, the former professional officer, considered his Stahlhelm the army of the new Germany which could only be ruined by the National Socialist bandits; while Seldte, bourgeois intellectual and World War captain, began to turn inwardly toward the movement of the armed intellectuals. Whether all too human motives played a part in this renegacy may later become clear; but there is no doubt that, like Blomberg, Seldte was a personal victim of Hitler, an admirer and convinced retainer. The German Nationalists, who had formerly regarded the Stahlhelm as their private army, no longer trusted it and tried to build up a small private army of their own, the 'German Nationalist Combat Ring (*Kampf-ring*).' This group also accepted Social Democrats as members; but its leadership proclaimed that it was the 'duty and responsibility' of the new state to restore the monarchy — aimlessness and hopelessness all along the line. At the end of March, Göring began to arrest leaders of both the Stahlhelm and the Combat Ring and to disband entire groups; always on the ground that they had accepted 'Marxists' as members — at the very time when the National Socialist shop cells were taking in 'Marxists' by the hundreds of thousands.

For Seldte these 'Marxists' were the most effective bribe. National Socialism was in the process of capturing the working masses, and Seldte, as Minister of Labor, hoped to become the leader of these masses in the National Socialist state. But for that his relation to the National Socialist Party must become clear. In these negotiations Röhm again demonstrated his diplomatic gifts. Röhm had in good part been responsible for the founding of National Socialism; a year before, he had engineered the understanding with Schleicher and the fall of Brüning; now he had brought about the party's first serious inroad into the conservative world. Since the beginning of April Röhm had been holding secret talks with Seldte; by about the twentieth, the two reached an accord. In Seldte this was a conspiracy against his followers; on April 26, he announced that he had dismissed his comrade and second-in-command, the great-grandson of Abraham Duesterberg (which the by-laws of the Stahlhelm gave him no right to do). On the next day, Seldte joined the National Socialist Party and presented his astonished followers with the accomplished fact that their Stahlhelm was now taking orders from the Chancellor. 'Heil Hitler!' was the party greeting of the National Socialists; 'Front Heil!' that of the Stahlhelm. Seldte concluded his radio speech with 'Front Heil Hitler!' It was a political *coup* and a human betrayal.

To a frightening degree the masses themselves had lost their sense of loyalty; many showed a suicidal frenzy in breaking with their customary ideals, connections, parties, leaders. They looked on in silence as their political world fell into ruins, and tacitly acknowledged that a new, uncertain, but bold edifice was growing up. This was no sudden, general flocking to National Socialism, but a cynical lack of resistance — 'they have won out, that makes them right.' A million people would not have participated voluntarily in the National Socialist May Day celebration at the Tempelhofer Feld in Berlin; but the workers in the large factories let themselves be coerced with little opposition. The directors and managers had to march first, and this was called 'German Socialism.' In every city in Germany, the masses marched out to some meadow; in every city Hitler's voice, speaking to the million at the Tempelhofer Feld, thundered from loudspeakers.

For the first time Hitler spoke directly to the mass of the workers; to those whom he had only recently compared with a people at a low cultural level. Now he said that for him there could be no greater pride than 'to say at the end of my days: I have won the German worker for the German Reich.' If he had wished to tell the truth, he would have had to admit that what he wanted was power, and that for this reason he would take away their trade unions; it would have been a forceful, impressive lie if he had promised them a Socialist Germany, as the Engels and their comrades were doing throughout the country. But Hitler avoided the full truth and the downright lie. In the Reichstag he had already indicated that he expected German economic revival through a great effort on the part of employers; his government, he had declared, was not planning 'an economic bureaucracy organized by the state, but the strongest encouragement of private initiative with recognition of private property.' Even to the workers at the Tempelhofer Feld he declared that creative initiative must be liberated 'from the catastrophic effects of majority decisions, not only in parliament, no, but in economic life as well.'

Here Leipart might have cried out that Hitler was no Socialist! Hitler's own followers, his anti-capitalist and shop cell leaders, his Bruckers and Engels, may have looked on very sourly when he praised, as the embodiment of 'creative initiative,' what they themselves had called a 'heap of dung.' But Hitler knew the masses and their state of mind better than his critics. The masses wanted work, no state of the future; the crisis was a problem capable of solution; energy could solve it, and here was energy. Hitler's political gift did not express itself in drawing practical economic plans, which would have been hard for him, but in proclaiming that he would stand all concepts of social rank on their heads — by brute force if necessary. The old society, he said, had looked down on the manual worker; now that would cease; and in order to teach rich people respect for manual labor, it was 'our unbreakable determination to put every single German, whoever he may be, whether rich and well-born, or poor, into contact with manual labor once in his life, to make him acquainted with it.' This was the meaning of May First, the new festival, to be observed 'down the centuries': to bring the Germans back together, 'and if they demur, to force them together.'

In the long run, only those can be coerced who really want to be, and this was the secret of Hitler's whole policy of successful coercion. Hitler's task was to find work for masses who wanted work; desperately difficult as this had seemed at some moments, it would have been a thousand times more difficult to force masses to work who did not want to. If the people's determination to work were combined with an equal determination on the part of the government, the question of program, the method, was almost secondary. Actually, the government had as yet no National Socialist plan for shaping economic life; its economic policy was not directed by National Socialists; as under Schleicher, the most pressing task was to relieve the crisis, 'in opposition to the laws of economic reason.' In Hitler's speech of May 1, he did not promise any key project to revive the whole economic machine; but he did have a private plan intended to put some scores of thousands to work for meager pay: the construction of giant motor highways through the length and breadth of Germany. The country actually was deficient in highways, because it had comparatively few automobiles; it was Hitler's dream that a great increase of automobile construction would bring Germany the same blessings it had showered on the

United States ten years before. Behind this was the idea which National Socialism now cast with force upon the modern world: that the mysterious primal force of political economy, demand, or need could be created and guided from above, here discouraged and there driven forward. But the prerequisite for this was absolute authority, which seemed obtainable only from absolute power. And, therefore, on the morning after the great labor festival, the trucks filled with storm troopers were again rolling through the streets of Germany. This time they stopped in front of the trade-union headquarters; the Brown bands stormed in, arrested the leading functionaries, in Berlin as well as in the states. Leipart and Grassman were beaten, forced to run long distances and do knee-bends; the same occurred all over the Reich with such oppressive uniformity that for the first time the German public learned the full meaning of 'co-ordination.' In paralyzed wonder, the over-powered workers looked on at their own ruin. There was no fight. Robert Ley addressed a pathetic proclamation to the workers: 'Worker,' he assured them, 'your institutions are sacred and unas-sailable to us National Socialists. I myself am a poor son of peasants and have known poverty. Worker, I swear to you that we shall not only preserve everything you have; we shall extend the protective laws and the rights of the worker, in order that he may enter into the new National Socialist state as an equal and respected member of the nation.'

From these National Socialist acts of violence, a sense of power, well-nigh unaccountable to outsiders, spread to the German work-ers. Injustice, repression, and destruction were the order of the day; but the victims acquiesced and were contented. They ap-proved the power, even when it made mistakes and did injustice; for it was through lack of power that conditions had grown so bad. In the spring of 1933, the ideal of the age, a functioning social machine, was reflected in the barbaric joy of the German masses at the violence and energy with which the state and economic life had been set running again. With a stroke of his pen, Ley put an end to the historic state of affairs in which trade unions, with dif-ferent political views and different aims, had existed side by side; all were now fused into a single body, and the armed intellectual gave this body the military name of 'German Labor Front.' A worker was no longer asked if he wanted to belong to the Labor Front; he simply belonged; and within a short time twenty-three million German workers were enrolled in this section of the National Socialist machine. How it would function was still not clear; but in its founding congress of May 10, at Berlin, Hitler left no doubt that it would be merely one pillar, and by no means the only pillar, of National Socialist power: 'There must arise a state leadership representing a real authority, and not dependent on any one social group.'

With the creation of the German Labor Front, co-ordination became an elemental force, drawing all Germany in its wake. With sudden changes of name, the organizations of economic and cultural life co-ordinated themselves, and a country, which had always been rich in clubs and societies, was suddenly bristling with 'fronts.' Those milk producers, who in Schleicher's time had risen against the domination of Danish butter, formed a 'German Milk Front' and proclaimed an 'offensive of German butter'; a German Honey Front called for an offensive of its own, not to mention the 'Shoe Front' and the 'Bowling Front.'

Some of these fronts thought they could merely change their names and yet remain exactly as they were. Leadership in all of them was assumed by a National Socialist who, as often as not, had been something else the day before; but the goals, the demands on the state, the 'selfish aims,' were far from giving way to 'common aims.' To renounce freedom was not to renounce private egotism. All were ready to grant the state, which had shown itself powerful enough to destroy all, the right to command all and thereby help all. By adaptation and co-ordination many hoped to preserve their place and failed to notice that this very adaptation was their downfall. If their 'Heil Hitler' was a lie, it was themselves above all that they were deceiving; they did not believe in the storm because, themselves carried away by it, they could not feel the wind. There were the overly wise who, already on the downward path, persuaded themselves that they were riding the flood tide toward their great aims. Former Kaiser Wilhelm II, in his luxurious Dutch exile, said to an English journalist in the spring of 1933: 'Herr Hitler has done what no one else was in a position to do; he has inspired the whole German nation with a common spirit; he has sent a wave of national sentiment through Germany such as she has never experienced in all her history.' Taken literally, this was a resigned admission that the younger pupil of Houston Stewart Chamberlain, the man of the people, had accomplished what had been denied to the philosopher's contemporary, friend, and sovereign. But the dethroned monarch intended no modesty and resignation; to Hindenburg he wrote, some months later, that the time would soon be at hand to restore happiness in Germany by bringing back the monarchy. Wilhelm praised the elemental event because he had no fear that it would last; these men of the past had no feeling for the forces of a present that to them was far beyond future.

But the old historic forms had ceased to be Germany; they were at most channels corroded by the flood of the new spirit. Heine had predicted that Thor would rise from his millennial sleep and smash the cross and the Gothic cathedrals with his hammer. There was no need to disturb Thor. Matthias Groeber, the Catholic archbishop appointed by Rome, who had concluded his shrewd compromise with National Socialism the year before, now carried his shrewdness one step farther. He ordered his clergymen, who gave religious instruction in the schools, to use the Hitler salute — the gesture invented by Gabriele d'Annunzio, heathen and enemy of the Church. In reply the pupils were to raise their hand in the Hitler salute and say: 'Praised be Jesus Christ!' And the priest, with his hand still raised: 'Forever and ever, amen!'

Chapter XXIV

CONQUEST BY PEACE

AT THE BEGINNING OF THE TWENTIETH CENTURY, Houston Stewart Chamberlain had summed up his idea of a future German foreign policy in a letter to his friend, Wilhelm II: 'A race-conscious Germany, knowing its aims and unified in organization from its center to its extremities, despite the special character of its different tribes, would — even though less rich in population than the Anglo-Saxon and Russian worlds — by outward power and by inner spiritual superiority, dominate the world.'

Shortly after Hitler came to power, Alfred Rosenberg, the ambassador of the Wise Men of Zion and now the officially appointed 'spiritual teacher of the new Germany,' proclaimed the late Anglo-German the 'seer of the Third Reich.' He prophesied in a speech, 'What Germany has experienced will befall other peoples.' And Goebbels, speaking to the press in Hamburg, said: 'I am convinced that Germany has a world mission to fulfill. The present revolution in Germany will not be limited to two countries of Europe. Hitler's declaration of war on the democratic state is only the prelude. The end of the development will be a Europe organized along the National Socialist lines.' This meant that Germany would dominate Europe by 'inner superiority,' to speak in Chamberlain's terms.

Inner superiority would, by a stronger magnetism than sheer

force, raise Germany to the commanding position of the great land blocks, the United States and Russia, or of the rising Asiatic continental power to be dominated perhaps by China, perhaps by Japan. The new Fascist science of political organization would rise to its greatest heights if the old world 'culture territories,' hitherto split up into nations, were welded into such a unit by superior leadership, and their old abilities, trained and stored for centuries, were opposed to the still incompletely organized force of the half-empty American and Asiatic continents. The position of Germany, a land of industrial surplus, surrounded in a large arc by the Balkans and Russia, lands of agrarian surplus, seemed like the summons of history to organize this space politically as a 'productive unit' with a calculable demand and production potential — to use the terms of the economic age.

The economic part of the Versailles system had been buried by Hoover's moratorium of 1931, by the American and English protective tariffs. On December 15, 1932, the French Chamber decided that France, since she was receiving no further German reparations, would cease payments on her war debts to the United States. In vain did Premier Edouard Herriot argue with the Chamber, pleading that the most powerful friend France had in the world should not be offended; he resigned; his successor was Edouard Daladier. For the first time France was led by a man who had not been a politician at the time of the World War, but merely an officer at the front.

The system of Versailles was broken in body and spirit. After 1929, the great world question was no longer: defense of all against a German war of revenge, but the struggle of all, even of the defeated nations, against the common enemy, the crisis; though, to be sure, in the consciousness of certain groups, the common enemy was identified with the Communist menace.

For world economy to enjoy conditions of peace, armaments would have to be eliminated or at least reduced; for they were devouring the prosperity of nations and their menacing presence deprived the business world of all confidence in a peaceable future. If, therefore, England granted Germany equality of armaments in principle, it was not intended that Germany should have more armaments, but that Italy and particularly France should have less. One thing was certain: only a Germany left at peace to work out her economic recovery could be a bulwark against Bolshevism — the French Maginot Line could be no such bulwark.

Now, however, an equalization of the military strength of France and Germany, to which France herself had formally consented in Geneva, would inevitably deprive the ring of French alliances surrounding Germany of much, if not all, of its force; for none of France's small allies — Poland, Czechoslovakia, Yugoslavia, and Rumania — could place absolute reliance in a France which was barely as strong as Germany. What made the danger to them all the more menacing was that these 'succession states' of the old Habsburg monarchy inherited its main evils. They had formerly been the oppressed nations of Austria-Hungary, and now they themselves contained foreign minorities, hostile or indifferent to the new states (Germans, Slovaks, and Hungarians in Czechoslovakia, Croats in Yugoslavia, Hungarians and Germans in Rumania).

The Czechoslovaks were led by men of democratic, liberal, 'western' character (Thomas Garrigue Masaryk, President, Eduard Beneš, Foreign Minister); the country was proud of its parliamentary form of government. Under these leaders, Czechoslovakia, despite the disquieting turn of events, held fast in letter and spirit to the French alliance. Poland, however, had been distrustful since Locarno. Under the leadership of her armed intellectuals embodied in Joseph Pilsudski, she began from 1932 on to renounce the French alliance inwardly, though not formally, and for practical purposes to emasculate it.

Pilsudski was one of the most remarkable historical figures to emerge after 1918; first a Socialist, then founder of a military dictatorship — a combination which, from Napoleon III to Leon Trotzky and Joseph Stalin, has influenced European history again and again. A strange, somber figure, somewhat recalling Nietzsche with his immense mustache and deep-set eyes; in the last years of his life, troubled in spirit, living in mysterious solitude, almost unapproachable, nevertheless dominating a powerful political machine with uncontested authority. He violently combated the parliament of his country, which, like Mussolini, he had to tolerate in the first years of his rule. This armed intellectual bore a political responsibility which might well have given him cause for gloom. None of Europe's larger nations has, up to the most recent times, suffered so hard a fate as Poland. Through one hundred and thirty years she had not existed as a sovereign state, but as a mere victim, torn into three parts, owned and oppressed by Russia (which had the largest share), Austria, and Prussia. After her resurrection through the First World War, she had looked for protection to a military alliance with France and to the League of Nations; but Polish confidence had been weakened by Locarno, and destroyed by the failure of the League to protect China against Japan in 1931. Half in despair, Poland began to help herself. First, in July, 1932, she concluded a 'non-aggression pact' with the Soviet Union. Then Pilsudski dismissed August Zaleski, Foreign Minister, who still favored friendship with France, replacing him by a personal follower, Colonel Joseph Beck, who, in 1921, as a student at the French military academy, had been obliged to leave France because the French authorities regarded him as a spy. Wholehearted friendship for France was scarcely to be expected of Beck, and, indeed, immediately after his appointment in November, 1932, he made it known that Poland was prepared to conclude a pact of non-aggression with Germany as well as Russia. At the Geneva Disarmament Conference, Poland and France began to vote against each other. When the French consented to 'equal rights' for Germany, Poland again felt betrayed by France and exposed to the German menace; when finally France proposed the creation of a League of Nations army, the Polish delegation withdrew its support, for in Polish eyes the League was no more than a guaranty of unreliability, a pretext of the great powers to evade their own responsibility.

One of the few things that the League did do with a certain energy served only to make it more distasteful to the Poles: the League did take an interest in the welfare of national minorities. Poland, among her people of thirty-four millions, not only had millions of Ukrainians, White Russians, and Germans, but over three million Jews, the highest percentage of Jews in all Europe. This fact imbued many Poles with anti-Semitism and a mixture of race and class arrogance. It was the fear of a lurking danger, but also the arrogant contempt of her new leaders for French democracy and their secret admiration for National Socialist energy, which made Poland the weakest link in the ring of French alliances.

One of the first aims of German foreign policy was inevitably to shatter this ring; true, the attempt took time, but the final success was terrific and seemed to confirm Hitler's conviction that in the end domestic politics decided the foreign policy of a country. This finally proved to be true in the case of Poland as well as in that of Italy.

In several points Fascist Italy already supported Germany; both were agreed that the Peace of Versailles would have to be revised. Both nations possessed large quantities of that international dynamite known as 'national minorities,' and this gave their political strategy a certain similarity; moreover, both declared themselves to be have-nots, cheated by the plutocratic world. Italy's chief national dynamite was located in southern France, with roughly a million Italian-speaking people, and in the French protectorate of Tunisia; the German minorities extended from the Baltic and the mid-Volga region, through eastern and central Europe, down to northern Italy. Here a contradiction arose which seemed to cross the common interests of the two countries. To be sure, no German leader had sacrificed the quarter of a million Germans in the South Tyrol with such enthusiasm as Hitler; but at the same time, none had so emphatically claimed the right of self-determination for the seven million Germans in Austria.

Thus began a contest for Austria between Italy and Germany, and for a time it seemed uncertain whether the conflicting foreign interests of the two countries or the inner cohesion of fascism would gain the upper hand. When Hitler seized power in Germany, the two last parliamentary states of Central Europe, Austria and Czechoslovakia, found themselves surrounded by anti-democratic powers: Poland, Hungary, Italy, and now Germany. Austrian democracy survived German democracy by only a few weeks; however, it was not German but Italian fascism which took control, and the methods were not those of the German model but of the Italian. Austrian fascism did not fight by means of elections and plebiscites;

it had to govern against its parliament, first by trickery, finally by violence. Chancellor Engelbert Dollfuss, who had been legally chosen by the parliament, used a trifling breakdown of the parliamentary machine, in a dispute over house rules, as a pretext to send parliament home. This was on March 7, 1933, two days after Hitler's Reichstag elections. Czechoslovakia was left as the last democratic island in Central Europe, now utterly surrounded.

Dollfuss, a strict Catholic, based his rule increasingly and a little reluctantly on the Fascist *Heimwehren* (home guards). These *Heimwehren* were just what one would expect of a Fascist movement in the homeland of National Socialism; they were anti-democratic and anti-Semitic. Their leader, Prince Ernst Rüdiger Starhemberg, scion of a once wealthy and important family, is said to have bought his way into the leadership of the movement; otherwise he was a scatterbrained young man who had been a follower of Hitler some years before.

The Austrian *Heimwehr* can be said with far more truth than German National Socialism to have been a child raised by sections of industry, who organized and armed it to break the Socialist control over a part of Austria. Its opponent, Austrian Social Democracy, could also be said, with far more truth than its German sister party, to be a Socialist movement that took its socialism seriously; consequently, the Communist movement was insignificant in Austria. Austrian Social Democracy organized the workers of the city of Vienna with a determination undreamed of by the American trade unions; and in the sphere of public health, housing, schools, its work was remarkable — in view of the poverty of the country, unique. While in Germany, fascism could claim to be fighting for a socialism which the Marxists had betrayed, Austrian fascism had to attack a socialism in which the tenets of Marxism had been partially realized. Furthermore, Austrian fascism was no absolute defender and ally of the Church. The old 'away from Rome' attitude, the resistance to the 'foreign' papacy, also to the baptized Jews (the 'aroma of incense and garlic'), of which there were great numbers in Austria, was strong in the *Heimwehr* and made them an unreliable ally of the Catholic Dollfuss régime.

From 1918 to 1933, it had been taken for granted on both sides of the border that the Germans and the Austrians were 'one people in two countries.' In September, 1932, when Dollfuss invited his German co-religionaries to hold the next 'German Catholic Congress' in Vienna, he referred to the Austrian capital as the 'second German city'—the first being Berlin. At this Catholic Congress, Kurt Schuschnigg, then Minister of Justice, declared: '... German culture and German law must continue to set their clear imprint upon our country.' As Austrian Minister of Justice, Schuschnigg endeavored to unify German and Austrian penal law—one of the innumerable inconspicuous preparations for a future union of the two countries. In March, 1933, he went to Germany in order to reach an understanding with Hitler. Before an assemblage of German and Austrian jurists in Weimar, he proclaimed, 'The middle of Europe was and is German space, and in it stands Austria.'

Now Hitler's Austrian followers demanded a share in the Austrian government. This, they declared, would represent a way of carrying out the *Anschluss* almost noiselessly; the Austrian government would simply be 'co-ordinated,' though the borders would not be formally abolished. They showed that they were made of different stuff from the *Heimwehr* Fascists, by the demand that the parliament, mutilated by Dollfuss, must be re-elected, for after the contagious example of the German electoral success the National Socialists justifiably expected Austrian successes. Thus they invoked the right of national self-determination, the fundamental idea of the Versailles Treaty. In the foreign struggle even more forcefully than in internal German politics, the dictatorship wielded the weapon of democracy.

This was exactly the point where the split between Germany and Italy threatened. But greater issues, stronger common interests, finally kept them together.

In March, 1933, James Ramsay MacDonald, the Prime Minister of England, called on Mussolini in Rome with Sir John Simon, head of the Foreign Office. The purpose of the visit was to plan for peace and disarmament, without which the economic crisis could never be overcome. MacDonald brought with him for Mussolini's approval a plan for world disarmament, which he had submitted two days before to the Disarmament Conference in Geneva. In this plan Germany was again granted equal rights in principle, though they were to be realized only by stages. The plan was to give Germany an army of 200,000 instead of the previous 100,000 on the European continent; Poland, only half as large, would likewise have 200,000; Czechoslovakia, 100,000; Italy, 250,000, but 50,000 of these in the colonies, and France, 400,000, half of these likewise in the colonies; the distant Soviet Union, in spite of the Bolshevist peril, was granted no less than half a million. But: the great powers, like England and France, were granted heavy weapons; artillery, tanks, and five hundred airplanes each — no more and no less! — while Germany was not allowed a single one.

Nevertheless, England was ready to grant Hitler's Germany twice as many soldiers as the treaty of Versailles had permitted the republic of Weimar. What a step forward! And now Mussolini, the friend, added another step which definitely seemed to demonstrate that Germany had become a great power again.

Was it possible for security and equality to exist side by side? Must not equal rights inevitably mean anarchy, whether all had cannon or all had only cudgels? With this question in mind, Mussolini answered his English visitors with a counter-proposal which would practically supersede the League of Nations as well as the system of Locarno: the four leading powers of Europe should conclude a pact and agree to solve all the great problems of the continent in common and then force their solution on the rest of the world; Germany, whose right to military equality was no longer subject to doubt, should nevertheless promise to rearm only by stages. But the Versailles Treaty must be revised; even a new distribution of colonial possessions was cautiously hinted. The Englishmen were ready to accept the plan, but France opposed the clause on the revision of Versailles, thus dooming the whole four-power pact to practical failure, and though it was formally concluded four months later, it was never ratified and soon forgotten. But all the same, the first Fascist power of Europe had proposed a plan for a new form of continental domination by the four great powers which would have killed the League of Nations; none of the other great powers at once rejected the plan on principle; and one of the four powers was to be Germany.

Hitler eagerly seized on the proposal of the great man south of the Alps. He was willing to give any promise regarding the harmless nature and slow rate of German rearmament, especially as he had long since made up his mind that the question of German rearmament would not be decided at conference tables, but in Germany herself. The S.A., for which, as Hitler put it, 'the World War was not over,' continued this World War in Germany; built up, during 1933, a force of about three million men; subjugated the other half of the people, conquered the parts of the country that resisted, and forced the defeated to admire their own defeat. 'The rickety bones of the world are shivering with fear of the great war,' began the song of the S.A. 'But to us this fear means a great victory. Today Germany belongs to us, tomorrow the whole world.'

Europe at that time possessed a diplomatic organ which registered these wild songs most vividly: the Geneva Disarmament Conference. To the German delegates, struggling for 'equal rights,' the answer could be given: 'You already have an immense army — by right you would have to disarm rather than rearm.' The immense army was no army at all, the German military experts replied; the Reichswehr people call it a 'lousy mob.' True, but the Reichswehr, with its twelve-year period of service, the best-trained army in the world, and hence far more important than the figures indicated, could quickly train these raw masses into serviceable soldiers. For this reason MacDonald's plan provided — and France bitterly insisted — that the increased German army should cease to be an élite army of professional soldiers and become a militia with eight months of service for the individual soldier. The German delegates, however, fought tenaciously for the small model army that the victors of Versailles had unwittingly given them; and made the counter-demand that the others should first do away with their heavy armament; otherwise Germany, like everyone else, must have her planes, tanks, and heavy guns.

What an irony of history! The victors of Versailles now wanted to do away with the army of Versailles; the defeated now fought to keep it. This small army had been unimportant only as long as there had been a common front of the victors; hence the desperate efforts of France to restore this front.

At the end of April, Edouard Herriot, former French Premier who had resigned for the sake of American friendship, came to Washington. He talked with Franklin D. Roosevelt, the new President, and in Geneva, Norman Davis, the American delegate, expressed himself against the German demand for heavy weapons. The French newspaper, *Echo de Paris,* wrote that France had never dealt with so understanding an American chief of state as Roosevelt. Official America did not really take sides, only pointed out quite reasonably that disarmament could not begin with rearmament. But for a time France and England indulged in greater hopes: that the long period of American isolation would come to an end under the new President, and that America would throw her whole prestige into the cause of disarmament, pledging her enormous material strength to guarantee the security of a disarmed world; actually to guarantee the security of a disarmed France against a (perhaps) secretly rearming Germany. In other fields as well a re-entrance of America into European affairs was expected, for Ramsay MacDonald had invited the whole world to London for an economic conference in June, and Roosevelt seemed to expect great things of this conference and of America's participation in it.

New powers had appeared on the European scene. Soviet Russia, with her first five-year plan nearing completion, was beginning to be recognized as a great nation. The Socialist fatherland had long had its ambassadors in Berlin, London, and Paris, distrusted and sometimes snubbed, to be sure; now, in 1933, the United States recognized the Soviet government and exchanged ambassadors. Thus, within a short time, the United States, Russia, and Germany became important forces in European politics, and the whole picture was changed.

At the beginning of May, Hjalmar Schacht appeared in America. Hitler's Reichsbank president came primarily in order to prepare, as quietly and amicably as possible, the great blow which he intended soon to deal Germany's private creditors abroad: the curtailment, in a sense the cessation, of interest and capital payments. The new President of the United States had already taken the first New Deal measures; they put an end to the methods in use under

President Hoover, very much as the Nazi economic policy put an end to the frugality and retrenchments of Brüning. It was the great epoch of state credits, of boosted prices and wages, of confidence induced by artificially created purchasing power. Though there were many extreme differences between the German and American methods — in Germany, for example, no limitation of agricultural production was attempted — the aims, successes, and failures of this policy were similar in most countries. Therefore Schacht, when he arrived in New York, proclaimed that he was bringing 'the heartiest greetings of Reich Chancellor Adolf Hitler to President Roosevelt, whose courage and astute conception of the world's economic problems has aroused the greatest admiration on the part of the Reich Chancellor.' For Hitler 'admires the courageous and resolute American President; moreover, the situation of America is in many respects similar to that of Germany. The Reich Chancellor does not rule as a dictator, but obtained an immense majority in the elections, just as Roosevelt was elected by an immense majority and received extensive powers from Congress.' Schacht continued: 'This is the best kind of politics and democracy in its best form. You choose your Leader and follow him. In this way you make it possible for him to carry out his plans.' This, said Schacht, was the case in America as well as in Germany. He, Schacht, had been commissioned by Hitler and was prepared to listen attentively to Roosevelt's ideas and, whenever possible, to adopt them as his own.

Schacht was received by Roosevelt. If he really understood Hitler's ideas, he may have explained to the President that the new Chancellor must not be confused with the old German military party which was forever raising an uproar in Geneva and disturbing the peace; that Hitler by no means demanded the world's consent to rearm. Notwithstanding, Roosevelt expressed himself to Schacht in extremely clear and unmistakable terms on the threat developing to peace through the new German nationalism.

Just as Schacht was conferring in Washington, news came of a relatively unimportant symbolic occurrence in Germany, in which no one was beaten or harmed, but which nevertheless provoked a wave of disgust across the world. Students and other young people invaded private and public libraries, dragged out books of Jewish,

'Marxist,' 'Bolshevist,' or otherwise 'disruptive' authors, and publicly burned them; they spared neither the living nor the dead, neither classics nor unknown moderns, and the finest writing was mingled with real filth. In Berlin works of Karl Marx, Sigmund Freud, Walter Rathenau, Erich Maria Remarque, and Heinrich Heine were burned in front of the State Opera House. Goebbels made a short speech and it could be noted that he was not entirely at his ease; if students, he said, took upon themselves the right to burn trash, they must also be conscious of the duty to create something better. But then he added, with a glance at the burning books: 'Never as today have young men had the right to cry out, Studies are thriving, spirits awakening, oh, century, it is a joy to live!'

While incomprehensible and hideous things kept happening in Germany, which foreboded nothing good for the future of the rest of the world, Hitler's policy toward foreign countries was of a suppleness, indeed a compliancy, which should have aroused amazement, except for the fact that most people see only what they expect and perceive the new only after it has become customary. On all sides, Hitler stretched forth friendly hands, as he had predicted in his letters to Hervé and explained in his correspondence with Papen. Sometimes he met hands that were stretched out with the same doubtful sincerity. This was the case with Pilsudski's Poland.

The most resolute and ruthless among his enemies — whom he never met personally — exerted a secret spell over Hitler which the latter always felt in the face of genuine authority. In the spring of 1933, Hitler liked to quote Machiavelli's phrase that one must either destroy or conciliate an enemy; and this same clear, cold wisdom — perhaps even consciously — determined the steps of the Polish dictator. When France entered on negotiations about Mussolini's Four Power Pact, Pilsudski believed that the time had come for Poland to force a decision. For this pact was tacitly but indubitably directed against Soviet Russia, but Poland, which would be the chief sufferer in a conflict of all Europe against Bolshevism, had not been included. France, her alleged friend and protector, had nevertheless declared herself ready to confer on a plan which barred Poland from the council of European powers.

Pilsudski answered with a series of military demonstrations on the German border; with reinforcement of the little garrison Poland was allowed to maintain in Danzig; by commissioning his ambassador, Wysocki, to ask Hitler bluntly whether he desired peace or war; finally, by posing to France what might be called the 'question of Locarno.' When the S.A. and S.S. in the Rhineland appeared as 'auxiliary police' with revolvers, this could be interpreted as 'concentration of armed forces in the demilitarized zone'; Pilsudski informed the French government that if France marched Poland would join her. To start war in order to save peace? This was in strict opposition to French public opinion; indeed, it was against the whole psychology of the French alliance system, which was made to prevent war, not to hasten it. France, under the leadership of Edouard Daladier, refused to march.

After the attack on Germany had failed, Pilsudski decided abruptly for peace. Feelers had been sent out long before, and the armed intellectual on one side could easily guess what the armed intellectual on the other side would be willing to do.

The ring around Germany began to break, because at the decisive moment France would not close it. Hitler received Polish Ambassador Wysocki, while German Ambassador von Moltke called on Beck; the result was a communiqué of May 4, published with a certain solemnity by both sides. Germany and Poland expressed the desire 'to examine and treat the common interest of the two countries dispassionately; in this, the existing treaties should serve as a firm basis.' Definitely peace! A week later, on May 12, the National Socialists stormed the headquarters of the Social Democratic trade unions in Danzig. The Polish press, which under former circumstances would have raised a loud outcry, remained conspicuously indifferent.

True, this *rapprochement* was extremely unpopular in both countries. Nationalists in both Germany and Poland had for years regarded a final reckoning with the other as the great aim in foreign policy. Poland was the only one among the victors of Versailles that had taken German territories and people — for it was admitted that Alsace-Lorraine, taken by France, did not want to be German. All those nationalists in Germany, who set their hopes for the future in force of arms, thought primarily of war against Poland — and now Hitler was making peace with this main enemy.

But Hitler was a political strategist far superior to any emotional nationalist. This was why, even in his Reichstag speech of March 23, he had said: the fight against Communism is 'our domestic affair in which we never shall tolerate any interference'; but 'toward the Soviet government the Reich government is willing to travel friendly ways beneficial to both parties.' Three days previous, Göring had declared: 'It is no business of ours what happens in Russia, and it is no business of Russia's what happens in Germany'; he was firmly convinced that 'German-Russian relations will remain as friendly as in the past years.' No, even more friendly, as it turned out. For Germany renewed the Berlin friendship pact with Russia — which had been forgotten, after its expiration in 1931, by the Brüning government, the Papen government, and the Schleicher government. This took place on May 5, a day after the exchange of the friendly declarations with Poland. If Hitler could still say that German National Socialism was a bulwark against the spread of Bolshevism to westward, he nevertheless remained true to his words to Hervé: an armed western crusade against Soviet Russia under German leadership, as Papen had contemplated, was not in his plans.

Presumably with the intention of explaining to British leaders the peaceable, defensive nature of German anti-Bolshevism and German policy in general, Alfred Rosenberg went to London on May 1. Rosenberg then looked like the future Foreign Minister of Germany. The ambassador of the Wise Men of Zion had, on March 31, become head of the newly created 'Foreign Office of the N.S.D.A.P.' For those positions of state power which the National Socialists could not occupy with their own people, they created corresponding 'shadow offices' in their own party organization, in this way setting up a second state beside the state — by no means always to the pleasure of Hitler, who, however, could not deny this consolation to those of his 'paladins' who had been neglected in the distribution of booty. For the moment Rosenberg in his 'foreign office' could do nothing but draw up projects and memorials criticizing the official conduct of diplomatic affairs by Neurath and his career diplomats. But the content of memorials might tomorrow be the official foreign policy. Rosenberg's trip to London was in a sense a test of his diplomatic gifts, and its outcome was deplorable. The sight of this morose figure, the living embodiment of National Socialist race hatred, did much to intensify English distrust of the new Germany. From right to left Rosenberg found a hostile press; public incidents made his stay in England almost unbearable and he soon departed. England's response to Hitler's private envoy was broadly this: We can deal with Germany, but not with National Socialism.

This was a misunderstanding, and before the year was out British public opinion was to be better informed — for in reality it was the National Socialists who wanted to negotiate, not traditional Germany. The official and competent spokesmen of the traditional German foreign policy made no attempt whatever to court understanding and demonstrate Germany's peaceable intentions. At the Geneva Disarmament Conference, the German delegate Nadolny, a career diplomat and personal friend of Hindenburg, fought for German equality of armaments, at first impatiently insisting that the others disarm, then hinting and threatening that German patience was by no means inexhaustible. He condemned MacDonald's plan and — instructed by his superior von Neurath — replied with counter-proposals which, in the eyes of the whole conference, made Germany appear as a disturber of unity and peace. Neurath wrote a newspaper article in a similar undiplomatic tone, stating bluntly that if the Disarmament Conference should fail, Germany would in any case rearm. Great agitation in France! The words of Nadolny and Neurath were taken to mean that German rearmament had already been decided; if this rearmament were to be prevented by force, now was the time to do it. In England the liberal *News Chronicle* wrote that whatever steps France might undertake, England would stand behind her. On May 11, Lord Hailsham, the Secretary of War, declared in the House of Lords that an attempt at German rearmament would be a breach of the Treaty of Versailles and would be countered by the sanctions provided in that treaty, by which he meant invasion.

Things suddenly looked very grave for Germany despite the exchange of friendly assurances with Poland and Russia. Although the existence and the internal methods of the Hitler government had aroused world resentment, it was the old-style German career diplomacy with its boastful speeches which really threatened an explosion. To fill the measure of folly, Papen, who at home and abroad was considered Hindenburg's spokesman, made a speech full of childish bloodthirstiness to his electorate in Munster, May 13. ('To the German man, the battlefield is what motherhood is to the woman.') The career diplomats apparently believed that this was the new tone which the new master expected of them. Hitler convoked the Reichstag for May 17 and intimated that he would inform the whole world in detail of his aims in foreign policy.

On the day before Hitler's speech, a message from President Roosevelt suddenly reached the chiefs of state of forty-four nations; in it the President set down his position on the question of peace and disarmament. Such a declaration on the part of America had been expected since Herriot's conversations in Washington. President Roosevelt had made his opinions known before this: that equal rights for Germany must not mean German rearmament, but the disarmament of the others; he had implied that France must not be expected to sacrifice any part of her security. What optimists in England and France now hoped for was a further, more significant step. If a formula for disarmament should be accepted by a majority in Geneva, it must also be enforced; but this seemed possible only if the world banded together in a security pact to apply sanctions against any possible infringement. The spirit of 'collective security,' which had been thought dead, now reappeared; America, under the leadership of Roosevelt, was expected to find a formula for participation in a security pact. But of this there was not a word in the President's note.

This note declared a solution of the world economic crisis to be the indispensable basis for political pacification; the World Economic Conference must, therefore, convene in all haste; currencies, which had all been endangered by the fall of the British pound, must be stabilized; international action to restore prices was demanded. The President's disarmament proposals moved in two directions: no country must rearm beyond the limits established by treaty — this applied to Germany — and the obligation to limit armaments must be observed by all; but in expressing his approval of the MacDonald plan, the President indirectly approved the principle of equal rights for Germany. Almost more important, Roosevelt demanded the abolition of 'offensive weapons' by all nations; that is, abolition of bombing planes, tanks, and mobile heavy artillery. His explanation of this demand seems prophetic:

'Modern weapons of offense,' he said, 'are vastly stronger than modern weapons of defense. Frontier forts, trenches, wire entanglements, coast defenses — in a word, fixed fortifications — are no longer impregnable to the attack of war planes, heavy mobile artillery, land battleships called tanks, and poison gas. If all nations agree wholly to eliminate from their possession and use weapons which make possible successful attack, defenses automatically will become impregnable and the frontiers and independence of every nation will be secure.'

With this impressive description of the battle of the future, Roosevelt gave the French to understand that they, a people more or less dependent on pure defense, would do well to agree to the elimination of all heavy offensive weapons. As long as these heavy offensive weapons existed, Germany could not be prevented from having them some day — and then, God help the Maginot Line! This proud achievement of the French defensive art was, after three and a half years, virtually on the point of completion; and the stronger the Maginot Line grew, the weaker became the inner meaning of the French alliance system, for the more obviously and definitely the French army entrenched itself behind its 'concrete Pyrenees,' the less able and willing it inevitably became to help its allies in the east by a thrust into Germany. This incapacity of the French army to offer a military guaranty of the French alliances would have become final and irrevocable by acceptance of Roosevelt's proposal, and eastern Europe would have been drawn into the German orbit, and become one more object of conflict between a strengthened Germany and a strengthened Soviet Russia. But even if France withdrew her protection from her allies, and thus lost what protection the allies had to offer her, Roosevelt's plan accorded her no better protection in exchange; for in the President's message there was not a word of the hoped-for statement that after disarmament had taken place the United States would join in guaranteeing the new European state of peace.

Bitter feelings in London and Paris! The *Daily Telegraph* in London wrote that, aside from Hitler, all the statesmen who had received the President's message would view it with disappointment; the *Morning Post* declared that if Roosevelt was not prepared for warlike intervention, he could not secure peace. In France the same *Echo de Paris,* which only a short time before had been so enthusiastic about Roosevelt, bluntly stated that America understood nothing and had learned nothing. But the reaction of Rome was that Italy accepted the American President's proposal 'unconditionally.'

The next day Hitler said almost the same thing to an astonished German Reichstag and an astonished world. The world, and the German public as well, had expected a speech full of violent threats, a speech in which Hitler would outdo Papen's battlefield bombast. Instead of this, Hitler said:

'The proposal of the American President, of which I learned only today' — and which, it had to be admitted, granted Germany no heavy arms — 'obligates the German government to warm thanks. Germany is ready to agree without further discussion to this method for relief of the international crisis. . . . Heavy offensive weapons are exactly what Germany does not possess. . . . The only nation which might justifiably suffer from fear of an invasion is Germany. . . . Germany is prepared at any time to renounce offensive weapons if the rest of the world renounces them. . . . Germany is prepared to participate in any solemn non-aggression pact, for Germany does not think of an attack, but of her security.'

This was a complete reversal of the German foreign policy initiated by Schleicher. But it was not, as most of his audience and readers thought, a reversal of the foreign policy formulated by Hitler more than two years before. It was the continuation of his tactics formulated in his correspondence with Hervé and Papen. Two years before, he had warned his Sudeten German supporters that a war would only carry Bolshevism into Europe, and now he repeated that the consequence of a war, however it turned out, would 'be a Europe sinking into Communist chaos.' In his speech Hitler again stressed that Germany must protect the rest of the world from Communism. Regardless of how this might infuriate the Strasser clique in his own party, one of his government's chief aims, he said, 'was prevention of the threatening Communist revolution and construction of a people's state, uniting the different interests of the classes and estates, based on the concept of property as the foundation of our culture.'

How much of this peace speech had been discussed by the Reich cabinet is not known; but probably there was very little discussion or argument. Hitler's speech, in tone and attitude, was entirely his own, the continuation of a line he had been following for a long time; almost in every point it overruled his professional diplomatic advisers, just as he had formerly overruled his 'revolutionaries,' his Otto Strassers and Walter Stenneses. It was Adolphe Légalité, reassuring an anxious world, swearing to uphold peace. Perhaps in his more intimate circle, when he explained this policy, he varied his old formula about democracy and prophesied, 'Peace must be overcome with the weapons of peace.' If he discussed this policy with anyone, it was with Mussolini, for it was the wish of Mussolini as well as Hitler that Germany should under no circumstances arouse the world's distrust by premature demands for rearmament.

Hitler's reaction to MacDonald's proposal, that equal rights for Germany should be realized slowly, was quite different from that of Nadolny and Neurath. He called the English plan 'a possible basis for future agreement.' He himself proposed a transitional period of five years; only at the end of five years should the disarmament of the great military states be completed, and then — not until then — would Germany achieve her full equality. Meanwhile, he declared, no one need fear that Germany would secretly build up an army contrary to the treaties; for the S.A. — whatever might be thought of it abroad — was not such an army and never could be. Here Hitler was speaking the truth; the Reichswehr did not allow the S.A. to be an army. Hitler even offered to place the S.A. under foreign supervision if other countries (perhaps he meant Poland) would do the same with their own semi-military formations.

Still arguing almost explicitly against the German Nationalists — 'do not confuse us with the bourgeois world!' — he explained why National Socialism wanted to, had to, and would, dispense with war. War, he implied, was a method of purely political state formations, belonging to an outlived dynastic era, while National Socialism was the philosophy of the great European national revolution, and therefore extended far beyond state limitations; a philosophy of democracy among nations which must make it possible to create a system of international justice and renounce force. His clumsy and uncertain choice of big words indicated that the speaker himself only half-believed what he was saying, but at the moment wanted to believe it: 'Through many centuries,' he said, 'the European states and their boundaries arose from conceptions which were restricted to exclusively state lines. But with the victorious emergence of the national idea and the principle of nationalities in the course of the past century, and in consequence of the failure of states arisen from other presuppositions to consider these new ideas and ideals, the seeds of numerous conflicts were planted.' The Treaty of Versailles might have changed this unhealthy state of affairs; but it neglected to do so, 'partly from ignorance, partly from passion and hatred.' The speaker enumerated all the sins which rightly or wrongly he had for fourteen years been holding up to the Peace of Versailles. The peace, he declared, had brought Germany such misery that since the day of its signing, 224,900 persons had committed suicide, and 'Germany, contrary to the sacred conviction of the German people and their government was branded with the World War guilt.' Did Germany wish to wipe out the curse of this 'world peace' by a new war? Never! 'No new European war would be able to replace the unsatisfactory conditions of today by any better ones. On the contrary. Neither politically nor economically could the use of force produce a more favorable situation in Europe than that which exists today. Even if a new European solution by violence brought a decisive success, the end result would be only to increase the disturbance of the European balance, thus planting the seeds of new future conflicts and entanglements. New wars, new victims, new insecurity, and new economic distress would be the consequence [lively applause]. . . . It is the deep and earnest wish of the national government of the German Reich to prevent such an unpeaceful development by its sincere and active co-operation.'

What a change, what a reversal, since the days, not so far past, when Hitler had scoffed at General von Seeckt for his moderate pacifism, his faith in the limitation of armaments! Now it was the generals who did not want to believe in the limitation of armaments; now it was Hitler who corrected them from the plat-form of the Reichstag! And if one of them had argued back that the unlimited insistence on national claims by three dozen big and little nations in Europe was bound to cause war, he would have replied with an expression of almost Utopian confidence in the peace-promoting power of the right of national self-determination; a 'territorial reshaping of Europe in Versailles, taking consideration of the real national frontiers, would historically have been an ideal solution.' And even in the German East, he believed, though with-out revealing the secret of his ideal solution, 'a considered treat-ment of European problems would at that time have been able without difficulty to find a way which would have met the understandable claims of Poland as well as the natural claims of Germany.' The assignment of the Corridor to Poland — this he only intimated — was not such a way, for he regarded the Cor-ridor — unrightly — as predominantly German. But 'no German government will, on its own responsibility, carry out the breach of an agreement, which cannot be eliminated without being replaced by a better one.' For, according to his new and startling concep-tion, the peace-promoting power of absolute nationalism was that it inwardly rebelled against the rape of any foreign people: 'No state can have greater understanding for the newly arisen young national states and their vital needs than the Germany of the national revolution which arose from similar urges. She wants noth-ing for herself which she is not willing to give others.'

A classic formulation of a truly exalted principle. As long as Hitler kept giving mere assurances that Germany needed and desired peace, doubt could still counter with the one word: 'Now!' But then he explained his longing for peace with an idea which he seemed to have gathered from the depths of his political being;

with an argument combined of passionate faith and brilliant false-hood. And an extraordinary number of people were immediately convinced:

'National Socialism is a principle which as a philosophy gives a general and fundamental obligation. Because of the boundless love and loyalty we feel for our own nationality, we respect the national rights of other peoples, and from the bottom of our hearts we desire to live with them in peace and friendship. Therefore, we do not have the idea of "Germanization." The mentality of the past century, which led people to think that they could make Germans out of Poles and Frenchmen, is alien to us, and we passionately oppose any attempt at the reverse. We see the European nations around us as a given fact. Frenchmen, Poles, and so on are our neighbors, and we know that no event that is historically conceivable can change this reality.'

Hitler's unexpected message of peace, shedding sweetness and light on a world trembling in fear of war, the ingenuity with which he cloaked the incredible in a film of credibility, show Hitler as a master of expedient propaganda; as a political pathfinder, discovering ways out of apparently inextricable situations; as the true armed intellectual, who unscrupulously masters the means for the solution of the task in hand. Yet, in this case, he can scarcely be accused of lying to the world. What he said was objectively the pure truth: that the world, and with it Germany, needed peace. This was all the more incontestable as in the moment when he said it he probably believed it himself; and for this reason millions inside and outside of Germany believed him. With disarming forthrightness he admitted that Germany would leave the Disarmament Conference and the League of Nations if she were again denied equal rights; he also admitted that obviously Germany could not defend herself against an occupation of the Rhineland; only it was 'inconceivable and out of the question that such an act should obtain legal validity through our own signature.' Hitler stepped forward in the figure of an eccentric saint who apparently was slow to give his signature, but once he had given it, never broke his word. German refugees might attempt to prove the contrary with facts out of Hitler's past — facts were powerless against the tone of truth in Hitler's speeches.

For the first time since he had been making speeches, Hitler seemed to express the sentiment of the whole German people without distinction of parties; for the first time he found agreement without the slightest jarring note of opposition — if one overlooked the fact that one sixth of the Reichstag, the Communist fraction, was forcibly excluded. However, it was the party which up till then had come out for peace with the greatest conviction, which now found it hardest to support this peace speech. No Social Democratic Party could honorably have given its support on any point to a government of concentration camps and breach of the constitution, for any kind of support was bound to strengthen the tyranny. But Frick, shortly before the session opened, dryly said to the parties that they had better think carefully before voting, for in this hour of the fatherland's need, the life of the individual would be of no importance. This was intended to mean: anyone who votes against the government will be beaten to death, and his comrades in the concentration camps with him. A part of the Social Democratic leaders had already fled abroad, and between the émigrés and those who had remained at home a bitter struggle, not free of personal irritation, was going on about the line to be taken. While the exiles, headed by the party chairman Wels, claimed to represent the party leadership and wished to organize an unlimited underground struggle against the régime, those who had remained behind, led by Paul Loebe, former president of the Reichstag, and Carl Severing, were for carrying on 'within the framework of legal possibilities,' of course with great tactical caution. In line with this caution they decided after Hitler's speech to join in the Reichstag's declaration of approval; they comforted themselves with the thought that even if this were not exactly the bravest kind of resistance to the government, it at least served the cause of peace. The Reichstag expressed unanimous support of Hitler's peace.

With his peace speech Hitler had immediately become the most powerful and most widely heard speaker in the world. He was now a molder and disseminator of world views, to whom the whole earth listened, whether in agreement or hostility; he wielded an influence on public opinion such as history had seldom before seen.

And so began the campaign of spiritual conquest that Houston

Chamberlain had demanded and Goebbels had announced; it was the first trumpet blast of the 'great world mission.' National Socialism, said Hitler, had arisen from the same roots as the nationalism of the Poles and Czechs. If you listened attentively, a faint cry of 'Aryans of all nations, unite,' could be heard behind his words. Hitler might boast today that he was destroying democracy and tomorrow claim that he was bringing the 'true' or 'ennobled' democracy, as Goebbels put it; it was neither the first nor presumably the last time that despotism has called itself democracy. Since the dramas of Friedrich Schiller, the philosophy of Arthur Schopenhauer, and the operas of Richard Wagner, there had been no such effective attempt at the spiritual conquest, or 'Germanization,' of the world as in Hitler's peace speeches which were now to follow one another over a period of years. It is easy to see that the herald of peace literally followed the counsel of the Wise Men of Zion, 'always to appear outwardly honorable and conciliatory'; 'to accustom the peoples to take our IOU's for cash' and in this way lead them 'some day to regard us as the benefactors and saviors of the human race.' But the effect cannot be explained by mere oratorical sleight of hand. Hitler's speeches expressed a feeling shared by the post-war generation of all nations — and perhaps by the speaker himself at the moment — that the relations between nations must have a meaning which war could not have. For the world — H. S. Chamberlain had seen and expressed this — is a task capable of solution, and the great final solution is peace — for Chamberlain a 'German peace.' The last war, at its outbreak welcomed as a gift from Heaven and cheered with astonishing uniformity by nearly all nations, had turned out to be the greatest of all deceptions, a world horror that benefited the people of no country. No less had been the disillusionment of the peace, which did not bring with it the world order for which men had hoped.

Hitler with all his political powers was not the prophetic figure that could promise and make credible this world future which had hitherto failed to materialize, though he occasionally had something of the sort in mind — as he occasionally had everything in mind. Nevertheless in his speech — which in places, to use Hans Grimm's words, 'was more than himself' — there was the distant sound of a more peaceful future, even though he himself envisaged it at best as a future in the style of H. S. Chamberlain, a scientific world order of German organizational skill, brought about by National Socialist violence. Though broader of horizon than Napoleon, he was subject to the curse of all Napoleonic figures. 'All these wielders of power,' said Wagner, 'could not conceive of peace except under the protection of a good many cannon.' But when he stood before the Reichstag and the world on May 17, Fate, for a moment at least, put it in his power to say what the world felt. What makes his speech significant is not how he said it, but the fact that he had to say it, and despite its treacherous, dishonorable underlying purpose, it is a document of the political world sentiment of our epoch. Like Aristide Briand seven years before, he turned his back on cannon.

Actually Hitler, with his assurances of peace, spoke to the hearts of so many millions in the world, that at once a more peaceful mood permeated all relations. Most hesitant was the reaction of France, where the *Echo de Paris* sarcastically remarked that Stresemann must be applauding Hitler from his grave, meaning: Let us believe Hitler no more than we should have believed Stresemann. The liberal press of England was also reserved; but the *Daily Herald,* organ of the Labour Party, up till then full of the sharpest criticism of Germany's internal conditions, shifted its position abruptly and demanded that Hitler be taken at his word. The conservative weekly *Spectator* wrote with enthusiasm that President Roosevelt had held out a hand to Germany in the name of the world, and that Hitler had taken it. An immense responsibility, *The Spectator* continued, lay on the shoulders of France, a scarcely smaller responsibility on those of England; but Roosevelt and Hitler were drawing at the same rope. Almost ecstatically, the writer concluded that in the unity of these two lay a new hope for the haunted world.

As for President Roosevelt, he had listened to the speech over the radio. The German press reported that Hitler's words 'had been received with great applause in the White House.' The official Wolff Bureau quoted Roosevelt's secretary as saying: 'The President was enthusiastic at Hitler's acceptance of his proposals.'

Chapter XXV

HITLER VERSUS

NATIONAL SOCIALISM

IN THE FIRST BOOK OF HIS *DISCORSI*, MACHIAVELLI writes that a tyrant who wishes to establish absolute rule in a country not previously ruled by tyranny must change everything: officials, institutions, titles, even the location of the cities; yes, he must even move inhabitants from one province to another, 'as shepherds drive their flocks from place to place.' He, on the other hand, who wished to reform a state to the satisfaction of all, would do well to leave as many things as possible outwardly as they are, so that the changes are not even noticed. Measured by this rule, the National Socialists conducted themselves more like reformers than like tyrants in the first months, even years, of their régime; for although they thoroughly revamped the methods of government, they retained most of the traditional institutions from parliament, whose decisions they never failed to invoke, down to the subdivision into states.

Here Hitler appeared at the height of his fickle political technique. Power suddenly offered problems he had not expected and was by no means prepared to solve — a situation very different from H. S. Chamberlain's utopian scientific dreams. Yes, there were many problems to be left unsolved — for the moment, at least; issues to be left untouched, resistance unbroken.

The reason for this was no inclination or gentleness on Hitler's part; it was his appreciation of the inevitable. As long as he was fighting for power, his task, in his own words, was to incline the existing institutions to his purposes; now, after his seizure of power, he had to make them serve him. As long as they had a spark of power or utility in them, they must not be destroyed. Obeying this eternal law of political wisdom, the National Socialists again trampled one of their political ideals, embodied in point 25 of their party program. They abandoned the idea of giving Germany political unity. Hitler, who otherwise appreciated the power of existing institutions, struggled against this necessity; but it was a necessity, and it was stronger than ever. For the wheels and levers of the administrative apparatus were not in the Reich, but in the separate states; here were the central switches, here was the power over the public life of the nation. And for this reason nothing was smashed or altered; the apparatuses were taken over as they were; and Göring, as Premier of Prussia, attempted to make Prussia even stronger. In place of the provincial diet, which had lost all power, he gave his state a chamber of leaders; in the process he had, in the good National Socialist fashion, to crush a rival. Up till then a council consisting of higher officials and mayors, the so-called *Staatsrat,* had carried on a rather inconspicuous existence in the Prussian state administration; Ley had hit on the idea of 'coordinating' this body, of making himself its president, and from this vantage-point governing Prussia as Hitler's 'chief of staff.' This occurred at the end of April. Göring tolerated this state of affairs for two months, then he threw Ley out — it was Göring who made the laws in Prussia — and transformed the shadowy council of officials into an areopagus of powerful and celebrated names.

From now on party functionaries formed the core of the *Staatsrat*: the top leaders of the S.A. and the S.S., their group leaders and chief group leaders; and the Prussian *gauleiters* of the party. Up till then the party *gaus* in Prussia had more or less coincided with the provinces, the comparatively large administrative districts of which the Prussian state was composed. One of the shrewdest tricks employed by the National Socialists in their seizure of power was now to appoint many of the *gauleiters* presidents of these provinces; where this could not be done, the *gauleiters* became at least state councilors (*Staatsräte*), and the provincial presidents were required by law, before taking important decisions, to obtain the consent of the state councilors, especially in filling offices. In the smaller states, the *gauleiters* had everywhere become Reich *statthalters*; so that now, though the system was not entirely unified, a net of National Socialist provincial tyrants covered the whole Reich.

But the *Staatsrat* was also intended to be something else; an assemblage of the famous, calculated to enhance Göring's fame. It included church dignitaries, leading men of science and art; among its members were Wilhelm Furtwängler, the conductor, and Fritz Thyssen, the steel magnate. In addition, Göring used his *Staatsrat* as a means of feeding a number of hungry ravens in his political family. The members received a monthly fee of a thousand marks for doing next to nothing.

Thus, National Socialism made its way into every corner and pigeonhole of the administrative apparatus. Pleased with his new power, Göring cried triumphantly that Prussia would continue, as in the past century, 'to constitute the fundament of the German Reich,' that she would never surrender so much as the smallest strip of territory to other German states; that anyone who made any such proposal would be sent to a concentration camp. Hitler replied morosely that the task of National Socialism was 'not to preserve the provinces, but to liquidate them.' Although Göring loyally maintained that he ruled 'above all and primarily as the true paladin of my Leader,' from whom he had learned for over a decade, it was plain that he had not fully learned the lesson of obedience. When Göring solemnly opened his *Staatsrat* in the Berlin Castle, Hitler remained absent; the faithful paladin had taken an important decision of state in open defiance of his Leader's will. But he had the force of necessity in his favor, for the task was the conquest, not the destruction, of power.

The dividing line between conquest and destruction was often hard to find; at times it seemed impossible to snatch a valuable institution from hostile hands without damaging it. If it was not always easy for the supreme Leader to make the proper distinction, much less was it easy for his egotistic and disunited followers, with their eternal thirst for booty. This egotism was an indispensable force in the party, but it could not be left unchecked. A decision and reckoning were due some day. It was more than ten years since Hess, in his portrait of Hitler, had foreseen this decision and had calmly prophesied that to attain his goal the Leader would 'trample his closest friends.' For years Hitler had seen this type of crisis approaching; he had several times fought his way through similar crises. He had surrounded himself more and more with the type of supporter he would need in trampling his friends; in exactly such a crisis, he had drawn Hess out of almost total obscurity and raised him to the party leadership. Now, in the spring of 1933, he put Hess in charge of the whole party apparatus — once again demonstrating by his choice that the party was his property. After Hess had tacitly held this position for some time, Hitler appointed him, on April 27, 'my deputy, with the power to take decisions in my name in all questions relating to the conduct of the party.' In so far as ruling meant work, Hitler transferred his power and his worries to his industrious helper, a man conscious of his own limitations, almost enjoying them.

Thus there arose a new apparatus of leadership with the task of curbing, and if necessary breaking, National Socialism as a mass movement in conflict with the Hitlerian system of authority and obedience; both ostensibly one and the same thing, in reality two opposed principles. For while Hitler's policy was directed toward conquering and dominating the existing political conditions, within the National Socialist movement forces were still working which were out to destroy and break them; for some time they had their way because Hitler as yet did not see his own way clearly enough.

These were concerned with more than power; many were out for more than advantages. They wanted their life to have a new meaning, their existence in society a purpose; their value for their own people was the one thing that gave their careers on earth any value. To many, and not always the worst among them, only faith in their fatherland had retained any meaning, their own nation had become God; if they hesitated openly to declare themselves religious unbelievers, Hitler had provided them with a suitable formula: 'We know two Gods: one in heaven and another on earth; the second is Germany.' But 'we' are Germany, Hitler had said on another occasion, and 'we' meant 'I.' And so there were people who prayed to Hitler, perhaps without realizing that this was prayer.

But now there arose voices among the National Socialists, openly declaring that the new movement must renew the German belief in God — making it clear that God was embodied in the German people. Many insisted that German religion must free itself from the Jewish Biblical tradition — from 'Satan's Bible,' as Hitler eleven years before, in a conversation with Dietrich Eckart, had called the Old Testament. The New Testament was no better, said others, perhaps fewer in number. General Ludendorff, head of a politico-religious sect numbering several tens of thousands, which he called the 'Tannenberg League,' after his most famous military victory, rejected both the teachings and the person of Jesus, whom even Gobineau and Wagner had declared to be 'white,' that is non-Semitic. Hitler himself in his youth, as he told his friend Hanisch, had been convinced that the historical Jesus had been no Jew, but the son of one Pantherus, a Greek soldier in the Roman army. In Ludendorff's eyes, however, the Saviour was the embodiment of Asiatic magic, a force destructive to the Germanic peoples. And, it must be added, to him one of the most dangerous agents of the Roman priesthood was Hitler himself.

For it could not be denied that Hitler still belonged to the Catholic Church. In March, 1933, it is true, he had demonstratively remained absent from the services of his Church; there was the story that in his youth he had spat out the Host. But he was on terms of intimate friendship with several Catholic clergymen, such as Abbot Alban Schachleitner, former head of the Emmaus Cloister in Prague, who after 1918 had been driven out by the Czechoslovakian revolution. In his whole being Schachleitner was a fragment of that German national dynamite scattered through the whole of Central and Eastern Europe. It is possible that his faith in his people overshadowed his faith in his Saviour. Hitler, who in 1918 certainly still went to confession and communion, is even said later to have received the sacrament from the hands of this National Socialist abbot. At all events, on July 1, he let it be officially proclaimed: 'Reich Chancellor Hitler still belongs to the Catholic Church and has no intention of leaving it.'

Certainly, he had stated that '... the priest in politics we shall eliminate . . . we shall give him back to the pulpit and the altar.' And to satisfy him the party of the Catholic Church itself took care to eliminate the priest from politics; Kaas, the prelate, on May 6, retired from the leadership of the Center Party, went to Rome, and found a position in the Vatican. But Brüning, his successor, carried on, and had conferences with Hitler, who had not as yet revoked his bid for collaboration. Actually, the party of the Church did, for a few months, share the government with the National Socialists; in Bavaria Count Quadt-Isny, the new leader of the Bavarian People's Party, served as Minister of Economics.

Step by step, the Catholic Church abandoned political resistance to National Socialism. The same German bishops, who three years before had warned against the un-Christian movement, declared in a conference at Fulda, March 28, 1933, that after Hitler's Reichstag speech of March 23, with its conciliatory words for the Church, they felt justified in 'hoping that the above-mentioned general prohibitions and warnings need no longer be regarded as necessary,' and recommended obedience to the legal authorities. The prohibitions and warnings had been issued while the National Socialists were merely marching through the streets and issuing threats; they were withdrawn when thousands were murdered or beaten to a pulp in concentration camps.

By retreating on the political field the Church hoped to keep its spiritual power intact. But was this possible?

For centuries it had been true that the cleavage into two sects of approximately equal strength — if Austria was included — had helped to tear Germany apart. But now: 'As soon as a man puts on the brown shirt,' said Rosenberg, 'he ceases to be a Catholic or a Protestant; he is only a National Socialist' — and what else could this mean except that the National Socialist had ceased to be a Christian? At all events, this is exactly what Rosenberg had meant by his words. In a society where the individual was nothing and the nation was everything, God could be nothing unless he was the nation; this was no philosophical hair-splitting, but a state of mind prevailing among large masses. The church-weariness and faith-lessness of considerable sections of the Protestant church member-ship, especially in the big cities, was clear from the emptiness of the churches. But the beer halls and sport stadiums could no longer hold all the people who thronged to political meetings.

Yet in the spring of 1933, the Catholic Church was able to demon-strate its appeal to great masses in Germany. In the city of Trier, for the first time in many decades, a remarkable relic, contested even in church circles, was put on exhibition: the so-called 'holy mantle,' which Jesus supposedly wore on the cross; for days throngs of Catholics streamed into the moderate-sized city and followed their priests to the cathedral, where they passed six or eight abreast before the holy relic. The National Socialists could not have staged a more impressive mass spectacle; perhaps this demonstration of Catholic strength helped to make Hitler more receptive to a con-cordat with the Holy See, negotiations for which had been in prog-ress for some time.

The aim of the Vatican in these 'concordats' was to lend the Church the protection of an international treaty. Up till then the Catholic Church had concluded its treaties with the German states, consciously exploiting the political division of Germany; obviously, it could obtain more favorable conditions from predominantly Catholic Bavaria than from Protestant Prussia. Now, under Hitler, new negotiations were begun. One thing that was definitely ex-pected from a treaty between the Third Reich and the Pope was to prevent the Vatican — that is, a foreign power — from concluding a treaty with a separate German state; even if the existing con-cordats with the states could not immediately be eliminated. Kaas in Rome was urging conclusion of the Reich Concordat, with the idea that in this case Hitler would be forced to give one of his promises in writing — and not in an unsent letter, as in the case of his promise to collaborate with the Center Party. Papen, the Catholic nobleman, went to Rome as chief negotiator.

Hitler's idea was that the Reich Concordat would mean the defi-nite disappearance of the Church from German political life. The Church was no doubt ready to adjust itself to a non-parliamentary state. Hitler had once contemptuously predicted: 'I see the time coming when the Pope will be glad if the Church is taken under the protection of National Socialism against the parties of the Center.' Perhaps in reality it was not too hard a blow for the Pope, or at least for his Secretary of State, Cardinal Pacelli, that by the Concordat they would have to forbid the German clergy to engage in political activity; the Reich government promised in a codicil that it would also prevent the Protestant clergy from engaging in political activity. The treaty obligated the Holy See, before appointment of any archbishop or bishop, to inquire if the provincial *statthalter* had any objection to the candidate; also, the bishop had to swear loyalty to the German Reich and promise to respect the government.

In return, the government agreed that many of the Church's religious and social organizations, including the Catholic workers' clubs, would be tolerated. While this was being discussed, the Munich S.A. assaulted members of these clubs who had gathered for a national congress (June 11-12, 1933), and beat them severely, not far from the place where, fourteen years before, twenty-one Catholic workers had fallen beneath the bullets and rifle butts of the murderers' army. But the conferences on the Concordat went on.

In renewing the Berlin treaty of friendship, the 'godless Jews of the Kremlin' had been the first world power to hold out a hand to Hitler; the Vicar of Christ on earth became the second. Many German Catholics felt more humiliated than protected by this treaty. The majority of the bishops and the Holy See saw things differently. Not a few sons of the Catholic Church vacillated when confronted by the choice between obedience to their clergy and obedience to their secular leaders; the Church now was compromising to save spiritual values in the modern man, values which lay outside of all social relations. On the other hand, such profoundly earthly considerations as concern for church property — cloisters, schools, hospitals — and for the livelihood of the clergy must also have influenced the Holy See in its dealings with the Antichrist.

At the same time, the National Socialists tried to sever the Catholic Church from the active life of the nation, they made a serious and promising attempt to take possession of the Protestant Church which was a German Church to begin with. Here the task was entirely different: not to tear or lure believers away from their Church, but to lead unbelievers back. In June, 1932, some National Socialist clergymen had founded an organization calling itself the 'Faith Movement of German Christians'; at its head stood a minister named Hossenfelder. It was a minority group in the Protestant clergy; and the 'German Christians' could not even claim to represent the 'living church' — i.e., the mass of believing men and women — against 'alien' priests. For those leaders of the Protestant Church who resisted National Socialism were supported by the majority of the churchgoers. The National Socialist ministers replied that they alone could bring back the non-churchgoers, and that these lost sheep were what mattered.

These were the masses of 'involuntary' church members; those numerous laymen who, according to the State Church laws prevailing in Germany, were counted as belonging to the official Church and had to pay church taxes, although they had not seen the inside of a church for years. Only this 'State Church' system makes all the German church struggles comprehensible. Up to the fall of the German Empire in 1918, practically everyone had to belong to a religious community, either the Catholic Church or the Protestant State Church. In Prussia, the King was supreme head of the Protestant Church. After the founding of the German Republic, this state of affairs had ceased in principle, but only in principle. In practice the state continued to collect church taxes, and anyone who did not expressly leave the Church had to go on paying them; but as a rule, even those who had lost their faith did not expressly resign. It was principally these faithless church members who had now suddenly flocked to the 'German Christians.'

With the authority of National Socialism, the German Christian ministers were able to enlist considerable masses of the unbelieving or half-believing church membership. Among their leaders was Ludwig Müller, the army chaplain who had brought Hitler and General von Blomberg together; Hitler believed that he was performing a masterly stroke when he summarily dismissed Hossenfelder and made the friend of his Reichswehr Minister head of the German Christians. Müller did not fulfill expectations; in the middle of May, the leaders of the Protestant Church drew from him an admission that the Church must be 'free of state guardianship.' But he did make it clear that the Protestant Church must be run in accordance with the 'leader principle.' The very titles of the new leadership had for German Protestant ears an ugly ring of Papism: there would be a 'Reich Bishop' with a number of other bishops under him. Taking Müller by surprise, the majority of the Church body elected as their bishop a man of their ranks, Pastor Friedrich von Bodelschwingh, a widely respected Churchman and by no means a National Socialist. His election was an open insult to Hitler, because Bodelschwingh was the director of a famous home for the feeble-minded, caring for those people who, in Hitler's opinion, should have been exterminated for the good of the race.

At this point, open warfare broke out between the Church and the party. Almost anything might have provoked it, for these were two faiths which could not live at peace with one another. The most obvious cause for conflict was the racial question, for the German Christians demanded that only Aryans be admitted to the Church, and especially to the clergy. The number of German non-Aryans who had ceased to be Jews was later set by National Socialist statistics at one million; over this relatively small number the German churches of both denominations waged an intense struggle. The Church as such could not renounce these people, for Christ had said: 'Ye shall teach all the nations.' The Catholic Church went even farther, and refused to admit that non-Aryans had ceased to be Germans; in a pastoral letter of June 10, 1933 — the last of its kind for many years to come — the Catholic bishops declared 'that national unity can be achieved, not only by like blood, but also by like mentality, and that exclusive consideration of race and blood in judging state membership leads to injustice.' In the Protestant Church the German Christians, with their insistence on the introduction of the 'Aryan clause' into the articles of faith, stood two thousand years of church history on its head. For the history of the Christian Church had begun with the principle that all Christians must be circumcised Jews, and only when this principle was discarded did Christianity begin to grow and to 'teach all nations'; now, in 1933, it was no longer permissible for a Christian to have been a circumcised Jew. When Bodelschwingh and his clergymen resisted this idea, Göring ordered his subordinate, Bernhard Rust, the Prussian Minister of Education, to use force; hesitantly and reluctantly, Rust set a taskmaster over the Protestant Church, a civil servant by the name of Jaeger. High and low clergymen were thrown out. Müller was made head of the Protestant churches, and Bodelschwingh was forced to resign. On July 2, 1933, the swastika flags were raised over the Evangelical churches of Germany.

It was the flood tide of the Nazi revolution. In this moment it still seemed uncertain how far National Socialism would go in the breaking of resistance; whether it would submit to the limitations which Machiavelli advises the reformer to accept. Hitler himself was not clear how far he could go and how far he wanted to go. At first he had counted on a slow but persistent overcoming of resistance; but then there had been great and unexpected successes, and his confidence rose above all difficulties. On June 15, he assembled the National Socialist leaders in Berlin and commanded them to intensify their struggle against those adversaries who were still present. The last months, he said, had strengthened him in the conviction that the National Socialist government would master foreign and economic difficulties with the same success that it mastered domestic difficulties. It was his conviction, firm as a rock, that the mighty movement of National Socialism would outlive the centuries and that nothing could end it. But the watchword for the present was: 'The law of the National Socialist Revolution has not yet expired. Its dynamics still dominate the development of Germany.' He had learned much from Leon Trotzky, whose slogan of the permanent revolution he now adopted: 'The German Revolution will not be concluded until the whole German nation is given a new form, a new organization, and a new structure.'

He never called this new Germany by the name which had been made popular by Goebbels: the 'third Reich' — meaning that it came after the (first) Holy Roman Empire (962-1806) and the (second) Bismarckian Empire (1871-1918 A.D.). This perhaps was due to his desire to make a clean break with the past. It was a time when he thought of himself as leading a revolution against everything reactionary, whether it was the Church, the economic age, or the bourgeois parties. It was a wave which would carry away all these motley remnants of the past, and he was riding the wave. He knew that even when he struck at the Communists he was hitting Hugenberg and his crowd at the same time, for both still belonged to that past; to the Weimar Republic, the 'interim Empire.'

The German Nationalists, who really had profound contempt for every outward sign of democracy, still gave the Hitler government the few votes in parliament which it needed for a majority, but by this very fact, they prevented it from becoming a full and unlimited dictatorship. However, there were signs that this forced support would soon become superfluous. In the 'Free City' of Danzig, elections to the *Volkstag* (parliament) were held on May 28; and the National Socialists achieved what had previously been denied them in the Reich: an absolute, though scant, majority of the votes: exactly 50.03 per cent; but a safe majority of seats: 38 out of 72. As in Bavaria and in some of the Prussian provinces, the Nazis set at the head of the Danzig government a man who had been in the party only a short time. Hermann Rauschning was one of Hitler's so-called 'latelings,' a type mostly hated by the 'old fighters,' but absolutely needed to cover that unsavory crowd and their crimes with a respectable name.

What had remained in the end of Hugenberg's following was essentially a group of inadequately armed intellectuals, connected with Germany's large economic holdings more as business managers and administrators than as owners. With Hugenberg in the ministries of economics and food supply, this group thought that it held its hand on the most powerful levers. In reality they had chosen the weakest of all positions of power, for it was precisely in the economic field that the most perilous conflict developed. And it was not the National Socialist workers who were demanding revolution in the economic sphere; it was those who had passed as the defenders and beneficiaries of the existing economic order. The middle class, threatened with ruin by overwhelming competition, was enraged at big capital; the peasant proprietors, incited by the National Socialists, demanded no less than the destruction of the German credit system.

In the first months of the régime, the 'anti-capitalist longing' of

National Socialism had not been very vociferous; it had been drowned out by the fight against Communism. The stock exchange had received Hitler's first successes with good cheer; after the elections of March 5, stocks had risen sharply. Then, by his Jewish boycott, Hitler had suddenly scotched this hope and confidence and stocks had crashed; they remained low when one staggering law on racial purity and co-ordination followed another. The conquest of the trade unions did not relieve the fear of the capital. For after the radicalism of the workers seemed to be crushed for the moment, capital was faced with the possibly more dangerous radicalism of the armed bohemians.

This radical spirit took possession of the party when increasing political success failed to benefit the mass of the membership. It was impossible to satisfy immediately the avid masses who had harnessed their future to this party; and at the head of these disappointed masses stood some of the first men. Röhm, whom Hindenburg had refused once and for all to tolerate in the government, had been put off with the beggarly post of a minister without portfolio in Bavaria. Gottfried Feder, as though there were no National Socialist government, had to go on fighting bitterly and hopelessly for the main point in the party program he had helped to frame, the breaking of interest slavery; he had received no post at all. He had indeed a strong support in R. W. Darré, Hitler's prophet among the peasantry; but Darré himself had no position in the government. True, thousands were already provided for, but this aroused the envy of tens of thousands who had been left out in the cold, who felt that in view of their great services to the movement they had been kept waiting too long.

The chief dispenser of lucrative posts in the government was Göring, the Prussian Premier, who also headed the still mysterious Ministry of Aviation. In both capacities he provided for a swarm of personal friends, who for the most part were quite unknown to the party. There was Göring's friend Körner, who became Secretary of State in the Prussian Ministry of the Interior, hence the most powerful dispenser of patronage in the Reich. There was Erhard Milch, director of the *Lufthansa,* whom Göring appointed Secretary of State in his new aviation ministry, partly because

Milch had supported Göring in the old days when he had been short of funds. No one had ever heard that Milch was a National Socialist, while it could not be doubted that he bore a Jewish name; and when Erhard Milch, pursuing a custom which was beginning to gain wide popularity, claimed to be the fruit of his 'Aryan' mother's infidelity, his detractors found out that the maiden name of this supposedly Aryan mother allegedly had been Rosenau.

The thousand-headed swarm of job-hunters was the human reservoir from which the current of radicalism in the party was fed. But it claimed to speak in the name of the farmers and the shop-keepers.

Large sections of the rural population, stifling under a mountain of mortgages, were passionately awaiting the breaking of interest slavery. Darré wanted to reduce all agricultural credits to two per cent. Hugenberg, as Minister of Food Supply, thought he was infringing sufficiently on the sanctity of contracts when he reduced agricultural interest from its really insane level to four and a half per cent, and even canceled some farm debts by decree (June 1, 1933). Schacht, as president of the Reichsbank, violently opposed this reduction of interest, which seemed to Darré absurdly slight. Hugenberg clung to his plan; in addition, he threw Danish butter, which had done so much political damage in Germany, out of the country by means of high customs duties, thereby driving up milk and butter prices. Then Hitler justified this by saying that the peasantry was so important that for their salvation even unpopular measures, such as the raising of prices, must be taken.

Thus began the short-lived era of 'German Socialism.'

The different sections of the German economy were linked by a broad and varied network of organizations. There were the *Normenverbände* (associations for the maintenance of industrial standards); there were organizations for common purchase of raw materials, for distributing orders, for advising producers, for the rational organization of production, and for maintaining relations between complementary plants. This highly developed and efficient system of organizations culminated in the powerful cartels aimed at maintaining high prices. These associations not only did not disappear, but they seemed to the National Socialist planners like a ready-made framework for a future National Socialist economic order. Among younger men, it was almost a matter of course to call this future economic order 'socialism.' The twenty-six-year-old Baldur von Schirach, leader of the Hitler youth, who could boast of standing close to Hitler, declared bluntly in those revolutionary June weeks: 'A socialist and anti-capitalist attitude is the most salient characteristic of the Young National Socialist Germany.'

Despite the rhetoric, these words did express the sound sentiment that socialism, like every great political idea, demanded above all a mental attitude on the part of the people, and that objective conditions were only secondary. But if this socialism were to be described in economic terms, it was clear that it could not mean an egalitarian elimination of private property. On the contrary, private property was not to be eliminated, but restored; for in this view, capitalism was the real enemy of private property, while socialism meant that one man's property would be equal — in importance and dignity — to another's.

For private property — in Hitler's view — belonged, along with superior strength, superior intelligence, and higher discipline, to the characteristics by which the higher race is distinguished. The uneven distribution of wealth came from the same causes as the organization of nations; from the interaction between races of different 'value'; from the superiority of the stronger race over the weaker. As soon as these two racial types came together, or, in Hitler's words, 'as soon as this process of nation and state formation was initiated, the Communist age of society was past. The primitive faculty of one race creates different values from the more highly developed or divergent faculty of another. And consequently, the fruits of labor will be distributed with a view to achievement' — and with this ponderous and tiresome racial argument Hitler comes to the same result as the most common old-fashioned Liberals: 'The idea of private property is, therefore, inseparably bound up with the conviction that the production of men varies in essence and in value.'

This means: the 'better race,' because the more creative one, deserves more property. But only because it is the more creative one; property is justified by nothing else. For 'common good' always dominates private interest; this is 'socialism,' and property could not continue to exist without this socialism.

The intellectuals who led the National Socialist 'Combat League of the Middle-Class Tradespeople' now wanted to put this socialism into serious practice. Out of the existing economic organizations they wanted to create an apparatus which would give small capital the same advantages as big capital: lower operating costs, easier access to raw materials, wider information on the marketing situation, etc.; but would not destroy the independence of small business. At the same time, the monopolies were to be investigated, and where they could not prove their necessity for the 'common good,' they were gradually to be dissolved. In this brand of socialism, property would be retained and even protected, but only in so far as it could be shown that it served the 'common good.'

These economic control organizations, strengthening small business for competition with big business and controlling the operation of monopolies, have been termed 'estates,' or in Italy, 'corporations': the 'corporate state,' a favorite project of Catholic social politicians of the 'Quadragesimo anno' school, seemed to many the ideal economic form for the Third Reich.

The man who pressed these projects was Otto Wagener. He had been a major in the German Army, then leader of a Free Corps, which after the German collapse had fought independently against the Red Army in the Baltic; he now headed the economic section in the Brown House, which Hitler had wanted to dissolve at the time of Gregor Strasser's fall. It still existed to the great distress of Wilhelm Keppler, who, in Hitler's presence, had given Papen and Baron von Schroeder his word that National Socialism would engage in no foolish economic experiments.

Hitler personally had little understanding of the controversy. What attention he did give economic matters was directed toward great state projects such as motor highways; mass undertakings which would put masses of men back to work overnight. He personally hardly wasted a thought on the corporate state. His great goal for the future was the creation of a new man.

The idea that material conditions could mold the spirit of a generation was profoundly alien to him; on the contrary, he saw in material circumstances the product of a spiritual condition, of a *weltanschauung* as he called it. This urge to create a new *weltan-*

schauung gave the movement its religious streak, and in Hitler was a true religious passion. In his eyes, political activity was tantamount to educating people in a new faith; he did not seek to change the institutions of society, but its state of mind, following Machiavelli's counsel to leave outward conditions essentially in their old form, but to work on people from within. Although he claimed that he would protect and restore the institution of the family that had been damaged by the general social disintegration, he aimed really to uproot the youth and tear them away from their families; ' . . . and so we shall take the children away from you and educate them to be what is necessary for the German people,' he cried on June 17, to the 'isolated persons who think that they can no longer adapt themselves to circumstances.' Yes, perhaps they could no longer adapt themselves, but 'you will pass away, and after you will come the youth which knows nothing else.'

This attempt to dissolve the family found and molded the suitable human implements. On June 18, Hitler conferred on the leader of his 'Hitler Youth,' his friend, Baldur von Schirach, the title 'Youth Leader of the German Reich.' Schirach, like many others in the movement, was a renegade from Germany's former ruling class, in this respect comparable to Prince August Wilhelm. He was the son of a theater director in Weimar; his mother, the American-born Emma Middleton Lynah Tillon, claimed two signers of the Declaration of Independence among her ancestry. As a student, he had been obliged to resign, under unpleasant circumstances, from an exclusive fraternity, and from that time on he had hated the upper crust of his own generation. Although strikingly handsome, his face had the banal and inexpressive quality that characterized his verses; for he wrote verses in which he called Hitler 'Germany's greatest son,' and expressed amazement that this 'genius grazing the stars' had remained a man like you and me. He was violently opposed to the old Christian God and carried his devotion to Hitler so far as to marry his Leader's extremely youthful protégée, Henny Hoffmann, the daughter of the truncated and jocose photographer.

Schirach, like most of the National Socialist 'co-ordinators,' had the good fortune to find a people which had already been thoroughly organized into clubs and great centralized organizations. It has been estimated that toward the end of 1932 no less than twelve million young Germans out of a population of sixty-six millions were organized into youth associations, for the most part sport groups; these associations, in turn, were bound together in a 'Reich Committee of German Youth Associations,' a bureau with innumerable desks and card indexes. The co-ordination of the youth began, true to form, with the occupation of this office by some uniformed young men (April 5, 1933). 'A year ago,' even the *Völkischer Beobachter* lamented ironically, 'the Reich leadership had only two rooms, and not very large ones, in the Brown House in Munich. Today it is a whole four-story building, and even now it is too small for the apparatus, which is growing and growing . . .' Cheered by the growth of this apparatus, Hitler now began to make speeches in which he promised that National Socialism would endure for centuries, because it was more than a political movement. In a speech of March, 1934, he described what had really happened in the great revolution of the preceding spring. Not the conquest of power, not the creation of new political conditions, not the economic measures had been the decisive factor — no, 'decisive, in the last analysis, is that in this year we created the basis for a German rebirth, which will perhaps be realized in a hundred, two hundred, or three hundred years.'

It is such certainty of a blessed future that can give a man the strength for shameless deeds in the present. The National Socialists overran their 'friends' to whom, five months earlier, they had bound themselves by oaths and words of honor; on June 21, the S.A., pistol in hand, stormed the meeting places and offices of the German National Combat Ring throughout Germany; there were shooting and casualties; Göring had the leaders arrested by his police chiefs. Hugenberg sent a courier to Hindenburg in distant Neudeck for help, but Hindenburg did nothing to save any of the old parties, Left or Right.

Next day, Frick, the Minister of the Interior, suppressed the Social Democratic Party. From their exile in Czechoslovakia the party's committee built an underground organization, which at times attained considerable size, but lacked experience and suffered grave setbacks; yet, in spite of all weaknesses, the organization (at least up to 1938) was able to furnish the world with the most extensive and reliable information on occurrences in the factories and occasionally even in high government circles. The greater experience of the Communists in illegal work now made itself felt, but also led to actions of excessive rashness. It is likely that there was considerable treachery in the ranks, and even now, Social Democracy was regarded as the main enemy. Ernst Thaelmann, the Communist Party chairman, arrested on the day after the Reichstag fire, had been buried alive ever since, sharing this fate with many of his party comrades. The Social Democratic leader, Paul Loebe, disappeared into prison for a long term; others were sent to concentration camps for an unlimited period. Johannes Stelling, a member of the Social Democratic Party Committee, was murdered; several of the party leaders committed suicide.

On June 21, the S.A. had fired on Hugenberg's youth organization; the day after, it struck in Munich against the Bavarian People's Party, with whom the National Socialists shared the government. The Bavarian People's Party in Munich maintained connections with the Clerical Party leaders in Austria; the National Socialists spoke of treason, occupied the party offices of the Bavarian People's Party, arrested members and confiscated property. This was a token of what Brüning's Center Party might expect. It had been stipulated in Rome that Catholic priests might no longer belong to a political party; the National Socialists saw to it that there was no party to which they could belong.

The parties now quickly collapsed. Forsaken by Hindenburg, Hugenberg resigned from his two economic ministries on June 27; next day the German Nationalist Party declared itself dissolved. The Center under Brüning tried to carry on negotiations for another week; then Brüning resigned from the leadership, and on July 5 what was left of the party committee announced that the party had voluntarily dissolved itself. Hitler promised that several of its deputies might enter the National Socialist Reichstag fraction as guests. But then he immediately had prominent members of the Center arrested and tried for alleged embezzlements. They were dragged through the streets, forced to draw carts, and wear humili-

ating signs around their necks. Some of them were sent to concentration camps, as though they had been Social Democrats or
Jews. Those arrested included priests.

The great event, the 'second revolution' for which Röhm and his
followers had been clamoring for months, seemed imminent.
Churches, economics, political parties — nothing and nobody had
been able to resist. The 'reaction' seemed beaten on the whole front.
Again the goal appeared to be reached at last; eleven months after
Hitler had missed it first, stopped by Hindenburg. These times
were definitely gone; Hindenburg could no longer threaten him
with the big stick.

But he did. On June 29, the President summoned Hitler to
Neudeck, and made serious representations to him regarding the
initiated destruction of the Protestant Church. As he had done on
some previous occasions, for example before the fall of Groener, he
put his verbal reproaches in writing and published them. He spoke
of 'anxiety for the freedom of the Church.' If the attacks were continued, let alone intensified, they 'cannot fail to cause grave damage
to the nation and the fatherland, and national unity will inevitably
suffer'; Göring's dictatorship over the Church must cease. This was
the first public remonstrance Hitler had received from Hindenburg
since he had become Chancellor.

Now would have been the moment for Hitler to stick desperately
to his policy and his plans — if he had had a policy and a plan.
But he had only a tactical method. He had only tried to find out
how far he could go without resistance. Now, here was resistance,
and this resistance did not lie only in Hindenburg's limited insight
or stubborn will. The old man was fundamentally right. The revolution had reached the point where it could become a danger to its
leader himself.

Therefore Hitler obeyed Hindenburg at once. Church questions were taken out of Göring's hands and transferred to the more
moderate Frick. Hossenfelder vanished completely from the scene.
The German Christians gave up their insistence that only Aryans
could be Christians; they also abandoned their plan to fuse the
two main branches of German Protestantism, Calvinists and Lutherans, into a uniform German Protestantism. It was, however, con-

ceded to the Lutherans that one of their number would become 'Reich Bishop.' To the pious Christians it seemed a victory that the Holy Scriptures and the writings of the reformers would remain the foundation of the Protestant faith. But it was conceded to the German Christians that new elections be held for the democratic 'Church parliament,' the highest legislative body of the Church — the old method of conquering democracy through democracy. The 'German Christians' were successful and elected Müller 'Reich Bishop.'

On July 13, Hitler announced to his Reichs President that the 'German Christians' had reached an agreement with the Church and that peace had been restored. As a born politician, he had recognized the decisive instant between stubborn persistence and inevitable retreat more clearly than had his co-workers. Having withdrawn a step in the church question, he now realized that in economic matters National Socialism had at various points passed the limits of the possible. He adopted Keppler's policy and hastily commanded the waves to stand still.

True to an old custom, he assembled his S.A. leaders for this purpose in Bad Reichenhall, a spa near his mountain home (July 2, 1933). Here he declared, as though he had never so much as mentioned a continuation of the revolution: 'I shall proceed ruthlessly against a so-called second revolution, for such a revolution could have chaotic consequences. . . . ' And hinting that he feared opposition in his own ranks, he added: 'Anyone who rebels against the National Socialist state power will be seized with an iron fist, regardless what camp he is in.'

Here Hitler was speaking to the egotistic and faint-hearted band which in constant panic had urged him to retreat all through the year 1932, in order that the party should obtain a few comfortable jobs. Now it was he who demanded retreat; but again his meaning was: no jobs. For 'no second revolution' meant exactly this.

The mass of the armed bohemians had grounds for bitterness. With giant steps the Leader was passing over his most loyal followers, those Uprooted and Disinherited, whose sole remaining hope in life had been the party. True, R. W. Darré became Minister of Food Supply in place of Hugenberg; though not exactly an 'old fighter' (and for this reason blindly devoted to Hitler personally), he was a man with National Socialist ideas; but he was forced to forget all about his two per cent interest. Gottfried Feder, who had promised that rapacious capital would be brought to its knees, was lucky to get the post of undersecretary in the Reich Ministry of Economics — a humiliating position, for here Feder became the subordinate of another of National Socialism's unknowns. His new superior was almost a stranger to the party, but familiar to the stock exchange and the financial sections of the 'Jewish business press': he was Doctor Karl Schmitt, general director of the largest German insurance company. A more pronounced representative of rapacious capital would have been hard to find; Schmitt had spent his life lending money and collecting interest; he had literally bought his way into the National Socialist Movement by giving the party generous aid in hard times. In his new post he was really a substitute for a man whose name was a battle-cry against any kind of socialism and who even now refused to join the party: Doctor Hjalmar Schacht, president of the Reichsbank.

The new policy of July, 1933, was a counter-revolution, as far-reaching as the erstwhile revolution supposedly had been. The armed bohemians had been rebuffed; now the middle class was openly betrayed; both, because only in this way did it seem possible to satisfy the proletarian masses. As Hindenburg had said, the 'most urgent task was to solve the unemployment problem.' What Schleicher had desperately attempted 'in opposition to the laws of economic reason,' National Socialism had to deliver, if necessary in opposition to its own ideals and programs. The shortest road to this solution — as the Social Democratic unions had realized for years — was to set capitalism, or rather the capitalists, in motion again. The employers had to be persuaded to provide work; masses of jobs had to be improvised and available jobs broadly distributed. Life or death of National Socialism depended on making the workers workers again. And so, as it developed, the uprooted proletariat was the greatest obstacle in the path of a middle-class corporate state.

With all the strength of his changeable nature, Hitler led the campaign for the protection of the economic age he had so despised. Four days after his condemnation of the second revolution, he gathered his *statthalters* in the Chancellery. He roared at them that in future he desired no so-called economic revolutions; that the eternal 'co-ordinating' must cease; that there would be no corporate development, although he himself had promised it; and above all, that the job-hunters who had not yet obtained their piece of pie should not get the idea of taking it by force — if for no other reason, because many of them were know-nothings. It was a startling turn, comparable to the 'New Economic Policy' of the Bolsheviki in 1921. 'A businessman,' cried Hitler, 'must not be deposed if he is a good businessman but not yet a National Socialist; and especially not if the National Socialist who is put in his place understands nothing of economic affairs. By theoretical co-ordinations we don't get bread for one worker. We shall not eliminate unemployment by economic commissions, organizations, constructions, and theories. . . .' One would not have believed him to be the same Hitler who had cried out that economic affairs were 'something secondary' and must 'serve the nation.' 'We must not reject practical experience,' he cried, 'because it is opposed to some preconceived idea' — and it would have been hard to find any more annihilating criticism of the National Socialist idea. 'If we come before the nation with reforms, we must also prove that we understand things and can master them' — a reflection which would not have been irrelevant even before January 30, 1933. The prophet who had promised fourteen years before to die for his immutable program now abjured it with the banal justification: 'The important thing is not programs and ideas, but daily bread for seventy million people.' Two weeks earlier he had proclaimed the permanent revolution; now he said: 'The revolution is no permanent condition'; and the art was to halt a revolution 'at the proper moment.' 'People should not look around to see if there is something left to revolutionize'; they should conquer and secure the positions and 'gradually occupy them with the best talents.' This was an admission that his élite was anything but the best; in reality, the whole National Socialist method of forming an élite consisted, not in seeking out the best, but in the training of average — and often less than average — men to a certain political usefulness.

Up till then the National Socialists had 'behaved like fools, overthrowing everything'—and stolen and blackmailed in the process, he might have added. This must stop; and such methods were no longer needed because the party had already won uncontested power: 'The party has now become the state.' And so 'we can enforce our will everywhere.' But not—this was what he meant—in the asinine way we have been doing. For 'history will not judge us by whether we have arrested as large a number of business leaders as possible, but by whether we have created work.' Nothing was gained by destroying intellects and talents that resisted; the important thing was to make them stop resisting. The stream of the revolution, said Hitler, must be brought into the safe channel of evolution, and 'the main point in this respect is the education of the individual'; 'the people who embody the present state of affairs must be educated in the National Socialist state conception.' It is characteristic that this brand of education, seemingly so self-reliant but actually so supple and ready to compromise, began with a retreat.

This halt in the revolution was exactly what Machiavelli demanded of the state reformer who did not want to be a tyrant. The interruption of 'co-ordination' was soon expressed in action. Hess issued an order to cease molesting the department stores; Ley gave up the idea of forcing the employer's associations into the Labor Front. Wagener and his whole following were removed overnight from the party leadership, and Wilhelm Keppler, who was primarily responsible for the halt in co-ordination, officially entered the Brown House as well as the Chancellery as Hitler's personal 'deputy for economic questions' (July 13). Robert Ley, availing himself of his powers as organizational leader of the party, summarily dissolved the Combat League of Middle-Class Tradespeople early in August. Schmitt, the Minister of Economics, made it known on August 13 that the corporate development must be abandoned; Hess ordered an end to all talk of corporations, which he branded as high treason. This was bitter earnest. Wagener and several of his following were sent to concentration camps. This was not only because they had been too idealistic; it was also a case of the successful bandits locking up those who had been less successful.

After stormy weeks that shook its very foundations, the Third

Reich decided for peace and order. Intentionally, though not always very methodically, the revolution had been steered to a certain point and then held back. In any case, Hitler dominated the storm and made it clear that what he called revolution would not be an upheaval.

After his peace speech of May 17, critics abroad admitted for the first time that he had spoken like a statesman. Now, after a halt had been called in the revolution, voices arose in Europe saying that he really was a statesman. The first important treaty of the Third Reich with a foreign government matured in this mood. On July 8, the draft of a Reich Concordat was signed in Rome; twelve days later, the two parties exchanged letters of ratification. On the same day *The Times* of London, hitherto critical toward the Third Reich and even now less benevolent than the Rothermere press, devoted a thoughtful and friendly discussion to Hitler's speech against revolution and co-ordination. The article did, it is true, deplore the atrocities; but then it went on to say:

> Herr Hitler is certainly not devoid of ideals. . . . He undoubtedly desires to re-inculcate the old German virtues of loyalty, self-discipline, and service to the state. Some of the grosser forms of post-war demoralization have been checked under the new régime; and Herr Hitler will win support which may be very valuable to him if he will genuinely devote himself to the moral and economic resurrection of his country.

Moral aims were ascribed to the régime of concentration camps; and English support of all sorts — obviously economic and diplomatic — was promised if Hitler adhered to his policy of pacification and really put an end to the revolutionizing and co-ordination. He was even assured that there would be no objection to the secret German rearmament of which everyone was aware. 'Even the passion for "defense sports," which is bringing striplings and learned professors together at practice on the rifle range, will not altogether be condemned if the training be really confined to the art of defending their country — even although no other country is at least likely to attack it.'

As though in answer to these remarks, Hitler on the following

day made it clear to a gathering of S.A. men in the city of Dort-
mund that he meant to devote himself above all to the moral resurrection of Germany; the thing, he said, was to educate people, not
to stand institutions on their heads. And education, he declared,
faithful to his old theory of propaganda, meant a spiritual driving
of the masses, until they knew no will other than that of the leadership: 'The German people must put itself a hundred per cent in
the service of our idea. . . . We must educate millions of men to fit
into our state. . . .'

On July 14, the cabinet, which since March 23 had been making
all the laws without bothering the parliament or the President,
issued a decree 'against the formation of new parties.' The first
paragraph ran: 'In Germany the National Socialist German Workers' Party is the sole existing political party.'

The one-party system, which had been in power for years in
Russia, Italy, China, and Turkey, had come to Germany. This system has been called dictatorship, meaning despotism, but this does
not express its essential character. A despotism ignores the will of
the people; but these new states of the armed intellectuals take the
will of the people so seriously that they create it and shape it themselves — or so they think; Hitler called this 'education.' For this
they use the methods which they have preserved from the democratic surroundings of their origins. Although all other parties have
been destroyed, the concept of the party has remained; elections,
parliaments, messages to the people, consent of the legislative body,
plebiscites — continue to be the salient features of public life, and
have even acquired a higher solemnity. The outward forms seem
scarcely changed, and Machiavelli might well be pleased; for his
disciples, by using the methods of democracy more adroitly and
cynically than the democrats themselves, have fathomed the banal
secret that one can do what one wants with men, as soon as one
brings them to want it themselves.

But the course of history reveals a higher secret. At the height
of his victory, the victor retreated in many places, seemingly of his
own free will, changed his plans, disappointed his own followers,
adapted himself to necessity. And the true secret of political victory
is contained in this Hegelian necessity: to know what one wants,
and to want what the people want, but do not yet know.

Chapter *XXVI*

OTHER PEOPLE'S MONEY

IN THE SUMMER OF 1933, VERNON BARTLETT, THE British journalist, took a trip through National Socialist Germany, and on his return he published a book of impressions. 'I do not believe — and most emphatically do not believe — ' he wrote, 'that Germany wants war. Not yet! And it will not be her fault alone if she ever does.'

Hitler — this was Bartlett's conviction — was far too concerned with the internal, and especially economic, reconstruction of his country to think of war. The Englishman had astonishing ideas regarding the shape of this reconstruction: 'Hitler, like Gandhi, wants a return to the spinning wheel, not only because he is an economic nationalist, but because he believes in simplicity. The most important feature of the German Revolution is that it is, in essence, a reaction against excessive materialism.'

This was Bartlett's way of saying what many Germans, notably Schacht, had been preaching for years: that Germany must base herself on the home soil, save, live frugally, and work twelve hours a day, and this should continue for a generation, as Frederick the Great had demanded in his time. Schacht continued his sermon under the Third Reich: 'Economic self-abnegation and readiness to content ourselves with reduced luxury expenditures' — this, he declared on July 31 in a radio speech addressed to the United States, was the essence of the new Germany; today many were working voluntarily for the community at reduced wages. Writers like Oswald Spengler held up frugality and hard labor to the German people as the supreme blessing. In his campaign speeches of February and March, Hitler had appealed to the pride of his audience by promising them the greatness of a hard life. The fight for work, he said some months later, was Germany's war, and here victory was in the offing; Germany needed no other wars and victories.

Through want to greatness, through hunger to power — this was the interpretation put on the first economic measures of the National Socialists by several foreign observers; this was the only connection they could see between German economic policy and National Socialist power politics. At the end of August, John F. Thelwall, commercial attaché at the British Embassy in Berlin, reported to his government with scarcely concealed admiration that in many spheres the supporters of the new German government were willing, for the sake of their principles, to renounce economic and political advantage. The standards of a democratic, individualistic, and capitalist state like Great Britain, he said, did not apply; and what surely seemed most startling of all to a foreigner was that, where party ideals and economic necessities came into conflict, it was always the ideals that won out.

The persecution of the Jews seemed an outstanding example of Nazi indifference to economic expediency, and it is probable that Thelwall had this particularly in mind. In reality, the treatment of the Jews exemplified the extreme concern of the Third Reich with economic matters after the first revolutionary holiday. True, the Jews were expelled from some intellectual professions at the very start, and beyond a doubt German economic life and technology lost valuable workers without any pressing necessity, as for example in the field of chemical research where Jews were especially prominent. But these Jews were not driven out for reasons of political idealism; it was merely that unemployed National Socialist intellectuals wanted jobs. In the main, the régime distinguished for a long time between useful and non-useful Jews. Jewish lawyers and civil servants were mercilessly removed, but Jewish doctors received much better treatment; despite all the fury against the 'Jewish mind,' indispensable Jewish economic journalists long retained their positions on the business press; Jewish technicians kept their places in industry for an astonishingly long time; after the first boycott mood had cleared, Jewish businessmen were graciously as-

sured that they had nothing further to fear, and some were prevented by the authorities from emigrating or liquidating their businesses — for suddenly they had ceased to be Jews and become employers, and employment was what mattered most to the régime.
Consequently there was a tendency to persecute and dismiss Jewish
employees and white-collar workers.

In the middle of 1933, the first Jewish refugees appeared in foreign capitals with *exposés* of conditions in Germany. But from
within Germany, from the Jewish masses who had remained behind, the reports became more and more reassuring: things were
not really so bad. In some cities, it was true, as in Julius Streicher's
Nuremberg, the restaurants and cafés were closed to Jews and in
general it was made hard for them to leave their houses; these
cities achieved world fame by their brutalities. But in most towns
the treatment of the Jews became more moderate; and their businesses, like all businesses in Germany, were flourishing again in the
economic revival.

This was the end of the talk about hunger and frugality, saving
and simplicity, not to mention spinning wheels. The people should
have grounds for economic satisfaction with the new régime. Addressing German captains of industry in August, Hitler sharply attacked 'primitivism and frugality' as the expression of an 'envious
attitude.' In November, he boasted to Ferdinand de Brinon, the
French newspaperman: 'I have restored to the German people the
concept of their honor' — by means of National Socialist victory
celebrations. 'I will also give back to them the joy of living.'

He knew the sources of this joy of living. He had once promised
the unmarried women that under the Third Reich they would get
husbands; and he kept this promise. The story that National Socialism favored free love and illegitimate births is a childish fantasy.
Since 1933, the Reich has given young couples applying for it a
loan of a thousand marks on marriage, all or a part of which did
not have to be returned if a number of children were produced
within a specified time; during the first five years of the régime,
approximately 880,000 marriages were promoted by this financial
aid, at times as much as thirty per cent of all marriages, and actually
the greater part of this money was not repaid. Families were

founded, the birth rate increased; and these new families entering the life of the nation gave whole branches of industry, from the building trades to furniture manufacture to textiles, increased employment, not to mention the jobs which the young wives vacated or never required.

Much has been said about National Socialist hostility toward female labor. In reality, women did not have to relinquish their jobs in industry to any appreciable degree; although of the new jobs that were being made and distributed, they did receive fewer than the men. Between 1933 and 1936, women's share in industrial employment sank from 29.3 to 24.7 per cent. But the number of industrial workers rose in the same period from 4,100,000 to 6,100,000; in other words, the percentage of women among the employed fell, but their absolute number rose by one quarter — all this at a time when there was as yet no question of a total mobilization of the German people for war production, rather an artificial mobilization of production for the unemployed.

Adolf Hitler, the architect and builder, erected palatial buildings for his party in Munich, and everywhere in Germany his lieutenants began to beautify their cities, to tear down old buildings and erect splendid new façades. A few years later, in faithful imitation of Napoleon III, the régime leveled whole sections of Berlin to make room for mighty temples of the new deified state; the religion of greatness put bread into the mouths of the wrecking crews.

This battle of labor was not yet the battle of rearmament as many believed. In 1933, there was no sign of stripping off peacetime luxury, of renouncing superfluous comforts for the sake of military necessities, of saving materials and labor power for weapons and war supplies — despite the scarcity of raw materials. Instead of this, a public demand for luxuries was almost forcibly encouraged; theaters, museums, monuments were erected, merely to find employment for jobless hands.

Almost half of the potential of Germany's industry lay unused when Hitler came to power. The Reich Bureau of Statistics, using 1928 as a norm, estimated that in 1932 average production had fallen to 58.7 (and for a time lower). And even in 1928, German productive power had not been exploited to capacity, for in this year there had been an average of 1,400,000 unemployed. In the same period, from 1928 to 1932, while the index of German industrial production fell from 100 to 58.7, that of the 'world' — that is, those industrial countries of which statistics were available (exclusive of Soviet Russia) — fell only to 65.1, or, if the United States, especially hard hit by the crisis, were disregarded, only 73.4. Of all the large countries, Germany and the United States had, at the depth of the crisis, suffered the greatest loss in production; that is, they disposed of the greatest reserves in unused economic power. Both countries put a part of this unused power to work by great government projects.

In these efforts, National Socialist Germany possessed one resource of government orders which the United States lacked: she planned to build a new army. But to revive 41 per cent of Germany's productive power, to re-employ 6,000,000 people, the planned army of 300,000 with all its needs was far from enough. In Seeckt's view, the army should in peacetime not make full use of industry's power of armament production; for a premature mass armament was in danger of soon becoming obsolete; and by keeping industry too busy, it discouraged experiments with newer and better weapons. It may be assumed that Seeckt's view, despite possible modifications, had remained that of the High Command. Consequently, no 'war economy' was built up in Germany in 1933, as has been maintained abroad; what happened was merely that an economy capable of war was better utilized and to some extent speeded up; for the economy of the modern industrial state is in itself the strongest war machine, as soon as it comes into warlike hands, the hands of the armed intellectual.

In Germany this was the case, and the German army that was now being built with the help of German industry was the army of Seeckt, not of Röhm; no monster army with which the world could be conquered, but a weapon easy to handle, mobile and sharp enough to protect Germany effectively against all possible military threats. Germany's situation in the heart of the continent, in itself a weakness for the defensive on all fronts, became, through the presence of a relatively small army, an incomparable strength for the offensive on one front. Of the four great armies which had surrounded Germany in 1914 — the French, Italian, Austrian, and Russian — only the French still existed as a threat. But even France had in 1928 reduced her term of military service to one year; on paper she disposed of 428,000 soldiers at the end of 1933, but of these only 256,000 were in Europe; some 40,000 of these were no real soldiers, but only police — *garde mobile* and *gendarmes;* the rest, some 172,000, were in the Asiatic and African colonies, and more than half of these, or 87,000, were colored, native troops. Against this divided French army, a concentrated and fully equipped German force of 300,000 would have been a more than adequate counterweight, particularly as they would have been subordinated to a resolute and ruthless command, hampered by no political restrictions at home.

Aside from Germany and France, the sole military power on the continent was Italy. But Italy, in the long run, was the military equal of neither France nor Germany, and in any case represented more of a threat to France than to Germany. The armies of the other countries, even of Poland, did not count by themselves — and Hitler's task, which he had already begun to solve, was to make sure that they always remained by themselves. An unknown quantity was the Soviet Union. But in 1933, Russia was shaken by an economic crisis in which hundreds of thousands died of hunger, and the ruling group, under the leadership of Stalin, had to contend with serious resistance, if not worse, in their own party. Up to 1931, Hitler had publicly expressed his doubts of Russian strength, his contempt for the inefficiency of Bolshevism, his conviction that the whole régime was crumbling; it seems that up till 1933 he did not consider Russia seriously as a military adversary.

It was for an explicitly limited task — to make Germany superior to an isolated foe — that the German army was first planned and created; then, with changing political situations, this army several times changed its form, size, and aims. To provide weapons, uniforms, and lodging for this army in its first moderate form was a great economic task, but none which could have set all German industry in motion. Although expansion and rearmament of the German armed forces had been under way for more than a year, since Papen's régime, the German troops still used wooden cannon

and sham tanks in the autumn maneuvers of 1933. Göring and
Milch displayed tremendous energy in building an air fleet, but
even their work was limited for the present to the building or re-
modeling of factories.

The German *Luftwaffe* was long a menacing legend before it became serious reality. Reports on feverish German plane construction spread abroad, and were presumably inspired by the German
government in order to spread fear at a time when reality was none
too impressive. From the start the strongest element in German
aviation was its human material, a young generation filled with
enthusiasm for flying, which had learned a primitive flying technique in great 'air-sport associations.' Already, before 1933, these
air-sport associations, in some ways resembling the combat leagues,
had been a part of the German political picture. Even the Social
Democratic movement and the trade unions had had their flying
associations with membership numbering tens of thousands. In the
western countries there were no comparable organizations; they
existed only in the Soviet Union, and it seems that Göring, the
aviator, took Russia seriously as a military power long before Hitler. A special skill, widespread among the younger German fliers,
was that of gliding. Gliders made use of the rising columns of air
which the science of aerodynamics had discovered in the vicinity
of mountains, cloud formations, and even cities, with their steep
walls. Springing from column to column, these fliers could drift
and glide for hundreds of miles. The art of gliding was perfected
in Germany when the restrictions of Versailles made it impossible
for the air-minded youth to fly motored planes — one more example
of how obstacles produce great accomplishments; in this way large
numbers of young men had achieved a knowledge of winds, clouds,
and weather which later proved of immense benefit to motorized
aviation.

To create an adequate air fleet for these young men was an undertaking that took time; German industry, though highly efficient in
most fields, was backward in motor production; plane construction
on a large scale would require a great improvement in quality as
well as quantity. The most ambitious effort of German aviation up
to that time, the construction in 1929-30 of a plane capable of cross-

ing the ocean by the firm of Dornier (the so-called DoX), had failed as a result of weakness in motor construction; and in the end Dornier had recourse to American motors.

Production of internal combustion engines, primarily in fulfillment of state orders, was from the start a central point in Hitler's economic program. There are no statistics covering airplane construction, but the related field of automobiles shows an increase far above that of general production: in 1932 approximately 43,000 private automobiles were built; in 1933 more than twice as many, approximately 93,000, or nearly as many as in 1929; in 1934 the figure had risen to 147,000 — still none too impressive compared to the 4,500,000 in the United States in 1929, the 2,100,000 in 1934, or even the modest 256,000 in England in 1934.

The acceleration of machine construction points to an early and systematic motorization of the army. It could not be denied that German industry was working for this army; but it was only a fraction of its work, and the main problem remained unemployment. Konstantin Hierl, the National Socialist proponent of the mass army, was consoled with the leadership of the 'Labor Service' — seemingly a mass army for putting men back to work. Under Papen and Schleicher it had still been voluntary in form, but now — at the beginning of 1934 — it became formally compulsory, though in practice compulsory only for a section of the gradually diminishing unemployed. Formally, every young German of nineteen was to enter the Labor Service for half a year; since every year 540,000 young men became eligible, the service should have embraced 270,000 men. They led a military life, lived in camps, were commanded by officers, learned to stand, march, run, jump, climb, crawl, like soldiers. Their chief implement was the shovel, and in addition to its normal functions, they learned to handle it like a rifle; above all, they learned obedience and the fear of their superiors.

But the High Command kept insisting that all this was useless from a military standpoint: when the time came for the army itself to take over the young people, they would have to be taught everything from the beginning. For what few weapons were produced went almost entirely to the Reichswehr. With his stern belief in specialization, Hitler insisted that professional officers understood nothing of politics, but that the purely technical handling of arms could be put into no better hands. Therefore, the Labor Service was to labor; it performed those gigantic works which no one else performed because they held out no promise of profit. Woods were cleared and leveled for farm land, dikes built, marshes drained, dry land irrigated. When, with the passing years, normal economic life demanded more and more labor, the Labor Service lost its importance as a haven for the unemployed; and in time it was overshadowed by the troop organized by Doctor Karl Todt, which first built the new motor highways and later the 'West Wall.' The construction of highways began in September, 1933, with some thirty thousand workers, increasing in the next years to an average of seventy thousand; of a projected network of approximately seventy-three hundred miles of four-lane highway, about one quarter was opened to traffic by the end of 1938.

On May 31 (while Hugenberg was still Minister of Economics), the Reich government had decided to issue a billion in so-called 'work drafts' (*Arbeits-Schatzanweisungen*); these were negotiable certificates paid out to employers who undertook projects of 'replacement,' or 'maintenance projects.' Anyone who equipped a factory with new machines or who merely had his house repainted could finance his operations with these work drafts, and his taxes were even remitted; Fritz Thyssen declared his intention of opening two new shafts in his coal mines — while the coal still lay unsalable on the sidings. All in all, the public treasury poured out approximately three billion marks from various sources (railways, postal service, unemployment insurance) for projects which, according to the view hitherto prevailing in those times of crisis, were senseless or at least unnecessary — at any rate, gave promise of no yield; the expenditures of the Reichswehr are not included in this sum. The ideal of rational operation, through which the German economic machine had been raised to such high efficiency between 1924 and 1929, was abandoned; in many industries — though this was never made official — the government limited the working week to forty hours, in order to distribute the available work among more hands; in some industries, as in cigar or bottle manufacture, a law prohibited the use of machines in order to provide work for more manual workers. The employers' associations in the province of West Prussia declared that their members would, in disregard of petty misgivings, 'undertake new installations beyond what was economically necessary at the time.'

There is no doubt that greater emphasis was laid on production goods than on consumers' goods; greater emphasis on machines, farm tools, industrial semi-manufactures, than on articles going directly into consumption, such as clothing, furniture, etc. The index of employment for the production goods industries rose in 1932-34 — on the basis of the level of 1936 as evaluated at 100 — from 48.8 to 78.2, or approximately 60 per cent; that for the consumers' goods industry only from 78.5 to 94.2, or exactly 20 per cent; and this more rapid tempo in production goods continued in the succeeding years. Before Hitler came to power, relatively more had been produced for direct consumption, while now greater stress was laid on increased production of capital plant, machines, factories, and farm tools.

Nevertheless, in Germany the greatest, most concentrated effort at re-employment, that embracing the largest single group of workers, was made by an industry chiefly satisfying private needs. In the first years of National Socialism, no industry so increased its employment figures as construction and the related building material industry. Between 1932 and 1935, the index of employment in the construction industry rose from 19.2 to 70; in the building material industry, from 41 to 83.1; in the former an increase of over 350 per cent, in the latter of more than 200 per cent. Roughly 2,600,000 workers were involved (building trades, 1933 — 2,020,000, building material industry, 615,000). The construction of motor highways, with its employment of 30,000 to 70,000 workers, did not have a major effect on these figures. The main factor was that in 1932, 141,265 new dwellings were built, and in 1934, 283,995, or more than twice as many. Larger dwelling complexes than before were constructed, big buildings with more individual apartments; the statistical expression of this is that the number of buildings rises more slowly than the number of dwellings. At the same time the number of the new 'non-dwelling' constructions decreased, from 54,200 in 1932 to 52,600 in 1934.

Not by building of air fleets, but by building new housing, did National Socialism begin to revive German economic life and obtain a solid and lasting popularity. Foreign observers, it can well be understood, were more impressed by the millions of S.A. men in new uniforms. Scarcely anyone was willing to believe that the S.A. was not the coming German army, though it happened to be true. When Röhm, in an interview at the beginning of October, gave assurance that the S.A. was not an army but a new religion — 'as the early Christians were bearers and warriors of their new view of life, Christianity' — to most people it sounded absurd, though actually the thought behind his words was more ominous than any warlike threat. Hitler was grieved at foreign suspicions; with righteous indignation he asked visitors what in the world led foreigners to think he wanted war. 'I have a long domestic task before me,' he said to Ferdinand de Brinon, his French visitor, in the beginning of November. 'I shall need years to reach my goal. Do you think that I want to destroy my work by a new war?' Brinon published this and similar utterances in the Paris *Matin,* which Hitler had formerly called a hotbed of Jewish lies and which actually was in a sense the organ of the Jewish bourgeoisie of France. Hitler had also said that if he wanted peace, all Germany wanted peace, for 'I alone decide on German policy, and if I give my word, I am accustomed to keep it.' De Brinon remarked that Ward Price, Lord Rothermere's correspondent in Germany and his unofficial ambassador to Hitler, had called Hitler sincere, and, he added, Ward Price was right.

Strange how these foreign observers, themselves half-Fascist at heart, loved to speculate about Hitler's 'sincerity.' As though he could have been lying when he maintained that he needed many years more time for his internal reconstruction! The German people needed time to adapt themselves to a far-reaching social upheaval. The National Socialist economic policy meant a return to work for millions; for even more millions it meant the final liberation from the fear of losing tomorrow the little employment they still retained. The state now seemed able to protect its people from starvation; mankind seemed to have risen one step — that is the feeling which the National Socialist revolution gave to many people.

This progress had been bought with the loss of free suffrage, the renunciation of free speech, with a press dominated by lies, with concentration camps for a minority and atrocities that could not be concealed.

Did this price have to be paid? In 1933, unemployment began to decrease all over the world. In the United States, according to an estimate of the American Federation of Labor, unemployment fell from thirteen millions to ten millions. The official German Institute for Business Research (*Konjunkturforschung*) noted in July, 1933, that in Latvia unemployment had decreased by 31 per cent from the second quarter of 1932 to the second quarter of 1933; in Rumania, by 23 per cent; in Germany, only by 9 per cent — for the figure of two millions, apparently a third, or 33 per cent of the total unemployed, was misleading, since it could be ascribed mainly to regular summer rise in employment. In Great Britain, the labor market had registered an improvement of 6 per cent in the course of a year. According to the index of the International Labor Office in Geneva, the level of employment for nineteen large countries had fallen from 100 in 1929 to 75 in 1932; in 1933, it rose to 78; in 1934 to 84; in 1935 to 88, or an increase of 17.3 per cent in three years; during the same period the German level of employment, according to German figures, rose from 12,500,000 to 15,900,000, an increase of 27 per cent. In a word: the 'National Socialist miracle' was neither entirely National Socialist nor entirely a miracle, but largely a part of a world recovery; though in Germany, it must be admitted, this recovery was experienced with a passion equaled nowhere else. The German Institute for Business Research also found that of the two millions who had returned to work in Germany by the end of August, some 1,400,000 would have done so without the intervention of the state, in consequence of the usual summer revival; and roughly 300,000 to 700,000 in Germany owed their re-employment to the general world prosperity. The measures of the Hitler government, properly spoken — still according to the estimate of the Institute for Business Research — would only have sent 300,000 back to work.

But what was world prosperity? No longer a product of economic, but of political, forces; in most countries it had been accelerated, if not induced, by state intervention. The great world revival from which Hitler profited did indeed result from a general political exertion, from state intervention in economic life. And that conservative country in which the state hesitated to intervene suffered the consequences. In France, employment had fallen more slowly during the great crisis than in Germany, from 100 in 1930 to 80.9 in 1932; but while in Germany, England, America, and the world in general employment then began to rise, the French index continued to fall to 73.5 in 1935.

All over the world attempts to create separate national spheres of prosperity were in progress. The German developments were merely a part of this picture, though indeed the Germans were more methodical than anyone else in their international efforts. No other country was so adept at co-ordinating economic policy, diplomacy, and propaganda. The outside world, doubting more and more the wisdom of its past policy, was more receptive than before to German complaints. Already Schleicher had blamed — not entirely without justification — the decisions of Ottawa for the special distress of German agriculture; now Hjalmar Schacht began to complain of the foreign tariffs which forced Germany — so he said — to defend herself with the harshest and indeed most unscrupulous means.

From time to time in former years, the condition of German foreign trade had been disquieting; often imports had been billions in excess of exports; or, to speak in the language of private business, more had been bought than could actually be paid for. But in those days the whole world had been glad to lend Germany money and had not pressed for repayment. In 1928, German imports had amounted to 14,000,000,000 marks, while exports had been only 12,300,000,000; but the difference had been almost made good by foreign long-term loans to the amount of 1,460,000,000 marks, not to mention short and medium-term loans and stock flotations. But after 1930, no further long-term loans were offered, and where possible the short-term loans were called in; the mass of international trade decreased throughout the world, and prices kept falling. In 1932, Germany exported goods valued at only 5,700,000,000 marks, but imported only 4,700,000,000 — a complete upset of the trade balance; borrowed imports had ceased to exist, and every pound of imported goods was honestly covered by exports. There is a small source of error in these figures; up to June, 1932, they included the so-called 'payments in kind' with which Germany defrayed a part of her reparations; but the figures nevertheless reflect the general picture with fair accuracy. In 1933, the year of recovery, German exports continued falling to 4,800,000,000 marks; imports sank to 4,200,000,000.

Germany's exports and imports had fallen off by almost two thirds; the patient seemed to be scarcely breathing. And yet the figures are misleading; for the seemingly fatal blood-letting conceals a remarkable gain which became evident only beginning in 1932; a gain which was most helpful to National Socialist trade and decisively influenced the economic structure of the Third Reich. The diminishing trade figures of Germany and the other European countries did in one way present an exaggerated picture. For while the bulk of goods exchanged on the world market was dwindling, prices crashed at an even faster rate; consequently, if in one year exports were valued at 12,000,000,000 marks and in a later year only at 4,000,000,000, this does not mean that the bulk of goods had fallen to one third. Possibly it had not even been halved; the greater part of the decline in value must be ascribed to the fall in prices. In 1927, German imports had a value of 14,200,000,000 marks and a weight of 82,200,000 tons; when in 1933 their value fell to 4,200,000,000 marks, or considerably less than one third, their weight was still 45,800,000 tons, or more than half.

This discrepancy between value and weight gives only the roughest outline of the process. Using a subtler and more accurate method, the official German statistics revealed what an advantage Germany derived from the difference between bulk and prices. This method measured the value of exports and imports, not by their actual prices, but by the prices prevailing in 1928. The figures obtained in this way do not tell how much Germany actually had to pay for her imports in a given year or how much she obtained for her exports, but how much she would have paid or received if the prices of 1928 had still prevailed in this given year. These figures alone give a true picture of the quantities exported and imported. They provide a faulty picture of the sums paid, received, or owed; but this they are intended to do; their aim is to penetrate the 'veil of money' and reveal the true quantity of goods turned over.

And here a remarkable fact comes to light. In 1932, when everyone stopped lending Germany money, Germany had been obliged to curb her imports drastically, for otherwise she would have been unable to pay for them by her reduced exports, blocked by new customs barriers. In this year the financial yield of German exports had crashed to 5,700,000,000 marks from 9,600,000,000 in the previous year; and the value of imports fell accordingly to 4,700,000,000. These were the uncorrected figures for German foreign trade. But if these sums were transposed in terms of the standard price of 1928, so that they clearly represented the real quantities, it turned out that German exports in 1932 amounted to 8,100,000,000 marks — that is, the quantity of goods exported would have brought in 8,100,000,000 marks if the prices of 1928 had still prevailed; by the same scale, the imports of 1932 amounted to 9,500,000,000 marks instead of only 4,700,000,000. In other words, according to the prices actually prevailing, exports exceeded imports; according to the prices prevailing in 1928, imports would have been higher. This meant that the goods that Germany imported or purchased since 1928 had decreased in price more than the goods that she exported or sold. This disparity in prices was Germany's gain from an apparently desperate situation. German exports consisted largely of finished manufactures; her imports largely of raw materials. The variation in the decline of export and import prices can be seen by comparing the two pairs of figures: 8,100,000,000 and 5,700,000,000 for export; 9,500,000,000 and 4,700,000,000 for import; the prices of the goods sold by Germany had fallen by 29.9 per cent, or less than a third; while the prices of the goods purchased by Germany, largely raw materials, had fallen by more than half, or 50.5 per cent.

This was the unexpected advantage which the crisis brought to a country like Germany, operating with foreign raw materials: despite greater difficulties and reduced profits in selling her own products, she obtained easier and cheaper access to raw materials.

This happy accident pointed the way to German trade policy. In 1933, the first year of National Socialism, the helpful discrepancy between import and export prices remained almost as great as in the previous year, although in this year German foreign trade continued to shrink; exports reckoned at current prices fell to 4,900,-000,000 marks, imports to 4,200,000,000. But, according to the prices of 1928, the relation between exports and imports remained the opposite: exports, 7,600,000,000, imports, 9,300,000,000, and this meant that, though the prices of the goods exported from Germany had continued to fall and were now 35.5 per cent below those of 1928, the prices of imports had fallen even more and stood more than half, or 54.8 per cent below the level of 1928 — so cheap had become the treasures of the world, rotting behind the customs barriers.

It was the great moment for Germany to supply herself cheaply with raw materials despite the relatively small sums which her exports provided for the purpose. Every mark was precious — and how many precious marks were still flowing uselessly out of Germany, bringing in nothing! These 'useless' sums were the money spent by Germany in servicing foreign loans; in the eyes of Hjalmar Schacht a real outrage.

When the German banking crisis broke out in July, 1931, Germany had had 23,800,000,000 marks in foreign debts, of which 10,700,000,000 were in long-term credits. Of the 13,100,000,000 in short-term credits, 6,300,000,000 had been frozen by the moratorium of September, 1931, but smaller sums had seeped away in the course of time. In February, 1933, the total German non-political indebtedness to foreign countries (including loans taken up by German states and municipalities) was exactly 19,000,000,000 marks, 10,300,000,000 of which was on a long-term basis; 4,100,000,000 in short-term credits fell under the moratorium; the rest consisted of other short-term credits, subject to no limitation except the usual foreign currency control introduced in 1931. All together, Germany had, during the year 1932, paid on this debt in interest, dividends, and amortization a sum of 1,100,000,000 marks — which, if expressed in terms of raw material prices of 1928, meant more than 2,200,000,000. And the men who directed German economic life in 1933 thought only in terms of raw materials.

It was the first great accomplishment of Hjalmar Schacht to save this billion — or two billions — for Germany's raw material program and to take advantage of the low raw material prices while they lasted. He pointed to the continued decline in German export figures, and declared that if foreign countries would not buy German manufactures, they could not expect Germany to pay her debts. At first the continued difficulties of the German export trade greatly embarrassed National Socialist propagandists; they did not know whether to attack the 'Jewish boycott' abroad or to conceal its successes from the home population. Actually the boycott had little to do with the decline in German exports; at the end of June, 1933, the Congress of German Commerce and Industry noted a sharp falling-off of anti-German propaganda abroad, and thirteen months later, in July, 1934, the German Ministry of Economics published a statement to the effect that an investigation by the competent authorities had shown that the political boycott was not the decisive factor in the decline of German exports.

Shortly after Hitler came to power, Germany's foreign creditors had been forced to accept a reduction of interest on capital lent to Germany from an average of 7 to 8 per cent to an average of 5 to 6 per cent. At the end of May, 1933, Hjalmar Schacht invited representatives of the foreign creditor banks to Berlin and asked them virtually to renounce interest payments on their long-term credits. This the foreign bankers refused to do, but pointed out that in a few days the great World Economic Conference was to open in London and would solve the problem of German foreign indebtedness, like so many other problems.

The London Economic Conference of June and July, 1933, solved no problems. Conceived and summoned by Ramsay MacDonald, originally welcomed and approved by Franklin D. Roosevelt, it concentrated its efforts, after beginnings in various directions, on the question of stabilizing international currencies, on attempts to restore the lost sanctity of money. After the majesty of money had been shattered in Russia and in Germany, and had suffered grave damage in France as well, the most respected of all international currencies had begun to totter; England had taken the pound off the gold standard and reduced its value. Just as the Economic

Conference was beginning its work, the United States, under the new leadership of Franklin D. Roosevelt, followed the example of England; the Gold Repeal Joint Resolution of June 5, 1933, took the American currency off the gold standard. The dollar began to slip and was later officially devaluated. It was Germany, where so much wealth had been destroyed, which now clung desperately to her currency, stabilized only a few years before. For the sake of the currency, if for no other reason, said Schacht, Germany could no longer pay her debts to foreign countries who no longer purchased her goods.

Schacht insisted that the cessation of payments was a hard blow to him, and this may be believed; he knew the importance of international credit, and he would surely have been overjoyed if foreign finance had voluntarily declared a moratorium. But certainly the rule of finance capital was crumbling, and anyone who did not want to crash with it had to help in its fall. For this he found ingenious methods. First, all interest on foreign loans was reduced from 5 per cent to a maximum of 4 per cent; even of this amount only half could be paid to foreign creditors; the other half of the interest, as well as all sums destined for amortization, had to remain in Germany; not in possession of the debtor himself, but in a 'conversion bank' to which the individual debtor made payments. The conversion bank then tendered the foreign creditor a paper called 'scrip' which for practical purposes he could spend only in Germany; moreover, the scrip was subject to an immediate discount of 40 per cent. These measures were put in the form of a law, proclaimed on June 3, 1933; on July 1, they became valid. The foreign creditors had to submit.

It was a masterpiece of official bankruptcy; a systematic robbery of foreign finance; a brilliant victory of the new state over money. The limited utility of the scrip, the constant danger that Schacht might one day devaluate it to the vanishing point, made this paper a doubtful asset on the international stock exchanges. In time other sorts of paper appeared, all based on the conception that foreigners possessing wealth — claims, shares in businesses, bank deposits — should be prevented from disposing of it freely; special victims of similar regulations were the German Jews, who were also pre-

vented from freely disposing of their funds within Germany; especially the liquidation of their bank deposits was made virtually
impossible. In time there came to be a varied assortment of foreign
claims on the different kinds of half or wholly 'blocked' deposits in
Germany; these claims were traded abroad, bought and sold; they
had their prices and rates, which were almost always considerably
below their nominal value. For it was almost always doubtful whether
such a claim could ever be collected; at best, the money could only be
used in Germany; and expense, loss of time, and irritation were certain. For all these claims against blocked German accounts, the expression 'blocked mark' came into use, and the different kinds of
blocked mark became a currency devaluated by the state, side by
side with the pound, the dollar, later — for the second time within
ten years — the French franc, etc. The blocked mark repeated,
though in a much attenuated form, the downward course of the
German mark after 1919.

But only the blocked mark. The German domestic mark was
in no way affected by this devaluation; the domestic mark was not
devaluated, wages and prices were subjected to an iron control, and
even in the following years of prosperity, they rose only slightly.
And equally successful was the state control over the real German
mark in its foreign relations. For not only were foreign assets in
Germany blocked and controlled, property or claims held by Germans abroad were likewise blocked. Restrictions on such property
had been imposed by Brüning's law governing the flight of capital;
at one time or another such restrictions had — even in peace —
been imposed by almost all countries; but Schacht's legislation and
its mode of operation held a place by themselves. Germans receiving payments from abroad had to deliver their foreign notes to the
Reichsbank which gave them marks in exchange; if they wished
to make a purchase abroad, they had to obtain the necessary sum in
foreign credits from the Reichsbank, or rather its *Devisenstelle* (foreign draft office); and only if the foreign draft office regarded the
transaction as useful to the German economy did it provide the
precious foreign checks. It gave them more readily if the foreign
goods were to be purchased in a country with which Germany had
a favorable trade balance — that is, which bought large quantities of

goods in Germany. A German importer might be advised to buy silk in Italy rather than in France, or to purchase wool in the Argentine instead of in Australia; vacationers who wanted to travel abroad — unless they had good reasons to the contrary, or, what amounted to the same thing, high recommendations — were definitely restricted to Italy, or, possibly, Switzerland. In this way the funds flowing back and forth between Germany and foreign countries were closely regulated, and care was taken that they should remain in exact proportion to the stream of goods actually traded. Hideous penalties were proclaimed for taking cash out of Germany. Not a mark was to go abroad for any purpose that was not covered by German sales to the country in question, and which had not been approved in advance by the foreign draft office. The German mark vanished from foreign markets as an object of trade and speculation, but remained active in the international exchange of *bona-fide* goods and services. Like the currency of most countries, it dispensed without bad consequences with the gold coverage that had formerly been regarded as indispensable, and, like the currency of most countries, it had ceased to be real money — that is, a measure of value honored for its intrinsic value. It was merely a token of credit, strictly limited in its use, and worthless outside of its assigned sphere. This process went so far that German bills, except in connection with transactions approved by the Reich, ceased to have any real value outside of Germany. And so the mark, having ceased to be an independent measure of value, lost in part the two other functions usually ascribed to money: the functions of transferring and of storing value.

It remained questionable whether Germany had saved or destroyed her currency. In any case, she removed it from the international stock exchange and, far more drastically than England, subjected it to the state. By this step Germany definitely broke with the system of international free trade which the Economic Conference in London was trying to restore. But the German delegation was not needed to paralyze this conference. For on July 3, the conference was stunned to receive a message from President Roosevelt, which called things by their proper name and announced America's withdrawal from the plans for international stabilization of currencies. Three days after Germany had stopped payments in order to rebuild her industry by her own strength, though not without stolen money, the President of the United States told the assembled financial experts of the world that a nation's internal economy was more vital to that nation's prosperity than the state of its currency; moreover, stabilization of currencies would not solve the problem of world trade; and it was more important to break down trade barriers; America — the message implied — would help herself and recommended the same to all countries. This was the end of the World Economic Conference, and after a few days it 'adjourned.' Hjalmar Schacht, always at great pains to discover a similarity between the American New Deal and the economic policy of the Third Reich, gave an interview in London, on July 12, in which he said that the failure of the conference had been a good thing; that all these conferences were going the same downward path as parliamentarianism; that in world economy as elsewhere the general watchword was: no more prattling. And the world should be grateful to President Roosevelt for his withdrawal: 'For Roosevelt has in principle the same idea that Hitler and Mussolini have put into action: take your economic fate into your own hands and you will be helping not only yourselves but the whole world!'

Chapter *XXVII*

'FRANCE IS TO BLAME'

WHEN SCHACHT LAMENTED HIS OWN BITTER FATE, which compelled him to destroy Germany's credit as the only way of saving Germany, it was no mere hypocrisy. These pleas of Schacht designate the point at which Germany for the last time had the choice between two ways to win the place in the world that was due her: the hard and slow way of using her growing power for peace and agreement, or the more showy way of taking it by force; which inevitably must lead to taking more than her due. She chose the second way. This way, no doubt, had long ago been outlined in the plans of the new rulers; but it will always be a grave question whether a happier destiny in the preceding years would have preserved her from these rulers and their dismally skillful methods.

True, in the beginning, as in all politics, a thousand principles had to be sacrificed in order that one opportunity might be seized. In the conflict between Hitler's Germany and her neighbors, of which Schacht's trade policy formed a part, Germany tried again and again to keep the peace and transform hostilities into friendships, because only in this way could her position in the heart of Europe cease to be a weakness and become a strength. For instance, National Socialist diplomacy exerted great self-discipline in abstaining from setting off the 'national dynamite' scattered through eastern Europe. Germany might, by invoking the right of national self-determination (the justice of which was incontestable), have raised claims on nearly all her frontiers. There were the German inhabitants of Danzig and those in Poland; there were the three and a quarter million Sudeten Germans in Czechoslovakia, forming a ring around the rest of that country; a few Germans living under a mild Danish rule in the border district of Slesvig; the Germans in the small area of Eupen and Malmédy, given to Belgium in 1919; the Germans in the Italian South Tyrol. But nowhere did National Socialism, in its first years, make any attempt to bring these Germans 'home to the Reich.' Two years before, Hitler had proclaimed that the Czechoslovakian state would have to be smashed with the help of the Sudeten Germans. Now not a word of this. The relatively small National Socialist Party of the Sudeten Germans was dissolved by the Czechoslovakian government in October, 1933, its leaders fled to Germany, and thus perished the oldest of all National Socialist parties, the mother movement, twenty years older than the N.S.D.A.P. Many Sudeten German National Socialists were tried and imprisoned — but Germany took no notice and kept silent. From Poland came complaints about the persecution of German minorities — official Germany, in public at least, was silent. No loud word or unfriendly act toward any of the countries in the French ring of alliances; with iron self-control the Third Reich waited for its day, which had not yet come.

For in these countries the German minorities lived on the soil of proud and jealous national states. But Austria, in her mutilated post-war form, was solely and purely a product of that Versailles world which it was the main business of German policy to rend thread by thread. Sudeten Germany, the Vistula Corridor, and German-speaking South Tyrol were territories which Czechs, Poles, and Italians could regard as their own — no one except the Austrians themselves could regard Austria as his own. No diplomacy in the world could overlook the fact that large parts, even the majority, of these Austrians, wanted, or had at one time wanted, to be united with Germany. In the disputes between the German minorities and the national governments of Poland and Czechoslovakia, people were struggling against people; in Austria the people struggled mainly against bureaucracy and diplomacy. And so it was the internal condition of Austria which influenced German foreign policy — and not the other way around. Even those opposed to *Anschluss* admitted, in spite of themselves, how hard, indeed how impossible, it was for the little country to break inwardly with Germany. Chancellor Engelbert Dollfuss, for example, declared the aim of his government to be the establishment of a 'Catholic German state.'

In March, 1933, Hans Frank, Hitler's friend, now a Bavarian minister, took a trip around Austria making speeches against Dollfuss and the government as though he had been home in Germany, attacking Brüning or Severing; the Austrian government deported him, and the battle was on. The Austrian National Socialists, led by Theo Habicht, a German, and an Austrian named Frauenfeld, began to hurl bombs, mostly harmless, to be sure, at government officials and public buildings. The government answered with arrests and established a mild sort of concentration camp. Hitler countered with a serious blow: at the end of May, Germany exacted a payment of a thousand marks from travelers desiring to visit Austria. This virtually closed the frontier; Austria's Alpine provinces had largely lived on the German tourist trade. In answer, Dollfuss suppressed the National Socialist Party and arrested its leaders; Habicht, Frauenfeld, and thousands of their supporters fled to Germany.

These National Socialists were organized into an 'Austrian Legion'; equipped with arms, even cannon, they lived in camps, ready to march at any moment; planes regularly crossed the Austrian frontier and threw down proclamations. It was an international civil war, and the National Socialists conducted it with an efficiency that might have been the envy of the Communist International. But the German Foreign Office insisted that it was all an internal affair of Austria; the Austrian National Socialists had chosen Hitler as their Leader; this was their right and their own affair.

Dollfuss turned to the great powers for help. But the days were past when Germany could be frightened by frowns in London or Paris. As long as the world could come to no decision on disarmament, it would not go out of its way for Austria, and more than a protest in words was not to be expected. On July 5, in the House of Commons, Sir Austen Chamberlain described the international menace of National Socialism with epigrammatic sharpness: 'The

spirit shown within Germany to Germans is a menace to every
nation beyond her borders. . . .' But Sir John Simon, the Foreign
Minister, had nothing to offer Austria but 'the whole sympathy of
this country'; and the Four-Power Pact, just concluded between
England, France, Italy, and Germany, 'which I hope will be used
to assist that country. . . .' England did not promise embattled
Austria her own aid, but only that of all Europe — little more than
an empty word.

It was the English Left which in those weeks made a real attempt
to injure National Socialist Germany. On July 25, the Congress of
British Trades Unions and the Labour Party issued a call to their
members to boycott German goods. But on the conservative side,
the most influential makers of public opinion opposed the boycott.
In the first days of July, Lord Rothermere published another of
his enthusiastic articles on the new Germany in the *Daily Mail*; in
Germany, wrote the founder of the 'Empire Party,' youth had seized
the power of command, there had been a national awakening, an
example to all the world. With the same methods Mussolini had
made his country the best governed on earth, and he, Rothermere,
confidently expected Hitler, who had come to power at the age of
forty-three, to achieve equal successes in Germany. The simple,
unadorned patriotism of Hitler and his followers was, according to
Rothermere, a source of great agitation among British parlor Bolsheviks and 'culture Communists.' The most hateful detractors of
Nazis, he went on, were to be found in those very sections of the
British public and press which were most enthusiastic about Soviet
rule in Russia. These people had undertaken a loud campaign of
slander against what they called 'Nazi atrocities,' which, as everyone who visited Germany quickly discovered, consisted only of a
few isolated acts, which propagandists had generalized, multiplied,
and exaggerated in order to give the impression that Nazi rule was
a bloodthirsty tyranny. Rothermere did not refrain from remarking
that under the Weimar Republic there had been twenty times as
many Jewish officials as before the war; and, as though to prove that
he really knew nothing about conditions in Germany, he concluded
with the remark that Hindenburg and the Crown Prince, along with
Herr Hitler, constituted the center of the edifice. These three men

would go down in history as the founders of a new Germany; Hitler was a leader who had gathered together all the valuable elements of his country for the public welfare. . . .

The growth and consolidation of National Socialist power in Germany, the broad, confused, and vain efforts at understanding on the part of public opinion in the western countries, were the real historical content of this period. But through it all the diplomats kept up their dwarfish activities: notes, memoranda, official visits, the meaninglessness of which was suspected even by the participants. This became evident when finally an attempt was made to do something for menaced Austria. The Daladier government in France, though none too hopefully, attempted to take Sir John Simon at his word with his invocation of the Four-Power Pact and to frighten Berlin with an impressive protest. The Four-Power Pact broke down at once; Italy declared that she could participate in no common measures, since this would constitute an act of unfriendliness to Germany. On August 5, the Italian ambassador rushed to the German Foreign Office and 'in a friendly way called the attention of the Reich government to . . . ' and so on. In an equally friendly way, Neurath replied that the Reich government was willing to suppress Habicht's radio speeches; there would be no more planes throwing down leaflets; he hoped that there would be no explosions of paper bombs, but for this Germany could assume no responsibility. Rome, highly pleased, transmitted the German promises to Paris and London, and requested these governments to take no steps of their own.

But France insisted in London that at least France and England should take steps in common. England, indifferent to Austria and Central Europe in general, was, after the desertion of Italy, unprepared for joint action. On the morning of August 7, the French ambassador appeared alone in the German Foreign Office with his note of protest; not until the afternoon did the British chargé d'affaires put in an appearance. Both received a sharp answer such as a disunited Europe could not but expect. An official German communiqué on the incident approached the limits of diplomatic discourtesy:

The French ambassador stated this morning, with reference to

the Four-Power Pact, that, in the opinion of the French government, German propaganda with regard to Austria was not compatible in certain recent instances with existing contractual obligations. The ambassador was informed that the Reich government
did not consider appropriate the application of the Four-Power
Pact in this form; that no contractual infringements of any kind
had taken place on the part of Germany; Germany, therefore, did
not regard this interference in German-Austrian affairs as permissible. The English chargé d'affaires, who appeared in the same
matter in the afternoon, received the same answer.

This was possibly the most unfriendly diplomatic communiqué
which Germany had permitted herself since 1919 in her dealings
with the victor powers. The western powers accepted the diplomatic defeat and did not repeat their step; they consoled themselves
by stating in their press that, after all, Hitler had promised the
Italians to respect the independence of Austria. Thereupon a new
statement from Berlin (August 19), semi-official and even ruder:
nothing whatever had been promised to France and England; certainly Germany had carried on friendly conversations with Italy,
but these conversations were no concern of France and England;
their protest had been and remained rejected.

On the day when the Italian ambassador had so amiably discussed
Austria with Neurath, the Free City of Danzig and the Republic
of Poland signed a treaty regarding their future relations. Negotiated by Josef Beck, the Polish Foreign Minister, and Hermann
Rauschning, President of the Danzig Senate, it was the first formal
peace pact between Poland and National Socialism. Up till then
Danzig, within striking distance of Polish military power, had been
guaranteed by the League of Nations against any possible Polish
attack, and for this purpose a High Commissioner of the League
lived in the Free City. Now the Danzig National Socialists renounced the protection of Geneva; Danzig and Poland agreed to
settle all disputes among themselves and to cease presenting them
to the League.

This was the new German line. Peace with individual neighbors
— yes; peace with the whole world, as represented by the League —
no!

Actually this great peace of all with all was an impossible figment of the brain, unrealizable in the world of reality. To be true and possible, it should have penetrated far deeper than the outer edges where the peoples touched one another; it presupposed a certain intimacy in the social relations between the nations; the London Economic Conference had tried to achieve such an intimacy, but with inadequate means. What was needed was a new form of life among the nations; what was offered was at best diplomatic agreements in which no two diplomats meant the same thing. To most of its English proponents, for example, collective security meant a system in which England would not have to give much help, since her responsibility was shared with so many others. But for France collective security was a condition in which everyone would have to help her with all his forces.

In French internal politics, rearmament and collective security became opposed, hostile concepts. Collective security meant: no necessity to rearm; no necessity for a larger army; hence no necessity for going back to the system of two years' service.

Without doubt, the military spirit had an even harder time in France than in the Germany of the twenties, combating the opposition of the masses; the struggle of the armed intellectuals for the working class seemed utterly hopeless. In *Au fil de l'épée,* a book dedicated to Marshal Pétain, Lieutenant Colonel Charles de Gaulle had written in 1932: 'Could we, indeed, conceive of life without force? . . . It is the medium of thought, the instrument of action, the prerequisite for movement, the midwife of progress. . . . Cradle of cities, scepter of empires, gravedigger of decadence, force gives law to peoples and controls their destiny. . . .' It was a summons to the national élite to understand, not the inevitability, but the creative necessity, of violence and war; 'this abnegation of individuals for the benefit of the whole, this glorified suffering — of which troops are made — correspond most perfectly to our aesthetic and moral concepts: the highest philosophical and religious doctrines have chosen no other ideal. . . . It is time for the military élite to regain consciousness of its pre-eminent rôle, for it to concentrate on its objective which is, quite simply, war. . . .'

Collective security or rearmament — this seemed to be the choice that was left to France. Actually, there was not even a choice. When, on September 20, the British cabinet decided to cease pressing France to disarm, it seemed like a gesture of friendship and aid, but actually it meant that France would be left to her fate and her own strength; she must not count on England's help.

France tried to remain strong. She submitted a plan which would make German equality impossible for eight years: first, Germany would have four years in which to transform her professional army with its twelve-year period of service into a short-term militia; after another four years in which to manifest her good intentions, she would be allowed to increase her armaments somewhat, while the other powers would have to decrease their armaments accordingly — this eight-year armaments moratorium was to be substituted for the five years proposed by MacDonald and accepted by Hitler. Whatever might be said of this plan, it could in any case be expected to halt German rearmament and save the world from a general armament race; for this reason it met with the approval of the United States. This made such an impression on Italy that she supported the plan; Hitler was shamefully forsaken by the 'great man in the south.' On September 24, the French plan, bearing the signatures of America, England, and Italy, was presented to Germany.

So this was the success of Hitler's great policy which was to split the world: the whole world formed a front against Germany! Göring flew to Rome, but Italy did not change her position, not outwardly at least. And yet, in this apparently united front there was no real unity. It was at best an agreement on a plan, no common will to carry it through, to stick together. Even if the British cabinet had had such a will — which it decidedly had not — large sections of public opinion would not have followed it.

When in September the trial of the alleged Reichstag incendiaries began in Leipzig, a few Englishmen of the political Left, working in collaboration with German refugees, staged a 'counter-trial' in London. All sorts of persons, some with and some without authority, appeared as witnesses and testified why in their opinion, not the accused, but the National Socialists, and particularly Göring, had set fire to the Reichstag. The Communists had staged the affair behind a screen of supposed non-Communists; Willy Muenzenberg, a German Communist leader, had organized the whole undertaking. The results were what was to be expected. Even Sir Austen Chamberlain called the 'counter-trial' a shameless abuse of hospitality. Lloyd George, England's leader in the World War, co-author of Versailles, who had long deeply regretted his own work, said, on September 22, in a meeting at Bournemouth, that if the powers succeeded in overthrowing National Socialism in Germany, Communism would succeed it; and that the Communists in the whole world, from Russia to America, were praying that the western nations would drive Germany into a Communist revolution.

Against this world mood, shifting between rancor and hope, tormented by the fear of irrevocable decisions, National Socialist propaganda now undertook a great offensive. When the plenary assembly of the League of Nations met at the end of September, Goebbels was the German delegate. Neurath refused to let the propaganda minister appear as the spokesman of Germany in the assembly; but outside Goebbels found a wide audience. It was wrong, he told fellow journalists at a press conference, to believe 'that the peoples wanted to govern themselves. They cannot and they have no desire to, they only want to be well governed.' This was what National Socialism did, said he; consequently, the Third Reich was 'an ennobled form of democracy.' It seemed as though Goebbels had been sent to Geneva to abjure all National Socialist principles, for he firmly denied that National Socialism had a 'world mission' to fulfill and that it planned the fascistization of Europe; no, National Socialism was 'a typically German phenomenon which can be explained only on the basis of German environment, German character, and German distress'; in a conversation he said that National Socialism was something so good that Germany wanted to keep it entirely for herself.

A few days later, simpler, more forceful words were addressed — not to the world, but to France alone — by Göring; as one of the military leaders of National Socialism, he invited the military leaders of France to a conference. In an interview with Jules Sauerwein, the French journalist, he made a peace proposal couched in very general terms; it was published by *Paris Soir* on

October 5 and caused a great sensation. The gist of the conversation was that it would be easy to bring about peace if France were not hampered by inner strife and parliament. It was impossible, said Göring, that France and Germany should want to annihilate one another; neither of the two had ever been able to do so and never would. France had long taken offense at the line, 'Victoriously we'll defeat the French,' in a song sung by the German combat leagues. Now Göring said: I have given orders to stop singing it. He called on the French to send him a soldier, and with him he would arrive at an agreement on certain needs of a German *Luftwaffe*. In Germany, said Göring in conclusion, the Leader desired peace, and if the Leader desired peace, the whole nation would follow him — 'but have you such a man in France, despite your party conflicts and your parliamentary compromises?'

Daladier replied in a speech delivered at Vichy. He asked, not without sharpness, why Germany wanted armaments when she spoke so much of peace; why she 'trained her youth for war?' But he also said: 'No one contests Germany's right to existence as a great nation. No one intends to humiliate Germany.' Despite all the brevity and coolness of these words, they were more than a French statesman had ever publicly conceded Germany since Versailles; and even when Daladier asked: 'What does Germany want? Why all these masses marching and drilling . . . ?' it sounded like a question demanding a reply in a personal conference, a discussion between one chief of state and another — which was just what Hitler wanted.

But French foreign policy was still dominated by the party of collective security; on September 24, the great powers had agreed on the plan for an eight-year quarantine, and when the Disarmament Conference met in October, it would have this plan to deal with. On October 13, Hitler sent Hans Luther, his ambassador to Washington, to call on Secretary of State Cordell Hull, and, according to the official German news bureau, Luther learned that the American government was determined that no pressure should be put on Germany and that no decisions should be made contrary to justified German wishes. In fact, the American State Department 'expressly denied that any reports on German armament were at hand.' Perhaps the sanguine German ambassador had heard too much. On the fourteenth, the bureau of the conference met in Geneva and Sir John Simon, as spokesman of the British delegation, declared that he still adhered to the plan for an eight-year transitional period. Germany's protests were rejected.

In his great peace speech of May 17, Hitler had declared that if the other powers meant to 'do violence' to Germany by outvoting her, their sole purpose could be 'to remove us from the conferences.' But: 'The German nation has character enough not to force its collaboration on other nations in such a case; though with a heavy heart, it will draw the necessary consequences. As a people constantly defamed, it would be hard for us to continue membership in the League of Nations.'

Now Germany had been 'outvoted.' Here was a splendid opportunity to teach the world once and for all that the Leader's words must be taken seriously and to carry the fight over European foreign policy to the peoples themselves with an issue which, in England and in France as well, might stir up one political party against another; and with which he hoped to unleash within his own people a surge of popular enthusiasm even greater than in the spring. And it was a unique opportunity to show that the apparent unity of the world against Germany would not withstand a test.

On the night of October 14, Germany announced her withdrawal from the Disarmament Conference and the League of Nations.

It was one of those political blows in which Hitler has always been a master; a combination *blitz* which he hurled in three or four directions at once, almost always choosing the right moment, as a rule uncannily sure of success. In the same hour he dissolved the Reichstag; new elections were to be held November 12; only one list of deputies, the National Socialist list, with a few 'Hospitants,' as for example Hugenberg, was to be put before the voters; they only could say 'Yes' or 'No' — and the most were convinced that practically they could not say No. At the same time they had, by way of plebiscite, to state whether or not they approved Hitler's foreign policy — which on the bulletin of vote was explained as a policy to save peace. The great plebiscite, the irresistible instrument of Napoleonic propaganda technique, the use of which Hitler had

been announcing for ten years, but for which in the spring of 1933
his hands had not been sufficiently free, now descended on the
German people like a natural cataclysm. A question of overpowering simplicity was put to the voters: Do you want peace? And the
rest of the world was asked, more emphatically than before: Do
you want Bolshevism?

Once again it was the events and circumstances that had shaped
this propaganda and forged its cutting edge. For some weeks the
Reichstag fire trial, which in the spring Hitler had been unable to
prevent, had been in progress in Leipzig. The secret preparations
for this trial are not yet known, but their results are a matter of
record. In the presence of National Socialist power, German justice
did not have the courage to look for the officially unknown incendiaries; it took refuge in a procedure of formal correctness, merely
seeking to ascertain whether the accused Van Der Lubbe, Dimitrov, Torgler, Popov, and Tanev had set the fire; the preliminary
investigation left little doubt of the result. Unexpectedly, Georgi
Dimitrov proved one of the most courageous and adroit agitators of
the Communist International — though his captors remained unaware of his identity. In endless disputes with Buenger, the chairman of the court, with National Socialist witnesses such as Goebbels, Heines, and particularly Göring, Dimitrov effectively destroyed the National Socialist propaganda fable of the Reichstag
fire. He asked Göring if he were afraid of his questions; and
Göring roared back in uncontrolled rage, 'You'll be afraid of me
when you get out of here, you scoundrel!' — thus admitting that he
did not regard Dimitrov as guilty, but meant to have him killed regardless. Large parts of the German public were carried away by
the speeches of the Bulgarian despite his poor command of the
language; he made the trial one of the most effective performances
of Communist world propaganda.

But Communist propaganda it was; and it was Communist propaganda that had staged the so-called counter-trial in London; it was
Communist propaganda, said Hitler, that cast world suspicion upon
Germany and ascribed warlike intentions to his country; German
refugees, in particular, had been highly active in this: 'These ruinous and inferior characters have succeeded in arousing a world

psychosis,' he said in a radio speech on the night of October 15, a day after his withdrawal from the League of Nations. He called on the world to witness, by the example of the London counter-trial, what National Socialism had saved the world from: 'By saving the world from this menacing catastrophe' — the Red incendiary torch — 'the National Socialist Movement has not only saved the German people, it has also rendered an historic service to the rest of Europe.'

And now incendiary Communism was busy stirring up a warlike mood in Europe; but Adolf Hitler — or so he himself said — opposed it and offered Europe peace. He had, according to his speech, left the League of Nations and the Disarmament Conference in order that Germany might seek understanding with her former adversaries, between nation and nation, in a way far better than had been possible beside the Swiss lakes. Daladier had spoken his cautious, reassuring words. 'I take it as a sign of a noble sense of justice,' said Hitler, 'that the French Premier in his last speech has found words in the spirit of conciliatory understanding, and for this innumerable millions of Germans are grateful to him.' Hitler made more of Daladier's words than the speaker presumably intended; he spoke to the French with a mixture of pride and warmth of which Stresemann had not been capable:

> With hopeful emotion we take notice of the assurance that the French government, under its new leader, does not intend to trample and humiliate the German people. We are moved by the reference to the unfortunate sad truth that these two great nations have so often in history sacrificed the blood of their best youth on the battlefields. I speak in the name of the whole German people when I assure you that we are all filled with the sincere desire to do away with a hostility the victims of which are out of all proportion to its possible gain. The German people is convinced that its military honor has remained untarnished through a thousand battles and contests of arms, just as in the French soldier we see only our old but glorious adversary. . . .

Only a few years earlier, Hitler had publicly said that Germany must forcibly retake Alsace-Lorraine from France. This he now solemnly contradicted. There was only one relatively unimportant frontier question outstanding: that of the Saar Basin and its eight hundred thousand inhabitants. Legally — as not even the peace treaties denied — it was German territory; but the Treaty of Versailles provided that it was to be governed for fifteen years by a League of Nations Commission with headquarters in Saarbrücken; economically, it was included in the French customs zone; the currency was French, French goods dominated the markets; the coal mines, which constituted the chief industry, were administered by a French government consortium and French officials. The totally German territory was strangely permeated by the French language and French customs, and the French Tricolors waved over the coal shafts. The ultimate fate of the territory was to be decided by a plebiscite to be held in 1935 at the earliest. The Saarlanders were unquestionably Germans and wanted to be Germans; the majority of the population of Alsace-Lorraine probably did not; now Hitler said:

> As a National Socialist, I, along with all my supporters, decline, on the basis of our national principles, to acquire people of a strange nation, who cannot be made to love us, with the blood and life of those who are dear and precious to us. It would be a gigantic event for all mankind if both nations, once and for all, should banish force from their mutual relations. The German nation is willing! Just as I freely invoke the rights which are given us in the treaties themselves [he meant Versailles and Locarno] I will just as freely declare that, as far as Germany is concerned, there are no further territorial conflicts between the two countries. After the return of the Saar to Germany, only a madman could conceive the possibility of war between the two countries; from our point of view there can be no morally or reasonably justifiable ground for one. For no one could demand that, to achieve a correction, dubious in value as well as scope, of the present frontiers, a million human lives should be sacrificed.

These declarations of peace were now submitted to the German voter, and it was to them that the question referred which he was to answer at the polls: Do you, German man, do you, German woman, approve this policy of your government? Again Hitler drove and flew up and down Germany, and everywhere his word to the masses was: Peace, peace! 'When I say peace, that is what the whole German people is thinking,' he cried. 'Hence the plebiscite!' It was not true, he declared, that a spiritual preparation for war was being carried on in Germany, and the enemies of Germany ought to think up something better. Whenever he, Hitler, spoke of peace, the answer was: only he and his intimate staff speak like that, but in the people a wild warlike spirit is raging; and in the next breath he was accused of repressing the will of the people. Indeed, the stormy applause of millions at Hitler's peace speeches could not be ignored; in England, Lord Robert Cecil, chairman of the British League of Nations Association, said that German statesmen could not continuously speak of peace if they were not convinced that the German people, in the bottom of its heart, desired peace as much as every other people on earth; moreover, he, Lord Cecil, would not maintain that Germany had no reason for complaint.

It was from England that the most encouraging voices came. While a large part of the French press warned that Hitler wanted only to separate France and England, in England the opinion was widespread that France only wanted to incite England and Germany against each other. True, not every Englishman was as enthusiastic as Lord Rothermere, who, on October 18, sent his correspondent, Ward Price, to Hitler. 'There are signs,' said Ward Price, 'that since last Saturday' — day of the German withdrawal from the League of Nations — 'your popularity with the British public has risen amazingly. Lord Rothermere, with whom I spoke on the telephone last night, told me that when your picture was shown in the news reels Monday night it was greeted with lively applause.' Even the conservative *Morning Post* wrote on October 16 that France should not reject Hitler's outstretched hand; Neville Chamberlain, Sir Austen's brother, demanded what more or less amounted to the same thing: that people reserve judgment in condemning Germany. Lord Beaverbrook wanted England to denounce the Treaty of Locarno, because France (not Germany) by rearming had morally broken it.

Vernon Bartlett said over the radio that he was convinced of the 'almost foolish' sincerity of the Germans. Lloyd George, in many articles and speeches, prophesied the victory of Communism in

Germany if Hitler fell; Germany, he said, had fulfilled her disarmament obligations; the other nations' failure to disarm was an 'infamy,' the 'most flagrant example of breach of faith in history.' Passionate accusations against Germany were also heard, for instance, from Lord Alfred Duff Cooper, a member of the cabinet, and from Wickham Steed, former editor-in-chief of the *Times*. But the editors of the *Times* probably expressed the mood of the average Englishman in an article, published on October 18, which violently attacked the military spirit of the new Germany, yet added, referring to Hitler's speeches: 'In the German case thus set out there is much that is undeniably true, and some of the grievances are well understood.'

The absence of a world coalition for the defense of collective security became overwhelmingly evident within a very short time. In the United States, Hitler's step was defended by the Hearst press, which sounded a warning against America's becoming entangled in European affairs; in Geneva, Norman Davis, the American delegate, declared on October 16, upon instructions from Washington, that the United States was 'in no way aligned with any European power,' and that such unity of purpose as existed had been entirely on world disarmament matters. The Washington correspondent of the London *Times* stated that the Roosevelt administration clearly wished 'to withdraw firmly and at once from any position even of seeming solidarity with Great Britain and France' — except in their opposition to rearmament.

The world, even Europe alone, would have certainly been stronger than Germany, but there was no Europe. On November 7, Winston Churchill said in the House of Commons: 'We should not try to weaken great powers [he meant France] which are or which feel themselves to be in great danger. . . .' But this was only in order to prevent England from becoming involved in a European war; we should not, he went on, 'thereby expose ourselves to a demand that we come to their aid. . . . We should forthwith recognize that our rôle in Europe is more limited than hitherto. Isolation is utterly impossible [cheers], but we ought to practice a certain degree of sober detachment from the European scene. . . . We should be able in any case to maintain our neutrality — a neutrality from which we should never be drawn except by the will and conscience of the overwhelming mass of our people.'

Two days later Prime Minister Ramsay MacDonald replied that this meant war sooner or later. On November 9, in a speech at the Guild Hall in London, he said he knew that a point might be reached where the policy of disarmament could no longer be continued: 'But let none of us imagine that by so doing we are establishing peace. . . . Those precautions [he meant: rearming] may postpone the day of war' — that was all he hoped for.

Actually the policy of disarmament had come to an end. England decided to rearm in the air. But when, on November 29, the Marquess of Londonderry, chief of the Air Ministry, made a pessimistic speech in the House of Lords about the danger to which England was exposed in the air, he did not mention Germany in the first place; in fact, he did not name her at all. But France, he said, had 1650 military planes and was the strongest air power in the world; Great Britain had only 750 and occupied fifth place.

Ten days after Germany's withdrawal from the League of Nations, Daladier's cabinet fell in France, because it tried to cut salaries of the civil servants; Albert Sarraut became Premier in one of those innumerable cabinet changes behind which the petrifaction of French political life was hidden. At the same time Hitler's plebiscite was being prepared throughout Germany. National Socialist officials — the so-called 'block wardens' of the party — visited every family; and the slogans, 'Your vote for the Führer!' . . . 'Germany says Yes!' . . . 'To vote is a duty!' etc., were plastered in huge letters all over the walls, blared all day long over the radio, spread across the front pages of the newspapers, so that the idea of resistance could find no room in anyone's mind. On voting day, November 12, in many places, particularly in the small communities, the vote was public. Even voters who seemed to be alone in the booths often did not believe in their solitude, but imagined that they were being spied upon in some mysterious way. An idea of the way the plebiscite was conducted can be gleaned from the fact that ballots were cast in the concentration camps, and that more than ninety per cent of the inmates voted allegedly for Hitler. Yet all these details about the freedom and secrecy of the ballot do not explain what took

place. Actually it was the same situation that occurred in France
in 1851, when Louis Napoleon Bonaparte, after having dissolved
Parliament, shed blood in the streets, organized mass executions
and deportations, nevertheless obtained ninety per cent of the votes
for the maintenance of his rule: the voters realized that they had
no choice, that a protest could only harm them personally and in no
case help their cause; if they did not give their vote to the established
power, they would give it only to impotence. The attraction of
established power has always been great even in 'secret' plebiscites;
in 1933, the German voter who voted Yes gave his vote not only
to power, but allegedly to peace.

In fact, Germany was now the country which repeated the word
'peace' most consistently and most loudly; she even made the most
definite and tangible peace proposals to her neighbors; and in her
various pronouncements a general peace plan gradually began to
take shape. The peace plans of the other countries had not with-
stood the storm of German opposition; America had retreated;
thus the front which had imposed an eight-year waiting period on
Germany, in order to stop the race for armaments, collapsed. On
November 7, Göring again visited Mussolini and handed him a
letter from Hitler; one day before the German plebiscite, Count
Sorragna, the Italian delegate in Geneva, declared that henceforth
Italy would limit herself to the rôle of observer at the Disarmament
Conference. How completely Germany and Italy had brought their
methods into harmony was evident from Sorragna's remark that
continued consultations would only bar the way to future diplomatic negotiations between individual powers. Italy's withdrawal
from the dying Disarmament Conference gave it the *coup de grâce*;
this was so obvious to everyone that Arthur Henderson, its British
chairman, declared that he would resign, although in the end he
did not.

Thus, Germany's withdrawal from the League of Nations had
strengthened her position after a few weeks; and the German voter
felt this, too. In the plebiscite of November 12, the German people
supported their Chancellor and what he called his peace plans; more
than ninety per cent of them or — depending on the methods of
calculation — almost ninety per cent voted Yes. Ninety per cent

must be taken for the whole of the people, whether their motives were genuine agreement, fatalism, or partly even fear. Of the 45,178,000 people who had the right to vote, 43,053,000 votes were cast; 39,655,000 of these were for the National Socialist list of Reichstag candidates; 3,398,000 were against them, or, to express it in National Socialist electoral terms, their ballots were 'invalid.'

Within three days this peace plebiscite was crowned by a deed by which Hitler once again showed what he meant by peace. He received Mr. Lipski, the Polish ambassador recently named to Berlin, and a communiqué published by both parties stated that the conversation revealed 'the complete unanimity of both governments in their intention to deal with the questions touching both countries by means of direct negotiations and to renounce all application of force in their relations with each other for the consolidation of European peace.' Here was a pact from which the League of Nations and the principle of collective security were openly excluded — for this was the meaning of the carefully chosen words, 'direct negotiations' and 'relations with each other.' Thus crumbled France's political system in Europe — but was it still France's system?

Among the Frenchmen who no longer believed in the great hope of collective security was Edouard Daladier, the Premier who had just been overthrown. He served as Minister of War in Sarraut's cabinet and was closer to what was sometimes called in public debates 'militaristic thinking' or 'the policy of the generals' than other French politicians. Frivolous or half-serious private diplomats were traveling back and forth between France and Germany; the novelty of the German Reich attracted many French observers, and those among them who in their own country were of any importance or were thought to wield any influence could be sure of an attentive, even flattering, reception by leading National Socialists. The close cartel connections between German and French steel industry made such meetings unceremonious, natural. Thus, soon after the German plebiscite, Ferdinand de Brinon, a French journalist representing *Le Matin* and *L'Information,* came to Berlin to write a few stimulating articles; actually he had been sent by Daladier. Hitler received him and told him that Germany would not return to the League of Nations; but war? — that would be madness! 'It would mean the end of our races which are both élites; Asia would establish itself on our continent and Bolshevism would triumph.' France, he warned, should cease 'building her security on Germany's inability to defend herself. . . . The days when this was possible are over.' In other words: We are already so strong that the French system of alliance is dead; you can no longer pass over us to stretch out your hand to the Poles or the Czechs. But: 'If France wants to find her security in an agreement, I am ready to listen to everything, to understand everything. . . .' And for the first time Hitler told de Brinon quite clearly: 'Alsace-Lorraine is not a controversial issue.'

Agreement . . . understanding . . . ? This was the question which now was put in full earnest before the military men of France: General Maxime Weygand, the chief of staff; Gustave Gamelin, his designated successor; Gamelin's associate, General Georges — and above all, Marshal Philippe Pétain, the most revered military figure of the country, who had always been an admirer of German military achievement. These men, dependent on the good will of a not too benevolent parliament, must have been filled with envy at the ease with which Hitler could command the strength of his country.

Friedrich Sieburg, a German journalist, described the curiously tortuous policy of the French military in their struggle for their army as follows:

> Daladier looks at the German military policy with the same technical eyes as the French General Staff, which also holds the view that the moment is opportune for participating in the limitation of a German armaments program before it is too late, and for preventing the complete demobilization of the French army by this means. It is known that plans are being prepared in the War Ministry and the General Staff which are supposed to take the realization of the German armaments program and the consequent strengthening of Germany's military position into account. For some time the military even nursed the hope of being able to increase the service-period to two years. . . .

Two countries, two general staffs; one country the terror of the other, one general staff the pretext for the other! It would surely be an exaggeration to say that the French military rejoiced over German rearmament; but they obviously were of the opinion that France should attempt to reach an understanding about the purpose and limits of this rearmament directly with Germany, without the intermediary of the cumbersome Disarmament Conference. In November and December, there were negotiations between Hitler and François-Poncet, the French ambassador to Germany. Hitler proposed a solemn Franco-German agreement which would proclaim the reconciliation of the two nations for all time to come, after the model of the agreement which he tried, about the same period, to reach with Poland. This proposal to France was formulated in terms that went far beyond the cool peace declarations which Pilsudski finally agreed to make. Hitler suggested that he was even willing to renounce Italian friendship in return; he expected that France, as a sign of her conciliatory attitude, would renounce the Saar without a plebiscite. And since France intended to maintain her strong armaments, she surely could not object to a modest German army of three hundred thousand men.

From France came a curiously encouraging reply in the form of an obviously inspired article in *Le Temps* of December 17, which said: Either the German proposals will be rejected, which would mean sanctions and war, but England was against this; or 'It will be granted that Herr Hitler's proposals, although unacceptable on many points, offer a possible basis for discussion on many other points.' What was 'unacceptable' was doubtless the demand of a three-hundred-thousand-man army; but is it not the purpose of all diplomatic negotiations to try to reach an agreement on 'unacceptable points'?

However, the party which believed in the League of Nations and collective security gained the upper hand in France. Foreign Minister Joseph Paul-Boncour, one of the chief spokesmen of this party, announced this in the League Council on January 20, 1934, when he rejected in resounding terms Hitler's demand for the Saar. The League's interest in the Saar, he said, was more important for France than her own interest in it; to be sure, France could reach a direct understanding with Germany, but it was her duty to enable the inhabitants of the Saar to make a free decision. This was more than a noble attitude; actually France could not expect any advantage from a free decision of the Saarlanders, while a passionate plebiscite meant useless vexations and dangers to her.

On January 21, 1933, however, German and foreign fascism moved a little closer to each other in another quarter. Marshal Pilsudski approved the project of a treaty of reconciliation between Germany and Poland, which had been under consideration for months. The treaty did not imply that Germany recognized the Polish-German frontier, but she promised not to change that frontier by force. The real meaning of the agreement lay in the fact that both parties renounced the help of the League in settling their mutual affairs. 'Both governments,' ran the Polish-German declaration published on January 26, 'desire to settle by direct negotiations all questions of whatever nature which concern them. In the case of disputes which cannot be solved by direct negotiations, a solution shall be sought by other peaceful means, without prejudice to other methods such as are laid down in existing agreements. In no case shall there be an appeal to force.' The treaty also declared that no problems shall be discussed 'which, in accordance with international law, should be regarded exclusively as internal affairs of either state' — in these ambiguous terms Germany perhaps renounced the protection of her minority in Poland; Poland certainly wished to place that interpretation on the phrase. The treaty was to remain in force for ten years, and to be automatically extended unless denounced. That it was designed to end the hostility between the two countries and thereby detach Poland from the French system of alliances, for all practical purposes, was confirmed a few days later by a so-called 'propaganda agreement,' in which Germany and Poland pledged themselves 'to co-operate on all questions concerning public opinion in their respective countries to the end that mutual understanding may be increasingly awakened and that a friendly atmosphere may thereby be assured.'

On the same day on which Poland made peace with National Socialist Germany, she ceased formally to be a democracy. This was the result of a parliamentary procedure which was curiously similar to the suicide of the Austrian democracy on March 7, 1933. A new constitution which abrogated equal and universal suffrage was proposed by the government and stood under debate in a parliamentary committee; the opposition parties left the session in protest; at that moment the chairman hastily put the proposal to a vote, and it was adopted within a few minutes. The deputies of the government bloc, for the most part former members of Pilsudski's Legion in the World War, jumped from their seats and sang their battle song, the 'First Brigade.'

But the dream of collective security was not yet dead despite all these blows. While France insisted on a security plan because she was threatened from one side, another country now began to advocate such a plan, because it considered itself encircled from all sides. For fifteen years the Soviet Union had taken it for granted that Western European capitalism was its mortal enemy, especially as represented by France and England; hence her defensive alliance with German militarism. Then her relations with Germany cooled; her eternal fear of a capitalist attack had never seemed so justified as at the time of Papen's accession to power. The French Left temporarily removed this threat: Herriot rejected an alliance with the German reactionaries. In August, 1932, Russia concluded a non-aggression pact with Poland, although she regarded the Polish eastern provinces as a region stolen from her. At the end of November, 1932, she signed a similar agreement with France. Then Hitler took power in Germany; and although he sincerely wanted to improve his relations with Russia, his good intentions were doubted. Just as in May, 1933, at the height of the war danger, Nadolny and Papen poured oil onto the fire by their noisy speeches, Hitler was unmasked in the eyes of the Bolsheviks by that cumbersome and despised appendage, Hugenberg. Hugenberg used his last weeks of ministerial power to submit, in his capacity of German delegate to the London Economic Conference, a memorandum in which he demanded no less than the Russian Ukraine for Germany. Hitler hastened to disavow him, and soon after that, Hugenberg was out of office. But the Bolsheviks took Hugenberg's threat almost more seriously than they would have taken a threat from Hitler himself; in their eyes Hugenberg represented the big capitalists whom they believed to rule Germany, and Hitler was only their servant.

Among the Bolshevist leaders the conflict between the principle

of world revolution and the desire for national security still remained undecided. The Executive Committee of the Third International sitting in Moscow seriously proclaimed in its 'Theses' of
December, 1933, that in all the countries with which Russia had
recently concluded treaties and alliances revolution was imminent;
this revolution, as the 'Theses' stated explicitly, would be led and
inspired by Soviet Russia. In the Fascist countries — this was said
in full earnest — the chief enemy was not fascism, but still Social
Democracy. This remarkable document declared that 'the revolutionary crisis and the indignation of large masses against the domination of capital is growing . . . that as a result, the capitalists are
compelled to pass to open terrorist dictatorship and to unrestrained
chauvinism in their foreign policy, which is a direct preparation
for imperialist wars. In fascism, which has grown out of the womb
of bourgeois democracy, the capitalists see a means of saving their
system from collapse. Social Democracy continues to play the
part of the chief social support of the bourgeoisie, even in countries
under open Fascist dictatorship, by fighting against the revolutionary unity of the proletariat and the Soviet Union. . . .' For that
reason, the struggle against Social Democracy remained the chief
task of the Communists even under the rule of fascism: 'How soon
the rule of bankrupt capitalism will be overthrown by the proletariat depends on the success of the Communist parties in undermining the influence of the Social Democracy upon the masses.'
Everywhere the Committee discovered the handwriting on the wall:
'In China — war, intervention, and revolution. In Japan — growth
of the revolutionary forces and mobilization of the military-Fascist
forces preliminary to great class conflicts. In Spain — the struggle
between the revolution and the counter-revolution. In the United
States — a wave of mass strikes and a revolt of farmers against the
bourgeois program for solving the crisis. In present-day Germany
the revolutionary sentiment of the proletariat is assuming less open
forms; there an immense revolutionary energy is accumulating in
the masses, and the new revolutionary upsurge is already beginning. . . .' And so on. The Committee found 'an uncommon sharp-
ening of class relations in Czechoslovakia, Austria, Scandinavia,
Holland, Belgium, Switzerland'; it found 'mass strikes of workers

accompanied by great revolutionary actions' in Poland; it found railroad strikes and barricade battles in Rumania; it found the Bulgarian working class closing its ranks behind the Communist Party; and 'the principal fortress of the world proletariat, the mighty land of the Soviets, the land of the triumphant working class . . . by its immense socialist conquests inspires the toilers of all countries in their revolutionary struggles. . . . The international proletariat is confronted with the great task of transforming the crisis of the capitalist world into the triumph of the proletariat revolution.'

Shortly before this, Russia had concluded a special kind of peace treaty with her smaller neighbors. In February, 1933, Maxim Litvinov, People's Commissar for Foreign Affairs, had proposed that the Disarmament Conference in Geneva define the term 'aggression,' which was so frequently mentioned in diplomatic notes. The Disarmament Conference did not come to a definition; but in July, Russia concluded treaties with ten of her neighbors, including Poland, Czechoslovakia, Rumania, and Turkey, for the sole purpose of establishing what was meant by the term 'aggression.' What was significant in these treaties was that henceforth a state would be guilty of aggression if it maintained on its territory armed bands which might penetrate into a foreign country; and, conversely, it was agreed that the domestic conditions within a neighboring country could never be considered an excuse for an attack. Thus, the existence of the German S.A.-formations and the Polish Legions in Poland might constitute an aggression, but the Communist constitution of Soviet Russia could not serve as a pretext for aggression. But what if one state supported armed bands on another's territory? In many countries the Communist parties or sections of them were just that; but the treaties did not refer to them.

True, the Soviet Union, engaged in a gigantic economic and social reconstruction, certainly wanted peace with her large neighbors — whether she also wanted peace with her small neighbors was doubted, at least by them. While the Japanese conquest of Manchuria created suspicion and hostility at Russia's eastern border, her relations with the other great powers became more conciliatory. On September 2, 1933, she concluded a non-aggression treaty with Fascist Italy; on November 16, she was recognized by the United

States through an exchange of notes. Literally the same men who in their 'Theses' threatened these countries with the destruction of their social institutions, vowed peace and friendship for them in their diplomatic notes.

Sometimes they did this in one and the same document, in one and the same speech. In January, 1934, in his report to the Seventeenth Congress of the Russian Communist Party, Stalin said that world capitalism was in a crisis from which it would never recover. The bourgeoisie saw no other way out but war: 'Conditions are obviously tending toward another war.' The triumph of fascism in Germany, he explained, was only a sign of bourgeois weakness, but 'if the bourgeoisie chooses the path of war, the working classes of the capitalist countries, driven to despair by four years of crisis and unemployment, will choose the path of revolution. The revolutionary crisis is maturing and will go on maturing.'

But then Stalin suddenly changed his tone and now spoke as a bourgeois politician to other bourgeois politicians. There were, he said, 'common-sense countries,' which for one reason or another were not interested in disturbing peace and wished to develop their trade relations with a customer who paid as well as the Soviet Union. Stalin here broached a subject which gradually began to interest the Russian leaders more than world revolution: that of Russian exports, or the sale of Russian goods partly produced at very low cost and partly kept cheap on capitalist markets by artificial means. Of certain goods, like timber products, it was not unjustly said abroad that they were produced by 'slave labor,' cut and transported by labor gangs of political prisoners. Russia's exports had suffered as a result of the collapse of world trade, and between 1930 and 1932 they had dropped in value from $910,000,000 to $570,000,000 (the drop was less considerable in volume). The Russians held the capitalist boycott responsible for this situation, at least in part. National Socialist Germany, too, held the political boycott responsible for her export troubles; if this contention was true at all, German imports were throttled by Russia's government-directed trade more than by anything else. But now Stalin denied that Russia nursed unfriendly feelings toward Germany only because fascism ruled there: 'Certain German politicians say that the

Soviet Union has changed from an opponent into a supporter of the Versailles Treaty, and that this change is due to the establishment of a Fascist régime in Germany. That is not true. Certainly we are far from being enthusiasts of the Fascist régime in Germany. But fascism is not the issue, as is proved by the fact that Italian fascism, for example, has not prevented Italy from establishing the best of relations with this country. Nor is the issue the alleged change in our attitude toward the Versailles Treaty. Certainly it is not for us,' Stalin said with bitterness and scorn, reminding militaristic Germany of her own sins, 'who have suffered the humiliation of the Treaty of Brest-Litovsk, to sing the praises of the Treaty of Versailles. But' — and with the statement that followed Russia broke with her former policy defined as 'with militarism against capitalism, with Germany against Versailles' — 'we do not admit that because of this treaty the world must be precipitated into the abyss of another war!'

Stalin accused Germany of having changed her foreign policy; he declared that a party had come into power, which, like the former German Kaiser, wanted to seize the Ukraine and the Baltic States. True, he left the door open for an understanding by urging Germany to renounce her new anti-Russian policy and to return to the treaties of Rapallo and Berlin. But deafening applause greeted his words: 'Should anyone attempt to attack our country, we shall reply with a crushing blow that will teach him not to stick his snout into our Soviet garden.'

Why had Germany and Poland come to an understanding? What had become of the hearty handclasp between Germany and Russia through which Poland would be reduced to a little sweat produced by the contact of the two great hands? Hitler hastened to answer that he still desired good relations with Russia and that all his treaties were designed to further peace. On January 30, 1934, in his report to the Reichstag at the end of his first year of rule, he said that he wanted to take 'a conciliatory attitude toward all other countries,' and that he was ready to come to an understanding with them 'even in cases where great — yes, unbridgeable — differences exist between their concept of government and ours.' This applied to democratic and anti-democratic states, while with regard to Russia, Hitler even used the word 'friendship': 'Only thus was it understandable and possible for Germany to continue cultivating friendly relations with Russia despite the great difference between their ruling ideologies.' He admitted that the results were meager; that 'Mr. Stalin in his last great speech had expressed fear that forces hostile to the Soviets might be active in Germany' — but he, Hitler, would correct that impression: after all, Russia did not tolerate German National Socialism within her borders — and so Germany tolerated no 'Communist tendencies, let alone propaganda. The more clearly and unequivocally both sides respect this state of affairs, the more naturally can the interests common to both countries be cultivated.' He went so far as to welcome the stabilization of conditions in Eastern Europe 'by a system of alliances' if these alliances were truly intended to strengthen peace.

At any rate, Hitler declared, he himself had brought true peace to a region where for years a war had secretly been smouldering, threatening the peace of all Europe: the Polish-German border. Before he came to power an unsatisfactory state of affairs had prevailed between Germany and Poland, a constant irritation, and even something like hereditary enmity. In fact, Hitler might have added, he himself had fanned this enmity to its most intense heat when in many speeches he loudly demanded the return of the Polish Corridor. With great candor, as though he himself had never said anything about Germany's need for 'living space' in the East, the Führer proceeded to explain that there was no reason for such an hereditary enmity in either nation and that there never would be any reason for it: 'Germans and Poles will have to face the fact of each other's existence and make the best of it. Therefore, it is expedient to accept a circumstance which could not be removed during the past thousand years and which will not be removed after us, and to give it such a form that both nations will derive as much profit from it as possible.' Hitler did not deny 'the differences that doubtless exist' and indicated his regret that Pilsudski had so far avoided an interview with him; yet he was 'happy to find that the leader of the present Polish state, Marshal Pilsudski, had the same broadminded approach that he [Hitler] had himself.' If anything remained to be desired, it was the settlement of commercial and customs questions, of the competition between Polish and German coal and the importation of Polish agricultural products opposed by German farmers. But Hitler did not say a word about the fate of the German minorities in Poland.

However, he did say a great deal about the fate of the people from whom he himself had sprung, the Austrians. 'The assertion that the German Reich intends to take over the Austrian state by force,' he said, 'is absurd and cannot be proved.' The emphasis was on the words 'Reich' and 'state.' Hitler frankly acknowledged that National Socialism involved an international revolution and that Austria was a most logical place to start it. 'Of course, an idea that has taken hold of the entire German nation and stirred it to its depths is not going to halt at the frontier posts of a country that is German by race.' Whether National Socialism was German or not, it reached across borders: 'But even apart from that, this case is not an isolated one if we consider that practically all intellectual and revolutionary movements in Europe have spread beyond the borders of their countries of origin. Thus, the ideas of the French Revolution filled the imagination of people all over the Continent regardless of frontiers. It was, therefore, quite natural for the Austrian Germans to take up the National Socialist idea in complete unity of spirit with the whole German people.' Germany, he went on, would gladly offer the Austrian government an opportunity for a full agreement; but being an Austrian himself he knew the temper of his countrymen, and in his opinion the best thing the Austrian government could do was to take a vote among its German people in order to prove to the whole world how well it was carrying out their wishes. In other words, Dollfuss should call an election and he would get the surprise of his life. 'I believe that I may say this much: no government that is kept in power by force alone can last forever.' In his excitement Hitler went so far as to threaten Dollfuss with murder in no uncertain terms if he did not give in: 'Should the present Austrian government consider it necessary to suppress this movement [National Socialism] by taking extreme measures and applying force, that is, of course, its own business. But then it must assume *personal* responsibility for the consequences of its own policy and take what comes.'

Toward France his tone again was cordial, almost imploring; and since the question of the Saar 'is the only territorial issue between the two countries that is still unsettled,' Germany would be ready to make extraordinary concessions once this stumbling block were removed. In the Locarno Treaty, Germany had not only given up all her claims to Alsace-Lorraine, but had even renounced the right to fortify her own frontiers along the Rhine — and even with these conditions Hitler cheerfully promised to be satisfied; once the Saar was returned, 'the German government is ready and determined to accept the spirit of the Locarno Treaty as well as its terms.' With these words he promised something unbelievable: not to fortify Germany's western frontier.

It is true that when he made this statement he apparently had failed in his attempt to come to an understanding with France by negotiating directly with her; no interview had taken place between the leaders of the two countries — partly because no one could tell who was the real leader of France; the Premiers who were in power for only a few months at a time seldom measured up to such a task and never had enough authority for it. But if France did not come to an agreement with Germany, the other powers did. When it became clear that Hitler had no intention of making an army out of his three million S.A. men, but that he would be satisfied with three hundred thousand, many people thought that a great and unexpected step forward had been taken.

The French government insisted that it could not treat with Germany directly, but only through the League of Nations and demanded that Germany should therefore return to that body. The English and Italian governments then indicated, at the end of January, 1934, that they considered Germany's return to the League desirable. However, this was no longer the main issue. The main thing was that in the meantime England, as well as Italy, had quietly accepted Germany's rearmament. An Italian memorandum approved an army of three hundred thousand men for Germany; one of the reasons given for this was that with the National Socialist revolution Germany had embarked upon such far-reaching changes in her whole social structure that she would not be able to undertake important military projects — apparently Mussolini drew this conclusion from his experience in reorganizing his own country. Even England was willing to concede Hitler his three hundred thousand soldiers — 'two or three hundred thousand soldiers,' said a memorandum of the Foreign Office published at the end of January.

However, the truly important events of the period took place, not between the countries, but within the countries; the struggle was no longer among the nations, but among forces and parties that were present in every nation. The beginning of 1934 witnessed significant uprisings and successes of the 'armed intellectuals' in at least three different places. In Poland, dictatorship suddenly had overrun Parliament on January 26. Eleven days later, democratic France was the scene of a bloody, not quite unsuccessful, assault against Parliament; within another week, Austrian fascism smashed the organizations of the working class.

French democracy was the outcome of a century-old resistance of the people against the privileged classes. Born of class struggles, this democracy always has — or had — a marked class character. However deeply it influenced the history of France, French democracy was not so much a national institution, but rather a powerful party, which always had to defend itself against a hostile opposition. During the first decades of the Third Republic, this hostile opposition was actually in power several times. After the democratic tendency definitely gained the upper hand (about the turn of the century), the anti-democratic forces formed an opposition especially among the intellectuals; after the World War it found its most noisy and colorful expression in the *Action Française,* which was composed mostly of students and young academicians. It was led by two unusual intellectuals, Charles Maurras, a master of prose style, and Léon Daudet, a master of vituperative polemics. This movement was unequivocally anti-parliamentarian and anti-Semitic. The *Croix de Feu,* a movement born after the World War, which was comparable to the German Steel Helmets, gained a larger mass following. The *Croix de Feu* was originally a union of French veterans; after 1930, under the leadership of former Colonel Casimir de la Rocque, it began to intervene in politics. In their struggle against democracy and parliamentarianism, these groups found abundant occasions for mockery and accusations in a country where the term 'incorruptible' has always been regarded as the highest praise for a statesman.

France began to feel the first symptoms of the economic depression which reached her later than the other countries; her social backwardness was indisputable; the fact that she, who had once led Europe's technical progress, was now far behind was clearly realized by discerning minds. The nation also felt that its foreign policy must have been faulty if fourteen years after 'the war to end all wars' the German danger had arisen again. Behind all this was the obscure realization among the people that the existing state was no longer equal to the tasks confronting modern society; that a more decisive, more efficient and more powerful government was required. The example of foreign fascism was contagious; Mussolini enjoyed great popularity in high French society, his *Scritti e Discorsi* were read with almost religious devotion. Many pamphlets and posters of the French Fascists clearly followed the pattern set by the undermining, disparaging, slandering agitation of German National Socialism, particularly in their attacks against the Jews, Negroes, and foreigners.

Public irritation was finally brought to the point of explosion by a shady foreigner, a certain Alexander Stavisky, born in Russian Odessa. Stavisky's connections with French politicians; the public funds which they had put at his disposal and which he had embezzled; his suicide at the last minute before his impending arrest, regarded by many as a murder engineered by the police agents sent to seize him; the violent and never-explained death of the judge who had directed the investigation of the case — all this was the immediate cause of the bloody riots of February 6, which had no visible leader, but were obviously organized by the chiefs of the *Action Française* and the *Croix de Feu*. The avowed object of the attack was Daladier, who again had become Premier a few days before. The rioters massed on the Place de la Concorde and tried to cross a bridge over the Seine in order to storm the Parliament building. Everything depended upon whether a determined leader of the defending troops, the *Garde Mobile,* would dare to give the order to open fire. Such a leader was found in the person of the Minister of the Interior, Eugène Frot, a fairly young man, who obtained Daladier's permission.

The attack was repelled, but the political crisis was not liquidated. A few days later, big demonstrations of the trade-unions and working-class parties, sharpened by a short general strike, tried to quell the Fascist upsurge. The Fascist thrust ended with a half-success: Daladier was forced to resign and was branded as a murderer by the Rightists; Frot, a lawyer by profession, barely ventured to appear in the Palais de Justice; his colleagues publicly burned the gown of the man whose courage had perhaps saved the Republic. Both sides agreed that overnight the country had fallen into a severe crisis and that extraordinary measures were necessary. Former President Gaston Doumergue was made Premier. The General Staff and probably de la Rocque supported him, and his cabinet included prominent statesmen both of the Left and the Right, from Tardieu to Herriot; his Minister of War was Marshal Pétain. It was a cabinet before which Parliament would tremble — at least, such was the idea behind it. Now began the popular period of French fascism — although it never reached the size and influence of German National Socialism. The following of the *Croix de Feu* and the number of their public demonstrations grew rapidly in spite of Léon Daudet's envious jeering ('a herd of lions led by an ass'). The most popular weekly in France, read particularly among the well-to-do classes, incited hatred of the Jews, Freemasons, foreigners, British and Americans, and, of course, Parliament; this was done with more wit, but with almost the same unscrupulousness as by Streicher's *Stürmer* in Germany. The atmosphere prevailing in France during those days recalled that of Munich in 1923: it was a time of feverish preparation for a brutal decision.

In little Austria this period of preparation was over, and the brutal decision fell a few days after the bloody riots in Paris.

On February 12, the police and the *Heimwehr* stormed the headquarters of the Social-Democratic party. In a fierce struggle, the inadequately armed Social-Democratic organizations resisted at various places throughout the country, particularly in the large apartment houses erected in the suburbs of Vienna, which sheltered several thousand people (Goethe Hof, Karl Marx Hof). The attack of the *Heimwehr* failed. The regular army had to come to the rescue and fire upon the apartment houses with cannon. The battle lasted three days; those sections of the workers, who were determined to resist, fought much more vigorously than, for instance, the National Socialists in Munich in 1923. But only a small part of them resisted. In contrast to what happened in Germany in 1920, the historic weapon of the working class, the general strike, this time failed: the wheels did not stand still, the trains ran on schedule, and the electric lights burned as before. A few prominent leaders fled to Czechoslovakia; others, like Seitz, the Mayor of Vienna, remained defiantly in the city; several of the real leaders of the battle were hanged by the government, which had neither human feeling nor respect for their magnificent courage. This blood-bath seemingly broke the political power of the Social Democracy; but the movement was not destroyed, it continued as a brilliantly organized 'underground,' which even managed to hold Communist competition down. It may be doubted whether Dollfuss wanted all of these horrors; but it is a fact that he did not oppose them. Amidst the life-and-death struggle the Austrian government was waging against National Socialism, the destruction and alienation of the strongest anti-Nazi force in the country was a model of political short-sightedness.

Dictatorship continued to make headway in Europe. Its semicircle, extending from Moscow to Rome, was solidly filled during that year; first Germany, then Austria, were added to the ring; in Poland, terrorism, which hitherto had been only an instrument of the Fascist rulers, had been raised to the dignity of a constitution. The Hungarian semi-dictatorship came closer to fascism when Julius Goemboes, an avowed Fascist and anti-Semite, became Prime Minister — this actually took place four months before Hitler's accession to power. The western end of the semicircle, formed by the Spanish dictatorship, had at first been broken off by the resignation of Primo de Rivera in 1929 and the deposition of King Alfonso in 1931; but within a few years Spanish fascism, bloodier than ever, was to return to power. And the *Europa Fascista,* prophesied by Mussolini, had even raised its head in Paris. In England, too, Lord Rothermere supported Sir Oswald Mosley's movement which openly called itself 'Fascist.'

With half of Europe won for fascism, how could international politics remain democratic? The new system of bilateral agreements gradually dissolved the system of collective security which was more symbolized than realized in the League of Nations. Cardinal Hlond, Archbishop of Gniezno, head of the Polish Church and with Pilsudski the most powerful man in this almost completely Catholic country, praised the German-Polish pact in an interview with a French journalist; he expressed his belief in a slow but sure improvement of Polish-German relations and said — exactly as Hitler had before him — that this pact was a 'prelude to a future Franco-German pact,' which would complete the work of pacification in Europe.

In less mild and hopeful words spoke the chief of government of another small nation the existence of which for a century had depended upon the effectiveness of a system of European security, although this system had not been able to spare the country a terrible ordeal during the First World War. On March 6, 1934, Count de Brocqueville made a speech in the Belgian Senate which resounded throughout Europe like a cry of alarm. The Versailles Treaty, he complained, was an illusion which disregarded all historic lessons. The men of Versailles, de Brocqueville said, had believed that it was possible to keep a great nation like Germany in a state of permanent disarmament. But how could anyone imagine — and remarks full of the most elementary wisdom now followed — that the twenty-seven nations, which were allied when the treaty was signed, would preserve their harmony in the future and impose upon Germany what Napoleon I, the autocrat of almost all Europe, had been unable to impose upon Prussia alone? Who had ever seen such treaties survive the circumstances out of which they were born? The Germany of today was no longer that of November 11, 1918; and what had become of the common will of the twenty-seven nations which were supposed to defend the Treaty of 1919? An unchanging law of history decrees that the defeated shall rise again sooner or later. Germany's rearmament, de Brocqueville went on, could no longer be prevented, for the only way to accomplish this would be by immediate war; 'but I refuse to drive my country into such an adventure.' What could and should be prevented was a general race for armaments. It is true that here de Brocqueville found comfort in the thought that neither Germany nor the other powers could 'take upon themselves the incredible burden which an armament race would bring in its train amidst the present crisis.'

Yes, according to the laws of economic reason a world armament race was impossible; and even Germany seemed to admit this. On March 22, 1934, the German government quite candidly published its budget. It appeared that Germany's armaments expenditures were being increased by 352,000,000 marks, or about fifty per cent; and those who still believed in the authority of the Versailles Treaty which forbade these armaments were horrified. In fact, what these figures announced was rearmament in a moderate degree approved long ago by England's and Italy's diplomatic notes; and Germany could still point out that of all the great powers she was still the only one which was spending less on defense than before 1914. About that time the French government asked its Parliament for extraordinary armaments credits to the amount of three billion francs (in addition to the current expenses); the United States and Great Britain decided to bring their navies up to the strength allowed in the Washington Agreement; the British air fleet was increased; the gigantic Russian armaments, never denied by Russia herself, yet not believed in by many at that time, were a miraculous effort of which the efficacy was later confirmed by events. Thus, the armaments race de Brocqueville feared was under way, although still slow and hesitating. The immediate cause of this race was, in at least some measure, the indisputable armaments of the National Socialist government in Germany, which, for its part, complained bitterly that the armaments of the rest of the world forced it to arm against its will. While publishing its own armaments budget with seeming honesty, it suggested that these figures expressed a thrifty effort, consistent with the laws of economic reason; the figures might still increase somewhat when the three-hundred-thousand-man army was ready and began to train; but the whole German armaments experiment seemed to be remaining within tolerable limits.

And this was no small comfort to the leaders of British foreign policy when they tried, through their bilateral conversations, to find out the real situation on the European Continent. Captain Anthony

Eden, in his official capacity of British Minister at the League of Nations, in fact even then a second Foreign Minister slowly built up at the side of Sir John Simon, undertook such a tour of investigation in February, 1934, a strikingly young envoy of the conservative British ruling class. In a marked gesture of courtesy toward National Socialist Germany, the British Minister first visited Hitler in Berlin (February 21), and the courtesy was well received. Once again Hitler was on the whole satisfied with the British proposals; he was satisfied with the three hundred thousand soldiers which were to be allowed him. He insisted on planes, which the British had not foreseen, but he did not want bombers, only fighters for the purpose of repelling attacks; and even this German air force, intended purely for defense, would be only half as strong as the French air force. To be sure, if Germany agreed to such marked military inferiority, it was not for all time to come, but only for five years, and full equality must be achieved within ten years.

It seemed that Hitler's meeting with Eden was just such a success as the Führer desired. Perhaps for the first time he managed to convince a foreign statesman that the much-discussed and feared S.A. were not an army and that he did not want them to be an army. He seems to have promised Eden that he would do away with certain aspects of National Socialist Germany which were considered particularly offensive abroad, such as the terrorist rule of the S.A. At any rate, Eden left with favorable impressions, and these were perhaps strengthened when a few days later Mussolini joyfully told him that if Hitler made such acceptable proposals, the best thing to do was to take him quickly at his word. Three hundred thousand soldiers for Germany seemed to Mussolini a reasonable figure; and if Hitler renounced bombing planes for ten years, the Italian dictator — as he told Eden — hoped that by the end of that period bombing planes would have disappeared from the world completely.

Thus, negotiations and exchanges of notes went on between the powers. That there was still a high council of nations in Geneva was half-forgotten; no one any longer took the Disarmament Conference seriously; collective security was almost a fantasy, a chimera, something like perpetual peace or the elimination of poverty.

Eventually, when the powers did take a common step, its feeble-ness revealed their profound disunion. This came about when Dollfuss, shortly after the blood-bath of the Vienna workers, again appealed for help against the National Socialists and this time (February 17) succeeded in getting out of England, France, and Italy a common declaration stressing 'the necessity of maintaining the independence and territorial integrity of Austria in accordance with the existing treaties.' This was a phrase without punch, with-out teeth, and above all without meaning, because the National Socialist method of conquest from within seemingly did not violate independence and territorial integrity.

The truth is that there was no agreement among these powers concerning the protection of Austria, and this fact became clear within a month. In March, three Fascist statesmen, Mussolini, Dollfuss, and Goemboes, met in Rome and signed a common declaration of war against the French system of alliances in central and eastern Europe. The so-called Rome Protocols of March 18, 1934, provided for political and economic collaboration among Italy, Austria, and Hungary. By implication they were directed against Czechoslovakia and Yugoslavia, the states of the Little Entente; and if any stern words against Germany could be found in them, they were masked behind cryptic phrases like 'respect for the in-dependence and rights of all countries.'

Actually Fascist Italy had made her choice: she neither could nor would stand in the way of a Fascist Europe, embodied in Fascist Germany. Confusing temporary circumstances might for a short time veil this decision; nevertheless, it was founded on the facts and vital forces of the times. When Mussolini opened his heart to his people, he frankly expressed this view. On the night following the signing of the Rome Protocols, he made a speech before three thousand Fascists in the Rome Opera House. He gave only pass-ing mention to the Protocols; but he loudly defended Germany, the system of bilateral pacts and German rearmament; and with great sincerity he explained why he did this and had to do it. That the Disarmament Conference had failed, he said, was now completely clear; it was the only completely clear fact. It was simply impossible to forbid defensive armament to a nation like the Germans. 'Perhaps,' said Mussolini with a smile, and his three thousand listeners laughed happily and approvingly, 'this has already been outstripped by the facts.' Italy, too, must be strong militarily, for Italy had a great mission dictated by her geography and her history. 'Until the year 2000, Italy's historic objectives are Asia and Africa' — and this was followed by the significant words: 'In the North there is little or nothing to be gained.' Hitler had said the same things years before. But in the South, Mussolini continued, 'the political and economic expansion of Italy must not be stopped by the satiated and the satisfied.'

Among these satiated and satisfied powers at whose expense Italy wanted to expand in Asia and Africa, the first place was occupied by France. And Germany's 'great hour' of revenge against the French hereditary enemy, which Hitler in his earlier prophecies had expected from an alliance with Mussolini, now seemed to strike — at the very moment when Hitler was seemingly changing his course and seeking a reconciliation with France. The British government urged France to reconcile herself with him. Even those British friends of France, who advised her not to disarm but to arm, nevertheless intimated that in the last analysis France must rely only upon herself, not upon English protection. It was Winston Churchill who again expressed this view on March 8, 1934. To be sure, England was then, in Churchill's opinion, threatened only by Germany's rearmament; but no one 'proposes a preventive war to stop her from breaking the Treaty of Versailles.' It was clear that 'this very gifted people are capable of developing with great rapidity the most powerful air force for all purposes, offensive and defensive, in a very short period.' The day when Germany would be in a position to threaten the heart of the British Empire by air was perhaps only eighteen months, perhaps even only one year, distant. And this meant, said Churchill, that England would lose her freedom of action and be dependent upon the help and good will of her friends on the Continent. That meant France — and France's policies. But this was the very thing England should prevent at any cost, above all by creating her own strong air force. 'The next great object we must have in view is to secure our freedom of choice to remain outside a European war if one should break out. . . . We must have the effective right and power to choose our own path in accordance with the wishes and resolves of the nation in any emergency that may arise on the Continent of Europe. For this purpose we must be safe from undue foreign pressure. These are not the times when we can afford to confide the safety of our country to the passions or the panic of any foreign nation, which might be facing some grim and desperate crisis. We must be independent and free; we must preserve our full latitude and choice. We have never lived at any-body's mercy. . . . We have never entrusted the home defense of this country to any foreign power, never asked for any help from any-one. . . . We ought not to be dependent upon the French air force for the safety of our island home. The fact that we cannot defend ourselves and that our friends across the Channel have additional power makes an implication and a whole series of implications which very nearly approach the establishment of the condition of British dependence on overseas protection.'

With these words Churchill, who was certainly a friend of France, said almost the same thing that a less good friend, Lord Lothian, former secretary to Lloyd George and co-author of the Treaty of Versailles, expressed in a letter to the *Times* written at the beginning of May: 'The proposal that we should try to stabilize Europe by joining a defensive coalition against Germany, as in 1904, involves the liability to war whenever a European power is forced or blunders into war.' Instead, Lord Lothian warned Europe — and in fact he meant France: 'Europe itself should gradually find its own way to an internal equilibrium and a limitation of arma-ments by political appeasement. . . .' One of the most portentous slogans of the period was coined here. But England, Lothian in-sisted, must not interfere in this appeasement: 'We shall not assist that process [of appeasement] by taking sides. Indeed, by doing so we should be likely to delay it. . . .'

Did this presage a triumph for Hitler? Were England and France drifting apart while Germany and Italy slowly came close together? Would France, which had partially lost her Polish ally, one day be abandoned by England as well?

The Doumergue cabinet had given up Daladier's plan to attempt a separate understanding with Germany. Germany's rearmament had progressed too rapidly; and who could seriously hope to stop this process by conversations? A conversation, let alone an agreement, would have meant that France was openly abandoning the treaties, whatever these were worth. But this was the very thing which England now urged her 'friend across the Channel' to do.

The direction of France's foreign policy was in the hands of Louis Barthou, who may be considered the last classic statesman of the Third Republic. A white-bearded old man of seventy-two, an adroit opportunist in the domestic field, not exactly a creative mind in the field of foreign politics, he was a remarkable mixture of talent and energy and was inspired by a great guiding principle. This principle was his lifelong fear of the German danger. He also had a strong will to break this danger. He spoke German and was a highly educated man who had achieved the rare distinction of being elected to France's literary society, the French Academy of the 'Forty Immortals.' He had written a book about Richard Wagner, and liked to quote Heine's gloomy prophecy that Germany would become a great danger to the world once Thor awoke from his thousand-year-long sleep and began to break the churches and the Cross. Barthou thought that this historic day had come; he said that only two or three years were left in which the danger could be eliminated.

England, however, demanded that France negotiate with Germany; this meant that Hitler was to have a three-hundred-thousand-man army if he renounced bombing planes and accepted a transitional period of five to ten years. It might be possible to accept this plan; but who would vouch that Hitler would abide by it? Barthou asked England for *garanties d'exécution* (guaranties that the plan would be carried out)— which was only a different form of France's eternal demand that England support her if Germany violated the treaties. Embarrassed, England countered by asking what such *garanties d'exécution* meant concretely; and it was again France's turn to reply.

What England's idea amounted to was: We will grant Hitler his army, and the four of us — England, France, Germany, and Italy — will sit down around a table. We will determine the future armaments of Europe; and neither Poland nor Czechoslovakia,

France's old allies, nor Russia, her possible future ally, will be invited.

Russia had openly and deliberately come forward as a possible ally of France since her friendship with Germany had grown cold. By way of the League of Nations, which Soviet diplomacy had formerly regarded as an instrument of the bourgeoisie in its class struggle against the Socialist fatherland, Russia indicated her desire to form part of France's system of collective security. The decision in the struggle for and against the continuation of this security policy again depended upon the domestic political constellation in France.

Barthou, a man of the Right, wanted to accept England's proposal and negotiate with Hitler if England promised adequate *garanties d'exécution;* this, at the risk not only of alienating Russia, but also of weakening the French ties with Poland. But Edouard Herriot, who for years had favored a Russian alliance and wished to incorporate it into the system of general security, once more opposed negotiations with Germany. He was still the leader of France's strongest party, a kind of incarnation of French democracy; and Premier Doumergue yielded to his demands. Thereupon Barthou threatened to resign; Doumergue replied with the same threat, and he proved the stronger. The British plan for negotiations with Germany was rejected.

On April 17, Barthou received R. H. Campbell, the British chargé d'affaires, at the Quai d'Orsay and handed him a note complaining of Germany's rearming. The German military budget was cited; Germany, the note said, was openly showing that she now no longer intended to abide by the Treaty of Versailles. Henceforward France must think of her own security on which depended that of other nations, too; further negotiations were futile until Germany returned to the League of Nations. Therefore, 'France regrets that the action of a third party [Germany] should abruptly have rendered vain the negotiations undertaken by the two countries [France and Great Britain] with equal good faith and good will.'

This note was of historic importance: it put an end to the dream of a Franco-German agreement. No doubt German armaments had made such an agreement a very difficult task; but France under-

took to say in hard and unfriendly words that it was impossible —
while Hitler still was speaking of peace and reconciliation. The
decision to negotiate or not to negotiate with Germany involved for
France the choice between England and Russia as her ally. Now
she had chosen, and rejected England; yet in the end she was unable to retain her allies in the East.

A year and a half before, Hitler had demanded that if the disarmament negotiations collapsed again, France should be considered guilty of their failure in the eyes of the world — that is to say,
of England and America. This was the case now. Germany was rearming, but France was considered responsible for it. The estrangement between France and England had begun before that seventeenth day of April, 1934; but now it was to be final for years to
come.

At the beginning of June, 1934, Doctor Cosmo Lang, Archbishop
of Canterbury, in an address to the Convocation of Canterbury,
made a number of political remarks. Among other things he said
that 'he could not but deplore the attitude taken by M. Barthou,'
and rebuked France for having 'almost contemptuously rejected the
most reasonable proposals put forward by Germany.' As for Germany herself, Doctor Lang, while expressing his concern over the
growth of 'paganism' under the influence of the National Socialist
Movement, said that nevertheless 'he had the very greatest sympathy
with the immense, undoubted, and, on the whole, beneficent awakening which had come to Germany and German life in every
aspect, in the remarkable revolution associated with the name of
Herr Hitler.'

About the same time Schacht began to set up so-called 'control
posts' for raw materials throughout Germany. Questionnaires were
sent out to businessmen, who were invited to state before the middle
of May, 1934, the amount of aluminum, lead, chromium, cop-
per, magnesium, manganese, quicksilver, wolfram, zinc, and tin
they had in stock. Also the stocks of wool, cotton, skins, and hides
were to be listed. Germany began to take a census of her raw materials, to test her economic strength, and everyone knew that henceforward aluminum, quicksilver, cotton, and skins were no longer
merchandise, but weapons. This was the first step toward rearmament 'beyond the limits of economic reason.'

On May 29, at one of those belated and hopeless meetings of the Disarmament Conference — it was the 'General Commission,' to be exact — Norman Davis, in the name of the United States government, declared that his country was prepared to co-operate in efforts to secure a general disarmament — but: 'The United States will not, however, take part in European political negotiations and settlements, and will not make any attempt whatever to use its armed forces for the settlement of any dispute anywhere. . . . The policy of the United States is to keep out of war. . . .'

Chapter XXVIII

THE BLOOD PURGE

THE DREAM OF WORLD DOMINATION IS IN THE LAST analysis a dream of the subjects, not of the masters. Innumerable people think this world would be perfect if it were wisely governed by an all-powerful central brain; but who wants to be this central brain? At most, men who are aware that for them this can be no more than an irresponsible dream; in practice, the slightest contact with real power usually destroys the dream, quickly and thoroughly. Few continue the climb to the colder regions where there is no longer any tangible enjoyment, but where only the pride of the heights can recompense them for the icy burden of responsibility and the constant fear of downfall. Moreover, the real summits of world power are but thinly distributed in the landscape of world history, and demonstrably, none of the great world rulers has been happy.

All the armed intellectuals had heard that happiness was ignoble; perhaps from Nietzsche, for whom only the 'dangerous life' was worthy; from Goethe, who wrote that man cannot 'rule and enjoy at once,' for 'enjoyment makes common'; or more recently from Oswald Spengler with his 'joy in the heaviness of human destiny.' But this book-learning stood up poorly under the test of reality; as soon as the warriors became ministers, they wanted to live like bank directors and enjoyed themselves with a splendor and publicity unknown to any of the leaders of the Weimar Republic in their modest cottages. Hitler, who indulged himself in everything, was fortunate enough not to be plagued with conspicuous desires. His inclination to conceal his private life helped him to enhance

the legend of his monastic frugality, giving it a quality of the pitiful, saintly, and awe-inspiring.

Restless, insatiable, and longing for greatness as a public figure,
in private life he found his well-being in a mild uneventfulness,
and the inevitable apparatus of luxury that grew up about him was
calculated only to protect him from noise, disturbance, and compulsion. Even his crowded banquets were a kind of menagerie
which he attended as a spectator. Rudolf Hess, Heinrich Himmler,
Wilhelm Frick, resembled him in this; they were silent, fishlike
natures, with a taste for quiet and littleness. But the party leadership was also full of beasts of prey, the type which rends more than
it can consume, and which likes to take its pleasures beneath the
public eye. Göring and Goebbels were typical; Hitler was obliged
to attack them publicly, but could not improve them. They were
at all times ready, was their reply, to die for their Leader; but you
could not expect a man, who gave his life without stint, to stint himself in the pleasures of life. It seemed to afford these men a per-
verse pleasure to insult public opinion by a shameless exhibition of
their magnificence. There was a kind of sporting rivalry between
them in their experiments on the public patience: how long would
people continue to find mockery wonderful?

The band of armed intellectuals had at last come into money.
They flung themselves into lives of wild, indecent sybaritism, forever pursued by the secret anxiety that they might be dead tomorrow or sooner. Hitler tried to teach them that it was better to
'find bliss in commanding' rather than in stolen motor-cars, expropriated castles and villas, wild eating and drinking bouts, and
obscene distractions which sometimes occurred before the eyes of an
indignant public.

This conflict between the Leader and his lieutenants involved
more than dignified behavior. It was an attempt to remold the
character of the leaders, to cleanse them of the incalculability and
wildness of the years of struggle and give them the hardness and
sobriety which are needed in a ruling class. Ruthlessness in battle
and pleasure had given the armed bohemians force for the attack;
but to preserve and to mold, they would need the self-discipline
which makes the bohemian into an armed intellectual. The 'chosen

order of leadership' — and that is what Hitler wanted his party to be — must learn to discipline itself if it wanted to discipline the people; for 'what the people demand of the state, this order of sworn leadership will demand of itself and realize through absolute subordination to its own laws.' The National Socialist Party, said Hitler, was far more than a political movement, and anyone who believed that its aim was mere domination of the state 'has neither learned anything from the past nor understood the task of the future.'

The task of the future consisted in creating, by artificial cultivation, the nation of which Houston Stewart Chamberlain had dreamed, and 'scientifically drilling' it. The higher race, indeterminate in origin but in its essence clearly definable as 'Aryan,' should create and lead this nation; for this very reason, Heaven protect the German nation from the curse of so-called racial purity! Chamberlain had called racial purity a scientific monstrosity; Hitler thought that racial purity — though luckily it was an impossibility — would be a political misfortune. He first expressed these thoughts in all their breadth at a Party Day in Nuremberg in September, 1933. 'A glance at nature,' he declared, 'shows us that the creatures of a pure race are more or less equal, not only physically, but also in their nature and abilities. This equality is the greatest obstacle in the formation of higher communities ... a multiplicity of individuals must sacrifice their individual freedom and subordinate themselves to the will of an individual. But much as reason would counsel this, it would in reality be very difficult to explain to men who were entirely equal why, nevertheless, one man must ultimately raise his will above that of the others.' Strange! It would be hard to make noble equals understand why they must obey? Yes, up till then he had publicly preached obedience as a virtue; but in the circle of his intimates he had said the opposite; and now, 'after victory,' he admitted that the movement possessed a secret doctrine of which he had never spoken in public. Now he would do so for the first time; and so the masses of the movement learned that the opposite was true of what they had been hearing from their Leader up till then. It is the better man who commands, the inferior who obeys. 'The two concepts of commanding and obeying,' Hitler declared in 1933, 'assume an entirely different and compelling meaning as soon as men of different value clash or mingle and a common purposive bond is created by the stronger part. The higher race — higher primarily in the sense of organizing ability — subjects a lower race, and thus enters into a relation which henceforth comprehends unequal races. From this results the subordination of a multiplicity of men to the will of a few, deriving simply from the right of the stronger, a right which is seen in nature and which can be regarded as the sole conceivable, because solely rational, right.'

This is the rational, expedient, organized nation: the domination of a minority of good race over a majority of inferior race. According to this doctrine, the Germans are not a master race, but a people to be led by a master race; as foreseen by Houston Stewart Chamberlain: 'Only the few,' said the creator of the National Socialist racial theory, 'can conceive great politics and execute them with iron logic; it is absurd to think that a whole nation can carry on "politics" and particularly that politics of which only Germany is capable and which alone befits it. Today there is much talk of "people" and in the last analysis it is always by certain circles who want to seize power and use it in their selfish interests. Germany must not become an industrial, financial, or agrarian state; she must be ruled by circles standing outside all parties and special interests; only under this condition is a truly scientific policy possible.'

The independence of the new leader class from special economic interests is what Hitler calls 'socialism'; and it is this economic independence which safeguards for the 'state-forming master race' its domination over the 'born slaves.' In a speech which Hitler delivered in February, 1934, at Berlin he made no bones about his social concepts:

The primitive man will have no understanding for the needs of the spirit, but he begrudges them to no one. All the millions of small and hard-working citizens of a nation do not demand that the wise man should adapt himself to their knowledge or that the man blessed with artistic gifts should prefer their culture. They always grant him what is his, but they also demand, and rightly so, that in return for their co-operation in the community they be given that which is compatible with their nature. And therefore a truly superior leadership of a political nation must be filled with a high social understanding . . . [Social understanding means to give the lowly his pleasures, but not to desire them for oneself;] the political leadership of a nation must seek their essential distinction from the rest of the people, not in any low pleasures, but in a harder self-discipline. They must understand that only what removes them from the primitive man, raises them above him. And they must know that only those whom a man rightly feels to be above him will in the long run be recognized as above him. And those who are slaves of the most primitive physical needs can, in the long run, be no masters over the born slaves.

On August 6, 1933, Hitler gathered together the civilian functionaries of the party at his residence in Obersalzberg. He led his guests in goosestep along a narrow mountain path to one of the surrounding summits and there addressed them in a short but violent speech of which the gist was more or less as follows: Below them they saw Germany, and Germany was now theirs; but they must not imagine that they could do with it what they pleased; giving orders implied a terrible responsibility. Once more he tried to prove that no second revolution was necessary.

Röhm was not among the guests. On that same August 6 — it was a Sunday — he had ordered 82,000 S.A. men to march before him on Tempelhof Field near Berlin and made an inflammatory speech against the 'reactionaries' who had suggested that the time had come for the S.A. to disappear. He could have quoted many of these reactionaries by name, and the best known of all would have been Göring. Not that Göring wanted to dissolve the Storm Troops. S.A. leaders, however, had become police chiefs and as such they were under the orders of the Prime Minister of Prussia. But Röhm insisted that they were and must remain S.A. leaders first and foremost, and that his orders had precedence over any others. For a man like Edmund Heines, an *Obergruppenführer* of the S.A. who had become chief of police of the city of Breslau in Silesia and established a reign of terror there, Göring's orders meant nothing at all. The war between these National Socialist government leaders had now almost come out into the open. As early as

May, 1933, Göring had flatly forbidden his police officials to belong
to the S.A. or the S.S. (or even the Steel Helmets); in the beginning of August he took an unusual step and sent the whole S.A.
and S.S. auxiliary police home. This was the treatment accorded
the 'old fighters' who had conquered power for Hitler and Göring.
In helpless rage Röhm exclaimed on Tempelhof Field: 'Those who
think that the task of the S.A. has been accomplished will have
to accept the fact that we are here and intend to stay here.' They
were here 'to suppress the defeated enemy and, if need be, exterminate him.' And he would not let anyone gainsay him in this
matter.

This — among other things — was a conflict between the state
and the party over the right to practice terrorism. The Third Reich
could not endure without using force against a part of its citizens,
without at least frightening the others and threatening all of them.
This state was always hovering on a wave of inflamed emotion,
whether of enthusiasm or of fear. The S.A. considered terrorism
its monopoly; but on May 3, Göring had created a government
agency for the purpose of exerting terrorism, and given it the name
of Secret State Police (Geheime Staats-Polizei, abbreviated Gestapo).
This police was explicitly charged with those tasks which only a
few months before had been considered unlawful arbitrary acts
strictly forbidden by the constitution, and which, for that reason,
seemed reserved to the S.A. Henceforward the Gestapo, without
any individual orders from above, had the right to exercise the exceptional powers against people's lives, freedom, and property which
the Third Reich had granted itself on the night of the Reichstag
fire. Moreover, it was not a National Socialist to whom Göring had
given these extraordinary powers, at least not an 'old fighter' known
to the party — it was the same Councillor Werner Diels who had
once betrayed his State Secretary Abegg to von Papen. At first the
Gestapo had authority only in Prussia. It must be said that throughout Germany there had always been a 'political police' — an institution as old as history itself; in the French Republic it was more
powerful than Parliament; in Tsarist Russia it had forged *The
Protocols of the Wise Men of Zion,* in Bolshevist Russia it was one
of the pillars of the state. In the Weimar Republic, it had not been

quite as powerful. Had not a saboteur like Frick been for years
the head of the political police in Bavaria? Had not Hess, with
the support of this Bavarian police, been able to spy upon his own
party? That is why in Bavaria the party and the state merged more
rapidly and more intimately than in Göring's domain. One of
Röhm's subordinates assumed the direction of the entire Bavarian
police apparatus — this was Heinrich Himmler, who in his capacity
of Reichsführer of the S.S. was subject to the orders of the chief of
staff of the S.A.

Here was an extraordinary confusion. The National Socialists had
'conquered power,' but the struggle between the state and the party
continued. Hitler's way of describing this was that 'things were
left to grow organically'; the stronger, he implied, would win, and
this was how it should be. Nevertheless, some thought, the Führer
had clearly said that the party commanded the state! No, Goebbels
contradicted them publicly; the Führer had not said 'the party' but
'we'; and 'we' were something different — only the party comrades
whom the Führer had appointed to commanding posts. But how
many were they? And who were they? Almost all of them were
Hitler's tools or the tools of his tools; but people like Röhm, Feder,
Rosenberg, and Streicher held no important government posts.

Among the most bitterly disappointed of the National Socialists
was Hitler's personal favorite, the lawyer, Hans Frank, who had
hoped to become Minister of Justice over the whole Reich. There
was a stain on the escutcheon of this Frank, whose unsatisfied ambition was written in his face all his life. His father, who had also
been a lawyer, had been sentenced to prison for embezzlement several years before; he had been disbarred, but still practiced law,
taking care of his son's juridical business while pretending to be
his bookkeeper. No sooner had Hitler come to power than Frank
Senior was readmitted to the Munich bar with full honors. There
were National Socialist dignitaries with worse blots on their names,
but they did not demand to be made Ministers of Justice, of all
things. It is true that in Bavaria, where the party's Old Guard
flaunted themselves more impudently than in the capital of the
Reich, Frank and his friends disregarded all delicate scruples, and
the young man became Minister of Justice of that small country.

Even spatially this was limited authority, and Hitler's personal friend was forced to look on bitterly while in great Prussia a commonplace official without any academic background, one Hans Kerrl, was put at the head of the Ministry of Justice because he was Göring's bosom friend; while a lawyer from Kassel, a certain Roland Freisler, actually managed the Ministry's affairs as Kerrl's State Secretary; while later Freisler succeeded Kerrl, when Kerrl had proved too obvious a failure. But he, Frank, could not achieve the goal which for the leader of the National Socialist jurists was the highest, the only one worth desiring: the Reich Ministry of Justice, the office where the laws were really made.

Through their own experience these men slowly learned that the state and power were not necessarily one and the same thing. They had been brought up on the idea that all political executive power was concentrated in the state. Since the creation of the Spanish monarchy in the sixteenth century, this view had become dominant in continental Europe. Since Napoleon I, it had no longer been disputed. When financiers and industrialists exercised their power, they did it by influencing the government authorities; only the Church had its own sphere of influence in society. This state monopoly of political power was not shaken until after the First World War, and then in the very countries where one would have least expected it: the so-called dictatorships. In these countries the party — or, more accurately, the numerous organizations between the party and the state — competed with or surpassed the power of the government administration; and in a thousand concrete cases it was impossible to predict which of the two would be stronger and emerge victorious. It was an excess of power that burst all controls and for a limited time spilled over into a chaos of crosscurrents.

Thus, for instance, Frank, who had not become Minister of Justice, instead was appointed 'Reich Commissioner for the Co-ordination of Justice in the German States and for the Renovation of the Administration of Law.' This opaque title meant that he was to enlist all the officials entrusted with the administration of justice, including the judges, into the National Socialist organizations; for this purpose he rebaptized the 'League of National Socialist

Jurists,' which he had founded and of which he had been the head for several years, as the 'German Juridical Front.' Respectable old legal societies, such as the Prussian Judges' Union and the German Lawyers' Union, had to join this 'Juridical Front' in a body. It can be said for the German judges that, at least for a time, they tried to oppose the rape of the law by the National Socialists; the largest of their organizations, the 'German Judges' Union,' declared on March 19 that the German judge 'has always ordained justice in accordance with the law and his conscience. This must continue to be so!' Later these same judges declared that their mission was 'to protect the weak.' This was not at all the National Socialist idea, and Frank replied contemptuously: yes, previous justice did 'protect the weak and created a morality for slaves.' Now equal rights no longer existed for all, but only for those who, in Hitler's words, 'did not refuse their support to the government.' According to Kerrl the idea that 'objectivity must be the idol of jurisprudence' was a superstition; no, justice must not 'practice dead objectivity worship'; and Frank said: 'Law should not protect the weakling, but make the strong even stronger.'

The German judges' backbone was broken when the government broke down the security of their existence. As in England, the judges in Germany had held tenure for life and could not be removed from office. This privilege, designed to insure the independence of the courts, was eliminated by the National Socialists. For many months the German judges tried to preserve the principle of equality at least in the wording of the laws, and the old officials of the Reich Ministry of Justice insisted that murder must remain murder, and homicide, homicide, no matter who was the criminal and who the victim. The S.A. leaders were particularly bitter about this. As it was, the police and public prosecutors often did not dare to bring National Socialist murderers to justice; but the S.A. men demanded that their impunity be confirmed by law. For this reason, as early as March 21, the government of the Reich decreed an 'amnesty' covering crimes under the previous régime 'which were committed out of the best will for the good of the Reich.' At once the five murderers of Potempa were released from prison.

The National Socialist financial backers now also came forward
with their claims; the rich people who had supported the party during hard times and had helped the party leaders in many a financial
strait, often enough by methods which involved cheating the state
of taxes. Several big firms were threatened with proceedings for tax
frauds; but now it turned out that the little favors done for Göring
had been a good investment. The businessmen came to him complaining: of course, they had defrauded the state, but only in order
to save their enterprises and give their workers a livelihood. Göring
listened to them without wincing and wrote to Kerrl, his Minister
of Justice, that in former times in business actions were committed
'which, although they violated penal law, were not inspired by
selfish motives. The Bolshevistic taxes of the democratic state often
compelled people, in the interest of preserving their enterprises, to
enter upon paths which were not permissible from a legal point of
view, but which are comprehensible in the light of the conditions
prevailing at that time, especially as the rigorous economic conceptions of National Socialism had not yet become the common possession of all circles of our nation. The indiscriminate prosecution
of such offenses might often affect persons who, imbued with the
spirit of the National Socialist revolution, are now willing to collaborate in the development of our economy.'

In thus breaking the law and saving millions for the big businessmen at the expense of the state, Göring again collected his share of
the booty in the form of tens and hundreds of thousands of marks.
From a large department store with a Jewish name he bought old
furniture and precious rugs without ever paying for them; a Jewish
super-market enjoyed the dubious privilege of delivering wines and
delicacies to him gratis for years. In 1935, when he married, he said
in an affable way to one of the best-known German industrialists
that the Prussian state manufacture of porcelain had a valuable
table service worth sixty thousand marks for sale, and that it would
really be a nice gesture if this industrialist presented it to him as a
wedding gift. The man thus called upon to make a princely gift
was not particularly surprised; two years earlier, during a conversation about the new Minister, Göring, he had heard a business
acquaintance whisper rapturously, 'He accepts gifts!' The sixty
thousand marks' worth of porcelain was bought and given.

As for Hitler, he bought his house and estate at Berchtesgaden with his own funds, so to speak, acquired from the sale of *Mein Kampf* — even though the largest part of his income as an author originated in the fact that the German people had to buy *Mein Kampf* whether they liked it or not. But Göring, who wished to have his own estate in close proximity to his Führer, got the cabinet of the Bavarian state to give him a piece of land ten thousand meters square, about a hundred yards above Hitler's residence; as a matter of principle, he did not spend any money for this piece of German soil. In Prussia, which he ruled personally, he appropriated for his own use the state hunting grounds of Schorfheide near Berlin; and where a modest hunting lodge of the German Kaiser had formerly stood, he erected a sumptuous villa. He imported the body of his dead wife from Sweden and named the whole estate in her honor, 'Karinhall.' However, he was considerate enough not to declare all this magnificence his formal property. Year after year, the Prussian budget contained an item showing that the state hunting grounds of Schorfheide, the private residence and hunting domain of Prime Minister Göring, were maintained at a cost of a million marks out of the taxpayers' pockets.

The corruption of the Third Reich is connected with the worship of 'great men,' which is a sort of religious principle of the new state. According to this principle, the people owe it to its great men to give them rich gifts. German industry had presented Hindenburg, or, more accurately, his son, with the estate of Neudeck and helped him to pocket the inheritance tax. Later, it had given him an additional gift of almost half a million marks in order that he might lack nothing on the estate. But Göring gave the old gentleman a much more magnificent gift by presenting him — or again, more accurately, his son — with the government-owned neighboring estate of Langenau along with the state forest of Reussenwald. Fittingly enough, this was done on August 27, the anniversary of the Battle of Tannenberg (1914), which had actually been won by Generals Hoffmann, von François, and Ludendorff; the gift was made 'in fulfillment of the duty of national gratitude.' Four days later, the German people learned that Hindenburg, 'in recognition of his [Captain Göring's] distinguished services in war and

peace, had granted him the status of infantry general with the right
to wear the army uniform.'

Thus they handed each other public property or plundered great
private properties. This armed Bohemia managed to make itself
both agreeable and frightful to organized wealth and justified
Machiavelli's saying that soldiers are stronger than money, for
soldiers can always find money, but money does not always find
soldiers. The mass of rank-and-file National Socialists, however,
who had no share in this cool plunder, boasted of their revolutionary purity and called Göring and his clique 'reactionaries,' more
out of envy than political conviction. The kernel of the 'old fighters' among the three million S.A. men still fared as they had in 1923,
when Wilhelm Brückner described their desperate gamble: they had
staked their poverty and their lives on the great political undertaking in order to find jobs as paid soldiers or officers in the future
German army; and they had been waiting too long according to
their lights. When Hitler wrangled with England and France over
the size of the future army, he was, in the eyes of the 'old fighters,'
fighting for their most important personal interests. For the time
being, despite all the Führer's warning speeches, they still stuck to
the belief that within a short time they would be that army — from
the plain S.A. man up to the *Obergruppenführer* who had the rank
of a commanding general and who, according to an order issued
by Blomberg, was tactfully to be saluted like a general by the
Reichswehr soldiers.

On June 2, when Hitler gathered the S.A. leaders in Reichenhall
and once more forbade them in sharp terms to continue the revolution, he also hammered into them the idea that 'only the army
of the Reich is the weapon-bearer of the nation.' Several of the
brown chieftains comforted themselves with the thought that their
Führer spoke thus only because he was afraid of Hindenburg and
Blomberg; but Röhm certainly knew that Hitler had never spoken
or thought otherwise. His promise that the S.A. would 'form a
Guard and be the unshakable bearers of our ideological values'
meant little; the term 'ideological values' had to be translated for
these veteran mercenaries before they could understand it. With
their 'ideological values,' Hitler said, they would 'penetrate the en-

tire nation,' and as their reward 'the German revolution would mold the face of the future for centuries.' These were big words; but the S.A. leaders wanted big remunerations. In the beginning of October, Röhm had complained to a Dutch newspaperman that nearly two million S.A. men were forced 'to continue in their professions'; they were barely reimbursed for the expenses of their trip to the Party Day in Nuremberg. In his public speeches Hitler repeatedly explained that the S.A. should not demand anything at all; the great privilege of these embittered men was, on the contrary, to be a model of self-sacrifice and renunciation, for 'the people has a right to expect that its leaders will be just as heroic as they demand that the people be.' He knew that he was addressing men who had rarely gone far in their civilian careers; men 'who in their social and economic origin mostly occupied a subordinate, and frequently low, rank.' In compensation he tried to convince them that 'at some future day they would represent the leadership of the nation.'

But this was precisely their trouble — they represented something which they were not; what they had perhaps been for a short time, but what they had now ceased to be. They were completely unfit to lead the nation; and Hitler, who at the bottom of his heart was well aware of this unfitness, only hesitatingly found euphemisms like 'ideological values' and 'future leadership of the nation' to tell them so.

These veterans of the civil war, these armed men who for ten years had been and still were bohemians, were not even any longer the seasoned and useful soldiers they believed themselves to be. The older men among their leaders had left the army with the ranks of lieutenant, captain, or sometimes even major; several of them had for a time served in the police force; one or another might have calculated that with luck he would have been a colonel or perhaps major-general if he had been able to remain in the service. In reality these people frequently could not be used even as the lieutenants and captains they had been before. In their demonstration marches and meeting brawls, these political soldiers had lost contact with the genuine modern soldiers who were developing new military ideas. For the most part they were simply unfit for the posts to which they aspired.

More generally they were unfit to occupy any responsible position — and their supreme leader knew this. When Hitler was still engaged in his struggle against the state, he had appealed to the 'Uprooted and Disinherited' and praised them as his best troops. Later, in his speech of justification for the events that were to follow, he contemptuously told these S.A. leaders, now for the most part dead, that they were people 'who in 1918 had been shaken in their former relation to the state and uprooted, and had thereby lost all inner contact with a human social order.' They were people, 'who without realizing it had found their profession of faith in nihilism. Incapable of any real co-operation, ready to oppose any order, filled with hatred for any kind of authority, their excited and restless minds were appeased only by constant intellectual and conspiratory preoccupation with the destruction of existing institutions.' These were Hitler's own words about his faithful, to whom he had to be unfaithful, because power cannot be established without a breach of faith — a breach of faith both to people and to ideas.

For a few months these men had been admired by the nation as the sinister embodiments of a mysterious but indisputably impressive political force; as a Viking army which had suddenly emerged into the present from legendary times; as the host of freedom seeking the light, which they themselves thought they were. But gradually the character of these heroes became better known, and what scoundrels many of them were was demonstrated in a thousand individual cases to be. Frightening reports also trickled through from the concentration camps, and the public began obscurely to realize that the Führer's picked troops had organized artificial hells in Dachau near Munich, in Oranienburg near Berlin, in Duerrgoy near Breslau, and in Boergermoor in northwestern Germany; hells which surpassed in horror the former slave camps in Belgian Congo or Bolshevist Russia. It became known that in Oranienburg cement cells were built in which camp inmates were kept standing for many hours, sometimes days, in the darkness — upright standing stone coffins. It became known that in all the concentration camps flogging had been officially introduced as a punishment for light offenses; that for relatively innocuous violations of rules the penalty was execution by hanging — officially this was designated, not as a penalty, but as a disciplinary measure. It happened that prisoners employed in road-building were 'for fun' thrown into the rotating barrel of a concrete-mixing machine and kept there until their bones were crushed. It happened that one torturer with a sense of humor burned, with a cigarette, holes in the bare chest of his victim to make them look like uniform buttons. To throw prisoners into sewers or drains 'by oversight' was also considered a permissible pastime. The most gruesome tortures were often those in which outwardly nothing seemed to happen. Prisoners were compelled to stand erect for many hours under a torrid sun; they were forbidden to make the slightest motion, not even a quiver of a limb. Cases were reported of this torture being inflicted on hundreds of people for as long as eighteen hours. It happened that people were locked up in boxlike wooden closets, fed with salted herrings, and left without water or any other drink; of course death was the result.

These atrocities revealed the depravity of the 'old fighters,' and gave the more cool-headed National Socialist leaders food for thought. Frick and Epp occasionally tried to stop the horrors or call their perpetrators to account. Now and then even Göring intervened, and Hitler himself doubtless realized the injury caused to his own popularity by these crimes. After the initial noisy enthusiasm over the magnificence and energy of the new government had somewhat subsided, the cries of the martyred were heard more distinctly. Röhm admitted publicly that these things seemed unbearable to many people, but said that he saw no reason for stopping them. 'Many complaints are being lodged concerning the alleged excesses of S.A. men,' he declared in a statement which probably seemed witty to him; but 'if the supreme leadership of the S.A. investigated each individual complaint, its staff would have to be increased tenfold and a skyscraper erected over the Brown House' (August, 1933).

A curious thing happened: the S.A. began to feel afraid in the Germany they dominated. The brown figures in the streets still seemed to behave like conquerors and masters who could say, strike, shoot, and, in general, act as they pleased; but the limit had been reached where pride turned into doubt and brutality into cowardice. Röhm sent out memoranda to the other National Socialist leaders, pointing out that the S.A. were practically 'defenseless' in the hands of the 'commune of murderers,' since they had been sent home and forced to turn in their revolvers. In July, 1933, in order to reassure the trembling heroes, Hess warned: 'We are far from intending to treat the enemy with mildness'; and as Hess was a specialist in handling hostages and had often said that in political struggles ten innocent people had to suffer for one guilty one, he proclaimed now: 'that every murder of a National Socialist committed by a Communist or Marxist would be expiated tenfold by Communist or Marxist leaders.'

The widening gulf between the S.A. and the people became particularly apparent during the elections, when the National Socialist propaganda tried to blur the differences between the party and the masses as much as possible. Hess denied in moving tones that 'Germans who did not belong to the National Socialist Party must be considered second-class Germans.' Then, as though frightened by his own daring, he immediately corrected this statement, admitting that a category of Germans existed 'which deserved particular recognition: the category of old fighters.' These old fighters, he said, had risked death for their Führer year after year and 'played the same part in the domestic struggle as the front-line soldiers in the World War.' The other National Socialists must not imagine that they are as valuable, must not demand 'to be put on the same level as the old fighters and raised above their fellow countrymen.' Hess went so far as to grant that people who had not joined the party after the seizure of power because they did not want to seem to be jumping on the bandwagon 'were not among the worst.' But then he was again frightened of having perhaps said too much, and added hastily: 'I do not mean at all to accuse all those who joined the National Socialist Party after January 30, 1933, of lack of character and foolish opportunism.'

Because these men of 'after January 30,' men of normal usefulness and efficiency, to some extent had again taken the reins into their hands, the S.A. grumbled about a second revolution, although Hitler had forbidden his partisans even to use the term 'revolution.' On November 5, 1933, before fifteen thousand National Socialist officials gathered in the Sportpalast in Berlin, Röhm attacked the renewed insolence of the reactionaries: 'One often hears voices from the bourgeois camp to the effect that the S.A. have lost their reason for being.' But this is what he wanted to say to these gentlemen: the bureaucratic spirit, which had barely changed after January 30, 1933, 'must still be changed in a gentle, or, if need be, in an ungentle, manner.' By no means could the National Socialist revolution be regarded as completed. At this there was thunderous applause. Then Himmler appeared before the footlights and exclaimed that 'revolutions are triumphant only if every man who is sent to a post considers himself, not an official of the state, but of the revolution. And so must it be today in the National Socialist revolution.' Again there was thunderous applause. However, when Goebbels came forward and cautiously tried to contradict the two previous speakers, saying that the revolution had only one slogan: Germany; that the period of domestic political activity was over and that the time had come to settle matters with the world, but that 'we could do this only if the people are behind us,' the applause was much weaker.

Important elements in the party leadership had here taken a stand against stopping the revolution; and the wrath of these now forgotten men was stronger than Hitler's will. Great concessions were made to the 'old fighters.' By a law promulgated in the middle of December and entitled 'On the Unity of the Party and the State,' the chief of staff of the S.A. was made a member of the Reich cabinet with the rank of Minister; thus the burning grievance of the S.A., the disdainful treatment of Röhm, was at least outwardly removed. At the same time, the Führer's deputy, Rudolf Hess, was given the rank of Minister.

This late and hasty honor was conferred upon Röhm at a moment when the S.A. was suddenly and unexpectedly needed again. The 'reactionaries' had indeed gained ground. This became apparent when former Kaiser Wilhelm wrote, from his exile in Holland to President Hindenburg, that the time had come for crowning the reconstruction of Germany by the restoration of the monarchy. The personal relations between Wilhelm II and Hindenburg were tense; the former Kaiser believed that his field marshal had been the real cause of his overthrow; but Hindenburg doubtless had a vague idea that the National Socialist period would not last forever in Germany. The National Socialists got wind of the contents of this letter and replied with a cry of fury, 'We will not tolerate the interference of the High Gentleman of Doorn,' as Goerlitzer, Goebbels's closest collaborator, put it. When a group of ladies and gentlemen belonging to Berlin high society organized a public celebration of the ex-Kaiser's birthday (January 27, 1934), Göring's police broke into the hall and dispersed these faithful followers of Wilhelm II. Earlier than this, Hitler had made it plain that he did not intend to restore the monarchy. 'What is past does not come again. . . . The wheels of history cannot be turned backward. . . . This would not be desirable at all. . . .' The dynasties of German princes, he had said, had often 'given only mediocrities to the throne'; or, 'Republic versus monarchy — a serious issue? Millions laugh at it.' He had promised a great deal to credulous princes; foreign observers had regarded Hitler as the herald of a future monarchy and did not realize how serious he was when — as early as 1923 — he had declared that 'today the German no longer dies for the monarchy, but only for Germany's freedom.'

When the Reichstag assembled on the anniversary of the 'seizure of power,' Hitler took the opportunity to declare that the achievement of the German princes had been 'almost exclusively the selfish operation of a ruthless power politics in favor of their own dynasties,' and if these policies of the German princes 'did not definitely destroy Germany as a nation, this was not the merit of the authors of these policies. . . . Therefore, I should like to register my protest against the recently reaffirmed thesis that Germany could be happy again only under her hereditary princes.' The future head of Germany, whoever he may be, 'will be called to that office by the German people and will be obligated to it alone and exclusively.'

This meant that the future form of the German government would be determined by the National Socialists, by the dictatorship based on the plebiscite; and to remove the last doubts about this, a law was proposed at the same Reichstag session which gave the Reich government the important right — and thereby deprived parliament of it — 'to promulgate new constitutional legislation,' that is to say, to give the country a new constitution. This 'is perhaps the most important law for Germany's future,' said Göring, the President of the Reichstag; and so it was. After the National Socialist deputies had passed this revolutionary law in less than three minutes, there was, according to the official record, 'a movement of cheerful satisfaction with this quick work throughout all the rows.'

On the same day Hitler wrote Röhm a letter full of strikingly cordial phrases intended to honor and pacify the man he had so often disdained. Expressing his desire 'to thank you, my dear Ernst Röhm, for your unforgettable services,' he assured the homosexual murderer that he was extremely 'grateful to destiny for having given me the right to call a man like you my friend and comrade-in-arms. In cordial friendship and grateful respect, your Adolf Hitler.'

And on February 2, Frick once more sent a telegram to the states, this time ordering his officials immediately to dissolve all the organizations working for the monarchy. The Weimar Republic had left a few quaint privileges of the former princes undisturbed. Thus, the birth, marriage, and death records of the Hohenzollern family were not kept in the public registrar's offices, but in a private office which was called the 'Ministry of the Royal House'; Frick gave orders that this practice be stopped and that the Hohenzollern family records be transferred to the public offices, like those of any other Prussian citizen.

Urged on by Röhm and Hess, the all-powerful government now saw to it that the Uprooted and Disinherited were treated by all public agencies and particularly by the treasury on an equal footing with World War veterans. In February, 1934, it adopted a law with the clear, unadorned title: 'Concerning provisions for the fighters of the national movement.' These fighters — that is, members of the National Socialist Party and the Steel Helmets — upon request, were to be granted damages to the same amount as victims of the World War for sickness or injuries 'which they had suffered before November 15, 1933, in connection with the political struggle for the national movement'; thus, a National Socialist office clerk could say that he had got stomach trouble as a result of excessive work for the party. In the past, Hitler had often publicly declared to his S.A. men that they should not think too much about the hardships of their struggle, for every minute at the front in the World War had been a thousand times worse. Now, Hess's law proclaimed: The German people 'owe the old fighters the same gratitude and recognition for their heroic achievements as they owe their fellow countrymen who sacrificed their health and lives for the fatherland.'

In the struggle against the reactionary conservatives and the monarchists, the S.A. was once again given a task. Goebbels, who, as late as November, had tried with anxious words to talk the revolutionaries out of their impatience, suddenly became bold and radical, and this was surely not without Hitler's explicit approval. The S.A. with their greedy grumblings were right; he had often heard it said, he declared in an address to the *S.A. Standarte VIII* in Berlin, 'that old party comrades and S.A. men could not be used in government offices and departments because they had not taken any examinations. If so, I must say that while the stay-at-homes passed their examinations, we saved the Reich' — that is to say, marched through the country as armed bohemians. 'We consider it intolerable,' he continued, 'that the Old Guard should silently give way after having conquered the Reich. . . . It won't do to put our old vanguard fighters in a lower category than the home-birds or to place the home-birds above them.' 'The National Socialist struggle,' he said in another speech, 'has been a socialist revolution; it has been the revolution of a workers' movement, and those who have made it must today also be its spokesmen.' The workers — he explicitly addressed them — should trust the leaders of the revolution, because 'if these leaders are now looking on and are not taking any steps against the reactionary machinations throughout the country, it is only in order better to know the reactionaries.' Then Goebbels drew a truly Oriental picture of whimsical government: 'If one wants to catch mice,' he said, 'one does not strike at them constantly, but only from time to time, for otherwise they would creep into their holes. One strikes once, then one waits for a while till the mice become insolent again, and when they feel safe, one strikes them for the second time.' Fortunately, he thought, the people refused to have anything to do with these mice, rats, stay-at-homes, and reactionaries.

This was objectively false. The people were beginning to find the achievements of the régime which they had admired at first quite normal and even to see its drawbacks. True, the number of unemployed continued to decrease; in March, Hitler was able to announce that 2,700,000 out of 7,000,000 jobless had found employment. But once the miracle of decreasing unemployment had been recognized and accepted, the people felt even more bitter about the still wretchedly low wages. Hitler, who a year and a half ago had reproached von Papen for expecting the workers to live on wages of a hundred marks a month, was now forced to admit that the wages of too many workers were still around that figure. Robert Ley, always open-hearted, called some of the German wages 'starvation wages'; but, he added, for the moment it could not be otherwise.

At this point Hitler and Goebbels had the unfortunate idea that more abuse, ridicule, and persecution of the dissatisfied might improve the popular mood and at the same time give a new goal and line to the party which had become purposeless. A campaign against the so-called 'bleaters, alarmists, and professional critics' was opened in May. Hitler shouted: 'Only those have a right to criticize who can solve a problem better. But we have attacked the solution of the German problem better than our opponents of the past and our critics of today.' Goebbels echoed him: 'As we National Socialists are convinced that we are right, we cannot tolerate anyone beside us who declares that he, too, is right. . . .' On May 2, Röhm, before his assembled sub-leaders, promised in his customary tart tone that the S.A., because they were disciplined, would 'fulfill every task given them by their Führer, Adolf Hitler, in thorough and exemplary fashion.'

The dissatisfied classes of the population were to be reminded of their insignificance and the S.A. of their importance and superiority. If anyone dared to say a deprecatory word about the new order on a street corner, life was made hard for him, to say the least. In a village near Mainz a housewife said to her milkman that actually nothing had as yet improved in Germany; as a punishment she was forced, for many months, to appear every morning at party headquarters and say in a loud voice: 'Much has been improved and even more will be improved in Germany.'

This campaign against the alarmists was an enterprise of exceptional shortsightedness on Hitler's part. The masses of the people grew so embittered that in the middle of June even Göring, in an address to his Prussian Council of State, admitted that 'the mood was deteriorating and dissatisfaction had broken out here and there.' Nor were the S.A. chieftains happier now that they were once again being called on to stand by and help while the 'philistines' were admonished, just as they had done for years. Everyone felt that the final decision concerning the leadership and the form of the new state was still pending.

If Hitler really had been the conscious framer of political plans that he seemed in his own and the world's eyes — 'the great strategist of the revolution,' as Hess once called him, who 'acts after ice-cold reflection' — he would have begun his preparations for the inevitable struggle for power at that very moment. It lies in the nature of things human that unused power passes imperceptibly from idle hands into more active ones; it was in the nature of this state that various ambitious absolute powers should struggle over its only half-used power; it was characteristic of Hitler to watch the ebb and flow of power and the struggle for it until a sudden danger cleared the situation like a flash of lightning and precipitated a decision. Thus groups arose in the National Socialist Party which prepared themselves for the bloody break-through to full, unrestricted domination, and all of them counted on carrying Hitler with them. Outwardly, the greatest force among these planners and makers of preparations was Röhm; he gathered around him a staff of people who were particularly devoted to him, not all of them among the oldest party members, but certainly all old Free Corps fighters, especially from the Rossbach unit. This group had personal points of support scattered throughout Germany: There was Count Wolf Helldorf, the leader of the Berlin-Brandenburg *Obergruppe* (that is, an organization of about a hundred thousand men) and, at that time, chief of police of Potsdam; there was Karl Ernst, Helldorf's friend and immediate subordinate, the Group Leader of Berlin, who came from the dregs of the lower classes just as Helldorf came from the dregs of the upper classes; there was the murderer, Edmund Heines, in Breslau; there was

Fritz Krausser, a friend of Röhm's, who had been ennobled by the King of Bavaria for outstanding bravery in the World War. Other members of the group were Manfred von Killinger, Prime Minister of Saxony; ex-Colonel August Schneidhuber, chief of police in Munich, and Reiner and Count Spreti, Röhm's aides-de-camp.

It was a group which fully deserved the epithet of Uprooted and Disinherited. Helldorf was perpetually bankrupt and had borrowed money from a certain Steinschneider who wanted his favor. This man was probably of Jewish origin and earned a great deal of money in theaters as a 'clairvoyant' under the pseudonym of Hanussen. In April, 1933, by order of Helldorf, he was kidnapped from a theater entrance and murdered in a woods near Berlin. Georg Bell, a former intimate friend of Röhm's who had broken with him, fled to Austria and from there threatened to make revelations concerning the Reichstag fire. By order of Röhm he was pursued by a group of assassins who discovered him in a border village and murdered him in his hotel room. The ideas and aims of these men can hardly be better described than by the words which Plato in his *Banquet* put into the mouth of one of their ilk: 'If it were possible to form a state or an army exclusively of homosexuals, these men would direct all their emulations toward honors, and going into battle with such a spirit would, even if their numbers were small, conquer the entire world.'

A curious appendage to this group was Goebbels, who, from an old habit, was always on the side of the dissatisfied S.A. so long as he believed that in the end Hitler would do what they wanted. With Helldorf he formed a kind of political leadership of the bloc around Röhm; he gave Röhm publicity; he gave him opportunities to speak before foreign diplomats; he put the S.A. leaders' complaints into words more eloquent than Röhm himself could have done; he praised him in speeches and writings. In the April edition of his so-called diary he still gave Röhm credit for the chief contribution to the 'seizure of power.'

Should it ever come to a revolutionary settlement, such a clique would need troops ready to strike at a moment's notice. In order to move quickly, this force must not be numerous, nor did it have to be numerous; for the party which, within a short time, could lay its hands on the geographical key points of government authority (government office buildings, centers of communication), would thereby enjoy the benefits of securing legality and power and draw the masses to its side. For that reason the National Socialist leaders had so-called 'staff-guards' around them. Hitler had his 'body-guard'; Göring kept a particularly formidable group near Berlin half-concealed in a building where he had been trained as an officer in his youth: this was a police group of several thousand men, formed 'for special services,' and called the *Landes-Polizeigruppe General Göring*. They were commanded by a certain Major Wecke who was quartered in the former Cadet School at Lichterfelde.

All these groups were silently supervised by a kind of armed 'black cabinet' which constantly kept the entire movement under control; it was composed of the most unostentatious high party officials and was completely in Hitler's hands. The leading person-alities in this group were Rudolf Hess, Heinrich Himmler, and former Major Walter Buch, chairman of the Party's Control Com-mittee.

Since 1920, when Hess joined Hitler, his job had been to spy on the party and keep it in order. For the supervision of the S.A. he had a particularly suitable human instrument, a certain Martin Bormann, an 'old fighter,' who was endowed with all the qualities and experience of the armed bohemians, including a year spent in prison for participation in a political murder. Bormann had been Captain von Pfeffer's right hand when the latter was the supreme leader of the S.A. When in 1930, Pfeffer was crowded out by Röhm's clique, Bormann left the leadership of the S.A., but re-mained director of the 'Relief Fund,' an institution which could also be called the bribe fund. At its headquarters the lamentations and grievances of the malcontents which the leadership would not listen to were loudly reiterated; and Bormann, full of bitter resent-ment against the 'gang of fairies' around Röhm, collected heaps of material. Its content was communicated to Hess; and Hess began to din into Hitler's ears that the conditions created by Röhm's male harem within the S.A. were gradually becoming unbearable. A similar complaint was brought by Walter Buch: he claimed that Röhm had built up around himself a peculiar staff, completely devoted to him personally, but dubious, to say the least, from the point of view of the party and its Führer. What seemed particularly objectionable was that Röhm's collaborators were in part men unknown in the movement; that their patron had chosen them for personal reasons, and that therefore they placed their personal loyalty to him above everything else. Actually Göring and Goebbels had always done the same thing — it would have been inconceivable if they had done otherwise; even Hitler himself had done it — thus, in April, 1934, he had got Hindenburg to appoint his translator, Joachim von Ribbentrop, 'deputy in disarmament problems,' thus making him, over Rosenberg's head, the first National Socialist expert on foreign politics.

At first, as he himself later admitted, Hitler ignored all these accusations. But the S.A. themselves suffered from the widening wedge which Hitler had deliberately driven into them from the beginning — and now this was to prove one of his shrewdest and most far-reaching measures. Outwardly, the Black S.S. was still subjected to Röhm's supreme command; among the S.S. leaders Himmler still appeared as one of the S.A. leaders; and when the old fighters grumbled and threatened publicly, Himmler was among the loudest of them. This situation continued seemingly undisturbed until well into May; it was as though the old fighters had triumphed — and perhaps they had when, at the beginning of April, Göring was forced to dismiss Werner Diels, his chief of the secret state police, and once a very useful traitor, and replace him by Heinrich Himmler. Himmler was already chief of the 'political police' in all the German states while remaining Reich leader of the S.S.; now he was given the strongest police machine in the Reich and he merged it, with the help of his collaborator, Reinhard Heydrich, with the police organizations of the other German states. Staffed by selected S.S. men, permeated with their silent arrogance and cold indifference toward humanity, this police body gradually became the most frightful organization of its kind in modern history.

The meaning of such shifts of power as Himmler's promotion to the post of chief of the Gestapo is rarely as clear at the moment to the persons most closely involved as it is later to outside ob-

servers. This is because those who act rarely know exactly what
they want. Only three months later, it looked as though Himmler
had been bought by Göring in April and thus detached from
Röhm; but Röhm himself may have believed at that time that the
growing power of Himmler, whom he had first elevated and who
was his subordinate, would be his own power, too. Moreover, he
knew that his own humiliation and dissatisfaction were the humiliation and dissatisfaction of the party; when he grumbled and made
demands, he did it at bottom for Hitler; even if he was trouble-
some, it was only — as he saw it — because of excessive zeal and
excessive loyalty. Even if Hitler sometimes liked to scold him,
there was nothing to show that he would eventually 'trample him'
as Hess had prophesied.

But in May, it became clear that Hindenburg would not live
much longer. Increasing senility had even earlier gradually removed the eighty-seven-year-old man from the actual business of
government. This left the National Socialists more freedom than
they would have obtained from the President in his better days.
But his imminent death put them in the greatest embarrassment:
the problem of his succession had to be solved.

Strangely enough, it did not occur to many well-informed people
that his successor could be Hitler. This idea was farthest removed
from the President himself. At the beginning of May, he wrote a
political testament which later, after its publication, bore the date
of May 10; in it he cast a retrospective glance over his life; he declared that the Empire had to be restored; referring to the immediate present, he gave 'my Chancellor, Adolf Hitler, and his
movement' high praise for their achievement, but explicitly avoided
designating the Führer as his successor. More than that, the whole
tenor of the document clearly gave the impression that Hindenburg
did not wish Hitler to be the future President of the Reich — nor
did Hitler later call himself President. The writer of this testament may have been even more explicit about this in passages
which were suppressed before its publication.

Soon rumors began to circulate that Hindenburg wanted a 'Reich
Regency' after his death, a régime with a leader of greater authority than Hitler had. It was said that the Regent should be a

Hohenzollern prince, and the most benevolently disposed toward the National Socialists thought of August Wilhelm, who addressed Hitler with reverence as 'My Führer.' Others mentioned the half-English Prince von Cumberland, former Duke of Brunswick and the ex-Kaiser's son-in-law. Still others — who had become accustomed to an old Marshal — staked their bets on Field Marshal August von Mackensen, an illegitimate offspring of the Hohenzollerns, who, during the World War, had been built up as Hindenburg's rival by the jealous Kaiser. At bottom all these were fantasies, without any serious basis; but they showed that, in the circles which secretly manufactured a good part of the nation's public opinion, Hitler was not envisaged as Hindenburg's successor.

Within a short time Hitler would thus be confronted with the task of overcoming the resistance of his dead predecessor and a very much alive public opinion, especially the resistance of the small upper crust whose influence had always been excessive in moments of uncertainty, and of making himself head of the state by force. But where was this force? Röhm could point at his S.A. and say: Here it is; the same could be said by Himmler of his S.S., and even Göring of his 'police groups'; but Hitler knew better: only the Reichswehr wielded real power. 'If the Reichswehr had not been on our side in the days of the revolution,' he used to say, 'we would not be here.' But the Reichswehr — more accurately, Blomberg and Reichenau — had supported him because they believed that the majority of the people supported him or, at any rate, would support him within a short time. Could he still count on this support when trying to become head of the German Reich? In this matter a majority of fifty-one per cent of the votes, which Hitler knew he certainly would get, especially by forbidding any other candidates to run, would not be satisfactory; ninety-nine per cent were required in order to enable his régime to represent what it claimed to represent: the unity of the German people. This could be achieved only if all resistance were silenced or put out of the way; and for this Hitler needed the collaboration of the 'only armed force in the state.'

At that very moment Röhm began a dispute with Blomberg and Reichenau; more accurately, he resumed the old dispute as a result of which he had been driven out of the Reichswehr ten years before, and which, since that time, had stood like a black cloud between the S.A. and the Reichswehr and kept even the relations between Röhm and Hitler in a state of constant although silent tension; the dispute over the question of whether the S.A. should form the bulk of the future army. Von Schleicher, as Minister of the Reichswehr and Chancellor, had envisaged such a plan when he wanted to surround the small professional army with a mass 'militia' and use the S.A. and Steel Helmets for this purpose. As a private citizen, he had continued to regard the Reichswehr as his own affair and his own creature; the plan for a mass militia obviously seemed to him an ideal solution at the moment when the negotiations with the Western powers about the increase of the Reichswehr came to a deadlock. Whether it is true — as Hitler maintained — that he intended to appoint Röhm Minister of the Reichswehr and himself Vice-Chancellor, and then brilliantly solve the problem of German rearmament by introducing his militia, is still impossible to verify; but he doubtless played with many projects, possibly with this one, too.

Röhm, as a member of the Reich cabinet, now raised his voice and demanded that the S.A. be made a part of the Reichswehr. Even if only a fraction of the three million S.A. men, most of whom were engaged in civilian activities, could become soldiers, as many S.A. leaders as possible were obviously to become officers, and this with a rank more or less corresponding to their S.A. rank. Thus, one fine morning these armed poultry farmers or department store porters would wake up with the rank of general or at least colonel, just because they had won the titles of S.A. group or brigade leaders as a result of various scuffles in beer-cellars or back alleys. Blomberg sharply rejected Röhm's demands.

By his aggressive move, Röhm gave the 'enemies of the S.A.' their long-desired occasion to blame and deride what almost everyone in Germany knew about the S.A. and their degenerate leaders; they particularly attacked Röhm's newly organized Berlin headquarters as the scene of extravagant and obscene orgies. At the beginning of June, Hitler, according to his own account, had a five-hour conversation with Röhm, from the afternoon until past midnight, in which he submitted to him the complaints gathered by Hess and Buch, demanded the liquidation of his male harem, and, more generally, a complete change in his system of leadership. From Hitler's subsequent explanations, it appears that Röhm refused to be intimidated, that he contradicted him stubbornly, and that his attitude was not respectful. Probably the conversation went far beyond the points Hitler mentions; Hitler must have demanded that Röhm show greater complaisance with regard to the Reichswehr and discussed with him the grave dangers created by Hindenburg's imminent death. Röhm may have replied that this very fact offered the historical opportunity for which the S.A. had been built through long years of work; but Hitler's conviction that he could achieve supreme power only with the help of the Reichswehr was unshakable.

From that moment on the fate of the S.A. and their leaders was sealed from an historical point of view; Hitler had to separate himself from them, 'trample them to dust,' if he were to become supreme chief of the Reich. Röhm was suddenly isolated, his *entourage* of followers, advocates, and companions quickly disintegrated; Goebbels and Himmler, who only recently had called for a new revolution or the continuation of the old one, grew silent. On June 7, Röhm took a furlough which was certainly a real sick-leave; he went for treatment to Wiessee in Upper Bavaria, where he lived in the 'Hanslbauer' sanatorium; Heines, too, went there, to restore his apparently failing health. Röhm could prove that he had really put himself in the hands of physicians; but obviously Hitler had insisted that he disappear from Berlin for some time. Before leaving, Röhm wrote a farewell message to the S.A. announcing that his S.A. men should take a four weeks' furlough on July 1; as for the 'enemies of the S.A.,' who circulated the rumor that this meant the disbandment of the brown army, 'they would be given a suitable answer in due time and in whatever form is necessary.' This warning was followed by an equally threatening concluding sentence: 'The S.A. is and remains Germany's destiny.' There was no 'Heil Hitler'; the Führer was not mentioned at all.

Hitler was in a difficult position, made even more difficult by Röhm. His Austrian policy was being criticized with increasing sharpness from many sides; without doubt, National Socialism had stupidly driven Germany's sister-country, Austria, once so close and friendly to the Reich, into the arms of the Italians. Among the critics of Hitler's Austrian policy was Röhm; in fact, he went beyond criticism and made it known in Vienna that he disapproved of Hitler's attacks on Austria. From this point on, Hitler evidently began to feel that Röhm was betraying him.

Amidst all the plans, conspiracies, and armed preparations carried on in various places and more and more clearly orientated toward the expected great event, the death of the old man of Neudeck, there were opportunities for dubious actions, actions that were treasonable or at least bordered on treason. Von Schleicher, a good friend of François-Poncet, the French ambassador, had already under Brüning used his good offices to prepare Paris for the coming change in Germany, and Hitler was certainly acquainted with these questionable activities because he himself had drawn the greatest advantage from them. Now it became known that during a session of the League Council in Geneva, Louis Barthou, the French Foreign Minister, had said in a private conversation that it was futile to negotiate with the present German government because it would soon be replaced by another. It was easy to draw conclusions from such a report, although difficult to check, let alone prove them — and Hitler never gave a single piece of evidence for the accusations he made in connection with the events that were to follow. True, some people involved in the affair admitted that during the month of May, François-Poncet met a varied group of German politicians in the home of a Dutch financier: but subsequent events showed that this meeting was harmless.

One of the German politicians present had been von Schleicher, who did not need any Dutchman to introduce him to François-Poncet; another was Gregor Strasser, who had been out of politics for a year and a half and was active as an adviser on labor relations for a chemical company and — a point which was not immaterial to him — earning much more in this capacity than ever before in his life. The third politician present had been Röhm. The meeting seems to have been imposed on all these three men rather than desired by them. Strasser had been compelled to promise his employers that he would no longer dabble in politics, and his salary was generous enough to make him keep this promise; he had a wife and two sons and did not carry much life insurance. Von Schleicher had asked his host to see to it that nothing leaked out about this meeting which he had not desired; he seemed deliberately to have spoken about unimportant matters — at least that is what François-Poncet later told the Foreign Office. After the events we are studying, Hitler kept the French ambassador in Berlin for many years and treated him with conspicuous kindness, which would not have been the case if this Frenchman, forgetting his diplomatic duties, had been involved in a conspiracy against the government to which he was accredited. A commission of German officers later investigated the matter and established that von Schleicher had acted honorably and had not committed treason. But Hitler later summed up his motives as follows: when three traitors meet with an ambassador of a foreign power and conceal the fact from him, Hitler, 'then I give orders to have these men shot, even should it be true that at such a meeting, hidden from me, only the weather, ancient coins, and similar subjects were discussed.'

Hitler made this declaration in cutting tones on July 13 when he spoke in the Reichstag; but in the same speech he said that he had not thought of the shootings until late in the night of June 30 — that is to say, at a time when he must have known of the meeting with François-Poncet for a long time. This was one of many cases in which his intelligence service got wind of part of a perhaps important incident, but failed to get hold of the decisive element in it which was later falsely added by inference. What is characteristic of Hitler's methods in this affair is that such pieces of half-information completed by inference were not used as a basis for justifiable preventive measures, but for the most far-reaching decisions concerning the life and death of hundreds of people and the morale of the entire nation. On June 30, says Hitler, he resolved to take extreme measures only at the last minute, under the pressure of extreme danger — after having said that he took these measures because the meeting with François-Poncet had aroused his suspicions. These two declarations are inconsistent — but actually Hitler's entire explanation of the events described below is inconsistent; it is contradictory on essential points, is based on thoroughly implausible assertions, and even the plausible ones remain unproved.

If a net of dangers was really being woven around Hitler, he obviously failed to discover it until the end of June. On June 14, he felt secure enough to leave Germany and visit Mussolini; this trip to Italy had been prepared by Ribbentrop, who had gone to Rome toward the end of May. For the first time the 'great man of the south' and his northern admirer met: the herald of *Europa Fascista* beheld the prophet who called upon Aryans of all nations to unite. The ostensible purpose of the meeting was to settle the question of Austria, over which National Socialist Germany and Fascist Italy had been wrangling. The real purpose, at least as far as Hitler was concerned, was to explore the possibilities of a close understanding between the two countries. Hitler landed from his plane in Venice, dressed as a civilian in an unpretentious raincoat; Mussolini received him in his gold-braided uniform, with a dagger at his side. As Hitler walked toward him, the Italian dictator is alleged to have said: *'Non mi piace.'* The visit lasted two days. Important matters were discussed in *tête-à-tête* conversations, and Mussolini politely made use of his fairly fluent German.

Despite Hitler's zealous wooing of the Italian dictator, his visit failed to create a cordial personal relationship between the two men. However, they had an extremely frank exchange of views; the premises of their ideas were so similar that they could not conceal much from each other. No concrete results were achieved, nor had Hitler expected any; Mussolini, who wanted to receive reassuring promises about Austria, got what he wanted. It would have been surprising if Hitler had refused to give a promise so earnestly desired by his respected host, especially as he knew at bottom that a statesman can always find an adequate excuse for breaking his word under compelling circumstances.

Mussolini frankly told his guest that the persecution of the Jews made it difficult even for him to be completely friendly toward Germany and tried to prove to Hitler that his anti-Jewish paranoia was unjustified. A leading Jewish-Italian rabbi, Mussolini said, had asked him not to rebuff Hitler, but on the contrary to cultivate the best possible relations with him, because Italy might thus have an opportunity to ease the sufferings of the German Jews. There is no doubt that Mussolini, older, successful for a longer time, and outwardly still more powerful than Hitler, told him what he disliked in the new Germany. The maxim that a great usurper must trample even upon his friends probably was invoked. In his autobiography, the Italian dictator had written that 'normally, a revolutionary movement can be channeled into legality only by means of forceful measures, directed, if necessary, against the personnel of the movement. . . . At certain historical hours, the sacrifice of those who were the deserving lieutenants of yesterday might become indispensable for the supreme interest of tomorrow.'

Hitler left Italy with the feeling that he had seen his rival at the climax of his power, but that his rival had seen him as a beginner entangled in the most inextricable difficulties, whose enemies were still too strong and whose own friends were disloyal to him. As though to confirm this impression, upon his return from Italy, on June 17, he was given the text of a speech in which von Papen, on the same day, had unsparingly attacked the National Socialist régime before an audience of professors and students at the University of Marburg; von Papen made only slight efforts to present his speech as a friendly criticism. The campaign against the 'bleaters' had taken on repulsive forms and filled many people with indignation; at times it degenerated into murderous propaganda against the two Christian churches. The man largely responsible for this was Alfred Rosenberg whom Hitler had commissioned (on January 31) 'to supervise all the spiritual and philosophic training and education of the party,' in order to compensate him for his political disappointments. Now National Socialist philosophy was being forcibly hammered into the minds of the young generation. At the universities, young S.A. or S.S. men gave so-called lectures on philosophy (*Weltanschanung*) which the students were compelled to attend. Doors were locked, nobody could leave the room; then the youthful teachers, who were often completely uneducated, demanded that the students memorize bloody gibberish such as the following verses:

> Wetzt die langen Messer an dem Buergersteig,
> dass sie besser flutschen in der Pfaffen Leib! . . .

Und kommt die Stunde der Vergeltung,
Stehn wir zu jedem Massenmord bereit![1]

Before the students of Marburg, von Papen declared threateningly
that the question whether the German Reich would be a Christian
state or not was still to be fought out. The everlasting lecturing of
the people must stop, he said. The situation was serious, the laws
were defective, the people were suffering from economic distress,
they were tired of hearing everything painted in glowing colors!
Propaganda, he went on, does not create great men, nor is propaganda alone sufficient to maintain the confidence of the people; the
absolute rule of one party could only be a transitional state of
affairs.

Von Papen's speech aroused Germany as no other speech had
aroused her for a long time; it expressed what millions were feeling
and what even Hitler himself had to recognize at the bottom of
his heart. True, on the same day, in a speech before his followers
in the city of Gera, he abused von Papen (although without mentioning his name) as a worm and ridiculous dwarf whom the
Führer 'would crush with the fist of the entire German nation' if
he engaged in serious sabotage; but there was nothing serious in
these grumblers who believed that they could slow up the gigantic
renascence movement of the people with a few figures of speech;
'this state is in its first youth, and you may be sure that in a thousand
years it will still stand unbroken.' But it could not be denied that
von Papen had spoken the truth and that, once more, he had proclaimed publicly what Hitler himself knew was true. And von
Papen had received a congratulatory telegram from Hindenburg.

It would have been more than a miracle if after von Papen's
speech, Röhm and his friends had not begun preparing for the
great settling of accounts or at least for a decision in the near future.
When Hitler spoke in Gera he still believed that the decision, which in
fact had been made, would not look like a decision; he thought that
his cheated followers would accept the fraud and that the politically
killed, just to please him, would pretend they were still alive. But

---

[1] Sharpen the long knives on the sidewalks, so that they can cut the clergymen's bodies better. . . . When the hour of retribution strikes, we will be ready
for mass murder.

they did not. After the Gera speech, the higher S.A. leaders seem to have discussed at great length Hitler's irresolution and lack of insight. Doubtless Röhm and his comrades thought about ways of compelling their Leader to make a decision; as Röhm put it, this time they would not be satisfied with 'Adolf's tears.'

The strife between the armed gangs not only separated the S.A. from the rest of the National Socialist party, it also divided the S.A. themselves into a group gathered under Röhm's peculiar leadership and other slighted and dissatisfied groups which were by no means always morally better. Among these latter elements was the *Obergruppenführer* of Hanover, a certain Viktor Lutze, an ex-officer severely wounded in the World War and one-eyed. Lutze was an intimate friend of Goebbels's who had brought Hitler himself to his home. Another malcontent was Count Helldorf, that former intimate friend of Röhm's, who had since quarrelled with him because Röhm had not sufficiently protected him from the unfavorable publicity which followed the murder of Hanussen. Whether the reports brought to Hitler by Lutze and Helldorf were of major or only of secondary importance will perhaps be established at some future date; at any rate, among Röhm's intimates, Helldorf was the only one to have survived him and to have even been given an honorable promotion.

When these groups got ready for the fight, this meant — among other things — that they had drawn up lists of persons to be 'liquidated' the moment action began. During the long-drawn-out years of struggle before 1933 there had been time to prepare such lists. The various fractions of the party had noted the names and addresses of their enemies, and the enemies of one group were not necessarily the enemies of another; the enemies of the supreme S.A. leadership were not necessarily those whom Reinhard Heydrich had singled out in the name of the S.S. Reich leadership; Hess's 'liaison staff' and Göring had quite different lists of their own. In some places bloodthirsty fanatics had compiled endless lists of proscripts; in others, following orders from above, only a few inevitable victims had been designated. Personal feuds often proved fatal. There were lists of various kinds, of persons to be eliminated under any circumstances and of persons to be eliminated only under certain circumstances; also purges of different degrees had been provided for: some in which the victims were to be killed at once, some in which arrest would be sufficient. This criss-cross system of lists and purges of various types seemed to work out on paper; but in reality bloody confusion was almost inevitable, especially when former executioners were suddenly to be designated as victims.

This mass of stored-up murder considerably added to the bloody confusion of the subsequent events; persons fell who had absolutely nothing in common with Röhm and his circle, and against whom there existed no tangible suspicion, let alone an accusation calling for the death penalty. Furthermore, the whole idea of a Schleicher-Strasser-Röhm conspiracy was little more than an invention, and the empty and embarrassed words which Hitler later used to describe this alleged plot suffice to prove this. True, the dissatisfaction of the S.A. and their readiness to go into action were much more serious; but all the facts later revealed by the victors or made known against their will show that on June 30 no immediate danger threatened. The brutal repression which inevitably caused the death of many innocent people was thus unnecessary and unjustified.

On July 1, the S.A. were supposed to take a furlough; the supreme leadership issued orders to this effect and even transmitted them to the press. During this furlough they were forbidden to wear uniforms and to organize meetings, even private meetings; so-called 'celebrations' were also forbidden, and lower officials were advised to avoid, as far as possible, sending written reports to their superiors during that period. Whether this very thoroughness aroused the suspicions of the opposing groups or whether they had better reasons to be suspicious, on June 25, Blomberg proclaimed a so-called 'little' state of alarm to the Reichswehr, which meant that every soldier had to be at the army's disposal, even if he were on leave. The same kind of state of alarm was proclaimed by Himmler for the S.S. troops. Karl Ernst, group leader of Berlin, twice telephoned Göring inquiring whether this state of alarm meant anything. Twice received 'No' for an answer.

It is certain that on June 25, when the state of alarm began, Hitler already envisaged the deposition of Röhm; but it is unlikely that this perpetually wavering will already had taken the final decision on that day. On June 26, through Hess, he made an offer to forgive Röhm his indiscipline, abuse of power, evil intentions and scandalous behavior — provided he renounced the 'second revolution.' Such revolutions, Hess said in a speech at Cologne, could not be made in Germany 'after the model of the annual little revolutions in small exotic republics,' referring to Röhm's career in the Bolivian army. But no bad feelings! 'An old National Socialist,' said Hess, 'must be generous toward human peculiarities and weaknesses in National Socialist leaders if these go hand in hand with great achievements. And because of the great achievements he will forgive the little weaknesses.'

Röhm was still with Heines, Count Spreti, and a few other friends in the Hanslbauer at Wiessee; not in a fortified headquarters building, but in a wing of a hotel accessible to anyone and supervised by physicians. For the most part the guests were people not involved in politics. Röhm was even without his usual staff guard which was quartered in Munich. He had invited a number of S.A. leaders from various parts of the Reich to Wiessee on Saturday, June 30, for a so-called 'leaders' conference' and had also ordered the staff guard to come on this occasion. Hitler was not expected to come, although Röhm desired his presence. He had ordered a Hungarian artist in Munich to prepare a bookplate which he intended to present to Hitler on the next appropriate occasion; it showed the book *Mein Kampf* with a sword on it, and two clasped hands above the book and the sword.

This conference at first does not seem to have aroused Hitler's suspicions. Far worse was the fact that Röhm had left Hess's peace offer unanswered. In Hitler's eyes Röhm's principal crime was perhaps that during these feverish days when Hitler expected a satisfying explanation, Röhm just did nothing, said nothing. From the vague partisan utterances of his victorious adversaries it cannot be reliably established whether or not, at the last moment, he made a desperate attempt to strike back; but it is certain that until this last moment all the first steps had been taken by his enemies.

Toward the end of June, Hitler said later, he decided 'to put an end to an intolerable situation,' that is to say, to depose Röhm, whom, according to these words, he still could not reproach with anything definite. Even if this step was exaggerated, it would be fully justifiable as a preventive measure; the only thing that can be said against it is that it was not carried out. If during these days of June 26 to June 28, Hitler had performed the normal duties of a statesman; if he had openly intervened and deposed, arrested and legally prosecuted the real or alleged rebels, the whole affair would probably have been significant historically, but not dramatic or even repulsive. He did the exact opposite: he buried himself in an inspection tour of the labor camps in northwestern Germany, 'in order to lull the rebels into security,' as he later boasted.

The rebels were those who even as late as June 26 were accused only of 'little weaknesses and peculiarities'! It is almost certain that a few hours before the catastrophe, the most serious element in the alleged state of danger was the rulers' fear of their own following. 'Working had become almost impossible,' Göring later said in the Reichstag, 'because at almost every moment we had to fear that we might be kidnapped by a gang of rebels.' Hitler's restless trips from one end of Germany to another — on June 25, he was in Bavaria, near the southern German border, inspecting a new Alpine road; two days later, he was almost in the extreme northwest — represent his attempt to conceal from himself the decision which events had already taken for him.

Up to the last minute he was not clear in his mind about his purpose nor the means of achieving it. According to one of his own statements he had ordered Göring, who was in Berlin, to proceed with 'analogous' measures at his, Hitler's, 'cue.' This 'cue,' as can be inferred from another of his utterances, was simply the report made to Göring that he, Hitler, was now striking out. The strength and extent of the blows to be delivered were not yet determined even after blood had been shed. On June 28, Göring and Himmler made preparations as for a civil war; they ordered their police commandos and their S.S. special troops to hold themselves in readiness. On June 29, Karl Ernst, the S.A. group leader in Berlin, seems to have got wind of these preparations; from a private report of one of Röhm's followers it appears that he interpreted them as a sign that the 'reactionaries' were making ready for the long-expected decisive blow against National Socialism; obviously it did not occur to him that Hitler himself desired this blow; on the contrary, he believed that his Führer would be the first victim. For that reason, on the afternoon of June 29, he proclaimed a state of alarm for the Berlin S.A.

While this went on — toward the evening of June 29 — Hitler stopped at Godesberg on the Rhine. He sat on the terrace of a hotel which belonged to a personal friend of his, a former war comrade named Dreesen. On the lawn in front of the hotel, men of the labor service organized a torch procession in his honor. Some thousand of them stood there, forming a gigantic blazing swastika.

By that time Goebbels had arrived from Berlin bringing disquieting reports about the S.A.'s activities; probably he had heard the latest ones from Helldorf. The following day, the S.A. were supposed to go on furlough; allegedly Goebbels and Hitler thought it 'alarming' that for the time being they were still at their posts. Lutze was summoned from Hanover by wire; the momentous decision was made during consultations with him, Goebbels, and Otto Dietrich, the 'press chief.' Hitler finally made up his mind to go personally to Wiessee on the following day and arrest Röhm and his staff at noon, but for the time being not to inflict any punishment upon him. He wired Röhm that he was on his way, and Röhm seems to have felt glad and honored; simultaneously Hitler ordered most of the high party officials to be in Munich the next day; obviously he was planning a kind of party trial of Röhm and his followers.

This was the political decision that had become inevitable, the choice Hitler was compelled to make between the S.A. and the Reichswehr, which he had for a long time tried to avoid and which he now made. It was also the end of a friendship, which had really foundered because one of the two friends refused to recognize the elevation of the other to a godlike status, because he wanted to remain on an equal footing with him, made him feel his weaknesses and repeatedly displayed his own self-confident strength in the most offensive manner. Whether Röhm still believed that at bottom he was loyal to Hitler, perhaps even more loyal than Hitler himself, was beside the point; he certainly was disobedient in refusing to be the victim of Hitler's Reichswehr policy; it is true that he had been disobedient in this sense again and again in the course of the last fifteen years.

But Hitler's decision implied more than this personal settling of accounts. He put an end to the weakness in himself, the weakness of having a friend who considered himself the Führer's equal; by a deed which went beyond normal human standards he definitively raised himself above normal human beings. His belief that he was a sort of Providence given to his people in human form was no trifling matter; his sincerest admirers took this belief in deadly earnest. Baldur von Schirach, the leader of the 'Hitler-Youth,' declared that his altar was not the church, but the steps of the *Feld-herrnhalle* drenched in blood in 1923, and he indicated that in his opinion this was the altar where Hitler had made his divine appearance. Only a few days before, Hess had once again proclaimed: 'We believe that the Führer follows a higher call to shape the destiny of Germany. . . . He has always been right, he always will be right.' A man as mundane as Göring, speaking on Hesselberg mountain in Franconia, an old pagan place of worship, before thousands of people, shouted contemptuously in the face of the churches: 'When was there ever deeper and more passionate faith in Germany than there is today? What faith was ever aroused more strongly than our faith in the Führer? Never has a greater miracle happened than in our time. The Almighty made this miracle through Adolf Hitler!' At the beginning of 1934, when Hess swore in the entire party to Hitler in a mass spectacle which brought millions of people in thousands of German towns and villages to the microphones, he said to them, before administering the oath: 'By this oath we again bind our lives to a man, through whom — this is our belief — superior forces act in fulfillment of Destiny. Do not seek Adolf Hitler with your brains; all of you will find him with the strength of your hearts. Adolf Hitler is Germany and Germany is Adolf Hitler.' — And, in Hitler's own words, 'Germany is our God on this earth.'

Twelve years earlier, when he had to serve a month in prison, he had said that he went to his place of punishment like Christ to Golgotha. Now he had gone farther than Golgotha, farther than

Christ. In his own lifetime he had become a faith and comfort for millions; they demanded greatness, and he was this greatness. This was not just a fantasy of his: the forest of raised hands, the endless sea of ecstatic faces, had confirmed its reality a hundred times.

This piece of divine will staring at the blazing swastika from the terrace at Godesberg was now doomed to do something horrible because he had for months neglected to do what was necessary. Accustomed to considering himself extraordinary, Hitler interpreted contradiction, let alone resistance, as a sign of depravity which had only itself to blame if it was destroyed on the spot; and everything he did was right, because the faith of millions could not be mistaken. Once a foreign diplomat asked Göring for a favor to which Hitler might have objected, and the great man hesitated. The foreigner asked: 'Are you really afraid of him?' Göring thought for a while and said: 'Yes, I think so. . . .You don't know him!'

Soon after midnight new reports arrived from Berlin about the disquieting state of alarm in the S.A. A similar report came in from Munich; Hitler should have been struck by the fact that the states of alarm in the two cities were separated by several hours and that no reports of this kind had come from other cities. Had he seen at this moment what was going on in Wiessee, he would have been forced to doubt that Röhm had planned and prepared a centrall directed rebellion of the S.A. Röhm was still in his sanatoriv without troops, almost without arms; he expected Hitler's visi following day. A banquet had been ordered in the Munich the Four Seasons, and a vegetarian menu for Hitler had n forgotten; on this occasion Röhm intended to present Hi his bookplate. To an industrialist whom he consulted on questions and who came to see him that day — Frid good-naturedly: 'Why don't you stay until tomorrow coming, too.' The industrialist did not stay, whic lucky for him.

For the day after the leaders' conference, a Su reserved a steamship for an excursion on the A tween Munich and Wiessee; Hitler was to hours there amidst his faithful. It was possib

which, despite the small distance involved, would have cut the company off from the world for a few hours, something might have happened in the rest of Germany. It is very likely that Hitler had given this interpretation to the plan; the excursion looked extremely like a temporary arrest. It has never become known whether the suspicion was justified; for all Hitler's dislike of exact facts, it is hardly credible that he would have concealed such a picturesque and convincing detail, when he later attempted to describe the 'plot' in a public speech. Actually he did not go beyond vague, even though hair-raising, insinuations. But it is conceivable that the report of the planned steamship trip clinched the matter in his mind: he was in personal danger; they wanted to capture Germany, perhaps even kill the great faith of our time.

By one o'clock, Hitler was finally convinced, as he put it later, that 'only ruthless and bloody blows might still succeed in throttling the extension of the rebellion.' At that moment, he said, he had no need 'to investigate if all or some of these conspirators, inciters, wreckers, and well-poisoners of public opinion might suffer too hard a fate,' for 'at all times rebellious divisions have been brought back to order by decimation.' Decimation meant, as Rudolf Hess explained in a speech made about the same time, 'that every tenth man, without any investigation, whether innocent or guilty, was struck by a bullet.'

With this bloody decision in his heart, at two past midnight Hitler flew from the Hangelar airdrome near Bonn to Munich in order personally to direct the decimation. He had made up his mind that 'only one man could and had to confront the chief of staff. He had broken faith with me, and I alone had to call him to account for it.' But the great secret of Hitler's political method, which he had only occasionally hinted at in words — the fact that he vaster the politician's field of action, the more he can expect one ifficulty to be superseded and thus solved by another — was now prove hideously true.

or even before Hitler appeared on the scene, the opposing forces ' clashed. In Munich, Walter Buch and Minister of the Interior lf Wagner had formed an action group, to which belonged stian Weber and Emil Maurice as well as Joseph Berchtold,

Hitler's old friend and shock troop leader. But Franz von Epp, general and governor, Röhm's old superior, did not suspect anything. From Hitler's account it can be inferred that local groups such as these in Munich acted on their own initiative; had so to act. Göring received at least a hint that he now should do what he pleased and proceed to put his death lists into effect. As for Wagner in Munich, even before he had received an order from Hitler, he summoned Schneidhuber, the *Obergruppenführer* of the S.A. and chief of police, along with his assistant, Wilhelm Schmidt, to the Ministry of the Interior, that old building abounding in staircases and corners, situated on the Odeonsplatz; there they were suddenly surrounded by a bunch of gunmen, among them Christian Weber and Emil Maurice; Wagner informed his prisoners they were under arrest. At first they thought it was a joke, and later, a mistake. Schneidhuber had just attended a vaudeville show; the question remains to what extent the whole report about the Munich S.A. was true at all.

At four o'clock Hitler landed at the Oberwiesenfeld airdrome near Munich. He was accompanied by Goebbels, Viktor Lutze, and Otto Dietrich.

Hysterical scenes followed. Hitler wept on the bosom of his old friend, Joseph Berchtold, and bewailed Röhm's breach of faith, as he called it, and the end of their fifteen years of comradeship. Then he rushed upon Schneidhuber and Schmidt and tore off their epaulets. Schneidhuber cried excitedly that Hitler could shoot him if he liked, but that he should keep his dirty fingers off his person. The flyer Ernst Udet, chief of the S.A. air force, was among those arrested; he ran up to Hitler and asked him in a fierce bellow whether he was not enough of a soldier to know the meaning of discipline. How could he punish soldiers for obeying the orders of their superiors? — and until now Röhm was still their superior. Udet was spared.

At seven in the morning, Hitler and his party sped southward in a long column of automobiles, in the direction of Wiessee. Goebbels, Lutze, Dietrich, and Buch were with him; Christian Weber, the fat brawler and murderer in his black S.S. uniform with its sinister skull and crossbones, was there, too, as well as Emil Maurice with his black hair and lurking black underworld look. According to Goebbels's account, Hitler was silent; but, according to the same account, if during the trip from Bonn to Munich the feeling of a real danger had allegedly weighed upon the little group of airplane travelers, now, after Hitler had stared into the faces of the first arrested victims, this feeling apparently yielded to one of omnipotence. 'In those hours, the supreme tribunal of the German nation — myself . . .' — thus Hitler later described his rôle and feelings. If this *coup* succeeded — actually it had already succeeded — the silent man even now wielded more power than the old man of Neudeck, whose imminent demise had been the cause of this whole undertaking. The man who now made this death-dealing pilgrimage had traveled a long and sinister road since the day, only eighteen months before, when he was forced to look on impotently while Gregor Strasser almost destroyed the party. He had grown so big now that he had an antidote for every difficulty, even if the name of this antidote was murder. An armored Reichswehr car was in the column; nor had Hitler forgotten to bring his press agent, Dietrich, who was to describe the planned blood-bath.

Against a background of dark green mountains shone the placid surface of the Tegernsee, illumined by a gold-blue morning sky. In the wing of the Hanslbauer, Röhm lay wrapped in deep sleep. Hitler and suite entered, deliberately silent, almost on tiptoes.

Count Spreti was the first prisoner to be brought in. He made a gesture which Hitler interpreted as an attempt to reach for his gun. The Führer hit him on the head with the iron end of his heavy whip, and kept hitting the young man's face and skull until he collapsed. Then he hammered at Röhm's door with his fists, shouting to him to open up. Röhm's sleepy voice was heard: 'What, you here already?' According to Dietrich's account, Hitler entered the room alone; Röhm submitted to his arrest and listened to Hitler's furious abuse without uttering a single word. Other accounts tell of a great scene between the two and of Röhm's rage; according to them, Hitler personally pressed a gun into Röhm's hand and invited him to commit suicide — at the obvious risk that Röhm would shoot him. This is scarcely credible.

'Heines's room, directly adjoining Röhm's,' says Dietrich's account, 'presented a disgraceful picture. Heines lay in bed with a homosexual boy. The disgusting scene which took place during the arrest of Heines and his friend defies description.' Hitler ordered Major Buch 'ruthlessly to exterminate this pestilential tumor.' Heines and his companion were dragged out and shot in a car by Maurice and Weber: they were the first dead.

They were literally buried in mud. A storm of public defamation descended upon these dead men, which described their unnatural tendencies with the most loathsome details; Goebbels's propaganda made it almost their principal crime that they had defiled the Führer's pure movement with their dirty practices — which only four days earlier Hess had termed 'little weaknesses.' Hitler hastily went back to Munich ordering Röhm's staff guard to precede him. This guard had appeared shortly after the arrest of their leader and did not make any attempt to free him — another sign that at least the troops were not prepared for a rebellion against Hitler. On his way back, Hitler intercepted car after car full of S.A. leaders on their way to the conference at Wiessee; he ordered some of them to follow him and signified to others that they were arrested — and no attempt to resist was reported. Followed by a long file of dismayed prisoners and frightened henchmen Hitler returned to Munich.

As Hess later suggested, these arrests were fairly arbitrary, made chiefly on the basis of feeling — and Hitler's feeling seems frequently to have been based on a suspicion that the person concerned had homosexual tendencies. This suspicion, Hess admitted, was not always justified and some of the arrests were the result of 'tragic entanglements,' that is to say, the victims were innocent. In the speech which Hitler made before the non-arrested party leaders at noon on June 30, he chiefly accused Röhm and his men for their loose or depraved conduct and declared that for this alone they deserved to die. To Lutze, whom he had appointed Röhm's successor, he sent an order comprising twelve points, which dealt almost exclusively with parties, drinking bouts, automobile trips, squandering and unnatural lewdness indulged in by Röhm and his gang — and stressed the necessity of putting an end to all that.

For the space of ten years he had known and tolerated these

things, publicly branded them as lies, admitted them among his intimates, excused and justified them — and the fact that Röhm had
compelled him to do this was probably his most heinous crime in
Hitler's innermost thoughts. He, the 'miracle,' 'the instrument of
higher powers,' was dishonored by his own instrument — this was
probably the treason which Hitler could not forgive his chief of
staff.

Dishonored by his instrument? Actually he was dishonored by
himself. True, Hitler had not shared Röhm's particular depravity in
a physical sense, but he had been the chosen leader of these depraved men; to them he owed his greatness. Yes, he was the product
and the creature of decay and degeneration, a flame kindled from
foul gases. These had been his 'élite.' And it was the painful
memory of his own weakness, now doomed in the person of Röhm
and his arrested clique, that he ordered sent to the Stadelheim
prison near Munich.

On the morning of the same June 30, Göring and Himmler
struck in Berlin. The police commandos for special services, led
by Wecke, thundered on motorcycles and trucks — making a detour
to mislead the adversary — from Lichterfelde via Tempelhof into
Berlin, surrounded the S.A. headquarters and penetrated inside
without encountering resistance. A few minutes later, when Göring
arrived, he found the S.A. leaders standing with arms upraised in
front of Wecke's riflemen; he ran through the rooms on every floor,
pointing at individuals and shouting: 'Arrest him . . . arrest him
. . . arrest him. . . .' Those whom he did not point out were free and
returned to life. The arrested men were taken to Lichterfelde in
Wecke's trucks. In the course of the morning approximately one
hundred and fifty prisoners were herded there.

Within the walls of Lichterfelde and Stadelheim, and to a lesser
extent at several other places, there now began a massacre which
surpassed in horror the May, 1919, executions in Munich, which
Hitler had helped to organize; it was probably the most hideous
incident in modern German history. In Munich, Walter Buch
directed the executions. He shouted: 'The Führer wills it. Heil
Hitler! Fire!' A fourfold salvo thundered, and against the wall fell:
August Schneidhuber, ex-Colonel, now *Obergruppenführer* and

chief of police in Munich; Fritz von Krausser whom the King of Bavaria had ennobled for bravery; Hans Hayn, old Free Corps fighter from the Rossbach unit, one of Röhm's most intimate friends; Peter von Heydebreck, who had lost an arm in the World War, later fought against the Poles in Upper Silesia and in honor of whom a Silesian city had been named Heydebreck; Group Leader Wilhelm Schmidt; Staff Adjutant Reiner; Group Leader Koch; Group Leader Lasch, Brigade Leader Kopp, *Standarte* Leader Uhl . . . and many many others.

The endless salvos under which his friends fell dead were probably the last thing of which Röhm was conscious in this world. For the second time in eleven years he was locked up in a cell in Stadelheim prison. He had spent a short time there in 1923-24, because he had planned and led a military mutiny and street fight which caused many fatal casualties; but his life had not been at stake then, he was sure of that. To dispel the boredom which was the worst feature of that imprisonment he had written poems in hexameters; one of these was dedicated to Ernst Haug, Hitler's chauffeur, whose sister, Jenny, had been deserted by the Führer after a long-drawn and tender affair. Possibly because Haug had been upset about this, Röhm exhorted him:

> Always be faithful to Adolf Hitler, our friend and great leader!
> Let the cowards trample you; our triumph will be the brighter.

Now he was reaping the fruits of his loyalty: he was again in Stadelheim, and his prospects were much more terrifying than the first time. The death which Röhm now faced with certainty was undeniably his own work on which he had spent a life marked by daring, cunning, energy, blood-thirstiness, and faith. So this was the purpose for which he had originated the armed political party, given it his soldiers and weapons, won the favors of the powers that be for its leader, pushed him into a decisive position shortly before the *putsch!* This was the purpose for which, after the first collapse and the long years of painful failures, he had rebuilt his 'Brown Popular Army,' without which Hitler would never have triumphed — to be murdered in an obscure cell! Adolf Hitler, his creature, had given orders to leave a gun on the table of his creator, for him to commit suicide with — he had been given ten minutes to do this. Röhm declared that 'Adolf himself should do the dirty work,' and let the ten minutes pass. Then the door opened, and from outside bullets were pumped into the cell until Röhm was dead. He was buried in the prison yard; the exact spot is unknown.

While this went on, about one hundred and fifty top S.A. leaders awaited their death at Lichterfelde. They had been locked up in a coal cellar of the Cadet School; one of them who escaped by accident has provided us with an account of the events, from which the following details are drawn.

At intervals of about fifteen minutes, four names were called out; this meant death for the four men named within a few minutes. The mood of the prisoners was not really dejected. Most of them realized that these were definitely their last hours of life. The whole thing lasted twenty-four hours, and there was a night's pause. It took all that time to slay the hundred and fifty men, except for five or six who were pardoned at the last minute. Many of them tried to be gay, and sometimes succeeded; at certain moments the whole group was in a solemn frame of mind; but with one exception there were no nervous breakdowns.

The prisoners had a completely false idea of the general situation and the reasons for which they were being murdered. It did not occur to them that they were to be shot by Hitler's orders; on the contrary, they believed that their supreme Leader was imprisoned like themselves, perhaps already dead, a victim of the 'reactionaries' among whom they counted Göring and Goebbels.

These doomed men in their coal cellar had a curious instinct for destiny. Whose name would be called out next, whose turn was it to be slaughtered? They tried to guess; in three or four cases they guessed right. From a window in the cellar those who still remained behind saw their comrades being led to a wall across the yard. Those who were being marched away kept their eyes on the window. The men in the cellar looked into the eyes of their departing comrade; this was a last charitable service which they rendered each other by silent agreement, a comforting exchange of glances during the last two minutes that separated life from death.

The victims were stood in a row against the wall. An S.S. man opened their shirts over their chests and drew a black circle around the left nipple with a piece of charcoal: this was the target. Five to six yards from the wall stood eight S.S. men with rifles. Four of the rifles were allegedly loaded with blank cartridges so that no one knew whether his bullet was the deadly one.

Then the order to fire rang out. Here, too, it was: 'The Führer wills it. Heil Hitler! Fire!'

Among the men stood against the wall at Lichterfelde was Karl Ernst. When he left the cellar he was still firmly convinced, just as his comrades were, that Hitler himself was a prisoner. Whether he heard, understood, and believed the order to fire, no one will ever be able to say. At any rate, he threw up his arm and shouted 'Heil Hitler!' He died with his Führer's name on his lips.

The shots, from a distance of five to six yards, tore out the flesh of the victims. Especially the spot where the bullet left the body under the left shoulder was transformed into a gaping hole, and the bullets dragged out parts of the body. The observers in the cellar could see bloody pieces of flesh stuck to the wall after the victims had dropped, and the darker heart fragments were clearly discernible. The wall was not cleaned in the intervals between the executions; hence, after a short time, it was completely covered with blood and human flesh.

Among the men in the cellar was *Standartenführer* Gehrt — 'little Gehrt,' as our account calls him. In the World War he had been a captain in the air force; he had been decorated with the highest Prussian order, 'Pour le Mérite'; during the last years of the war he had belonged to the Richthofen squadron commanded by Göring.

Gehrt's name was called out and he left the cellar, but apparently was not taken to be executed. Had Destiny intervened at the last moment? Those remaining inside assumed that Göring's personal friendship had saved him. But two hours later, Gehrt returned to the cellar, completely broken, and told the following story:

An S.S. officer told him: 'Go home, wash and shave, put on your gala uniform with all your medals, and report to Prime Minister Göring!' Gehrt left the barracks. He was free. Overwhelmed by this apparent last-minute escape, he went home, did as he had been told, washed, shaved, put on his gala uniform with all his medals, and reported to Göring's headquarters in Prinz Albrecht Street. It took some effort on his part to get through all the guards, but he was stubborn and finally reached his old comrade-in-arms whom he wanted to thank warmly for his release.

Göring received him surrounded by his staff. He approached Gehrt, tore off his 'Pour le Mérite' decoration, tore off his other medals, and said to the people around him: 'I gave orders that this filthy pig be brought here because he once belonged to my squadron. Take him away!'

Gehrt was taken back to the coal cellar. After that, our informant tells us, he collapsed, allegedly the only man who did not keep up his nerve. He had to be pushed to the wall.

Most of those who fell during this slaughter were little known to the world. Very few people outside the S.A. had ever heard of Group Leader Georg von Detten or his life; but whatever could be said of him, good or bad, during his lifetime, in the hour of his death he made an extraordinary impression on his comrades in the cellar. He delivered a farewell speech which opened — as our report puts it — a gate into a world they had never known. The path that they had taken, he said, was false. What must and would come about had a significance far greater than Germany's fate alone; a league of the thousand best men of all nations, classes, and creeds, who would take the fate of the world into their hands and give peace to the earth. To our informant his words seemed great, but so new and strange that it occurred to him that Detten must have secretly been a Freemason. Actually his words contained a faint reminiscence of 'Aryans of all nations, unite!' But Hitler had no room in Detten's last thoughts; he referred to the Führer as a disappointment and spoke of him 'with contempt.' This did not prevent his listeners from being thrilled by his speech. The account tells of a solemn mood, which descended upon the men and made death easier to bear for many.

Our informant insists that almost all the victims went to their death calm and dignified. Goebbels maintained the opposite: in a confidential communication to the S.A. he said that the 'rebels' were led to the wall pale and trembling. Our account indignantly attacks this assertion. But, according to it, the nerves of the S.S. firing squads could not stand the strain very long; they had to be frequently changed; and after each change, the shooting was accurate the first time, but at the second or third execution many shots went wide of the mark. The victims lay on the ground, but were still alive; the commanding S.S. officer had to finish them off with a revolver shot in the head.

From time to time a horse-drawn tin-lined truck, which obviously belonged to a butcher and served for transporting meat, entered the yard. The corpses were thrown into this truck and carted away.

How many such corpses had been carried away by July 1 was never known. In his Reichstag speech Hitler mentioned a figure which means nothing: he said that there were more than seventy-seven. There were certainly many hundreds. Executions like those at Stadelheim and Lichterfelde also took place in Stettin, Dresden, Breslau, and other cities. But not everywhere were such masses dragged to the slaughterhouse. Many victims were hunted down individually, and more than one man in those gruesome days took advantage of the general freedom to shoot in order to satisfy his private hatred, lust for revenge, and sometimes the most hideous murderous instincts. There is no doubt that Göring himself sent the six assassins in mufti who on the morning of June 30 appeared at von Schleicher's villa, rang the bell, quickly broke in, and shot the former Chancellor in front of his wife and niece. Von Schleicher died on the spot. He had reached for his gun, and the six assassins had killed him in self-defense — this was the version Göring at first tried to circulate; but later Hitler in his Reichstag speech made no attempt to maintain it. One bullet, allegedly by mistake, hit Frau Elisabeth von Schleicher, who died half an hour later; the six murderers drove away in their car one minute after they had carried out their mission.

Göring took advantage of the vagueness of Hitler's orders and the confused state of the death lists to slaughter a number of enemies other than the rebellious S.A. leaders, but he certainly did not go against Hitler's intentions in doing this. For in Munich, too, where Hitler gave direct orders, people were murdered who had nothing in common with Röhm. To justify these crimes, the story of a 'reactionary' plot was put into circulation, a plot which was even more incredible than the alleged revolt of Röhm. General von Bredow, a friend of von Schleicher's, was dragged out of his apartment at night and apparently shot in his abductors' car; Gregor Strasser, arrested at noon on June 30, fell like Röhm under bullets fired through the window of a prison cell. The reason for these murders was not only a reason of state, but probably also a personal one; Göring bitterly hated von Schleicher and Strasser. He would have gladly dispatched a third enemy, von Papen; but von Papen was not only 'Vice-Chancellor,' he was also a personal friend of Hindenburg's, who at least in the flesh was still alive. So, Göring summoned von Papen on the morning of June 30 and told him to stay at home and above all not to show himself in his office, for decisions concerning the fate of the nation and the Reich would be carried out on that day. Von Papen remained at home; whether he could not or would not warn his assistants is uncertain. At any rate, three S.S. men appeared at the Vice-Chancellery where von Bose, von Papen's unsuspecting aide, was engaged in a conversation with two industrialists from the Rhineland. Von Bose was politely asked to step into the adjoining room. The visitors heard shots. The three S.S. men departed. Von Bose was dead.

Toward noon, two S.S. men broke into the office of Erich Klausener of the Ministry of Communications and declared him under arrest. Klausener, a leader of the 'Catholic Action,' founded by Pope Pius XI, willingly followed them, certain that the obvious misunderstanding would presently be dispelled. No sooner had he walked two steps than two bullets hit him in the nape of the neck. The heavy-set man fell on his face and lay there with his hat on until he bled to death.

In Munich, seventy-three-year-old Gustav von Kahr, who eleven years earlier had crushed Hitler's *putsch* and had lived in retirement since then, was dragged out of his home; a few days later, his horribly disfigured corpse was found in a swamp near the Dachau concentration camp. Kahr was not shot; he was hacked to death with pickaxes.

Fritz Beck, director of the Munich Students' Welfare Fund, a Catholic like Klausener and von Bose, was taken out of his apartment by two S.S. men, on June 30; two days later, his naked corpse was found in a woods near the town of Pasing. He was identified by a papal medal he wore around his neck; his face was a formless mass.

Father Bernhard Stempfle lay with a broken neck and three bullets in his heart in a woods near Harlaching, a suburb of Munich. Willy Schmidt, the music critic, died only because his name was Willy Schmidt; the murderers confused him with Colonel Schneidhuber's assistant, Wilhelm Schmidt. The fiancée of Doctor Voss, a Berlin attorney who was Gregor Strasser's counsel, anxiously asked the police to find her vanished lover; they replied, 'Do you really think he is still alive?'

People were murdered whose only crime was that they had had a quarrel over a copyright with Max Amann, Hitler's publisher. People were murdered to whom Hitler had promised his personal protection. Among those who were saved by Hitler in the last minute was Manfred von Killinger.

These murders extending beyond the S.A. circles would have been impossible if Hitler had not been absolutely sure of Blomberg's and Reichenau's personal devotion. With von Schleicher fell their sharpest critic and opponent; and Reichenau's joy at his death was proved a few days later when he declared that von Schleicher had long ago ceased to be a soldier, that he was a born conspirator who had sunk so low that he even had relations with the S.A. Blomberg would have approved anything that Hitler did; the general blindly admired the Führer. And so it was not surprising that on July 3, when Hitler reported to the cabinet on the blood-bath, Franz Gürtner, his eternal silent guardian angel, who fourteen years earlier had been unable to discover the political murderers of that day, stated now that there had been no murders at all, and introduced a law, immediately adopted by the cabinet, which proclaimed that the deeds of June 30 were 'justified as a measure of state defense.' A congratulatory telegram arrived from Hindenburg.

The following story was told about one of Gregor Strasser's boys. A Frenchman living in the neighborhood, who was superficially acquainted with the family, met him a few days after the murder of his father and could not resist asking him what he now thought of Hitler — who, by the way, was the boy's godfather. The boy swallowed, and staring ahead of him said: 'He is still our Führer!'

Thus the prophets' words had at last come true. The Führer had 'trampled on the bodies' of his best friends; along with his enemies he murdered these friends in the most criminal and the most frivolous fashion; and for that very reason he was admired by the people — including those of his victims who escaped death. Once again greatness had come cheaply as soon as he could bring himself to be great; and the mass character of the horrors silenced the question of good and evil, justice and injustice, in men's souls, leaving them only with the feeling that a hideous necessity had worked itself out. By his gruesome deed of June 30, 1934, Hitler, in the eyes of the German people, definitely assumed the dimensions of an historical, superhuman being, whose rights and reasons could no longer be questioned. 'There won't be another revolution in Germany for the next thousand years,' he proclaimed.

The belief in the necessity of evil, which slumbers in the lowest depths of the human soul, had been awakened by Hitler as by no other man in the history of Europe; the fact that he could do what he had done seemed like a confirmation of Hess's fanatical words: that through Hitler higher powers were fulfilling man's destiny. Hitler now began to do frightful things easily, and the more frightful they were, the more easily he did them. He discovered the secret law of history which has made all bloody figures like himself bigger than life-size when the times were favorable: the law by which the most horrible deeds become less heavy to bear, the more monstrous and numerous they are, because in the end each horror wipes out its predecessor in the minds of the people.

Hitler had known this for a long time; his own career, the deeds that had raised him to leadership, had proved it to him many years before. The piles of corpses on June 30, 1934, must have given him the final proof that since 1919 his path of murder and violence had been the right path to greatness.

A few days after June 30, at midnight, Hitler, exhausted and disheveled, appeared at the Reich Chancellery in Berlin and shouted: 'I must work until tomorrow at noon, and I must not be disturbed!' He locked himself up in his room. A quarter of an hour later, his voice was heard again: he wanted a plane. At almost the same hour as a few days before in Bonn, he left for Munich. At daybreak, his car took him from the Oberwiesenfeld airport to the Brown House in Brienner Street. Impetuously he leaped up the steps to the Hall of Honor, hung with banners and flags, including the 'bloody banner' of November 9, 1923. Silently he stared at the banners for a while, then ran down the steps, entered his car, and hurried back to the airport.

Postscript

This book has related from its beginnings a story which has not yet come to an end.

In it, I have shown — or tried to show — the roots of Hitlerism and the growth of that sinister philosophy of force which seemed, at one time, almost destined to overshadow the earth.

There is a double question this book has tried to answer: What sort of people were they who were capable of committing the crimes here described; and (even more urgently) what sort of people were capable of submitting to them?

The question cannot be answered with a definition or a formula. Great events can be understood only when they have been experienced or suffered, at least in spirit; and to know something deeply is to experience it. This book has attempted to let the reader share the experiences of a generation; its story is the reader's own.

The ending I have given it — the days when the blood purge gave Hitler absolute mastery of his party and of Germany — is less arbitrary than may, perhaps, appear. For by that time, the pattern was set and the weapon forged. Having enslaved his own people, Hitler was ready to use the techniques he had learned — which I have here analyzed — to enslave the continent. The shots in the Stadelheim Prison were the first shots of the Second World War.

Hitler was able to enslave his own people because he seemed to give them something that even the traditional religions could no longer provide; the belief in a meaning to existence beyond the narrowest self-interest. The real degradation began when people realized that they were in league with the Devil, but felt that even the Devil was preferable to the emptiness of an existence which lacked a larger significance.

The problem today is to give that larger significance and dignity to a life that has been dwarfed by the world of material things. Until that problem is solved, the annihilation of Naziism will be no more than the removal of one symptom of the world's unrest.

Index

Index